D0214437

Political Violence and Trauma in Argentina

The Ethnography of Political Violence

Cynthia Keppley Mahmood, Series Editor

A complete list of books in the series is available from the publisher.

Political Violence and Trauma in Argentina

Antonius C. G. M. Robben

PENN

University of Pennsylvania Press

Philadelphia

9 8 7 6 5 4 3 2 1

Published by
University of Pennsylvania Press
Philadelphia, Pennsylvania 19104-4011

Library of Congress Cataloging-in-Publication Data

Robben, Antonius C. G. M.
    Political violence and trauma in Argentina / Antonius C. G. M. Robben.
        p.   cm. (The ethnography of political violence)
    ISBN 0-8122-3836-2 (cloth : alk. paper)
    Includes bibliographical references (p.   ) and index.
    1. Political violence—Argentina—History—20th century.   2. Argentina—Politics
and government—1943–.   3. Argentina—Social conditions—1945–1983.
4. Argentina—Social conditions—1983–.   I. Title.   II. Series
HN270.Z9 V555   2005
303.6′0982—dc22   2004052007

To Ellen,
Oscar, and Sofia

Contents

Preface

This is the story of a country of great natural wealth and economic promise torn asunder by violence and trauma. Decades of mounting political violence cost the lives of more than ten thousand people, inflicted unimaginable suffering on many more, and traumatized society in the process. This traumatization was not apparent to me when I visited Argentina in 1978 during a break from fieldwork in Brazil. In retrospect, I understand that the deceptive calm of public life in Buenos Aires had been imposed by state terror and concealed a national tragedy. The atmosphere was entirely different in April 1983, when, again away from fieldwork, I became swept up in the popular effervescence of a protest march against the transitional military government that had replaced a military junta discredited by losing the 1982 Falkland/Malvinas war.

On 16 April 1983, twelve thousand people joined the March for Human Rights to present the military government with a petition demanding that they bring back the disappeared alive, return the abducted babies, and dismantle the repressive apparatus. What I remember most vividly is my shock at the display of force when we reached the intersection of Avenida 9 de Julio and Avenida de Mayo. It seemed as if a human stockade had been stacked against the advancing crowd to prevent its direct passage to the presidential palace. An assembly of policemen on horseback stood in front, closely followed by rows of riot police, behind them bumper-to-bumper squad cars, and finally a barrier of armored vehicles with gun-toting soldiers on top. As the protesters veered toward the right, away from Avenida de Mayo and into a narrow parallel street, several mounted policemen charged into the crowd. Like everyone else, I shrank away and felt a tremendous surge of anger because of this intimidation. I quickly entered Hipólito Yrigoyen street. Each side street was blocked by armed policemen and soldiers. The crowd was cheered from the balconies, and finally arrived at the Plaza de Mayo. Prominent human rights leaders, among them Nobel Peace Prize laureate Adolfo Pérez Esquivel, approached the Casa Rosada presidential palace to hand over the petition, supported by more than two hundred thousand signatures, but there was no government official to receive them and the doorman refused to accept any papers. "Murderers!

Murderers! Murderers!" the crowd chanted incessantly. This was my crowd baptism in Argentina.

When seven years later I began conducting research for this book and read the newspapers of the 1970s and 1980s, studied military riot control procedures, and listened to the participants of historic crowd manifestations like the 1945 Day of Loyalty, the 1969 uprising in the city of Córdoba, the deadly 1973 confrontation among Peronists at Ezeiza airport, and also the 1983 March for Human Rights in which I had participated, I became convinced that at least one key to the political violence and traumatization of Argentine society was to be found in the extraordinary importance of crowds in Argentine political culture. As one protagonist of those turbulent decades has commented, Argentine street mobilizations are "like hinges where years of history are compressed, and where one sees history turning a page to start a new chapter."[1]

Another key to the political violence and especially the disappearances relates to an earlier experience. The memories are much vaguer, but several troubling and indelible images still come to mind. Strolling across the Plaza de Mayo in April 1978, where Evita and Juan Domingo Perón had addressed their incendiary speeches to huge Peronist crowds, I was suddenly approached by several women who spoke anxiously about their disappeared children. Before I could realize what was happening, they had already been taken away by police. These mothers were obviously a second key to Argentina. The guerrilla insurgency and the systematic torture in secret detention centers of the Argentine police and military provided the third and fourth key toward understanding the country's spiral of violence and trauma.

More than two years of fieldwork were carried out in the city of Buenos Aires, its outskirts, and surrounding towns between April 1989 and July 1991. Additional field trips were made in 1995, 2000, and 2002. I realize that Buenos Aires is not representative of Argentina and that I have missed out on the richness of provincial capitals, regional towns, and the vast countryside. When I arrived in April 1989, less than six years after the fall of the military regime, it so happened that most protagonists of the decades of violence were living in Buenos Aires, whereas the few who resided elsewhere would visit the city often enough to set up a meeting. Furthermore, as the nation's federal capital, Buenos Aires housed most human rights organizations, political parties and organizations, labor union centrals, military headquarters, and ecclesiastic authorities. Buenos Aires was therefore a hotbed of political activity and thus the most suitable place for my research.

The length of the historical period covered, the complexity of Argentine politics, and my ambition of trying to understand political violence from various ideological sides demanded a variety of research methods. I conducted more than one hundred in-depth interviews with many protagonists of the historical period under scrutiny and analyzed newspapers, court records, clandestine publications, secret documents, and the writings and speeches of the principal political actors, many of whom died tragic deaths. Participant observation was conducted at exhumations, funerals, reburials, commemorations, parades, and especially many crowd gatherings like the political rallies, street demonstrations, and protest marches so typical of Argentine political culture, and so mesmerizing to the Argentine people and their leaders.[2]

The analysis of political violence and collective trauma in Argentina during five turbulent decades in an equally turbulent century is a daunting undertaking. I have resisted the temptation to begin this book in 1976 when state terror hit Argentina with full force. The dirty war did not come about all of a sudden. A comprehensive understanding of this most tragic of Argentine political convulsions must therefore start much earlier because the historical roots are long and convoluted. Some Argentines advised me to start with the return of Perón from exile in 1973 or with his overthrow in 1955. Others pointed at the 1969 mass uprising in the industrial city of Córdoba, while still others harked back to the 1919 Tragic Week when police killed striking workers. Some even emphasized that political violence had been endemic to Argentine society since the civil wars following Argentina's War of Independence against Spain during the early nineteenth century. I have chosen 17 October 1945 as my starting point, the day when the Argentine working class marched on the presidential palace at the Plaza de Mayo, became a crucial player in Argentine politics, and made crowds essential to Argentine political culture. The predicament of this working class motivated many young people to grab arms in the 1970s to achieve a social revolution. This political radicalization persuaded the Argentine armed forces to use military force and state terror to defeat the guerrilla insurgency, disassemble the radicalized political opposition, subjugate the working class, and reeducate the Argentine people.

This book's narrative structure combines historical chronology with social complexity, separating out particular social domains in distinct periods to interpret Argentina's multilevel political violence and traumatization. Taken together, these four parts demonstrate how various strands of violence arose at different times and interlocked in the 1970s to create an overdetermined traumatized whole that had penetrated four levels of social complexity. Part I analyzes the development and decline of political crowds between 1945 and 1976. It pays close attention to the ambiguous relation between political crowds and military regimes, and how the repression and traumatization of protest crowds led to political radicalization and revolutionary violence. Part II focuses on the comings and goings of armed violence between 1955 and 1979. I analyze the dynamics of the guerrilla insurgency and the mimetic response by the Argentine armed forces. The relation between increasing levels of violence and the traumatization of the

Peronist resistance movement and the guerrilla organizations becomes apparent here. Part III covers the state terror between 1976 and 1983 when the Argentine military believed that neither the repression of crowds, the proscription of political movements, nor the annihilation of the guerrilla organizations were sufficient to cure Argentina of its political ills. The military were convinced that their just war had to continue into the hearts and minds of their political enemies through torture, disappearance, captivity, and either assassination or reeducation. Finally, Part IV focuses on the period between 1976 and 1990, when family members, mothers in particular, embarked on an interminable search of disappeared relatives. The growing working-class and human rights protests, together with the British victory over Argentine troops in the Falkland/Malvinas war, brought down the military regime by 1982. The rise of democracy in 1983 ended the armed violence and state terror but not the political turmoil as the post-traumatic sequels of decades of abuse and suffering dominated Argentina into the twenty-first century.

Part I
Groundswell: The Rise and Fall of Argentine Crowds

Workers expressing their loyalty to Perón, 17 October 1945. Courtesy of Archivo General de la Nación.

Chapter 1
Changing the Course of History: Dignity, Emancipation, and Entrenchment

"That's the morgue," she said calmly, having removed the padlock from the gate that gave access to a walled off wasteland surrounding a drab building. The morgue of Avellaneda cemetery near Buenos Aires consisted of three rooms. One room contained the skeletons of the exhumed bodies, another held various tools, while the central room was dominated by a stainless steel table. Autopsies used to be performed on the table years ago, but it served now to reassemble the remains of the disappeared. After taking off our coats, we walked to an area of ten by thirty meters overgrown with grass, some mounds of recently disturbed soil, and a large open pit protected from the autumn rains by a corrugated roof.

The site turned gruesome when I helped lift the boards that rested across the mass grave: not just because of the exposed skulls, but because most skeletons had been covered with blankets and sheets to protect them from the weather. It seemed as if they were asleep, only to be awakened by a gentle touch. Their place of rest was only temporary. They waited to be reunited with their relatives after exhumation, after having been abducted, tortured, disappeared, assassinated, stripped naked, and dumped at night in this mass grave in a concealed corner of Avellaneda cemetery.

Darío arrived soon after Patricia and I had removed the coverings. We tried to separate a tumbled collection of at least four bodies from section E-D 2. After brush strokes by Darío, a skull appeared. Luis arrived, and the three forensic anthropologists moved to section C 8 to a body that had been burned around the legs and head. Both legs appeared to have been broken with a club or stick and then cut with a knife or machete. One part could not be located. The remains were difficult to identify by age and sex, but indicated a man in his mid-twenties.

Piece by piece, Luis and Darío removed the skeleton and handed the bones to Patricia, who placed them in numbered bags which identified the anatomical contents. The brush swept away morsels of gray clay mixed with traces of rust. Burns on the skull and thigh became visible, but it was uncertain whether they were inflicted before or after death. The skull, weakened by the fire, had been crushed under the weight of the soil when the provisory grave was closed about eleven years ago. The anthropologists searched the soil for clues about the cause of death and the identity of the person—bullets, pieces of clothing, glasses, hair, and teeth—tossing the soil into a bucket. Once several were full, they were taken away in a wheelbarrow. After five hours of diligent work, one skeleton from section C 8 had been exhumed. The coded plastic bags were placed in a cardboard box for later study. We covered the mass grave again, and left.

The identification of the skeletal remains of 278 persons, including nineteen fetuses and babies, in the mass grave at Avellaneda would take years of painstaking work. Meanwhile, the multiple traumas of Argentina's past kept intruding on society as more mass graves were opened, adopted children asked about their biological parents, and perpetrators made chilling confessions about torture, disappearances, childbirths under hooded captivity, and death flights by night.[1]

The Avellaneda mass grave and the pain and suffering of the searching relatives are the result of an all-out war in which the Argentine military outterrorized and outtraumatized the guerrilla insurgency and the country's radicalized political opposition. Just as the guerrillas attempted a social revolution, so the military were determined to protect Argentina's cultural heritage. Two large guerrilla organizations made daring attacks on army bases, and political assassinations were happening daily by 1975.[2] Argentine military rulers became convinced that their antirevolutionary war was a necessary shock therapy to heal a society ridden with violence, corruption, immorality and defiance of authority. General Alcides López Aufranc wrote in late 1975 that the political violence in Argentina, "concerns an infection of the minds, a gangrene that runs the risk of killing the free, democratic and plural Argentine social body if it is not attacked decisively and energetically."[3] The Argentine military felt that Argentina's whole way of life, its entire cultural, moral, and social universe were at stake in this war. They decided in 1975 to stamp out this threat with ruthless resolve.

The political violence that led the Argentine military to assault their own society and disappear thousands of people did not come about suddenly. To understand how Argentine society became traumatized and why around ten thousand dead came to inhabit hundreds of mass graves, we have to uncover the historical roots of the cultural war that raged in the 1970s. We have to reach back to a time when the V-Day celebrations in Europe and North America at the end of World War II echoed in the euphoria of hundreds of thousands of Argentine workers who took to the streets of Buenos Aires on 17 October 1945 in defense of their leader Juan Domingo Perón.

Fear among the Argentine military and the middle and upper classes of a social revolution on Argentine soil began with this one crowd in 1945.

It raised hopes for a better future among the working class and provoked anxieties among the vested interests. All recognized the revolutionary potential of this new political movement, but where some saw the 17 October gathering as a celebration of social emancipation, others feared that a demagogic leader might unleash the crowd's irrational violence on the established social order. Mobilizations became a fertile political practice on which violence was grafted. A spiral of violence was set in motion that produced multiple social traumas suffered throughout Argentine society. The traumatizing fallout of tens of thousands of dead, disappeared, and tortured citizens affected Argentine society at large, and eventually engulfed the perpetrators themselves.

Crowds became a constant in Argentine political culture during the reign of Juan Domingo Perón from 1945 till his military overthrow in 1955. Perón manipulated the deep-seated fear of the crowd that existed among the middle and upper classes, and continued to mobilize his following in a crowd competition when the opposition to his government became greater. Crowds became the groundswell of Argentine political life, creating and toppling governments and dictatorships, inspiring fear and raising hopes.

An Enormous and Silent Force

The founding myth of the Peronist movement tells us that on the morning of Wednesday 17 October 1945, hundreds of thousands of workers began to walk the many kilometers from the factories, meatpacking plants, and working class neighborhoods on the outskirts of Buenos Aires to the Plaza de Mayo at the heart of the nation's capital. They carried makeshift signs and shouted slogans in favor of Perón. "I had the impression that something very powerful and even mysterious was happening," observed Ernesto Sábato years later, "the impression that, almost underground, an enormous and silent force had been set in motion."[4] Perón had become Secretary of Labor and Social Welfare in October 1943 and helped pass labor legislation that improved salaries, social benefits, and workers' rights. Under pressure from hostile conservative forces, Perón was forced to resign on 9 October 1945, and was interned on the island of Martín García on 12 October. This confinement would lead five days later to protests of Argentine workers in the entire country.

The 1969 account of this day by historian Félix Luna has sustained the founding myth of the Peronist movement. According to Luna, the leaders of the national confederation of labor unions (CGT), had planned a general strike for October 18 to demand free elections and the protection of workers' rights. With great drama, Luna writes that just as the union leaders were going to bed, the ordinary people were getting up to take to the streets and demand the freedom of Perón.[5] Nothing could stop the masses advancing on Buenos Aires. They crossed the Riachuelo river on rickety rafts when policemen opened the bridges to stop them. Streetcars were rerouted, and trucks and buses were ordered to drive to the Plaza de Mayo. This spontaneous protest arose throughout Argentina. Everywhere, workers converged on towns and cities as if moved by an instinct or collective mind.[6] The image of workers giving rest to their tired feet in the fountain at the Plaza de Mayo became a lasting symbol of Peronism. This Day of Loyalty (Día de Lealtad) to Perón, as it became known, has provided the Argentine working class with an interpretation of history in which they became its protagonists; an inspiration on which they have drawn in times of repression and times of protest.

The Argentine workers took destiny in their hands by mounting the peaceful protest, so the myth goes, and expressed their loyalty to the hastily released Perón in a spiritual reunion at the Plaza de Mayo. Most Peronists believed in the historical protagonism of the crowd, and this conviction made Peronists believe in themselves as a movement, not an ideology or political party. The protesters were regarded as the authentic voice of the Argentine people who had a right to determine their destiny. This belief was carefully cultivated. On 17 October, according to Félix Luna, "the people had corrected the course of history."[7] In this founding myth, Perón and the Peronist movement gave birth to each other on 17 October 1945. The masses were "driven by a dark and undetainable instinct, almost without leaders or a prepared plan."[8] In this rendition, nothing stood between the emotions of these humble people and their call for Perón. But was the popular mobilization of 17 October 1945 really so spontaneous?

The intellectual debate about the events on 17 October 1945 has crystallized into three positions. Gino Germani emphasizes the irrationality of the mass protests, and attributes the success of the Peronist movement to the able manipulation of impoverished, ignorant, and leaderless rural migrants by the charismatic Perón.[9] Murmis and Portantiero argue, on the other hand, that the mass support of Perón was entirely rational and self-interested. The unions asserted their political might and mobilized the workers to defend a leader who had championed their rights and delivered social reforms and better working conditions.[10] Finally, Torre and James have provided in my opinion the most accurate account. They show that the worker mobilization was prepared by the union confederation and instigated by local representatives.[11]

Torre and James explain that under pressure from locally declared strikes in Rosario, Greater Buenos Aires, and the province of Tucumán, the CGT union central decided on 15 October to call for a national strike on 18 October. Everywhere, workers were prepared for action by union representatives to give expression to their feelings of exploitation and social exclusion. However, on 16 October, it became clear that the protest could no longer be contained. Meatpacking plants were picketed at daybreak, workers in other branches of industry were alerted about the upcoming strike, shopkeepers were warned not to open their establishments, and several street protests erupted in the outskirts of Buenos Aires. The 17 October mobilization occurred because the rank and file had already been put on the alert by the CGT decision to strike on 18 October.[12] Even though the precise moment of the mobilization was not orchestrated, the strike directive of the CGT and the grass roots work by local labor representatives had been essential.[13]

The image of 17 October as a popular feast has been debunked by Daniel James. Félix Luna speaks of a "festive atmosphere," a "great party," and an "orgiastic, triumphant" event.[14] Myth and reality are again at odds. James reveals the secular iconoclasm of the day. He interprets the mass mobilization as a Bakhtinean ritual reversal of traditional hierarchies in which workers danced in the streets as in "a form of 'counter-theatre,' of ridicule and abuse against the symbolic authority and pretensions of the Argentine elite."[15] There were outbursts of violence against the symbols of hierarchy. Buildings were stoned, stores pillaged, and windows broken in 167 major incidents. Centers of leisure, like the Jockey Club, offices of conservative newspapers, and student bars and lodging houses, were favorite targets in various cities. There was at least one death to mourn. Stones hurled at the offices of the antiPeronist newspaper *Crítica* were answered by gun fire, killing one seventeen-year-old demonstrator and wounding forty.[16]

Daniel James and Juan Carlos Torre have given the most accurate account, with a sharp eye for the feelings of worker resentment that built massive adherence to Peronism, but they pay little attention to actual crowd experiences. However, these profound feelings are indispensable to understand the founding myth. It was the crowd experience that remained most vivid to participants, and that gave the day its mythic quality. I therefore turn again to 17 October, asking four questions related to the formation of the crowd. Why would workers respond to a call for mobilization? How did they experience being in the crowd? What conception did activists have of the crowd as a political phenomenon? Why did the representation of the crowd as a spontaneous protest become the hegemonic version of 17 October?

It was not just the threat of economic and social deprivation or the strike preparation by the labor unions that drove people to the streets, but rather the injury to the feelings of dignity articulated effectively by Perón. The decades before the rise of Perón were marked by exploitative and humiliating labor relations. Perón's policies tried to remove the origins of these "stings of command," to use Elias Canetti's trope, but it was at the 17 October crowd gathering at the nation's capital that these resentments and humiliations were emotionally shed en masse. "For that period at any rate they were free of stings and so will always look back to it with nostalgia."[17]

Canetti's thought is suggestive, and can be supported historically because the stings of command were real experiences of oppression. The violence directed at the symbols of oppression can only be understood in conjunction with the joy of throwing off the yoke of exploitation and the fraternal equality felt by the workers. Peronists drew strength from the event for decades on end, and its spirit made them soldier on in times of repression.

Another reason why people responded to the mobilization was the existence of a rival crowd. Street demonstrations in Argentina often become a competitive show of force between opposing crowds. The first major street mobilization by workers, on 12 July 1945, protested a proclamation by landowners and industrialists against Perón. The opposition responded with street demonstrations on 9, 10, and 11 August whereupon the military government declared a state of siege.[18] The fire of opposition was kindled. On 19 September, the middle classes demonstrated for free elections and against the Farrell-Perón military government. The march expressed anger at the junta that had been contained since May of that year. As V-Day crowds in Europe were celebrating, street celebrations were forbidden in Argentina. The police declared that they had discovered a communist plot to create disturbances, unleash a revolutionary strike, and overthrow the government.[19] The end of World War II was openly celebrated on 31 August, and this street mobilization soon developed into a call for a return to a constitutional government in Argentina.

The public resentment at the Farrell-Perón military government culminated on 19 September 1945 in a peaceful crowd of roughly one-quarter million people who walked from the National Congress to Plaza Francia, singing the Marseillaise and shouting "National unity hurts Perón" and "From corporal to colonel, let them return to the barracks."[20] The march was described as a spontaneous mobilization, surprisingly similar to that of the upcoming 17 October crowd. "The people of Buenos Aires experienced yesterday one of its greatest days. Lacking means of transportation, they mobilized, organized, engaged in and won a great battle for the cause of democracy. . . . The need to walk five or ten kms. to keep an appointment with their own honor as citizens didn't scare away men and women determined to much more than that. . . ."[21] The newspaper *La Prensa* observed that the streets of Buenos Aires had never witnessed such a large crowd. 17 October was going to rival this crowd as in a contest. Both crowds fought for freedom, but freedom meant different things to the two social groupings. The middle class wanted freedom of speech, an end to the state of siege, and the restoration of civil liberties. The freedom of the working class was emancipatory, observed Luna, "to look upon the foreman as an equal, to feel protected by the union representative, not to hear every moment the bark of misery. . . ."[22] 17 October was thus an outpouring of feelings of oppression by the working class in rivalry with the middle class.

How did the participants experience 17 October as a crowd? Canetti has suggested that, "It is for the sake of this equality that people become a crowd and they tend to overlook anything which might detract from it."[23] 17 October was not by chance both a celebration and a riot. Just like in carnival, it became a ritual reversal of hierarchy and an expression of equality. Working-class people appropriated a public space that had been the privilege of "decent people," the *gente decente* who had demonstrated on 19 September. They did so in defiance of established codes of dress and conduct as they danced in the streets in their working clothes, and refreshed themselves in the fountain of the Plaza de Mayo.[24] Seen from Canetti's perspective, the mixture of violence and elation is therefore not as contradictory as it might seem. The 17 October crowd was not one homogeneous mass but was comprised of several crowds with several causes and objectives. Many celebrated the freeing of Perón, others experienced a sense of personal dignity, while still others turned with violence on the symbols of oppression. The violence was an expression of anger directed at the sources of subjugation. The euphoria came from the removal of the stings of command, and the sense of equality that was experienced in the crowd. These feelings became inscribed in people's crowd memory and touched each following Peronist crowd with its mythic unity and aggrandizement.

Why did the founding myth of Peronism as a spontaneous movement in search of Perón become hegemonic, despite many indications to the contrary? Belief in a spontaneous mobilization is most attractive from a political perspective and most persuasive emotionally. It invokes effervescence and feelings of equality which only derive from the crowd itself, not from external forces. Understandably, the evocation of the spontaneity and equality of 17 October gave way to nostalgia when the political fortunes of the Peronist movement turned, when demands were no longer met, and the overall living conditions of the working class worsened. Peronists of succeeding generations continued to long for another 17 October of fraternization, hope, and dignity that became so indispensable to the Peronist identity.

Politically, the myth was attractive because it could accommodate various interpretations that suited Peronist leaders, supporters, and opponents alike. Each party to the event cherished its own account of the mobilization. Union workers considered the demonstration as the purest expression of the popular will. The rank and file recognized themselves in the throngs of ordinary people accompanying them to the Plaza de Mayo. In turn, Peronist union leaders saw 17 October as legitimizing their pivotal role in the Peronist movement by channeling the feelings of discontent into an organized protest. Perón himself stated that the Day of Loyalty took place because he had prepared the Argentine working class for his leadership. The spontaneous mobilization was his harvest.[25] Surprisingly, the Peronist founding myth was also embraced by anti-Peronists. For the opposition, the protest was ominous evidence that a political movement could either turn into tyranny or mob rule. This hostility to Peronism was fed by a fear that popular crowds were driven by deep-seated irrational and violent instincts. Perón's opponents portrayed the 17 October crowd as irrational, primitive, and moved by bestial outbursts.[26] In sum, 17 October 1945 could readily be interpreted in different ways. Competitive versions of crowd conceptions must be examined further because the post-World War II crowds became such formidable players in Argentine politics from then on.

The Fear of Popular Crowds

The perception of the crowd as either a mass of people ruled by a strong leader or a mob threatening the established order has been common among political philosophers since antiquity.[27] This fear was given a theoretical foundation during the late nineteenth century, when mass psychologists like Tarde and Le Bon reflected on the political significance of the riots and insurrections of their times. Their ideas about the irrational and violent nature of popular crowds found willing ears in a turn-of-the-century Argentina where labor unrest was growing rapidly, and combative unions were being formed. In 1899 the physician José María Ramos Mejía published his book *The Argentine Crowds*. Ramos Mejía relied heavily on Le Bon. He drew an analogy between the individual and society, comparing the crowd with the body and the elite with the brain. In addition, he associated the crowd with madness and the elite with reason, concluding that "the day when the rabble is hungry, the organized socialist crowd will be relentless, and the leading agitators will be the perfect example of this virulent mob that will contaminate everything."[28]

These ideas pervaded Argentine police and justice departments. The image of a violent and culturally regressive crowd threatened to become reality as Argentine workers were becoming a distinct, class-conscious sector of society. Argentina was modernizing rapidly, attracting many European immigrants between 1865 and 1880. Exiles from the Paris Commune established an Argentine branch of the First International in 1872, and workers began organizing themselves in unions, boosting their demands with strikes and street protests. Anarchists and socialists multiplied during the last decade of the nineteenth century, and raised the class consciousness and combativeness of the workers.

A second immigration wave between 1900 and 1908 brought nearly two million people to the shores of the River Plate. These impoverished Europeans added social ferment to the labor movement. They had fled economic exploitation, and arrived in Buenos Aires with high hopes, only to find a sprawling capital in which workers received no better treatment than in their homeland. Political agitation and street protest were forms of resistance familiar from the old country.[29] The working class was coming of age, and popular crowds had become such a force in twentieth-century Argentine politics that Hilda Sabato talks of a "culture of mobilization" among disenfranchised Argentines. The streets and squares of Buenos Aires became "an arena of mediation between certain sectors of civil society and political power, through which relatively large numbers of people were involved in various forms of politically consequential public action."[30]

These mobilizations did not arise exclusively from a disaffected working class but were also organized by the middle class demanding universal suffrage for all men. This right was finally gained in 1912. In other words, there existed among the ruling elite a great suspicion of crowds in general, but of working class crowds in particular because of their revolutionary potential. Confrontations with the guardians of order were just a matter of time as the police began to fight strikes and protests with increasing force.

The first major strike was in 1902. The repression of the 1909 May Day celebrations led to the death of a dozen workers, and renewed protests in 1910 made the authorities declare a state of siege in Buenos Aires.[31] The police repression of striking metal workers in January 1919 cost the lives of four men. The confrontation by army and police of the protesters accompanying the funeral killed around thirty workers during what became called the Tragic Week (Semana Trágica).[32] At this time, workers were already carrying banners which demanded "dignity," a slogan that became Perón's rallying cry.

It was the fear of either mob rule or the manipulation of the masses by a dictator that frightened the middle and upper classes most, only months after the Allied victory over fascism in Europe. Thus, the 17 October 1945 protest did not come unexpected, while the ideas of Le Bon and Ramos Mejía about the irrationality of crowds provided a scientific framework to explain the events. The panicked reaction by some cabinet members on 17 October, upon hearing that column after column of workers was marching on downtown Buenos Aires, expressed their fear of the crowd. Navy Minister Admiral Vernengo Lima ordered an army captain to shoot at the crowd, but War Minister Avalos refused to ratify the order. General Avalos believed that the people would disperse quietly once word was out that Perón had been released.[33]

The negotiations between Colonel Perón and General Avalos during the late-afternoon of 17 October are unknown but possibly they agreed that only Perón's able manipulation of the crowd might avoid street violence and prevent a radicalization of the working class. The military's fear of a violent crowd taking revenge for Perón's political death was greater than the price of his reinstallation. Their belief in the likelihood of a social revolution had already been exploited by Perón in 1944 when he explained to Argentine industrialists how his aggressive policy of unionization had rescued the working class from the clutches of communist agitators.[34] Still, however opportune the temporary alliance with Perón might have been on

17 October 1945, the fear that some day he might incite these workers against the established conservative forces, or that the masses would disentangle themselves from his control, kept feeding the mistrust of Peronism among the elite and the majority of conservative military officers. Their understanding of crowds convinced them that this fear was justified when Perón tightened his grip on Argentine society, and the violence surrounding his fall from power in 1955 made them feel that their suspicion had been right all along.

Perón and the Masses

Perón's appearance at the balcony of the presidential palace at the Plaza de Mayo on 17 October 1945 was certainly one of the greatest political comebacks in Argentine history. His political career had begun three years earlier after a sojourn in Italy as a military attaché to the Argentine embassy in 1939 and 1940. Upon his return to Argentina in December 1940, he became a military instructor in Mendoza, and was assigned in March 1942 to the inspectorate of mountain troops in Buenos Aires.[35] Once in the capital, Perón founded a secret military society called the United Officers Group (Grupo de Oficiales Unidos). It consisted of twenty officers who were strongly anticommunist, wanted Argentina to remain neutral in the Second World War, and were appalled by the fraudulent politics of President Ramón Castillo. The Castillo government was overthrown in the coup of 4 June 1943, that would be the springboard for Perón's rise to prominence.[36]

Perón's leading role in the military lodge and his support for General Farrell as Minister of War in the new cabinet of General Ramírez resulted in his 7 June 1943 appointment as Undersecretary at the War Ministry. However, it was his appointment on 27 October as head of the National Labor Department that would bring Perón his greatest political windfall. He transformed the regulatory agency into the Secretariat of Labor and Social Welfare, and won the trust of the unions by taking their demands seriously. Farrell replaced Ramírez in February 1944 as Argentina's president. Perón became the new Minister of War, and was appointed as Farrell's vice-president in July 1944.[37] His sympathy among the working class and the political support from the labor unions were to be decisive when oppositional forces succeeded in ousting him from power on 9 October 1945.

Perón's rise from army instructor in 1941 to president-to-be in 1945 was meteoric. How much of the military instructor was still in him when he assumed power? How did he perceive his role as a national leader, and what was his relation to the working class? These questions are important to understand the Peronist movement, the suspicion of his control of the working class among his opponents, and the factional struggle that would lead three decades later to an incipient civil war.

Perón's acquaintance with fascism during his 1939–1940 stay in Europe has often been mentioned as a formative influence on his political style and ideology.[38] Perón was proud of his alleged contact with Mussolini, and may have even heard of his admiration for the French mass psychologist Le Bon. The sight of Mussolini's rallies must have convinced Perón of the transformative power of crowds.[39] Even after his fall from power in 1955, Perón's faith in the historical destiny of the masses remained firm. He wrote on 14 September 1956 from his exile in Caracas: "The Russian Revolution, Mussolini, and Hitler demonstrated to the world that the people and especially the organized masses are the politics of the future with which they buried the political parties that the countries still preserve as a vice from the twentieth century."[40] The crowd was for Perón the acme of the masses, and became a crucial weapon at decisive moments in his political career.

Perón saw it as his mission to prevent the radicalization of the Argentine working class. He rejected communism but also capitalism. Perón pursued a Third Position (Tercera Posición) that opposed class conflict and pursued social justice through a pact of capital and labor. His stay in Europe had made him realize that the political emancipation of the working class was an historical inevitability, and that unions were playing a growing role in achieving social demands. The simultaneous rise of fascism and communism taught him the important lesson that organization superseded ideology in mobilizing the masses. After all, both movements had equally drawn on the working class. As Perón wrote: "Le Bon anticipated us quite some time ago: 'The age we are entering will truly be the "age of the crowds.'" 'The destiny of nations is not created through the advice of princes but in the soul of crowds.' 'The divine right of crowds will replace the divine right of kings', etc."[41]

Le Bon's crowd theory had a great influence on Perón, whereas the works by Ramos Mejía and Taine were widely read in the nationalist circles of the 1930s that influenced Perón.[42] Like Le Bon and Ramos Mejía, Perón believed that the popular masses would turn violent without a leader, especially when they formed a crowd. "When a mass does not have any sense of leadership and one abandons it, it is not capable of going on by itself, and great political cataclysms will follow."[43] This view is consistent with his 1944 warning that an unorganized, inorganic mass is a dangerous mass. Since masses are by nature impulsive and destructive, they need to be educated to become organized masses. This education is the task of a leader, "because the masses do not think; the masses feel and have reactions that are more or less intuitive or organized."[44] When he became Secretary of Labor in 1943, Perón set himself the task to curb the potential violence of the masses and use their force to achieve long-term objectives. The spontaneous crowd had to be domesticated and harnessed into the mold of the

Peronist hierarchy. Perón perfected his mass control upon his political rebirth on 17 October 1945.

Perón drew on his military experience for political leadership, and perceived a structural similarity between the army and the organized masses.[45] He emphasized qualities like discipline, obedience, loyalty, camaraderie, and modesty, also found in the military, but set these in an emotional frame that exalted the honor and dignity of the Argentine worker. Part of his appeal came from tapping into and voicing the hidden injuries and injustices, resentment and exploitation of the Argentine working class.[46]

Perón did not want to instill workers with a combative class consciousness but to inculcate a leader-crowd model that stimulated their personal identification with him as their leader. "The first thing one has to do," Perón said, "is to awaken the sense of leadership in the masses. People can be better led when they are willing and prepared to be led."[47] Perón set out to disseminate his political doctrine among the Argentine workers and inculcate his ideas during crowd assemblies.

The complexity of Perón's political philosophy consists of his emphasis on both the equality of all Peronists—and by extension all Argentines—and on their fundamental hierarchical dependence on Perón and the party structure through unquestioned loyalty and discipline. Perón wanted to create an organization in which "there is nothing better for one Peronist than another Peronist." He tried to tie followers to him as their leader, while at the same time presenting himself as one of them, very much as a commander calls himself above all a soldier. The refrain of the Peronist march sums it up best: "Perón, Perón, How great you are. My General, how valuable you are. Perón, Perón, how great you are. You are the first worker." As a general, a soldier, and a worker, Perón institutionalized the popular crowds in Argentine politics. In his historic speech on 17 October he asked the crowd gathered at the Plaza de Mayo to create "a common bond that will turn the alliance between the people, the army, and the police indestructible."[48]

Perón had prepared the Peronist masses during his two years as Secretary of Labor and Social Welfare. He regarded himself as the only Argentine politician who had instilled the people with a sense of leadership, and this cultivation of an obedient mass made 17 October possible. "If the masses wouldn't have had the ability they had when the 17th of October lost its command and leadership, then they wouldn't have proceeded the way they did. The masses acted by themselves because they had already been taught."[49] In other words, the mythic spontaneity of the 17 October crowd had been sown by Perón during the preceding years. Expressing the dual quality of the crowd as both vertically and horizontally structured, he said "One doesn't lead a mass, but the mass only goes by reaction to where one wants it to go, thus fusing two factors: the individual will of the leader and the will of the mass which he knows to interpret at the right moment."[50]

The belief that there was true communication between Perón and the Peronist crowds is another ingredient of the 17 October myth. The people cheered for more than ten minutes when Perón arrived on the balcony of the Casa Rosada, the presidential palace at the Plaza de Mayo. After they had sung the national anthem, Perón greeted them with a single word: "Workers!" According to Luna, "From then on one wasn't hearing a speech but a dialogue."[51] Luna referred in particular to the insistent questioning of Perón by the crowd, "Where were you? Where were you?" Perón shunned the question because he did not want to refer to his stay at the island Martín García as an imprisonment. He responded that he had been making a sacrifice for the Argentine people which he would make a thousand times over if necessary.[52] This exchange became legendary and was followed by others that cannot be properly called dialogues but were rhetorical discourses in which Perón asked a question, used a slogan, or selected a cue from the crowd and incorporated this adroitly in an impromptu speech.

Spontaneity, peaceful demonstration, and dialogue between leader and crowd became the essential qualities sought for in all subsequent Peronist demonstrations. These ingredients had particular value for a new generation of Peronists born after 1945. Their interpretation of Peronism—a Peronism that had been proscribed since 1955—was that its essence rested in the dialogue between Perón and the crowd, and in the convergence of people and leader in the person of Perón.[53] Perón voiced and personified the genuine will of the people. Crowd and leader were believed to accomplish this spiritual and political alignment during the Peronist rallies. The magazine of the Peronist Youth described in 1974 this public dialogue as follows: "Between Perón and his people there is always this phenomenon of mutual nourishment: the crowd creates, Perón incorporates, Perón creates, the crowd recreates, and so the movement advances. . . ."[54]

Still, as is typical of all myths, they are rewritten whenever opportune to their believers. At the beginning of 1974, as the breach between Perón and the second-generation Peronists became clear, they began to circulate the unlikely story that Eva Perón had been the driving force behind 17 October, inciting the workers to take to the streets. Evita was represented as a revolutionary who preferred the worker masses over the Peronist Party and labor union bosses, beckoning them to overthrow the conservative oligarchy by force.[55] Yet, it was not through Evita's incendiary speeches but under Perón's tutelage that the Peronist crowd began to use violence as a means to achieve political goals.

The Violence of Popular Crowds

The fear that someday the Peronist masses would turn violent was always present among the Argentine middle and upper classes. The working class had become a political force that could no longer be ignored. Perón's brand of populism was tolerated because the elite believed that he might prevent a radicalization of the Argentine workers. The violent Tragic Week of 1919 was still fresh in their minds, and the Cold War had made a Soviet-backed resurgence of communism in Argentina a real possibility. The brazen-faced working-class crowds entering the heart of Buenos Aires might become easy prey to revolutionary agitators without the presence of Perón. These misgivings were shared by the Argentine Catholic Church because it was after all the Church which had monopolized the mobilization of popular crowds in processions and pilgrimages.

Initially, the relations between Perón and the Church hierarchy had been fine. The Church had supported his presidential candidacy in 1946, and Perón had embraced the Church's Social Doctrine and approved legislation that guaranteed religious instruction in public schools. What precisely sparked the disaffection between Perón and the Church is hard to determine, but in 1950 Perón began to state publicly that Peronism embodied the essence of the Christian faith, namely defending the poor, the down trodden, and the oppressed. His pronouncement that there was a spiritual unity between the Argentine Catholic Church and the (Peronist) State raised the suspicion that Perón was usurping the Catholic community.[56] In fact, Peronist youth and workers' organizations were depleting similar Catholic organizations of their membership. Furthermore, Evita Perón's Foundation which provided social assistance to the poor undermined the Catholic charity organizations.[57]

The Peronist crowds were even more unsettling to the Argentine Catholic authorities: they undermined the natural hierarchy deemed sacred by the Church, and provided a formidable competition to the religious crowds. 17 October had demonstrated what this subversion of hierarchy could do to people. The ritual reversals and the occupation of a public space hitherto reserved for the upper and middle classes undermined authority and their divinely given right to rule.

The threat of usurpation was an additional worry to the Church. The Peronist movement organized large crowds in an atmosphere with spiritual overtones. This became clear after the death of Evita Perón in 1952, and caused a considerable deterioration in the relations between Perón and the Argentine Catholic Church. The refusal of Rome to canonize Eva Perón added chagrin to the conflict, but it was the spiritual mobilization of the Argentine people for a dying Eva Perón without the involvement of the official Church that accelerated the crisis.

On 20 July 1952, the CGT union central organized a mass at the Plaza de la República to pray for Evita's health. One week later, on Saturday 26 July, she died of cancer. There was an outpouring of public mourning. People erected small altars in the streets in her memory and, for two weeks, more than one million people passed by her body in state at the CGT headquarters in Buenos Aires.[58] The Catholic crowds of the 1934 Eucharistic Congress led by the Argentine ecclesiastical authorities had been replaced by the 1952 Peronist crowds praying for Evita's recovery, and later mourning her death.[59] "The pastoral role of the Church seemed threatened," Lila Caimari has observed, "and its monopoly on massive religious mobilization became seriously questioned."[60]

There was an increased crowd mobilization after Eva Perón's death. There were torchlight processions in remembrance of Evita, demonstrations supporting Perón, and welcome crowds as he returned from foreign visits. Embattled by anti-Peronist forces and amidst an economic crisis, Perón called for a show of force on 15 April 1953. Overconfident because of a massive working-class backing in the 1951 elections (in great part made possible by Evita's efforts to obtain female suffrage in 1947), he threw in his lot with the working class and alienated his middle class supporters. In a radio address, he threatened "the internal and external enemies" of Argentina, while the CGT ordered a general strike and organized a crowd mobilization at the Plaza de Mayo. A notorious rhetorical exchange developed when Perón responded to two bombs that suddenly went off nearby: "Comrades, comrades! I think we're going to have to go back to the days when we went around with garrotes in our pockets." The crowd chanted, "Perón! Perón! Punish them! Punish them!" And Perón replied, "This thing about punishment you are telling me to do, why don't you do it?"[61] Even though Perón asked the crowd to return home quietly, the message was clear. Irate Peronists attacked the seats of the Radical party (UCR) and the Democratic National party, and burned down the headquarters of the Socialist party and the Jockey Club, the exclusive meeting place of Argentina's landed elite. Police and firemen were standing by passively as the fire burned priceless libraries and art treasures. The greatest loss was caused by two anonymous bombs that killed seven people and wounded ninety-three at the Plaza de Mayo. The arrest of around four thousand anti-Peronists intensified the polarization in Argentine society.[62]

Two weeks later, during his speech at the 1 May demonstration, Perón tried to rein in the street violence by asking the crowd to leave matters to him. However, he also threatened the opposition with unleashing the crowd's destructive force: "I ask you, comrades, not to burn down anything anymore, not to do those things. Because when something needs to be burned down, then I will go ahead of you. But then, if this would be necessary, then history will record the greatest bonfire that humanity will have lit until today."[63] The fears of those weary of 17 October seemed to be coming true. Perón had the people in his grip. He had inculcated a leader-crowd model that allowed him to manipulate the popular masses. Perón's militant language drove his opponents into one camp, a camp that became reinforced with the powerful Catholic Church when Perón directed his attention to Argentina's youth.

Perón repeated often that the youth held the future of the Peronist movement, and his words proved prophetic in the 1970s.[64] The Union of High School Students or UES (Unión de Estudiantes Secundarios) was the principal organization to captivate the youth. The UES was conceived in 1953 as a sports organization with separate branches for boys and girls. The combination of rumors about Perón's more than normal interest in the adolescent girls using the sport facilities of the presidential summer home at Olivos in January 1954, and the annoyance of anti-Peronist parents at the growing hold of the State on their children, led to the charge that the Peronist rule was morally corrupt. When priests advised parents from the pulpit to keep their daughters away from the UES clubs, time was ripe for a showdown in the streets of Argentina.[65]

The crowd became an obvious choice of weapons in a society in which "to win the street" (*ganar la calle*) had been a successful Peronist tactic since 17 October 1945. The Student Day celebrations on 21 September 1954 in Córdoba became the first major occasion for a public contest. The march of the Peronist UES drew an estimated 10,000 high school students, while the rally organized by the Catholic Action (Acción Católica) gathered 80,000 participants.[66] This shocking defeat worried Perón. On 10 November 1954 he pointed an accusing finger at Córdoba's Bishop Lafitte as an enemy of the government and threatened to release the Peronist masses into the streets.[67]

The surprising defeat of the Peronist mobilization in Córdoba was followed by an even stronger blow in Buenos Aires. On 8 December 1954 the Church was to celebrate the Feast of the Immaculate Conception and the end of the Marian Year. That same day, the Argentine people were invited to accompany Perón to the Aeroparque airport for a homecoming welcome of Pascual Pérez, the new world champion boxer. The arrival of the flyweight boxer had been deliberately planned to coincide with the religious ceremony at the Plaza de Mayo. A crowd of 100,000 to 200,000 faithful greatly surpassed the reception crowd of 4,000 at the airport. The people overflowed the cathedral and inundated the Plaza de Mayo.[68] The crowd had symbolically ousted Perón from the square he had dominated for nine years. In revenge, Perón annulled the 1946 legislation that had made religious education compulsory in public schools.

No longer able to win the street, Perón harassed the Church by legalizing divorce and prostitution. These reprisals drove larger crowds of disaffected Argentines into the streets, and coalesced an array of anti-Peronist forces around the Church. In the ten months following the Immaculate Conception victory, twelve large Catholic demonstrations took place in Buenos Aires. These crowds formed generally after mass in the cathedral at the Plaza de Mayo, often resulted in violent confrontations with Peronist supporters, and ended in the arrest of Catholic demonstrators. Meanwhile, the retaliatory exchanges between the Peronist government and the Argentine

Catholic Church continued unabated. Perón declared on 20 May 1955 the official separation of Church and State. The Church responded with a pastoral letter postulating the divinity of the Church and prepared for a massive show of force that developed into a tragic crowd contest.[69] Many factors contributed to Perón's downfall in 1955, such as a lackluster economy, military discontent, the restriction of civil liberties, and Perón's growing authoritarianism, but most scholars agree that the ongoing power struggle with the Argentine Catholic Church was the most important cause.[70] This conflict was fought out prominently in the street as crowd competitions between Peronists rallied around Perón and anti-Peronists galvanized around the Church.

June 9, 1955, was the day for the traditional Corpus Cristi procession around Plaza de Mayo. Pretending concern about the disruption of traffic in the business center, the archdiocese asked for permission to postpone the procession to Saturday June 11. The real objective was to maximize attendance. The request was denied but the Church went ahead as planned. A combative Perón responded to this challenge: "For every person our enemy can bring out, we shall bring out ten."[71] The boxer Pascual Pérez was enlisted to draw the competing crowd. Pasqualito had successfully defended his title in Tokyo, and a celebration was organized on June 11.

Perón's bluff ended in total failure. Only a small Peronist crowd appeared at the Luna Park celebration against 100,000 to 250,000 people who gathered at the Plaza de Mayo. The crowd walked in silence through Avenida de Mayo to the National Congress, carrying the yellow papal flag and waving white handkerchiefs.[72] The crowd was religious in name but political in nature. Even noted anti-Catholics participated in this demonstration congregating anti-Peronists from all political persuasions and walks of life.[73]

The Peronists had to respond to this public humiliation. An analogy with the 19 September 1945 Constitution and Liberty March was forced upon them. Perón warned that "those who sow winds can reap storms," and added fuel to the situation by expelling two bishops from Argentina for inciting the troubles of 11 June. The CGT union central announced a 24-hour strike on Tuesday 14 June as a show of support to the government, and began to prepare its members for mobilization.

On Thursday morning 16 June 1955 Perón was warned of a possible navy insurrection. In fact, the coup d'état had been in the making since February but the organizers had not succeeded in gaining enough support from the army, even though there were widespread anti-Peronist sentiments in the force ever since the failed rebellions of September 1951 and February 1952. The discovery of the plot demanded swift action. An air strike on the presidential palace had been planned for 16 June at 10:00 A.M. to assassinate Perón. Armed civilian groups would move in to secure the seat of government. The attack planes would take advantage of a fly-over planned in tribute to the Argentine flag which had allegedly been burnt during the Corpus Cristi demonstration.[74] Dense fog prevented the planes from taking off on time, but when they finally did and released their fragmentation bombs at 12:40 P.M., the devastation among the people assembled to watch the fly-over was horrendous. One bomber made a direct hit on the Casa Rosada. The first civilians were killed by the shattered glass of the Treasury Ministry. Many more casualties fell when a bomb hit a trolley. Perón was unhurt. He had taken refuge in the War Ministry that morning after hearing of rebellions at the Navy Mechanics School (ESMA) and Ezeiza international airport.[75]

A second bombardment was carried out at 1:10 P.M. which again caused many deaths. Meanwhile, groups of Peronists began arriving at the Plaza de Mayo. Shouting "Perón, Perón," they gathered in front of the Casa Rosada. Was this crowd spontaneous or organized? A parallel appears with 17 October 1945. The rank and file had been put on the alert and acted when the crucial moment arrived. A small crowd had already congregated at the Plaza de Mayo before the call for a general mobilization went out. At 1:12 P.M., the CGT issued an urgent broadcast: "Comrades, the CGT gave a slogan on Tuesday: On the alert! The moment has arrived to carry it out. All workers of the Federal Capital and Greater Buenos Aires must gather immediately near the CGT building [Independencia and Azopardo streets]. All means of transport must be taken, willing or unwilling. Comrades! Instructions will be given at the CGT building. The CGT calls upon you to defend our leader. Gather immediately but without violence!"[76] Within half an hour, a large number of people had congregated at the CGT building. The same Avenida de Mayo, where five days earlier the silent Corpus Christi procession had taken place, was now filled with vehicles carrying workers coming to the rescue of Perón, as they had done one decade earlier. A number of workers were killed by machine-gun fire as they arrived at the Casa Rosada.[77]

The final aerial assault took place around 3:30 P.M., when a squadron dropped their bombs and killed many soldiers and civilians in the zone of action before the pilots fled to Uruguay. Army troops loyal to Perón succeeded in reconquering the Plaza de Mayo. The toll of the four-hour insurrection was 355 dead and more than 600 wounded.[78] For the first time in Argentine history, a popular crowd had been attacked with weapons of war. Peronists were dumbstruck. The boundless Peronist crowd had revealed its weakness, and this awareness had a traumatizing effect that changed forever the self-perception of Peronist street mobilizations. The excessive violence, the hundreds of dead and the impunity of the attacking forces would be recalled in future decades whenever a Peronist crowd was under the threat of repression.

Perón was equally shocked. He had been dismayed earlier that day by the call of mobilization. "Go back to the CGT," he told a messenger, "and tell the CGT that not one worker should go to the plaza."[79] However, it was only after the fighting had ceased that Perón's message was received. Clearly, Perón had temporarily lost control over the Peronist crowd. Even his plea to the workers, in his 6:00 P.M. radio address, to control their anger, and reseal the indestructible bond of people and army, fell on deaf ears. The acute social trauma incurred by the brutal killings made the Peronists seek revenge.

The metropolitan curia at the Plaza de Mayo was the first target of the angry crowd. The interior was destroyed and its valuable archive torched. Reminiscent of the assault on churches by rioters upon the assassination of the popular Colombian leader Jorge Gaitán in April 1948 or the icono-clastic attacks by the Republican Left on the Church during the Spanish civil war, the demonstrators mutilated statues and dressed themselves in sacred vestments. Seventeen churches were ransacked and partly destroyed by fire as police and firemen looked on.[80] The gutting of the curia of Bue-nos Aires on 16 June 1955 became the symbolic reversal of 17 October 1945. Here was finally the true face of the popular crowd, according to the political opposition. Typical LeBonian terminology pervaded their lan-guage. The editor of the Catholic magazine *Criterio* described the protesters as subhuman, "totally immoral, without sensitivity, without education, with a smell of alcohol, living off women, gambling and theft. . . ."[81] The crowd had finally raised its ugly head and revealed its true nature.

Street protests continued to be a means of political pressure and legitimi-zation in the months ahead. John William Cooke, the head of the Peronist party, favored street mobilizations and the formation of an armed militia with the slogan "Another 1945" (*volver al 45*).[82] Perón began to have grave doubts about his power base. He admitted to having curtailed civil liberties, declared the end of the Peronist revolution, and promised to be president of all Argentines.

Perón's offer of a truce was too late. The Church hierarchy continued with its critique, dissident officers were planning another coup, and anti-Peronists held frequent street demonstrations. Perón had a daring answer. He announced his resignation on 31 August 1955. The CGT union central had been privy to Perón's decision, and had already planned a large dem-onstration at the Plaza de Mayo to express the support of the Peronist work-ers. Once more, 17 October 1945 cast its shadow over the crowd.

The people were in a joyous mood on 31 August, eating the soup, bread, and oranges distributed by the Eva Perón Foundation.[83] The tone of Perón's speech contrasted sharply with the crowd's peacefulness. Perón said that he had offered his hand to the opposition during the two-month truce, but that they had responded with violence. Now, there were only two roads open: the government must repress the subversion, or the people must retaliate. Unleashing his following and giving free reign to violence,

Perón authorized every Argentine to kill whoever undermined or con-
spired against the public order. "And from now on we establish as permanent rule for our movement: Whoever in any place tries to disturb order
against the constituted authorities, or against the law and the Constitution,
may be killed by any Argentine. . . . The watchword for every *peronista*,
whether alone or within an organization, is to answer a violent act with
another violent act. And whenever one of us falls five of them will fall."[84]
Perón's terrible threat and the CGT's insistence on the formation of an
armed militia convinced his opposition within the armed forces that the
time was ripe for a final assault.

The Liberating Revolution (Revolución Libertadora) was launched on
16 September 1955 when General Lonardi rose in rebellion in Córdoba
together with all major naval bases. Perón declared a state of siege but did
not advance on the rebels with loyalist troops. On 18 September, Rear-
Admiral Rojas broke the stand-off by threatening to bomb the oil deposits
in Buenos Aires harbor and the oil refinery in La Plata. The next morning,
naval salvos destroyed the oil deposits in Mar del Plata. Perón feared a further escalation, delegated his army command, and took refuge in the Paraguayan Embassy on 20 September. Later, he moved to a Paraguayan gun
boat anchored in the harbor of Buenos Aires, and finally left Argentina on
3 October by a twin-engine flying boat with Asunción as its destination.[85]

Why did Perón give up his presidency so easily? By late August 1955, only
a handful of the around ninety generals were committed to Perón's overthrow. Once the rebellion got under way, Lonardi's rebel troops were surrounded and outnumbered ten to four by General Iñíguez's loyalist
troops.[86] Close associates advised Perón to open the weapons deposits and
arm the workers but Perón dreaded the idea of civil war and the scenes of
destruction he had seen in Spain in 1939.[87] Instead, he placed his hopes
on a peaceful solution by mobilizing his Peronist following as he had done
a fortnight earlier, on 31 August. Yet, the people remained at home. Perón
realized that he had lost the crowd contest with the opposition.

The crowd mobilizations of 17 October 1945 and 16 June 1955 had
shown that something more was needed than a union directive to make
people take to the streets. Somehow, the feelings were no longer there
among the people to motivate another massive show of force at the Plaza
de Mayo. We can only guess at the passiveness of the Peronist workers, but
it is reasonable to assume that the bombardment on 16 June 1955 had traumatized the Peronist crowd. The crowd had responded with retaliatory violence, but could not redress the real and symbolic losses incurred. The
bombardment had revealed the vulnerability of the street crowd, demolished the edifice of invincibility and historical destiny erected by Perón,
and raised fears of future attacks. After the initial rage against the metropolitan curia at the Plaza de Mayo, the Peronist masses demobilized as if a
defeated army. The memories of the hundreds of dead were still too fresh

to carry through a massive resistance. Personal feelings of self-preservation, a lack of faith in Perón, and a sense that the tables had turned made most Peronists stay at home. There were small violent demonstrations in Buenos Aires on 23 September and in Rosario between 24 and 28 September but the repressive response of army and police ended the protests swiftly.[88]

The Coming of Age of Argentine Crowds

The figure of Perón looms large in the history of Argentine crowds. The streets and squares of Argentina became the scene of a variety of crowd demonstrations after the end of World War II. There were protest marches, religious processions, strike crowds, election rallies, commemorations, celebrations, belligerent crowds, and festive crowds.[89] Mass mobilizations had also occurred before World War II, but they only became a constant in Argentine politics when the populist leader Juan Domingo Perón came to power in 1945. The year 1945 marked a watershed in the history of Argentine crowds because it saw the birth of the working class as a principal player in the public arena.

The crowd on 17 October 1945 that rose to the defense of Perón was a cathartic crowd that shed an "infamous decade" (*década infame*) of frustration and disenfranchisement in a liberating identification with Juan Domingo Perón. Perón transformed the popular masses into impressive crowds which took center stage in Argentine political life. He provided the Argentine working class with a public forum to express their resentment of social, economic, and political wrongs. He established a link between the dignity of Argentine workers, their rights as full citizens of Argentine society, and their assembly in crowd mobilizations. The Peronist crowds affirmed and renewed these newly won privileges by gathering periodically in the symbolic heart of the nation, at the Plaza de Mayo with its Cathedral, presidential palace (Casa Rosada), and town hall (*cabildo*) where Argentina's independence from Spain had been secured.

The importance of the physical assembly of the Peronist following in a crowd cannot be overestimated. The Peronist crowd was essential for the transformation of injustice into dignity. According to Elias Canetti, crowds evoke irresistible feelings of unity and equality.[90] "It is for the sake of this equality that people become a crowd and they tend to overlook anything which might detract from it. All demands for justice and all theories of equality ultimately derive their energy from the actual experience of equality familiar to anyone who has been part of a crowd."[91] These sensations relieve people temporarily of society's "stings of command" left by institutional inequality and exploitation, precisely the social injustices and restrictive civil rights which Perón addressed. Such stings of command leave residues of resentment which can be shed temporarily in a crowd.[92] In other words, people can give free rein to their innate aversion of unjust authority and social injustice when gathered in a crowd. Even though Canetti's imagination took flight in essentialism and romantic extravagance, his suggestive ideas about society's stings of command help us understand the collective experiences of oppression, injustice, and exploitation that existed in Argentina at the end of World War II when V-Day celebrations were forbidden by an authoritarian regime fearful of a popular insurrection.

The 17 October crowd took on the mythic proportions of a popular mobilization which emancipated the Argentine workers, united them with fellow Argentines behind the banner of social justice, and represented for every Peronist the most supreme manifestation of identity, belonging, togetherness, dignity, and equality. These gatherings gave Peronists a sense of comradeship and community that transcended narrow class boundaries. The momentous 17 October 1945 and the tragic 16 June 1955 framed an era in which crowds made their presence felt in Argentine politics. Within one decade, Perón had inserted the working class into national politics and had turned the crowd into a familiar tool to achieve political ends. Winning the streets with a large crowd became an equally favorite weapon of power and legitimization for Peronists as well as nonPeronists.

Perón's crowd manipulation was condoned as long as he curbed the political radicalization of the Argentine working class. This tolerance ended when Perón became increasingly authoritarian and threatened to turn the Peronist crowds loose on the middle and upper class establishment. The presence of the Peronist crowds had been so great between 1945 and 1952 that political opponents could not help but enter into a crowd competition to dispute their dominance in an attempt to oust Perón. One segment of the Argentine people tried to protect Perón and the recent social gains, while another segment wanted greater civil liberties. This growing political opposition to Perón drove the middle classes into the streets, while the hitherto rigidly organized Peronist masses erupted inside Argentine society in uncontrollable ways, ways which would eventually draw the country asunder in massive violence.

Chapter 2
The Time of the Furnaces: Proscription, Compromise, and Insurrection

"There hung a murmurous atmosphere resembling the sea," one reporter wrote of the crowd that celebrated the installation of General Lonardi as Argentina's new president on 23 September 1955, "a constant surf of sounds: shouts and applause."[1] The people were in a festive mood on this warm first day of Spring. Some fainted from the heat and the crowd's pressure, while others refreshed themselves in the fountain at the Plaza de Mayo. The reporter compared the crowd to the Peronist crowds that used to monopolize the square, and asserted that never "has there gathered such a dense crowd as the one which yesterday tried to find a place at [the Plaza de Mayo] and overflowed into the converging avenues. . . ."[2] Perón had consecrated the Plaza de Mayo during ten years of mobilizations as the nation's foremost political arena where the Argentine people and the authorities determined their destiny. Packing the square with an immense crowd became henceforth a proof of political legitimacy for every future Argentine president and dictator.

The 23 September crowd expressed as much its support for the military government as its aversion of Peronism. The final years of Peronist rule with its increasing suppression of public speech, imprisonment and mistreatment of political opponents, curtailment of civil liberties, and the confrontation with the Catholic Church had blown deep divisions in Argentine society which had manifested themselves in several crowd competitions. The 23 September crowd marked only the first of several street mobilizations that legitimized the Liberating Revolution. There were crowds on 11 January 1956 to support the new Aramburu government, on 10 June 1956 to listen to President Aramburu after a failed Peronist rebellion, and on 16 September 1956 to celebrate the anniversary of the Revolution. Finally, there was a massive farewell on 21 October 1957 for a military junta which was voluntarily abandoning power through general elections in February 1958.

The repression of Peronist crowds after the 1955 coup became particularly harsh when the moderate Lieutenant-General Lonardi was pushed aside in November 1955 by the hardliners General Aramburu and Admiral Rojas. Four months after the palace coup, the Peronist party was declared illegal. Systematically, the Peronist Organization was dismantled and with it the dignity of the working class.[3] What became now of the leaderless Peronist masses? How would they be able to recapture their feelings of dignity, unity, and power without the presence of Perón, and what would motivate them to take to the streets and brave the repressive climate?

The prohibition of Peronist mobilizations had a tremendous impact which compelled Peronists to remember the 1945 Day of Loyalty through sabotage and undo the bombardment of the Plaza de Mayo with acts of defiance. Bombs exploded every 17 October and slogans were painted hastily on the walls. Canetti's stings of command accumulated again, not only in the working class, but also among a younger generation that had been raised with stories about the glorious days of Perón and Evita. Some guerrillas of the 1970s were only children in 1956 when they had their first brush with violence and repression. Ernesto Jauretche recalls how deeply the search for his mother affected him when she was arrested after the failed Peronist rebellion of June 1956. "The first time they took my mother, they also disappeared her. For one month, we searched for her everywhere but they told us: 'She's not here, she's not here.' We searched for her at military bases, everywhere. Executions were taking place and we didn't have any news about my mother, we didn't know where she was. The history of the disappearances is indeed very old."[4] Jauretche believes that this episode and the frequent visits to his incarcerated mother caused a profound class hatred that fed his political activity during the rest of his life.

These experiences were shared by many Peronists, and contrasted with happier and increasingly idealized memories of the Peronist years. Hardship and happiness shaped militant Peronists who romanticized about Eva Perón helping the poor and the sick, the jubilant Labor Day crowds at the Plaza de Mayo, and the holidays at the seaside resorts built for the workers. Added to these memories came the traumatic bombardment of the Peronist crowd on 16 June 1955 and the frustration of not being able to manifest the loyalty to Perón and his ideals, because if the crowd was not the progenitor, then it was certainly the womb of the Peronist movement. As Perón wrote on 3 November 1956 to John William Cooke: "I have given them an organization, a doctrine and a mystique. I have worked eleven years to politicize the masses. I have prepared them to fight against a reactionary response and I have left them with an example of how to achieve important reforms."[5] The leader-crowd relation stood at the origin of the mystique of Peronism, and the obstruction of the public expression of that sentiment, either in crowds or in votes, added fuel to its manifestation in surrogate forms such as strike mobilizations, protest marches, illegal gatherings on commemorative days, public disturbances, and street violence.

In this chapter, I concentrate on the attempts to express Peronist sentiments in public by establishing a diverse presence in the streets of Argentina's large cities. These public manifestations had an emotional and a political component. The protests arose in reaction to the repression of Peronist sympathies and from a grass roots belief in popular insurrection as the best strategy to restore Perón to power. Strike crowds and small public outcries of Peronist sentiment were at their most intense between 1956 and 1959, only to come to a standstill after increased police and military repression. The labor movement fractured into several segments which each pursued its objectives with different political instruments, only to reappear again with revolutionary fervor in 1969.

Retreat and Reconquest

The leaders of the Liberating Revolution saw Peronism as a belated outcrop of fascism. Its elimination would grant Argentina the same post-war prosperity as Europe and the United States. Decree 4161 of March 1956 prohibited all references to Perón, Evita or Peronism. President Aramburu only spoke of Perón as "the monster," and newspapers identified him as "the fugitive tyrant." The display of his pictures and books, the singing of Peronist themes, and the commemoration of days important to the Peronist movement were forbidden. The expression of Peronist sentiments and identity markers was banned from public space. Any violation was punishable by a prison sentence, and would bar the violators from assuming a political or union office.[6] These anti-Peronist measures were experienced by Peronists as anti-working-class measures. The Argentine workers were expelled politically from the city centers to their poor neighborhoods in the periphery.

Decree 4161 turned the shouting of Perón's name in public into a small act of resistance in which, at least for a few seconds, the street was retaken. There were many such instances, and they turned into a civil disobedience that became more violent with the day. Jorge Rulli became involved in the political struggle after the failed Peronist rebellion of June 1956. He attended the silent protest marches in Buenos Aires that attracted two to three thousand people, and felt the brunt of the revolutionary civil commandos that had emerged in the resistance against the Peronist government in 1954 and 1955. These commandos were workers affiliated with the Socialist and Radical parties. They took over Peronist union branches and suppressed public expressions of Peronism. In 1956 and 1957, young Peronists began to dispute the center of Buenos Aires with these civil commandos. Their motto was to win the streets for Peronism.

Public space was conquered through physical confrontations with bludgeons or bare hands. For example, Rulli's group would hang a photo of Perón at the corner of Corrientes and Esmeralda Streets in Buenos Aires, and lie in wait for their victims. Every person who tore down the image was severely beaten. Thus, they intimidated passersby into not reacting at all on any public expression of Peronist sentiment. They sang the Peronist march and shouted "Viva Perón."[7] The shouting of Perón's name united the orphaned Peronists in their yearning and enhanced their desire to manifest their allegiance together. These protests were the response of a dispersed crowd in search of something or someone around which to gather.

Perón himself continued to have faith in the masses.[8] Civil resistance would wear out the government and organize a general strike paralyzing the country and inciting a mass insurrection. He emphasized that it is important to hit "when it hurts and where it hurts" as well as to learn to "throw a stone and hide the hand."[9] However, the majority of the Peronist following was not receptive to such insurrectional disobedience. John William Cooke, Perón's head of resistance in Argentina, complained in June 1957 that there was considerable sabotage and widespread aversion of the government, but that "This mood doesn't translate, however, into a total civil resistance in the way that we would like."[10] Cooke's assessment was correct at that particular moment, but unjustified when seen over a longer period of time. Strike mobilizations became the hotbed of political militancy that fed into an insurrectional movement of slow maturation. Peronists would have to wait fourteen long years before the moment for insurrection appeared.

Strikes and Barricades

The first major strike after Perón's fall occurred between 13 and 16 November 1955 to protest the usurpation of union locales by non-Peronist unionists. These confrontations between Peronist and non-Peronist workers demonstrated that the Liberating Revolution had cut right across class lines. As James has observed, an anti-Peronist (*gorila*) could just as well be an oligarch as a fellow worker.[11] Many Peronist workers adhered to the November strike, but did not manifest their protest publicly. Workers and union delegates were arrested, and an inspector-general appointed by the government took control of the CGT.[12] One worker recalled years later that "there were no protest marches, nor assault groups . . . it was a calm, peaceful strike as though the workers had still not got over the shock caused by the fall of the Leader. . . ."[13] Perón's fall had a devastating effect on the Peronist movement which had deemed itself almighty.

Compared to the previous five years, there was a great willingness to strike in 1956, but this disposition declined significantly in 1957, only to increase rapidly in 1958 and 1959.[14] The national elections of February 1958 had been won by Arturo Frondizi of the Radical party (UCR) thanks to the Peronist vote ordered by Perón. Frondizi extended his hand immediately to the unions by withdrawing the inspector-general from the CGT union central. Nevertheless, major strikes struck his government after July. Most strikes in 1958 were organized by non-Peronist unions. Peronist union leaders were still supporting Frondizi because of his conciliatory attitude and legislation that reinstated the Peronist supremacy in many unions.[15] When Frondizi implemented a wage freeze in late 1958 to resolve a serious imbalance of payments, the unwritten pact with the Peronist unions was broken.

The year 1959 became a watershed for government and labor. In confrontation upon confrontation, the two parties were staking out their territory and redefining the rules of engagement. The unions were defending worker employment and the principal tenets of Peronism, namely social justice and national sovereignty. Instead, Frondizi wanted to diminish Argentina's dependence on agricultural exports and develop its industry by attracting foreign capital and raising labor productivity. The privatization of the Lisandro de la Torre meatpacking plant on 14 January 1959 fitted perfectly in his development plan. However, there were strong nationalist and Peronist sentiments attached to the plant. Like the railroads, the Lisandro de la Torre plant had been nationalized by Perón. Its privatization was felt as another retreat from the Peronist policies and a sell-out to foreign capital.

Upon hearing the news about the privatization, nearly nine thousand workers gathered in general assembly and decided to occupy the plant. Solidarity strikes erupted throughout the country through grass roots activism, instead of union leadership. On 17 January, fifteen hundred policemen, gendarmery, and soldiers accompanied by four Sherman tanks assaulted the Lisandro de la Torre plant.[16] What concerns me here are not the mass arrests and the eviction of the workers, but the street protests that broke out afterwards and their interpretation by the Peronist resistance movement. This local insurrection in Buenos Aires (known as the *porteñazo*), showed that strikes about labor issues might easily escalate into political confrontations attracting the solidarity of other social groups. Behind each general strike, there lurked the danger of an insurrectional crowd.

The Frigorífico Nacional Lisandro de la Torre was located in Mataderos, a working-class neighborhood of Buenos Aires. The police assault was received with indignation. Mataderos and adjoining neighborhoods turned into a barricaded zone of resistance as had never been seen before in Argentina. According to the clandestine Peronist National Command or CNP (Comando Nacional Peronista), thousands of young workers joined the struggle. A new generation of Peronists had become incorporated into the Peronist movement. They cut the street lights, overturned trees, and erected barricades.[17] Meanwhile, Mataderos was enveloped in the stench of rotting flesh from the corrals surrounding the meatpacking plant. Due to the insurrection, the animals had been left without care in the high summer temperatures.[18]

The CNP document exalted the combativeness of the Argentine working class, and regarded the general strike as a confirmation of the central position of the Peronist masses in the struggle for national liberation. Only the Peronist rank and file had thrown itself entirely into the struggle to protect the national patrimony, while many union leaders had struck unacceptable compromises with the government.[19] Here, a conflict surfaced that had been brooding for several years between on one side the so-called integrationist unions which pursued an accommodation with the government to save what there was to save of the embattled labor conditions, and on the other side the intransigent unionists and the vanguardists. The intransigents rejected all deals and engaged in sabotage, while the vanguardists of the CNP tried to organize a guerrilla insurgency. The events in January 1959 led the CNP to believe that they and the intransigents, not the integrationists, were in step with the people.

The CNP report mentioned also the mass appeal of the general strike. Not just the workers of Lisandro de la Torre, but workers from other branches of industry as well as students and shopkeepers joined the protest. Yet, the general strike was never at any moment an insurrection because of the absence of a recognizable political leadership which could have planned the general strike, provided armed support, and thus achieved more success.[20] Nevertheless, the Lisandro de la Torre protests fed dreams of future insurrections, taught valuable lessons about how to better organize the popular defenses, and added one more episode to the memory of the Peronist resistance movement.

Frondizi took the strike movement very seriously. He had already declared a thirty-day state of siege on 9 November 1958 to deal with the Mendoza oil workers' strike, and kept renewing it till a military coup ended his government on 29 March 1962. The state of siege did not prevent workers from striking throughout 1959, but the protests met with little success.[21] The Lisandro de la Torre plant continued in private hands, and only half of the nine thousand workers were rehired. Strikes of bank employees and textile and metal workers were broken, and street protests were facing new tough repressive measures as the Frondizi government installed the CONINTES Plan (Plan de Conmoción Interior del Estado) on 14 March 1960. This Plan of Internal Upheaval of the State had been put in place by Perón on 16 September 1955 to make headway against the growing opposition that would end in the Liberating Revolution. Now, the same repressive measures were used to curtail the Peronists. The CONINTES Plan gave extensive powers to the armed forces dealing with public disturbance. The country was divided into defense zones and subzones; an organizational structure which was used again during the 1976–1983 dictatorship. The police was placed under the command of the armed forces, and the country became subject to martial law on 16 March 1960. The CONINTES measures were suspended on 2 August 1961, but the state of siege continued unabated.[22]

The labor strikes dropped dramatically in Buenos Aires city from over ten million working days lost in 1959 to 1.6 million in 1960, and then declined rapidly to less than three thousand days in 1967.[23] Thousands of militant unionists had been blacklisted, and factory managers were granted extensive powers over their workers. Rising unemployment in a worsening economy, the CONINTES repression, and the realization that the strikes and street protests of 1959 had accomplished little, had disillusioned the rank and file. Understandably, many workers drifted into the orbit of integrationist union leaders who could at least achieve some modest material advances through their negotiations with the government. Occasional street protests became instrumental means during negotiations instead of emotional manifestations of political sentiment. The street presence became always related to sectorial interests, and only seldom acquired the transgressive quality of the previous five years. During this period, a division developed between integrationists who pursued a strategy of pragmatic negotiation and intransigents who continued with a grass roots resistance. The intransigents would eventually split into those who tried to incite a mass mobilization that intended to overthrow the ruling powers, and those who joined the vanguardists and propagated a guerrilla insurgency.

Integrationism, Intransigence, and Vanguardism

The 1959 tug of war between the unions on one side and the government, armed forces, and industry on the other, disconnected the political goals from the economic objectives of the Peronist workers. The call for Perón's return had been a motivating force in the labor disputes since 1955, but became a remote ideal as more pressing economic concerns arose after the 1959 defeat. The façade of Peronist militancy was maintained in order not to betray the hardships suffered by the rank and file, but a new style of union politics was taking shape. The years between 1961 and 1966 were times of institutional pragmatism.[24] Institutional pragmatism implied a strategy of "hit and negotiate" (*golpear y negociar*) in which strikes, work stoppages, and factory occupations were used as bargaining tools.[25] It led to the growing isolation of militant union activists from the majority of the Peronist workers organized by the integrationist unions. Sabotage never ceased entirely, but it was the work of small groups. Militant Peronists were admired by their co-workers for their tenacious resistance to the authorities, but their political intuition was no longer trusted.

The dominance of the integrationists pushed the intransigents to the margins of the Peronist movement. Most former activists joined the unions in their move towards political moderation. Intransigent workers in Buenos Aires were ousted from Peronist unions, and reorganized over the years into two small groups.[26] The most militant intransigents became involved in guerrilla warfare. The other group continued with their sabotage and political work in factories and neighborhoods. These intransigents-turned-insurrectionists hoped for a return to the crowd mobilizations of the Peronist era, and became convinced that nothing should be allowed to stand between the masses and Perón. However, despite their rhetorical appeal to the myths of the past, they lacked a clear conception on how to mobilize the masses, and wean the rank and file from the bosom of union clientelism.[27]

Many workers recognized that the institutional pragmatism had reaped material results. The integrationist union leaders summoned a large following, and had the means to maintain people in a clientelistic relation. They controlled the union dues and pension funds, maintained health clinics, gave jobs to loyal members, and acted as brokers between labor, management, and the government. In return for swallowing rationalization schemes, greater managerial control, and an overall depolitization on the work floor, the workers received fringe benefits such as maternity benefits, bonuses for years of employment, and furloughs on social occasions.[28] Still, the workers rejected the personal life styles of the union leaders, the corruption, bodyguards, expensive cars, and imported whiskey. Rubbing shoulders with politicians and captains of industry, union leaders stood at a growing distance from the oppressive climate on the work floor. The workers were also bitter about the fraudulent union elections, and the removal of shop floor union representatives considered too radical. A clear indication of this withdrawal was the declining participation in union elections. In other words, the pragmatic stance of the workers conflicted with how they experienced this process emotionally.

This unresolved tension between material gains and emotional losses worked itself out in a crowd demobilization. Labor conflicts in the first half of the 1960s were increasingly confined to the work place, and did no longer transbord into the streets and squares of the major industrial cities. The Peronist workers had lost their leader in 1955, yet his ideas continued to be of collective inspiration, but his place remained vacant and was not occupied by either integrationists or intransigents. The crowd as a political means in a conflict and as an emotional force for its participants failed therefore to materialize.

The gap between intransigents and integrationists was as much vertical as regional. The integrationist union leaders dominated labor politics in the city and province of Buenos Aires and at the national level, but they were less influential in the city of Córdoba. Córdoba had become Argentina's second largest industrial center since the arrival of Fiat in 1954 and the IKA car manufacturer in 1955. Local unions kept their independence from the overbearing union centrals based in Buenos Aires and cultivated an internal democracy which maintained an active participation of the rank and file in union politics. Attempting to prevent the Peronist union establishment from dominating the newly founded auto industry of Córdoba, the Aramburu government had granted in 1956 the union rights of the IKA auto workers to the tiny garage mechanics union SMATA (Sindicatos de Mecánicos y Afines del Transporte Automotor), and not to the Peronist UOM metal workers union (Unión Obrera Metalúrgica). The embattled UOM in Córdoba adopted therefore a more hard-line, intransigent position than both the Buenos Aires UOM and the UOM union central.[29]

The SMATA auto workers union in Córdoba pursued a line relatively independent from the national union centrals. Peronists commanded only a small majority in SMATA, and had to tolerate a critical communist presence. SMATA succeeded in raising the number of shop stewards on the work floor and organized open assemblies at which workers could express their opinions. Various governments did not succeed in preventing the politicization of the auto workers. Grass roots participation forged the workers' identification with the union and with each other. This solidarity would become crucial in the considerable crowd mobilizations of 1969.[30]

The bloc of Independents, a group of unaffiliated unions not subject to the Peronist union centrals, played a pivotal role in Cordoban union politics. Many members were anti-Peronists with strong Radical, socialist or communist sympathies. The bloc stood under the inspired leadership of Agustín Tosco, the secretary-general of the light and power workers union Luz y Fuerza. Despite a membership of less than three thousand members, the union occupied a strategic position in Córdoba because of its ability to cut off the city's power supply. The militancy of the electricians can be attributed to their grass roots involvement in union issues cultivated by Tosco and the inability of the union centrals to assume control over the Cordoban working class. The prominence of the Independents in Cordoban labor politics prevented local Peronist unions from slipping into the soft-line strategies of the Buenos Aires unions, and made Luz y Fuerza spearhead an uncompromising position towards the government.[31]

So, at the beginning of the 1960s, there were two major currents in the Peronist labor movement: intransigents and integrationists. The intransigents were mainly based in Córdoba. They were more prone to take to the streets to lend force to their demands, and were ready to enter into loose alliances with non-Peronist Independent unions to further their interests. The intransigent union leaders were not averse to pragmatic negotiations to achieve concrete gains, but did not give in entirely to the integrationism of the Buenos Aires-based union centrals.

Peronism Without Perón

In control of the majority of the Peronist workers, the integrationist union leaders in Buenos Aires began to acquire political aspirations. Augusto Vandor, the leader of the powerful metal workers union, succeeded in placing unionists on the provincial election slates. The resounding victory on 18 March 1962 of Peronist candidates in nine provinces, including the province of Buenos Aires, triggered the downfall of the Frondizi government.[32] The armed forces did not tolerate a Peronist victory, let alone the return of Perón to Argentina. The elections were annulled on 19 March, and Frondizi was arrested on 29 March. José María Guido was sworn in that day as head of the transitional government. General elections were held on 7 July 1963.[33]

The 1963 elections were won by Arturo Illia of the Radical Party (UCR) with only 25 percent of the total vote because the proscribed Peronists cast blank votes en masse.[34] In the eyes of many Peronists Illia lacked the legitimacy to lead the country, while the union leaders feared his desire to cut their clientelism and improve the internal union democracy.[35] The opposition to Illia's government began with nationwide Peronist demonstrations on 17 October 1963 to commemorate the Day of Loyalty and proclaim a popular mobilization. The protesters demanded new general elections, the withdrawal of all repressive measures, an embargo on the export of capital, extensive nationalizations, and the return of Perón.[36] Perón had declared on New Year's eve of 1963 that he would return to Argentina before the end of 1964. Economic and political demands merged again. The political climate added increased credibility to the slogan "Perón returns" (*Perón vuelve*) which began to appear on street walls throughout Argentina. A massive rally was held at Plaza Once on 17 October 1964 attended by more than one hundred thousand people. On the economic front, almost four million workers participated in the occupation of eleven thousand factories during seven operations between 21 May and 24 June 1964.

Ironically, it was Perón's attempt to return to Argentina which provided Augusto Vandor with an opportunity to displace him from the pinnacle of the Peronist movement.[37] Perón tried to enter Argentina on 2 December 1964 but the Argentine military asked the Brazilian authorities to deny him free passage. Perón was ordered to disembark in Rio de Janeiro, and forced to await the return flight to Madrid.[38] The failure of Operation Return gave Vandor an important political victory. He had demonstrated his unfailing loyalty by accompanying Perón on his ill-fated trip, and could now return to Argentina with the laurels of his heroism.

Vandor tried to use his newly gained prestige to consolidate his political influence in the Peronist movement during the March 1965 congressional elections as he maneuvered his candidates into the key tickets of the Peronist Unión Popular. When the votes had been counted, there were seventy seats in the House of Representatives for Illia's Radical party UCR and fifty-two seats for the Unión Popular.[39] For the first time since 1955, Peronists returned to Congress, now under the tutelage of the UOM leader Augusto Vandor. The victory would be short-lived because a military coup on 28 June 1966 deposed President Illia and brought retired General Juan Carlos Onganía to power.

The Onganía dictatorship proclaimed the beginning of the Argentine Revolution which sought to consolidate the nation's moral and spiritual values, jump-start the stagnant economy, improve labor relations, and uphold the ideals of dignity and freedom which were the patrimony of Argentina's Christian and Western civilization.[40] These ideals were implemented by closing Congress, dissolving the political parties, and dismissing the Supreme Court.[41]

The coup was initially welcomed by the principal union leaders José Alonso and Augusto Vandor because the Onganía government suspended many measures of the Illia government intended to curtail the political power of the labor unions.[42] The Cordoban union leader Tosco stood practically alone in his condemnation of the military takeover, while Vandor and Alonso were prominently present at the swearing in ceremony.

The first blow to the unions came in August 1966 when the government imposed obligatory arbitration on labor conflicts and denied collective bargaining and the right to strike.[43] In line with the hitherto successful hit and negotiate strategy, Alonso and Vandor organized strikes. In Córdoba, auto workers went on strike and the Independent union leader Tosco organized work stoppages. The Onganía government, on the instigation of the National Security Council (CONASE) headed by General Osiris Villegas, responded with surprising harshness. Unions were placed under the control (*intervenido*) of inspectors-general, bank accounts frozen, and strikes and street demonstrations prohibited. In 1967 there were only six strikes in Greater Buenos Aires, in which no more than 547 workers participated.[44]

In the two years following the defeat of the union protests, the union leadership disintegrated into a collaborationist, a participationist, and a combative bloc. The collaborationists, headed by Juan José Taccone and Rogelio Coria, were willing to submit workers to the government's tutelage. Instead, Vandor and Alonso wished some degree of participation in the collective negotiations with the government to bargain for more favorable labor conditions. Finally, the combative union leaders condemned the accommodating attitude of the other two blocs and demanded a return to active resistance. In their opinion, the pact between labor, government, and capital had led the labor movement away from the class struggle and the pursuit of a socialist revolution. The combative unionists provoked a breach within the CGT union central in March 1968 and formed the CGTA (Confederación General de Trabajo de los Argentinos), also known as the CGT de Paseo Colón, under the leadership of Raimundo Ongaro. The

CGTA received the support of most unions in the provinces, including Tos-co's electricians union and the UOM metal workers union in Córdoba.[45] The collaborationists and the participationists constituted the CGT de Azo-pardo under the control of Augusto Vandor.[46]

The incendiary speech in Córdoba on 1 May 1968, by CGTA leader Ong-aro, had all the tenets of the revolutionary discourse of the coming unruly years. He denounced the growing power of foreign multinationals and the dependence on the IMF and the World Bank. He condemned the high infant mortality, the slums on the outskirts of Buenos Aires, and the many infectious diseases that troubled the poor. He verbalized the images of an impoverished Argentina many had seen in Fernando Solanas' impressive 1966 documentary *The Hour of the Furnaces* (*La Hora de los Hornos*).[47] Ongaro called upon students and intellectuals to join the workers in combating the nation's social ills.[48] Precisely in this period, the struggle of the combative Peronists took a revolutionary turn, as Carlos Villagra testifies: "The revolu-tion became possible for us and we began to talk about organizing our-selves in a totally different way. The people wanted to fight, wanted to confront the system. . . . It wasn't just the return of Perón, it was no longer throwing a stone or placing a pipe bomb. We said already that the system had to be changed, that a revolution had to be made. People were already saying that the struggle was going to be long and extensive. Peronism must make a revolution, yes or yes."[49] The CGTA combatives embarked on a col-lision course with the Onganía dictatorship that culminated in June 1968 in a series of street protests in Argentina's major cities.

After initially backing Ongaro for mobilizing the Peronist following, Perón became suspicious of the Marxist leaning of the combative CGTA and had in the end more faith in the institutional continuity of the old union establishment than a revolutionary union leadership which was hard to control.[50] However, the CGTA had put a militant momentum in motion which was hard to stop. Perón sensed the widespread resentment and emphasized in September 1968 the importance of a civil disobedience and mass protests comparable to Gandhi's anticolonial struggle in India.[51]

Vandor also sensed the growing discontent among the rank and file. He declared war on the dictatorship in May 1969, and began to regain some of the ground lost after the partition of the CGT in March 1968. The influ-ence of the CGTA dwindled rapidly. Their street mobilizations were repressed, they lost the support of Perón, and Vandor's new oppositional strategy preempted their struggle. Nevertheless, the combatives continued to be a power to reckon with in Córdoba.[52]

The institutional pragmatism and participationism of the 1960s had pro-vided basic subsistence needs to many workers in times of political disen-franchisement.[53] Yet they had also created enduring hatreds within the labor movement. Vandor and Alonso were assassinated in 1969 and 1970 by hit squads of the revolutionary left for being traitors to the Peronist movement. The reign of the imposing union bosses had come to an end, and it was up to the rank and file to take the initiative again. A new generation of mostly young Peronists began to take the crowd initiative which the pragmatic union leaders had abandoned in the early 1960s. These revolutionary Peronists succeeded in dominating the streets with large demonstrations that would eventually contribute to the return of Perón in 1972. They created the means for an expression of Peronist sentiments submerged for a decade. Crowds gave the participants an identity and esprit de corps that could never be attained in equal emotional measure by institutional pragmatism, clientelism, and participationism. The political vigor was in the hands of a new generation of Peronist leaders who were untainted with the comforts of a union office, and who dreamed of seeing Perón raising his arms in salute from the balcony of the presidential Casa Rosada. The longing for these crowd sentiments was nowhere stronger than among the young second-generation Peronists who had never experienced them.

Crowd Alliances: Students, Workers, and Peronists

The involvement of young Peronists in the street conquests during the second half of the 1950s, as described earlier in this chapter, came to an abrupt halt in 1960. The crackdown on the Peronist worker resistance also imprisoned many youth leaders and incapacitated the Peronist Youth organization or JP (Juventud Peronista) founded in late 1957.[54] Surprisingly, their place was taken by the student body, an unsuspected segment of society that had always shown an aversion to Perón and his mass movement.

The rapprochement of university students and young working-class Peronists was rooted in the student protests against Frondizi's 1958 proposal to allow the foundation of private universities. Rectors and students opposed the legislation because it would lead to the creation of private Catholic universities with a conservative curriculum. Street fights took place around the National University of Buenos Aires as rival groups of students in favor or against the legislation tried to occupy the buildings. Many students and young Peronist working-class activists received their fire baptism together in these clashes. So also did an adolescent Ernesto Jauretche who came from a family of militant Peronists, and became impressed by the battles with the police near the Medical School: "There, I saw the police back away for the first time. I saw the police run, I saw them fall under a shower of stones. For the first time I saw what a street fight was. There I began to learn throwing stones, to fight. . . . to see them withdraw was thrilling, to see the police run away suddenly gave a rush of happiness. It was marvelous. I think that this was for me the beginning of almost a linear process and so it was for almost all the other activists. . . . We began to discover there that they were not invulnerable."[55] The street opposition culminated on 19 September 1958 in a protest crowd of about three hundred people who listened to speeches by politicians and student and union leaders. Frondizi's bill was defeated in the house of representatives, amended and approved in the senate, and finally adopted by Congress.[56]

The social and ideological rapprochement of workers and students intensified considerably in the early 1960s as increasingly more students began to have leftist political sympathies. This radicalization was world-wide, and had to do with the rebellious mood of the times. The radicalization of students in Argentina had its roots in the development of an intellectual new left which stood initially under the influence of Sartre's existentialism and later became attracted to Marxism. Sartre argued that the objective structures of exploitation did not predetermine people's consciousness, but that people were active subjects who produced history. Volition entered the political thought of Argentine intellectuals, a volition demonstrated in practice by the Cuban revolution.[57]

These heterogeneous influences fell in fertile soil among the Argentine students of the early 1960s. They were a disenfranchised generation which felt politically gagged by the proscription of Peronism, the repeated military coups, and the paternalism of the authorities. The former Montonero guerrilla commander Fernando Vaca Narvaja recalls the growing social consciousness of his student days: "The university begins to embrace Peronism, begins to nationalize itself in the sense that the student breaks with his own isolation, his own environment and begins to develop . . . a social commitment with his people. . . . We became close to the working-class neighborhoods through social work."[58] Student leaders wanted a curriculum that addressed social rather than purely scientific problems, and a research agenda that relieved the poor health and social distress of the underprivileged classes. The working class was, in the eyes of students and intellectuals, the only social sector in Argentine society with a true revolutionary potential. Solidarity with the working class in their struggle against the ruling powers was an inevitable step, even if many workers were Peronist and not socialist.

The July 1963 amnesty of Peronist activists incarcerated in 1960 gave a new impetus to the political alliance of students and young Peronists. The Peronist Youth held its first national congress on 27 October 1963 and elected Héctor Spina, Envar El Kadri, and Jorge Rulli as the executive committee. Perón supported the insurrectional convictions of these leaders. He reiterated in a letter of 20 October 1965 that the JP must "Have a close relation with the masses—the tactics and strategy must fuse with the masses—never forget that the combatants emerge from the masses and that revolutionary work is impossible without support from the masses."[59] Similar ideas were heard in the prisons of Caseros and Villa Devoto where militant Peronists were held. John William Cooke invited university students to join the Peronist movement because they could help raise the revolutionary consciousness of the working class.[60] The time of dialogue had passed. Time had come for a revolutionary takeover. This revolution had to be fought with all means at its disposal, and should not shun the use of violence.

The rapprochement of students and workers was watched with growing concern by the military. Soon after Lieutenant-General Onganía came to power in 1966, he sought to curb the student radicalization by assuming control over the universities. Presidents, rectors and deans lost their autonomy and became administrators in service of the Ministry of Education. The law of 29 July 1966 stipulated that student centers were forbidden to engage in political activities.[61] These repressive measures provoked a nationwide protest of students and faculty.

At 10:00 P.M. on 29 July 1966, about two hundred students barricaded themselves with benches and desks inside the Faculty of Architecture and Urban Studies in Buenos Aires. Similar occupations occurred at other faculties of the National University of Buenos Aires (UNBA). The Infantry Guard of the federal police responded eagerly.[62] On the evening of 29 July, policemen ordered students to vacate the Faculty of Exact Sciences within fifteen minutes. After the time was up, the men forced their way in with tear gas while angry students pelted them with all sorts of objects. Once inside, the students were forced to walk the gauntlet with their arms held up high while policemen wielded their rubber batons on the protesters.[63] Warren Ambrose of MIT, who was a visiting professor at the time, gave the following eyewitness account to the *New York Times:* "The police entered firing tear gas and ordered everyone to face the wall with our hands up. . . . As we stood blinded by the tear gas against the walls of the classrooms, the police then began hitting us. Then one by one we were taken out and forced to run between rows of police spaced about 10 feet apart. That is when I got seven or eight wallops and a broken finger. No one resisted. We were all terrified, what with the curses and gas."[64] This incident gave the event the memorable name the "Night of the Long Sticks" (la Noche de los Bastones Largos). The police authorities claimed that their actions had been provoked by the student violence. Their press release emphasized the political character of the occupations stating that Marxist literature and contribution slips to the communist party had been found at the Faculty of Architecture.[65]

The Night of the Long Sticks spoke to the imagination of all Argentine students, and came to stand not only for the beatings and the hundreds of arrests, but also for the exodus of thousands of professors abroad and into private research institutes. The long-term economic and intellectual loss of this brain drain is hard to assess but the political cost became clear immediately. Students and faculty were driven to the political opposition by a dictatorial government whose repressive measures, authoritarianism, and budgetary neglect of the universities contributed to the escalation of violence in Argentine society.[66] Four years later, Onganía confessed that his approach to the universities had been a serious political error: "It was our first big mistake. And we committed it thirty days after getting into power through a coup."[67] The public beatings, arrests, interrogations, and incarcerations during the Onganía dictatorship became markers of political initiation for students that made them kindred in spirit to Peronist activists and intransigent unionists, radicalizing them towards armed resistance.

The repression of the student protests was also a mistake from a crowd perspective. The police drove the students literally and figuratively speaking into the streets. Members of the Peronist Youth entered the university to forge the ties between workers and students.[68] The crowd began to supersede the unions and student organizations as the principal social collective to which people adhered and through which they expressed their anger. As Moyano has observed, the first step to political involvement consisted often in attending a solidarity meeting, a protest rally, or a street demonstration in the company of friends.[69] Such experiences had a radicalizing effect, especially if accompanied by police violence.

The student-worker alliance erupted with full force in 1969 with three memorable crowd events in Rosario and Córdoba. The day of street fighting in Córdoba on 29 May has become known as the Cordobazo.[70] This violent crowd will be discussed in the next chapter because of a historical significance which places it on a par with the epoch-making 17 October 1945. Here, I discuss the events of one week earlier in Rosario because, unlike the Cordobazo, the Rosariazo on 21 May 1969 was initiated by students instead of workers.

As is so typical of major crowd gatherings in Argentina, the events in Rosario of May 1969 had been preceded by months of small street mobilizations. Since the beginning of the year, students had been objecting to the curtailment of student enrollments. These protests were successful in the faculties of Philosophy and Letters, but restrictions continued in other disciplines. Although not all demands were met, the students realized that their demonstrations were effective, and that the authorities were tolerating the street protests. It was in this turbulent climate of May 1969 that student restaurants were privatized, and meal prices raised.[71]

The student opposition arose in the northeastern provinces of Santa Fe, Corrientes, and Entre Rios.[72] Classes were boycotted, student restaurants were occupied, and daily street protests were held in the towns of Rosario, Corrientes, and Resistencia. The students understood that the authorities had no intention of reversing the price hike, and began to approach social sectors sympathetic to their demands. Students in Resistencia sought the support of progressive forces in the Catholic church, while students in Corrientes asked for help from Ongaro's combative CGTA and Tosco's electricians union. Of particular importance was the labor unrest among metal workers in Rosario where three hundred workers were confronted with a lockout. The UOM called for a general strike on 23 May 1969.[73]

The tense situation escalated when police in Corrientes attacked a street demonstration on 15 May, wounding four students, and killing the nineteen-year-old Juan José Cabral.[74] The indignation was nationwide, and unions condemned the disproportionate police response. The UOM national headquarters expressed its solidarity with the students in Corrientes and the striking workers in Rosario, while continuing to strengthen the links between the two sectors: "We refuse to accept the hunger to which they are submitting us, and the violent repression of every form of protest. We already know that the regime kills, here in Corrientes, in Córdoba, or in any other place. They are killing the best we have: our young students and workers."[75] The protests multiplied in all major Argentine cities, and a student strike was announced for Tuesday 20 May. The students intensified their protests during the intervening days when another casualty fell to police bullets. Rosario was this time the location of police brutality.[76]

On 17 May, there were the usual daily demonstrations in Rosario. The Night of the Long Sticks was casting its shadow over the protests when protesters linked the death of Juan José Cabral two days earlier to that of Santiago Pampillón, a student and part-time auto worker who died in September 1966 during a student protest in Córdoba. Some activists were carrying molotov cocktails and shouted the slogan "Cabral and Pampillón, the martyrs of the road to freedom."[77] That afternoon, groups of students were throwing stones at the police and at several financial institutions in Rosario, when police officer Lezcano stepped out of his car and shot the student Adolfo Ramón Bello through the head. According to a police communiqué, the victim was part of a group that had cornered the officer, thrown molotov cocktails, and tried to overturn his car. The officer drew his pistol in self-defense and fired an accidental shot which killed Adolfo Bello.[78]

The killings provoked a public resentment impossible to appease. The students called upon everybody to repudiate the deaths of Cabral and Bello in a silent protest march on 21 May. The demonstration was called for six o'clock in the evening at the Plaza 25 de Mayo in downtown Rosario. The trajectory of the march was to run for twelve blocks from the square to the headquarters of the CGTA. As an indication of the alliance between students and workers, secretary-general Raimundo Ongaro promised to address the crowd at the end of the protest march. On the way to the CGTA building, the demonstrators intended to pass by the shopping center where Adolfo Bello had been shot four days earlier.

At this stage of the month-long demonstrations, the authorities were faced with a crowd that was no longer concerned with the conflict over expensive meal tickets, but wanted to mourn their dead in a collective gathering and control public space as a political protest. Police and military mounted an impressive force at three core locations. Their defense capability of fire engines and assault cars was concentrated around the Plaza 25 de Mayo. The force wanted to prevent the protesters from gathering there before they proceeded to the CGTA offices where also several radio stations, the court, the university's administrative center, and the police and army headquarters were located. The march through the city symbolized a political supremacy which the security forces were not willing to concede.

At six o'clock in the evening, about two thousand protesters are circulating around the Plaza 25 de Mayo. Many are students, but there are also blue- and white-collar workers. They try to enter the square in small groups but are immediately dispersed by the police, whereupon they try to circumvent the barrier through another passage. The tug of war undulates back and forth through the streets of Rosario until the police decides to attack. They launch large quantities of tear gas into the streets, and charge on horseback towards the protesters. The crowd disperses but regroups seven blocks away from the square in the direction of the CGTA headquarters.

A new element is added to the volatile situation when people begin to burn papers in the street, initially to neutralize the tear gas. Fires can be seen at various places and are even fed by local residents who throw paper onto the street. The protest begins to acquire an insurrectional appearance when barricades are erected to halt the advancing security forces. Buses are overturned and building materials are taken from construction sites to reinforce the improvised obstructions. The protesters even go on the offensive. They attack the mounted police and throw them off their horses. At 9:20 in the evening, the police withdraw from the area in the direction of their headquarters near the CGTA offices. The jubilant crowd can finally form a whole, and begin to advance on their trajectory, shouting slogans about the unity of students and workers. Protesters force their way into the LT8 radio station, and destroy the furniture when they cannot enter the studio. Others try to advance to the CGTA building, but are stopped by a barrage of tear gas and gunfire from the police. The fifteen-year-old metal worker and high school student Luis Norberto Blanco is killed. The crowd disperses at midnight, and Rosario is placed under martial law.[79]

The high price for maintaining public order in Rosario was two dead adolescents, many wounded, and the much-feared alliance of students and workers.[80] The inordinate police repression of the student-worker crowd evoked a mutual identification with each other's suffering and forged a new social configuration through collective violence. The protest crowds were fast on their way to becoming insurrectional crowds which in the political heat of the times threatened to consolidate into a revolutionary movement.

The Resurrection of Peronist Crowds

By the end of 1969 Peronist crowds had finally resolved the social trauma of the 1955 bombardment, overcome the fear of violent repression, let go of their dependence on Perón, and become once again aware of their strength. The yearning for expressing discontent in the presence of tens of thousands of equally indignant protesters, and the moral example of uncompromising Peronist workers resisting oppression, had slowly swayed a growing segment of the Argentine working class towards an historic crowd alliance with a politicized student body in Argentina's radicalized universities. These crowds were summoned by grass roots mobilization and lacked national leaders. The fear of the revolutionary crowd among the military, upper, and middle classes was becoming a reality.

The Argentine military had tried to rein in popular crowds in various ways after 1945. Their strategies arose from two assumptions: first of all, crowds are irrational by nature and potentially subversive of the established order, and second, the Argentine people had an inbred tendency toward crowd mobilization. The popular mobilizations between 1945 and 1955 were tolerated in the belief that Perón could control the passionate crowd and prevent its political radicalization. The strategy changed to selective repression between 1955 and 1960. Middle class crowds were encouraged, whereas Peronist crowds were forbidden. The occasional street demonstrations during the crowd interlude between 1961 and 1969 can be characterized as strike crowds because they were in most instances directly related to major labor disputes. Negotiation had taken the place of repression by 1961 as pragmatic union leaders obtained material benefits for the rank and file without taking resort to street protests. This crowd demobilization strategy worked until 1969, when street crowds returned with a vengeance.

Chapter 3
A Breeze Turned into Hurricane:
The Apogee of Crowd Mobilization

The revolutionary insurrection of tens of thousands of workers and students, raising hundreds of barricades and fighting off police and army during two days of pitched battle on 29 and 30 May 1969 in Córdoba, constitutes the second crowd myth of twentieth-century Argentine history. Lieutenant-General Alejandro Lanusse recalled in 1977: "I sensed on that difficult 29th of May in 1969 that something was happening in the country, something new whose uniqueness I tried to gauge within the framework of my greater worries. I couldn't know in what it would end, how I would react to the events, or what were the indirect and deeper causes. But I became convinced that other elements, unusual until then, were entering the political reality and the way in which we were living this reality."[1] These "other elements" were snipers belonging to a tiny communist party with grand ambitions.

The tragedy of May 1969 consists of the widespread myth that the events in Córdoba were the beginning of a revolutionary process that could only be advanced or stopped with violence. This fatal conclusion gave a decisive impulse to an urban guerrilla insurgency intent on leading the masses to victory and an entrenched military determined to halt the revolutionary process through indiscriminate repression. The outburst of collective violence in Córdoba became known as the Cordobazo, and has been hailed and condemned as the beginning of a social revolution that ushered in a decade of mass mobilizations, guerrilla insurgency, and a deadly factionalism within the Peronist movement ending in the coup of March 1976.

The military and the radicalized left did not doubt that the Cordobazo signaled a revolutionary moment in Argentine history. Lieutenant-General Onganía declared that: "The tragic events in Córdoba responded to the actions of an organized extremist force intending to produce an urban insurrection."[2] The Marxists interpreted the Cordobazo as an expression of class consciousness: "On May 29, 1969, the people of Córdoba flung themselves into the streets to reveal all the hatred accumulated during years of misery, exploitation and humiliation. . . . The just fury of the people poured like burning lava through the city streets, demolishing whatever vestige of exploitation crossed its path, trapping and harassing the police which, overrun by the crowd, left the city in the hands of the working class and the people."[3] The Workers Revolutionary Party (PRT) concluded that the latent yearning for revolutionary change on 17 October 1945 became redirected into the reformist program of Perón, but that the Cordobazo signaled a qualitative jump towards a social revolution. "The breeze has turned into a hurricane. History, the real history written by the people, is in motion."[4] The working class had liberated itself from its patronage by Perón, and would finally realize its revolutionary mission.

The Cordobazo marked a watershed in mass mobilization. The rank and file took the initiative without Perón or the national union leadership. The street demonstrations between 1969 and 1972 arose from uncontainable grass roots resentments, while national union leaders tried in vain to hold their grip on the disgruntled working class by negotiating better labor conditions with the dictatorial government.

The Cordobazo also demonstrated the cracks in the vertical discipline and ideological purity of the Peronist movement. A decentralized unionism with political overtones of shop floor mobilization had developed. Ideological differences between Peronist and non-Peronist workers made space for a common opposition to the government. Labor demands continued to be made after 1969 but they must always be understood within a larger political framework that created an alliance among various social sectors. The working class became increasingly militant and was joined by middle class students. It was this grass roots protagonism that was feared most by the military. As Perón had already said in 1944, a leaderless crowd was dangerous to society because it could be taken advantage of by agitators and revolutionaries. The military, the union leaders, and the revolutionaries all concluded that the Cordobazo revealed that the fighting spirit of the Argentine working class remained unbroken despite years of military repression, and that its capacity for resistance had neither been domesticated by the Peronist hierarchy nor paralyzed by Perón's prolonged absence. On the contrary, the Cordobazo showed that the people could become violent, that the violence might be spontaneous, and that this collective violence was begging for the direction of a revolutionary vanguard. Those who succeeded in captivating the potentially violent collectivity could overthrow all principal institutions of society.

Cordoban Violence and Euphoria

The months preceding the Cordobazo had been turbulent. The Cordoban unions associated in the combative CGTA union central had held numerous street mobilizations against the deterioration of worker rights and called for mass mobilizations and armed resistance.[5] Cordoban students were protesting the restrictions on student enrollment, the raise in meal tickets, and the deaths incurred in Rosario and Corrientes. Metal workers were complaining about the unfavorable pay scale differences between Córdoba and Buenos Aires, while auto workers were angry about the increase of the work week by four hours. Cordoban bus drivers were intermittently on strike about a planned reorganization of public transport, and electricians were opposing the privatization of the provincial electricity company. Finally, Córdoba's middle class was upset by the higher property taxes imposed in early 1969.[6] Each social sector had its ax to grind with the Onganía dictatorship, but they shared a resentment of the abuses and injustices suffered. Their specific economic grievances were framed in a dissatisfaction with the political proscription and cultural patronizing by a dictatorial government which even forbade certain types of bathing suits.[7] Working class, middle class, and student resentment coalesced in May 1969. Two events in the streets of Córdoba set the tone of the protests and established the practice of violent engagement that was to erupt on an unimaginable scale.

The rescindment of the English Saturday was received with much indignation by the Cordoban auto workers. The English Saturday (*sábado inglés*) meant that certain categories of industrial workers in several provinces received a forty-eight-hour remuneration for a work week of forty-four hours. This privilege had been won in 1957, and the auto workers of the SMATA union assembled on 14 May to decide about their protest strategy. In the middle of a heated debate, the police launched tear gas into the enclosed space. Six thousand asphyxiated workers ran for the only major exit and once in the street were attacked. The workers responded with such force that the police fled from the scene.[8]

The second violent street confrontation occurred during protests against the death of Juan José Cabral in Corrientes. Together with workers from various Cordoban labor unions, thousands of students took to the streets on 23 May. Just as had happened a week earlier at the auto workers assembly, the police attacked with tear gas to disperse the crowd. The students retreated to the Clínicas neighborhood in downtown Córdoba and began to erect barricades. The police tried to overrun the makeshift obstacles but were repelled with molotov cocktails. It would take until the early hours of the next day before the police succeeded in conquering the area.[9] These two street victories enhanced the confidence of workers and students, sealed their political pact, and motivated them to press their demands with even more vigor. Street battle practices—mobilizations, barricades, molotov cocktails—that were established then were used with even greater intensity a week later.

On 28 May, student and union leaders met to coordinate the massive protest of 29 May. They anticipated a considerable police repression and divided the city into four zones of contestation in order to disperse the security forces. The workers of Luz y Fuerza (electricians), the UOM (metal workers), SMATA (auto workers), and UTA (bus drivers) would march upon the center of Córdoba from two directions, while the students were planning to gather near the university buildings in the city center or join the worker columns along the way. The final meeting place was the center (*casco chico*) of Córdoba where all major political, financial, and cultural institutions were located. The SMATA and Luz y Fuerza unions would supply their men with metal bars, ball bearings, caltrops (*miguelitos*), molotov cocktails, sling shots, and small firearms in case the police would try to repress the street mobilization.[10]

At around eleven o'clock on Thursday morning, 29 May, a column of four thousand auto workers depart on foot under the leadership of the Peronist SMATA leader Elpidio Torres from the IKA-Renault plant at Santa Isabel, eight kilometers outside the city. Their number swells with thousands of students and workers as they walk on the Avenida Vélez Sarsfield to the CGT union central headquarters in downtown Córdoba. Other groups of students advance from Avenida Colón together with the electricians and bus drivers, but are forced to take an alternative route when the police blocks their way. Elsewhere, workers abandon factories and also converge on the city. Meanwhile, the two principal columns are informed by motorized workers about the police forces ahead of them. Unlike the case of the Rosariazo where the police tried to prevent the crowd from taking shape, the police forces in Córdoba are determined to defend the center against the penetration of the advancing protesters. The situation escalates when the auto worker column reaches the Plaza Vélez Sarsfield several blocks from the CGT building, and only five blocks from Plaza San Martín. A large police force lies in wait. A confrontation becomes inevitable. The police shoot tear gas at the protesters, and are pelted in return with homemade tear gas bombs. As the crowd diverts to another boulevard, the police open fire and kill the worker Máximo Mena. Indignation reverberates through the crowd and angry protesters charge at the police who withdraw in haste to the Plaza San Martín.

The other column of workers and students headed by Agustín Tosco also encounters stiff police opposition. They are attacked at their gathering point outside the headquarters of the electricians' union. They succeed finally in crossing the six blocks that separate them from the autoworkers near the Plaza Vélez Sarsfield.

At one o'clock in the afternoon, the united crowd turns violent. Union leaders Tosco and Torres try to get a grip on the collective violence, but to no avail. Cars are overturned to erect barricades. Furniture is taken from stores and offices to reinforce the obstructions. Middle class residents participate actively in the protest, and throw paper on the street to feed the inflamed barricades. Every large display window in sight is smashed. When a car dealer tries to prevent his cars from being burnt in the street, one of the participants responds: "No complaints, sir. If you have so much money, then you must have taken it from the people. We are destroying what is ours. Because we can't take it home, we simply smash it to pieces."[11] The violence of the people is specifically directed at the symbols of repression and privilege: banks, government buildings, police stations, foreign companies, and luxury stores.

Tosco remarks that afternoon: "This can't be possible. This is incredible. The people went by themselves. Here, the leaders died. . . . the people went by themselves. Nobody is in charge now. It all slipped through our fingers."[12] The same day, an official communiqué reads: "The city of Córdoba has been ruined by popular hordes that destroyed everything in their way, without respecting private property and without taking fundamental differences between large, small and middle-size businesses into account."[13]

A quarter after one o'clock in the afternoon, the commander of the Third Army Corps of Córdoba, General Sánchez Lahoz, installs martial law and orders the protesters to abandon the barricades and return home. Many workers leave but others remain to witness what is to become an outbreak of collective violence only comparable to the 1919 Tragic Week and the 1959 Lisandro de la Torre street battles. An estimated crowd of fifty thousand people occupy the adjoining student neighborhoods Barrio Clínicas and Barrio Alberdi, while snipers assume positions on roof tops to detain the advancing military. As they had done one week earlier, students begin to build barricades. Barrio Clínicas with its hospital buildings and private clinics is the center of resistance. Orators incite people to resist the military force converging on the city. The military arrive at about five o'clock in the afternoon at Barrio Alberdi, and take the area street by street. The neighborhood consists of narrow streets of two-story houses with wrought-iron balconies and flat roof tops providing an optimal mobility to protesters and snipers. Sniper fire is returned with machine gun bursts, and student boarding houses are combed for activists.

The confrontation of crowd and army takes an unexpected turn when at eleven o'clock in the evening of 29 May, a small group of Luz y Fuerza workers shuts off the electricity to the city. The blackout severely disrupts the communications among the various military units. Students, workers, and local residents win valuable time to reinforce the barricades. A small group attempts to incinerate the national bank. The army resumes its assault when power is restored at one o'clock in the morning of 30 May. Meanwhile, the street occupation spreads to the city's periphery where the military presence is not so prominent. In addition, the unions most closely associated with the CGT union central proceed as planned with their twenty-four-hour general strike and protest march. The workers hinder the troop movements considerably and the final military assault can only begin at around six o'clock in the evening. The Barrio Clínicas is retaken in one hour, even though incidental outbreaks of collective violence continue to flare up in other parts of Córdoba. Gas stations are assaulted to obtain fuel for molotov cocktails, more stores are ransacked, and railways are obstructed.

The union leaders Torres and Tosco were arrested earlier that day. They were immediately court-martialed, and sentenced to prison terms of four to eight years, but were released in December 1969. The official toll of two days of collective violence was sixteen dead, even though figures as high as sixty have been mentioned. There were hundreds of wounded, and over six hundred people were arrested. About four thousand policemen and five thousand soldiers had been mobilized to control the insurrection.[14]

General Lanusse visited Córdoba on Monday, 2 June, and observed that the turmoil was not exclusively the work of an organized extremist force, as President Onganía was to declare two days later. "Subversive elements acted and at some moment marked the beat. But in the street one could see the dissatisfaction of everybody. For what I could see and hear . . . I can say that it was the people of Córdoba, in either an active or passive way, who showed that they were against the National Government in general and the Provincial Government in particular."[15] General Lanusse sensed the beginnings of a broad-based rebellion which might turn into a social revolution if the direction of the Argentine dictatorship would not change soon.

The Historical Cordobazo

There are three explanations of the Cordobazo. They are all situated within the context of a repressive political climate, deteriorating economic conditions, years of labor resistance, and the student opposition to the Onganía dictatorship. The emphasis of the three approaches lies respectively on the maturing class struggle, the resistance to authoritarianism, and grass roots militancy.

Ernesto Laclau and Beba and Beatriz Balvé emphasize that the Cordobazo marks a stage in the mounting class antagonism in Argentine society. Parts of the middle class (students, professionals, progressive priests) united with the working class against capitalist exploitation and political oppression, while pursuing a new morality and social order.[16] Delich, Lewis, Munck, and Smith attribute the Cordobazo to the decline of the Cordoban auto industry, a divided middle class, combative labor unions, and the authoritarianism of the national and local government. Unable to express their dissatisfaction through democratic channels, the discontent exploded, as if in a pressure cooker, into collective violence.[17] Finally, Brennan and James interpret the Cordobazo as a combination of diverse economic grievances of the workers, political forces within local unions, a fierce rank-and-file militancy, and rising frustrations among multiple layers of Cordoban society accumulated during the Onganía dictatorship. The large Cordoban student population added fuel to the widespread resentment about the authoritarian government, and contributed to the insurrectional atmosphere.[18]

Brennan and James are most convincing with their sophisticated understanding of the complexities of the Cordoban working class. Nevertheless, all three analyses fail to account for the crowd dynamic of the Cordobazo and its social consequences. The strike and march that preceded the events had been carefully planned by militant union leaders, but the massive adhesion, the violent response to the repression, the raising of barricades, and the attacks on police stations were not. These manifestations cannot be explained by delineating the structural or political conditions of the social sectors among which the protest arose. Instead, the analytical lead of Brennan and James must be followed into the crowd itself.

The protest march on 29 May was carefully planned, including the tactical decisions to distribute defensive weapons and to approach the center from various directions preventing a concentration of police forces. However, as had happened on 17 October 1945, the street mobilization developed a distinct crowd dynamic once the protesters stood face to face with the heavily armed police. The union leaders Torres and Tosco tried to prevent an escalation into violence, but were overtaken by the more militant protesters. The collective violence manifested feelings of repression among the mass of Argentine society, among workers, Peronists, and students. Their anger was released in the crowds and transformed into a sense of empowerment.

In their public declarations, the authorities portrayed the Cordobazo as an irrational outburst of collective violence. Yet the protesters were never entirely out of control. For example, the fire brigade was allowed free passage when the fire at the Xerox corporation threatened to consume the homes of residents. Policemen were stripped of their helmets and weapons, but five policemen who had been briefly taken hostage were released unharmed.

Several eyewitnesses described the protesters as festive and euphoric. Around noontime on 29 May, an area of about one hundred and fifty blocks was in festive turmoil. The pastries and hams taken from expensive upper class stores were eaten with delight.[19] The piano at the junior officers' club was dragged outside and became the center of an impromptu dance. The sabers were taken off the walls and used to parody medieval duels. One of the participants remarked later: "But do you know why there was also so much happiness as the events progressed and the whole city was being taken? Do you know why the emotions ran so high at Plaza Colón when we were having the party? Because everyone was also settling a personal score. The Radical against the coup against Illia, the Peronist because he rejected once more the coup against his leader and was fighting for his return to the country, the leftist because he felt that he was taking revenge for so many exiles, prisoners, and dead comrades since times unknown. . . ."[20] Another experience by one witness makes this emotional release even clearer: "Very special moments were lived at Plaza Colón because there men of seventy years old embracing youths of fifteen, and they both cried. The youngest because he had been born under repression and felt that he was liberating himself; the older because after many years he felt that it was possible to win."[21] These stings of the past did not motivate the general strike, but they did emerge during the crowd mobilization and were temporarily relieved through the outbursts of collective violence and euphoria.

The collective violence was not the work of an irrational horde, but was highly organized. The shop floor politics and grass roots participation, so distinctive of the Cordoban unions and student organizations, found their expression in the street actions. A division of labor emerged in building barricades which resembled the typical organization of any production process. There were groups specializing in the extraction of raw materials from construction sites, their transformation into suitable components for the barricades, their distribution and transportation to the various barricades, and the actual building of the obstacles. Other groups were specialized in making molotov cocktails, while messages and molotov cocktails were distributed by motor bike to various locations. Logistic support was provided to supply young activists at the front lines with a continuous supply of bricks to throw at the police. Small groups of women prepared food for the various teams. These small production and defense teams emerged throughout Córdoba without any preestablished plan.

The spontaneity of the grass roots movement and the rapid organization of the resistance undermined the repressive state. The Cordobazo gave people confidence in the power of mobilization, the strength of their number, the ability to organize a protest, and the force to make the government change its authoritarian policies. Particularly worrying to the military junta was the presence of snipers, and the attempt of a revolutionary vanguard to organize the protests and assume its leadership. The nightmare of a revolutionary insurrection was becoming a likely reality for the Argentine military, and they intended to discourage future protests with massive displays of force. The military junta did not just move into action to protect property and lives but to quell the challenge to their authority and the order which they sought to impose on society. These deeper motives become clear after a close examination of military crowd control tactics.

Military Conceptualization of Crowds

The Cordobazo was military doctrine come true. Contemporary field manuals of the Argentine army explained that vanguardism and mass mobilization were the two principal strategies of revolutionary warfare.[22] Attempts had been made in the 1960s to start a guerrilla insurgency, but they failed because of the lack of resonance within Argentine society and the energetic military response. The Cordobazo proved to the military and the left that the consciousness of the working class was ripe for a mass insurrection.

Army instructions on how to control violent crowds began with the assumption that mass mobilizations were inevitable because every society has malcontents. The causes of popular dissatisfaction and collective violence identified by Argentine military analysts and revolutionary thinkers such as Marx, Lenin, Mao, and Guevara were remarkably similar: social and economic inequality, authoritarianism, frustrated expectations, and relative deprivation among large segments of the population. The roots of mass protest were subdivided into economic, social, psychological, and political causes.[23] Typical of the Argentine army field manuals was the complete absence of any reference to concrete situations or historical events. The instructions were presented in an objectifying language as if they built on universal and timeless knowledge, but behind the neutral, almost clinical, descriptions rested a keen awareness of national circumstances.

The social, economic, and psychological causes of popular dissatisfaction relate largely to the unequal distribution of wealth in society: widespread poverty, high unemployment, and an unjust concentration of land and capital. Social factors, like stark class divisions, high illiteracy rates, a poor educational system, and inadequate health services, will make people feel frustrated and hopeless. These feelings translate psychologically into a lack of faith in the government. People have a profound feeling of injustice and believe that the government does not intend to make amends. There reigns uncertainty and anxiety about the future provoking alternatively aggressive and apathetic behavior.[24]

Finally, the Argentine army manuals identify the political causes of unrest: a repressive government which does not respond to the aspirations of its people, proscribes certain political interests, and does not tolerate a political opposition. The field manuals indicate furthermore the danger of a polarization in society between the middle class and an extreme right and left wing.

Did President Onganía recognize the political situation in Argentina of the late 1960s in this diagnostic instrument devised by the staff of Army commander Lanusse? Onganía ruled in an authoritarian fashion, Peronism was proscribed, a large part of the Peronist movement was swinging to the political left and talking about class struggle, while there was also a noticeable growth of right-wing nationalist splinter groups. Furthermore, there was widespread indignation about the proscription of political parties, the concentration of wealth, thwarted social mobility, an unjust land tenure system, the dependency on multinationals, and rising unemployment.

Finally, the feelings of injustice pervading the angry protests in Córdoba resonated throughout the country.

Why did Onganía not change his political course? Onganía decided to follow his original long-term strategy for transforming Argentina. One of his principal advisers, General Osiris Villegas, convinced him that the development of Argentine society was a matter of national security. The communist incursion in Argentina would have less chance if the government stimulated the country's industrial, regional, political, scientific, and military development.[25] Onganía envisioned a three-stage development that began with a rapid modernization of the economy, was followed by economic growth allowing for a period of social reforms, and eventually led to a mature democracy.[26]

The only problem was that these changes could take as much as twenty years. Many Argentines were unwilling to wait so long, and this impatience might stimulate the rise of a revolutionary movement. In this situation, the army field manuals stated that insurrection movements could only be prevented from taking root when "the original causes have been removed or attenuated, or when the repressive action has been sufficiently effective and energetic to discourage new subversive actions."[27] Lieutenant-General Onganía chose repression rather than reform to deal with civil unrest.

What does a crowd try to obtain, according to the Argentine military specialists?[28] The crowd wants to display its strength in public, demonstrate its popular support, intimidate the authorities, and demoralize the security forces. An outburst of violence provokes panic among the people, paralyzes their normal activities, and challenges public order. It may create a revolutionary climate and be used to test the strength of the legal forces. The emergence of an urban insurrection consists of two main phases and one subsidiary phase: the gathering of a large multitude, the organization of civil disturbances and, if the occasion arises, the creation of martyrs.[29] The armed and security forces must focus their repressive action on these three phases.

The army field manuals stated that crowds do not arise spontaneously, but that they are summoned by activists and professional agitators. These agitators infiltrate labor unions, student organizations, or political movements, and then inculcate revolutionary ideas creating a fertile climate for civil disturbance. They translate the people's legitimate demands into a discourse that coincides with their hidden political aspirations. They try to create a common enemy, like the military dictatorship, foreign imperialism, or the capitalist system. Once the idea has caught on that a street demonstration is necessary, then the leading activists choose a public space such as a park, square, or avenue to hold a protest. There, they provoke the collective violence and trigger the crowd's psychological mechanisms. During the street fighting "seemingly fanatic or insolent elements (so prepared to act) will contaminate in an irrational manner the persons who are near them, influencing the mood of the crowd and pulling along the moderates and undecided."[30] The crowd is thus seen as the fertile soil of collective violence and revolutionary action, so public gatherings must be forbidden during times of military repression.[31]

According to the field manuals, all civil disturbances are tightly orchestrated. They write about the crowd as if it were a regular enemy force carrying out a tactical plan with military precision. There is an external crowd commander who observes the protest area and confrontation from an apartment or office building. The external commander gives orders to an internal commander about when and where to incite the collective violence. The crowd commanders are located near mail boxes and street signs or wear visible signs so that they can be identified easily. Most multitudes contain activists who carry banners, placards, and protest signs conveying the grievances, and are aided by an agitation group shouting slogans. Their place will be eventually taken by other activists who will incite the demonstrators to violence.

Protest crowds organize their offensive and defensive capabilities. There are shock groups which distract or pin down the legal forces, so that other protesters can proceed to the gathering place. These shock groups may throw stones, incinerate cars and buildings, smash windows, and provoke people into ransacking stores. There are supply groups providing bombs and arms to the activists, and security guards who protect the internal commanders and prepare their flight from the scene of confrontation. There may also be snipers who try to detain the legal forces or provide cover to retreating comrades.[32]

After the collective violence has waned, the army field manuals continued, the protest leaders will exploit the loss of life to create martyrs. One field manual explained further that deaths may occur during the disturbances, either by the use of force to which the legal forces have been provoked, or by assassinations carried out by the activists themselves. "The creation of martyrs will try to aggravate the emotional state of the crowd, will seek to attract sympathizers to the movement, discredit the legal forces and drag along the protesters in an insane frenzy, thus ensuring the success of the riot."[33]

The instruction manuals recommend an array of repressive means (megaphones, tear gas, war dogs, snipers, artillery, armored vehicles, helicopters) and tactics (patrols, blockades, entrapments, incursions, ambushes, hand-to-hand combat) to deal with the collective violence. The field manuals also suggest that snipers should "eliminate the leaders located in a crowd."[34]

Despite occasional references to its irrationality and emotional discharge, the crowd is treated as a rational organization in which the various groups (agitation groups, shock groups, supply groups, security guards, internal and external command) are hierarchically linked. As an authoritative text on crowd control stated, "In general, the same principles of war which govern the movements and disposition of large armies in the field may be applied in controlling rioting mobs."[35] It seems as if the military strategists tried to get a grip on a collective phenomenon that bewildered them and imposed a familiar organizational form that made leaders responsible for the crowd's actions. Crucial in the thinking of the military was that revolutionary leaders ride the wave of popular resentment.

The resentment about declining labor conditions, political repression, authoritarianism, and the proscription of Peronism reached unprecedented proportions in 1969. The decision to repress mass mobilizations, instead of taking away the grievances through a political solution, galvanized the opposition. An editorial in *Criterio* summed up the political balance of the Rosariazo and the Cordobazo: "And so, in fifteen days, the government's political leadership achieved what the opposition could not in three years. It succeeded in uniting the two CGTs [labor union centrals], the different student groups, the students with the professors, the students and professors with employees and workers, and Catholic universities with public universities. And all of them against the government, as became clear at the successful strike of the 30th of May."[36] The link between workers, students, and middle class professionals was recognized as a broad-based alliance in Argentine society with ominous prospects.

Second Rosariazo and Liberation Syndicalism

The civil unrest stirred up by the Cordobazo refused to die down. Strikes and protest marches were held throughout the country.[37] A student was shot down by police during a demonstration in Córdoba, and the once powerful union leader Augusto Vandor was assassinated by a guerrilla hit squad on 30 June 1969. Lieutenant-General Onganía declared that same day a state of siege which would only be lifted on 23 May 1973. The authority of the military government had been severely damaged by the unabated strike and protest activities. Four months after the Rosariazo and Cordobazo, a second Rosariazo took place.

The street violence in Rosario was triggered by striking railroad workers placed under martial law and ordered back to work. Striking workers and students marched together at ten o'clock in the morning on 16 September towards the city center with every intention of attacking the police forces frontally. The strategy of a combined police force of three and a half thousand men was to prevent the crowd from gathering strength by thwarting its assembly. The tactical plan consisted of positioning a defensive cordon around the city center. I will not enter into a detailed description of the second Rosariazo, but what was remarkable in comparison to the Cordobazo was the offensive nature of the crowd mobilization.

Rosario was transformed into a battlefield. About thirty thousand demonstrators, including four thousand students, defended the territory covered with barricades. Commercial buildings were torched and stores were ransacked in an area the size of ninety street blocks. At 1:30 P.M., the police had only secured an area of six blocks comprising the radio stations, army and police headquarters, the courts, and the principal government buildings. One worker died from police bullets in the afternoon of 16 September and a twelve-year-old boy was killed by an armed civilian.[38] At nine o'clock in the evening, the Second Army Corps moved into action, and the quiet of martial law descended on the city.

The organization of the second Rosariazo had been far more complex than that of the Cordobazo, and resembled the crowds described in the army field manuals analyzed above. In Rosario the crowd proceeded in a well-planned offensive and was not a runaway crowd, as the authorities tried to make the Argentine people believe. The second Rosariazo manifested a crowd consciousness, an awareness of its power. The protesters realized that their superior number and determination to undo the many injustices that united them could provoke a legitimacy crisis for the military dictatorship.

What is noteworthy about the Cordobazo and Rosariazos of 1969 is that the name Perón was not mentioned, even though the essence of the Peronist doctrine (social justice, economic independence, and political sovereignty) appeared in several proclamations.[39] The majority of the workers maintained their Peronist sympathies, but Perón was no longer indispensable to summon a large crowd. Years of resistance and repression had not only emancipated the Peronist following from Perón, but had cultivated a class consciousness. It became impossible to conceive of a pact among capital, State, and labor similar to that of the 1945–1955 Peronist rule. The labor conflicts of the following fourteen years, the repression by successive military governments, and the free reign given to foreign multinationals—most visible in the Cordoban auto industry—made the subjugated social layers aware of Argentina's class nature. The Cordobazo and Rosariazos revealed this class consciousness in a most forceful way, and gave rise to a radical ideological current in the labor movement, known as *clasismo* or liberation syndicalism (*sindicalismo de liberación*).

Clasismo began in the Cordoban auto industry with the demand for honest union representation and shop floor democracy, and evolved ideologically in a Marxist direction under the influence of nascent revolutionary organizations. Its Marxist agenda was in 1970 even too radical for Agustín Tosco, who preferred combative trade unionism over divisive class-struggle unionism. Clasismo was at even greater odds with Peronism. The idea of an open class struggle to bring about a socialist revolution did not find broad acceptance among Peronist workers, while the demand for greater union democracy did of course not find any support among the verticalist union leaders, such as Vandor's successors Lorenzo Miguel and José Rucci. Most militant union protests during the 1969–1973 period therefore took place in Córdoba, and not in Buenos Aires.[40]

What united the Cordoban labor movement was an active opposition to the Onganía dictatorship, and continued crowd mobilizations as the principal tactic to force the government to its knees. This resistance was reinforced in 1970 with the radicalization of the Fiat auto workers unions SITRAC and SITRAM. The Fiat workers had shunned union activism for many years, and had not participated in the Cordobazo. The prominent role of their IKA-Renault colleagues inspired the Fiat auto workers to demand a genuine union democracy with honest elections and leaders willing to confront management. This objective made the Fiat workers an ideal target for grass roots revolutionary activity. Organizations such as the Revolutionary Communist Party (Partido Comunista Revolucionario), the Communist Vanguard (Vanguardia Comunista), and the Workers Revolutionary Party (Partido Revolucionario de los Trabajadores) did their best to create an ideological foothold in the auto industry by distributing pamphlets at factory gates and taking blue collar jobs in auto plants.

The strategy of the revolutionary parties proved successful. On 12 May 1970, Revolutionary Communist Party activists persuaded the workers at the IKA-Renault tool and die factory to occupy the plant and take the French supervisors hostage after management tried to replace left-wing candidates in the shop steward elections by more conciliatory Peronist candidates. The reinstatement of the original candidates was an important victory, but even more important was the introduction of hostage-taking as a new combative tactic besides work stoppages, strikes, street mobilizations, and plant occupations.

The Fiat workers followed suit. The members of the two company-controlled Fiat unions SITRAC and SITRAM demanded new union elections after more than a decade of docile union leadership. The Fiat workers elected a steering committee to prepare new elections. Years of frustration, subjugation, unfair treatment, and underpayment were shed that night in the decision to take matters into their own hands. Still, it would take an unprecedented three-day factory occupation of the Fiat Concord factory, starting on 15 May 1970, at which Fiat officials were taken hostage, before the Ministry of Labor allowed the elections to take place. Colleagues at another Fiat plant followed suit on 3 June. On the same day, IKA-Renault auto workers also took hostages and occupied various plants to pressure management into reopening labor contract negotiations. The crisis ended when the Cordoban police broke into the IKA-Renault tool and die factory and arrested around two hundred and fifty workers.[41]

The Cordobazo and Rosariazos, and the factory occupations and hostage-taking in Córdoba, had evaporated Onganía's authority. Street mobilizations had taken place despite police ordinances. Railroad workers had defied martial law and had refused the military order to return to work.

Rank-and-file union members had dismissed government-imposed union leaders, and militant union leaders had gone on hunger strike. The street had been Onganía's Achilles heel. Civil disobedience could cripple even a curfew, the most far-reaching crowd control measure, as army manuals admitted, "Civil disobedience en masse will be the only effective action against a curfew. . . . "[42] The kidnapping of retired Lieutenant-General Aramburu by the Montoneros guerrilla organization on 29 May 1970, exactly one year after the Cordobazo, gave the final blow to Onganía's precarious position. He was deposed on 8 June 1970, and General Roberto Levingston became the new president of Argentina.

Calm did not return to Córdoba after the changing of the guard in the presidential palace. The strikes, occupations, and street mobilizations continued unabated. At their root rested a complex array of demands about higher wages and better working conditions, more honest union leadership, and an end to the military dictatorship. The clasista practice of open assemblies and internal union democracy contributed significantly to the permanent state of mass mobilization. The Cordobazo had paved the way for numerous grass roots crowd mobilizations and provided a fertile environment for the development of the clasista internal union democracy.[43]

On 1 March 1971, the conservative Dr. José Camilo Uriburu became governor of the province of Córdoba. Two days later, the CGT of Córdoba declared a general strike, and refused to negotiate with the new authorities: "Action and Struggle. The people in the street are invincible."[44] Uriburu was determined to cut off with one slash, as he called it, the head of the poisonous snake directing the militant activism.[45] The indignation at Uriburu's scoffing at what many workers saw as legitimate protests was great. Factory occupations and a street mobilization of Fiat workers in downtown Córdoba followed on 12 March 1971. Several barricades were erected and set afire. The police launched large quantities of tear gas into the crowd, and began to shoot at the protesters. They killed eighteen-year-old worker Adolfo Cepeda. As so often before, a violent death precipitated more intense protests.[46]

On Sunday, 14 March, thousands of people accompanied the funeral of Adolfo Cepeda. One union leader called upon the mourners at San Vicente cemetery to "turn pain into hatred, into hatred and combat against the exploiters," and take revenge for Cepeda's death.[47] The next morning, two thousand Fiat workers marched to downtown Córdoba in protest against the police violence. At 12:30 P.M., the protesters began to erect barricades. A second Cordobazo was in the making. Several neighborhoods were taken, including the Barrio Clínicas and Barrio Alberdi where around two hundred barricades were raised in defense, securing an area of five hundred and fifty blocks for a period of twelve hours. This collective violence was to a much larger extent the work of the Cordoban working class, and in particular the nonaffiliated and unemployed workers. The students and middle class had a far less notable presence than during the Cordobazo. Particularly troubling to the authorities was the sniper support given by members of the People's Revolutionary Army or ERP (Ejército Revolucionario del Pueblo), the armed wing of the Workers Revolutionary Party or PRT. Clasismo had forged close ties among the most radical unions and several revolutionary organizations which were sealed on the barricades of Córdoba.

At nightfall, the police had not yet moved into action. A special antiguerrilla brigade was flown in from Buenos Aires which advanced rapidly in the early hours of 16 March from barricade to barricade under the light of star shells. The security forces were again in control of the city at sunrise. Governor Uriburu resigned the same day, and a Cordoban newspaper printed a cartoon that depicted a viper (víbora), satisfied after having devoured the ill-fated Dr. Uriburu. This second Cordobazo became known as the Viborazo. On 18 March, Córdoba was put under martial law. A warrant for the arrest of Tosco and other union leaders was issued, and hundreds of workers were detained.[48]

Once more, an Argentine president was forced to resign because of collective violence. General Lanusse ousted Lieutenant-General Levingston on 22 March 1971 and assumed full powers four days later. The Cordobazo and the Viborazo drove Onganía and Levingston from the seat of power because they failed to make haste with a democratization process that might have defused the popular anger and increased the political participation of the Argentine people. Within a period of less than two years, the string of crowd mobilizations changed the national course from an ill-coined and ill-conceived Argentine Revolution without clear time limits to a speedy return to democracy.

The crowd mobilizations and the collective violence did not cease. Lieutenant-General Lanusse's call for national unity and promise of democracy were taken as an encouragement. The strikes and street mobilizations by combative and clasista workers in Córdoba continued for several months after the Viborazo, but quickly subsided in October 1971 when the military arrested the principal SITRAC-SITRAM union leaders and occupied the Fiat factories, and management fired the union representatives. The center of street mobilization shifted from the interior to the nation's capital, and students took over the crowd initiative from the workers, principally through the activities of the Peronist Youth.[49]

The Hour of the People

Lanusse envisioned a two-pronged strategy to pacify Argentine society: the call for national harmony was his carrot, and counterinsurgency his stick. Lanusse launched in July 1971 his Great National Accord (Gran Acuerdo Nacional) among Argentina's principal social sectors (political parties, unions, industry, financial institutions). This plan came too late because Argentina's principal political parties had already joined forces on 11 November 1970 in a document entitled The Hour of the People (La Hora del Pueblo). Peronists, Radicals, socialists, and conservatives had demanded free elections and the right to political expression. The politicians did not want to commit themselves to the Great National Accord and neither did Perón, who became once more an active player in Argentine politics.[50]

Lanusse's counterinsurgency strategy was only in part successful. Even though all principal guerrilla commanders had been imprisoned by mid-1972, and their influence on the labor movement curtailed by a crackdown on the clasista unions, their revolutionary ideology had a captivating effect on many young Argentines. They came to swell the ranks of a radical and often violent political opposition. The rise in crowd mobilizations had become so dramatic, and the fear of an unstoppable revolutionary process so great, that the armed forces were deployed with every threat of collective violence.[51]

Immediately after his ascendance to the presidency, Lanusse opened a dialogue with Perón. Despite these overtures, Lanusse sought to demystify Perón as an old man in poor health and to coax him into denouncing the guerrilla movement. However, Perón refused to play along with Lanusse's game. He operated on several political fronts and used different weapons to strike at the embattled military government. As he was negotiating with Lanusse's representatives about a return to democracy, Perón instructed Peronist politicians to take a tough stand against the government and cultivated contacts with army officers susceptible to overthrowing Lanusse. Perón also praised the violence of the Peronist guerrilla organizations and encouraged the Peronist Youth to maintain an active street presence.[52]

The year 1972 marked the end of the violent street protests (azos) that began in May 1969. There were labor conflicts and public disturbances during the months of April and July 1972 in Mendoza, San Juan, San Miguel de Tucumán, Córdoba, and General Roca.[53] Yet the crowd momentum had shifted from the labor unions to the Peronist movement as the prospect of free elections dominated the political scene. The CGTA had virtually disappeared in 1970. Many Independent union leaders, among them Tosco, were imprisoned in 1971. The SITRAC-SITRAM Fiat auto worker unions had lost their legal status in October 1971, and clasista shop stewards were fired. The union bureaucracy with its Vandorist tendency towards verticalism began to accumulate strength again in 1972.[54] The UOM and CGT union centrals pursued a nonconfrontational course in order not to endanger the elections. The crowd initiative was left to the Peronist Youth and the students.

Anger, Flight, and Celebration of Argentine Crowds

The violent crowd protests of 1969 marked the second watershed in Argentine crowd history, October 1945 being the first. The Cordobazo, Rosariazos and Viborazo arose from local union conditions and economic grievances, but their political significance was nationwide. The 1969–1972 period witnessed insurrectional crowds that emerged from uncontainable grass roots resentments and sought structural changes in Argentine society. Collective violence was a reaction to the violence of disenfranchisement, economic exploitation, the loss of worker privileges, social injustice, and outright military repression. The guerrilla insurgency sprouted from the collective violence. The crowds did not cause the emergence of the guerrilla organizations in a direct way, but provided a medium in which they could grow and mature.

Radical sectors of Argentine society attributed a revolutionary meaning to the 1969 crowd demonstrations which they did not possess. The Marxist guerrilla organizations pictured themselves as the vanguard of the working masses on the move, shunned a direct involvement in crowd politics, and concentrated on building a revolutionary army. The revolutionary Peronists believed that the popular masses were the propelling force of history, whose most authentic political expression was found in the assembled Peronist crowd clamoring for dignity and social justice. They tried to place themselves at the head of the Peronist crowd and transform its spontaneous force into a collective insurrection. This was not an easy task because time and again Argentine crowds had disengaged themselves from their leaders and disintegrated into outbursts of rage, only to reorganize into a violent grassroots resistance. This combination of spontaneous and calculated collective violence, and the rage, euphoria, and sudden panic that could come over crowds, turned street mobilizations into an unpredictable political instrument for revolutionary organizations.

In his groundbreaking study of South Asian crowds, Stanley Tambiah explains their characteristic oscillation between attack and flight as a dynamic of anger/rage and fear/panic. The South Asian ethnic crowd becomes violent towards another ethnic group because it feels harmed in its well-being and identity. Such destructive rage may suddenly turn into panic and hysteric flight. Encouraged by rumors, the violent crowd fears the retaliation from a rival group defined as dangerous and threatening. The heightened sense of power experienced by the violent crowd is thus inextricably tied to a sudden awareness of its vulnerability.[55]

Anger/rage and fear/panic have also been qualities of Argentine crowds but, unlike in South Asia, the most direct threat in Argentina did not come from a rival group but from the State. The panic provoked by the bombardment of the Peronist crowd at the Plaza de Mayo on 16 June 1955 is the most dramatic example of the recurrent threat posed by police and armed forces. The key to understanding this panic lies in the crowd's dual qualities as violent and euphoric.

Both in South Asia and in Argentina, crowds often turn festive while engaged in destruction. According to Tambiah, the jubilation arises from "their temporary sense of homogeneity, equality, and physical intimacy, their sense of taking righteous action to level down the enemy's presumed advantage and claim their collective entitlements."[56] In other words, violence and euphoria constitute a pair opposite to fear and flight. What unites these two pairs is, according to Tambiah, the loss of restraint by people in a crowd.

This loss of restraint is caused by the boundless sociality experienced in crowds, a sociality which Durkheim described as social effervescence and Canetti identified as the feeling of equality. Euphoria emerges from the sense of unity, equality, and the shedding of injustices in a crowd; a powerful feeling which may make the crowd turn violent towards perceived sources of social injury. The vulnerability of crowds, their propensity towards panic, and their potential traumatization lie precisely in this feeling of aggrandizement. People in a crowd lower their personal defenses as they surrender to its collective emotions. A violent repression causes an emotional overload because people have their guard down in the crowd. In other words, the boundary loss that is so liberating in a euphoric and violent crowd also exposes its vulnerability when subjected to indiscriminate repression. People can no longer rely on the power of their number, or the justice of their demands, and run for their lives.

Such social injury can make people reluctant to gather again in street mobilizations. Repeated repression made Argentine people at times reluctant to attend street demonstrations, as happened between 1961 and 1969 and would happen again between 1975 and 1982. Argentine crowds had incurred several social traumas by 1974. The euphoria and invincibility of victorious crowds were transformed into defeat and traumatization. Repressive violence damaged people's belief in the force of social association and wounded the crowd as a political force in a society used to manifesting its political convictions through street mobilizations.

The Cordobazo became a watershed in Argentine crowd politics not only because of its revolutionary promise but also because it demonstrated that the Argentine people seemed to have overcome the social traumas of past crowd repressions. In 1969 Argentine crowds became able to shed their spontaneous, passionate, and chaotic quality by quickly organizing a tenacious resistance against the security forces through the erection of barricades, the coordination of counterattacks, the disruption of communications, the preparedness for a lengthy siege, and a readiness to face a trained and disciplined opponent.[57]

This mastery over traumatization was hastened by the specific nature of

Argentine crowd politics. Unlike the South Asian ethnic crowds, Argentine protest crowds were generally mobilized in opposition to local and state forces.[58] Argentine protesters entered into crowd competitions with the advancing police and army by imitating their discipline and organic composition. Argentine crowds therefore tried to show their power by gaining control over public space. In clear awareness of the state's repressive capabilities, crowds entered into a tug-of-war with the advancing forces and withdrew, rather than flee, when the repression became too overwhelming.

In mid-1972, the Argentine protest crowds were still full of confidence and in awe of their own historical force. Protest crowds railed successfully against the Lanusse dictatorship and allowed Perón to return to Argentina from his exile in Spain. Paradoxically, the Peronist electoral victory of March 1973 offered a greater opportunity for revolutionary change than the Cordobazo of May 1969. Broad layers of Argentine society felt the relief of casting off years of political proscription. New civil servants peopled the ministries, educational reforms were made in the universities, the arts blossomed, and the economy was booming. The willingness to rebuild the country was great, but the myth of the Cordobazo kept haunting the nation.

Chapter 4
Crowd Clashes: Euphoria, Disenchantment, and Rupture

On Friday 17 November 1972, a seventy-seven-year-old Juan Domingo Perón steps on Argentine soil after an absence of seventeen years. Tens of thousands of Peronists walk through the rain to Ezeiza airport to welcome him, but they are stopped by a barrier of police cars, armored vehicles, tanks, and an army force thirty-five thousand strong. Numerous tear gas shells are spent to detain throngs of people trying to make their way to Ezeiza along railroad tracks or wading across the brooks and streams surrounding the airport. Only a select group of three hundred spectators and fifteen hundred reporters are present to witness Perón's historic return. A loyal following, including his wife Isabel and his private secretary López Rega, accompany him on the flight from Rome to Buenos Aires. Surprisingly, the representatives of the Peronist Youth are absent from Perón's entourage.[1] Yet the crowd that tries in vain to welcome the aged leader home consists mostly of young, second-generation Peronists whose street mobilizations and guerrilla activities forced Lanusse into accepting Perón's return to Argentine politics.

Upon arrival, Perón is not allowed to leave the morose Ezeiza airport hotel until dawn of the following day, supposedly for security reasons.[2] It is only in the afternoon of Saturday 18 November 1972, that thousands of young Peronists can finally see Perón as he appears in the window of his temporary residence in Vicente López, a suburb of Buenos Aires. Initially, the police block Gaspar Campos Street but they withdraw after Perón complains that the people are being kept away from him. A festive mood surrounds the villa, with ice cream vendors, bass drummers, and young Peronists who serenade the leader to sleep with lullabies. Perón is deeply moved.[3] The next morning, he confirms the growing political influence of these young Peronists: "If the past is history and the present struggle, then the future is the youth. . . . the Peronist Organization has already for a long time begun with its generational rejuvenation. . . ."[4]

Peronist Youth leaders blamed not just the military but particularly the Peronist right wing for the foiled reception at Ezeiza. They had kept Perón from meeting with his people to prevent the leader-crowd dynamic from taking place that had characterized the Peronist rallies of the 1940s and 1950s. The Peronist Youth interpreted Perón's demand for free access to his residence as an indication that he himself tried to break the isolation imposed from the inside. This tug-of-war about the public access to Perón remained the central focus of the crowd competitions between the Peronist left (Peronist Youth and Montoneros guerrilla organization) and the Peronist right (Peronist party and labor unions) until Perón's death in 1974.

The Peronist left saw their mobilizations as the means to carry the Peronist revolution forward because historical change was forged in the physical encounter of leader and crowd. This covenant about political rule and power through popular assembly had been sealed on 17 October 1945. As older Peronists had told their children, the people entered into dialogue with Perón during rallies in which for instance the crowd shouted its disapproval of a particular union leader, or answered "yes" or "no" to a question from Perón.[5] The second-generation Peronists interpreted these verbal exchanges as expressions of the true union of people and Perón in which they shaped one another's political direction. Hence, the strategy of the Peronist Youth consisted of enhancing its political influence on Perón through the mobilization of large crowds.

This conception of historical change has three important implications for political practice. One, only a frequent reunion of crowd and leader guarantees their political attunement under ever changing national and international circumstances. Two, competing political groups and factions need to show their might continuously at rallies to influence the leader. Finally, if the crowd really possesses the power of legitimacy then a disaffection between people and leader will dethrone the leader.

This chapter focuses on the turbulence within Peronist crowds between 1972 and 1975 with respect to these three implications. The belief in the crowd as the impetus of history propelled many, mostly young Peronists, to risk beatings, imprisonment, and even death. The collapse of the military government demonstrated the importance of crowd mobilizations and the force of the masses. The Peronist left tried to persuade, if not force, Perón to embrace their radical political project. Convinced that most Peronists supported their revolutionary ideals, they believed that the leader-crowd dynamic would turn the tables in their favor. This continuous crowd mobilization and its tutelage by growing guerrilla organizations raised the apprehension of the military and contributed in an important degree to the coup of March 1976.

Crowd Offensive and Generational Rejuvenation

The reunion with Perón at Ezeiza airport on 17 November was to have been the culmination of the increasing crowd mobilizations of the Peronist Youth or JP (Juventud Peronista).[6] In July 1972, the Peronist Youth had spearheaded the Fight and Return (Luche y Vuelve) campaign to allow the exiled Perón to return to Argentina and hold free elections.[7] The JP mustered a grass roots power which battled the Lanusse dictatorship with continuous street mobilizations and provided support to Peronist guerrilla organizations, such as the Montoneros. The young, second-generation Peronists rose to political prominence by the inclusion of Rodolfo Galimberti in the Superior Council of the National Justicialist Movement in early 1972, and the appointment of Juan Manuel Abal Medina as secretary-general of the Peronist Organization in late 1972.[8]

Perón used his month-long 1972 sojourn in Argentina to negotiate the elections of 11 March 1973. Before returning to Madrid, he hammered out a coalition of the Peronist party with most other political parties. As head of the Justicialist Liberation Front or FREJULI (Frente Justicialista de Liberación), Perón appointed Héctor José Cámpora as the presidential candidate. Perón could not lead the Peronist ticket because he was living in Spain and thus not a permanent resident of Argentina.[9] Meanwhile, he played the roles of warmonger and peacemaker. He instructed the JP and the Montoneros to maintain pressure on the military government with mass demonstrations and guerrilla attacks, but at the same time promised to resolve the discord within Argentine society.[10] Perón was playing with fire by encouraging the Peronist guerrilla groups to attack the Lanusse dictatorship, but believed that he would be able to control them once in power. Perón and Lanusse understood very well that hell would break loose if the elections were canceled or the victory of Cámpora was annulled.

An important source of inspiration for the political involvement and Peronization of many young Argentines had been the documentary *Political and Doctrinal Actualization for the Seizure of Power*. This film was made between June and October 1971 by Fernando Solanas and Octavio Gettino, and consisted of an interview with Perón cast in fashionable revolutionary language. Frequent references to Mao Zedong and the liberal use of terms such as national liberation, Argentine socialism, imperialism, and revolutionary war from the mouth of the aged leader made a great impression on a young generation raised with the conservative speeches of Lieutenant-General Onganía.

What also made the interview attractive was that Perón accorded the younger generation a leading role in the political transformation of Argentina.[11] This so-called generational rejuvenation (*trasvasamiento generacional*) was called upon by the Peronist Youth, and especially the Montoneros, to see themselves as the political and ideological heirs of Perón. This entitlement was formalized by the creation of a youth branch of the Peronist Organization—in addition to the political, women's, and labor branches—assigning it twenty-five percent of the offices under electoral dispute. The candidates were mostly hand-picked by the Montonero leadership.[12] This unprecedented chance for a new generation of Peronists to exert political influence in Argentina gave a unique élan to an electoral campaign surrounded by incessant street demonstrations and frequent guerrilla operations.

A Taste of Revolution

Héctor Cámpora won the elections with nearly fifty percent of the vote.[13] He attributed his victory to the incessant street mobilizations: "The reality is that Peronism had won over the street and that there wasn't any space left for anybody else. . . . we were certain that our method was preferable: take direct contact with the people through mobilizations and popular gatherings."[14] The elections had returned the Peronist crowds to center stage after eighteen years of repression and proscription. These crowds, however, did not consist of the first-generation Peronists who had suffered the disenfranchisement but mainly of young, revolutionary Peronists who demanded their share of the victory. Miguel Bonasso wrote during these expectant days in his diary: "Happiness exists. I believe that this is the happiest moment in my life. . . . [because of] the unsurpassed sensation to participate in a collective project of real historic significance."[15]

The Plaza de Mayo was filled with an immense crowd on 25 May 1973, the day of Cámpora's inauguration as president. The placards of the various labor unions were dwarfed by the display of banners by the Peronist Youth and the guerrilla organizations FAP, FAR, and Montoneros. Was this a sign that Perón's special guerrilla formations were now laying down their arms and entering the democratic fold or did they wish to demonstrate their political strength and preparedness to grab power by force?

If anything was an indication of the times ahead, then it was not the torching of several automobiles in downtown Buenos Aires or the hasty departure of most military officials by helicopter from the roof of the Casa Rosada, but the shouting and shoving match between orthodox and revolutionary Peronists. The chants of the left for a Socialist Fatherland were answered by the right with a call for a Peronist Fatherland. The mounting tensions between the left and right wings of the Peronist Organization were still contained by the electoral victory but they would soon ignite.[16]

The revolutionary Peronists in general, and the JP and Montoneros in particular, sensed their influence on Cámpora, and succeeded in occupying many mid-level administrative positions in the national and provincial governments.[17] They constituted the Revolutionary Tendency (Tendencia

Revolucionaria) which had in Cámpora its most important official ally, but was ruled by the Montonero leadership.

The right-wing Peronist union centrals and first-generation politicians may have had to admit to a defeat in the crowd competitions but they had won the struggle for supremacy within the Peronist Organization and in the new government. The appointments of Perón's private secretary López Rega as Minister of Social Welfare, López Rega's son-in-law Raúl Lastiri as president of the Chamber of Deputies, and the integrationist union leader Ricardo Otero as Minister of Labor, as well as the signing of a Social Pact on 8 June between the government, the employers' organization CGE and the union central CGT, confirmed the growing influence of the right wing.

A volatile contest had erupted between left and right within the Peronist movement. The tensions found their most concrete expression in the administrative and political seizure of hospitals, cemeteries, universities, high schools, scientific institutes, prisons, ministerial departments, holiday camps, cooperatives, radio and television channels, and state-owned enterprises such as the railroads. Ostensibly, these seizures were carried out to depose the authorities that had been appointed under the 1966–1973 military rule, but factionalism was responsible for their haste. Takeovers were carried out at gunpoint, and extensive security measures were mounted to prevent counter-takeovers.[18]

The reception of Perón at Ezeiza airport on 20 June 1973 would be the ideal occasion for a showdown between the revolutionary and orthodox Peronists. Whichever wing succeeded in mobilizing the largest crowd would reap political power and would influence the ideological direction of the Peronist movement. The unshaken belief in the leader-crowd dynamic stood behind the efforts of both wings to try to dominate the historic reunion of Perón with the Peronist masses in one of the largest crowds ever to gather in Argentina.

The Ezeiza Tragedy

Perón was to arrive at Ezeiza international airport in the late-afternoon of 20 June 1973. Eighteen thousand pigeons would be released upon his arrival, one thousand for each year spent in exile. Since the previous day, people had been gathering near the highway overpass where the reception stage had been built. Small tents were raised in a makeshift encampment, and people passed the time singing the Peronist march and preparing barbecues. The day had been declared a holiday, and public transport was free throughout the country. At daybreak of June 20, hundreds of buses, trucks and cars jammed Avenida Ricchieri to Ezeiza airport. Most passengers abandoned their vehicles and continued on foot. The newspaper *La Nación* spoke of "genuine human rivers," as if to express the tendency of crowds to grow without bounds.[19] More than one, two, some claim even four, million people were converging on the reception stage from which Perón was to address the crowd.

The mood was festive and expectant, but not free of tension. The contest between the right and left wings of the Peronist movement continued unabated. The organizing committee consisted of retired Lieutenant-Colonel Jorge Manuel Osinde as head of security and the four committee members José Rucci, Lorenzo Miguel, Norma Kennedy, and Juan Manuel Abal Medina, representing each of the four branches of the Peronist Organization.[20] This composition seemed reasonable from an organizational point of view, but was highly unbalanced from a factional and political perspective. The revolutionary youth organizations were outnumbered four-to-one with only Abal Medina as their representative, while all others pertained to the orthodox right wing. Furthermore, the orthodox wing also controlled the security of Perón's reception.

The ongoing contest between the two Peronist factions soon turns violent. The first incident takes place near the podium at 3:00 A.M. on June 20 when left-wing Peronists begin chanting "Perón, Evita, the Socialist Fatherland," and the right-wing Peronists reply with "Perón, Evita, the Peronist Fatherland." The shouting match provokes an exchange of gunfire that leaves three persons wounded. A second incident occurs at 10:00 A.M. In their urge to be as close as possible to Perón, a group of young revolutionary Peronists presses towards the stage. They are repelled by the security people with blows, kicks, and gunfire. More people are wounded. Later that morning, the podium is transformed on the orders of Lieutenant-Colonel Osinde. The open rostrum with its three large canvas portraits of Perón, Evita, and Isabel is replaced by a closed stand with bulletproof glass.

The conflict escalates at two o'clock in the afternoon. Large contingents of young people, carrying banners of the FAR, Montoneros, and ERP 22 de Agosto guerrilla organizations, converge on the stage. At 2:35 P.M., the clamor between the proponents of the Socialist Fatherland and the Peronist Fatherland erupts again. An intense exchange of gunfire bursts loose. According to the reconstruction by *La Nación* newspaper, the podium is taken under fire with carbines, machine guns, and pistols by gunmen hiding in a forest about 150 meters away. The security guards at the podium return fire. Frightened bystanders fall on the podium floor for protection, while the throngs of people near the reception area run for cover. The firing lasts for forty minutes. Meanwhile, the eighteen thousand pigeons are released. The newspaper *La Prensa* reports that at 3:40 P.M. a group of five hundred Montoneros try to take the podium by force. They are thrown back by the security guards, whereupon they flee to a nearby forest and suddenly turn around to shoot at their rivals. Another intense exchange occurs at 4:30 P.M. when security people fire at snipers hiding in the trees close to the podium. The most intense exchanges take place between 6:00

and 7:00 P.M. The crowd disperses when the firing finally stops. The official casualty count at 7:00 P.M. is thirteen dead and 250 wounded.[21]

Once again, after the obstructed reception of November 1972, the Peronist crowd failed to reunite with its leader. The violence at Ezeiza airport obliged the plane carrying Perón from Madrid to Buenos Aires to land at Morón air force base. Perón touched Argentine soil at 4:49 P.M., was taken for the night to the presidential residence at Olivos, and left the next day for the villa in Vicente López where he had stayed in 1972.

There are conflicting interpretations of the Ezeiza tragedy. The orthodox Peronists accused the revolutionary Peronists of using their numerical superiority to overtake the reception platform in a pincer movement with heavily armed shock troops, and opening fire when their attempt was frustrated by official security personnel.[22]

The most detailed analysis of the so-called Ezeiza massacre has been written by Horacio Verbitsky in a style that resembles the investigative journalism of his mentor and fellow-Montonero Rodolfo Walsh. He writes that on the fated morning, columns of Peronist Youth and Montoneros were advancing towards the airport but were forbidden to pass behind the reception stage to move to its front. These people came from southern Greater Buenos Aires, and would have had to make a detour of six to twelve hours by way of the Federal Capital if they wanted to approach the north-facing stage from the north. The column organizers suspected political motives when their maneuver was forbidden. So, they decided to ignore the order, approach the stage from an eastern direction, and circle around the overpass. Once behind the platform, they were fired upon. The Peronist Youth security people responded with small arms they were carrying for personal defense but were struck down by a barrage of heavy weapon fire. Verbitsky, whose interpretation of events is the same as that of the Peronist left at the time, concludes that "the massacre was premeditated to displace Cámpora and grab power."[23] The JP and Montonero leaders stated that the Peronist right had provoked the violence to prevent Perón from meeting his people because such an encounter would have persuaded him that his power base did not rest with the right-wing unionists but with the revolutionary Peronists.[24]

Whether the confrontation was provoked by left or right, whether one or the other took advantage of a shouting match that arose spontaneously, or whether the shootings were the accidental spark in a factional powder keg cannot be determined with certainty. Conspiracy or not, what matters are the political conclusions that were drawn from the Ezeiza tragedy, the strategies that were devised, and the traumatization of the crowd, factors which all together influenced the political events of the following months. The Peronist right had earned a public and political victory over the revolutionary Peronists. They had ingratiated themselves with Perón, had a strong ally in the overbearing presence of Perón's secretary López Rega, and had interrupted the crowd mobilization of the revolutionary Peronists.

The events at Ezeiza reminded the military once more of the dangers of popular crowds. The pincer movement by the Montoneros column on the reception stage showed most vividly the level of organization reached by the revolutionary left. The discipline of the column, the dutiful execution of the order to advance, the tactical engagement with adversary groups, and the mobilization of hundreds of thousands of sympathizers betrayed a revolutionary potential of menacing dimensions. Such crowd operation could only be achieved by a vanguard which had far from dismantled its organization upon the return of democracy but was craving for more power.

The leaders of the revolutionary Peronists concluded that Perón was surrounded by a cordon that prevented him from reuniting with the Peronist masses. They believed that the orthodox Peronist union leaders, the Peronist political right, and Perón's secretary López Rega acted in collusion to isolate Perón from the people and take control of the Peronist government after the leader's death. The Peronist left was convinced that the right wing had resorted to violence at Ezeiza because they had been unable to mobilize their following in equally large numbers. They disturbed the welcome party to prevent the left-wing majority from pulling Perón into their camp and proceeding with a revolutionary line of government that had been initiated by Cámpora.[25]

Breaking the Cordon

The cordon theory fitted like a glove around the crowd conception with which young Peronists had been raised. Their interpretation of Peronism rested on the dialogue between Perón and the crowd, and on the belief in a spiritual and political alignment of people and leader during Peronist rallies.[26] This public dialogue was described as follows: "Between Perón and his people there is always this mutual nourishment: the crowd creates, Perón incorporates, Perón creates, the crowd recreates, and so the movement advances. . . . The same happened with the Peronist doctrine. Perón proposes and the people pick up and reshape this proposal. And Perón finally synthesizes it and puts it into practice. Let us remember those extraordinary dialogues between Perón and the People assembled, there the President heard what the people wanted."[27]

The cordon conspiracy obsessed the leaders of the Peronist left. They wanted to outmaneuver the right wing by showing Perón that they could mobilize much larger crowds than the labor union centrals, and believed that this convocational power translated into political power. The superior numbers of Peronist Youth, FAR, and Montoneros that covered Ezeiza with flags and banners had to be demonstrated again and again until Perón became convinced that most Peronists belonged to the left wing. As in 1972, the key phrase became "to win the street" (*ganar la calle*), but this time the mobilization was not directed at Lanusse, but against the so-called reactionary forces within the bosom of the Peronist movement.

Perón clearly wished the street mobilizations to end. First, the conflict with the military dictatorship was over and now Argentina had to get back to work. Second, verticality had to reign again within the Peronist Organization, and the youth organizations, guerrilla formations, and their leaders had to subscribe to the party line. Third, the Peronist revolution was not going to happen by way of a grass roots movement, but by Perón leading the people. This demobilization would mean the death blow to the revolutionary Peronist left and prevent the social revolution from taking place at a moment of high political consciousness. Perón wanted to consolidate the Peronist Organization, head a pragmatic government based on a social pact of labor and capital, and appease the political violence that disrupted Argentine society.

On 13 July 1973, President Cámpora presented his resignation to Congress. Raúl Lastiri was sworn in as president until the general elections of 23 September 1973.[28] Cámpora's withdrawal was widely expected, and kept the promise of the electoral slogan "Cámpora into the government, Perón into power." The Montoneros had their own explanation of events. In a public statement on 17 July titled "Perón confronts the conspiracy," they quoted Perón as saying that Cámpora's forty-five days in office had been excellent. Perón had thus no reason to end Cámpora's presidency. Nevertheless, Perón felt forced to step in, so the Montoneros reasoned, to curtail the growing power of the conspiratorial Peronist right.[29] A public display of support was the most effective means to aid the aging leader.

This show of support was made on 21 July 1973. A column of eighty thousand Peronist Youth members marched on Perón's residence at Gaspar Campos Street. Perón was not at home but invited four representatives to meet him in Olivos.[30] The JP leaders felt that they had finally gotten through to Perón, but soon after their departure, the government press agency announced that Perón had appointed the right-wing López Rega as his go-between with the Peronist Youth.

A new public display became now the only recourse to break the cordon, and tip the balance in favor of the left wing. The opportunity arrived on 31 August 1973 when Perón reviewed a parade in support of his presidential candidacy from the balcony of the CGT union headquarters. The Peronist left regarded this parade both as a showdown with the labor unions and as an opportunity to convince Perón that their political line mustered the greatest popular support.

The extraordinary importance given to the crowd competition can be inferred from the meticulous reporting by the Peronist Youth magazine *El Descamisado* about the amount of time each column spent passing before the CGT headquarters. The labor unions took two hours and forty-five minutes, while the Peronist Youth groups marched for two hours and forty-two minutes in much tighter columns and at a faster pace.[31] The Peronist left believed they had won the contest and broken the cordon around Perón. The revolutionary process could start afresh.[32]

This belief was strengthened by the visit of the FAR and Montoneros leaders Roberto Quieto and Mario Firmenich to Perón on Wednesday 5 September, and again three days later in the company of the principal leaders of the Peronist Youth. Unbeknownst to them, Perón was playing a Machiavellian game with stakes he soon failed to control. He raised their expectations because he needed their support for the upcoming elections, but had already cast his lot with the unions, the traditional vertical backbone of the Peronist movement. As Perón remarked at the beginning of September 1973, the time had not yet come for a generational rejuvenation because the country's reconstruction would take several years: "the boys will be in charge three years from now."[33] But the revolutionary Peronists were unwilling to wait three years while the Peronist right continued its advance into power.

Perón into Power

The presidential elections of 23 September 1973 were won overwhelmingly by Juan Domingo Perón.[34] Perón had not toured the country during the election campaign, and there were no massive rallies. The victory was as expected, but the ballot needed to be ratified by a massive Peronist crowd at Perón's inaugural speech at the Plaza de Mayo. *El Descamisado* expressed this sentiment of 12 October 1973, as follows: "The square almost came down when he said 'Comrades.' How much did that moment cost, that word and spoken from up there, from that balcony. . . . Many felt a shiver running down their spine. There were tears. Embraces. Others shouted like crazy. And some even lowered their head. This 'Comrades' was, crystal clear, the end of 'the battle of eighteen years.' And those present in the square were the witnesses of the signing of the triumph of this first battle."[35] The deaths of Ezeiza and Cámpora's resignation seemed forgotten when Perón dedicated a special word to the second-generation Peronists: "I want to send our deepest affection to these young people who are our hope, together with the most sincere appeal that they should work and become qualified. Because young people will be the artisans of the future we are dreaming of."[36]

These words gave new hope to the revolutionary Peronists. The cordon had been broken, Perón was now in charge, and the generational rejuvenation remained firm in place. The leader-crowd dynamic was once again the compass of Peronist rule. Perón told the crowd that "following an old Peronist custom, I will present myself each year on the first day of May at this same place to ask the people gathered here whether they agree with the government we are leading."[37] Little did Perón know that the belief of the second-generation Peronists in the mythical leader-crowd dialogues would precipitate their falling out with him on 1 May 1974. Nevertheless, in October 1973 the crowd romance was still in full bloom, and the revolutionary Peronists were convinced that their tireless crowd mobilizations had paid off.

Once Perón was in power, the Peronist Youth and Montoneros realized that he did not accept their radical proposals. He continued to advocate a pact among labor, capital, and government, while rejecting the class struggle.[38] Perón stated that the labor unions constituted the vertical backbone of the Peronist movement, and he passed legislation which increased the power of the Peronist union centrals at the expense of the more radical Independent and clasista unions.[39] The revolutionary Peronist left was dumbfounded and concluded that Perón was surrounded again by traitors and bureaucrats incapable of defending the true essence of Peronism. In their eyes, the political situation of 1973 resembled that of 1955, and they were not going to stand by passively and watch the revolution being crushed. They also concluded that street mobilizations had outlived their political usefulness.

Crowd mobilizations were abandoned and replaced by two tactics: grass roots organization and guerrilla actions. The grass roots work consisted of recruiting new members, developing local organizations in neighborhoods and slums, and founding new chapters (*unidades básicas*).[40] The guerrilla actions entailed an increased harassment of labor union chapters, and the elimination of union leaders. A deadly feud developed between the Peronist right and the Peronist left which will be discussed in chapter seven.

Crowd Rupture with Perón

The tense relationship between Perón and the revolutionary Peronists deteriorated further between late 1973 and early January 1974. Five elements contributed to this situation. One, the government proposed in December 1973 tougher laws on political violence.[41] The Montoneros declared that Perón had always maintained that the violence from above generates the violence from below. If a truly popular Peronist government had been in power, then there would not have been any cause for political violence.[42] Two, Perón stated on 10 January 1974 that he would "impose the Social Pact" if need be.[43] The revolutionary Peronists felt betrayed. In their eyes, Perón was making common cause with the Peronist right, the oligarchy, and the multinational corporations. Three, on 19 January 1974 the Marxist People's Revolutionary Army (ERP) attacked the Azul army base. Perón was furious, and insinuated a complicity of the governor of Buenos Aires, Oscar Bidegain. Bidegain sympathized with the Revolutionary Tendency, and was replaced by his vice-governor Victorio Calabró, an important right-wing union leader. Four, the guerrilla attack gave Perón further reason to pass his tough laws on political violence. He cowed eight left-wing Peronist congressmen into stepping down in case of dissent.[44] The congressmen resigned on 24 January, and the new legislation was approved on 25 January. The next day a dozen Peronist Youth chapters were bombed. The political position of the Peronist left was caving in rapidly with the loss of governor Bidegain, the eight congressmen, and the assaults on local branches. Finally, the Peronist Youth leaders had a personal falling out with Perón on 1 February. When Perón invited thirty-six representatives of an array of youth organizations, including many small right-wing groups, to reopen a dialogue, the Peronist Youth leaders refused to attend. This affront worsened the relations even more, and the pressure increased on the Peronist left in the party, the movement, and on the street. Prominent leaders were arrested, the left-leaning Peronist governor of Córdoba was deposed, the popular magazine *El Descamisado* was forbidden, and street demonstrations were repressed.

To make matters worse, the Peronist left was also weakened from the inside. Political differences made several groups turn away from the principal Peronist Youth and Montonero leaders in January 1974. One dissident group expressed its unswerving loyalty to Perón, a second group favored grass roots mobilization, and a third wanted a more confrontational opposition to the Peronist right.[45] The Peronist left was falling apart and losing political ground. They embarked deliberately on a collision course with Perón. Aside from guerrilla operations, their principal weapon became once again the crowd. They were going to demonstrate their power of mobilization at Perón's appearance at Plaza de Mayo on 1 May 1974.

The 11 March demonstration in the Atlanta soccer stadium was the general rehearsal for Labor Day. Twenty-five thousand people gathered to listen to the political state of affairs. The anxiety and defiance with which people went to the rally foreshadowed the confrontation with Perón: "We went with clenched teeth. With anger and prepared for everything. We knew that this was not going to be just another assembly. This was different. We had to show many things. Assert ourselves. We had to find ourselves again with our best weapon: the mobilization."[46] The tone of the upcoming May demonstration was summed up by *El Descamisado* in the title of the account of the Atlanta gathering: "What's happening, General. . . . The Popular Government is full of anti-Peronists [gorilas]." In this mood, they were going to the 1 May meeting, and asking Perón to account himself for his failed policies. The belief in a leader-crowd dialogue as the heart of political activity, where policies are forged among conflicting social interests, remained firm.

The long-awaited day finally arrives. The unmistakable sound of the large bass drums leaves no doubt that this is a Peronist event. The first small groups arrive at 10:00 A.M., and policemen check them for concealed weapons. The square is adorned with flags, and two large podia for invited guests have been erected in front of the Casa Rosada, bearing a CGT emblem. The official slogan is: "We agree, my General." The first large JP and Montonero columns arrive at 3:30 in the afternoon. Rivaling chants are shouted across the invisible division between the two factions, and intermittent skirmishes occur when the youth columns press against the labor union columns to occupy the left side of the large square facing the Casa Rosada. Both parties had accepted a lengthwise division of the Plaza de Mayo to prevent another Ezeiza tragedy and agreed to display only Argentine flags and union signs.[47] In a surprise move, they lower the Argentine flags and quickly spray-paint "Montoneros" on them.

The atmosphere becomes tense when Perón appears close to five in the afternoon on the balcony of the Casa Rosada, accompanied by his wife Isabel and López Rega. The military band plays the national anthem. As the last sounds die out, the public announcer asks one minute of silence "for comrade Evita and the dead of the struggle for liberation." As the quiet descends over the Plaza de Mayo, the Montoneros begin a roll call of their most illustrious dead: "Fernando Abal Medina . . . Present! Carlos Gustavo Ramos . . . Present! José Sabino Navarro . . . Present!"[48] The band strikes up the Labor March (Marcha del Trabajo). As the music dies down for the second time, Vice-President Isabel Martínez de Perón crowns the Labor queen, but the tens of thousands of revolutionary Peronists shout that they do not want a carnival but a popular assembly.

Finally, Perón steps up to microphone and, to his fury, is welcomed with the chant: "What's happening, what's happening, what's happening, General? That the Popular Government is full of anti-Peronists [gorilas]?" Perón is beside himself with anger, and after recalling that twenty years ago on this same spot he had asked the labor organizations to discipline themselves, he lashes out at the Peronist left: "I was saying that throughout these twenty years, the labor unions have remained standfast and that today some beardless young men pretend to have more merit than those who fought for twenty years. For this reason, comrades, I want that this first reunion on Labor Day will pay homage to those organizations and prudent, wise leaders who have maintained their organic strength, and who have seen their murdered leaders fall without yet having meted out punishment."[49] The revolutionary Peronists feel trampled. Perón humiliates them by calling them immature, while he embraces the orthodox labor unions that have been harassing the Peronist left with increasing intensity.

Some labor union columns begin to chant "Let them leave. Let them leave." And depart they do, chanting "Sawdust, sawing [Aserrín, aserrán], these are the people leaving" as well as "We agree, we agree, we agree, General. The anti-Peronists agree, and the people are going to fight."[50] Tens of thousands of Peronist Youth and Montoneros vacate the left side of the Plaza de Mayo in the most dramatic crowd rupture in Argentine history. Skirmishes flare up in the streets surrounding the Plaza de Mayo but fortunately there are no fatal casualties. The situation returns to normal at 7:30 P.M.[51]

Perón's political life has come full circle. Rescued by a crowd on 17 October 1945, he is now repudiated by a new generation of Peronists who has contributed most to his political resurrection. The deadly factionalism within the Peronist movement has extended into the Plaza de Mayo, can no longer be contained by the charismatic leader, and causes the first crowd defection in Perón's long political career.

The larger political conditions had been conducive for a rupture but Perón's humiliating remarks were the catalyst that drove people away. The torn feelings of identification and betrayal were profound. People turned their backs to the man for whom many had risked their lives and some endured years in prison. Rebelling against Perón was in a way reneging on the years of struggle and hardship. Political violence became the outlet for the crowd humiliation, and soon this violence was not just directed at the Peronist right but at an Argentine society which had rejected them.

From the crowd perspective I have been developing in these last four chapters, the 1974 Labor Day break with Perón was the sundering of the Peronist crowd along lines of conflicting horizontal and vertical loyalties. The horizontal identification among the rebellious second-generation Peronists was greater than the vertical identification with Perón. Comradeships nurtured during the Fight and Return campaign of 1972, the joint mourning of the fallen, and the growing embattlement from the Peronist right were centrifugal forces which drove them off the Plaza de Mayo when publicly humiliated by Perón. The Peronist crowd, divided since the day of Perón's arrival in June 1973, parted ways on 1 May 1974.

The crowd division had its origin in different types of identification. The Peronist left exalted Perón the revolutionary, to whom they attributed many of the radical ideas they had acquired during the fight for his return. The Peronist right adhered to Perón the justicialist for bringing dignity and social justice to the Argentine working class. The left had as its example the insurrectional crowds of 1969–1972, while the right cherished the leader-inspired crowds of 1945–1955. The 1973–1974 crowd rivalries, albeit violent at times, were part of the political process of a movement trying to find its proper course. Perón's alignment with the Peronist right meant an end to the crowd contest. The hegemonic Montoneros turned their backs to Perón and delivered themselves to a guerrilla warfare against the union hierarchy and the Argentine military. Perón had lost his aura as a revolutionary savior. From now on, as the editors of the leftist magazine *De Frente* concluded, "only the people can save the people."[52]

But how could the people save themselves? Faith in the voting booth had been lost, and the Labor Day tragedy had dismantled the crowd as a political instrument. It drove the *movimientista* Montoneros to vanguardism, elitism, and military action which quickly increased their distance from their popular backing. Instead, the *alternativista* groups, such as the Columna José Sabino Navarro from Córdoba, called for strengthening the grass roots organization in factories and working class neighborhoods. It is dubious whether this grass roots strategy would have been successful. The relation between the Montoneros and the masses had been affective rather than organizational and ideological. People were drawn to their crowds by the defiant "Montoneros, dammit!" chant, by the intoxicating bass drumming, and by an awe for their armed resistance against the Lanusse dictatorship. Still, the average Peronist worker was too firmly attached to the labor unions, whether orthodox or combative, to follow the lead of the Montoneros. Once the emotions of the crowd gatherings waned, the political support was gone. In the international mood of the times, vanguardism won out, and urban guerrilla warfare was embraced as the tit-for-tat killings with the right-wing death squads increased at an eerie pace.

The Final Farewell

The pressure on the Peronist left intensified on all sides after the Labor Day crowd rupture. Right-wing death squads continued to eliminate revolutionary Peronists and increased their bombings of local chapters. The left also lost administrative ground. After the forced departure of Bidegain and Obregón Cano in early 1974, three more governors with sympathies for the Revolutionary Tendency were dismissed.[53]

The political situation was not much better in the street as several public demonstrations were prohibited by the police. In fact, there were not any significant crowds during May and June of 1974. There was, however, one exception. On Wednesday morning 12 June, the aging Perón gave a televised speech to the nation, criticizing union leaders, businessmen, and the conservative press alike for endangering the Social Pact. Rumors about food shortages had led to sudden price hikes, while workers had demanded substantial salary increases. The strike activity was picking up again, and inflation was on the rise. Perón threatened to abandon the presidency if these political attacks on his government did not cease.

In a last masterful stroke, Perón orchestrated his final crowd gathering. The CGT leaders had been notified in advance of Perón's threat to resign, and called for a mass mobilization at the Plaza de Mayo in his support. Hundreds of buses were waiting at factory gates to transport the workers. A large crowd gathered that afternoon in the cold winter weather of 12 June. The labor union centrals had not lost their power of mobilization, as the Peronist left had believed, but continued to count on the support of most Peronist workers.[54] Perón was certainly warmed by the welcome as he appeared on the balcony at 5:15 in the afternoon. He took in the chants as if they were a political nourishment, and confessed: "I carry in my ears what to me is the most remarkable music of all, the voice of the Argentine people."[55] It was to be his last crowd appearance, and it seemed as if the Peronist crowd had died with him.

For weeks, Perón had been suffering from a cold contracted on his 6 June visit to Paraguay. The 12 June speech on the freezing balcony of the Casa Rosada had deteriorated his condition. Bedridden for a week, Perón delegated his presidential powers on 30 June to the vice-president, his wife Isabel Martínez de Perón. The seventy-nine-year-old Juan Domingo Perón died of cardiac arrest on Sunday 1 July 1974 at 1:15 P.M. at the presidential residence in Olivos. The funeral was held on Tuesday 3 July at the Metropolitan Cathedral on Plaza de Mayo, after which the remains lay in state at Congress. The line of mourners stretched for many blocks in the pouring rain, but "Neither the cold drizzle, nor the wet clothes stopped the crowd from saying goodbye to the president's remains."[56] Unlike the wake of two weeks after Evita's death, the grieving public was given less than forty-eight hours to pay their respects. The principal Peronist Youth and Montonero leaders also bid farewell to Perón, giving a V-victory salute.[57] Despite their falling out with Perón, they could not afford not paying homage. It would have been political suicide, and most important, they were as profoundly grief-stricken as all Peronists, left or right. Miguel Bonasso confessed in his diary at the day of Perón's death: "Several of us have cried this afternoon. For him and for ourselves. Because we were his soldiers and his children and his chosen and his rejected ones. . . . we felt that the old bastard, whom we had loved and hated as one loves and hates a father, was taking our own youth with him into his crypt. We knew that difficult times were ahead. . . ."[58]

Two generations of Peronists had come of political age since Perón founded his popular movement in 1945. Their political identities were as much linked with Perón as with the victories they reaped and the defeats and hardships they suffered in his name. Many Peronists might have lost faith in Perón's political ability to govern a country rapidly falling apart through political violence, but their Peronist identity stood firm. This Peronist identity had been shaped by the crowd and by resistance, by street mobilizations and collective violence. Mobilization and violence continued again as important expressions of political practice after Perón's death, even though the first was more rhetorical and the second frightfully real.

The transference of power to Vice-President María Estela Martínez de Perón on 1 July 1974 might have been constitutional, but it was not accepted by the Peronist left, which considered itself the true political heir of Perón.[59] On 6 September 1974, the Montoneros declared that a new period of Peronist Resistance had begun, and that their organization would go underground to resume the armed struggle. Their crowd mobilizations ceased entirely. The state of siege declared on 6 November 1974 further discouraged mass meetings. Public demonstrations between July 1974 and March 1976 consisted either of small crowds in support of Isabel Perón or street protests by striking workers. These strikes and protests were mostly about internal union disputes, shop floor democracy, poor working conditions, and deteriorating wages.

After Perón's death, the UOM and CGT union centrals, which counted on the support of the Ministry of Economy, the federal police, and the death squads headed by López Rega, began a crackdown on Independent and clasista unions. The arrest of combative labor leaders, like Ongaro, Tosco, and Salamanca, was ordered, the legal status of Independent and clasista unions was taken away, militant workers were assassinated, and union locals were bombed. Strikes and factory seizures declined rapidly because of this repression.

The first stand in this retreat was made in Villa Constitución. On 25 November 1974, steelworkers voted en masse for a clasista slate in the UOM metal workers union elections. Combative local union leaders began to demand better safety measures, higher wages, and control over production speeds. On 20 March 1975, a security force of over four thousand men entered Villa Constitución with helicopters and assault cars, and arrested the forty principal labor leaders on the charge of organizing a subversive plot to paralyze the regional industry.

The workers mounted a massive strike that lasted for fifty-nine days until several union leaders were released. This spirited protest awakened the worker opposition in Argentina. The ensuing open confrontation of forces led to the only significant crowd eruption between Perón's death in July 1974 and the military coup in March 1976 as a last gasp of the groundswell of mass protest which had begun in 1969.

On 27 June 1975, the CGT organized a demonstration to ask Isabel Perón to ratify negotiated wage increases of up to 150 percent. The crowd filled the Plaza de Mayo to capacity and turned rapidly against Isabel Perón, López Rega, and the Minister of Economy Celestino Rodrigo. President Isabel Perón announced the next day that only a 50 percent wage correction would be granted. The CGT declared a forty-eight-hour strike for 7 and 8 July. This national strike triggered a series of wildcat strikes and factory occupations called the Rodrigazo. Thousands of workers took to the streets in Argentine cities to voice their disenchantment with the Peronist government. The protest was successful. Once more, a popular crowd shook the foundations of the Argentine government. Celestino Rodrigo resigned on 18 July, López Rega was forced out of the country two days later, and Isabel Perón ratified the negotiated wage raise after all.[60]

The crowd had won a Pyrrhic victory because the Rodrigazo further destabilized the Peronist government: a government which had already lost the support of various factions within the Peronist movement and was now also facing a fractured and hostile working class as inflation skyrocketed to an annual rate of 335 percent in 1975.

The year 1975 had been the most combative year in Argentine labor history in terms of strike activity and loss of working days. The crisis was heightened in January 1976 by work stoppages, factory seizures, the threat of more strikes, and more wage demands. Rather than rallying at the Plaza de Mayo under the tutorship of once powerful union leaders, the Argentine workers were organizing in independent, grass roots coordinating committees (*coordinadoras*) of shopfloor activists and workers' commissions. A lockout of workers on 16 February 1976, organized by employers dissatisfied with the government's new economic policies, shut down newspaper stands, grocery stores, and small commercial establishments.[61] The military takeover was only weeks away.

The Demise of Argentine Crowds

Crowds exert a strange attraction on people. They are menacing and enticing, inspire fear and incite captivation. What lured the Argentine people during the second half of the twentieth century to streets and squares in increasing numbers, often at the risk of death? And what made Argentine military rulers so fearful of and at the same time so fascinated by large crowds? Is it that unpredictable power of the dense crowd packed shoulder to shoulder and hip to hip that both fascinates and frightens, threatens and beckons? The crowd seems possessed of a strange, passionate quality which when dominated invigorates their masters with omnipotence, but when unleashed paralyzes them with fear. What made crowds so mesmerizing to both Argentine leaders and the Argentine people?

Argentine crowds had created and toppled governments and dictatorships since the end of World War II. Crowds brought Perón to power in 1945, supported his deposition in 1955, contributed to the palace coups against Onganía in 1970 and against Levingston in 1971. Finally, popular crowds accomplished the downfall of Lanusse in 1973, and enforced Perón's return to power that same year. Argentine crowds have of course also often failed to achieve their objectives because of their severe repression by police and military. The defeated crowd stands in stark opposition to the victorious crowd. Fear takes the place of aggrandizement as people fall left and right, and the crowd flees in panic. Whether victorious or defeated, the crowd constituted between 1945 and 1975 the groundswell of Argentine political life.

Argentine crowds have during the third quarter of the twentieth century been leader-inspired, vanguard-inspired, mass-inspired or issue-inspired. The crowds between 1945 and 1958 were leader-inspired. People assembled in crowds till 1955 because of the presence of Perón. As I demonstrated in Chapter 1, Juan Domingo Perón drew on his knowledge of crowds to mobilize a political following in the 1940s and played on wide-spread fears about either a leaderless rioting crowd or a revolutionary insurrectional crowd to silence his critics. As an army officer, he sensed bet-ter than anyone else the ambiguous feelings about crowds among the Argentine military and conservative civilian circles. Yet Perón believed that he had the political acumen and charisma to domesticate the crowd and prevent the popular masses from falling victim to the enchanting call of communism.

After Perón's fall in 1955, the Argentine middle classes gathered in leader-inspired crowds to support the military junta that had deposed Perón. The forced exile of Perón left the Peronist movement without its leader but not without the desire to express its political convictions and protest its disenfranchisement.

The year 1959 witnessed several major protest crowds that arose around matters of economic policy. These issue-inspired crowds would most likely have continued to appear were it not for the harsh repressive measures taken against street protests in 1960, and the increasing ability of union leaders to negotiate settlements before major strikes and street marches would break out. The period between 1961 and 1969 was by and large a crowd interlude with only a few leader-inspired outbreaks of Peronist senti-ment in 1963 and 1964, and occasional issue-inspired street marches by striking workers.

The issue-inspired crowds evolved by 1969 into mass-inspired crowds mobilized by grass roots organizations. Slowly, the notion began to emerge among Peronists that the initiative for crowd formation did not come from the leader but from the people themselves. The period from 1969 to 1972 was characterized by mass-inspired crowds. Students and workers took entire city centers in an insurrectional atmosphere, despite the efforts of union leaders to discourage such collective violence.

The revolutionary left interpreted the belief among Argentine workers in the grass roots crowd model as a sign of an emerging class consciousness. Leaning heavily on Leninist insurrectional theory, the revolutionary left embraced a vanguard crowd model. The vanguard-inspired model implied that the popular masses would arise in protest against the injustices of capi-talist society but needed the guidance of a revolutionary vanguard to be successful in overthrowing the exploitative socioeconomic order. The grass roots and vanguard crowd models both departed from the understanding that leaders did not elicit and dominate crowds but that crowds allowed leaders to usurp and feed on them. In other words, behind each leader-inspired crowd lurked the force of a spontaneous and uncontrollable mass-inspired crowd.

The period between 1972 and 1974 gave rise to composite crowds that were partly leader-, partly vanguard- and partly mass-inspired. The pres-ence of Perón drew his following into the streets and squares of Argentina, but these people were equally impelled by the grass roots mobilization of the Peronist left, and the appeal of a revolutionary Peronist vanguard. Finally, issue-inspired crowds appeared again in 1975. Perón had died in 1974, the grass roots organizations of the Peronist left had been dismantled, and the revolutionary organizations had decided to wage a guerrilla insurgency. The worsening economic situation became therefore the central focus of worker protest in 1975.

Twenty-five years of crowd mobilizations had formed a mold in which other political expressions matured. Strikes, sabotage, armed struggle, factionalism, guerrilla insurgency, and state repression occurred in a climate of crowd mobilization which shaped Argentine political culture. The roles accorded to leader and crowd were recognized by all but were weighed differently by opposed social sectors. Conservative and right-wing segments— the military, landowners, industrialists, and political elites as well as corporatist labor leaders—regarded leaders as the architects of history who organized the at heart irrational masses. The revolutionary and political left considered the masses, the people, as the driving force of history— whether or not this force was delegated to a revolutionary vanguard.[62]

It is on these two political practices, mass mobilization and vanguardism, that the Argentine armed forces began to concentrate their repression when they took power in 1976. As the Generals Martínez and Jáuregui declared at a press conference in 1977: "The subversion develops two lines of action to obtain power: armed action and the insurrectional action of the masses. The Army, with the support of the other two armed forces, is defeating the executive organs of the armed action and the activists of the insurrectional action of the masses."[63]

The military strategy was guided by a multidimensional conception of crowds. Each dimension corresponded to one of several relations between armies and crowds. First of all, there was an instrumental conception based on repressing crowds, irrespective of their origin or objective. Military field manuals gave the same tactical directions for a disorderly soccer crowd, a strike crowd, or a crowd of people in a state of panic after a major natural disaster. The instrumental treatment of crowds by the Argentine army was built on classic notions of crowd psychology, and was almost identical to the tactical instructions used by other armed forces, and in particular the U.S. army.[64]

There was also a political conception of crowds. Crowds were evaluated in terms of their political origins and objectives. This analysis was more directed towards preventing and redirecting future crowd demonstrations than repressing them in the present. The political conception varied much more with the ideological mood of the times than the instrumental treatment. In the late 1960s, the understanding of crowds was framed by the Cold War, the Cuban Revolution, and the political radicalization of broad layers of Argentine society. The political crowd conception was geared towards understanding the revolutionary potential of popular protest crowds.

The instrumental and political crowd conceptions were anchored in a cultural conception. This conception was seldom spelled out, but can be understood by analyzing the complex relation among army, crowd, and society. This perspective owed much to nineteenth-century thinking about crowds as irrational, destructive, and vulnerable to deceit. Popular crowds were believed to be antithetical to Argentine society, and a denial of its natural hierarchy.

In chapter 1, I mentioned how Perón's understanding of crowds carried the stamp of Gustave Le Bon, and how the fear of crowds by the Argentine ruling class was fed by a rendition of Le Bon's ideas in the work of Ramos Mejía. Le Bon, and his late nineteenth-century contemporaries Taine, Sighele, Fournial, and Tarde, feared the irrationality and unpredictability of the crowd. The individual in the crowd was reason transformed into passion, and identity into animal anonymity. Swept away by mass hysteria, the individuals in the crowd acted as one and could be driven to destruction by their collective mind.[65] The concern of nineteenth-century mass psychologists was not merely the violence of a rioting crowd but a much deeper fear of the dominance of the multitude over the individual. These conservative social scientists feared that Western civilization might be torn asunder by violent popular masses determined "to destroy utterly society as it now exists, with a view to making it hark back to that primitive communism which was the normal condition of all human groups before the dawn of civilisation."[66] They regarded the popular riots in nineteenth-century Europe as symptoms of a deep cultural and moral crisis of Western civilization, very much as the Argentine military perceived the incessant street mobilizations of the 1970s.

Still, the Argentine military were less worried by the destructive capacity of the violent crowd itself—a fury which could never surpass the army's capacity for repression—than that people would disengage themselves from hierarchy and authority, and negate the vertical structure of society by feelings of equality and solidarity generated among crowd participants. The Argentine military had an ideological mistrust of crowds. Imbued by a Thomist world view, as will be shown in Chapter 9, they believed firmly that society was an expression of a divine hierarchy. The leaderless crowd subverted the divine social order temporarily as in a ritual reversal.

The military commanders who took power in 1976 wanted to end the cycle of recurrent political conflict incited by violent street mobilizations because they feared that the crowds might come under the influence of revolutionary leaders. The junta wanted to inoculate the Argentine people against their subversion in future crowd mobilizations.[67] The conviction that the antiauthoritarian tendency of spontaneous crowds had to be broken for the good of the nation by inculcating notions of hierarchy led the military to stage parades, religious processions, commemorations, and celebrations of military victories.

The military's fear of the revolutionary potential of crowds was complicated by a fascination with their spiritual cohesion and dogged resolution. Such force made Argentine dictators beam with an air of potency and invincibility in the sight of a crowd chanting their name; a crowd that was excited yet disciplined. There seemed among Argentine rulers a need to measure their power by freeing a leviathan which thereupon was dominated. It is this fascination with the gift to harness crowds that made these leaders fond of summoning them. The crowd empowered them by submitting to their authority. The everexistent danger that the crowd might turn against them, as happened several times in Argentine history, enhanced their appeal as proofs of legitimization, power, and authority.

In a series of thirty-four communiqués on 24 March 1976, the military junta declared first its total control over the country, and in its second communiqué prohibited all street demonstrations and crowd formations. "With the objective of maintaining order and calm, the population is reminded that the state of siege is in effect. All inhabitants must abstain from assembling along public routes and from spreading alarming news. Those who disobey this communiqué will be detained by the military, security or police authorities. It is forewarned, likewise, that any street demonstration will be severely repressed."[68]

Silence fell. The streets were empty. Now, an entirely different crowd stood in the wings to impress its stamp on the streets and squares of Argentina. The armed forces were determined to end the internecine fighting between right and left in the Peronist movement, the increasingly audacious assaults by the guerrilla organizations, and the legitimacy crisis of a crippled government. This repression was not merely antirevolutionary or a measure of state security, but it rested on a profoundly different conception of the place of leaders and crowds in Argentine society. Crowds were feared for creating an uncontrollable horizontal solidarity among people which threatened to disentangle them from the powerholders. Therefore, crowds had to be domesticated so that they would uphold authority and reproduce the hierarchical values of the natural order. Thus, an attempt was made at social engineering, at altering people's sociality away from a unifying gregariousness and towards obedience, discipline, respect for God, and awe of the nation's military leaders who had saved the country from a communist revolution and the loss of its Western, Christian civilization.

Part II
Utopia Lost: Guerrilla War and Counterinsurgency

Apartment of Vice-Admiral Lambruschini, destroyed by Montonero guerrillas on 12 August 1978. Courtesy of *Diario Clarín*.

Chapter 5
Shots in the Night:
Revenge, Revolution, and Insurgency

The execution of eight workers at the garbage dump of José León Suárez in June 1956, after a failed military rebellion against the leaders of the 1955 coup against Perón, remained an enduring social trauma of the Peronist movement. The 1957 account by Rodolfo Walsh nestled itself firmly in the popular sentiment, and inspired militant Peronists for decades. Walsh had initially supported the Liberating Revolution, but the sight of a survivor's face, "the hole in the cheek, the largest hole in the throat, the injured mouth and the opaque eyes where the shadow of death remained floating," compelled him to investigate the killings. His discovery of the true circumstances made him embrace Peronism.[1]

Walsh narrates that a group of fourteen men were listening to a boxing match on the evening of the 9 June rebellion, when the police burst into the house. The commanding officer asks about the whereabouts of General Tanco and, after receiving no answer, gives the order to take the men to the police station for aiding the rebels. Only the house owner and two visitors are vaguely connected to the rebels, all others are unaware of the conspiracy. Early next morning, after the military rebels have already been defeated, the head of police of Buenos Aires province, Lieutenant-Colonel Fernández Suárez, gives orders to execute the men. They are driven to the garbage dump of José León Suárez and summoned out of the truck. "They make the persons under arrest walk by the edge of the vacant lot," narrates Rodolfo Walsh. "The guards push them with the barrel of their guns. The pick-up truck enters the street and lights their backs with the headlamps. The moment has arrived."[2] A few men realize that they are about to be shot and walk away slowly from the headlights. The others still cannot believe that their end has come. As one man falls on his knees and pleads for his life, the first shot rings out. Three men succeed in fleeing under the cover of darkness, while three others survive by playing dead. The remaining eight are assassinated. "In the glare of the headlights where the acrid smoke of the gun powder boils, a few moans float over the bodies stretched out in the garbage dump. A new crackling of gun shots seems to finish them off."[3]

These summary executions became known as the massacre at the garbage dump of José León Suárez. The assassinations symbolized the repression of the Peronist movement during the second half of the 1950s. The narrative talent of Walsh and a general indignation kept this tragedy alive for future Peronist generations. Months after the failed 1956 rebellion Perón remarked about the military rulers: "The hatred and wish for revenge which these despicable persons have awakened among the people will one day burst into the street as a moving force and only then will it be possible to think about the pacification and unity of the Argentine people."[4]

The assassinations were so traumatizing because they revealed the defenselessness of the Peronists and the regime's willingness to use excessive violence against political opponents. The massacre became commemorated in the decade thereafter through impromptu street protests and the detonation of homemade pipe bombs reliving the trauma by seeking redress through violence. The proscription of Peronism, worsening labor conditions, mass arrests, and the repression of Peronist sentiments resulted in strike protests, civil disobedience, and sabotage.

The Peronist resistance movement wanted to take revenge and punish the repressive forces for bombing the Plaza de Mayo, executing workers, and overthrowing Perón. Perón shared these feelings because of his call for boundless violence. He suggested the creation of thousands of temporary secret groups which were to kill the principal opponents, harass their families, and incinerate their homes. "We must make them feel the terror themselves. . . . The more violent and intense the intimidation campaign will be, the more certain and faster will be its effects. . . . The greatest violence is the general rule."[5]

Perón also proposed the organization of a cellular structure of permanent, secret cells covering every province, city, village, and labor union in Argentina. The members were the dispossessed, the persecuted, and the relatives and friends of persons killed by the repression. They would pass through an initiation ceremony swearing eternal hatred towards the people's enemies. Members would wear hoods to hide their identity, and receive a number and pass word. Each sect would have a list with the names and addresses of their enemies, with the coup leaders Aramburu and Rojas at its head. Traitors received the death sentence.[6] Little came of this popular retaliation and one must seriously consider whether Perón's proposal was an instance of psychological warfare. Nevertheless, Perón's call for violence did encourage the emergence of small sabotage groups in the so-called Peronist Resistance, and the first hesitant steps of a Peronist guerrilla insurgency.

This chapter discusses the Peronist Resistance, and the appearance of an incipient guerrilla insurgency under the influence of the 1959 Cuban Revolution. Peronism was adopted in the 1960s by a new generation of Peronists trying to achieve through armed struggle what the older generation had tried to accomplish with massive strikes, crowd mobilizations, and economic sabotage. These diverse outcrops of political violence in Argentina, the determination of Fidel Castro and Che Guevara to export their revolution to the Latin American continent, and the guerrilla training received by young Argentines in Cuba, made the Argentine military prepare themselves for an impending counterinsurgency war.

The 1956 Peronist Rebellion

On 9 June 1956 Generals Juan José Valle and Raúl Tanco rose in rebellion. They demanded free elections, the restoration of civil and political liberties, and the reincorporation of dismissed officers. Although Valle and Tanco seem to have been driven more by resentment than by Peronist fervor, the belief that the rebellion tried to return Perón to power attracted many militant Peronists.[7] These civilians were to move into place once the rebellion got under way. However, they never received the weapons that had been promised, and many were arrested without having come into action.

The Valle-Tanco rebellion was doomed to fail because the military intelligence service had detected the plan weeks in advance.[8] Lieutenant-General Aramburu had already signed undated decrees to proclaim the state of siege in his absence and establish martial law. Admiral Rojas went to Navy headquarters when the rebellion took place and ordered Lieutenant-General Aramburu to pass from the presidential yacht to a naval vessel for his own safety. Next, Rojas communicated to all commanders not to execute anybody without his written approval.[9]

Lieutenant-Colonel Fernández Suárez, the commanding officer of the operation at José León Suárez, declared later that he had received information about the hiding place of General Tanco. However, arriving too late, he found only fourteen men armed with Colt pistols. In the early hours of 10 June, according to Fernández Suárez, he received an order from the Executive Office to execute the men.[10] Walsh denounced the execution as murder because the men had been arrested on 9 June at 11:30 P.M. more than one hour before martial law was announced publicly by radio on 10 June at 12:32 A.M., so the death penalty for aiding the rebels should not have been applied to them retroactively.

Admiral Isaac Rojas stated thirty-four years later that around midnight on 9 June, he had sent the order that nobody could be executed without his official permission. Unfortunately, Lieutenant-Colonel Fernández Suárez never received this order, and thus acted on his own authority against "a large group of troublemakers with fire arms and abundant means of communication."[11] Walsh, with his usual irony, appraised the actions of Fernández Suárez differently: "Everybody knows the drive with which his troops defeated the enemy; the heroism with which his Mausers triumphed over the clenched fists; the 45 caliber pistols over the moans. Your victory was overwhelming . . ., Colonel."[12]

The rebellion was quelled within twelve hours, and its leaders arrested. General Tanco sought refuge in the Haitian embassy, but General Valle surrendered voluntarily to the police.[13] The death toll of the rebellion was thirty-four. Most deaths were caused by execution, because only seven died in combat. These executions were openly publicized to intimidate any rebels at large, prevent an escalation into a civil war, and discourage future rebellions.[14] General Valle was executed three days after the start of the rebellion. Rojas confesses having been instrumental in the execution. Lieutenant-General Aramburu wanted to give Valle a life sentence, but Rojas disagreed. " 'President,' I say, 'I totally disagree. . . . the first who must be executed is General Valle because he is the leader of the thing.' And so it went. This decision was taken . . . and Valle was executed."[15]

The execution of Valle and the summary executions at José León Suárez as well as the hundreds of arrests gave a new impetus to the Peronist Resistance. Perón had strongly condemned the Valle-Tanco rebellion as naive, and suspected them of acting out of personal ambition. On 12 June 1956, he wrote that not a coup but civil resistance was the only road to success. "From now on, we must organize a total struggle at all costs. Every man, every entity, every labor union, every organization must have the struggle as its purpose. But it is necessary that the struggle will basically be a guerrilla struggle. The reactionary force must never know where to hit but must receive the blows of the resistance each and every day. . . . We have to oppose the arms of the people to the arms of usurpation."[16]

This call to arms resonated well with thousands of militant Peronists already engaged in sabotage on their own account since the Aramburu-Rojas palace coup against Lonardi. Perón's call for revenge in the January 1956 directive gave an important justification for the use of violence. "We must take revenge for our assassinated brothers in all of Argentina. We must take revenge for the thousands of comrades scoffed at and imprisoned by the reactionary force."[17] With each new death, and each new wave of arrests, new traumatizing experiences were added to existing ones, and new causes for revenge arose.

Peronist Resistance and Guerrilla Insurgency

The rank-and-file sabotage erupting after Perón's overthrow increased considerably when the moderate Lonardi government was replaced by the hard-liners Aramburu and Rojas in November 1955. The new government took measures to raise the productivity of Argentine industry, such as the reduction of worker participation in management decisions, less favorable labor conditions, and the introduction of incentive schemes. Some changes cut deep into the everyday working climate. For instance, Alberto Belloni recalls how workers at the Rosario shipyard no longer received protective masks, special clothing, and a free pint of milk when cleaning the engine rooms.[18] Workers felt that such labor measures were tarred with the brush of *revanchismo* or vindictive retaliation. The policies added more fuel to their resentment about Perón's ouster and intensified the worker resistance at the shop-floor level. Perón supported the intensification of violence, and proposed in his January 1956 directive three forms of opposition: individual civil resistance, collective civil resistance, and guerrilla warfare.[19]

The individual resistance was to consist of civil disobedience, such as leaving the water running at night, withdrawing savings, sending hate mail, making offensive phone calls, creating bomb scares, painting slogans, and spreading rumors about strikes, corruption, political deals, and troop movements. The damage done by a casually dropped cigarette, a piece of wood thrown into a machine, and the wasting of electricity at the work place would be considerable. We have no way to assess whether or not many people followed Perón's call for individual civil disobedience, but the prevailing mood was certainly conducive to such sabotage.[20]

Collective civil resistance was to take place in the social, economic, and political domains. The social and political resistance, already described in chapter 2, tried to destabilize public life and question the government's legitimacy. Strikes were organized, and the streets became the terrain of public protest by young Peronists. Neighborhood-based groups of rabble-rousers would soon disintegrate under the growing repression and their interest in guerrilla warfare would be awakened.

Economic resistance aimed at undermining the government's economic policies through sabotage.[21] The most militant workers in each plant were to form small groups operating also outside the work place. Trains were to be derailed, grain deposits set on fire, power stations outed, and locales of the political opposition torched. This resistance movement attracted considerable support. There were more than two hundred groups operating in Greater Buenos Aires with an estimated ten thousand participants.[22]

Between September 1955 and June 1956, there was a predominance of fire bombings and other forms of arson, while the period from July 1956 to January 1958 was characterized by the use of pipe bombs (*caños*). Around seven thousand explosive devices were detonated between September 1955 and February 1958.[23] There were periods of greater and lesser intensity, but a general level of political violence continued for years on end. Between 1 May 1958 and 30 June 1961, there were 1,022 incidents with explosive devices, 104 cases of arson, and 440 instances of sabotage. There were 17 deaths and 89 wounded attributed to the violence.[24] However, as James observes, the extent of the Peronist Resistance was exaggerated by the Peronists intent on demonstrating their strength and by the authorities eager to justify their repressive measures.[25] As was explained in Chapter 2, government repression and the institutional pragmatism of integrationist union leaders ended the Peronist Resistance in the economic sector by 1961.

Perón ordered guerrilla warfare as the third form of opposition once civil resistance had destabilized the dictatorship. The guerrilla insurgency would aim at military installations, public utilities, and human targets.[26] In a letter of 3 November 1956, Perón left no mistake about the nature of the violence: "The more violent we are the better: terror can only be beaten by greater terror."[27]

Perón had one insurmountable problem. He was too far from the theater of operations to direct the Peronist Resistance. He relied mainly on John William Cooke. Cooke had been a Peronist congressman and had shown his unwavering loyalty to Perón in September 1955. He was imprisoned, tortured, and subjected to mock executions. Despite these abuses, Cooke conducted the Peronist Resistance from his prison cell in Río Gallegos. Perón had so much faith in Cooke that he had even designated him in November 1956 as his successor in case of a premature death. Cooke succeeded in making a spectacular prison escape to Chile in March 1957.[28]

Perón and Cooke shared the belief that a general insurrection would bring down the Aramburu-Rojas government, but disagreed on how to achieve this objective. Perón stated that a guerrilla war should only be initiated after civil resistance and a paralyzing general strike failed to bring down the military government.[29] Cooke, instead, believed that only a combative and devoted vanguard, the "backbone of civil resistance," could instigate a mass uprising.[30]

In June 1958, Perón decided that the time had arrived to lash out at the Frondizi government which had failed to keep its promise to protect worker rights. Perón proposed both violent and nonviolent resistance. He founded the CNP or Peronist National Command (Comando Nacional Peronista) to direct the multipronged offensive. This organization functioned as a clandestine general staff to Perón. The CNP was presided over by General Iñíguez and integrated several small guerrilla organizations.[31] These groups consisted principally of retired military officers who were suspicious of civilian activists and reluctant to provide them with weapons.[32] The failed November 1960 coup by General Iñíguez, and the subsequent arrests, ended the organized involvement of these retired Peronist officers in the Peronist Resistance.[33] With the role of the retired Peronist military played out, Perón's loyal second John William Cooke came to embody the armed resistance, and would become an inspiration for the Peronist guerrilla organizations of the 1970s.

After his escape from Argentina in 1957, Cooke tried in vain to organize the armed resistance from his exile in Chile and Uruguay. The Peronist Resistance remained a rank-and-file affair that never reached the organizational level of a guerrilla organization. Cooke shuttled between Chile and Uruguay from 1957 to 1960, entering Argentina clandestinely several times in attempts to organize the Peronist Resistance, especially during the 1959 Lisandro de la Torre insurrection, until he departed for Cuba in 1960. Before his departure, Cooke gave his approval to a rural guerrilla insurgency in the remote hills of Tucumán.[34]

In mid-1959, Argentina's first rural guerrilla force arose, supported by tiny groups of young Peronists assaulting police stations to obtain weapons. The guerrilla group intended to overthrow Frondizi and pave the way for Perón's return to power. The main force in Tucumán was a poorly armed group of about twenty men, under the command of Manuel Enrique Mena, calling themselves Uturuncos. Uturunco was the Quechua word for a legendary man who transformed himself into a tiger to avenge social injustice. The timing seemed right because the industrial working class continued in a combative mood, even after the military repression of the Lisandro de la Torre insurrection in January 1959.

The thoughts of the Uturuncos must certainly have gone out to the revolutionary victory in Cuba earlier that year. The terrain was comparable to the Sierra Maestra, the population consisted also of poor peasants, and Castro's original group that began operations in December 1956 agreed more on their common opposition to the dictator Batista than on ideology. The Uturuncos were also ideologically divided, and only united in their common opposition to Frondizi. They were mostly former students coming from the left-wing JP or Peronist Youth (Juventud Peronista) and the right-wing ALN or Nationalist Liberating Alliance (Alianza Libertadora Nacionalista), as well as the PSRN or the Socialist Party of the National Revolution (Partido Socialista de la Revolución Nacional). The Peronist participants demanded the return of Perón, the nationalists opposed the drilling concessions made to foreign oil companies, and the socialists wanted more worker rights.

The small guerrilla force established two camps in northeast Tucumán, and hoped eventually to secure a liberated zone, a strategy that had proven successful in the Sierra Maestra. Their only feat of arms was the seizure of a police station in the hamlet of Frías on Christmas Day of 1959. The unexpected action received the public support of the Peronist Organization, but behind closed doors the violence was believed to be too radical and too threatening to the political space being negotiated with Frondizi. Weakened by internal divisions, ideological disagreements, and desertions, the group was finally trapped by a police force of several hundred on 10 January 1960. Three men were caught. The rest escaped to Bolivia and the city of Tucumán.[35] Even though the guerrilla insurgency had been a military failure, the die had been cast. The Uturuncos demonstrated that political protest in Argentina was not restricted to strikes, occupations, crowd mobilizations, street violence, and sabotage, but that a small group might engage the state's security forces in armed combat.

Jorge Rulli and his street fighters were impressed by the Uturuncos. "I believe that we allowed ourselves to be seduced by the armed struggle. What happens is that we were already on the pathway of violence, and it becomes then very difficult not to escalate further."[36] Some of Rulli's friends entered the Peronist guerrilla groups, but most found a new basis in the unions and joined the resistance in factories.[37] Revolutionary dreams were kindled by the contrast between the noncombative institutional pragmatism of the unions in Argentina during the 1960s, and an international context of heightened tension between East and West due to insurgency and national liberation movements in Algeria, Angola, the Congo, Vietnam, and, of course, Cuba.

The Cuban Revolution

The 1959 Cuban Revolution sent political shockwaves through the American continent. Within months after seizing power, Castro implemented radical agrarian reforms, strengthened the ties with the Soviet Union, and trained foreign revolutionaries in guerrilla warfare. The initiative for exporting the revolution was taken by the Argentine Ernesto "Che" Guevara. His so-called Liberation Department trained combatants for incursions in Guatemala, Nicaragua, Panama, Venezuela, Peru, Argentina, Haiti, and the Dominican Republic.[38] Still hesitant to admit openly to the Revolution's socialist course, Fidel Castro ordered during his April 1959 visit to Washington the rounding up of Nicaraguan trainees in Cuba, while Che Guevara declared that Cuba was exporting the revolutionary idea but not revolutions because revolutions were fought only by the exploited themselves.[39] Guevara was of course hiding his real intentions, but he was right that revolutions do not prosper without a local resonance. The failure of the Uturuncos had demonstrated this all too clearly. As we shall see, neither the Argentine revolutionaries of the 1960s and 1970s nor Guevara himself would heed this advice. Guevara embarked on a fateful and ill-conceived adventure in Bolivia, while Argentine rural guerrillas would time and again fight their losing battles without the support of local peasants.

The Cold War between the United States and the Soviet Union was heating up within one year of the Cuban Revolution. The Soviet Union had gained a foothold on the Western hemisphere, less than a day's sailing from the U.S. coast. To add insult to injury, Cuba expanded its efforts to spread the revolutionary faith in Latin America. Driven by a desire to combat American imperialism and protect the Cuban Revolution, Guevara hoped to duplicate the Cuban scenario all over Latin America. He drew three fundamental lessons about revolutionary warfare from the Cuban experience: "(1) Popular forces can win a war against the army. (2) It is not necessary to wait until all conditions for making revolution exist; the insurrection can create them. (3) In underdeveloped America the country-side is the basic area for armed fighting."[40]

Guevara's second lesson has had the most far-reaching consequences for Latin America. It is known as Guevarism or foquism, and became a license for any small group to grab arms in the hope of creating the conditions for a revolution. Guevara was blind to the unique regional, national, and international circumstances enabling the success of the tiny Castro group. He believed that they had created the conditions for their own victory, downplaying the importance of the Cuban communist party, the urban resistance network, and the assistance from radical sugar workers.[41]

Guevara and Castro may have been the first to use the term "foco" to describe their guerrilla strategy, but the Frenchman Régis Debray made it a household word among the Latin American left, and led them to believe that the Cuban Revolution could be repeated in Latin America.[42] Debray defined the foco as a nucleus of guerrilla insurgency, not a liberated zone but a small group of armed men determined to create a revolutionary front that eventually would engage a professional army in combat. A number of metaphors were used that spoke more to the imagination than to reality: the foco is a detonator, a small engine that jump starts the large engine of mass insurrection, that spreads itself like an oil patch across the nation and, the most famous of all, "For the prairie to catch fire, it is necessary that the spark should be there, present, waiting."[43]

Once volition entered the political field, it overshadowed everything else. Not the painstaking building of grass roots support as had been the practice in Peronism or the strengthening of the party apparatus as was the custom among traditional communist groups, but foquism became the most appealing revolutionary practice. Pedro Cazes Camarero reminisces how after years of standing at factory gates in the industrial belt of Buenos Aires, trying to pass out pamphlets which few workers accepted, he was immediately taken by the example of Che Guevara. The idea that the revolution was within reach through sheer will power proved irresistible. "The echoes of the Tragic Week, of the Rebellious Patagonia, of the 17th of October came back to us. We had no longer the sensation that we would have to wait forever, in a curve of history, for this vehicle that would maybe never come."[44] The participation of the intellectual left no longer consisted of high-flown discussions in Café La Paz in Buenos Aires but meant a struggle "with vile acts, with blood, with sweat, and with human lives."[45] The young revolutionary left in Argentina saw themselves as the authors of history, and the anonymous masses as their subject matter, a reticent and retrograde mass which needed to be awakened by spectacular armed actions.

The People's Guerrilla Army

Castro's landing on Cuba in December 1956 did not draw much attention in Argentina. Argentina was too occupied with the failed Valle-Tanco rebellion and the Peronist Resistance. It was not until the Argentine journalist Jorge Ricardo Masetti interviewed Fidel Castro and Che Guevara in March 1958 that Argentina began to take notice.[46] The Peronists were at first at a loss about what to make of the Cuban insurgency because the Argentine middle class applauded the resistance against Batista, whom they likened to Perón. The Argentine military even sent weapons to Castro because the overthrow of Batista would be one corrupt dictator less in Latin America. This support meant that, in a knee jerk reaction, the Peronists and the working class adhered to Batista.[47]

Masetti returned frequently to Cuba, came under the wings of Guevara, and received military training in Cuba, Czechoslovakia, and Algeria.[48] Guevara urged Masetti and the Argentine exiles in Cuba to set aside their ideological differences, and start a revolutionary insurgency in Argentina, eventually under the general command of Guevara himself.[49] Guevara chose the province of Salta in northern Argentina as the first theater of operations.

On 21 June 1963, Masetti and his men, including several Cubans, made their first foray into Argentine territory. The group called itself the People's Guerrilla Army or EGP (Ejército Guerrillero del Pueblo). They had great difficulty scaling the inhospitable terrain, but their largest problem was to secure the support from the local population. Unlike the Sierra Maestra, the remote Salta region did not have the type of peasant brokers who had been of decisive influence for the survival of Castro's rebels providing local recruits, guides, couriers, and supplies.[50] Masetti and his group were shocked by the economic deprivation and ideological backwardness of the poverty-stricken peasants. As Ciro Bustos, one of the surviving members, remembers, "You couldn't even call these people *campesinos* [peasants]. These were people who lived in little bush clearings, full of fleas and dogs . . . and snot-nosed kids, with no links to the real world, nothing."[51]

The tiny People's Guerrilla Army also faced adverse national conditions. The July 1963 presidential election of Arturo Illia undermined the legitimacy of the guerrilla struggle. Even though the Peronists had abstained from voting, Illia was a democratically elected head of state who tried to lessen the political repression in Argentina. The Peronist movement was gaining strength again with street demonstrations on 17 October 1963, and with Perón's promise that he would return to Argentina in 1964. Nevertheless, Masetti sent a communiqué to President Illia, berating him for accepting the electoral fraud, and vowing to do battle for the liberty of Argentina.[52] Unlike Cuba during the late 1950s, Argentina had several more plausible roads to power available than an unpredictable guerrilla insurgency in a remote region of the country.

Meanwhile, Masetti and his group were going through some tough times of their own in the forested mountains of Salta. They were continuously short on supplies and faced internal problems. Two young middle class recruits had been executed for lowering morale and not measuring up to the high standards of a guerrilla fighter. Still, Guevara sent his trusted José María Martínez Tamayo in late September 1963 to prepare for his arrival. This Cuban army captain told Masetti that Salta was unsuitable for a guerrilla insurgency, that the group should be more mobile, and that a new front had to be opened in Tucumán.[53] By November 1963, local cattle ranchers tipped off the Argentine border patrol to the guerrillas' presence.

Masetti decided to take the initiative on 18 March 1964 when the CGT union central planned a general strike against the Illia government. Multiple attacks on several rural military posts would express the guerrillas' solidarity with the workers' cause, and would deceive the military about the real strength of the tiny group. Masetti hoped to secure enough weapons to arm a second guerrilla group in Tucumán. These Armed Forces of the National Revolution or FARN (Fuerzas Armadas de la Revolución Nacional) would be led by the Cuban-trained Angel Bengochea. However, Bengochea never arrived in Tucumán. He and four comrades, as well as six residents of the building, were killed by a massive explosion in May 1964 while manufacturing bombs in a downtown Buenos Aires apartment.[54]

Masetti went ahead as planned. His group was reinforced with five new recruits from Buenos Aires who had a falling out with the Soviet-leaning Argentine communist party. Unbeknownst to Masetti, two combatants were undercover agents of the Argentine secret service. Around the same time, local gendarmes discovered a meeting point along the Salta-Orán road where the guerrillas came to pick up supplies. Soon, they captured the first guerrillas, among them the two undercover agents. Ricardo Rojo recalled that five captives were tortured with mock executions and by submerging their faces in the intestines of their dead comrades.[55]

The net closed rapidly around Masetti's group. Several men died on 18 April 1964 in an ambush, including a former Cuban bodyguard of Che Guevara, while a starving Masetti and three companions wandered around aimlessly in the mountains. The group decided to split in two. After their departure, one man fell to his death, and his companion was captured by the gendarmes. By late April, there were eighteen men in custody who would eventually all receive lengthy prison sentences.[56] Masetti and his companion were never again heard of. His former comrades in arms have provided three possible explanations: suicide, starvation, or their assassination by the gendarmes who stole the twenty thousand dollars in Masetti's possession.[57]

The feelings of many young Argentines about the demise of Masetti's military adventure were voiced by Juan Gelman in his poem "Deeds" ("Hechos").

I would like to know
what am I doing here below this roof safe from
the cold the heat I want to say
what am I doing
while Commandant Segundo other men
are pursued to death are
given back to the wind to the time that will come
and the sadness and pain have names
and there are shots in the night and I can't sleep[58]

There was an intense soul searching among Argentina's post-World War II generation about what to do, what life to lead, and how to bring about change. Young, politically conscious Argentines perceived an analogy between the American semi-colonization of Cuba with its brothels, casinos, and impoverished peasantry and Argentina with its landed gentry and conservative ruling class. The presence of Che Guevara added a special flavor to their state of mind. They romanticized Fidel's Cuba, its Revolution, its deliverance from exploitation and injustice, its stimulation of the arts, its Caribbean exuberance, and its promise of a New and morally superior Man. The 1966 coup in Argentina and its crackdown on the freedom of thought, together with the death of Guevara in 1967 and the murky involvement of the U.S.A. in Vietnam, turned self-reflection into action.

The gauntlet had been thrown in Argentina's political arena. Guevara's dream of liberating his native Argentina ended in 1967, but his ideas about revolutionary violence would outlive him for at least a decade.[59] The Uturuncos and the People's Guerrilla Army might have failed but an urban guerrilla insurgency, which was much more appropriate for an industrializing nation, was already brewing at the time of Guevara's death. This guerrilla insurgency emerged within the Peronist movement, and bore the ideological stamp of John William Cooke, an early admirer of the Cuban Revolution. Cooke's militant past and proximity to Perón allowed him to draw upon the Peronist following for the grass roots support which Masetti and Guevara had lacked. Cooke's revolutionary Peronism became firmly implanted among young Peronists, and his works would be the second most sold Peronist books in 1973, only those of Perón ahead of him.[60] Cooke's enduring contribution to the revolutionary Peronism of the 1970s was his strategic shift from crowd mobilization to vanguardism, and his ideological development from Peronism to socialism.

Cooke's Provocation

John William Cooke arrived in Havana in mid-1960 to share in its revolutionary vigor. He learned that a truly national liberation, traditionally desired by Peronism, could not be accomplished without a social revolution. Peronism and Castrism were national expressions of the same anti-imperialism, and he even invited Perón to move from Madrid to Havana.[61] Perón never responded, and the two grew apart ideologically.

Cooke's awareness went hand in hand with his interpretation of Peronism as a movement of social emancipation arisen in response to a crisis of the Argentine bourgeois system. He emphasized that the Peronist movement was a heterogeneous, multiclass movement which contained within itself a struggle between opposed class interests. The orthodox segment, represented by the pragmatic union leaders, held back the revolutionary potential of the Peronist masses. The struggle between reformists and revolutionaries would eventually be resolved in a dialectic fashion, and be won by the revolutionary Peronists.[62] The development of a revolutionary Peronism without Perón was only a matter of time. Just as Peronism became wed to socialism, and Perón became replaced by the revolutionary vanguard, so the Cuban Revolution became a model of inspiration for Cooke. Guerrilla insurgency was to replace the Peronist crowd mobilizations as the principal political instrument of change.

In 1964, Cooke founded the Peronist Revolutionary Action or ARP (Acción Revolucionaria Peronista). Cooke justified the use of violence by arguing that the bourgeois state was founded on the structural violence hidden in its institutions and crystallized in its laws. The guiding principle behind the words of vanguardists, such as Cooke, was the belief in a political *Verelendung*, the conviction that a violent deterioration of the political process would persuade the armed forces to militarize the conflict and respond with excessive violence.[63] This escalation would reveal the true repressive nature of the Argentine regime and provoke an insurrection. In more Peronist terms, the structural violence from above would provoke the armed violence from below which, in turn, would result in more repressive violence from above. This dialectical process would raise the political consciousness of the working class, undermine the legitimacy of the State, and end with a revolutionary insurrection.

Despite Cooke's call for a guerrilla insurgency, his group never came into action, this to the chagrin of several members who decided to split off in late 1966. The dissidents included future Montoneros such as Fernando Abal Medina and Norma Arrostito. They converted Cooke's ideas into practice.[64] John William Cooke was not to witness the revolutionary surge of the 1970s of which he had been one of the intellectual fathers. He died of cancer in September 1968, at the age of forty-seven, in Buenos Aires.

Despite Castro's threat to turn the Andes into the hemisphere's Sierra Maestra, Cuba's assistance to Argentine revolutionaries consisted only of the basic training of a hundred or so Argentines and limited support for Masetti's People's Guerrilla Army.[65] Nevertheless, this Cuban connection troubled the Argentine military. Analyzing national threats in geopolitical terms, they perceived an international conspiracy of a magnitude that vastly surpassed reality. Nuclear deterrence between East and West had moved the battlefield from Europe to Asia, Africa, and Latin America, so they argued. World War III would start there as the communists tried to achieve world hegemony.

The fear of an Argentine social revolution was not new. As I explained in Chapter 1, similar fears had been voiced since the beginning of the twentieth century, and especially after the Russian Revolution. The Cuban Revolution resuscitated these worries. Many Latin American officers doubted whether the United States had the political capacity and military capability to protect the world from communism. Cuba, the Berlin Wall, Vietnam, and the unstoppable decolonization of the Third World were all signs that the West was losing ground. Democracy and Christianity were on the retreat, and the Latin American nations had to unite their efforts in combating the communist aggression.[66]

The Latin American military rejected the professionalism of the American armed forces and harked back to a nineteenth century Hispanic tradition in which the military were the nation's moral guardians. They emphasized tradition, authority, spirituality, honor, abnegation, and austerity, all values which the Argentine armed forces had upheld in a more glorious past. They deplored the materialism, individualism, sexual permissiveness, and moral corruption of the Western world. Crucial was their belief in the gift of leadership (*don de mando*), an inbred, near-mystical, charismatic quality, which obliged them to lead the nation through turbulent times. A national security policy emerged which integrated national defense with economic development, political consolidation, and ideological combativeness.[67]

The military's belief in their historical protagonism became cause for action when democratic Latin American governments began to suffer from guerrilla insurgency, labor unrest, economic recession, and legitimacy crises. The 1964 military coup in Brazil was the first stance made in Latin America to halt the process of deterioration and implement a national security plan. Brazil's example would soon inspire similar takeovers in many other Latin American countries.[68]

The concern with national security in Argentina was voiced by General Osiris Villegas, one of the principal experts on revolutionary war. He wrote already in June 1961 that this new type of warfare was invading all domains of society by making people their battleground, seeking the destruction of their personalities and trying to convert them into a depersonalized mass under the guardianship of a socialist State.[69] These same ideas were expressed by General Juan Carlos Onganía on 6 August 1964 at the Fifth Conference of the American Armies at West Point Military Academy. The speech was largely written by General Villegas. Onganía declared that the armed forces had the constitutional mission to secure the country's internal peace when domestic enemies, under the influence of foreign ideologies, threatened its republican institutions.[70] The armed forces could not become the obedient instruments of an illegitimate authority which violated the democracy they were supposed to protect. In the end, the Argentine military owed a loyalty to the Constitution, but not to the ruling parties and elected politicians.[71]

The sting of the West Point address was in the self-adjudicated obligation to "defend the spiritual and moral values of Christian and Western civilization."[72] This clause gave the military a safe-conduct to grab power whenever they believed that Argentine culture was under threat of "foreign ideologies." The West Point address tied the defense of civilization to domestic military intervention, and labeled political opponents as enemies of Western culture.

Two years later, retired General Onganía succeeded President Illia after a military coup. The new regime was called the Argentine Revolution, and the Marxist infiltration in Argentine society figured prominently among its justifications.[73] General Villegas explained to me twenty-four years later how the decision about the military takeover was reached. "There is a national atmosphere that cries out for a solution, involving a group of men, the general staffs of the forces, the academies, and certain important clubs such as the Jockey Club. As these men who know each other are talking—they are friends—they begin to arrive at a certain conclusion."[74] In other words, a small group of civilians and officers at high levels decided in 1966 whether or not the elected government still had the confidence of the Argentine people.

The government's acid test of legitimacy was the presence or absence of crowd mobilizations in support of the embattled head of state. Villegas mentioned the overthrow of President Illia as a case in point. "The people went on with their daily activities as if nothing had happened. . . . The question is then: was this man really representative for the people? Was he the governor of these people who didn't bat an eyelid?"[75] The 1966 Argentine Revolution promised to put Argentina again on the tracks of progress. The subordination of the unruly labor unions, the disenfranchisement of the Peronist movement, and the building of a national defense against foreign ideologies and guerrilla insurgents were high on the agenda.

Guerrilla Resurgence in Argentina

Two international conferences held in Cuba in 1966 and 1967 were clear proof to the Argentine military that a guerrilla insurgency was becoming likely.[76] These conferences aimed at coordinating the guerrilla insurgencies in the developing world. The January 1966 conference was attended by nearly five hundred official delegates and six hundred observers and invited guests. John William Cooke was there, representing various factions of revolutionary Peronism, while Héctor Villalón acted as Perón's representative.[77] More important than the resolutions and speeches were the behind the scenes contacts among radical groups. Surprisingly, Che Guevara did not attend the conference. He was bogged down in a hopeless effort to unite the rebel forces in the former Belgian Congo.[78] However, Guevara had prepared a message to the conference containing a chilling threat: "How close we could look into a bright future should two, three, or many Vietnams flourish throughout the world with their share of deaths and their immense tragedies, their everyday heroism and their repeated blows against imperialism, impelled to disperse its forces under the sudden attack and the increasing hatred of all peoples of the world!"[79]

The August 1967 conference was again attended by Cooke and other Argentines and was mainly concerned with creating focos in Latin America. Che Guevara was once more absent, but was elected its honorary president. Guevara was of course in Bolivia, fighting his way to a new dawn whatever his immediate success on the battlefield. One month later, Guevara was dead, but his spirit was very much alive. As Castro said in his eulogy one week later, "Che has become a model of what men should be, not only for our people but also for people everywhere in Latin America. Che carried to its highest expression revolutionary stoicism, the revolutionary spirit of sacrifice, revolutionary combativeness, the revolutionary's spirit of work."[80]

Castro was right. Within less than a decade of the 1959 Cuban Revolution, the political landscape of Latin America had undergone a cataclysmic change. This situation was in large part due to the socioeconomic and political conditions of the Latin American countries themselves and to the military response to the Cuban Revolution, and only to a lesser degree to the active Cuban assistance in training and arming would-be insurgents.

Castro's eulogy to Guevara had not gone unnoticed in Argentina but, to the dismay of the Argentine military, the resurgence of a rural guerrilla foco in Argentina did not come from Cuban-backed Marxists. At dawn, on 19 September 1968, a large police force overpowered fourteen guerrillas. The group was caught by surprise as they were returning to base camp after a long march. The secret encampment was situated twenty kms. east of the small town of Taco Ralo, in the extreme south of Tucumán province. Most guerrillas were between twenty-five and thirty years of age. The setting closely resembled Guevara's encampment in Bolivia: the remote ranch was bought by one of the guerrillas; it functioned as a training ground, had a shooting range for target practice, a storage place for arms, communications equipment, two years of canned food supplies, surgical instruments, and even some cages with carrier pigeons. Most disconcerting was that the thirteen men and one woman did not identify themselves as communists but as Peronists, and called themselves the Peronist Armed Forces or FAP (Fuerzas Armadas Peronistas). They were planning to come into action within one month, on historic 17 October.[81]

This tiny foquist insurgency by militant Peronists troubled the Argentine military. If there was a rapprochement of Peronism and Guevarism, then this would have tremendous consequences because these guerrillas might much more easily receive the help of rank-and-file Peronists than a Marxist insurgency. The connection between Marxism and Peronism had already been made ideologically by Cooke, Hernández Arregui, and other revolutionary Peronist thinkers, but the FAP guerrillas were the first proof that those ideas were being acted upon.

Several small Peronist groups had tried since 1964 to organize a guerrilla insurgency but none of them ever came into action. Still, these groups did more than just go through the motions of insurgency. Valuable relations were forged among would-be combatants of very diverse political backgrounds, ideological discussions strengthened their resolve, tactical disagreements sharpened their knowledge of guerrilla warfare, and occasional military training prepared them for action. The FAP members captured at Taco Ralo exemplified this process of maturation. The fourteen members came from Cooke's ARP (Peronist Revolutionary Action), the Uturuncos, the MJP (Peronist Youth Movement), and Palabra Obrero.[82]

In a November 1968 communiqué from their prison cells in Buenos Aires, the guerrillas stated: "We belong to a new Peronist generation born of the struggle amidst the thundering noise of the murderous bombs of the 16th of June 1955 at the Plaza de Mayo and the executions of the 9th of June 1956 of General Valle and his brave comrades."[83] They declared having taken up arms to fight for the happiness of the Argentine people and the greatness of the nation. There was no option left but the armed struggle to overthrow Onganía, and achieve economic independence, political sovereignty, and social justice.[84]

Reading about the factionalism of the early years of the armed struggle, one comes to the conclusion that personal sympathies and petty politics played a much greater role in the internal divisiveness of the many small guerrilla organizations than any real strategic differences. They all desired the overthrow of the Onganía dictatorship, all rejected crowd mobilizations as ineffective, and all were convinced that armed violence was the only means to achieve their objectives. They were inspired by the Cuban revolution, most groups regarded themselves as the vanguard of the Peronist movement, and these same groups all demanded social justice and the return of Perón to power. Finally, they were all moved by anger.

The capture of the fourteen FAP guerrillas at Taco Ralo showed for the third time that a rural insurgency was not possible in a highly urbanized Argentina. Soon, the strategy changed to urban guerrilla warfare. But the Argentine military were lying in wait. Even before one shot had been fired, they were convinced that Argentina was the next target of a global revolutionary war. At the beginning of 1969, both the urban guerrillas and the military counterinsurgency were poised for action. About three thousand Argentines had received at least some guerrilla training during the 1960s, while Argentine military commanders had received counterinsurgency instruction in the United States.[85] The Cordobazo and Rosariazos of May 1969 were the starting signal. These crowd mobilizations were read by guerrillas and military as a popular surge of revolutionary consciousness that would now justify a call to arms.

Chapter 6
The Long Arm of Popular Justice: Punishment, Rebellion, and Sacrifice

On the morning of 29 May 1970, at the first anniversary of the Cordobazo, Fernando Abal Medina and Emilio Maza ascend to the eighth floor of 1053 Montevideo Street and ring the bell of former President Aramburu's apartment. His wife opens the door and beckons the two young men posing as army officers to enter. An impeccably dressed Aramburu enters the room, drinks coffee with the two officers, while the men offer to improve the general's security situation. At 9:30 A.M., the two men rise to their feet and ask Aramburu to accompany them outside. Aramburu is neither surprised nor alarmed. Possibly, he thinks that a coup against Onganía is finally occurring, and that he will be invited to become Argentina's new president. Aramburu is taken to a white Peugeot, and later transferred to a van. After another vehicle change, he is driven to a small ranch near the hamlet of Timote in Buenos Aires province. The ranch belongs to the family of Carlos Ramus.

On the evening of 29 May, Aramburu is led before a revolutionary court composed of three guerrillas. "The first charge we made against him was the execution of General Valle and the other patriots who rose with him on the 9th of June 1956," recalled Norma Arrostito and Mario Firmenich in their chilling 1974 account. "In the beginning he tried to deny everything. He said that he was in Rosario when that happened." They read the death sentences signed by Aramburu and describe the executions at José León Suárez. "He was without an answer. Finally, he admitted: 'All right, we were making a revolution, and every revolution executes the counter-revolutionaries.'"[1] Aramburu is asked about his involvement in a possible coup against Onganía, and he admits to the need for a transitional government. When the guerrillas ask about the fate of Evita's embalmed body, he responds that it is buried in a Roman cemetery under the Vatican's care.

At day break on 1 June, Fernando Abal Medina gives Aramburu his sentence: " 'General, the Tribunal has sentenced you to death. You are going to be executed in half an hour.' He tried to affect us emotionally. He spoke of the blood that we, young kids, were going to shed. We untied him when the half hour was over, made him sit on the bed and tied his hands on his back. He asked us to tie his shoes. We did so. He asked if he could shave himself. We said that we didn't have the implements. . . . He asked for a confessor. We said that we couldn't bring a confessor because the roads were being checked."[2] They take Aramburu to the basement, stuff a hand-kerchief in his mouth, and put him against the wall. Mario Firmenich returns upstairs to hit with a wrench on a vise to dissimulate the shots. At 7:00 A.M., the twenty-two-year-old Fernando Abal Medina, who had received military training in Cuba in 1967, shoots the sixty-seven-year-old former President Lieutenant-General Pedro Eugenio Aramburu in the chest, and then gives three coups de grace. The body is buried in the basement, and discovered by the police six weeks later.[3]

The assassination of former President Aramburu by a guerrilla group of young Peronists rocked the nation. Many Peronists regarded the execution as a justified vengeance for his 1955 coup against Perón and the 1956 exe-cutions at José León Suárez. They were having barbecues in celebration. After all, Perón himself had said in 1956: "The day that Aramburu, Rojas, and the last of their murderers have died, we will have taken not only revenge for our brothers but then the Republic can sleep peacefully, free of the tremendous nightmare that weighs it down. Killing these infamous men is not only a matter of patriotism but also of self-defense."[4]

Other sectors of Argentine society were horrified by the merciless act and worried that a new threshold had been crossed involving the country more deeply into a violent descent begun the previous year with the Cordo-ban worker and student insurrection. Aramburu's abduction meant the decisive blow to a government already seriously destabilized by the crowd violence of 1969. Ten days after the abduction, President Onganía was forced out of office by army strongman General Lanusse and replaced by General Levingston. The Argentine military consider Lieutenant-General Aramburu as the first victim of the revolutionary violence of the 1970s.[5]

Aramburu's execution signaled, in the eyes of many young Peronists, an end to the impunity of Argentine political leaders and made room for many more future Aramburazos. Any high-ranking military or police offi-cer was now fair game, and there were hundreds of young Peronist and Marxist revolutionaries ready to reap the glory of an act of popular justice. One tiny group of determined young Peronists had shown that the military were not invincible. This encouraged others to join the armed struggle, carried forward by the groundswell of worker and student protest in Cór-doba and Rosario.

The wheels of violence had been set in motion by the anger, hatred, and humiliation accumulated during nearly two decades of Peronist proscrip-tion, the succession of military dictatorships, the imprisonment of thousands of political opponents, and the deaths inflicted by the military. The repression was suffered by young and old alike, but the younger generation felt particularly oppressed by the disciplinary military regime. Still at the start of their lives, they were more inclined to rebel. Imprisonment, torture, and even death could not detain the young revolutionary left. The personal costs were known to all, but were regarded as inevitable sacrifices of the political struggle. The Aramburazo showed that retaliation was possible, and this gave a tremendous boost of confidence in the ability to change the country's political direction.

Assassinations and executions had become legitimate political methods to enforce the transition from dictatorship to democracy, and these radical measures were supported by Perón, the Peronist leadership, and the young middle class. A tiny group of guerrillas, many of whom were too young to have had a personal recollection of Aramburu's decisions, tried to undo the suffering of their parents' generation. They became emotionally so tied up with those injustices that these resurfaced again and again, and could not be appeased. The young generation had become part of a social trauma which, furthermore, was fed by new humiliations, injustices, and traumas as they were hunted, abducted, and tortured in the early 1970s. New causes for violence were added to old ones. These emotions became enmeshed with ideological convictions that rationalized the use of violence in the pursuit of political objectives.

In this chapter, I describe the emergence of Peronist and Marxist guerrilla organizations, and demonstrate how they saw their violence as redemptive and retributive. I do not elaborate on the complex factionalism, internal squabbles, breakaways, temporary coalitions, and personnel changes within the revolutionary left.[6] Instead, I organize the guerrilla insurgency into Marxist and Peronist guerrilla organizations, of which the PRT-ERP and the Montoneros became the most prominent after 1972.

Anger, Liberation, and Social Justice

The touch of a dead baby changed Luis Farinello's life. Father Farinello remembers himself as a timid, unworldly young man who visited the slums near his parish in Quilmes weekly out of a sense of obligation. One day in 1968, he saw an ambulance waiting outside a small shack and heard a woman crying inconsolably. Father Farinello stepped inside and was handed a dead baby. "I looked at him. He was big, skinny and dark. I pressed him tightly to my chest. Never had I held a dead infant in my arms."[7] The twenty-seven-year-old Luis Farinello could not sleep for days, asking himself what it really meant to be a priest and wondering about the world he was living in which allowed people to go hungry and their babies to die of malnutrition. The step to joining a movement of progressive Third World priests was small and obvious.

The awareness of Argentina's social injustices awakened in Father Farinello arose with equal strength among middle class youth in the mid-1960s. Worldwide, there reigned a spirit of rebellion. The desire for radical change existed among young people of all political persuasions but its translation into concrete objectives depended on national circumstances. What for young Americans was the Vietnam war and the civil rights movement, and for young Europeans the radical reform of the universities and the approach to the working class, was for young Argentines the Cuban Revolution, the Cordobazo, and the Onganía dictatorship. This historical context defined them as a generation.[8]

The young middle class, left and right, felt suffocated by the Onganía government. They could not participate in politics because Congress had been closed, political parties dissolved, and universities placed under strict administrative control. In this repressive political climate, the rebellion surfaced first in music, art, literature, and film; often borrowing from similar cultural expressions in Europe and the United States. A cultural space within the authoritarian Argentine state was created which soon expanded into the political arena. Mostly young people began demanding the same freedom of political imagination which they had opened in the cultural realm. The power to create a new political reality and shape Argentina's future became desired with increasing intensity and force.[9]

The embrace of vanguardism during the 1960s had initially more to do with the general appeal of armed action than with an ideological affinity with the Cuban Revolution. Even Andrés Castillo and his Peronist friends, who condemned the Cuban Revolution for its socialist course, wanted to reach for weapons. They decided in 1959 to join the falangist Tacuara movement which glorified violence and sacrifice. "Tacuara embraced violence as a form of activism and this was wonderful to us, something in which we really believed. . . . We joined because of the nationalism, the violence, because of the truth of fists and pistols over reason. All this took hold of us."[10] Violence became for them the only road available to influence the political direction of Argentine society in a time of repression, proscription and disenfranchisement.

Independent of the right-wing Tacuara, a left-wing Tacuara organization, called MNRT or Tacuara Revolutionary Nationalist Movement (Movimiento Nacionalista Revolucionario Tacuara), was founded in 1962. The MNRT robbed a bank in August 1963, in which two guards were killed and $100,000 was taken. The group disintegrated in 1964, but the organizational links between the middle class nationalist, Catholic youth and the lower class nationalist, Peronist youth had been forged.[11] These links were reinforced ideologically by a movement of progressive priests emphasizing the Christian duty to care for the poor and combat social injustice. Encouraged by the progressive encyclical *Populorum Progressio* of March 1967, Argentine priests founded in May 1968 the Movement of Priests for the

Third World (Movimiento de Sacerdotes para el Tercer Mundo).[12] The movement represented around four hundred Argentine priests, out of a total of five thousand. Its 1968 manifesto spoke about the "unjust violence" of hunger and exploitation, and the "just violence" of the oppressed seeking liberation, and was personified by the Colombian guerrilla-priest Camilo Torres.[13]

Hundreds of young Catholic nationalists were radicalized under the intellectual influence of Juan García Elorrio and the tutorship of the Jesuit Carlos Mugica. Mugica was the spiritual advisor of the National School of Buenos Aires (Colegio Nacional). This high school was attended by Fernando Abal Medina, Carlos Gustavo Ramus and Mario Firmenich, the founders of the Montoneros. The students accompanied Mugica in 1964 on his visits to the shanty towns of Buenos Aires and the impoverished countryside of Santa Fe province.[14]

Like the founders of the Montoneros, thousands of young people, especially high school and university students, became moved politically by compassion and solidarity with the downtrodden. They initiated literacy campaigns, set up rudimentary medical posts, distributed clothing, and taught mothers about hygiene, still without any clear ideological motivation. Such motivation would soon develop as the military junta cracked down on the revolutionary outcrops of this youthful fervor for social change, and exposed the deep emotional scars that had been accumulating since Perón's removal from power in 1955. Angry at the proscription, the incarceration, the beatings, and the torture, they worked only for the return of Perón. As David Ramos, one of the few survivors of a 1968 rural guerrilla group recalled in 1988: "And facing all this [anger], the armed struggle begins to appear as the only possible, the only valid, the only way that remained to be traveled."[15]

Following the trajectory from right to left within Catholic nationalism and adding the influence of the progressive Catholic priests, the rapprochement of the middle class youth to Peronism becomes understandable. What better movement to embrace than Peronism, a working class movement which was repressed by consecutive military regimes and held social justice high in its banner? The progressive youth came into contact with seasoned Peronists who had experienced the anti-Peronist repression in their own flesh and could tell them of the bombardments of the Plaza de Mayo and the executions at José León Suárez. Many guerrillas might have had middle class and conservative backgrounds, but they were profoundly influenced by the suffering and combativeness of their working class comrades. Vengeance and the ensuing restoration of society under Peronist rule were emotional forces that reinforced the wish to participate in the political process. There arose the desire to undo the harm done to the older generation of Peronists and to the working class, and to create a better society based on human dignity and social justice.

The change from meting out punishment and exacting justice to embracing socialism was another small step. Peronism and socialism became natural partners in the fight against oppression and exploitation. Peronism had always propagated the pursuit of social justice and socialism pursued an equality for all humankind. Both ideologies rejected capitalism and imperialism. Socialism had thus a strong appeal for Peronists who were just as willing to take up arms to reinstate Perón to power as were Marxist revolutionaries who rejected Peronism as a reformist or even fascist mass movement. Despite their ideological differences and political projects, the young Peronists and Marxists preferred vanguardist violence over crowd mobilization as a means to achieve their objectives.

The majority of the persons who joined the guerrilla organizations between 1969 and 1972 belonged to the middle class and were in their early and mid-twenties; 20 percent were female. These revolutionaries were precisely not the ones who had felt the brunt of the post-1955 repression. Theirs was a call for revolution born from the idealization of the Cuban Revolution and a rebellion against middle class complacency. Those who entered after 1973 were in their late-teens, 30 percent female, of more varied class background, and many of them university students rather than workers.[16] They shared a sense of loss, anger, and humiliation with many workers and Peronists. For the youth, Catholic as well as revolutionary, working, middle, and upper class, the military junta had lost all credibility.[17]

Peronist Armed Propaganda and Political Rejuvenation

The mobilization of twenty-two thousand men to hunt after Aramburu's abductors prompted the Montoneros to mount another spectacular operation to mislead the authorities about their real strength.[18] In mid-1970, they consisted of no more than two dozen overconfident members divided between Buenos Aires and Córdoba.

On an unusually cold 1 July 1970, at 7:30 in the morning, fifteen guerrillas arrive at La Calera, a small town 18 kms. northeast of Córdoba. Two other guerrillas, posing as a married couple, had arrived earlier to register a complaint with the police. Soon, three guerrillas disguised as police officers enter the police station. The five guerrillas subdue the policemen, force them to sing the Peronist march, and destroy books and police records. The assailants steal several weapons, and leave for their next assault on the public institutions of La Calera. Three guerrillas enter the local telephone office, identify themselves as Montoneros and cut all communications. Fifteen minutes after the start of the operation, about nine guerrillas turn their attention to the bank. They rear-end the police car stationed in front with their pick-up truck and hold the two policemen at gunpoint. Within twenty minutes, the guerrillas empty the cash registers and safety-deposit boxes, leaving with about $26,000. At the same time, a few guerrillas enter the post office and run off with large quantities of stamps. One policeman, who had been wounded in a robbery carried out by the Montoneros at the same bank in December 1969, is shot again. As the group departs, they throw large quantities of caltrops to cover their retreat.

Cut off from all communications, one policeman drives to the headquarters of the Third Army Corps, and notifies the authorities. Federal police and army depart immediately for La Calera, and seal off all roads. Meanwhile, another policeman and one civilian have embarked on a hot pursuit of the guerrillas. They succeed in detaining Luis Lozada and his companion. After an intense fire fight six guerrillas, among them a gravely wounded Emilio Maza and a partially paralyzed Ignacio Vélez, are arrested.[19] The snapshot of a slightly wounded but broadly smiling Luis Lozada, his long hair trailing in the wind, and the boldness of reducing a police station, gave the operation and the guerrillas a legendary aura.[20] More correctly, the La Calera operation was a political success, but a military failure.

The arrests were disastrous for the budding Montonero organization. Emilio Maza, who had impersonated an army captain in Aramburu's abduction, was believed to have been tortured to death by the police. The interrogation of the other guerrillas and the raids on their homes led to safe houses, weapon deposits, and a blueprint of the organization's cell-like structure. The authors of Aramburu's abduction were now known to the police. Wanted posters were distributed throughout Argentina. On 16 July 1970, the half-deteriorated body of Aramburu, covered in lime, was found at the farm house of the Ramus family in Timote.[21]

More misfortune would soon strike the Montoneros. After lying low for two months, Fernando Abal Medina, Carlos Ramus, and several comrades robbed a bank on the outskirts of Buenos Aires. One week later, on 7 September 1970, Fernando Abal Medina, Carlos Ramus, José Sabino Navarro, and two other comrades were meeting in a pizzeria in the town of William Morris. The owner recognized the first two from the wanted posters distributed in July, and notified the police. Sabino Navarro escaped, but Ramus and Abal Medina, both only twenty-two years of age, died and three policemen got hurt in the fire fight.[22]

The shootout at William Morris, the ill-ending La Calera operation, and the dozens of arrests surely decimated the original Montoneros force, but it swelled the ranks with sympathizers. Solidarity calls went out from combative labor unions, the Peronist Youth, and the Movement of Third World Priests.[23] The political climate in Argentina was explosive. Auto workers in Córdoba had occupied the Fiat factories in May and June of 1970 and had taken company officials hostage. The police responded with mass arrests and a violent entry into one of the plants. There were numerous strikes and crowd mobilizations protesting the mass firings. No wonder that the funeral of Emilio Maza was attended by three thousand people, and that money was collected in factories, slums, and universities to support the imprisoned Montoneros. Likewise, the funerals of Ramus and Abal Medina at Chacarita cemetery in Buenos Aires attracted many people, and even Perón sent a wreath.[24]

The Aramburu assassination and the La Calera operation were galvanizing public opposition against the military dictatorship, but the Montoneros were in shambles. Other Peronist vanguard organizations now took the lead. The crowd violence of 1969 in Córdoba and Rosario had accelerated their formation. In 1969, they acquired military experience, bombed commercial establishments, stole weapons and explosives, and assaulted banks. 1970 was the year in which Argentina's guerrilla groups went public.[25] The Peronist Armed Forces or FAP (Fuerzas Armadas Peronistas) had recuperated from their 1968 defeat at Taco Ralo and attacked three police posts and two military installations in 1970.[26] The FAR or Revolutionary Armed Forces (Fuerzas Armadas Revolucionarias) launched on 30 July 1970 an attack on the town of Garín, in Buenos Aires province, duplicating the La Calera operation.[27] Still, the FAR did not fare much better than the Montoneros. By the end of 1970, several members were dead and many more were in prison. Again, as they had done for the Montoneros, the FAP came to the rescue by offering shelter to FAR guerrillas on the run.[28]

Perón looked with satisfaction upon the guerrilla insurgency. He had successfully ingratiated himself with a new rebellious generation which was initially more drawn to Che Guevara and Fidel Castro than to the aged leader in exile. Perón was quick to jump on the revolutionary band wagon when Guevara was assassinated in Bolivia, and recommended him as an example for the youth of Latin America. He concluded that the days of revolutionary speeches were over, and that the time of action had arrived.[29] In a September 1968 tape recording, Perón returned to his 1956 instructions to the Peronist Resistance, and proposed a "fight of vanguards" which needed to wage a "phantom war" of thousands of small battles based on the principle "hitting where it hurts and when it hurts: nothing where the force is; everything where the force is not."[30]

Still, Perón was careful not to privilege the guerrilla struggle over crowd mobilizations. The greatest danger of a vanguardist struggle was the demobilization of the Peronist movement. Perón therefore designed a three-pronged attack on the Lanusse government. He would negotiate free elections, bless the guerrilla violence, and encourage both angry street protests and peaceful crowd gatherings. Thus Perón stimulated the creation of a heterogeneous Peronist movement in order to reach the presidential seat.

Behind the struggles for Perón's return to Argentina, there was also a factional struggle between the guerrilla formations and the labor union hierarchy about the control of the Peronist movement. The union leaders wanted to recapture their role as Perón's brokers, and return to the corpo-ratism of the 1945–1955 government. Instead, the radical left wanted to become Perón's army and install a socialist government. One month after the Cordoban revolt, a guerrilla commando eliminated Augusto Vandor, the once powerful integrationist union leader. Vandor was assassinated in his office on 30 June 1969 by the National Revolutionary Army or ENR (Ejército Nacional Revolucionario). The assailants shot him twice in the chest, once in the side, and pumped two final shots in his back.[31] The writer Rodolfo Walsh, who had immortalized the 1956 massacre at José León Suárez, was one of the five persons carrying out Vandor's elimination. The ENR commando accused Vandor of having collaborated with the various anti-Peronist governments, built a union bureaucracy which controlled the rank and file through intimidation, and dampened the combativeness of the working class. Vandor's elimination was therefore code-named Opera-tion Judas.[32]

José Alonso was the second prominent union leader to fall victim to the bullets of the ENR hit squad. He was shot fourteen times on 27 August 1970 while traveling in his car.[33] The assassination of union leaders continued until 1975. These executions strengthened the belief that violence was the way to solve political differences. It was the politics of deed, not of action. What mattered was the political pressure of vanguards, not of crowds. Despite their similarity in method, the assassinations of Vandor, Alonso, and Aramburu corresponded to different political objectives. One agenda was to harass the armed forces, police, and military government. The other was a violent factional dispute with the Peronist right for the leadership of the Peronist movement.

The Montoneros regarded themselves as the life blood of the Peronist movement and the most politically conscious expression of the people's will, as proven by the sympathy for their operations. These convictions enhanced their sense of entitlement to the leadership of the Peronist Orga-nization, and strengthened their belief that such political rejuvenation was imminent.[34] In 1971 and 1972 the Montoneros began to legitimize their claim to power by usurping the leadership of grass roots organizations, notably the Peronist Youth, and were thus able to summon large crowds in their support.[35] Other Peronist guerrilla organizations were less astute at the politics of infiltration and cooptation, and could thus never muster the same mass appeal as the Montoneros. These organizations would all merge with the Montoneros by the beginning of 1973.

The Peronist guerrilla organizations marked the beat of political vio-lence against police, military, and the Peronist right, but the political situa-tion became considerably more complex with the appearance of the Marxist People's Revolutionary Army or ERP (Ejército Revolucionario del Pueblo). The ERP would become one of the key players in the spiraling insurgency violence. All in all, the total number of armed operations in

Argentina, of which almost half were anonymous bombings, had risen from 141 in 1969 to 434 in 1970. These numbers increased further to 654 in 1971. This rise was in particular due to the work of the Marxist PRT-ERP.[36]

Marxist Guerrilla Apprenticeship

The Workers Revolutionary Party or PRT (Partido Revolucionario de los Trabajadores) was founded in May 1965.[37] Mario Roberto Santucho, who had received military training in Cuba in 1961, would become its undisputed leader. In 1967, Santucho had a fundamental disagreement with secretary-general Nahuel Moreno. Santucho wanted to begin a guerrilla insurgency, whereas Moreno pursued the long road to popular insurrection. The party broke in two in January 1968, and Moreno left with one-third of the PRT members.

Now, Santucho had his hands free. The party congress of February 1968 declared that guerrilla warfare was the surest way to revolution. The worker-student alliance at the Cordobazo convinced Santucho that the party was right. Revolutionary times seemed ahead, and the emphasis on armed struggle led to a vanguardist view of insurgency at the expense of nurturing grass roots support.[38] The Vietnamese people were Santucho's great example because of their unceasing battle against American imperialism. The guerrilla war had to develop from small to large, from simple to more complex actions, and from vanguard violence to violence by the masses. The strategic plan consisted of a rural insurgency operating together with an urban guerrilla force. This war of attrition was intended to break the offensive capability of the armed forces and was supposed to end with a general insurrection.[39]

When the Peronist guerrilla organizations began stockpiling weapons in 1969 and assaulting banks to finance their operations, the PRT decided to join them. Bank robberies and the theft of arms and vehicles were the preparatory steps towards guerrilla warfare. Pedro Cazes Camarero remarks that, "Disarming policemen was like taking candies from a child. Through the years, they never, never resisted. They didn't resist. You talked to them with enough authority and they surrendered."[40] Cazes Camarero claims to have trained hundreds of comrades. Disarming a policeman was an important rite of initiation for new guerrillas because it demystified the state's security forces and convinced the young recruits that they were all-powerful.

In October 1969, the PRT planned a rural guerrilla war in Tucumán, but the preparations were detected and Santucho was arrested in late November. His escape from the prison hospital on 9 July 1970, and his decisive role in the party's national congress, put the party back on track.[41] The Fifth PRT Party Congress of 28–30 July 1970 voted in favor of creating an armed wing with the name People's Revolutionary Army or ERP.[42] Mario

Roberto Santucho remained PRT's secretary-general and became ERP's commander-in-chief.[43] The long-awaited revolutionary war had finally arrived. The jubilant delegates returned to their members and transmitted the message from the party congress. "The activists cried from happiness, they embraced one another and the enthusiasm raised the spirit."[44] The utopian dream of a new world and a new human being, free of the shackles of exploitation, repression, and imperialism, was a powerful motivating force.

The first ERP operation consisted of an assault on a police station in Rosario in September 1970. The guerrillas succeeded in briefly raising their white and blue flag with its red five-pointed star over the building. Two policemen died in the confrontation. The ERP leaders realized that such casualties might provoke a backlash among the working class. Armed operations had to be better planned, and more directed towards gaining popular support. The distribution of food to the poor was chosen as the ideal method. Food distributions were surprisingly simple. Several guerrillas would force a truck to a halt, and the driver was ordered to distribute the milk, chicken, and other foodstuffs to a poor neighborhood. Later, pamphlets were handed out, and the people were asked to collaborate with the ERP. More than half of around five hundred ERP operations between September 1970 and September 1973 consisted of operations intended to benefit the popular masses.[45]

In 1971 the ERP kidnapped the manager of a meatpacking plant in Rosario, obliged the company to distribute food, and received a ransom of $250,000. They tried but failed to kidnap General Alsogaray and sprung comrades from two prisons. One prison assault cost the lives of five prison guards. ERP guerrillas also attacked several police stations, robbed banks, and bombed many commercial establishments. The year 1971 also saw several joint operations with Peronist guerrilla groups, namely assaults on police stations, and one execution.[46]

The PRT was triumphant. "Argentina is living through crucial times. The process of revolutionary war has begun that will lead to the victory of the socialist revolution, to the final solution of the diverse and painful problems of our fatherland and our people."[47] The increased repression by the security forces was interpreted as a sign that the revolutionary war was heading towards victory. Now was the time to conquer the leadership of both the guerrilla insurgency and the working class.

However, for all the talk about urban guerrilla warfare, the over twelve hundred armed operations carried out between 1969 and 1971 were little more than armed propaganda because no sustained attempt was made to confront the Argentine armed forces. Violence was seen as pedagogic, as conceiving a revolutionary consciousness. Its success was measured by the degree of public support. A 1971 survey revealed that 49.5 percent of the

Argentine population justified the armed struggle. Surprisingly, the approval came principally from the middle and upper classes.[48]

This broad support attracted many new faces to the guerrilla organizations.[49] Crowd manifestations were generally the first step towards a growing involvement. One former member recalls how he became enwrapped in student politics after a street protest in 1970. Next, he was invited to a student demonstration. "So I went to the appointed place . . . the place looked very peaceful and suddenly I heard this ferocious roar and two thousand got going. I was terrified. But I loved it, and next time I was carrying the molotovs."[50] The PRT-ERP participated in crowd protests to attract new activists and then initiate them into the armed struggle with the disarming of policemen.[51]

Even though there is not a causal relation between crowd protests and armed operations, the year 1971 was at least quantitatively the peak year for both violent street protests and armed operations during the 1969–1973 period. There were about 700 incidents of collective violence and over 650 instances of guerrilla violence in 1971.[52] The ERP participated in the March 1971 street protests in Córdoba with snipers keeping the police at bay. The party reported enthusiastically that the crowd had closed the armed vanguard in its bosom and concluded that the mass adherence of the proletariat to the revolutionary war had forced the military to overthrow President Levingston and replace him with General Lanusse.[53] The combination of crowd protests and armed operations had destabilized the military dictatorship to such an extent that a democratic transition seemed inevitable. The new President Lanusse initiated talks with the Peronists, and began to pave the way for national elections. With the promise of democracy in place, Lanusse felt he had the political room to crack down on the guerrilla organizations.[54]

The military government had repressive measures at its disposal dating from the Onganía dictatorship. The police were on 6 July 1966 authorized to conduct house searches and detain civilians up to ten days without charge. Special War Tribunals (Consejos de Guerra Especiales) were instituted on 28 May 1969 to try and convict civilians. The state of siege was in operation from 30 June 1969, and the death penalty was reinstated in June 1970. President Lanusse added several new measures. Maximum security prisons were established in early 1971 to isolate guerrillas from common convicts. The Federal Penal Chamber (Cámara Federal en lo Penal de la Nación) was instituted on 28 May 1971 to deal with acts of political violence. Finally, the armed forces were authorized on 16 June 1971 to participate in the prevention and repression of terrorism.[55]

The vigorous pursuit of the guerrillas by the police forces, joined in 1971 by the Army, was very effective. This success was in great measure due to many indiscriminate house searches, the use of torture, and the inexperience in combat and security of the guerrillas. The year 1972 saw a dramatic decline in guerrilla violence with 352 armed operations, down from 654 operations in 1971.[56] A contributing factor was the relatively small number of guerrillas. Moyano estimates that the number of combatants increased only from 200 in 1969 to 600 in late 1972, many of whom were by then in prison.[57] These setbacks did not detain small guerrilla units from continuing their assaults, preferably with spectacular operations, such as two ERP operations that led to the death of Fiat president Oberdan Sallustro and General Juan Carlos Sánchez on 10 April 1972. These deaths filled Argentine society with horror and were condemned by Perón.

With most seasoned leaders in prison, and having lost 80 percent of their armament, the PRT-ERP tried to abandon its militarism and return to raising grass roots support. The party even contemplated participating in the elections with candidates presented by neighborhood committees. With an ingenuous ignorance of the massive support of the general elections by the overwhelmingly Peronist working class, the party suggested that the people must be given the choice between the "electoral farce" and a revolutionary war.[58]

The Dead of Trelew

The principal leaders of most guerrilla organizations, Peronist as well as Marxist, were in prison by mid-1972. The deaths of Oberdan Sallustro and General Sánchez worsened their prison regime. ERP commander Santucho was moved to the maximum security prison of Rawson after masterminding Sallustro's kidnapping from his Villa Devoto prison cell. Many FAR, ERP, and Montonero guerrillas as well as combative union leaders like Tosco and Ongaro followed his trail to Rawson, the small capital of the province of Chubut, about fifteen hundred kms. south of Buenos Aires. Far from any major urban center and hemmed in by the icy south Atlantic ocean on one side and the wind-swept plains of Patagonia on the other, the prison seemed escape-proof. In mid-1972, there were around two hundred political prisoners at Rawson.[59]

The guerrilla commanders felt the need for a spectacular action to jumpstart the armed resistance, free valuable comrades, and demonstrate that they were far from defeated. They decided upon an escape from the Rawson prison. The audacious operation was placed under the command of ERP leader Mario Roberto Santucho, and took months of planning.[60] In fact, escape plans were developed in every Argentine prison, and helped to forge close bonds among inmates from different political extractions. Notably, the Rawson escape facilitated the fusion of the Peronist guerrilla organizations FAR and Montoneros in October 1973.[61]

On 15 August 1972, at about 6:15 P.M., one guerrilla calls a prison guard to register a complaint. The guard approaches the cell, is immediately subdued, and a group of 116 guerrillas begin taking the prison rapidly, guard by guard, room by room, and pavilion by pavilion. After fifteen minutes about seventy guards have been subdued by the time all eight pavilions have been occupied, except the front gate.

The front gate is guarded by Juan Gregorio Valenzuela, and he becomes suspicious when he fails to recognize the guerrilla disguised as a prison guard. Immediately, Valenzuela orders his arrest, but the guerrilla kills Valenzuela, and wounds the other guard. The guerrillas open the front gate and wait for the four vehicles—two trucks, a pickup truck and a passenger car—to transport them to the Rawson airport. However, only the passenger car arrives due to a serious misjudgment. Already doubtful about the feasibility of Santucho's plan, his comrades outside the prison assume that the operation has failed when they hear the gun shots that kill Valenzuela. The three trucks turn around and flee.[62]

Santucho decides to proceed as planned to Rawson airport, situated about twenty-five kms. from the prison. The six highest ranking persons, Mario Roberto Santucho, Domingo Menna, and Enrique Gorriarán Merlo of the ERP, Roberto Quieto and Marcos Osatinsky of the FAR, and Fernando Vaca Narvaja of the Montoneros leave immediately. The remaining nineteen guerrillas waiting at the Rawson prison gate order four taxis. The car with the six guerrilla leaders continues to the airport and arrives at 7:15 P.M. where a passenger plane is to make a scheduled stop on its flight from Comodoro Rivadavia to Buenos Aires. Four guerrillas are on board to hijack the plane once it lands at Rawson. Precious minutes tick by as the group of six wait on board for their nineteen comrades. Santucho decides at 7:30 P.M. that they have to leave for Chile, while the fourteen men and five women, including Santucho's eight-months pregnant wife and Vaca Narvaja's companion, are forced to remain behind.[63]

As soon as the taxis reach the Rawson prison, the group of nineteen leaves for the airport. They arrive there at 7:45 P.M., and take control of the terminal. After four hours of negotiations, pressed by the army's declaration of a state of emergency, and surrounded by a marine infantry unit ready for assault, the group finally surrenders. The commanding officer Navy Captain Sosa must have felt humiliated by the negotiations because even the conscripts snicker behind his back. One naval officer expresses his frustration to a journalist: "I'm disappointed. We came to liquidate them all and they're alive. If they would have felt like firing even one single shot, then we wouldn't have left one [alive]. . . ."[64] A physician examines the guerrillas to ascertain their good health, and in the presence of a judge, a lawyer, and the journalists, they lay down their weapons. They demand to be returned to the Rawson prison but this facility is still in the hands of their comrades, and the nineteen are therefore taken to the nearby Trelew naval airbase Almirante Zar.[65]

At Trelew, the guerrillas are kept in eight cells located on both sides of a narrow corridor. They are heavily guarded, interrogated, and mistreated, but not tortured. One week after their arrest, on 22 August, at 3:30 A.M., the prisoners are awakened. They hear Navy Captain Sosa saying, "They will see what it means to pick a fight with the Navy." A few minutes later they hear Navy Lieutenant Bravo saying: "Now they will see what antiguerrilla terror means," as well as "One combats terror with terror."[66] The guerrillas are forced out of their cells and ordered to form two lines with their heads bowed. As the last inmate steps into the passageway, fire is opened upon them with two machine guns. Several prisoners throw themselves into their cell to escape the shots.

Alberto Camps, one of the three survivors, tells about the moment the firing stopped: "When they stop, one hears the moans, the death rattles of the comrades, even curses. And then isolated shots begin to sound. I realize that they are finishing them off. Someone even says: 'This one is still alive,' and immediately afterwards one hears a shot."[67] Camps is shot in the stomach by Lieutenant Bravo, and vomits blood. Next, René Haidar is shot in the chest by another naval officer, while María Antonia Berger is shot in the face.

The three survivors and three mortally wounded comrades played dead until help arrived. The heavy gunfire had apparently startled some persons not privy to the massacre. It would still take half an hour before the paramedics arrived. The three gravely wounded guerrillas died for lack of attention. The three survivors were flown the next day to Bahía Blanca for treatment, and were eventually taken to the Villa Devoto prison near Buenos Aires. Outraged by this brutal turn of events, President Allende refused to extradite the six escaped guerrilla commanders and their four accomplices, allowing them to continue to Cuba on 23 August. Allende would be overthrown two weeks later by a military coup.

This account is largely based on the testimonies of María Antonia Berger, Alberto Camps and René Haidar on the eve of their release from prison on 25 May 1973.[68] Their suffering did not end there. Humiliated by the events, the Navy pursued the three survivors of Trelew with an uncommon tenacity. Camps disappeared in 1977, Berger in 1979, and Haidar in 1982.

The official version of events was presented by Rear-Admiral Hermes Quijada. According to Quijada, the guerrillas were ordered out of their cells at 3:30 A.M. for a general inspection. When Captain Sosa ended the review and returned to the entrance of the corridor, Mariano Pujadas, a martial arts expert and of La Calera fame, grabbed Sosa from behind in a judo hold and took his pistol. In the ensuing scuffle, two guards opened fire. Pujadas fired three shots that missed their target, while his comrades advanced toward the firing guards. In the heat of the moment, the two guards emptied their weapons on the prisoners, killing thirteen and wounding the remaining six. The wounded were given immediate medical assistance, and military personnel donated blood.[69]

I checked this official version with three key players, namely former President Lanusse, Rear-Admiral Horacio Mayorga, and former Montonero commander Fernando Vaca Narvaja. Mayorga, in 1972 a navy captain, was the commander of the navy airforce base Almirante Zar at Trelew where the nineteen guerrillas were taken. Mayorga began our conversation by pointing out the precise circumstances of the Rawson escape. He stated that the guerrillas had threatened to harm the wives of some prison guards, saying, "'Today your wife is visiting such a person in such a place, if you don't open the cell then we'll kill her.'" The doors were opened, but the prison guard Valenzuela sensed that something was wrong. "Valenzuela goes and strikes the buzzers that sound in the naval base, giving the alarm that something is happening in the prison. Santucho's wife kills him. She pumps in fourteen shots; with this I say everything about the delicateness of female guerrillas."[70]

After the six guerrilla commanders escaped to Chile and the nineteen remaining comrades were taken to Trelew, Mayorga left the express order that if any hostages were taken, then the guards should open fire at both hostages and guerrillas. He knew that Trelew was a security risk because the cells were only calabooses to discipline soldiers, not to incarcerate guerrillas. When the naval guards suspected that the guerrillas had arms hidden in their cells, Mayorga continues, they ordered them out into the passageway. "They begin to revise everything, searching for weapons, but they don't find any because they don't have weapons. More military arrive at this moment, isn't it so? They ask, 'What's happening?' And in the middle of the shouting and everything, [one officer says] 'I was looking for weapons,' which the others understand as, 'He has weapons,' with the result that they plant themselves in front of those [prisoners] arranged into two lines. The fire fight takes place when Pujadas and the entire group rush forward, he takes the pistol from the commanding officer, and shoots at the guards."

Mayorga arrived two and a half hours after the shooting. "My shoes were sticking to the blood in the passageway. The people were still in a cataleptic state. There was a smell of gun powder in everything." Rear-Admiral Mayorga concludes that if the Navy had really wanted to kill the guerrillas, then they would have done a better job, and taken them outside to simulate their flight, instead of shooting them in a narrow corridor and afterwards saving the lives of three of them.[71]

Another major player in the Trelew tragedy, Lieutenant-General Lanusse, recalls that he gave orders to return the prisoners from Trelew to the Rawson prison because he knew that the Trelew naval base did not have the proper facilities to incarcerate guerrillas. Lanusse: "And precisely what I feared happened. A clumsy episode, clumsiness by one, clumsiness by the others and, well, the reaction was to spend all bullets, all the cartridges that were in the weapons. But one thing was very clear, namely that they didn't try, didn't want to kill everybody, because it would have cost nothing to kill them all. Nevertheless, three were wounded, they were alive, and every-thing possible was done. They succeeded in saving their lives. They took them to a hospital in Bahía Blanca and everything. This is to say, it is mad-ness from a military viewpoint on this [counterinsurgency] struggle to leave people like that alive."[72] Lanusse's last judgment is as shocking as it is revealing because it demonstrates the belief that the guerrillas did not deserve to live, that keeping them in prison would be a waste. Maybe Lanusse is here unwillingly speaking his mind about the true course of events at Trelew. Whether revelation or wish, this was a mistake the military vowed never to make again.

Fernando Vaca Narvaja, who got away safely from Rawson with the other five guerrilla commanders, vehemently refutes the official version about Trelew: "First, none of us is suicidal. It is known that the possibilities of, for example, an escape are studied and analyzed. In the second place. . . . try-ing to escape from a military base at which they arrived at night, without knowing the watch, the building, the features, is madness. We never com-mitted those kinds of follies. That is to say, rationally, there is nothing which supports this. In the third place, the comrades surrendered them-selves openly, filmed by television, with lawyers and judges present."[73] Why would the guerrillas risk their lives in an unprepared escape from an unknown prison, when only one week before they went to lengths to guar-antee their safety? And why would the Navy tirelessly hunt down the survi-vors of Trelew? Simply, says Vaca Narvaja, because they were the only surviving witnesses of the infamous massacre.[74] And why did the Navy not orchestrate a more credible scheme by taking the prisoners outside and shooting them there? Because, says Vaca Narvaja, there were hundreds of conscripts at the naval base who would become unwilling witnesses to the mock flight. And why, finally, were the guerrillas assassinated at Trelew? Vaca Narvaja gives two reasons: taking revenge for the daring Rawson prison escape and eliminating these experienced guerrillas as "a strategic investment" in counterinsurgency warfare, as one military officer called it.[75]

Weighing the different versions, reading the conflicting testimonies, examining the forensic autopsy reports, and talking to three of the princi-pal actors, I am just as convinced that the Trelew killings were a deliberate execution as were the Argentine human rights organizations, lawyer associ-ations, professional associations, and the international press at the time.[76] However, the importance of Trelew does not stop at ascertaining the cor-rect course of events. Each version has an internal coherence which makes it convincing when placed in a compatible context and political discourse.

The official version convinced the armed forces and their political allies because it fitted in perfectly with their perception of similar violent events. The military account emphasized the treachery of the guerrillas (register-ing a complaint under false pretense, posing as prison guards), their disregard for innocent civilians (intimidating prison guards by threatening their wives), and their blind ferocity (Santucho's pregnant wife killing prison guard Valenzuela). Furthermore, the flights to Allende's Chile and Castro's Cuba demonstrated that Argentina's guerrilla insurgency was not a domestic affair but part of a global revolutionary strategy. As far as the military themselves were concerned, they emphasized their commitment to maintaining law and order, their correct treatment of the prisoners, their compassionate donation of blood, the due process given to the guerrillas by holding an official investigation, putting them on trial, and allowing lawyers to defend them. This contextualization did not just preach to the converted but constructed—together with many similar renditions of the executions of the Generals Aramburu and Sánchez, the occupations of Garín and La Calera, and the bank robberies and numerous fire bombings—a political discourse which hardened into an uncompromising stance. This discourse served to legitimize the position of the military in Argentine society, convince them of the value of their own sacrifices, entrench them in an irreconcilable position, and justify the use of force.

Likewise, the rendition of the revolutionary left served to portray them as sacrificing their lives for the future of Argentina. It showed their dedication to the struggle (Santucho and Vaca Narvaja leaving their wives behind), their brilliance and creativity at devising the escape plan (occupation from within instead of an assault from the outside), their daring (ordering taxis to the prison), the camaraderie in prison (cooperation of Marxists and Peronists), their professionalism, discipline, and compassion (not taking civilian hostages at the airport). They paint the military as incompetent (the easy takeover of Rawson prison), ruthless (planning to attack the airport despite the presence of civilians), cruel (tormenting the prisoners), cowardly (giving coups de grace to several wounded prisoners), and without military honor (delaying medical assistance to the wounded). This political discourse was just as convincing to the revolutionary left, the Peronist following, and the labor union rank and file as the official version was to the military. The Trelew executions or, as they became known, the Trelew massacre were for them one more tragedy in a long list of ignoble acts of military repression beginning with the 1955 bombardment of civilians at the Plaza de Mayo.

The designation of the executions at Trelew as the "Trelew massacre" was not just a descriptive term but established a resemblance to the "José León Suárez massacre." Both served the same military objectives of repression, punishment, and intimidation. The social trauma of the 1956 tragedy was given a new posttraumatic content on 22 August 1972. The two massacres were recontextualized by one another, thus enhancing the traumatic load of both. Trelew and José León Suárez were from then on mentioned in one breath, and foreshadowed new tragedies and new massacres.

Trelew demanded revenge. Old and new accounts had to be settled.

According to the leftist press, Mayorga had been one of the naval pilots who had bombed the Plaza de Mayo in June 1955, and now he was involved in the Trelew massacre.[77] Rear-Admiral Mayorga is still haunted by the chant, "Soon you will see, soon you will see, when we avenge the Trelew dead," a chant that obsessed all military because the chance of a revenge killing was real. "You are talking to an ordinary admiral. They tried to kidnap my daughter, they came looking for her at her high school. They shot my guard here at the watch, and they let me know from Puerto Belgrano that an ERP guerrilla had picked up my maid at a catechism class in the church next door, so that she would place a bomb [under my bed] as has happened to Cardozo. . . . The Navy made me change destinations every fifteen days when I retired, from Puerto Belgrano I went to Salta, to Ushuaia, to Rio Gallegos and so on. And this may all seem very amusing, but there comes a moment when it uproots you from everything, and it makes you afraid, it makes you afraid. This is what happens."[78]

Rear-Admirals Emilio Berisso and Hermes Quijada were less fortunate than Rear-Admiral Mayorga. Berisso was shot as revenge for Trelew on 28 December 1972 outside a supermarket in Lomas de Zamora. Three days later, Perón gave his approval to the execution with the remark that he would have done the same if he had been fifty years younger.[79] Quijada met a similar fate on 30 April 1973. He was assassinated in downtown Buenos Aires by six bullets fired through the window of his car by ERP guerrilla Vítor Palmeiro. Palmeiro was shot by Quijada's driver as he fled away on a motorcycle. He died several hours later.[80]

The assassinations worried the armed forces greatly. The navy high command said in a communiqué that "this is not a war between terrorism and the Navy or the Armed Forces. This is a fight between two ways of life: democracy and a totalitarianism without a fatherland, where death is a means to achieve utopic objectives."[81] How would peace ever be restored when these killings continued even after free elections, and the upcoming transition to democracy?

Redemptive and Retributive Violence

Political violence was for the Peronist and Marxist guerrillas inevitable to change the dictatorial state of affairs of the late 1960s. For the Marxists, violence replaced the class struggle as the engine of history. Humankind was, according to Lenin, in a continuous state of war.[82] Likewise, Guevara had said that violence was "the midwife of new societies."[83] This conviction dismissed strikes, sabotage, and street protests as well-intended but inferior forms of struggle. The singular focus on violence, without the arduous task of grass roots mobilization, made Guevarism equally appealing to Marxist and Peronist guerrilla organizations. Nevertheless, they differed in their understanding of the morality of violence.

Revolutionary violence was redemptive for the Marxist guerrillas because it transformed them into Guevara's New Man even before socialist society had arrived. Dreaming about this future from their prison cells in Rawson, ERP commanders wrote an inspiring essay about revolutionary morality. Humility, patience, sacrifice, decisiveness, tenacity, generosity, and compassion were the values of this New Man.[84] These qualities were acquired through the guerrilla struggle itself because practice determined consciousness. "We cannot even think of winning this war when we do not decide to start immediately with the practice of war, the construction of the New Man, the Man capable of fighting and winning this war."[85] Heroism and sacrifice were particularly important because they would awaken among the masses admiration, solidarity, and the desire to follow the example set by the combatants.[86]

The morality of violence depended according to Marxist doctrine on its objective. The class struggle contained both evil (exploitation) and justified (resistance) violence. Even though the casualties of revolutionary war were people of flesh and blood with families, parents, and children, "They are but mere representatives of two irreconcilable orders. . . . It is not individuals that are placed face to face in these battles, but class interests and ideas; but those who fall in them, those who die, are persons, are men. We cannot avoid this contradiction, escape from this pain."[87] This revolutionary thought dehumanized people by subjecting them to the forces of history, forces with their own rationale and justification. Human beings degenerated into means toward the achievement of higher ideals. Furthermore, such violence was redemptive because of the millions of lives that would be saved from the hunger and disease inflicted by capitalism and imperialism. This position made the guerrillas feel absolved from any personal responsibility for the violence. There is no room for innocence and guilt in Marxist-Leninist theory. As Hannah Arendt has pointed out, the victims are simply in the way of the inevitable march of history, and the perpetrators are only executing historical laws to which all mankind is subject.[88]

For the Peronist guerrillas, individuals did matter. Lieutenant-General Aramburu and union leader Augusto Vandor were not dispensable pawns crushed by the forces of history. Aramburu was personally responsible for the executions at José León Suárez and Vandor for the ills that had befallen the Argentine working class. Their elimination through retributive violence was a step forward in the struggle towards a more just society. The execution of repressors and traitors was regarded as a duty that unburdened the traumatic load of the Peronist movement.

This duty to undo past injuries was fed by an emotional aversion to exploitation, was manifested in hatred of the ruling class, and translated into anger and violence. Hatred was just as much a motivating force in guerrilla warfare as the desire for a better future. This hatred was not in the first place based on the class struggle but on real hardships. The belief that "one had to fight to conquer something, that nothing was given freely" was not accidental, but conformed to the experience of Argentine historical reality where democratic processes had been repeatedly interrupted, labor strikes repressed, worker privileges rolled back, and universities deprived of their academic freedom.[89]

All faith in nonviolent protest and street demonstrations had evaporated. Power had to be disputed at the barrel of a gun, as can be read from a romanticized account of how Fernando Abal Medina and Carlos Ramus founded the Montoneros in 1967. "To accompany that immense disarticulated army that was suffering from misery, repression, the sadness of having its leader in exile, the heart-break of not being able to visit Evita, and of knowing that they had mistreated her. The mounting anger was no longer enough. There was more that could be done. They had done everything to us. We had to begin to prepare ourselves in a different way, better organized: the hour of the guns had arrived."[90] This mounting anger was as strong as the sense of social justice that motivated young people to enter the files of the Montoneros, unaware of the price they would have to pay for their anger. Violence could not just change society but also traumatize its people.

The belief that violence could redress a social trauma hit home hard in Argentine society when in 1970 the still unknown Montoneros abducted Lieutenant-General Aramburu. His execution was intended to neutralize the injuries incurred by the 1955 coup, the 1956 José León Suárez massacre, and the 1957 disappearance of Evita Perón's embalmed body through vengeance and reparation. Tellingly, Aramburu's executioner was only eight years old when the 1956 executions took place. If crowds allowed people to shed past injuries through the collective emotion of unity and equality, then guerrilla violence exacted a payment in blood for the social traumas inflicted by past repressive regimes.

Aramburu's death was the first of a string of executions, assassinations, and reprisal killings which traumatized the armed forces. Every military officer feared a sudden attack, experienced the risks to his men, and was worried about his family. The posttraumatic reaction to this violence raised their group cohesion, and prepared them mentally and emotionally for a state of war. They decided to defend themselves with excessive, traumatizing violence intended to take away the guerrilla threat once and for all.

Chapter 7
Revolution Postponed: Anger, Frustration, and Entitlement

The mood in Villa Devoto prison was euphoric the day before President Cámpora's inauguration. Common and political prisoners took the pavilions in mutiny, mattresses were set on fire, and flames enwrapped the barred windows. The rebels were singing the Peronist march, making flags, painting slogans on prison walls, and preparing elaborate meals. The evening of 24 May 1973 was experienced as one big party because the political prisoners were promised amnesty. Relatives were visiting, and some prisoners even had their small children with them.

After the newly sworn-in president had spoken to the people gathered at the Plaza de Mayo, tens of thousands of young Peronists and Marxist revolutionaries marched to Villa Devoto to demand the immediate release of the prisoners. Juan Manuel Abal Medina, secretary of the Peronist Organization and brother of Aramburu's executioner Fernando Abal Medina, played a crucial role. Outside the prison, he noticed an aggressive group of ERP members. Inside, he was confronted with an explosive situation of hundreds of common prisoners either drunk or high on drugs. There and then, he ordered the prison director to open the gates.[1]

The Devotazo had taken place. Francisco Urondo described what followed: "This so special climate of brotherhood and happiness blossomed in the street. This need to be with people, to talk with people we didn't know, only because they were there, holding us by our hands."[2] The released prisoners felt empowered for having defeated the military government in four years of armed struggle. They believed that the victory was theirs and the future their reward. The generational rejuvenation was finally taking place. Yet within one year the political tide would turn against them and within three years more many of them would be dead.

The euphoria among the revolutionary left contrasted with the dread among the military. The military read the release of the convicted guerrillas as a sign of the turbulent times ahead. The military felt violated in their sense of justice by the Devotazo. They objected that the guerrillas had been released before the presidential pardon and amnesty law had been passed, and that Cámpora was blind to the guerrillas' own admission that they would return to the armed struggle once free.[3] The Devotazo became a watershed in their thinking about counterinsurgency. Aware of the unpredictability of Argentine politics, they decided that they would never make such a mistake again. Not incarceration but annihilation would be the future objective of counterinsurgency.

Departing President Lanusse relayed two grave concerns to the new government: the threat of revolutionary war waged by the guerrilla organizations and the escalation of sectarian political violence within the Peronist Organization.[4] The revolutionary Peronists recognized these same problems, but in a different context. Their cooperation with the Marxist guerrilla organizations between 1970 and 1972 had made them appear as of one stock in the eyes of the military. The revolutionary Peronists had difficulty dissociating themselves from the Marxist organizations which had decided to continue the guerrilla warfare after the turn to democracy.

The second problem was that the revolutionary Peronists could now participate in Argentina's political process. The transition from the transparency of weapons, with their immediate results and clear objectives, to the swamps of Argentine politics with its wheeling and dealing, was not as easy as it seemed. Political decisions could no longer be forced with the use of violence but had to be accomplished through persuasion, negotiation, and the electoral mobilization of the Argentine people.

The shift from arms to administration was complicated by an unsolvable tension between crowd and vanguard politics as two contradictory means to achieve political ends. The revolutionary Peronists believed that Perón was isolated from the masses by a coterie of right-wing Peronists. The desire to break this cordon implied a vigorous crowd mobilization, as was explained in chapter 4. Once the Montonero leaders succeeded in entering in a dialogue with a Perón unwilling to embrace their revolutionary project, they abandoned crowd politics and engaged once more into vanguardism. The large crowds of 1972 and 1973 had convinced them that the masses were behind them, and that they were just one step away from assuming power. This one step was to become a leap into a pool of intrigue, betrayal, and vengeance. Violence was embraced as the principal means to satisfy the obsession for power. Motivated by a sense of entitlement to the seat of power wrenched away from them, the Peronist revolutionaries embarked on a military campaign without clear plans, tactics, and strategies, with only their anger to guide them.

This chapter focuses on the separation of crowd and vanguard, and the political violence between the turn to democracy in May 1973 and the official military involvement in the counterinsurgency in February 1975. Violence escalated in this period because of a confluence of two relatively independent struggles. The violence of the ERP rested on the belief in the historical certainty of a social revolution. The Montoneros, on the other hand, were moved by the factional struggle with the orthodox labor unions. The violence intensified in late 1973 when an extreme right-wing organization entered into a temporary alliance with the orthodox labor unions and attacked the revolutionary left, Marxist as well as Peronist. Vengeance killings became the dominant mode of engagement in a spiral of violence. Each assassination added to a growing social trauma in which the political and physical existence of the parties in conflict were threatened.

Liberation and Regrouping

The freeing of all political prisoners had been one of the principal campaign issues of the elections, and Cámpora dutifully decreed a presidential pardon (*indulto*) before midnight of 25 May 1973. The political prisoners of Villa Devoto were already free by then, and those in Rawson, Córdoba, and several other places followed in the wee hours of the next morning. Cámpora's decree was seconded the next day in Congress by an amnesty law supported unanimously by all political parties, including the opposition. Election campaign promises, pressure from the revolutionary left, and the conviction that the armed resistance had been a legitimate struggle against an unconstitutional government, were the principal motives for the amnesty.[5] Within three days of Congressional debate, the counterinsurgency legislation was dismantled, the Federal Penal Chamber dissolved, the violence covered with a mantle of oblivion, and the imprisoned guerrillas, and union, student, and youth leaders freed. A total of 372 political prisoners were released, including 180 in Villa Devoto and 173 in Rawson.[6]

The military were shocked. They could not and still cannot comprehend how tried and convicted terrorists were now being released.[7] They felt that the amnesty allowed an unrepentant subversive element back into Argentine society which would once again poison the political process. They remembered well the chanting during the Devotazo: "The people will free them, the struggle will be awaiting them. A gun is waiting for every guerrilla."[8] Horacio Mayorga had warned in early May 1973 against "the presence of a violent left that can sink us into a killing process, and if the dead are ours then it will be the law of the jungle."[9]

The military suspicion was not unfounded. On 28 February 1973 the ERP had attacked the Communications Battalion 141 in Córdoba while its troops were away on maneuvers. The guard on duty was subdued by a conscript belonging to the ERP. The guerrillas took hundreds of weapons, including five grenade launchers. The conscript defected to the ERP and was duly decorated.[10]

The ERP promised in May 1973 that they were not going to attack the elected government and the police if they remained neutral but that guerrilla units would continue to harass the armed forces, the praetorian guards of a capitalist order.[11] Notwithstanding its defiant war cry, the ERP did not carry out any major attack during the seven weeks of Cámpora's government. The task of rebuilding the organization was more urgent. Within days of the amnesty, the PRT-ERP leaders met in Córdoba to evaluate the near total defeat in 1972. They concluded that the ERP had taken a misguided militarist turn, and that the party had failed to rally political support among Argentina's workers. A change of course was promised.[12]

Yet the PRT-ERP leaders were of two minds about their strategy. For all the talk of grass roots penetration, the clandestine activities took precedence over legal political work. Unlike the Montonero leaders who addressed large crowds at political rallies, they shunned any contact with the masses. All public political activities were relegated to only one member of the eight-man Political Bureau, while three members were assigned to union work.[13] Mario Roberto Santucho did not speak at public gatherings and only seldom met with other revolutionary leaders. The security risk of such appearances was one factor, but more significant was a general lack of faith in grass roots work. And once grass roots support began to grow, it was misinterpreted as a demonstration of the general revolutionary spirit of the Argentine working class.

Militarism raised its head again on 6 September 1973, at 1:30 A.M., when the soldier Hernán Invernizzi orders the guards to open the gate of the Comando de Sanidad in Buenos Aires, the army's medical base, to allow the delivery of supplies. Instead, a truck with eleven ERP guerrillas enters. One lieutenant and one soldier are wounded as they try to prevent the assailants from taking control of the base. At a leisurely pace, the men load 150 FAL rifles, uniforms, and large quantities of medical supplies into the truck. The operation falters when two conscripts succeed in notifying the police. At 5:35 A.M., the guerrillas are ordered to surrender but instead, they ask for the presence of judges, lawyers, congressmen, and the press. Their request is denied and at 6:30 A.M., several shots are fired at the guerrillas. Ten minutes later, Lieutenant-Colonel Juan Duarte Hardoy and fifty commandos assault the premises. Hardoy is killed, but the operation ends at 6:55 A.M. with the surrender of the eleven ERP combatants. Hernán Invernizzi and another conscript are arrested for aiding the guerrillas. It would take almost six years before they were sentenced to 16–22 years in prison.[14]

The ERP stated with its usual optimism that the exploited masses approved of the action and admired the courage of the combatants, yet the Argentine people were dumbfounded.[15] The military were in the barracks, democracy reigned, and Perón was about to be elected to the highest office. The Peronist Youth and Montoneros declared that the days of the armed struggle had passed because the masses had been mobilized through free elections.[16] A decisive response from the Peronist government to the renewed guerrilla insurgency became inevitable. On election day, 23 September 1973, the ERP was declared illegal, and its publications forbidden.[17] Mario Roberto Santucho concluded that this was "a true declaration of war on the guerrilla, placing the government thus decisively in the camp of the people's enemies, together with the oppressing army and the exploitative enterprises."[18] The police had also forfeited their immunity by interfering with guerrilla operations, and were from now on regarded as legitimate targets for reprisal killings.

In 1973 the ERP collected over twenty-two million U.S. dollars in ransom with the kidnapping of six company executives.[19] Guerrilla organizations staged in 1973 205 operations before and 208 operations after Cámpora's inauguration on 25 May.[20] Most operations were carried out by the ERP. Clearly, Perón was unable to control the political violence. On the contrary, guerrilla operations were evolving from assaults on civilian targets between 1970 and 1972 to attacks on military installations in 1973. The ERP had set the trend with its attacks in Córdoba and Buenos Aires. The attack on the Azul army base in 1974 was to surpass the two previous assaults by far.

On Saturday evening 19 January 1974, at 10:15 P.M., about seventy guerrillas launch an attack on the military base at Azul in Buenos Aires province, giving quarter to two thousand servicemen of an armored cavalry regiment and an armored artillery group. Combatants disarm a sentry and enter in three groups, two intending to steal weapons, while the third group will try to kidnap the base commander. Meanwhile, three trucks enter to carry away the booty. The assault is discovered and a pitched fire fight ensues in which two trucks are destroyed and the first two groups of guerrillas are repelled. The third group proceeds to the residential quarters of the military base and runs into several officers who have been alarmed by the shooting. Colonel Camilo Gay draws his weapon and is killed, whereas Mrs. Gay and her children are taken hostage. (According to military sources, she was later executed by the guerrillas; while the ERP declares that she was killed by military gunfire.) When the fighting stops, three guerrillas, a sentry, and Colonel Gay and his wife are dead and Lieutenant-Colonel Ibarzábal has been kidnapped.[21]

An incensed Perón appeared on television the next day, dressed in his military uniform and surrounded by his cabinet and the three commanders of the armed forces. He denounced the guerrillas as delinquents who were helped by foreign mercenaries. "The annihilation of this criminal terrorism, as soon as possible, is a task which concerns all who long for a sovereign, free, and just Fatherland. . . ."[22] Perón sacked Oscar Bidegain, who happened to live in Azul, as the governor of Buenos Aires province, for tolerating the guerrilla operations and pressured eight leftist Peronist representatives into resigning from Congress for opposing tougher legislation on political violence. On 22 January 1974, Perón made it known in no uncertain terms that he would root out the Marxist guerrillas: "We will proceed in accordance with the necessities, whatever the means may be. If there is no legislation, then we will do it outside the law and we will do it violently. Because the only thing that one can oppose to violence is violence itself.''[23]

This official call for repression was music to the ears of Mario Roberto Santucho. Perón had made the counterrevolutionary war a center piece of his administration and thus polarized the political forces. Santucho believed that the successful attack on the Azul army base would convince the working class that the ERP had the strength to wage a victorious war against Argentina's best-trained troops.[24] However, the effect of these armed interventions was exactly the opposite. Long months of diligent recruitment work by the PRT were erased in one hour of fighting. The regional grass roots organizations disintegrated beyond recuperation, and one local leader remarked bitterly, "Our ways part. It is very difficult for us not to regard this type of action as a provocation.''[25]

Despite the disintegration of the grass roots organizations, the PRT grew considerably in 1974, according to one-time secretary-general Luis Mattini, and the ERP improved its combative capability.[26] In contrast to the 1970–1972 period when the guerrilla organizations and their popular support grew in unison, there was now an inverse relation between the growth of the PRT-ERP and the support of the working class. With all its talk about the masses, there was a considerable disdain about worker demands like better salaries, working conditions, and social benefits. The Marxist revolutionaries wanted a radical transformation which would solve all these small, in essence bourgeois, problems with one blow.

In September 1974, Santucho decided to create worker militias and construct a regular revolutionary army with divisions, battalions, companies, platoons, and squads, and with a hierarchical command structure of officers and troops in olive green uniforms.[27] There were graduation and decoration ceremonies, and a training program at ERP's military academy. But, for all its outward appearances, the military preparation was insufficient. The ERP threw itself at military bases with inexperienced commanders, combatants without proper training in conventional warfare, and poor operational communications at the cost of many lives and the loss of important quantities of weapons.[28] To top this off, the PRT-ERP decided to launch a rural guerrilla insurgency, which will be analyzed in the next chapter.

The frontal assault on the armed forces coincided with the increasingly violent confrontation between the right-wing and the left-wing of the Peronist Organization. The rapid growth of the opposed forces within the Peronist movement made this polarization lethal. There are no reliable figures, not even estimates, about the size of the right-wing forces, but there must have been at least one thousand persons willing to resort to violence for political ends. They ranged from the bodyguards of orthodox

Peronist unions and members of right-wing youth organizations to death squads.[29] The strength of the left-wing forces, Marxist and Peronist, is better known. Whereas the total number of guerrillas had not exceeded six hundred in late 1972, their numbers increased throughout 1973 and 1974 to an estimated five thousand combatants in 1975.[30] These guerrilla organizations attracted also tens of thousands of sympathizers but at the same time alienated millions of Argentines.

Violent Factionalism Within the Peronist Movement

The PRT-ERP was upfront about its continuation of the armed struggle after May 1973, but the Peronist guerrilla organizations were more secretive about their real intentions. They had hailed the elections as their victory and succeeded in placing many revolutionary Peronists in mid-level positions in the Cámpora government, but they did not hand in their weapons. The fusion of FAR (Revolutionary Armed Forces) and Montoneros on 12 October 1973, the day of Perón's inauguration, was a public message, if not political affront, that they were determined to conquer power within the Peronist Organization.[31] They claimed to need these weapons to protect their local chapters and administrative posts, sensing that right-wing union leaders might take revenge for the assassination of Vandor and Alonso.

Perón was aware of the factional struggle inside the Peronist Organization, and exhorted the youth to patience, harmony, and moderation.[32] On 27 August 1973, a FAP hit squad assassinated union leader Marcelino Mansilla to commemorate the execution of union boss Alonso three years earlier.[33] An angry Perón lectured several leaders of the Peronist left: "Revolution has always two ingredients: blood and time. You save time if you spend a lot of blood; you save blood if you spend a lot of time. This is the only thing we can say, but [revolution] is always a struggle."[34]

The Montoneros had of course already made their choice: they wanted rapid change, a bloody change if necessary. There was haste to implement the revolution, but also a strong dislike for the unexciting work of negotiating policies, implementing administrative measures, and long hours in the dull offices surrounding Plaza de Mayo. As one Montonero told the journalist Pablo Giussani about the assassination of union leader Rucci: "It was something we needed . . . Our people were becoming bourgeois inside the offices. Occasionally, we have to save them from this danger with a return to military action."[35]

José Ignacio Rucci was the Vandor of the 1970s. He had begun his working life cleaning intestines in the slaughterhouses of Rosario, and later became a metal worker in Buenos Aires. He helped organize the Peronist Resistance in the 1950s and rose in the ranks under Vandor's tutelage.[36] When Rucci became head of the CGT union central in July 1970, he began to hobnob with the Argentine upper class, buying expensive clothing and fancy automobiles. According to his critics from the left, he placed his men in key union positions through election fraud, was eager to kick the revolutionary Peronists from the Peronist Organization, and organized shock troops to confront them in the street.[37] In the eyes of the revolutionary Peronists, Rucci was the epitome of the union bureaucracy. The time had arrived to bring the revolutionary struggle to the heart of the Peronist movement and eliminate its enemies. "Our first task will be to clean our own camp a bit," it said in the favorite magazine of the Peronist left.[38]

At ten past noon on Tuesday 25 September 1973, Rucci leaves a borrowed apartment on the outskirts of Buenos Aires, where he passed the night for security reasons after receiving several death threats. As he crosses the sidewalk toward his car, he is shot in the neck by assailants hiding on a roof. Rucci falls on the pavement and his two bodyguards take cover behind the parked cars to return fire. Suddenly, Rucci and his guards are shot in the back from an abandoned house. The forty-seven-year-old Rucci is killed and one guard severely wounded. The nine to eleven attackers flee the scene of this political crime.[39]

There was uncertainty about which organization had assassinated Rucci, but all fingers pointed at the Montoneros because they had three obvious motives. One, the Montoneros wanted to send a clear message to Perón, who had been elected two days earlier, that they were willing to eliminate anybody who obstructed their leadership of the Peronist Organization. Two, Rucci was becoming an important political leader with his own power base. Rather than building their own rank-and-file support in opposition to Rucci, the Montoneros wanted a quick solution, a violent solution that would enlarge their political space. Three, the elimination served the factional struggle within the Montoneros between the movimientistas who wanted to form a revolutionary Peronist vanguard and the loyalists (la Lealtad) who advocated a vertical obedience to Perón. The execution of Rucci would shift the balance of power irrevocably to the movimientistas.[40]

Rucci was buried in the presence of Perón, the commanders of the Armed Forces, and all major union leaders. The Minister of Labor Otero said at the funeral: "We did not come here to cry for you, but to swear that we will achieve the Peronist fatherland and eliminate the traitors on the right and the left."[41] The Peronist Youth leader Enrique Grynberg was assassinated the same day in revenge for Rucci, and several JP chapters were bombed.[42] The attacks were intended to dissuade the rank and file from visiting these neighborhood locales, and thus destroy the grass roots penetration of the Peronist left.[43] This was the start of what the revolutionary left called the white terror from death squads operating with the tacit approval of the authorities. A covert counterinsurgency campaign was being waged against the Peronist left with increasing intensity.[44]

Perón was profoundly shaken by the assassination of his personal friend and prominent political ally. Apparently, he had not been able to assert his authority on the Peronist left, and he became determined to eliminate them from his political movement.[45] He declared in November 1973 that the labor unions were the backbone of the Peronist Organization and that their violence was self-defense. "How are these self-defenses generated? It is very simple. The microbe that enters, the pathological germ that invades the physiological organism, generates its own antibodies, and these antibodies are the ones that act in self-defense. The same happens in the institutional organism."[46]

By late 1973, there were four groups responsible for Argentina's political violence. The left consisted of the Peronist Montoneros and the Marxist PRT-ERP. The right was composed of the ultra-nationalist Anti-Communist Alliance or AAA (Alianza Anticomunista Argentina) and a bloc of orthodox Peronist labor unions. Left and right harassed each other with the bombing of offices and neighborhood chapters, assassinations, inflammatory editorials, and even hit lists in their periodicals. Aside from the importance of revenge as a means to assert power and conquer more political space, the assassinations served also as propaganda to measure the degree of popular support. The Argentine people were made a referee in the conflict, but without the power to stop this spiraling violence.

Soon revenge lost its tit-for-tat equivalence and became an equity of horror, suffering, and excess. Nevertheless, there was no equity for the parties involved. A comrade's death could never be appeased through the death of an enemy because there is a chasm between the emotional values attached to both lives: one is priceless, the other worthless. The death of comrade after comrade traumatized each party because it weakened the organization and threatened to end its political existence and identity.

Right-Wing Violence

Juan Domingo Perón met the Argentine nightclub dancer María Estela Martínez in Panama in December 1955. She was performing under the stage name of Isabel. Less than a month later, the two were living together.[47] Isabel followed Perón to Spain, where they married in 1961. It was during a political mission to Argentina in October 1965 that she met José López Rega.

After his retirement as a police corporal, José López Rega had become a watchman at Perón's Buenos Aires residence till 1955. One decade later, he offered his services to Isabel Perón and within one year more he was walking the dogs at Perón's house in Spain. López Rega became Perón's private secretary, and by the time Perón returned to Argentina, the former police corporal had become Isabel's principal advisor and the pivotal middleman between the aged Perón and his political interlocutors.[48]

López Rega had long-standing ties with right-wing nationalist circles in

Argentina, and drew immediately on these contacts when Perón's return became imminent. He was a virulent anticommunist and was determined to drive back the advancing Peronist left; an objective which he pursued vigorously as the Minister of Social Welfare in Cámpora's government. The right-wing attack on the Peronist left at Ezeiza airport on 20 June 1973 was carried out with his approval, if not direction. At the end of the day, there were 13 dead, 365 wounded, and hundreds of thousands of Peronists who became too intimidated to attend any future crowd mobilizations.

Cámpora's removal from power was the next item on López Rega's agenda. Cámpora was replaced on 13 July 1973 by Raúl Lastiri, the president of the Chamber of Deputies, and López Rega's son-in-law. López Rega became one of the most influential persons in the new government and backed up his power with a parapolice force run from his Ministry, AAA, which consisted of death squads modeled after those operating in Brazil.[49]

The AAA made its first public appearance with the 21 November 1973 attack on Hipólito Solari Yrigoyen, a senator of the Radical party UCR and a vocal critic of the government's labor legislation. The previous day he had received a letter with the single inscription "AAA." The next day he shifted his car into gear and a bomb went off. Solari Yrigoyen survived the assault as well as six surgical operations, only to endure another attack on 15 April 1975.[50]

Vicious rhetoric had presaged the arrival of the Triple A on the political scene. The first issue of *El Caudillo*, the AAA's unofficial public voice, declared on 16 November 1973 that the orthodox Peronists had won their first victory when the revolutionary Peronists were kicked off the Ezeiza reception stage. "Comrades, the fight is clear. There are only two fronts: that of the allies and that of the enemies. That of the people and that of the anti-people. . . . Perón is our caudillo [military strongman]."[51] Two months later, the traitors to Peronism were ordered to leave the Peronist Organization and the country: "There will be another warning, but one that you will be unable to read or hear. I'll leave you cold, I assure you."[52] Death lists were published and anyone who did not heed the advance warning could expect an attempt on his or her life. Many left the country in a hurry, only to return when the military government stepped down in 1983.

The parapolice organization took flight when the counterinsurgency expert Alberto Villar was appointed in April 1974 as chief of the federal police and López Rega as its commissioner-general. Three groups were operating within the Triple A. López Rega and Villar each had their own circle of trusted assistants and, in addition, there was a small group of right-wing Peronists headed by Brito Lima and Norma Kennedy who had participated in the Ezeiza attacks.[53] The Triple A was composed of active service and retired policemen and military personnel, employees of the Ministry of Social Welfare, labor union bodyguards, common criminals, and even firemen who deactivated bombs on duty and assembled them off-duty.[54]

Whether or not the AAA had the approval of Perón is a moot question given the liberty with which López Rega and his death squads operated. Perón did nothing to stop them.[55]

The number of deaths inflicted by the Triple A proper has been established at 212 but the total number of assassinations by right-wing death squads during the democratic rule between May 1973 and March 1976 is estimated at 1,165 deaths.[56] Nearly half of these deaths were not claimed by any group, so it is safe to assume that the Triple A alone can be held accountable for at least 425 killings.[57] By comparison, the number of deaths caused by Peronist and Marxist guerrilla organizations was 480.

There was a clear division of labor between the orthodox Peronist unions and the Triple A as far as political violence was concerned. The unions specialized in the seizure and bombing of the offices of combative unions and the locales of the Peronist left, but carried out few assassinations. Kidnappings, torture, and executions were the trademark of the right-wing death squads. Victims were arrested by men carrying police badges, taken away, and then tortured and executed. Death squads were operating freely thanks to the police protection offered by Villar and López Rega.[58]

The cooperation of the orthodox labor unions and the ultranationalist death squads was a matter of expediency. They collaborated at Ezeiza in 1973 and during the crackdown on combative labor unions in Córdoba in late 1974. Yet, there was always an undercurrent of tension about who controlled the right wing of the Peronist Organization, a conflict already existing between Rucci and López Rega. The orthodox Peronists and the ultranationalist Peronists parted ways when the unions opposed the economic policies of Isabel Perón and López Rega in mid-1975. This conflict demonstrated that, unlike the labor union leaders, the Triple A did not have a rank-and-file following but only well-connected allies among right-wing military and police circles to give them fire power.

The ascendance of Perón's widow María Estela to the presidency in July 1974 turned López Rega into Argentina's strongman. The assassinations became more frequent and the right-wing discourse more violent: "Euthanasia for them. Nothing else, not even justice."[59] Although both camps were violent, the right-wing death squads cannot be equated with the equally deadly guerrilla forces because organizations such as the Triple A operated from within the bosom of a democratic government. Their principal objectives were eliminating political and ideological opponents, taking revenge, and intimidating politically active persons to make them abandon the public arena. Rather than pursuing guerrillas, the Triple A went after easy targets, such as former employees of the Cámpora government, journalists, artists, lawyers, and academics.

In mid-August 1974, the Montonero commanders began to prepare their following for an all-out fight with the Peronist right. Mario Firmenich accused the government of waging a "dirty war" (*guerra sucia*) against the people, and invoked a favorite phrase by Perón: "One has to choose where to hit, one has to hit where it hurts them most and where they least expect it."[60] The Montoneros carried out several revenge killings in the first week of September and decided to assassinate once more a person who had been inextricably tied to Perón and their own birth: Lieutenant-General Aramburu.

Mario Firmenich and Norma Arrostito published their detailed account of Aramburu's execution in the 3 September 1974 issue of *La Causa Peronista* as a means to rehabilitate themselves after their break with Perón.[61] However, this symbolic assassination did not vindicate them, but contributed to the ire of the military and a growing dissociation from the Peronist masses. Their rendition did not evoke the image of a callous general who had overthrown Perón and ordered the execution of defenseless Peronist workers at the garbage dump of José León Suárez, but painted a dignified, defenseless old man wanting to tie his shoes, have a shave, and confide his last thoughts to a priest before being shot to death.

The Road to Vanguardism

The move underground by the Montoneros combined feelings of anger, abandonment, and arrogance: anger at being deprived of the leadership of the Peronist Organization, anger at the increasing attacks by the right, abandonment by Perón's death, and the arrogance of regarding themselves at the center of a popular process and the masters of historical truth. Still, the decision to resume the armed struggle was not without controversy, and was preceded by months of public debates about which course to follow in the conflict with Perón.

In January 1974, there existed three political currents within the Montoneros: the loyalists (la Lealtad), the vanguardists (movimientistas), and the insurrectionists (alternativistas). The loyalists advocated an unconditional obedience to Perón, and separated from the Montoneros in May 1974 when the Plaza de Mayo crowd ruptured in two. The vanguardists and insurrectionists were both determined to achieve a Peronist revolution without Perón. They differed on how to attain their objective.

In late January 1974 the insurrectionists placed doubts on Perón's revolutionary disposition, and questioned the vertical obedience to Perón. "As if the 17th of October, the Cordobazo, and the fights against the Dictatorship had been ordered vertically!"[62] They believed that the working class was the only true revolutionary segment of the Peronist movement, and put a much greater emphasis on crowd protests than on vanguardism. When Perón turned against the revolutionary Peronists in May 1974, and the crowd mobilizations lost their effectiveness, the insurrectionists turned to grass roots organization, while the vanguardists turned to political violence.

In March 1974, the vanguardist Montoneros lost faith in Perón as a revolutionary leader. National leaders, from Aramburu to Onganía and Lanusse, had always been dictators who repressed the people. Perón had been that one charismatic exception who had their interest at heart. "This was a mistake. The mistake of believing that one man alone could change the entire situation or part of the situation."[63] Not a leader, but only a vanguard could direct the masses. Perón no longer represented the will of the people because he had lost touch with his popular base and was out of sync with the extraordinary revolutionary times Argentina and the world were living. The Montoneros regarded themselves as the people's vanguard and thus the equals of Perón. The decision was made, not only to dispute the leadership of the Peronist Organization, but also the leadership of the nation.

Perón's death was received with torn emotions. Hopes for the leadership of the Peronist Organization were mixed with a profound sadness at the loss of their leader. The Montoneros and the Peronist Youth were unable to free themselves from a Perón who had nestled himself firmly in their innermost selves, and they felt an enormous anger so fundamental in Peronism. "Anger. That marvelous anger. That anger which the Peronists know so well. That comes from our insides. Peronism is massively demonstrated anger. Anger of the people. Against the oligarchy. Against imperialism. Against the unforgettable oppression and persecution during eighteen years. That anger ours for the absence of the leader concentrated in every 'Viva Perón' which we shouted in the face of the repression of the dictatorship. . . . Anger, yes, anger dammit! Until our sovereign, free, and just fatherland."[64] This anger translated into a claim to power and a turn to violence.

The breach between vanguardist Montoneros and insurrectionist Montoneros increased after Perón's death. The insurrectionists stated in September 1974 that the socialist fatherland could only be reached through a mass insurrection, and that the most urgent task at hand was to organize a popular front of labor unions, peasant leagues, factory assemblies, and grass roots organizations in preparation of that moment. A guerrilla insurgency was premature because the revolutionary process had not yet arrived at its military stage but was still in its political stage. Hence, there was no reason for the Montoneros to go underground.[65]

Instead, the hegemonic vanguardist Montoneros believed that they were the most conscious part of the working class. They felt illuminated by the revolutionary fire, and were convinced that their armed struggle would radicalize the working class and make them join the revolutionary forces. In political practice, it meant that the vanguardists considered that all other forms of resistance had been exhausted and that violence was the only viable response to the right-wing terror.

The vanguardist Montoneros won the internal battle, and attracted a greater following because of their revolutionary appeal. The willingness to risk their lives for larger ideals elevated them to a higher moral plane in the eyes of many sympathizers. Furthermore, they simply imposed their vanguardism on the entire revolutionary left by inexplicable acts of violence, such as the assassination of Arturo Mor Roig for being the Minister of Interior in the Lanusse government and the architect of the GAN (Great National Accord).[66]

On 6 September 1974, Mario Firmenich announced that the Montoneros were going to return to the armed struggle because "all legal forms of carrying on the struggle have been used up."[67] The Montoneros wanted, as Hannah Arendt has said in another context, "access to history even at the price of destruction."[68] The revolutionary vanguard created an unbridgeable distance from the Peronist following. They had alienated themselves from the orthodox Peronist workers by assassinating union leaders, while many sympathizers were unwilling to risk their lives in crowd demonstrations, let alone in the armed struggle. As Fernando Vaca Narvaja admitted fifteen years later: "When we passed [into illegality] we began to harden our politics of resistance against Isabel Martínez because of the confrontation with Perón. We see this reflected in the decreasing capacity for mobilization. . . . Clandestinity ends up closing the link with the mass fronts."[69]

The decision to enter into the Second Resistance—the First Resistance was defined self-servingly as the Peronist protests between 1955 and 1973—was intended to protect the Montonero forces against right-wing attacks and be more effective in harassing enemy forces. This defensive withdrawal had three objectives: "1) To avoid that they annihilate us. 2) To accumulate strength. 3) To prepare a general offensive."[70] This move underground left tens of thousands of ordinary members and sympathizers completely unprotected. Alcira Argumedo calls this retreat a murder of the masses. "It's a murderous decision because they knew very well that they were condemning these people. . . . because these were people of the neighborhood, these were people who couldn't move, who had their children, who were workers, who had no means at all. They were giving them to the repression."[71] A surrender while awaiting better times would have been the most astute political strategy, argues Ernesto Jauretche retrospectively, but this was not contemplated at the time. After all, the Argentine people had forced each and every military regime to its knees. Why would it be different now? "How to imagine that the army could develop the unheard of cruelty, the brutality, which it developed? Extermination had never come to our minds. How could an extermination have ever occurred to us? It wasn't in our rationality, it belonged to another rationality. . . . We knew all the counterinsurgency strategies, and none of them contained this brutal component."[72]

The existence of various political options demonstrates that the move to vanguardism was not inevitable. Nevertheless, it was a decision shared by a substantial segment of the Montonero rank and file. The deeper reason for this support was the feeling that the second-generation Peronists had been cheated out of their share of political power and thus felt entitled to Argentina's future. Surrender was unimaginable, and a return to crowd mobilizations undesirable. There was no turning back in the minds of the guerrilla commanders and their rank and file. Revolutions were won by an unwavering belief in one's own strength, the historical correctness of the chosen course, and a reliance on a proven past performance.

Grass Roots Retreat and the Montonero Army

On Thursday morning 19 September 1974 at about 7:30, the Ford Falcon de Luxe carrying the brothers Jorge and Juan Carlos Born was directed by a policeman to a side street off the main thoroughfare Avenida del Libertador. The accompanying car with three bodyguards followed. As the two cars completed a left-hand turn onto a one-way street, they were hit by two pickup trucks and immediately surrounded by seven guerrillas. The driver and a passenger in the first car were riddled with bullets on suspicion of resisting the assault. The brothers Born were kidnapped by the Montoneros, and taken to a people's prison nearby, at the residential town of Martínez on the outskirts of Buenos Aires.

The whole operation involved nineteen guerrillas, some of them dressed as policemen, others as telephone workers.[73] The abduction had been planned and executed by Roberto Quieto, the former FAR commander who had participated in the 1972 escape from the Rawson prison. The operation was codenamed Twins, and planning had begun already in January 1974. The growing conflict with Perón must have made the Montoneros think that a return to guerrilla warfare was becoming inevitable.

Jorge and Juan Carlos Born were the sons of the president of Bunge y Born, one of Latin America's largest multinationals. Ostensibly, the brothers were put on trial for harming the interests of the Argentine people and convicted to a one-year people's prison term. Months of negotiations followed. Juan Carlos Born was released for health reasons after six months, while Jorge Born ended his sentence on 20 June 1975 during a press conference with Montonero leader Mario Firmenich. The Montoneros released Jorge Born unharmed after $U.S.64 million dollars had been paid and food and clothing had been distributed to the poor. The Montoneros became the richest guerrilla organization of Latin America. The mobilization of the Montonero Army could begin.[74] The ransom allowed them to build a well-armed guerrilla force, and maintain an infrastructure of safe houses, printshops, and weapons and ammunitions workshops, even though most arms were still acquired through theft.

After their move underground, the Montoneros intensified their attacks on the orthodox Peronist labor unions, the nationalist right, and the police. A dynamic of retaliation developed between September 1974 and

August 1975. On the left, congressman Rodolfo Ortega Peña, PRT lawyer Silvio Frondizi, and Julio Troxler, survivor of the José León Suárez massacre, were assassinated.[75] On the right, the ideologues Bruno Genta and Carlos Alberto Sacheri were assassinated by the ERP, while the Montoneros assassinated federal police chief Alberto Villar and his wife Elsa Marina by detonating an explosive device attached to their small yacht.[76] The result of this last vengeance killing was the institution of a state of siege on 6 November 1974 which would only be lifted in 1983.

The tit-for-tat vengeance killings served three purposes: they were part of a naked dispute for power, exposed the opponent's vulnerability, and paved a road of no return for the members of one's own organization. For example, the assassination of Rucci removed an influential right-wing union leader, demonstrated the strength of the Montoneros, and precluded a political settlement with the orthodox labor unions. Thousands of Montoneros were thus forced into an armed confrontation, including many sympathizers who were organizing neighborhoods, factories, and universities in support of a more progressive politics. But vengeance killings were more than a retaliatory routine, as if two deaths were valued the same. The revenge cycle continued spinning because of the accumulating social traumas and entailed violent posttraumatic responses. Each party had to endure the death of comrades and the extinction of its political force and identity. Such social traumatization fed the retaliatory practices, the militarization of the conflict, and an increase in security measures.

The Montoneros soon realized that they could not sustain a large guerrilla army in hiding, so they decided to divide the armed force into combatants and militias. A minority of combatants was organized into platoons dedicated full-time to military operations with the most advanced weapons. The majority would be militias holding regular jobs and using only hand guns and molotov cocktails. The militias were supposed to represent the organic link between the revolutionary vanguard Montoneros and the Peronist workers. They would assist combatants in certain operations, harass the security forces with demonstrations and disturbances, or strike out on limited missions themselves. The combatant forces were replenished from the militias.

In late 1974, the Montoneros were organized geographically into eight regions. Some regions were subdivided into zones because of their population size. Each region or zone harbored one column. Each guerrilla column had a commander responsible for all operations, and contained a military, political, logistic, and propaganda branch. The military branch was comprised of combat platoons and combat militias. The combat unit was the basic cell in a structure designed to provide maximum security and secrecy: individual members only knew their unit comrades and could thus not reveal the identity of others when tortured. This whole structure was headed by the National Command which used its tens of millions of dollars as political means to enforce a hierarchical obedience by withholding funds from recalcitrant columns. In addition, there were the elite Special Combat Groups operating anywhere in Argentina, and conducted directly by the national commanders.

The Politico-Military Organization Montoneros, as it was now called, began to look more like a regular army with military ranks, uniforms, insignia, a flag, and formal regulations.[77] These structural and organizational qualities led to a growing militarization in which professional combatants pulled all strings and the gap with the political front organizations became almost unbridgeable. The time when guerrillas, grass root organizations, and crowds composed one organic whole was only two years ago, but seemed in a far and distant past.[78]

The overall Montonero strategy was, understandably, greatly influenced by their successful opposition to the Lanusse dictatorship. The Montoneros hoped to precipitate the downfall of the Peronist government through grass roots organizations, electoral participation, and armed harassment. "The clandestinity allows us to hide from the enemy, to continue with our grass roots work and always be present with our political beliefs. It would be suicide to hide our politics."[79]

However, precisely this three-pronged strategy proved suicidal. The association of grass roots activists and party members with clandestine Montoneros made them into vulnerable targets. The idea that grass roots organizations "must be the 'eyes, ears, and voice' of the militias" to discover suitable military targets, turned these civilians into legitimate enemies, at first of their right-wing opponents and later of the Argentine military.[80] Few Argentine workers were therefore willing to participate in the Montonero grass roots organizations.

The belief that an armed struggle and an electoral campaign could be waged side by side was even more unrealistic. The Authentic Peronist Party (Partido Peronista Auténtico), founded on 11 March 1975, suffered a devastating defeat in the provincial elections of Missiones. Still, on 6 September 1975—foolishly chosen to commemorate the anniversary of the Montoneros' move to illegality—the national Authentic Party (Partido Auténtico) was founded. This electoral strategy proved disastrous. Party registration requirements exposed the names and addresses of forty thousand Montonero supporters, only to have the party outlawed on Christmas Eve of 1975.[81] The militarization of the armed struggle isolated the Montoneros from their dwindling political base instead of inserting them more firmly.

The Montoneros were at their maximum strength in 1975 with at least three thousand guerrillas, counting both combatants and militias.[82] In addition, there were around five hundred people dedicated to subsidiary tasks like forging documents, providing medical care, gathering intelligence, and manufacturing ammunition and weapons.[83] The year 1975 was to be decisive because of the military confrontations between guerrilla organizations and the Argentine Armed Forces. It was a particularly violent year with nine hundred political deaths to mourn in the country. The majority fell on the left side. The chaos in Argentina with the deadly retaliation between the right-wing AAA and the left-wing Montoneros, the attempt by the ERP to create a liberated zone in the north as well as its attacks on military bases, were important although not the major reasons why the armed forces decided to grab power. In February 1975, the foundation was laid for a systematic assault on the revolutionary left by a secret decree ordering the Army to annihilate the encampments of Marxist insurgents in Tucumán.

From Rebellion to Revolution

In 1971, Perón had decided that the struggle for a return to power should be waged on three fronts: crowd protests, guerrilla warfare, and political negotiations. The guerrilla organizations became Perón's preferred son because of the effectiveness of their means and the sacrifice of their lives. The Peronist guerrilla organizations spearheaded the resistance with robberies, kidnappings, assaults on police stations, and selective executions. The combination of armed violence, massive street protests, and Perón's able political manipulation made the military dictatorship fall within a few years.

With Perón once more at the helm in 1973, the revolutionary Peronists expected a considerable portion of the power to carry out Perón's 1971 call for an Argentine socialism. Instead, Perón sensed the danger of a revolutionary Peronist faction backed by barely demobilized Peronist guerrilla organizations. He strengthened his ties with the orthodox Peronist labor unions to outflank the Peronist left. The revolutionary Peronists felt cheated out of what they considered their legitimate right to power, and waged a violent struggle with the Peronist unions for the control of the Peronist Organization, at first through crowd competitions and later by assassinating their rivals.

The Marxist and Peronist guerrilla groups that emerged in 1969 had different objectives, but nevertheless coordinated their actions between 1970 and 1973 because of their common goal of overthrowing the military junta. The Marxists pursued a revolutionary course while the Peronist guerrillas only wanted a rebellion. The Marxist guerrillas rejected Peronism but rode along on the shoulders of general resentment against the dictatorship. Once the junta fell, they dismissed the democratic government as bourgeois, and continued with their attacks on the Argentine military. In contrast, the Peronist revolutionaries abandoned the violent struggle for power once democracy returned to Argentina, at least between mid-1973 and mid-1974. Their guerrilla activities had contributed to the return of Perón and had opened an avenue towards political power and participation.

The death of Perón in July 1974 made the Peronist left turn again to violence. This violence was motivated by a sense of entitlement to power in the Peronist government, but now they lacked the approval of the broad spectrum of Argentine society which had supported their armed operations between 1970 and 1973. Like the Marxists, the Peronist guerrillas began chasing after their objectives in isolation from Argentine society. The Peronist crowds quickly dwindled as the violence increased and the guerrilla organizations turned into militarized vanguards. The resumption of guerrilla warfare made the Peronist revolutionaries again join hands with the Marxist guerrillas. The guerrilla warfare developed its own dynamic through its engagement with right-wing death squads and later with military counterinsurgency forces. Violence was seen as the only recourse, and social trauma the inevitable price of survival and lasting happiness.

Chapter 8
The Shadows of Death: Improvisation, Counterinsurgency, and Downfall

On Sunday 1 December 1974, at 1:15 in the afternoon, Captain Humberto Viola arrives with his pregnant wife and two little daughters at his parents' home in San Miguel de Tucumán. He barely succeeds in squeezing his car between two parked taxis, and asks his wife to open the gate to the driveway. The moment Ms. Viola steps out of the car, fire is opened by several assailants. A badly wounded Viola abandons his car and staggers away with his wounded five-year-old daughter María Fernanda in his arms. One guerrilla approaches him and shoots him through the head. The three-year-old María Cristina remains gravely wounded in the back of the car and dies later in the hospital.[1]

At a time when government forces were tightening their grip on the insurgency, the ERP decided to carry out reprisal killings, of which Captain Viola was the tenth.[2] The belief was that such measures would intimidate the armed forces into lessening the repression, and make them respect the Geneva conventions regulating the treatment of prisoners of war. The direct cause was the execution of fourteen guerrillas on 11 August 1974. "As long as the oppressing army doesn't take guerrillas prisoner, the ERP will not take officers prisoner, and every assassination will be answered with the indiscriminate execution of officers."[3]

I believe that a functional explanation of the reprisal killings fails to grasp their emotional significance for the parties in conflict. The guerrillas were shaken by the harsh repression, the torture and summary executions. In turn, the reprisal killings traumatized the security and armed forces. By attacking individuals at random, whether these were field commanders or traffic policemen, they made everyone fear for his or her life. This sensation of defenselessness enhanced the military's corps spirit, strengthened the corporate identity, and increased the resolve to continue with the search-and-destroy missions. The indiscriminate attacks by the parties in conflict traumatized them both, even though the capacity to seek redress through violence differed greatly. Whereas the ERP and Montoneros had difficulty maintaining their guerrilla forces at strength, the Argentine government in 1975 gave the armed forces unlimited powers to use all their might against the insurgency. The traumatization of the former increased proportionally with the violence of the latter. In contrast, the armed forces celebrated victories which recontextualized their losses as a sacrifice for the good of Argentine society and lessened their social trauma.

This chapter describes the growing militarism of the ERP and Montoneros, and the mimesis between guerrilla organizations and armed forces. The ERP and Montoneros began to resemble regular armies, while the Argentine national army responded by mimicking not only the operational organization but also as the culture of guerrilla warfare. The tit-for-tat killings fed into the violence-trauma-violence dynamic that became increasingly harder to stop as more deaths fell on both sides. Such tragic victims as Captain Viola's three-year-old daughter made growing numbers of officers emotionally ripe for a return to arms and convinced them that the guerrillas could only be stopped by outterrorizing them.[4] The attempt by the ERP to create a liberated territory in northwestern Argentina resulted in 1975 in a counterinsurgency war to interrupt a scenario proven so successful in Cuba and Vietnam.

Rural Guerrilla Insurgency and Operation Independence

The People's Revolutionary Army had played since early 1973 with the idea of starting a rural insurgency and sent eight men on a reconnaissance trip to Tucumán, but the political situation was not yet ripe for such escalation.[5] The return to the armed struggle by the Montoneros convinced Santucho that a military coup was becoming inevitable, and that the revolutionary situation was maturing.

When the ERP failed to secure rural guerrilla training from Cuba and Vietnam, Santucho decided to take forty combatants to Tucumán and lead the instruction himself.[6] The nucleus was called the Ramón Rosa Jiménez Mountain Company, named after an ERP guerrilla from Tucumán killed by the police. As had happened to the Uturuncos in 1959, Masetti's EGP in 1964, and the FAP in 1968, the guerrillas were soon detected by the federal police. They made a successful escape and on 30 May 1974 attacked the village of Acheral. The company occupied the police post, the telephone office, and the railway station and controlled the main access roads for some time.[7]

The operation was celebrated as a qualitative jump in the revolutionary struggle, and the outcome of two fundamental principles of guerrilla warfare: "the development from small to large and the incorporation of the masses in the war."[8] In true foquist reasoning, a stepped-up armed struggle would result in a "consequent deepening of the political consciousness of the masses."[9] In reality, the masses were not even trickling in small numbers to the guerrillas, because the violence was condemned by most Argentines.[10]

In August 1974 the ERP Mountain Company carried out two assaults on military installations in neighboring Catamarca. These attacks led to the first large-scale involvement of the army in counterinsurgency since the fall of the military government in 1973. A military force combed the hills of Tucumán, but only two guerrillas were apprehended.[11] Six months later, the army would launch a full-scale attack on the ERP guerrilla insurgency with thousands of men, complete with reconnaissance planes and helicopters with air-to-ground missiles.

With considerable dramatism, the counterinsurgency campaign in Tucumán was called Operation Independence (Operativo Independencia) named after Argentina's declaration of independence made in 1816 in Tucumán province. Directive 333, the first tactical plan of the counterinsurgency campaign, was drawn up on 23 January 1975.[12] Its constitutional basis was provided on 5 February 1975 when President Martínez de Perón and key cabinet members signed Decree 261 authorizing the armed forces to annihilate the rural guerrilla insurgency in Tucumán.[13] Even though the campaign was to last six months, the army impressed on its troops "that the fight against the subversion is a long, slow process that demands great sacrifices, tenacity, patience, and perseverance, and that successful results are not easily achieved."[14] The extended struggle against the Tupamaros in Uruguay, Che Guevara in Bolivia, and the decades of counterinsurgency against Colombian guerrilla forces were given as examples.

The troops in Tucumán consisted of the national gendarmery, police forces, and the Third Army Corps. The Fifth Infantry Brigade would carry out the operations under the command of General Acdel Vilas. Officers and NCOs who were commissioned on 5 February 1975 were to be relieved on April 2. The tours of duty were fifty-five days.[15] The infantry brigade was reinforced on 9 March 1975 with three army corps units taking turns after a tour of duty of thirty-two days.[16] Every army corps sent personnel so that as many officers as possible could gain combat experience.[17]

The military mission consisted of occupying the urban zones followed by offensive actions against the insurgency in rural areas. The maneuvers would begin by isolating the civilian population from the guerrillas. Next, the military would carry out reconnaissance missions to become familiar with the terrain, followed by actions against the urban rearguard and a progressive incursion of army patrols to provoke guerrillas into combat until they were eliminated. The battle plan noted that the guerrilla assaults of military installations and the attacks on military officers "have created strong aggressive feelings among the troops which translate into a desire to operate against the enemy."[18] There would not be any spectacular victories but the enemy had to be pursued until "the subversion no longer finds any hiding place on the soil of the Fatherland, other than the shadows of death."[19]

The Military Campaign in Tucumán

Mario Roberto Santucho hailed Operation Independence as proof of the steady advancement of the revolutionary process and the growing support for the rural insurgency among the peasants of Tucumán. Santucho was not only guilty of wishful thinking but also of misinterpreting the counter-insurgency tactic. He expected an encirclement of the ERP Mountain Company, between fifty and ninety guerrillas strong. He ordered its division into four groups, intended to entice the army into an inhospitable, humid terrain in the foothills of the Andes and then wage dozens of small battles through surprise and movement. Thus, the armed forces would become demoralized. This victorious struggle would attract rural workers and poor peasants and earn the support of the people in the region.

However, General Acdel Vilas did not chase after the guerrillas but established his command in the town of Famaillá, and stationed his troops in the hamlets strung along Interstate 38 which bordered the guerrilla zone.[20] General Vilas inverted Mao Zedong's dictum that the guerrilla fighter had to operate like a fish in the water. His repressive tactic consisted of killing the fish by draining the water. Vilas admitted years later that he had ordered the summary execution of combatants out of a lack of faith in the justice system, while only passing harmless suspects to the courts.[21] Many repressive practices of the dirty war (abduction, torture, disappearance, assassination) were first tested in Tucumán, and later adopted throughout the country.

The first confrontation between army troops and guerrilla forces took place accidentally near the Pueblo Viejo river on 14 February 1975. The task force Chañi had days earlier detected some guerrilla movement and dispatched a combat unit on patrol. The platoon was led by First Lieutenant Héctor Cáceres, and also included one lieutenant, two NCOs and six soldiers. Returning to base after an unsuccessful search, one corporal spotted the impression of sandals.[22] A military account described the scene as follows: "And the search began. The listening. The attention to everything, to every possible sign. The advance was made slowly because all traces disappeared in the hills and appeared only in the clearing, which worried the group a little, especially because there wasn't much experience then."[23] Suddenly, the men were shot from behind by a group of fifteen to twenty guerrillas. The corporal collapsed wounded to the ground. First-Lieutenant Cáceres ran to his aid and became severely wounded. The remaining lieutenant, "stretched out and paralyzed on the ground, manages in a desperate move—which proves his combative capacity, will and valor—to throw a hand grenade and succeeds in knocking down one [guerrilla] who was escaping."[24] The wounded corporal and his lieutenant repelled the attack. Soon, helicopter support dispersed the guerrillas. First Lieutenant Cáceres died of his wounds, and so did two guerrillas.[25] This fire baptism was regarded as the army's first experience with "a new war. Different. Strange. Maybe the military instruction that was received did not entirely prepare the troops for these exigencies."[26]

Reading the final army report about Operation Independence with quotes from the secret communications between Santucho and Mountain Company commander Irurzún, seeing the extensive lists with the names of the combatants, one realizes the impossible odds at which the ERP was operating and can only shudder at the interrogation regime to which the captives must have been submitted.[27] The new counterinsurgency strategy transformed the theater of operations into a diffuse environment of suspicion, where any person might be accused of collaborating with the enemy. Torture was the judge that decided the fate of people, and fear was the punishment meted out to all alike.

The PRT-ERP in Argentina was by mid-1975 comprised of around 600 combatants, 2,000 active supporters, and more than 20,000 sympathizers. The mountain company consisted of ninety men and ten women, but the military have claimed that the actual strength was 170 guerrillas.[28] Santucho established a rural military school and installed a powerful radio transmitter which never went on the air. Very much like the Montoneros, the ERP developed all the features of a regular army with war flags, uniforms, and decoration ceremonies. Santucho insisted on strict discipline, instituted target practice, trained the men and women physically, and instructed them tactically by studying the military feats of other guerrilla organizations.[29]

At the end of August 1975, the army discovered the rural guerrilla headquarters, and Santucho fled to Buenos Aires. Dozen of small combats were waged during the following year at which the ERP combatants generally incurred more casualties than the army. The only dramatic blow to Operation Independence was dealt by the Montoneros when they attacked a C-130 Hercules plane transporting a special counterinsurgency unit. Five men died in the assault, which will be described below. The ERP mountain company was now constantly on the run, had lost many experienced combatants, and was forced to replace them with guerrillas with less combat experience, less ideological instruction, and less revolutionary zeal. The army extended the six-month campaign and erected check points at provincial borders to prevent guerrilla reinforcements from arriving.[30]

October 1975 was the decisive month in the counterinsurgency campaign, a month in which the government gave the armed forces extensive powers to combat the guerrilla insurgency in the whole country. The army decided to change its tactics in Tucumán. Aside from controlling roads, hamlets, villages, and towns, the army had until then only made day-long incursions into guerrilla territory with small units, but it would from now on harass guerrillas progressively. The task forces Ibatín and Aguila remained permanently in the inhabitable hills of Tucumán, continuously shifting base, searching for and ambushing guerrillas.

One important combat occurred during the evening of 5 October as an army task force received information about a group of thirty guerrillas waiting for two days to ambush an army truck. The army sent out several patrols. One platoon walked into an ambush, suffered two casualties, and fled. A wounded sergeant narrated later how he survived by playing dead, "one of them ordered: 'Go and take the armament from those two in front, and finish them off if they are alive.' When I heard the sound he was making while approaching me, apparently dragging himself close to me, I cut my breath at the moment that the individual was taking my weapon with one jerk, while he kicked me immediately in the side of my body. Then he pulled my head up and shouted: 'this one is dead meat'. . . . They left me there till darkness came."[31]

The army was now on the trail of an important group of guerrillas. Several ambushes were mounted and helicopters were ordered to strafe the sugar cane fields. The tracer ammunition set the fields on fire, and the guerrillas took refuge in the surrounding shrubbery. They accused the army of using explosive bullets, which left deep lacerations and were forbidden by the Geneva conventions.[32] Three commanding officers, among them Santucho's brother Asdrúbal, and ten combatants of the ERP Mountain Company died between 8 and 10 October.[33] There were fifteen confrontations in October 1975 at which forty guerrillas found their death.[34]

The combats were few in November and December of 1975, but the army decided to step up their counterinsurgency in January 1976. Operation Lamadrid combed the mountainous zone and destroyed the network of guerrilla camps. Thirty-two small encampments were discovered and three guerrillas killed during the first twenty days of the campaign.[35] The Ramón Rosa Jiménez Mountain Company was nearing its end, when a small impulse came from an unexpected side. The Montoneros had always rejected a rural insurgency as unsuitable for a highly urbanized Argentina. Nevertheless, the Montoneros decided in January 1976 to send about twenty combatants for training to Tucumán in an attempt to broaden the front for the Argentine military and oblige them to disperse their forces. The first Montonero to be killed was Juan Carlos Alsogaray, the son of General Julio Alsogaray who had been President Onganía's commander-in-chief.[36]

The March 1976 coup allowed the army to deal the deathblow. Ambushes killed the remaining guerrillas roaming in the hills and through sugar cane fields. The death of Mario Roberto Santucho in July 1976, described in chapter 10, signaled the end. Three combatants of the Mountain Company were killed in mid-October, and the last surviving member was traced and killed in early November 1976. The PRT-ERP admitted to having lost around eighty combatants during Operation Independence, while the army had lost twenty-four men on combat duty during the 1975–1976 Operation Independence. The total number of military and police casualties from 1975 to 1977 in Tucumán reached eighty-four.[37]

Militarism of the People's Revolutionary Army

The rural exploits of the Ramón Rosa Jiménez Mountain Company had been carried out alongside frontal attacks on army bases by urban guerrilla units. These strikes at the "heart" of the enemy, at its centers of power, sought to inflict traumatizing blows, blows which demoralized, blows which would expose the vulnerabilities of the Argentine armed forces, and cause them to admit to their defenselessness against future attacks. Such loss of mastery was traumatizing for an armed forces accustomed to imposing its will on Argentine society.

On 11 August 1974, at 1 A.M., a guerrilla force of about sixty combatants attacked the ammunition plant (Fábrica Militar de Pólvora y Explosivas) near Villa María, near Córdoba. They surprised a sentry, and received help from three comrades in military service. There were isolated fire fights, but the resistance was small because many servicemen were on holiday leave. The guerrillas departed rapidly, stole large amounts of weapons, and took Major Larrabure hostage. The operation had cost the lives of three guerrillas, one policeman, and one corporal. The ERP considered the action a success and decorated the guerrillas with the Heroes of Trelew medal.[38]

At the time of the assault on the Villa María ammunition factory, seventy guerrillas of the Ramón Rosa Jiménez Mountain Company were poised for attack on the 17th Airborne Infantry Regiment of Catamarca. The operation failed because just after midnight two cyclists observed eight guerrillas changing into their uniforms. Army and police succeeded in pinning down a group of twenty-seven guerrillas trying to return to their base in Tucumán. The group was detained after a fire fight of several hours. The army declared that fourteen combatants had been killed in action, while the ERP stated that they had been arrested, tortured, and finally executed.[39] A combined force of four thousand servicemen and federal policemen under the command of General Luciano Menéndez combed the hills around Famaillá but only two men and some weapons were located.[40]

The Catamarca debâcle made the ERP institute reprisal killings as a pedagogic weapon in the unfolding guerrilla war.[41] Just as the Montoneros believed that the violence from above generated the violence from below, so the guerrilla commanders placed a misguided faith in their principle, "The more general and savage the repression, the greater will be the resistance."[42] But the Argentine armed forces had no intention of playing by the Geneva conventions. The executions and kidnappings of officers made them use more rather than less brutal forms of repression. In particular the abduction of officers, like Lieutenant-Colonel Jorge Ibarzábel and Major Julio Larrabure, infuriated the military.

Major Argentino del Valle Larrabure was a chemical engineer who specialized in explosives. He was kept in a Cordoban people's prison after his abduction on August 11, but was moved in November 1974 to Rosario. The windowless cell contained a cot and a portable toilet. It was located in the basement of a small dry-goods store. A ventilator connected to two plastic tubes refreshed the place with air.

Larrabure was allowed to keep a diary and could occasionally write a letter to his family. They responded with letters in the newspapers. Suffering from asthma, Larrabure had nightmares about dying of asphyxiation. He became disoriented, could not tell night from day, and floated between despair, depression, and religious exaltation. He suffered from emotional ups and downs, insomnia, hallucinations, lack of appetite, stomach pain, and an acute bladder infection. He was clearly suffering from a psychic trauma. One guerrilla offered him freedom if he agreed to work in their weapons workshop, but Larrabure refused.

Major Larrabure's diary stopped abruptly in early 1975: "I feel agitated and anguished today, a deep sorrow oppresses my chest. I feel extremely tense and nervous. My mind is disturbed and seems to perceive I don't know what whole of extrasensory sensations. I am invaded by a desperate desire to cry or scream, to kick the thin wall of my cell while the vigilant eyes of the young hooded man watch my nervous movement in this mouse trap closely."[43] On 19 August 1975, after more than one year in prison, Larrabure died from asphyxiation, at the age of forty-three. According to the ERP, he hung himself during an unguarded moment. The military autopsy report suspected torture and death by strangulation. His body had lost more than forty kgs. of its original weight.[44] The appearance of Major Larrabure's mangled body on 23 August 1975 contributed significantly to the resolve of the military to end the political violence. It was indicative that the press was banned from the official wake. One newspaper interpreted this ban as a sign "that the institution has begun closing itself with the intention to settle the matter single-handed when the process reaches its highest point."[45]

With plenty of money and arms to continue the armed struggle, thanks to numerous extortive kidnappings, the PRT-ERP leadership decided to step up the formation of a guerrilla army with squads, platoons, companies, and battalions.[46] In January 1975 Mario Roberto Santucho was solemnly appointed as the ERP's commander-in-chief, and as the PRT's secretary-general.[47] A demonstration of the newly formed army was given on Sunday 13 April 1975. In less than one hour, a unit of about fifty combatants assaulted the 121 Arsenal Battalion (Batallón de Arsenales 121) at Fray Luis Beltrán. After seventeen hundred light rifles and smaller quantities of heavy weapons had been loaded on a school bus, the guerrilla force abandoned the military base, leaving behind two dead comrades and one dead army colonel.[48]

This success encouraged the PRT-ERP to involve more party members in the revolutionary struggle. In early 1975 the PRT had given new impetus to the creation of a cellular structure to bridge the gap between the party and the masses. There were three kinds of cells: party cells (*células de aparato*), front cells (*células de frente*), and sympathizer cells (*células de simpatizantes*). Party cells supported the revolutionary activities of the PRT-ERP directly. These cells were dedicated to providing armament, false documents, propaganda, publications, health care, and so forth. Front cells organized street protests and grass roots activities in neighborhoods, slums, factories, schools, and universities. Each cell had generally three activists for reasons of security. Sympathizer cells demonstrated the penetration of the PRT among the masses.[49] An individual was considered a sympathizer (*simpatizante*) when he or she received the magazines *El Combatiente* or *Estrella Roja*, and sold at least one copy to another person, known as a reader (*lector*). An individual became an activist (*militante*) when he or she brought along at least four sympathizers. New activists were welcomed with an admission ceremony in which they expressed their dedication to the party and the revolution. They were given their tasks, and were registered on personnel file cards. Each cell of three activists was thus to be supported by a cell of at least twelve sympathizers. Sympathizers could be called upon for assistance, such as providing temporary shelter to party members and combatants. The PRT-ERP commanders hoped that this pyramidal structure would enhance their organic penetration among the Argentine people.

In January 1974, the PRT Youth (Juventud del PRT) was founded to attract high school students. The PRT central committee emphasized that "the road of the popular war for our final liberation is hard and long" and that was why the party needed a strategic reserve of thousands of well-trained young militants "who will form the combat detachments of the people's forces."[50] The organization changed its name to Guevarist Youth (Juventud Guevarista) in mid-1975. The Guevarist Youth was to be a front organization engaged only in public protest, but the ERP recruited the most mature members as guerrilla combatants. The spirit of sacrifice of the youth was perceived as invigorating the PRT-ERP but also led to unforgiving tragedy when the military repression tarred them with the same brush as the guerrilla combatants.[51]

In October 1975, when the counterinsurgency war was extended nationwide, the ERP decided to launch its greatest attack ever. The target was Argentina's largest arsenal (Batallón de Arsenales 601 Comandante Domingo Viejobueno) at Monte Chingolo, about twenty-five kms. from downtown Buenos Aires. The first objective was to transport thirteen tons of weapons to Tucumán to arm a six-hundred-man rural guerrilla force. The second objective was to demoralize the armed forces and discourage them from staging the anticipated coup against President Isabel Martínez de Perón. Santucho assumed that the military would only grab power once the guerrilla insurgency had been defeated.[52] Secret military sources estimated their strength at around five hundred combatants nationwide.[53]

The José de San Martin Battalion guerrilla force consisted of around three hundred men and women under the command of Benito Urteaga. There were 130 experienced and well-armed combatants, and 130 poorly armed party activists without combat training ordered to erect a defense ring around the theater of operations by barricading bridges and access roads. There were also twenty-five security guards checking on the retreating force after the assault was over. Finally, seven health posts manned by twenty physicians were established nearby to attend the wounded. Meanwhile, the army was put on the alert by an informer, and reduced its troops to a minimum to pretend that the operation had not been detected.[54]

On Tuesday 23 December 1975, at 7:00 P.M., fifty ERP guerrillas invade the Hotel Molino Blanco, take nine vehicles from the parking lot and follow a large truck in the direction of the military base. A hail of machine gun fire meets the caravan at 7:40 P.M., just before the Mercedes Benz truck rams the entrance gate of Arsenal Battalion 601 and the nine vehicles fan out across the base. One pickup truck reaches an armory but is repelled by the guards, killing eight guerrillas. The army resistance is so great that the guerrillas fail to make progress but continue exchanging fire for two consecutive hours. Meanwhile, the inexperienced PRT activists begin to harass two police stations and erect barricades on half a dozen bridges leading to the combat zone.

A helicopter arrives at 8:30 P.M. for a reconnaissance flight. At 9:20 P.M., three armored vehicles bring fresh army troops, while several helicopters strafe the area. At 10:00 P.M., ERP field commander Urteaga decides to retreat but his order fails to reach the combatants. Three hours after the fighting started, the guerrilla units begin their confused withdrawal. They leave behind their vehicles, dead and wounded, and depart on foot. The Navy employs light Canberra planes to bomb the surrounding shantytowns where the guerrillas are supposed to be hiding. The army has by 11:30 P.M. gained total control over the military base. The operation cost the lives of forty-nine guerrilla combatants, the highest number of casualties for any operation in Argentina. Most of the dead were between twenty and twenty-five years of age. Four civilians died accidentally in the crossfire. The army incurred four losses and the police suffered two dead.[55]

The father of one guerrilla wrote about the state in which he found his son's body at Avellaneda cemetery: "The bodies stretched out on the ground at noonday. All piled on top of one another, mixed together helter-skelter. They had left them in whatever position. They were mutilated. It is a lie that they had taken their hands only to identify them. Their arms were cut off at different lengths. . . . My son had fortunately died instantaneously. He had only half his face left. . . . They were all naked except my son and another kid whose head was destroyed. They all had a number painted on their chest and some the ERP initials. My wife said that this was sowing hatred among the Argentines because of the lack of respect. But I think furthermore that these assassins want to break the relatives."[56] The majority of the dead were not returned to their relatives. In a public plea, a group of relatives asked for the remains of twenty-three persons and inquired about the whereabouts of nineteen disappeared persons.[57]

A depressed Mario Roberto Santucho told his brother Julio next day on Christmas Eve: "something is really going wrong, Julito, we are making mistakes."[58] His reaction was entirely different three days later at a political bureau meeting. After a reconstruction of events, and after some members wondered whether or not the Monte Chingolo attack had been an instance of adventurism, Santucho concluded surprisingly that the attack had been a military defeat but a political victory since the coup had been postponed and the Argentine people could now prepare for a popular resistance.

The Monte Chingolo disaster did not in any direct sense mark the ERP's military defeat. In fact, the ERP was in late 1975 militarily speaking stronger, better equipped, and more experienced than in late 1972. However, the armed forces were also in a different state of preparation. The military now had their hands free to hit the guerrillas without restraint. According to Luis Mattini, Monte Chingolo marked the beginning of the PRT-ERP's defeat because it revealed the inability of the leadership to critically examine its own strategy. A Marxist-Leninist belief in its own pseudo-scientific analysis of the objective forces of history clouded the perception of the political and military reality. Less than four months after the 24 March 1976 coup, and at a time when thousands of people were disappearing, an internal PRT bulletin wrote that "Such is the state of war that our Party is living, at the start of an already initiated and generalized popular revolutionary war, that will culminate in the total and final victory of the socialist revolution."[59]

Mario Roberto Santucho and two other commanders were killed on 19 July 1976, leaving the guerrilla organization in disarray (see Chapter 10). Finally, in April 1977, the PRT-ERP concluded that they had been defeated, and the members were ordered to retreat into exile, first to Brazil and then to Europe and Mexico. The PRT-ERP in exile disintegrated into several groups without much support from the demoralized cadres. These revolutionary Marxists realized that their defeat had been in the making since 1973 because of their vanguardism, militarism, and lack of appreciation for the political space afforded by democracy. Furthermore, they had underestimated the Argentine armed forces, alienated the middle classes and the Peronist working class, and had failed to realize that Argentina was not ripe for the coming of a socialist dawn.[60]

Revolutionary Creativity and Montonero Militarism

The militarization of the Montoneros occurred in late 1974. Calls for mass mobilization and the conquest of political power through electoral victories were hollow phrases defied by the embrace of violence. The Montoneros drew their strategic insight no longer from the guerrilla warfare theorists Guevara, Guillén, and Marighela, but from two generals beyond suspicion: Juan Domingo Perón and Carl von Clausewitz. Von Clausewitz taught them that war is "a continuation of political activity by other means."[61] This implied for the Montoneros not just that the military and political struggle were each other's complement, but more importantly that military actions and victories were justified as political advances.[62]

The Montoneros had learned from Perón that "one hits there where it hurts and when it hurts."[63] This principle was carried out to the extreme in the realm of individual killings and contributed greatly to a degeneration of the guerrilla warfare. Executions ranged from active duty military officers and policemen to politicians, union leaders, and business managers. They were as pointless from a strategic standpoint as the ERP reprisal killings. The two organizations began to resemble each other closely in their militarism and tendency towards terrorism. These assassinations certainly did not bring the victory any closer, but only helped to incite the ire of the Argentine military.

The Montoneros waged three military campaigns of many small actions between January 1975 and March 1976, while occasionally carrying out large operations intended to demonstrate their might and military ingenuity as true artists of war. "In sum, the fight for liberation has a scientific basis, but is an art. Improvisation, audacity, and intuition are often necessary ingredients."[64] Unlike the Marxist revolutionaries, the Montoneros always placed a great emphasis on the creativity of its members. Numerous writers and poets were prominent Montoneros, such as Francisco Urondo, Juan Gelman, and Rodolfo Walsh.

This notion of the creative force of the revolutionary struggle resonated well with the belief in violence as constructive rather than destructive. Violence would remedy the ills of Argentine society and create a "new human being," free of selfishness and willing to sacrifice his or her life for the happiness of others.[65] One might even say that the very use of violence demonstrated that the combatant was already this new human being. The creativity of violence was very much present in the Montonero operations. Their actions were always more inventive than effective. They spent disproportionate amounts of time and resources on spectacular feats as if the tactical importance of surprise attacks was extended into the realm of creativity.

The January–March 1975 campaign involved numerous bombings and vengeance killings, totaling 150 operations. The four objectives were to train new combatants in larger and more complex operations, to demonstrate openly the unbroken operational capacity of the Montoneros, to harass the security forces, and to demonstrate that the armed forces could not repress the armed insurgency without satisfying the demands of the Argentine people.[66]

The July–October 1975 campaign began with attacks on police stations and the temporary seizure of urban neighborhoods. The experience gained in this campaign prompted the Montoneros to announce the formation of the Montonero Army. This decision was another move towards militarization, consisting of three steps: (1.) the creation of an organization specialized in combat with heavy arms, and the additional training of militias; (2.) the incorporation of militias in large operations; and (3.) the expansion of the logistic and political support structures among the masses.[67]

Unlike the ERP, the Montoneros waged most of their operations in Argentina's large urban centers. The urban population was believed to have the highest political consciousness, and the city was ideal to create grass root organizations among the Peronist working class.[68] Montoneros and ERP had agreed upon a division of labor in which the latter concentrated on the military, while the former attacked the Peronist right, the police, and multinational corporations. The Montoneros had always regarded the police, and in particular the federal police, as their principal adversary because they were most responsible for repressing Peronist workers.

The division of labor ended with a daring sabotage on 22 August 1975 of the Santísima Trinidad, a missile-carrying frigate and the pride of the Argentine Navy. The objective was not strategic but psychological. Explosive devices were attached to the hull during a three-and-a-half hour operation of Montonero frogmen. The successful attack was to commemorate the Trelew massacre, and demonstrate that the Montoneros were capable of striking anywhere in the country, even at a well-guarded naval base.[69] A similar audacity was displayed on Thursday 28 August, when a C-130 Hercules was struck by a remote control detonation at the airport of San Miguel de Tucumán. The transport plane was carrying 116 members of the national gendarmerie returning from a counterinsurgency mission. Four persons died instantly and twenty-five were wounded by the blazing fire. One person died later in the hospital.[70] But the Montoneros were still on to greater things. Operation First Fruits (Operación Primicias) involved fifty-five combatants, nineteen vehicles, two aircrafts, and the coordination of actions in four locations. This was to be their only major military attack on the Argentine army.

Operation First Fruits begins when four guerrillas hijack a Boeing 739 departing from the downtown Buenos Aires airport at 3:15 P.M. on Sunday 5 October 1975 with destination Corrientes. The guerrillas redirect the plane to Formosa, where it arrives at 4:45 P.M. A group of nine combatants on the ground takes control of the Formosa airport, refuels the Boeing, and takes possession of a four-seater Cessna. Meanwhile, a second group secures a private airstrip on a ranch in Santa Fe province.

At 4:00 P.M., a guerrilla force of twenty-six combatants enters the 29th Mounted Infantry Regiment in Formosa, a city 930 kilometers north of Buenos Aires, after one guard has been subdued by a soldier who is a member of the Montoneros. The group enters with five vehicles but is surprised by heavy MAG machine-gun fire. The guerrillas nevertheless succeed in entering the garrison. They allow conscript soldiers to leave, but these immediately assume position and return intense fire. Most guerrillas die in this confrontation. Several guerrilla platoons shoot their way to the armory and succeed in taking fifty FAL rifles. Officers and soldiers have by now organized a fierce resistance and the guerrilla combatants make a narrow escape by truck to the Formosa airport. They load the stolen rifles in the cargo, board the hijacked plane, and depart at 5:25 P.M. They fly to the ranch in Santa Fe, while the Cessna heads with several guerrillas for Corrientes.[71]

The army reported ten dead soldiers and sixteen dead guerrillas, including the soldier who helped the Montoneros on the inside. The Montoneros registered eleven dead guerrillas and between forty and fifty dead soldiers and officers. General Díaz Bessone was the commander of the Second Army Corps at the time.

I was the corps commander, and I went there. I arrived when the hostilities had already ended, but I saw the dead and I saw the wounded. Well, the dead. Soldiers of the base, NCOs, and officers were being covered up in one place of the barracks, and there were mothers. I remember the mothers of the soldiers, how they were distressed from the immense pain of their dead sons. And the guerrillas were on the other side and there was not one relative present. Why? First, because it was impossible to identify them, because their finger prints had been erased. They erased them with acid or pumice stone. . . . Second, the documents were false. They were carrying documents that said whatever. Furthermore, some parents were ashamed and didn't even want to go and inquire; others were afraid, a silly fear because we handed over the body if they came.[72]

Again, the rationale of Operation First Fruits was psychological rather than strategic. Apart from acquiring fifty rifles, the assault served no other purpose than to humiliate the Argentine army with a spectacular action. The general public was baffled about the sense of it all.[73] Furthermore, the Montoneros were having increasing difficulties persuading sympathizers to enlist. The attrition rate was high and a definite victory was nowhere in sight. The principal threat to the Montoneros no longer came from right-wing death squads but from police and army.

The number of combatants dropped rapidly by late 1975. The Montoneros were incurring great losses, such as the abduction of Roberto Quieto on 28 December 1975. Quieto was the third-in-command of the Montonero national leadership. Within weeks of his disappearance, two guerrilla bases and many safe houses were raided, while dozens of comrades were abducted. In February 1976, Roberto Quieto, the same Quieto who had escaped from the Rawson naval base in 1972 and masterminded the 1974 kidnapping of the Born brothers which had filled the Montonero war chest to capacity, was found guilty by the Montonero leadership of informing and desertion in action, stripped of his rank, and sentenced to death in absentia.[74]

In January 1976 the Montoneros were aware that the military were determined to annihilate them.[75] The head of Montonero intelligence, Rodolfo Walsh, had informed the Montonero commanders Firmenich, Perdía, and Quieto already in early December 1975 about the March 1976 coup. The son of retired General Julio Alsogaray had opened his father's safe, copied a draft of "Battle Order 24 March," and passed it to Walsh.[76] The Montoneros described this war as a "dirty war" (*guerra sucia*) consisting of "abductions, assassinations, and generalized torture" with specialized task forces.[77] Intent on preserving their strength, Montonero activists were ordered to create an impression of normality by moving to a new residence and living a life indistinguishable from the neighbors, while hiding their weapons, spray paints, communication equipment, and revolutionary literature.

Nevertheless, the Montonero commanders proceeded with their March 1976 campaign. The campaign was aimed specifically at the police. In reaction, workers and Montoneros were incarcerated, razzias held, and students were tortured and assassinated. Still, the Montoneros were elated about the results of the campaign's first week with sixteen dead among the various police forces.[78]

Within the Montoneros and ERP, there reigned the belief that action contained its own justification in times of repression. Commitment to a cause, the willingness to participate and risk one's life (*se jugar*) for a better future, validated violent action, moralized all means, and reaped the admiration of the supporters. The sincere moral commitment of thousands of young people to improve life in Argentina, participate in the political process, and enhance justice and social welfare, were cynically exploited by guerrilla commanders who saw themselves as the political leaders of Argentina's revolutionary future.

The order to use a cyanide capsule to escape detention reveals the extent to which the Montonero organization had degenerated its guerrilla ethic to the extremes of voluntarism. The practice also expressed the depths of immorality. By obliging the rank and file to sacrifice themselves for the organization, the Montonero commanders violated the human integrity and personal autonomy of their members by taking away the possibility to survive, their right to choose how to surrender, and even how to die.

Rodolfo Walsh criticized the Montonero commanders for their militarism. He recommended a withdrawal among the Argentine people to regain their trust, and a return to grass roots resistance against Argentina's economic infrastructure.[79] By 13 December 1976, Walsh concluded that the Montoneros "have suffered a military defeat in 1976 that threatens to turn itself into an extermination. . . ."[80] Four months later, he suffered this extermination himself. On 25 March 1977, he was ambushed by a navy task group. When Walsh realized that he was being captured, he ran away and took out his 22 caliber Walther pistol. Navy Lieutenant Alfredo Astiz failed to tackle Walsh, and Walsh wounded one of his pursuers. The avalanche of bullets from the navy task group killed Walsh instantly.[81]

Unlike the ERP which admitted defeat in 1977, demobilized its forces and awaited better days, the four-man Montonero leadership in exile (Firmenich, Perdía, Hobert, and Yäger) continued their harassment of the military, supposedly to provoke a mass insurrection.[82] General Cesáreo Cardozo, head of the federal police, was assassinated on 18 June 1976 by a time bomb placed under the matrimonial bed. His wife and daughter were wounded.[83] A powerful artifact hidden in a suitcase was left on 2 July 1976 during lunch time in the dining hall of the Security Branch of the federal police. Eighteen persons died and sixty-six were wounded. Eleven policemen perished in Rosario on 12 September from the impact of a car bomb. The building of Navy intelligence was rocked on 15 December by a powerful bomb killing fourteen persons and wounding eighteen.[84] The Montoneros claimed to have carried out four hundred operations in 1976, inflicting three hundred casualties.[85] However, such actions failed to earn the mass support so sought after because the Montoneros lacked any real presence among the Peronist working class. Most workers refused to throw in their lot with the guerrillas because of the real danger of military reprisals and a lack of trust in the Montonero leadership.

The Montoneros did not lose their audacity in 1977 with failed assassination attempts on the lives of President Videla and Vice-Admiral Guzzetti.[86] Even though the Montoneros claimed to have carried out six hundred actions in 1977, the overwhelming majority was insignificant and failed to harm the Argentine armed and security forces.[87] A handful of spectacular actions concealed their decimation through the relentless military repression. According to a calculation by Ernesto Jauretche and Jaime Dri, made in November 1977, there were only four hundred active combatants left who responded directly to the Montonero National Leadership. This number coincided with the military intelligence at the time, estimating their number at 370 in May 1978.[88]

The Montoneros regarded the World Cup soccer tournament of June 1978, held in Argentina, as a golden opportunity to draw attention to the military repression and their own resistance. However, the dozens of attacks on homes and buildings failed to raise much press coverage.[89] The most publicized feat of 1978 was the bomb blast on 1 August 1978 that killed the fifteen-year-old daughter of Vice-Admiral Lambruschini. A Montonero communiqué stated that the Vice-Admiral was targeted for being responsible for the secret detention center at the Navy Mechanics School.[90]

In late 1978 the Montonero leadership planned a counteroffensive for 1979 which demonstrated the extreme to which the Montoneros had adopted a military perspective. The idea of armed resistance weighed more than the lives of the combatants. Graciela Daleo, who was held captive at a secret detention center, was told at the time by naval officer Perren, "We know that they're going to return, they're going to return in the middle of the year, and we're going to be waiting for them with a butterfly-net."[91] Around 140 guerrillas were captured, including María Antonia Berger who had survived the 1972 Trelew massacre. Only about sixteen survived. The others were either killed or disappeared.[92]

Juan Carlos Scarpati and his wife Nilda Haydée Orazi carried a very somber message away from Argentina. Scarpati had escaped from an army detention center in 1977, while his abducted wife Nilda Haydée Orazi was allowed to go into exile in mid-1979. Once in Spain, the reunited couple wrote a bitter reflection about the defeat of the Montoneros. They stated that about six thousand comrades had been imprisoned between 1976 and 1978 in the Campo de Mayo and Navy Mechanics School secret detention centers: "only five percent of this figure fell through intelligence or by accident, the other ninety-five percent were the result of direct or indirect collaboration."[93] They attributed the general inability to withstand torture to the low combat morale and a lack of faith in the success of the guerrilla war. "This low morale before the enemy is a common denominator, not just of the Montoneros but of the members of all armed organizations in the country, because they all have one thing in common: *defeat.*"[94] The military rationalization "low morale" was nothing other than a social trauma.

The Montoneros began to go asunder in 1979. Rodolfo Galimberti, Juan Gelman, and 200 to 250 members of the Northern Column broke with the Montonero leadership in February 1979.[95] Another group, whose most prominent members were Miguel Bonasso, Jaime Dri, and Ernesto Jauretche, departed in April 1980.[96] The 1982 Falkland/Malvinas War dealt the deathblow to the Montoneros. The organization split in two when the Montonero National Leadership offered to supply troops to fight the British, even though in reality they were unable to supply even one company of combatants. The opponents argued that the military were trying to make amends for the dirty war with the invasion, and regain lost support among the Argentine people. Patriotism and betrayal stood diametrically opposed to one another and left permanent scars in what remained of the Montoneros.[97] The Peronist Montonero Movement was formally dissolved in December 1983. The supreme Montonero commander Mario Firmenich, who had ordered his combatants to commit suicide with a cyanide capsule when caught, surrendered voluntarily to Brazilian authorities on 13 February 1984 without having fired one shot.[98]

Mimesis and Attrition

The militarization of the ERP and Montoneros began in late 1974 when they tried to transform their loose assemblies of guerrilla units into armies with a commander-in-chief, general staff, and a hierarchical chain of command. Officer ranks and army units were given the same technical names as those of standing armies throughout the world, while the regional divisions corresponded to the zonal structure of the Argentine national army. In addition, troops were given uniforms and military insignia and greeted with military salutes. This military culture manifested itself also in recruitment, graduation, and decoration ceremonies as well as in military tribunals.

These formal structures and regulations reflected of course more their aspirations than their real military strength. The ERP units which had assaulted seven military bases were generally platoons of thirty men, seldom reached company strength of eighty combatants, and only formed a battalion of three hundred combatants at the ERP's last major and most disastrous attack at Monte Chingolo. The Montoneros operated only once on company strength, namely at the attack on the Formosa base. Most often, the guerrillas would operate as squads of a dozen combatants. In practice, this meant that the squads functioned with considerable operational freedom, and could maximize the hit-and-run guerrilla tactics. The incorporation of combat units in a cellular structure further enhanced their independence from the national guerrilla command.

The Argentine armed forces traveled the opposite mimetic road, adopting the organizational forms of the guerrilla forces. Combat squad became pitted against combat squad in Tucumán, laying ambushes and constantly on the move to surprise the ERP guerrillas.[99] The urban counterinsurgency assumed a cellular structure operating parallel to and independent of the standing armed forces. These task groups wore civilian dress, used unmarked cars, and had a great freedom of operation.

Both the guerrilla organizations and the armed forces began using a bellicose discourse which raised the level of violence and expanded the enemy definition beyond that of combatants. No distinctions were made between civilians and combatants, officers and employers, or enemies and opponents. The entire society became a battlefield and everyone a potential target. The counterinsurgency was recognized by the military and the guerrillas as a dirty war in which torture, disappearance, and execution became the preferred practices.

Both parties talked about annihilating the other, even though large-scale torture was the exclusive domain of the Argentine military. They embarked on a war of attrition, determined to destroy the other. The Argentine military and the guerrillas also believed that the confrontation was going to take many years. The guerrillas talked about a long and hard struggle until the popular forces would be victorious, while the military stressed that the Argentine people should not expect quick results because the subversion had many faces.

Of course, this mimesis in no sense implies that the two parties can be equated in terms of strength, objectives, ideology, popular support, position in Argentine society, or number of casualties. The importance of the mimetic process rested in the singular focus on warfare as their principal mode of engagement. The guerrilla organizations and the armed forces were not two demons who had dragged Argentine society into a cesspool of political violence, but Argentina was also not engaged in a civil war with large segments of society fighting on opposite sides. The guerrilla and armed forces carry the greatest responsibility for the escalation of violence, for the thousands of deaths, but they were also part of a society which was struggling in a highly conflictive manner to define its social, political, and cultural parameters. Violent crowd mobilizations, street protests, and labor strikes had been continuing forces of contention, while the repression, incarceration, and torture of political opponents by police and armed forces, as well as the repeated military coups, further enhanced and legitimized the use of violence. The opposing guerrilla and military forces, pitted with anger and rage against one another, were the most violent exponents of this search. Their mimesis established a social contract of annihilation around the pursuit of a moral community by destroying the enemy, and imposing its own cultural order. In the uneven battle, the physical, psychological, and social annihilation was carried to unimaginable extremes in which the entire Argentine society became involved.

Violence, Injury, and Social Trauma

The guerrilla insurgency had long and diverse roots in the traumatizing political violence that had reigned in Argentina since the mid-1950s. The Argentine revolutionary movements were determined to undo those injuries through violence, protect the Argentine people against further traumatization, and construct a new and more just society. The bombing of Plaza de Mayo in June 1955, the overthrow of Perón in September 1955, and the executions following the failed 1956 Peronist rebellion, had inflicted great harm on the large Peronist following, and made violence endemic to Argentine political culture. The Argentine working class, overwhelmingly

Peronist, responded with strikes, protest crowds, urban insurrections, and sabotage against Argentina's economic infrastructure. Consecutive governments responded with repressive violence which demoralized and further traumatized the Peronist movement.

The social traumas from the past became vessels of suffering whose posttraumatic effects increased with every new violent act intending to undo past hurt and preempt future victimization. Every violent act carried an emotional price. Each new acute social trauma was understood in the context of past traumas which, in turn, were given new meaning by later tragedies. The various social traumas reinforced one another, as one was interpreted as a duplication of the other. The trauma of the afflicted group became therefore a layered, oversaturated phenomenon that could never be mourned, accepted, or relegated to the past. The much-heard chant "shed blood will not be negotiated" expressed the endurance of the social traumas incurred through the decades. The common practice of guerrilla organizations to commemorate past acts of violence as well as traumatizing events with more violence is a clear indication of the enduring relation of violence and trauma. The reexperience of the past in the present is as much a characteristic of a social trauma as the insatiable demand to redress past wrongs with vengeance killings.

Since injustice and suffering were believed to be endemic to Argentine society, only violence could end it. The spiral of excessive violence and the ensuing social traumas and posttraumatic sequels caused by periodic mass executions, torture, imprisonment, and military interventions required a revolutionary change which could break the pattern and establish a new society. The old had to be destroyed to construct the new. The revolutionary left believed that the structural and volitional violence of Argentine society would disappear once a new, just society had been created.

Under influence of the 1959 Cuban revolution, several small groups tried to develop a guerrilla insurgency in Argentina during the 1960s but failed for lack of popular backing. The 1969 urban insurrections in Rosario and Córdoba triggered a resurgence of guerrilla violence counting now on the support of the Peronist working class and large sectors of the middle class, while receiving the blessing of an exiled Perón. This insurgency consisted of Peronist and Marxist organizations which recruited their following from a disenfranchised younger generation and took inspiration from the Cuban Revolution and the Peronist Resistance of the 1950s.

The young generation of the 1960s had tried desperately to participate in the reconstruction of their country but had been excluded from the political process by the reigning authoritarian regimes. The pursuit of social justice became a propelling force of their political activism. And what was more appealing than an ideology that pursued social equality for all humankind, abolished divisive property relations, and banned economic exploitation? The Cuban Revolution, the anticolonialist struggles in Vietnam and Algeria, and the personal example of Che Guevara were irresistible sources of inspiration as the effervescence of street fighting in Córdoba and Rosario further raised the hopes for revolution.

Executions, eliminations, and assassinations became means that served two goals: power and punishment. High-ranking military officers and union leaders were executed because they occupied positions of influence and because they needed to be punished for past offenses. These assassinations were often accompanied by explanations describing the wrongdoings of the executed, and calling for more vengeance to neutralize the traumatic injuries. The execution of Peronist civilians after a failed military rebellion in June 1956 and the slaying of sixteen guerrillas at a naval base in August 1972 were experienced as related social traumas of the Peronist movement. Narrative accounts of suffering were passed from one generation to the next, became part of a social memory, and were embraced as social traumas which influenced political action.

In 1975 the Argentine military entered into the same dynamic of vengeance, reparation, and redemption that motivated the guerrillas: vengeance for the officers killed, reparation of Argentine society, and redemption for their salvation of Western, Christian civilization. A mimetic hostility developed between guerrillas and armed forces in which each party began to resemble the other. According to Girard, "The more a tragic conflict is prolonged, the more likely it is to culminate in a violent mimesis; the resemblance between the combatants grows ever stronger until each presents a mirror image of the other."[100] Although I subscribe to Girard's description of the mimetic process, I disagree with his view that this mimesis is symmetrical. Opposed combatants are mirror images only in form and desire, in the violence they use and the determination with which they try to achieve their objectives, but not in their effects. Each tries to outdo the other by inflicting a greater trauma, but one's own trauma can never be neutralized by the severity of the opponent's trauma, in particular because the enemy has been dehumanized and debased.

What made the military and the guerrillas so willing to use violence? Were there no moral inhibitions? Hannah Arendt's profound analysis of totalitarianism provides a suitable perspective. Arendt writes that the exaltation of mankind at the expense of ordinary human beings justified the killing of millions of individuals believed to be dispensable, all for the good of a greater cause. When violence becomes the cradle of utopia, then people become mere obstacles to be crushed by the forces of history. Guilt, innocence, and morality are irrelevant when humankind is surrendered to superhuman historical forces. Violence and terror, argues Arendt, are intended to accelerate these forces of history.[101]

Something similar occurred in Argentina. The guerrillas were willing to embark on an escalating civil war and the military resorted to increased state terror, sacrificing human beings for greater causes. Vengeance killings set a violence-trauma-violence dynamic in motion. The avengers did not believe that their victims would in any way make up for their own losses but sought retribution for having been damaged, tried to restore and strengthen their defenses, and to master the volatile situation. A loss of control was particularly traumatizing because it threatened the group and everything that it cherished with extinction. In Argentina, each party tried to hit where it hurt most, as both the Argentine military and the guerrilla organizations propagandized.

The Argentine military understood intuitively that severe traumatization ended an enemy's willingness to fight. After all, Clausewitz had defined the true aim of warfare as to "render the enemy powerless" and "make him incapable of further resistance" by the "maximum use of force."[102] Of course, the Argentine military did not verbalize their dirty war in terms of traumatization but their tactical actions and strategic objectives were guided by the principle that terror only ends by greater terror. This terror served to paralyze the revolutionary opposition, combatants as well as non-combatants. Counterinsurgency decimated guerrilla organizations and state terror traumatized society to such an extent that only a few were willing to resist with nonviolent protests. The Argentine military were so desirous of victory that they were willing to cross moral boundaries that had kept earlier regimes in check.

Part III
Breaking Hearts and Minds: Torture, Self, and Resocialization

Parade by military junta leaders Videla, Massera, and Agosti, 9 July 1976. Courtesy of *Diario Clarín*.

Chapter 9
The War of Cultures:
Hierarchy Versus Equality, Christianity
Versus Marxism

"To the people of the Argentine Republic: The country is passing through one of the most difficult periods in its history. With the country on the point of national disintegration, the intervention of the armed forces was the only possible alternative in the face of the deterioration provoked by misgovernment, corruption, and complacency."[1] Ten days earlier, on Wednesday, 24 March 1976, the Argentine armed forces had taken power. Videla's opening sentence failed to mention the guerrilla insurgency, for the simple reason that the coup served primarily to construct a new foundation to Argentine society, and only secondarily to wage a more effective counterinsurgency war.

The military had already been granted extensive powers to combat the armed violence in October 1975 and did not need a coup to defeat the guerrillas. Not a military but a perceived cultural threat required an absolute political control unobtainable under a democratic government. The military's sacred mission involved a deep penetration into Argentine society, and even into the selves of its people, to reap a lasting victory. As Lieutenant-General Videla never tired of saying, this was "A fight that we neither sought nor desired, a fight that was forced upon us, but which we accepted because nothing more and nothing less than the national being was at stake."[2]

The military rule between 1976 and 1983 has been described with a confusing array of names, each revealing different causes, conditions, and consequences. The military used terms like dirty war, antirevolutionary war, and the fight against subversion. Human rights groups talked about state terror, repression, and military dictatorship. Guerrilla organizations coined the term dirty war and also spoke of a civil war, war of liberation, and anti-imperialist struggle. Whether the period is described with the term antirevolutionary war, civil war, or state terror is important because each designation implies a different moral and historical judgment turning patriots into oppressors, victims into ideologues, and heroes into subversives.

"War," writes Elaine Scarry, "is . . . a huge structure for the derealization of cultural constructs and, simultaneously, for their eventual reconstitution. The purpose of the war is to designate as an outcome which of the two competing cultural constructs will by both sides be allowed to become real. . . ."[3] The revolution which the Argentine guerrillas tried to achieve, and the social and political institutions which the military were trying to reinstall, were seen as irreconcilable cultural projects. Theirs was not just a contest about power but a contest about the space of culture, about the cultural confines and social conditions within which the Argentine people were supposed to lead their lives.

The military perceived Argentine history as a struggle between primitive and advanced cultural forms. The nineteenth century witnessed the development from barbarism to civilization. The twentieth century was facing a new challenge with the rise of a communist ideology harking back to primitive notions of collectivism and social equality. "The subversive war. . . . is the clash of two civilizations," stated General Galtieri, "ours and the Marxist, to determine which one will be dominant and thus inspire or direct the future organization of the world. More concretely, it is about discovering which scale of values will serve as the foundation of such organization."[4] The Marxist guerrillas held on to a classic model of an antagonistic class struggle and the revolutionary advance from capitalism to socialism. The revolutionary Peronists emphasized the emancipation of the popular masses and hailed Justicialism as their ideology. In the 1970s, all three parties legitimated violence as the price of progress.

Victory could only be achieved at the cost of great sacrifice. The Argentine revolutionaries and military officers were willing to risk their lives, all that for which they stood and all that gave meaning to their existence, to come out on top. If several parties saw each other as a serious threat, defined operational targets, proclaimed an all-out war, and suited action to word with violence, then intentions and expectations were bound to meet in deadly decisions. This armed conflict was not a war in strict legal terms, but the conduct, perception, and stakes gave the confrontation the unmistakable characteristics of war, in my opinion, a cultural war.

I prefer the term cultural war because the objectives were ultimately cultural, and so were the effects on the Argentine people. Furthermore, the term cultural war is ideologically neutral in ways the terms liberation, revolutionary, and antirevolutionary war are not. Finally, the term cultural war allows us to extend its historical time frame beyond the 1976–1983 dictatorship.

The cultural war of the 1970s was regarded by both sides as a just war, pitting good against evil. According to the Marxist PRT-ERP there were only two types of war: "just wars and unjust wars. The bourgeoisie and its armed forces, determined to defend and preserve their privileges founded on exploitation and oppression, are launching all their repressive troops against the people. . . . Against that war, against that violence by the exploiting class, the masses put up their own war, the just war of popular resistance."[5] Argentine military, like General Díaz Bessone, spoke also of a just war: "The entire Christian tradition, of Saint Thomas and others, speaks of a just war. . . . we haven't violated the law of God. . . . For me, this is a just war because we weren't the ones who attacked."[6]

The cultural war legitimized whatever violence was necessary to reap a victory. Thirteen years after the date General Díaz Bessone is still convinced that this cultural war was inevitable. "I maintain that when the values are completely opposed, then war follows. There is no other solution. One cannot live together. . . . Subversion means the change of values, the change of national culture. Culture is not just art and painting. No, no. Culture is everything."[7] Its objective was therefore not only to defeat the guerrilla insurgency but to stamp out a hostile cultural construct. The theater of operations was Argentine society, and this battle of men and minds called for unconventional methods requiring an absolute control over the highest seats of power.

Now, the Argentine military were certainly justified in defending themselves against the guerrilla attacks, but did this give them the freedom to use indiscriminate means? As Michael Walzer has stated: "It is right to resist aggression, but the resistance is subject to moral (and legal) restraint."[8] The reasons of war may be just, but its means unjust, and the other way around. Even those who fight just wars are accountable for their actions, because "justice itself requires that unjust killing be condemned."[9] The perception that the revolutionary insurgency was striking at Argentine culture made the military emphasize that victory had to be attained at all costs and justified extreme measures.

Walzer has reasoned convincingly that the conditions are seldom so adverse and the consequences of defeat so devastating that winning a war becomes all-important. Walzer mentions two criteria to justify unjust means: the imminence of danger and the nature of that danger.[10] The Argentine military failed to measure up to both criteria. There was not an immediate threat because the ERP and Montoneros had been largely defeated by early 1976, nor was there a serious threat because neither the guerrilla organizations nor revolutionary thought had substantial popular support. The moral gravity of the dirty war became thus quadrupled. The rhetorically erected state of urgency was an excuse to justify the elimination of an entire social sector believed to constitute an eventual threat. This amputation was considered a precondition for a fundamental reorganization of Argentine society bringing lasting prosperity and protecting national culture and identity.

The moral constraints of war applied of course also to guerrilla insurgents. The reprisal killings, the kidnapping of officers and businessmen, and the assassination of public officials qualify as significant moral offenses.[11] Yet, they stand in no comparison to the disappearances and assassinations carried out by the Argentine armed forces. The reasons for the guerrilla attacks on military bases might have been unjust, but the means themselves did not violate the conventions of war. Instead, their gravest moral offense consisted of placing noncombatant supporters and sympathizers at risk. The guerrillas often disguised themselves as ordinary citizens and thus undermined the war conventions which they wanted the Argentine military to uphold. Such disguise was of course the quintessence of urban guerrilla warfare, but invited the military to violate the rights of all civilians.[12] So, the guerrillas could not have it both ways; if they disguised themselves as civilians then they could not claim a status as regular combatants. Be this as it may, even as unlawful combatants who did not wear uniforms or openly display their weapons, the Argentine guerrillas deserved some form of due process in courts of law or military tribunals, denied to them by the Argentine junta.

This chapter delineates the ideological foundation of the cultural war. I pay close attention to the military junta's cultural project, called the Process of National Reorganization (Proceso de Reorganización Nacional). Argentine society had to be refashioned in ways similar to the near-mythical heyday of the late nineteenth century when the country was heralded as the promise of the New World.[13] The armed insurgents and a political opposition ranging from radical students and combative union leaders to avant-garde artists stood in the way of the junta's grand design. They were not only regarded as obstacles to Argentina's glorious future, but had been subverting the nation's Christian values and Western cultural heritage. Their annihilation was the rationalization for a repressive regime in which torture and disappearance became commonplace war practices.

Prelude to the 1976 Coup d'Etat

The coup of 24 March 1976 was preceded by the progressive enclosure of the Peronist government. Operation Independence had given the military unlimited powers in Tucumán in February 1975 which were extended in October 1975 to the entire country. General Videla had been designated as the new army commander on 28 August 1975 with the overwhelming approval of most generals. General Roberto Viola became the new army chief of staff.[14] Videla's principal objective was to enhance the cohesion of the army, and then coalesce the armed forces into a corporation insulated from the corrupting influences of civil society. He strengthened his command further by sending generals with Peronist sympathies into retirement, and making the army take charge of the counterinsurgency war.[15]

President María Estela Martínez de Perón was powerless against the encroaching military. She had been deeply affected by the hasty departure of López Rega under pressure from the armed forces and the Rodrigazo protest crowd.[16] On the edge of a nervous breakdown, she took a leave of absence in the Cordoban mountains, and was temporarily replaced on 13 September 1975 by the president of the Senate, the Peronist Italo Argentino Luder. On 6 October 1975 Luder signed the fateful decree 2772 bestowing on the armed forces the power to annihilate the guerrilla insurgency in Argentina. General Videla affirmed on 23 October 1975, "In Argentina, if need be, all persons necessary to achieve the country's security must die."[17] President Isabel Perón reassumed her office on 16 October but her days were numbered.[18]

The October 1975 Montonero attack on the Formosa army base and the persistence of the ERP insurgency in Tucumán, together with nationwide labor unrest, the tensions within the Peronist Organization and the faltering government of Isabel Perón, created a political atmosphere in which the military began to think seriously about a coup. Equally important, a coup could prevent a political rupture within the army threatening Videla's objective for a greater corporate cohesion. Videla and Viola headed a majority faction, known as conditional legalism (legalismo condicionado), which tolerated the democratic government as long as the political crisis did not deteriorate further. The Generals Suárez Mason, Díaz Bessone, Riveros, and Menéndez, four of the five army corps commanders, were the hardliners accusing their commander Videla of passiveness in face of the country's many crises. They favored a military coup. The planning of Operation Aries began in late October 1975 at navy headquarters, and the go-ahead signal for a coup was given by late December 1975.[19]

The military and civilian forces were heating up between January and March 1976 for the upcoming coup. A military task force met daily at navy headquarters, and a team of civilians under the leadership of José Martínez de Hoz, the future Minister of Economy, worked out a comprehensive economic plan. Attempts to persuade President Isabel Perón to resign voluntarily failed. Ricardo Balbín, the respected leader of the Radical party (UCR), and most important landowners and industrialists gave the military their blessing to seize power. Meanwhile, the social chaos in Argentina continued with continuous labor strikes and lockouts orchestrated by the employers' organization headed by Martínez de Hoz.[20]

The immediate reasons for the coup were the government's inability to solve the economic crisis, the rising inflation and growing unemployment, the deterioration of its political legitimacy, the fragmentation of the Peronist Organization, and the unwillingness of the opposition to come to the rescue. In addition, there were tensions within the labor movement, growing waves of strikes, and a lack of faith among the business sector in the economic plans of the Peronist government. Finally, the military believed that the Peronist government was undoing the counterinsurgency successes. Not only would the deteriorating economy incite more popular unrest and be a fertile soil for revolutionary ideas, but several governors and judges were releasing suspected guerrillas detained by the army.[21] There was even a fear that the unstable government of Isabel Perón might withdraw the blank cheque given to the armed forces to combat the insurgency.

General Videla escaped death on March 15 when the Montoneros detonated a car near army headquarters in Buenos Aires. One civilian truck driver was killed by the debris, and twenty-three persons were wounded.[22] On the evening of 23 March 1976, President Martínez de Perón ordered a helicopter to take her from the Casa Rosada to her residence in Olivos, but the pilot flew to the Aeroparque city airport instead, claiming mechanical failure. Isabel Perón was detained on 24 March at 12:45 A.M., and was moved to a villa in the Andean province of Neuquén.[23] At 3:32 A.M., on 24 March 1976, the military junta communicated to the Argentine people that "the country is under the operational control of the Joint Chiefs of Staff of the Armed Forces."[24]

Many Argentines sighed with relief, and welcomed a military government restoring law and order. The PRT-ERP also rejoiced because it interpreted the coup as a sign of desperation. The increased military repression would make the popular masses join the revolutionary forces and lead to an insurrection. The Montoneros thought that the coup meant that the guerrilla insurgency had forced the armed forces to initiate a dialogue. They could conduct this dialogue from a position of power, so they argued, as Peronists had done successfully in the past, in 1958 with Frondizi, in 1969 with Onganía, and in 1972 with Lanusse. However, a point of no return had been reached for the military: "We only speak with bullets because we think that a synthesis has been reached: no more words, only defeat and annihilation."[25] There was no room for negotiation and dialogue, only extermination.

The Process of National Reorganization

The thirty-three communiqués to the Argentine people on 24 March established the public parameters of military rule. People were forbidden to congregate in public places; all air, sea, and river transport was suspended; factories came under military control; a bank holiday was declared; schools and universities were closed; the media were censured; cinemas and theaters were not allowed to open doors; and a midnight curfew was enforced. The Argentine people were ordered to hand in all weapons within forty-eight hours, and acts of violence against the government forces were punishable by death, while Permanent Special War Councils (Consejos de Guerra Especiales Estables) were instituted to try suspects.[26]

At 10:40 A.M., Lieutenant-General Jorge Rafael Videla, Admiral Emilio

Eduardo Massera, and Brigadier-General Orlando Ramón Agosti swore before a public notary to take charge of the government as members of the military junta, obey the Argentine Constitution, and realize the objectives of the Process of National Reorganization (Proceso de Reorganización Nacional). Unlike previous military dictatorships which had assigned one commander at the helm, the three commanders would equally share all powers and responsibilities. Army commander Videla would also act as president of Argentina. The triumvirate would rule for three years and make decisions by majority vote.[27] The mandates of María Estela Martínez de Perón and the provincial governors were canceled, Congress, provincial legislatures, and Supreme Court dissolved, and political parties, labor unions, and employers' organizations suspended.[28] The military junta was the same day recognized by Spain, Malta, Ecuador, Perú, Brazil, and Chile.

The junta's proclamation declared that the armed forces felt obliged to lead the Argentine state because the constitutional government had exhausted all means to resolve the country's many crises. There was a tremendous power vacuum which might have ended in disintegration and anarchy. There was no popular support for the government, no coherent political strategy to deal with the subversion, a total lack of ethical and moral conduct, an irresponsible management of the economy, and generalized corruption.[29] The armed forces were determined to eradicate the vices troubling Argentina, "Through order, work, the full observance of ethical and moral principles, justice, the complete realization of man, and through the respect of his rights and dignity. . . ."[30] They failed to inform the Argentine people about the cost of this cultural construct.

The Argentine military felt that they had the right and the obligation to reorganize the country as they saw fit because they had stood at its birth. Not the people, but the military had liberated Argentina from Spain during the Independence Wars. The army had also conquered the Patagonian pampas during the 1870s in its domestic war against the indigenous population and thus laid the foundation for its agricultural export economy. The prosperity of the final decades of the nineteenth century rested on the 1852–1862 national organization during which the Republic was formed, a national constitution written, Congress instated, formal education organized, and the domestic market opened to foreign investments and products.[31] The Argentine presidents most responsible for the economic success, Mitre, Sarmiento, and Roca, had all three made their career in the Argentine army, and the 1976 commanders must have seen themselves mirrored in their illustrious predecessors.[32] The 1976 military junta felt itself destined to repeat the economic miracle of the nineteenth century, reestablish domestic peace, and turn Argentina once more into a nation under God.

The Process, as the political program and historical period between 1976 and 1983 became popularly known, had as one of its principal aims the restoration of "the essential values that serve as the foundation to the comprehensive rule of the State. . . ."[33] This objective proved so central, and is at the same time so vague, that it requires some elaboration. According to General Díaz Bessone—a noted hardliner, commander of the Second Army Corps between 1975 and 1976, Minister of Planning between 1976 and 1977, and considered one of the ideologues of the Process—the national values of Argentine society are formulated in the Preamble of the National Constitution, their rock bottom foundation. The Preamble states that the Constitution's objectives are the maintenance of justice and domestic peace, the provision of a national defense, the advancement of general well-being, and the protection of freedom. "Good, very well," explained the general, "I say that definitely among these values there are transcending values, that is to say, values that are undeniable. And basically I find liberty, justice, and peace among them." But how should we interpret these three supervalues? "The interpretation of liberty, justice, and peace exists in the light of respect for the natural law, all of which God is illuminating."[34]

The concept of natural law derives from the thirteenth-century Saint Thomas Aquinas, who argued that all actions should be based on the principle, "Good should be done and sought after; evil is to be avoided."[35] This principle entails a particular moral conduct and assigns certain fundamental rights to people through their place in the natural order created by God as a way to continue his absolute governance over the universe.[36] The French Neo-Thomists Jacques Maritain and Etienne Gilson, and the Argentine Bruno Genta, were mentioned by several Argentine army officers as important sources of inspiration. Bruno Genta, the conservative Catholic and ideologue of the nationalist faction of the Argentine military, expressed Aquinas's ideas as follows: "The inferior exists at the service of the superior; the inert mineral to what has life; the life of plants to that of animals; all this is subject to the rationality of man, and man is subject to God who is the beginning and end of all that exists. . . . All human works, theoretical and practical, must express this unity, order, hierarchy, service of the inferior to what is superior . . . thus manifesting the universe created by the Creator."[37]

The Argentine military interpreted the National Constitution as the worldly translation of this divine order into law.[38] Given the constitutional right to defend those laws, the military believed that they could not remain aloof from the political deterioration threatening this order and the revolutionary attempts to change the foundation of Argentine society.[39] As one navy officer told the Montonero Jaime Dri: "You want to corrode like acid the natural order, the principle on which Western, Christian civilization rests."[40]

The notion of a divine hierarchy touches upon three fundamental differences between revolutionaries and military about the future of Argentine society, and explains why their violent confrontation was a war of cultures. Whereas the military believed in the naturalness of the social hierarchy, the revolutionaries believed in the naturalness of equality. Second, the military perceived society as an organic whole and therefore talked frequently in medical terms about extirpating the subversive cancer from society, while the revolutionaries saw society as a whole characterized by the exploitation of one social class by another. Finally, the military believed in an eternal order, a permanent essence, while the revolutionaries believed in the historical development of society through the dialectics of class antagonism. The conflict between revolutionaries and military derived from their entirely different image of an ideal society, respectively expressing the fundamental equality of human beings or manifesting the divine order.

The Thomist world view translated into a political program emphasizing the importance of the nuclear family, paternal authority, private property, Catholic school education, and the right and duty of the military to protect the Fatherland when its Christian culture was under siege. The term Fatherland (*Patria*) referred to a shared material and spiritual legacy, including the Spanish language, Christian culture, and Roman Catholicism. The revolutionaries, so argued the military, wanted to do away with private property, abolish the nuclear family, forbid religion, and replace the Argentine armed forces with a revolutionary militia. General Riveros painted Argentina's bleak future if the guerrillas would win the war: "Everything in disorder, without God, without family, without freedom, without hope, with little bread, without a concept of the beginning and end of Creation, and with Satan at its head."[41] The armed forces believed that they had the constitutional right to defend Argentina's cultural heritage, and rekindle lost values.[42]

Even though most commanding officers embraced free-market liberalism as their economic ideology, they certainly did absorb many notions about religion, society, and politics from Argentine Catholic nationalist thinkers like Julio Meinvielle, Leonardo Castellani, Jordán Bruno Genta, and Carlos Sacheri.[43] Evidence of their influence was the appointment of many Catholic nationalists to key posts in education, justice, and the Central Bank.[44]

Jordán Bruno Genta, in particular, deserves mention since he taught a course in counterrevolutionary warfare in 1962 to air force officers in Córdoba and to army officers at the Campo de Mayo base. The course was cut short because of a factional struggle within the army leading the military away from politics and back to professionalism.[45] However, Genta found a new audience. Army officers, such as Aldo Rico and Santiago Alonso, were members of a substantial group of cadets taking private classes in political philosophy at the home of Genta during the late 1960s and the early 1970s.[46] Genta created for them a conceptual order in turbulent times, carving up the world into good and evil, and assigning the young officers to the holy mission of achieving a total victory over communism.[47] He compared the officers to Christ because they sacrificed their innocent blood for the good of the nation.[48]

Bruno Genta found a responsive ear among Argentine officers because of their Catholic upbringing, their formation as soldiers, and the political circumstances of the decade. The Cold War between East and West, fears about the Cuban Revolution, their experience with the Argentine guerrilla insurgency, strong religious convictions, and deeply inculcated notions of order, hierarchy, discipline, and obedience made them receptive to a vulgar Thomist and extreme Manichean discourse.[49] The Manichean religious-ideological framework helped the military wage a cultural war and demonize fellow Argentines into enemies.[50]

The Argentine military believed that the Third World War, a final confrontation between Christianity and communism, had begun with Argentina as its first battleground. General Galtieri explained on 3 November 1981: "The First World War was a confrontation between armies, the Second was between nations, and the Third is between ideologies."[51] World War III reminded the Argentine military of the nineteenth-century fight of the budding Argentine nation against the indians and gauchos. This Manichean view was expressed first by Sarmiento in his influential book *Civilization and Barbarism*, and was now echoed by Vice-Admiral Lambruschini, a future junta member. "In a moment of our history one confrontation, not political but existential, was defined as the antinomy between civilization and barbarism, and it is appropriate to ask: Are we not witnessing today a resurgence of that confrontation? Isn't civilization to protect liberty, democracy, the pluralism of ideas, and the right to disagree? Isn't civilization to wish for a creative, respected, and culturally modern country? And, on the contrary, isn't barbarism to hate life, and to adopt murder as a branch of political science? Isn't barbarism to threaten, corrupt, manipulate consciences, and to animalize human beings? Aren't there still groups of fanatics of destruction left who only know the language of bullets and bombs?"[52]

What had begun officially in October 1975 as a counterinsurgency campaign had turned within less than one year into a cultural war against barbarism and subversion to protect Christian values and a Western way of life. This cultural Manicheism made war for the Argentine military, steeped in vulgarized Thomist theology and rabid nationalist thought, the only viable course of action. The military saw themselves as the only saviors of the Argentine nation left in a culturally corrupt society.

Cultural War and Counterrevolutionary Warfare

Argentine counterinsurgency warfare was initially influenced by French and later by American military thought. The American and French doctrines were in turn shaped by their experiences in Indo-China. The French were faced with Ho Chi Minh's liberation army after the end of World War II, and suffered a devastating blow at Dien Bien Phu in 1954. Colonel Lacheroy and General Chassin were the first French officers to analyze the defeat in Indo-China. They talked about a new kind of war, a revolutionary war that demanded a new military doctrine. This revolutionary war was a total war because it "throws all children, all women, all old people . . . and all forces of hatred into the war. . . . it is a war that takes souls as well as bodies and submits them to obedience and to the war effort."[53]

The understanding of revolutionary warfare was also affected by the colonial war in Algeria. Unlike the North Vietnamese guerrilla forces which quickly formed a conventional army, the Algerian liberation movement (FLN) fought in the narrow streets and alleyways of the Casbah in Algiers, mixing easily with the local population. General Massu was called in to reestablish public order. He appointed Indo-China veteran Colonel Roger Trinquier as head of intelligence.[54] The French were determined not to make the mistakes of Vietnam. Massu and Trinquier unleashed a counterinsurgency force which did not eschew the use of torture to extract information from detained Algerians.

Trinquier arrived in Algiers in 1957. He divided the city into sectors, subsectors, blocks, and buildings. Block wardens were appointed to report any suspicious activity.[55] Torture gave General Massu's paratroopers victory in the 1957 Battle of Algiers after Algerian separatists had begun placing bombs in bars frequented by the French.[56] Yet, Massu lost the war. Torture dismantled the network of fourteen hundred operators in the bombing campaign, but the brutal repression motivated many more to join the liberation front. Around three thousand Algerians disappeared after dying under torture. Their bodies were interred in mass graves or dumped at sea by helicopter.[57]

Colonel Carlos Jorge Rosas introduced the French counterinsurgency tactics into Argentina in 1957 as subdirector of the Superior War College. He had just graduated from the French War Academy.[58] The two French Lieutenant-Colonels Patricio de Naurois and François Pierre Badie, who had links to the right-wing OAS hit squads in Algeria, gave advice.[59] In 1960 their ideas helped to update the 1955 CONINTES Plan for the repression of civil unrest. Argentina was divided into zones and subzones, and commanders were given considerable freedom of action, following Colonel Trinquier's Algerian strategy.[60]

The military involvement in Vietnam made the Americans develop their own type of counterrevolutionary warfare. The Cuban revolution had spawned the creation of the Alliance for Progress program intended to improve economic conditions in Latin America to reduce civil tensions. Hundreds of millions of dollars were given in economic aid, but the military assistance proved more influential. The first Inter-American Counterrevolutionary War Course was held in October 1961 at the Superior War College in Argentina, while other courses in domestic repression were given at the International Police Academy in Washington, D.C.[61] In 1962, the U.S. army organized counterinsurgency courses at the army special forces of the Southern Command in Panama, and at Fort Bragg in North Carolina. Argentine officers, among them Generals Videla and Viola, brought the American counterinsurgency doctrine to Argentina.[62] CIA agent Felix Rodríguez—who had ordered Che Guevara's execution upon his capture in Bolivia—was assigned to Argentina's First Army Corps as an advisor on counterinsurgency warfare.[63]

The French and American counterinsurgency doctrines consisted of separating the civilian population from the guerrillas. The French taught the Argentines that an urban insurgency was fought best through intelligence gathering, not through territorial control. Nevertheless, according to General Ramón Camps, the French and American doctrines had to be altered because of their defeatist undertone.[64] Having lost Algeria and Vietnam, those doctrines were based on unsuccessful military operations deployed on foreign soil, among foreign peoples with different national cultures. Instead, the Argentine military were fighting on familiar terrain and, confident about the support of most Argentines, thus pursued an aggressive, offensive, and not a defensive counterinsurgency war.[65] Already in 1967, an Argentine officer stated that "Although it is true that the objective of the subversion is the mind of man, it is no less true that it uses weapons in addition to ideas for its conquest. As a consequence, there are two areas in which the subversion develops itself: the mental battle and the armed battle."[66] Argentine military analysts criticized the French for privileging the military aspects of counterinsurgency while relegating the social, political, and mental dimensions to a secondary plane.[67]

The Argentine military began to develop their own military doctrine. Lieutenant-Colonel Leoni Houssay played an important role as professor in counterinsurgency warfare at the Superior War College between 1965 and 1970.[68] Leoni Houssay delineated three phases of revolutionary warfare. The first phase was characterized by agitation and propaganda aimed at the ideological conquest of the people. The second phase tried to undermine the government by guerrilla foci, liberated zones, and armed violence, while the third phase consisted of the formation of regular rebel forces entering into direct combat with the legal forces.[69] The revolutionary war was in his view: (1) a global war with international support structures; (2) a multiform war in which revolutionaries have no moral or material constraints in attaining a victory; (3) a permanent war; and (4) a total war which develops in all realms of life.[70] These four characteristics delineated clearly the areas of engagement for the Argentine military in their cultural war of the 1970s.

The geopolitical dimension was foremost in the minds of the Argentine military. The insurgency training of Argentines in Cuba during the 1960s was taken as a telling sign of the international threat. The Argentine military neglected to say in public that the material assistance from Cuba, Vietnam, China, and the Soviet Union was negligible, and that the political violence in Argentina was largely due to domestic circumstances. Nevertheless, when the military victory over the guerrillas was declared in 1978, Brigadier-General Agosti emphasized that "What we have won was a nonconventional war and not a simple war game. We have won it inside national territory, but the aggressor is just one tentacle of a monster whose head and whose body are beyond the reach of our swords."[71]

The revolutionary war was not a confrontation of armed combatants but a multiform war, as Lieutenant-General Videla explained in 1976: "The fight against subversion is not only a military problem: it is a worldwide phenomenon which has a political, economic, social, cultural, psychological and also a military dimension."[72] As a consequence, the counterrevolutionary war needed to be fought on many planes, as Vice-Admiral Lambruschini emphasized: "The fight which the Argentines are waging against those enemies develops itself in three large theaters: We can call the first one operational, the second ideological and the third emotional."[73]

The revolutionary war involved Argentina in a permanent war because it existed "in a semi-dark zone that envelops all of humanity with the anxiety of hate, incomprehension and disaster."[74] There would never be definite victories or final defeats. The war did not stop when the enemies had been killed, but had to continue into all realms of society. Brigadier Graffigna, a member of the second military junta, considered the Argentine counterinsurgency war "the most remarkable and successful anti-guerrilla campaign of modern times in the entire world. . . ." but he nevertheless doubted if the cultural war would ever end. "The war continues. The enemy will change tactics and terrain, once and again. It will appear that they are withdrawing, away from combat, but they will reappear in the remotest places. They will try to infiltrate in class rooms and universities, in all sorts of organizations, and in all areas of national life which they will use again as a base for their extermination and subjugation campaign."[75]

Finally, the revolutionary war was a total war that could only be won when the civilian population could be mobilized on behalf of the armed forces. "This is the hour to risk oneself for Argentina's destiny," declared General Santiago in March 1977. "This fight is worldwide and total, touching all areas of the national being. No one can be left out; the population must join the ranks of the legal forces. . . ."[76] Three years later, General Menéndez reiterated: "I say again that this war, like all wars, is total. One loses the war which one doesn't wage in a total way."[77]

Clearly, the Argentine military believed itself to be on a divine mission to preserve the natural order and Christian civilization against the neverending assault of Godless ideologies. This subversion was as total as the cultural war the military were waging. War became a process involving all Argentines, a continued fight without end, without clear objectives, targets, and time limits.

Mobilizing Argentina

The military junta emphasized time and again that this antirevolutionary war was not between armed forces and guerrillas, but between the Argentine people and the subversives, be they combatants or not. The military painted an apocalyptic picture of the cultural war. Who could remain outside this struggle when the future of Argentine society and culture was at stake? "It is suicidal pretending to stay at the side. This is the hour of truth and to risk one's life for Argentina's destiny."[78] The antirevolutionary war was a total war in which the entire population needed to be mobilized to ensure victory. The junta's proclamation on 24 March 1976 stated literally: "There is a combat post for every citizen at this new stage. The task is arduous and urgent."[79] General Acdel Vilas reiterated in 1976: "This is a dirty war, a war of attrition, dark and sly, which one wins with decisiveness and calculation, and principally with the help of the people supporting the cause being defended."[80]

The military and the guerrillas regarded an enemy-foe division of Argentine society as the inevitable outcome of their struggle. Both tried to rally the Argentine people behind their cause. There was no legitimate middle ground. "The worsening of the repression and the beginning of a generalized civil war will polarize the camps and eliminate intermediary positions," the Workers Revolutionary Party (PRT) stated.[81] Armed violence was intended to accelerate this polarization. Nobody could remain neutral in this confrontation. Indifference spelled complicity. General Nicolaides said that "Every one must choose his side, this one or the one opposite, there are no positions in between. The indifferent cannot exist in our country. . . ."[82] General Ibérico Saint-Jean, the governor of Buenos Aires province, went so far as to declare in May 1976 the ominous threat: "First we will kill all the subversives; then we will kill their collaborators; then . . . their sympathizers, then . . . those who remain indifferent; and finally we will kill the timid."[83]

The rhetorical inclusion of the frightened, the timid, and the indifferent as enemies reveals the apprehension about an opposition proclaimed as fundamental. These people undermined the moral hierarchy of good versus evil so insistently emphasized by military and revolutionaries alike. It also demonstrated the importance of a discursive reinforcement of enmity in Argentine society, because the military realized that most people were not particularly forthcoming with information. Many people had already in 1974 turned their backs to the political violence, while the majority was plainly afraid and simply wanted to survive the turbulent years unscathed.[84]

Such aloofness was understandable because the people were not incited to participate in a war against a foreign enemy but against their fellow citizens, the very sons and daughters of Argentina. Yet, in the eyes of the military, the subversives had lost their membership in Argentine society. Videla stated categorically that "I want to point out that the Argentine citizenry is not the victim of repression. The repression is against a minority which we do not consider Argentine. . . ."[85] The enemy was a person without a fatherland (*apátrida*) because he or she denied the existence of a national cultural heritage, and made the world his or her battlefield.[86]

The absolute otherness of the guerrillas was described by General Bignone after General Cardozo, chief of the federal police, had been assassinated on 18 June 1976 by a bomb under his bed: "those who killed you do not have God, do not have a Fatherland, do not have friends, act by impulse, for hatred, for revenge and for matter."[87] By demonizing the guerrillas, the Argentine commanders elevated the counterinsurgency war to a spiritual plane and converted their troops into God's army on earth.

Subversion and the Argentine Self

Enemies come into existence when the fear about a perceived threat is channeled into violent action against a specific target. The Argentine military regarded the threat as geopolitical but the enemy as domestic. Subversion was a key word in the military discourse about the cultural war. Lieutenant-General Videla was unequivocal: "We understand by subversion the attempt to alter our essential values inspired by our historical tradition and Christian conception of the world and of man. This man who inherited from God his freedom and dignity as a person as his most precious good."[88]

But who was trying to alter Argentina's essential values and how could he or she be identified? A speech in November 1978 by Brigadier-General Agosti revealed that such identification was not as simple as it might appear.

When the crisis of 1976 produced itself, the Argentine situation revealed the existence of an identity problem. We no longer knew who we were, where we had come from, where we were, at what we aspired, in what we believed, that is to say we did not know our own self. . . . Neither did we identify the enemy. That is to say, we had alienated ourselves for lack of an identity, and for lack of a vocation of greatness. We had forgotten that we came from a Western culture, the cradle of Christianity; and that we had been a Nation of free human beings. . . . Now we identify our enemies, we know how they act and we know their objectives. We recognize that they are fundamentally different from us, some in their behavior, others conceptually and ideologically. At those occasions in which we have doubts about our identity, we can find it by analyzing our enemy's identity.[89]

The enemy had advanced to the perimeters of the self. In doubt about their own political and cultural identity, the military sought the contours of their self in its negation. One was what the other was not. The enemy was not just the one who attacked society, but the negation of the self.

Admiral Massera took one step further and included the Kingdom of God: "What is certain, what is absolutely certain is that here and all over the world, at these moments, there is a fight between those who are on the side of death and those who are on the side of life. . . . Because of this we, who are on the side of life, are going to win. . . . We are not going to fight until death. We are going to fight till victory, whether this is beyond or before death."[90] According to the military triumvirate, the cultural war had successively entered the cultural domain (Videla), the self (Agosti), and now even the hereafter (Massera). The war's multiform nature turned everybody into a suspect, and pulled the conflict into a shadowy struggle about national culture and identity.

The military's enemy definition broadened as the years progressed. In 1975, the guerrilla combatants were still the principal target, but in 1976 they began to include ideologues and sympathizers. General Vilas declared in August 1976: "The fight against subversion in subzone 51 [Bahia Blanca] has been carried on until now against the visible head, the subversive delinquent, but not against the ideologue who generates, forms, and molds this new class of delinquents."[91] The military were aware that this sweeping enemy definition implied a considerable adjustment of public opinion which still viewed war as the confrontation of armed combatants. Beginning in 1977, ideologues were said to be even more dangerous than combatants. In July 1978, Brigadier-General Agosti considered the enemy as defeated but not annihilated. They had moved their operations to the ideological plane.[92] General Chasseing emphasized that "I am much more worried about an ideologue than a combatant; the combatant is dangerous because he destroys, because his bomb may end many lives. But the ideologue is the one who poisons, who robs children, who destroys the family, who may create chaos."[93]

But who were those ideologues and sympathizers? Did they include the political strategists of the Workers Revolutionary Party or the editors of clandestine newsprints? Jaime Swart, a Minister of the provincial government of Buenos Aires, denounced as ideologues "politicians, priests, journalists, professors on all levels of education. . . ."[94] Everyone who was involved in any sort of political activism, everyone who called publicly for social justice could be branded as an ideologue. Sympathizers were all those feeling an affinity with the utopian ideals of the revolutionary left.[95] Many disappeared who were labeled as ideologues and sympathizers, had never brandished a weapon or participated in an armed assault but were considered responsible for spreading subversive ideas or were believed to be potential recruits of the guerrilla organizations. In fact, the ideologue was considered the larger threat and therefore a legitimate target, so the military reasoned, because the violent insurgency was the brainchild of the ideologues and the combatants their pawns. After all, the revolutionary war was above all a cultural war, and the first and final skirmishes were conducted with ideas. The human spirit was the preferred battlefield of the Third World War, said Admiral Massera.[96] General Villegas held the same opinion: " 'The 'spirit of man' is the terrain of action imposed by the Marxist enemy."[97]

Any participation in groups that mobilized persons for particular social or political causes was subversive. Young women teaching shantydwellers to read and write were accused of organizing the poor, and thus stirring up political trouble. The priest Yorrio was told upon his abduction: "You are not violent. You are not a guerrilla, but you have gone to live with the poor and, living with the poor, you unite them and uniting the poor is subversion."[98] In another bizarre case, a handicapped man was tortured to reveal the names of his co-workers in an organization for the disabled. This organization was accused of being a front for international Zionism.[99]

Since the cultural war was waged on the battlefield of the mind, the Argentine military believed that psychologists and psychiatrists were particularly suspicious, not just because some of them were also guerrillas. Timerman hypothesizes that the intelligence services had discovered during interrogation that guerrillas were receiving counseling. So, they surmised that such treatment served to make them cope better with the pressures of guerrilla warfare and thus improved their battle readiness. As a result, numerous psychotherapists and psychiatrists disappeared.[100]

Artists could also qualify as subversives because they created new ways of looking at the world, influenced people's feelings, and thus became the heralds of political ideas seeking to change society. Vice-Admiral Lambruschini enumerated the vast cultural terrain in which the revolutionaries were operating: "the press, protest songs, cartoons, cinema, folklore, literature, academic courses, and religion. . . ."[101] Art works were considered an interpretation of God's creation, namely the cosmos and human beings. Art could thus be religious or antireligious. Religiously inspired art expressed the natural order and celebrated the glory of God, while subversive art undermined and ridiculed God's creation.[102] This is not to suggest that artists were specific military targets—even though artists have disappeared for their political sympathies—but to demonstrate that the obsession with subversion was not purely military but cultural.

When subversion is detected in every nook and cranny of Argentine society, and enemies are defined in such a broad manner, then one understands immediately that the cultural war against subversion was without end for the Argentine military. One army intelligence officer said that "for us, a subversive ranges from the greengrocer charging ten cents too much for a carrot to the one who brandishes weapons. . . ."[103] The military notion of cultural war as permanent became a justification for annihilation because the subversive enemy would always continue to fight, if not with weapons than with ideas, alternative lifestyles, and artistic creations.

The Argentine military had convinced themselves by 1976 that the imprisonment of subversives, whether guerrilla combatants or ideologues, would not end the ills of Argentine society. In the words of General Díaz Bessone, the guerrilla organizations were "strange bodies" which had to be extirpated "however hard the surgery may be."[104] The recent past had shown that convicted guerrillas would be released prematurely if the national government changed, as had happened in May 1973 and again in November 1975. Meanwhile, the elusive subversion would continue in its devious Gramscian ways. Radical measures were needed, argued General Galtieri. "We all wish to be cured with medicines, but if the Nation's authorities so desire, the Armed Forces will operate, and in that case, let nobody have any doubt that all evil will be extirpated; and to extirpate all evil, all cells will have to be extirpated, even those about which we are in doubt."[105] In other words, the scalpel had to cut through healthy social tissue to be certain. The sacrifice of innocent victims was deemed necessary for the greater good of the Argentine nation.

War, Mind, and Self

The Argentine military visualized political violence as an infection and portrayed the revolutionaries as a cancer that metastasized in society. If broad layers of society accepted the subversive ideology then a revolution became unavoidable, and the Western, Christian culture of the Argentine nation would be torn asunder. The military agreed that surgery on the diseased social body should accomplish the physical, psychological, and social destruction of Argentina's revolutionary forces. Many political opponents, whether guerrilla combatants, radical student union members, or combative labor union representatives, were assassinated while numerous others were mentally, emotionally, and socially crippled through lengthy imprisonment and captivity.

The Argentine military arrived at these war practices after rejecting French and American counterinsurgency doctrines for their too singular emphasis on military strategy at the neglect of the social, political, psychological, and cultural aspects of guerrilla warfare. General Vilas, the commander of Operation Independence, wrote in the aftermath of military rule: "When in Tucumán we began to investigate the causes and effects of subversion, we arrived at two inescapable conclusions: (1) Culture was really the motivating force, among other causes. The war that we were confronting was eminently a cultural war. (2) There was a perfect continuity between Marxist ideology and subversive practice, whether in its armed military aspect, or in the religious, institutional, educational or economic domains. Subversion had therefore to be dealt a mortal blow in its deepest essence, in its structure or, that is to say, in its ideological foundation."[106] General Osiris Villegas, one of Argentina's most influential counterinsurgency experts, had concluded already in July 1969 that a counterrevolutionary war could only be won on the terrain of the mind through the conquest of people's psyches.[107]

These ideas about waging war in the enemy's mind must be taken literally because according to General Vilas: "If the military would have allowed the proliferation of disintegrative elements—psychoanalysts, psychiatrists, Freudians, etc.—who stirred up the consciences and put doubt on our national and family roots, then we would have been defeated."[108] The revolutionary forces could not be defeated by simply killing all subversives. The military had to break the enemy's willingness to fight by entering their minds, getting inside their ideological convictions, political beliefs, emotions, and unconscious.

As a consequence, the cultural war was waged on various fronts and against a wide range of enemies. Part I of this book explained the repression of oppositional crowds feared for their unpredictability, collective excess, revolutionary potential, and subversion of a divine social hierarchy. Part II demonstrated how the Argentine armed forces tried to prevent the emergence of a revolutionary movement through political disenfranchisement, widespread repression, and military coups. They escalated their use of armed force when Marxist and Peronist guerrillas tried to transform Argentine society with violent means. The Argentine military decided to outterrorize and outtraumatize the revolutionary forces. Part III shows how the theater of military operations expanded from the guerrilla organizations into Argentina's political opposition, and into the minds and selves of their enemies. The demobilization of popular crowds and the military assault on the guerrilla organizations and the radicalized political opposition turned out to be just the first and second stage of a comprehensive cultural war. The mind and the self were the next battlefield on which the Argentine military tried to gain their victory.

Chapter 10
The Wheelworks of Repression:
Assault, Abduction, and Annihilation

"I would leave in the morning, and wouldn't know whether I'd return alive in the evening," I was told by General Rivas as he showed me the scar on his hand inflicted by the teeth of a female Montonero combatant. General Rivas was the commander of the Campo de Mayo army base, and had invited me to visit the Major Juan Carlos Leonetti Museum of the Fight Against Subversion, founded there in October 1978.[1] The commander spoke with admiration of Leonetti who had died in a fire fight with Mario Roberto Santucho in July 1976. Naming a museum after Leonetti demonstrated that the army regarded Santucho's death as a turning point in the counterinsurgency war. In the entrance, there hung a photograph of the posthumously promoted Major Leonetti and his diploma from the Military Academy. Further down hung Santucho's picture with a copy of his accountancy diploma. A show case displayed Leonetti's brown boots, a pair of jeans, and his bullet-hole-ridden brown sweater.

Leonetti had died without knowing that he had shot Santucho because the ERP commander was disguised to leave that day for Cuba. A gravely wounded Santucho was taken to Campo de Mayo, and was welcomed by the head of the interrogators: "You lost here, I'm not going to be satisfied with your telling me one hundred percent of what you know, I want one hundred and ten percent of what you have to say."[2] Santucho was taken to surgery but died within minutes, just after intelligence had discovered his true identity. Santucho's body was preserved for two years and shown to the military visitors of the museum.[3]

The museum had walls covered with captured weapons and a large library with books by authors like Lenin, Marx, Mao, Giap, Marighela, Debray, Che Guevara, and also Erich Fromm and Herbert Marcuse. The collection contained a device to make plastic explosives and a van used by Montoneros to interfere in radio and television programs with political messages. Even a people's prison, in which guerrillas held abducted businessmen and officers, had been reconstructed. The prison was hidden below a writing desk. The attending officer invited me to experience the people's justice. I descended the ladder a few steps but politely declined the invitation to crawl into the dark narrow space carved out into the building's foundation, and only remained there a few minutes with the hatch closed. As further proof of the kidnapping practices, the original blood-stained mattress and the metal case that had contained Major Larrabure's dead body were also displayed in the museum.

Argentina's guerrilla movement had become history by 1978. The museum was a memorial to the counterinsurgency war, even though the cultural war against the ideological subversion continued. The military victory had been accomplished through a mimesis that began in early 1975, was consolidated structurally in October 1975, and was institutionalized at the March 1976 coup. A nationwide web of special task forces arose determined to dismantle the guerrilla organizations and the radicalized political opposition. Major Masi had stated in 1967 that, "The best thing to combat a guerrilla is another guerrilla."[4] Brigadier Norberto Sciutto still echoes these words, explaining that mimesis was the crux of their success. "One had to combat the enemy with the same procedures. I am convinced of this. And it was the only way to defeat them, and I would say that Argentina is the only country that defeated the guerrillas because the guerrillas in Spain, the guerrillas in Perú, the guerrillas in El Salvador were not defeated. They were defeated here because . . . the Armed Forces adapted themselves to the enemy's impositions and they fought them with the same weapons."[5]

The task forces were given an independence of action that had never been accorded to any conventional army unit, not even the counterinsurgency squads deployed in Tucumán. "The commandos will have the greatest freedom of action to intervene in all those situations in which there may exist subversive activities," stated the army's tactical plan.[6] The task forces operated as plainclothesmen and moved in unmarked passenger cars, often under the cover of darkness. This operational flexibility was required to go after urban guerrillas disguised as civilians. Yet the number of armed confrontations with guerrilla units was small. Most people targeted as enemies were not combatants but either former members of revolutionary Marxist and Peronist front organizations or politically active workers, students, and union members. It was mostly through abduction, rather than arrest, that detainees were apprehended. Most captives were not treated as criminal suspects or as prisoners of war, and were neither formally charged nor officially acknowledged as in the custody of the government forces. They simply vanished into the hundreds of secret detention centers.

This chapter analyzes the secret battle plans of the Argentine military aimed at annihilating their enemies and delineates the visible and hidden structures of repression taking effect after the coup. I describe the military operations against the guerrilla organizations and the political opposition. Finally, I give a detailed analysis of the house raids and abductions, the first stage of the sequence abduction-torture-disappearance-captivity that was suffered by many Argentines.

Nationwide Repression

On 6 October 1975, President Italo Luder and six cabinet ministers signed three decrees establishing that a Consejo de Seguridad Interna would direct the counterinsurgency. The Internal Security Council was composed of the cabinet and the three commanders of the armed forces. This body delegated the strategic command to the Defense Council (Consejo de Defensa). The Defense Council, composed of the Minister of Defense and once again the three commanders of the armed forces, planned and coordinated the repression. Decree 2772 stated that "The Armed Forces, under the Supreme Command of the President of the Nation delegated to the Defense Council, will proceed to execute the military and security operations necessary to annihilate the actions of the subversive elements throughout the country's territory."[7] The Argentine military interpreted Decree 2772 as a blank check to kill, execute, or assassinate all guerrillas.[8] The tactical instructions in the 1976 army manual RC-9-1 stated unequivocally: "The subversive delinquent who brandishes weapons must be annihilated, because the Armed Forces must neither cease combat temporarily nor accept surrender once they enter into operations."[9]

The Defense Council adopted its first battle plan on 15 October 1975. The army presented its operationalization on 28 October, signed by General Jorge Rafael Videla. The navy also elaborated a tactical plan, entitled the Navy Internal Capacities Plan or PLACINTARA (Plan de Capacidades Internas de la Armada).[10] Although these plans were blue prints of the repressive structure, they spelled out neither the structure of special task forces nor the dirty war practices of abduction, torture, disappearance, and captivity. The army was given the primary responsibility for intelligence and combat operations, while the navy, air force, gendarmery, police, and penitentiary forces were subsidiary.[11] The tactical plans did not change after the military assumed power in March 1976, but the counterinsurgency war could now be waged more effectively because the chains of command were shortened and any legal restraints had been removed. The Internal Security Council became defunct and the Defense Council was replaced by the Joint Chiefs of Staff.

The military offensive aimed at restricting the freedom of movement of the revolutionary organizations, isolating them from their national and international support structures, and harassing them through permanent pressure. The maneuvers were to develop along four phases. The repression would hit Argentina's three major urban-industrial areas during the first phase. The guerrilla organizations had developed most prominently along three geographical axes: the Andean axis Tucumán-Córdoba, the riverine axis Santa Fe-Rosario-Federal Capital, and the coastal axis Greater Buenos Aires-La Plata-Bahia Blanca. Operations would focus during the second phase on the cities Córdoba, Rosario, and Santa Fe. The third phase concentrated on the industrial belts of Greater Buenos Aires and La Plata. The final phase would eliminate the remaining guerrilla organizations. Operation Independence in Tucumán was to continue throughout these four phases until the rural insurgency had been eliminated.[12]

The National Countersubversive Strategy (Estrategia Nacional Contrasubversiva) implanted in March 1976 consisted, on the one hand, of direct military operations and, on the other, of military support for operations directed at crucial social sectors of Argentine society. The frontal military offensive involved three principal actions: combat, intelligence, and psychological operations. The combat operations were directed at the actual elimination of guerrilla organizations, their militias, sympathizers, and whoever was deemed a direct threat to national interests. The intelligence efforts gathered information, mapped the social networks of the political opposition, and traced the cellular guerrilla organizations. The psychological operations intended to affect the opponent, consolidate the support of the civilian population and the military themselves, and favorably influence foreign public opinion.

The second objective of the National Countersubversive Strategy was to provide military support for civic actions and police operations. Civic actions were intended to win the adherence of the Argentine people. Police operations were directed at preventing the guerrilla organizations from regaining a foothold in factories, labor unions, universities, churches, and working-class neighborhoods through strengthening national values, eliminating Marxist influences, and addressing current problems.[13] The emphasis of the armed forces was on direct military action in 1976 and 1977, and began to shift to political action in 1978.

Defense Zones and Combat Areas

Argentina was organized into five defense zones (Zonas de Defensa). Four zones were under the jurisdiction of the four army corps commanders, and one zone pertained to the Military Institutes (*Institutos Militares*) at Campo de Mayo which housed institutions such as the Cavalry School, Infantry School, Communications School and School for Noncommissioned Officers.[14] The navy and air force offered support to the army. The navy controlled the sea, waterways, and harbors, as well as two areas in the Federal Capital. The air force commanded the skies and airports, and one subzone and three areas in Greater Buenos Aires.[15] The national gendarmery, federal police, naval prefecture, provincial police, and the penitentiary service were under the command of the Army High Command, but their operational control was delegated to the five defense zone commanders where they were stationed.

The territorial organization established five command structures with a far-reaching license to the defense zone commanders (see map). The army corps comprised the regular troops trained primarily for conventional warfare, whereas special task forces did the "dirty work." As Captain Mittelbach has emphatically stated, it would be a grave mistake to assume that the entire Argentine officer corps, their troops, and the combined police forces were involved in the torture and disappearances. The responsibility rested firmly in the hands of the military junta and the defense zone and subzone commanders, while the operations were carried out by specialized military intelligence personnel with assistance of the police. Not the sixty thousand conscript soldiers and twenty thousand officers and NCOs but several thousand task group members were directly involved in the repression.[16]

The decision to create a flexible structure of task forces with great freedom of action, parallel to the standing structure of the armed forces, was made in October 1975. Former Army Commander Videla claims in a 1998 interview that he had presented President Luder and his cabinet with four options to combat the counterinsurgency, ranging from gradual and formal to total and virulent. The latter option, "Implied attacking en masse, with everything, throughout the entire terrain, taking them from their hide-outs. And they chose this option."[17] As such, there was nothing unusual about the deployment of small, mobile special forces to combat equally small and mobile nonconventional forces.[18] Not the organization of the special forces but their tactics and mission made them abuse civil and human rights and violate criminal and martial law.

Commanding officers were conscious of the danger of giving task forces such extensive operational freedom. As one officer complained to Elena Alfaro: "You are released; in fact, you shouldn't have been abducted, but you know that sometimes things slip out of our hands, especially with the gangs [task groups]. This is one of the problems we have to resolve when the war ends, namely the impunity which we have given these people."[19] Patricia Derian, the former assistant secretary of state for human rights under President Carter, spoke in 1977 with the three members of the junta: "they all spoke to me about the difficulty to control the lower-rank personnel, especially those who had seen their comrades suffer by the hands of the terrorists; [Videla] explained that it wasn't possible to control them. . . ."[20]

The dirty war doctrine was elaborated by the Generals Videla, Viola, Suárez Mason, Menéndez, Martínez, and other top military brass. General Cardozo was entrusted with the editorship of the text outlining the repressive structure. This document became the battle order of 24 March 1976.

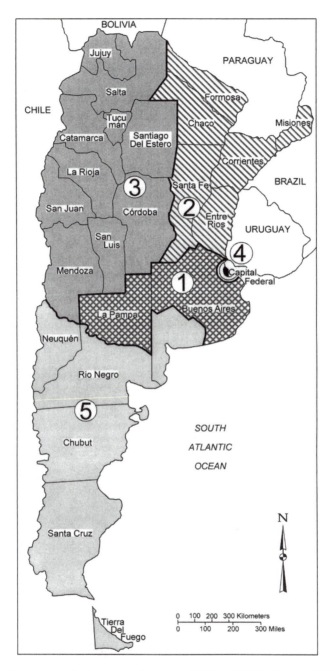

Military defense zones in Argentina between 1976 and 1981. Source: Mittelbach 1986: 10; CJE 1979, anexo 2–3.

Former police inspector Rodolfo Fernández revealed that a meeting of retired and active duty generals was held in April 1976 to explain the characteristics of the new war doctrine.[21] According to Bishop Justo Laguna, fifty-three generals attended of whom only three opposed the strategy. General Riveros confirmed during a visit to Washington, "We made war with the doctrine in our hand, with written orders from the superior commanders. We never needed the paramilitary organizations of which they accuse us. . . ."[22]

The task forces (*fuerzas de tareas*), subdivided into operational task groups (*grupos de tareas*), operated parallel to the regular troops and had independent command structures. Whereas the regular troops would man checkpoints, guard infrastructural facilities, or engage the dwindling rural guerrilla force in Tucumán, the task forces were in charge of the urban guerrilla counterinsurgency and the repression of political opponents. Joint operations made this parallel command structure visible. Whenever troops were called upon to seal off a neighborhood, then the officers and soldiers would be dressed in combat fatigues and arrive in licensed army trucks. In contrast, the task group or "gang" (*patota*) would be dressed as civilians and arrive in unmarked cars.[23] Upon completion of the operation, the troops withdrew to their garrison, while the task group departed with the captives to a secret detention center.

Combat operations were undergirded by intelligence operations. An Intelligence and Operations Center or COI (Central de Operaciones e Inteligencia) was created in May 1976 to coordinate the army intelligence activities of the five defense zones.[24] Each zone had an army intelligence battalion. Sections of each battalion were stationed in the subzones. In addition, there was Intelligence Battalion 601 which stood under the direct command of Army Commander Videla.[25] Detachments of this battalion, together with specialists from the army intelligence service SIDE, and federal and provincial police, were stationed in the five defense zones to facilitate the national coordination of the intelligence effort.[26]

The centralization of information was complicated by the fact that each armed and security force operated its own intelligence service, namely the army, the army high command, the navy, air force, federal police, national gendarmery, national naval prefecture, and the provincial police.[27] Even though the army stood at the helm of the national and zonal intelligence structures, each service was also subordinate to its own commander, say the head of the provincial police or the national gendarmery. Several lines of command were thus operating at the same time, even though they finally converged in the five defense zone commanders who were all army generals.

Each defense zone was divided into subzones.[28] Subzones were further divided into areas. The five defense zones were comprised of nineteen subzones, and a total of 117 areas. The subzones were the jurisdiction of the task forces, and stood under the command of a general. The areas were the operational territories of the task groups, and were commanded by a colonel, lieutenant-colonel or major.[29]

Air force and navy commanded their own task forces. For example, the navy controlled two of the seven areas within the subzone Federal Capital of defense zone 1. Task force FT 3.3 and task force FT 3.4 operated in sector 3a of area 3 and in area 6 respectively. The infamous navy task group GT 3.3.2, operative between March 1976 and December 1978, was based at the Navy Mechanics School, and operated in sector 3a.[30]

Naval task group GT 3.3.2. was divided into three subgroups. The logistics subgroup consisted of officers and NCOs who maintained the building where the disappeared were kept, administered the pillaged goods, provided food to the captives, and supplied money, automobiles, weapons, and ammunition to the operational team. The intelligence subgroup indicated the human targets, and later interrogated and tortured the captives. This team decided who would live or be assassinated. This team consisted of naval officers, and received support from NCOs, naval prefecture, and prison personnel. Finally, the operational subgroup abducted and guarded the captives. Members of the federal police and the naval prefecture, as well as retired army and navy officers, collaborated with active duty naval officers in these operations. There were task group members who only completed one tour of duty of forty-five days, thus allowing the greatest number of navymen to dirty their hands. There were also permanent members. The notorious Navy Lieutenant Alfredo Astiz belonged to an operational team as a permanent member.[31]

The dirty war was not a territorial war but above all an intelligence war in which gathering information about social networks and cellular organizations was paramount. These network structures were the object of what Argentine military called active intelligence gathering. Abducted suspects were questioned to discover their contacts. Torture was a standard procedure to speed up the interrogation process.

The military also carried out passive intelligence gathering. Clandestine magazines, secret reports, and photographs of protest demonstrations were analyzed to identify targets. Two particularly important sources of information were the ERP registration cards and the voter registration of the 1975 Partido Peronista Auténtico, a front party for the outlawed Montoneros. The names and addresses of forty thousand supporters of the Montonero party became available to the intelligence services in late 1975. The PRT-ERP had a personnel section (jefatura de personal) which kept statistics on its members, such as their class background. A card was prepared for each new sympathizer, party member, or combatant. A second card was made when the member entered a new party organ or combat unit. A third card was kept to monitor the comrade's progress. This card was updated every month.[32] The Political Bureau of the PRT-ERP seemed so blind to the security risk of this registration system that they sanctioned a member of the Buenos Aires regional secretariat with a five-day arrest for burning personnel files.[33] The card files were of course eagerly exploited by the Argentine intelligence services.

First Month of Repression

The Argentine armed forces directed their repression not just at guerrilla combatants but at any person or group regarded as subversive. The military ignored the difference between rearguard and combatants, because "the characteristic of revolutionary war, created and imposed by Marxism, is the absence of a rearguard and the impossibility of neutral positions: everything is 'front' and all will be treated as 'combatants,' whether they want to participate in combat or not."[34] The labor unions and grass roots organizations were first on the list of enemies in March 1976.

The Argentine working class was hit hard by the dirty war. The CONADEP calculated that of the 8,960 disappeared reported to the truth commission, 30.2 percent were blue collar and 17.9 percent white collar workers.[35] The military junta took full control of the largest unions and appointed military inspectors-general. The intelligence services had prepared lists of names with work and home addresses. Hundreds of union leaders, shopfloor representatives, and grass roots activists were either detained or abducted during the first days of military rule. Important orthodox Peronist union leaders, such as Lorenzo Miguel, were held in custody. Combative leaders, such as René Salamanca, disappeared. The military junta wanted to stamp out all opposition to its economic policies, prevent strikes and sabotage, and cut immediately the ties between workers and the guerrilla organizations.[36] They knew that the embattled guerrillas were retreating into the factories, taking menial jobs, and living in working-class neighborhoods to weather the first wave of repression, only to reassume their revolutionary activities at a later time. Many rank-and-file union people disappeared, often with the complicity of company management, while some might later reappear and be officially recognized as prisoners.

For example, sixty dockworkers were arrested on the morning of the coup d'état at the Astarsa shipyard in San Fernando and taken to the Tigre police station. The union delegate Rodolfo José Iriarte was also detained. His wife tracked him on his way through several police stations until she finally arrived at the Don Torcuato station. There, she received his blood-stained clothing, and was told to bring clean clothes, antibiotics, and medicines. She never saw her husband again.[37] Some dockworkers were released after one year, but many more were disappeared and assassinated.

The Cordoban autoworkers went on strike on the day of the military coup and were immediately repressed. Still, they had not lost their combativeness. Wildcat strikes over declining wages struck the auto industry in

September 1976. The strikes were not led by one particular leader but were a grass-roots initiative. The military responded with the visible presence of army troops and new legislation penalizing striking workers with a maximum prison sentence of ten years. Such high penalties did not prevent the electricity company workers in Buenos Aires from striking in October 1976 and January–February 1977 over the firing of 260 employees active in the union. The military arrested over one hundred workers during the October protests and dispatched twenty thousand disciplinary slips in February 1977. Light and Power Workers Union leader Oscar Smith was abducted and disappeared. The strike had been broken. The American embassy reported in mid-1977 that between 750 and 1,000 union activists were being held captive, of whom 500 were presumed dead. The embassy estimated further that between three and four thousand ordinary workers were in prison, of whom 750 had probably been killed.[38]

Still, the military did not succeed in entirely stifling worker protest. Slowdown strikes between October and December 1977 caused the Minister of Labor to accept oppositional unions as valid interlocutors. This small gain in union power did not kindle more protests. The strike activity declined by more than half in 1978. Only forty strikes were registered in 1978, as opposed to one hundred in 1977.[39]

Military Operations against the Guerrilla Forces

After the real and imagined ties with the Argentine working class had been cut, the military turned to the Montoneros and PRT-ERP.[40] The three armed forces combated both organizations, but the army concentrated on the Marxist ERP and the navy on the Peronist Montoneros, while the air force was put on the pursuit of smaller organizations.[41] The ERP operated more clearly as a guerrilla army, especially in Tucumán, and was thus the most suitable adversary for the Argentine army. Furthermore, the army was staunchly anti-communist, while the navy was rabidly anti-Peronist and therefore most tenacious in its pursuit of the Montoneros.

The enemy definition was crucial. The PRT-ERP was subdivided into three groups: PRT members (activists and aspirants), ERP combatants (officers, NCOs, and combatants), and members of the PRT youth organization, the Guevarist Youth.[42] The Montoneros were divided into two groups: members or *encuadrados* (officers, NCOs, and soldiers) and peripheral members or *periféricos* (activists, collaborators, and sympathizers).[43]

The Montoneros and PRT-ERP had gotten hold of the secret army battle plans through their own intelligence services, but were unaware of the parallel task force structure.[44] Familiar with American and French counterinsurgency doctrines, they expected the Argentine army to seal off entire neighborhoods, as had happened in Chile in 1973, and search for guerrillas and political opponents. "But what did they do?" asks former Montonero Ernesto Jauretche. "They launched a war technology that was totally unknown to us. They launched those famous pickup trucks in the street, the ones that had six soldiers in the back, one of whom operated a MAG, a MAG-30 machine gun which is something terrifying; the other five with FAL rifles; in front an NCO with a machine gun and grenades, and a driver. Every contact of one of our vehicles with one of theirs was four deaths for us. . . . We disappeared from the street very soon because the combat situation was totally uneven."[45]

The hunted Montoneros moved from one shelter to another and tried to maintain contact with their organization. Continuing to inflict casualties among the Argentine military and fighting till the end were ways to work through their own losses. It was their way of taking charge of their own destiny, a destiny towards defeat mined with torture, disappearance, the loss of comrade after comrade, and the brutal rupture of affective ties with parents, spouses, friends, and children. This growing social trauma about the fallen and the ongoing defeat of the living might lead to total passiveness, profound disillusion, and cynicism but also to seething anger, hatred, and a dogged determination to fight. In the end, the will to evade the tireless task groups and the mastery to choose death carried a strange empowerment which the surrender to state terror did not.

But where to go? Surviving Montoneros were completely disheartened by the abductions, according to Jauretche. "Everything produced an impressive demoralization in the heart of the organization. One couldn't walk in the street, nobody knew where it was safe because also your own comrades were informers."[46] The military had in fact imitated the guerrilla way of warfare: "Hit and run, wait, lie in ambush, again hit and run, and thus repeatedly, without giving any rest to the enemy."[47]

The misjudgment of the nature and extent of the repression had also to do with the Montoneros' Peronist identity. Since 1945, the Peronists had always succeeded in negotiating a deal with their adversaries. Violence was a means to force the opponent to the negotiating table and obtain the best outcome possible. As Ernesto Jauretche recalls his bewilderment about the military repression after the 1976 coup: "But we never ever imagined that this could be a project of physical annihilation of the political adversary, and the destruction of the economic, social, and cultural foundation from which the culture of revolution was being reproduced. The enemy's strategy was integral, it destroyed the universities, reduced the productive apparatus, and hit militarily all vanguards, and above all those that were part of the intermediary connections between the organized cadres of the [guerrilla] organizations and the popular grass roots."[48]

Mario Roberto Santucho, inflexible in his faith in the historical victory of communism, also misinterpreted the counterinsurgency strategy. He expected a repression similar to that of the Lanusse dictatorship.[49] Surprisingly, the army left the PRT-ERP largely untouched during the first week after the coup, and the ERP went immediately on the offensive.[50] In his editorial "Argentines, to arms!" Santucho wrote that "a river of blood will separate the military from the Argentine people," and this would result in a popular uprising, followed by a civil war.[51] Combatants were ordered to disarm two policemen a week, and attack a police station every month. This fatal tactic only facilitated the repression because the guerrillas and their rearguard exposed themselves. The PRT-ERP was attacked heavily in April 1976. First, the financial basis was taken away, and then the clandestine presses. The Montoneros came to the aid with money, weapons, and safe houses. Santucho's *Verelendung* theory was materializing but the final outcome was not what he had dreamed of because the army was hot on his trail.

On 29 March 1976, the ERP chief of intelligence was caught after a fire fight at which four guerrillas died, eight disappeared, and Santucho and over fifty guerrillas escaped unharmed. Much sensitive information was captured, and many high-ranking ERP officers were forced to change residence.[52] The army came down hard on the PRT in Córdoba in mid-April, and dismantled around one hundred of the 120 party cells in ten days. A total of three hundred men and women were abducted. Santucho was so affected by the losses that he was bedridden for almost a week.[53] Other regions were also attacked. Several hundred adolescents belonging to the Guevarist Youth disappeared in Zárate.

One member of the national PRT-ERP leadership after another fell into the hands of the task groups. The surviving members tried desperately, but in vain, to repair the tears in the guerrilla organization. "The survivors search one another, they meet in the street, check certain bars, and cross certain squares and specific streets at specific hours; everyone has his reference points and resorts to them driven by the need to know, to meet each other, and talk with others about the disaster."[54] Santucho and the members of the Political Bureau were having difficulties finding safe houses. Santucho admitted that he had completely underestimated the repressive capacity of the armed forces and had failed to foresee the withdrawal of popular support for the guerrillas. The idea matured that he had to leave Argentina, and that the remaining guerrillas would need to retreat among the working class, organize resistance committees in factories, and become involved in any emerging labor protest.[55]

Santucho took refuge in Domingo Menna's apartment, the number three of the PRT political bureau. He was scheduled to fly on Monday 19 July 1976 to Lima and, by way of Prague, continue to Havana. That day, Domingo Menna left his apartment in Villa Martelli around noontime to meet a friend. He was abducted by a task group and taken to the Campo de Mayo army base. Meanwhile, Santucho was waiting to be taken to a meeting with Montonero leader Firmenich to seal their cooperation within the Argentine Liberation Organization or OLA (Organización para la Liberación de Argentina). However, Santucho heard that Firmenich could not meet him because a liaison had been detained. Santucho was now ready to travel. He wore glasses and curly hair in disguise. Also present in Menna's apartment were Benito Urteaga and his two-year-old son, and the wives of Santucho and Menna.

At 2:30 P.M., Captain Juan Carlos Leonetti stepped out of his unlicensed Ford Falcon and walked to Domingo Menna's apartment, accompanied by three armed men. They ascended to the fourth floor, and hid themselves as the doorman knocked. Santucho's wife opened, and sounded alarm but the assault team was already inside, holding Santucho and Urteaga at gun point. As Leonetti searched Santucho for weapons, the ERP commander grabbed the captain by the throat, took his pistol and wounded him mortally. The three men accompanying Leonetti immediately opened fire. Urteaga was killed and Santucho seriously injured. Santucho was taken to Campo de Mayo where he soon died. The bodies of Urteaga and Santucho were displayed as trophies to the troops. The wives of Santucho and Urteaga were abducted to the Campo de Mayo army base, and assassinated. Urteaga's two-year-old son José was given to his paternal grandparents. Domingo Menna was tortured for months. According to former Campo de Mayo Sergeant Víctor Ibáñez, the torturers even hooked him to an automatic electric prod when they went out for lunch. Menna never spoke and was eventually assassinated.[56]

The PRT-ERP had in one day lost its three most important commanders. Luis Mattini became the new secretary-general. He went into exile in late 1976, together with fifty high-ranking guerrillas. Whereas in the late 1960s Lenin's optimistic *What Is To Be Done?* was the guiding text of the PRT-ERP, in 1977 it had become Lenin's 1904 crisis assessment *One Step Forward, Two Steps Back: The Crisis in our Party.*[57] The heavy blows by the Argentine military made the PRT-ERP fall into two groups. One group admitted total defeat and proposed the flight abroad of the surviving members. The second group favored the withdrawal of some comrades but felt that the majority had to insert themselves among the working class in Argentina.

The final blow took place in May 1977. After an eight-month stay abroad, a few commanders returned in late April to Argentina to jump start the resistance. Within three weeks, the army came down with all its might, except in the Federal Capital.[58] The military were playing a cat-and-mouse game with the ERP, paralyzing them with doubt about the next blow. Suddenly, the Federal Capital regional commander Osvaldo Soto was caught, and the whole cellular structure collapsed.

Meanwhile, an army intelligence report observed that the Montoneros "continues to be an extremely dangerous organization for the degree of its development and organization, for the combatants at its disposal, the acquired experience and fundamentally because its will to fight has not been broken."[59] Its strength was estimated on 28 February 1977 at around

2,850 members.[60] Defeat was not far off. In fact, Norma Arrostito, a founding member of the Montoneros, offered upon her capture to hold a press conference admitting that the Montoneros had been defeated. The commander of the ESMA (Navy Mechanics School), Rear-Admiral Chamorro, rejected this offer because it would make many guerrillas drop their weapons and save themselves.[61]

The way combatants responded to their capture differed considerably between the Marxist and Peronist revolutionaries. The Montonero leadership ordered all guerrillas to carry a cyanide capsule and commit suicide instead of being captured alive. Arriving at public places where the chance of detection was considerable, at train stations, subway stations, bus stations, airports, and ferries, the person would place the cyanide capsule in his or her mouth. However, the task groups were prepared for such an eventuality. They would inject him or her with an antidote or a substance provoking intense vomiting.[62] They went then to a hospital to empty the stomach. Abducted Montoneros were often deeply shaken by their survival. The task group commander emphasized that he had saved their life, whereas the guerrilla commanders had send them to death while living abroad in luxury. With this moral blackmail, the military tried to persuade their captives to collaborate in the hunt for their comrades.

The PRT-ERP believed this suicide practice to be counterproductive and demoralizing, a demonstration of the bourgeois attitude of the Montoneros. Instead, their combatants were ordered to fight till the end and, if captured alive, to continue the revolutionary struggle inside the torture room.[63] Whoever has the courage to commit suicide also has the courage to resist torture, so was the reasoning, while the weak-spirited will collapse under torture and also be too afraid to swallow cyanide.[64]

Military repression had decimated the guerrilla organizations in little over one year. The commander of the Third Army Corps and defense zone three, General Luciano Benjamín Menéndez, declared proudly in May 1977: "The armed part . . . has been totally annihilated in our jurisdiction."[65] The remaining guerrillas, continued Menéndez, were now trying to take shelter among the population by infiltrating in labor unions and even churches, but his men were determined to find them. A 10 May 1978 update of the national security situation stated that the military side of the counterinsurgency had been very successful with 90 percent of the guerrilla organizations annihilated. The following estimates were given of the guerrillas at large in Argentina: Montoneros (370 combatants), PRT-ERP (185 combatants), and Poder Obrero (16 combatants).

Operations Against the Political Opposition

With the guerrilla organizations considerably reduced, the emphasis of the cultural war shifted in April 1977 to the political terrain. The repression was directed at four targets: major industries, educational institutions, the church, and working class neighborhoods.[66] Workers, students, and clergymen were already being persecuted since the coup, but now they became the principal targets. Lieutenant-General Videla said it with so many words on a visit to Uruguay: "There remain other dimensions of the subversion, such as the possible infiltration in labor unions, student organizations, political parties, and even in the public administration. This is the reason for a systematic cleansing operation."[67]

The economic program of the Minister of Economy José Martínez de Hoz proved disastrous for the working class, and the military were well aware that labor discontent was a feeding ground for revolutionary organizations. So, after the first repressive wave in March 1976 aimed at cutting the ties between guerrillas and workers, the army embarked on a second mission against industries and state companies to eliminate labor conflicts. The operations sought to achieve "ideologically cleansed" business, labor, and state structures improving the economy's efficiency, productivity, and socioeconomic climate.[68]

The nationwide actions were directed at shop floor representatives sympathetic to the revolutionary cause. The operation consisted of two phases. Phase One lasted from April through December 1977, and was intended to diminish the revolutionary activities in the industrial zones and prevent mass mobilizations. Detentions were recommended to take place outside factory gates "in a more or less simultaneous and hidden way."[69] Meanwhile, new representatives and delegates were proposed to restore the labor structure. Phase Two lasted throughout 1978, and was intended to "cleanse" targets of secondary importance. Each defense zone was ordered to keep records on persons fired because of subversive activities during such operations so that future employers might check on the political histories of potential employees.

High schools and universities were, according to the military, hotbeds of ideological formation and recruitment for revolutionary organizations.[70] Intelligence and combat operations were determined to remove all political opponents.[71] The military believed that education was the foremost means to transmit the revolutionary ideology from one generation to the next and diminish the influence of parents and national leaders. They regarded Marx, Freud, and Einstein as the three principal ideological enemies of Argentina because they tried to destroy the Western concepts of property and society, spirit and family, and matter, time and space respectively. Their works certainly qualified for the book-burning pyre that was erected in Córdoba on 29 April 1976.[72] Furthermore, all subversive literature had to be removed from courses and libraries and be replaced with books expressing national values and the Christian worldview.[73]

The Roman Catholic Church was the third public target of the antirevolutionary war. The army stated that, true enough, the Roman Catholic

Church was overall sympathetic to the military junta, but the pastoral calling was sometimes abused by the guerrilla organizations. The army was therefore to establish a dialogue with all levels of the ecclesiastical hierarchy to gain their support for the antirevolutionary struggle. The greatest tact had to be displayed to eliminate political opponents from the church.[74]

The working class neighborhoods were the final target of the army. Since the guerrilla organizations had been forced to abandon their armed insurrection, they tried to incite a popular insurrection. According to the military, they were infiltrating sport clubs, religious organizations, cultural associations, folklore groups, rock bands, and support groups for political prisoners. They would try to sow discontent, reap sympathy for revolutionary causes, and eventually produce a mass insurrection. The army proposed a preventive operation at the municipal level, but also moved in on local leaders and infiltrators.[75] Many civilians were abducted from their homes, tortured, disappeared, and either released or assassinated.

Raids and Abductions

Most political opponents targeted by the Argentine military were neither guerrilla combatants nor support troops which gave shelter, provided logistic support for attacks, or assembled, hid, and transported weapons. The majority consisted of politically involved but unarmed civilians. They were sympathizers who distributed illegal pamphlets and painted slogans, Third World priests, critical journalists and defense lawyers, and left-leaning physicians and teachers. They were student and labor union representatives, political activists and grass roots workers, young men and women who taught slum dwellers literacy skills, ran a public dispensary, or provided social assistance to the poor. Most were never charged with any particular offense. Some people were abducted because they had relatives or friends considered subversive. As one army manual explained, one vulnerable spot of the guerrillas was, "Terror or the threat of violence to them and their relatives and friends. . . ."[76]

There were also several bizarre abductions, like that of twenty-year-old Rosa Ana Frigerio who was taken away on a stretcher because her lower body was in a cast due to a spinal operation. She disappeared and the naval authorities told her parents that she died in an armed confrontation between a task group and a squad of Montoneros.[77] The reasoning behind Rosa Ana Frigerio's disappearance must have been the same as given by President Videla when asked why the severely handicapped Claudia Inés Grumberg had been detained for being a subversive: "a person is not just regarded a terrorist for killing with a weapon or planting a bomb, but also for inciting other people through ideas contrary to our Western, Christian civilization, and possibly this young person has been detained in this capacity."[78]

Lilia and Lucas Orfanó are a typical example of the abduction of political activists. They belonged to the Peronist left, and Lucas was the president of the Argentine League for the Rights of Man.[79] Their two sons were Montoneros. Their house was first raided by police in June 1975. Their son Guillermo was detained for painting slogans and was released five days later. The federal police raided their house again in June 1976, but the two sons were not there.

On 30 July 1976, their eldest son Daniel was abducted. Lilia and Lucas were unable to sleep after that. After their fifth restless night, they received an unexpected visit. "They rang the door bell at dawn on the 3rd of August 1976. I had the lights on in the house. Lucas and I were there alone, and Lucas says to me, 'Lili, calm down.' I tried to calm down. He goes and opens the door, and they turn him around so that he won't see them, and they take him through the corridor of my house while screaming loudly. One said, 'Madam, the army, put yourself against the wall.' They put the two of us against the wall, grabbed a sheet, and hooded us both."

The assailants search the entire house, kick the dog into submission, and take some bottles of Coca-Cola from the refrigerator, handing also two bottles to Lilia and Lucas. Meanwhile, they beat Lucas Orfanó, asking him where the arms are hidden. Lilia is screaming all the while for someone to hear her. Suddenly, they are ordered to get dressed. "They drag us away, me and Lucas, dragging. They put us in a car, a small car, and take all the money we had. They put us together in a car, the two of us on the floor, together. . . ." Five minutes later, they arrive at the federal police headquarters. They are kicked out of the car, and their rings and wristwatches are taken from them.

Their names are asked, and Lilia says her name aloud, hoping that her son will hear her if he is there. When Lucas says his name, the policeman typing down their names says, "The family united." Their son Daniel is apparently also there. They are taken blindfolded to a large place with many other captives. Some are occasionally taken away for torture. "At one time we heard screams that were the screams of my son, and Lucas says to me, 'That's Dani who's screaming!,' and I go crazy. I call one of the guards and tell him, 'Sir, the one who is screaming is my son!' And he asks, 'What's your son's name?' 'Pantaleón Daniel Orfanó.' He leaves, returns, and says, 'No, it isn't your son.' It was a lie, it was my son, I'm certain it was my son."

Lilia and Lucas Orfanó were held blindfolded for fifteen days. They were given cold tea to drink and cold polenta, spaghetti, or boiled tripe to eat. When they were released, the attending officer told them that they had been arrested by mistake: "They didn't interrogate us but that was an even worse torture, the psychological torture of waiting till they come to torture you as they were torturing the other persons, you see? Afterwards, they threw us out of a car at four blocks from my house. There, begins the search for my son."[80] They were notified later by the court of Mercedes that their son Daniel had been found dead, but the body was not released. Their other son Guillermo was abducted on 2 December 1976, and remains disappeared.

What was a bewildering experience for the abducted was a standard procedure for the abductors. The house search had been developed by police for criminal investigations, and around 1970 was adapted for the detention of political suspects.[81] Most operations followed a raid plan (*plan de allanamiento*) delineating the various stages of the assault. The four principal factors were secrecy, objective, surprise, and speed. The assault was divided into two parts: the raid (*allanamiento*) and the search (*registro*). The size and composition of the assault group differed according to the anticipated resistance.

The assault group consisted of the siege team, the search team, and the support team. The siege team surrounded the house and provided protection to the search team against any external actions. The search team carried out the raid, looked for suspects and material evidence, and conducted a brief interrogation. The support team gave cover and assistance to the search team. Medical personnel was available to provide first aid.[82] These procedures were developed to reduce casualties in armed encounters with experienced and heavily armed guerrillas. Yet, they were applied with equal force to defenseless civilians, even though such raids were not considered as combat but as intelligence operations. Not personal safety but intimidation, terror, and social disruption were the reasons for the routine use of excessive force.

Generally, the task group notified police in advance to establish an emergency zone.[83] Operations could be carried out without such notification, but then the civilian-clad task group risked being arrested on the suspicion of being ordinary criminals. Likewise, incursions into the areas of other task groups were always communicated immediately to prevent any mishap because such trespassing violated the preestablished jurisdictions.

The raid began with a break-in to capture suspects and obtain proof of subversive activities. "When there is no other way to enter a building than through a closed door, then one can try to open it with a strong kick, directly below the lock."[84] However, the front door was as easily perforated with the shots of a machine gun in complete disregard of who might be standing behind.[85] A group of around eight men would bash into the home. They were seldom in uniform, although their identity might be betrayed by a pair of pants, a belt buckle, or boots. Sometimes, the men were disguised, as in the case of the abduction of Iris Etelvina de Avellaneda in April 1976: "Except for the one who was called Commissioner, and who conducted the procedure, the rest was ostensibly disguised with wigs, beards, and stockings covering their faces."[86]

The men would enter heavily armed, and would say, for instance, "Well, it stops here, the joke has ended."[87] Often, the task group asked "Where are the weapons?" in an attempt to justify the violent entry. Most occupants were immediately discouraged in deed and word to undertake action. "The entry must be made with weapons in hand," the raid manual stated. "Doors and windows must be crossed diagonally to prevent that one becomes dangerously silhouetted by the light from outside."[88]

"Nocturnal incursions present many risks, especially when one expects to find desperate, armed men."[89] Most of the time, however, the task groups only found terrorized parents and sleeping children. And precisely in these defenseless situations, the instructions were followed to the letter. "When a suspect is located in a room and one finds him sleeping in bed, one must shine a flashlight directly in his face when awakening him. The sudden glare will blind him when he opens his eyes. . . . Whenever possible, the approach must be made from behind the bed's headboard. This will put him in a position from which he will not be able to fire with precision when he wakes up."[90] The bewildered residents were at their most defenseless while fast asleep. When four armed men entered the house of Nemí Lebed around 5:00 A.M. on 30 September 1976, his twenty-four-year-old daughter María Susana was still sleeping, "my daughter was deep asleep when this man put a machine gun to her head and said while assuming a shooting position: 'Get up, Susanita, because if you don't, then this is the end.'"[91]

The search team would first body search the detained persons and then go systematically through everything in the house: cupboards, furniture, carpets, washing machines, radios, books, bottles, and lamps.[92] The task group took over the social routines of the house. The inhabitants had to ask for permission to go to the bathroom, were forced into the bedroom, had to stand against a wall, could not answer the phone, or were kept hostage. The men would wait till the sought-after person returned or they might oblige the hostage to drive them to where the son or daughter was staying. Thus relatives were implicated in a complex emotional tangle in which the person sought was held responsible for their suffering, and they were pressured to betray his or her whereabouts.

The raid procedures warned that "Female personnel may turn out to be as dangerous or even more so than the men, and one must therefore never take down one's guard."[93] Women could more easily hide weapons than men, and should therefore be searched carefully. "Women must be made to take off all clothing that does not affect their chastity (wigs, coats, jackets, hats, large belts, hand bags, etc.) which then will be searched separately and carefully without neglecting security. . . . One must always treat women with the greatest consideration and respect but with firmness, while avoiding all physical force not absolutely necessary. Military personnel must not allow themselves to feel threatened by insults or hysterical reactions."[94] Ana María Caracoche de Gatica learned the extent of this respect when the doorbell rang on the evening of 19 April 1977. Several men forced their way into the house, and one of them "grabs me by the head, takes me to a wall, and begins to beat me, to insult me and to ask me where my husband was; once they hit me on the back, kick my legs and hit me on my eyes, I feel that they are tying my arms behind my back. . . ."[95]

Generally, the abducted were only tortured in interrogation centers, but sometimes an impromptu session was given at home, and even relatives were abused to intimidate them, as happened to Carlos Alberto Campero: "My mother was taken to the shop, and threatening her life, they beat her in a way that should not even be used on wild animals. In the shop we had a ventilator fan. They cut the cable, plugged it in and used it to give her electric shocks. So that it would have more effect, they poured mineral water over my mother, whom they had tied to a chair. While they were committing this savagery, another one of them was hitting her with a belt until her body was bleeding and her face disfigured."[96]

Allen Feldman has interpreted the capture and incarceration of suspects in Northern Ireland as a social death in which the captive is violently isolated from the protection of family, friends, and community.[97] This important interpretation deserves, in the case of Argentina, to be understood additionally as a traumatizing assault on people's sociality, in particular because abductions often took place at homes. To be exact, 62 percent of the disappeared were detained in their homes, 24.6 percent in the street, and only 7 percent at work.[98] The abduction of Argentines from their homes and the humiliation of their relatives led to the violation of the physical, psychological, and symbolic safety of the home, the destruction of trust among parents and children, and the disintegration of personal boundaries. The raid was a disturbing intrusion of a threatening outside world and caused lasting damage to the self by the transgression of deepseated cultural values.

Most people acquire the differentiation between the home as an inner sanctuary and the outer world as a different physical and moral universe while growing up in their parents' house.[99] Winnicott expressed this superbly with his felicitous title, *Home Is Where We Start From.*[100] The home exudes trust and safety because these values were inculcated there during childhood. A forced entry is therefore an attack taking place as much on the physical and psychological as on the social and cultural level. A person's social trust is assaulted as much as the body's integrity, and intimate relations are damaged together with the symbolic order of society. As I shall demonstrate in the next chapter, the inner and social defenses that were battered by the abduction were further broken down under torture.

These violent assaults on the home transgressed the deep-seated opposition between the public and the domestic domain so common in Latin America.[101] Latin American societies have created many social, material, and symbolic barriers to prevent the two domains from mixing. The public sphere is seen as a polluted and dangerous place whose harmful influences must be stopped at the door-step. Thresholds, material demarcations, heavily locked doors, and symbolic divisions impede a free interchange between public and domestic, serving to transform people symbolically during their transition from one social sphere to another.[102] These sociospatial and symbolic divisions between domestic and public reinforce people's ego boundaries between self and not-self, between what is inside and what is outside. A forced entry is thus a personal attack, and violates the home's emotional protection. Children sense this infraction on the sanctity of the house immediately. When in November 1976 a task group broke into the house of Marta Lifsica de Chester at night to abduct her husband Jorge, the twelve-year-old daughter Zulema woke up and entered the living room. The surprised commanding officer asked her: "What are you doing here?" to which the girl responded: "I'm in my house. What are you doing here?"[103]

The assaults were also extended on the symbolic level to the objects that gave content and meaning to people's existence.[104] Paintings, photographs, porcelain, toys, and momentos were broken and urinated upon. Pillage further reinforced the violation of the home as emotionally valuable objects were stripped from their social surroundings. Theft was common, even though Army Directive 404/75 stated that strict measures would be taken to prevent the pillage and unnecessary destruction of private property not to lose the support of the Argentine people for the counterinsurgency war.[105] Task groups regarded the goods of their captives as legitimate war booty. Cars were stolen for use in operations. People were forced to sell their land, house, and in one case even the owner's race horses and vineyards.[106] The navy operated a real estate agency selling houses with false property titles. The Navy Mechanics School had a deposit, known as Pañol Grande (large storeroom), containing furniture, electrical appliances, electronic equipment, refrigerators, stoves, and large piles of clothes which had formerly belonged to assassinated captives.[107]

The aggression against the home went in one case to the extreme of tearing down walls and modifying its sociospatial arrangement. This happened to the home of Marta García Candeloro in the Andean capital of Neuquén. She and her husband had been abducted in June 1977. Her husband had died under torture. After her release six months later, Mrs. Garcia Candeloro decided to sell her home. To her dismay she discovered that a group of policemen from the interior were living there: "my house was completely sacked. They had destroyed the bookcases and even the walls. They had made compartments. The house used to have four rooms and with those compartments made out of broken bookcases, they had created about seven rooms in the dining room. . . ."[108] The dining room's restructuring into provisory bedrooms turned sociospatial functions and cultural meanings inculcated during childhood upside down.[109] The semi-public place where guests used to be received had now become confounded with the most intimate retreat of the house. The symbolic separations of body and community, intimacy and sociality, and inner and outer were all thrown together in a disturbing whole in which refuge was no longer possible.

The following account by Rubén Darío Martínez sums up the major elements of a typical house raid. "They detained me at home. A group of people, seven or eight persons, entered. . . . I was asleep. They broke down the door, covered me with a hood, put me against the wall, and began to inspect the entire place. They asked me where the weapons were, turned the mattress over, broke everything, and forced me to the floor. After hitting me inside my house, they put a pistol to my head, and then took me downstairs."[110]

The first stage of the disappearance had ended. Commonly, captives were registered, and the information sent to the defense zone commander and the High Command. A detention card would be drawn up that stated the name, age, and degree of danger (*grado de peligrosidad*) of the abducted person, when and in which zone and area he or she had been detained, where the person was held, and which security force was responsible.[111]

Abduction, Fear, and Traumatization

The Argentine military were convinced that their cultural war was a necessary means—a precise surgery into the diseased social body, as they called it—towards healing a troubled and chaotic society, a society whose sovereignty was in danger, politics was poisoned, economy was in shambles, family life was disturbed, and social organization had been undermined by moral decay. With this higher objective in mind, the military decided to terrorize and by extension traumatize the guerrilla forces and the radicalized political opposition. Fear and uncertainty were deliberate means of combat. "The first victory is achieved by instilling fear in the adversary. Thus, one task of the forces of order consists of instilling such fear among the guerrillas. Fear leads to mistrust and mistrust leads to uncertainty. . . . One loses fear when one knows the cause producing it. This cause must therefore always remain hidden, must constantly change if possible, and must in all cases be part of reality."[112] It is precisely the impossibility of knowing the causes of abduction, torture, and disappearance that can be so traumatizing.

The guerrillas and the oppositional forces were given no quarter, both in the sense of mercy and of a safe retreat. Inadvertently, Admiral Massera gave one of the best summaries of the state terror as he was describing the guerrilla insurgency: "Slowly, almost without us realizing, a horror machine unleashed its wickedness on the unprepared and the innocent, amidst the disbelief of some, the complicity of others, and the astonishment of many. War had begun. A different and devious war. A war primitive in its procedures but sophisticated in its cruelty. A war we had to get used to little by little because it wasn't easy to admit that the entire country saw itself forced into a monstrous intimacy with blood."[113] Civilians were abducted principally from their homes, thus transgressing the cultural boundaries between the public and domestic domain, violating the differentiation between self and non-self, and damaging the social trust between helpless captives and powerless family members. The home's violent invasion was only the beginning of a breakdown of people's personal defenses to achieve their psychological, social, and cultural dismantlement through torture and traumatization.

The Argentine military did not use the term trauma in the design of their repressive strategy but preferred such formulations as annihilating the ability to operate and breaking the enemy's will to fight. When the enemy is defined as a negation of the self and its threat is not material but mental then traumatization is the most effective means of annihilation short of assassination. Many abducted captives were assassinated, and most survivors were emotionally deeply shaken, while an unknown number suffered from acute psychic traumas and posttraumatic disorders. Psychic and social traumatization are pernicious but highly effective means of repression because the tenacious emotional disturbance may prevent individuals and groups from taking decisive action. They are given over to uncontrollable emotions, may have difficulty in organizing themselves, and may adversely affect the people in their surroundings.

The elimination of the guerrilla organizations and the defeat of combatants, ideologues, and sympathizers were just one stage of this drawn-out conflict. The cultural war continued through the practice of torture. Torture was not an epiphenomenon, a detail, the necessary dirty work, but an integral part of an overall strategy in which the battlefield extended onto the human body and into the self and the mind. Torture was to complete the victory on the ground into the minds and selves of the defeated, because it was there that culture was embodied most fully. Von Ludendorff's concept of total war acquired a whole new meaning as it was fought on the uncharted terrain of the human soul.

Chapter 11
The Operating Theater: Torture, Dehumanization, and Traumatization

Pablo Díaz was eighteen years old when he was abducted by a task group in La Plata, the capital of Buenos Aires province. Five days earlier, his friends Francisco López Muntaner (16 years old), María Claudia Falcone (16 years), Claudio de Acha (17 years), Horacio Angel Ungaro (17 years), Daniel Alberto Racero (18 years), and María Clara Ciocchini (18 years) had disappeared. History was repeating itself. Thirty years earlier, in 1946, four students and one worker had been abducted, disappeared, and tortured by police on the suspicion of placing bombs around La Plata.[1]

Pablo's friends were all members of the forbidden Union of High School Students or UES which had been a front organization for the Montoneros. Pablo Díaz used to belong to the UES but moved in 1975 to the Guevarist Youth (Juventud Guevarista), controlled by the Marxist PRT-ERP. Several friends had participated in literacy campaigns and solidarity groups seeking a better treatment for political prisoners. Their friendship was welded, and their fate sealed, when they met on 4 September 1975 for the preparations of a large street protest. The demonstration was intended to secure a bus fare discount for high school students. Pablo Díaz recalls that they were under constant surveillance: "We knew that there was a cop who wrote down our names and kept files on us."[2] More than three thousand students marched the next day to the Ministry of Public Works. Despite the exchanges of stones and tear gas, Pablo and his friends succeeded in talking to the authorities. One week later, the demand was granted. A flat bus rate was established, irrespective of the trajectory.[3]

The military coup did not stop the political activism of the high school students of La Plata. In fact, the PRT-ERP ordered the illegal Guevarist Youth in July 1976 to continue with its opposition to the junta with mass protests. The Montoneros sent similar signals to the UES.[4] Students met in school halls, bathrooms, and passageways, in bars, squares, and parks, and at home. Slogans were painted on walls, tiny ERP flags were left in buses entering the Campo de Mayo army base, pamphlets were distributed at factory gates, and clandestine meetings held. By June 1976, the student bus fare once again came under pressure as rates were more than doubled. Student protests began to organize in late August 1976.[5]

Colonel Ramón Camps, the commander of the provincial police, and police commissioner Miguel Etchecolatz decided to eradicate the persistent high school student opposition. Students were interrogated at the National College of La Plata, and nine students belonging to various student organizations were abducted by 4 September 1976.[6] Pablo Díaz's group sensed that their detention was imminent. The army task group started operations at 12:30 A.M. on 16 September, and by 5:00 A.M. six of the group of seven had been abducted. This night became known as the Night of the Pencils (la Noche de los Lápices).

At 4:00 A.M. on 21 September 1976, Pablo Díaz was taken from his home, hooded, thrown into a car, and taken to La Arana police station in La Plata. They interrogated him briefly about the upcoming student protest and his alleged guerrilla activities. They also brought in another captive, and asked him about Pablo Díaz. The blindfolded man did not know that Pablo was present and responded that Pablo Díaz sympathized with the Guevarist Youth, was a member of his high school student center, and had participated in the 1975 street demonstrations for the bus fare discount. "You proved your innocence," said the interrogator to Pablo Díaz, "Still, you're only going to live if I want you to."[7] Then, Pablo Díaz was taken to a torture room. After several days he was moved from La Arana police station to the Banfield secret detention center run by the Buenos Aires provincial police commanded by Colonel Camps. There, he finally met his high school friends again, blindfolded and tortured.

The abduction of the sixteen high school students from La Plata demonstrates clearly how wide the net of repression was cast, and that torture was an integral part of the cultural war. These adolescents and young adults were noncombatant members of illegal organizations. They had become politically active in their teens during the fall of the Lanusse dictatorship, and carried along by the enthusiasm of the 1973 Cámpora government, joined the tens of thousands of young people in all sorts of political and social associations to advance the country on the road to social justice. Many of the Argentine disappeared resembled these young people, while a minority consisted of experienced guerrilla combatants. Both groups were tortured because the Argentine cultural war and the junta's plan to reorganize Argentine society continued into the torture rooms of hundreds of secret detention centers.

Torture in Argentine History

The history of torture in twentieth century Argentina has evolved along two parallel but periodically intersecting lines. Whereas the torture of political prisoners served intermittently to repress attacks on the authoritarian state, the torture of common criminal suspects was a routine accompaniment of interrogation throughout the twentieth century. In times of political turbulence, the police would extend their repressive regime to the political arena and apply exactly the same torture methods to which criminal suspects were subjected.[8]

The emergence of the labor movement in the early twentieth century led to the abuse of incarcerated workers perceived as a revolutionary threat to the Argentine state. The 1930–1932 military dictatorship stepped up the physical repression considerably. Students, workers, and even dissident military officers were tortured by submersion in water, and the use of pincers, sandpaper, boiling water, and turpentine.[9] The invention of the electric prod around 1934 added a whole new dimension to the repression. Electric shocks to the genitals and the use of wet towels to enhance their intensity, so familiar in the 1970s, were already standard practices in the mid-1930s. These routines failed to disappear when Perón was elected in 1946.[10]

Perón's rise to power had created the expectation that a government founded on the pursuit of social justice would not tolerate torture. Unfortunately, the mistreatment of common and political suspects continued unabated. For example, four students and one worker were detained in La Plata in December 1946 on the accusation of organizing strikes and placing bombs. Although not yet in a systematic fashion, the practice of disappearances entered the repertoire of police repression already in 1946. When the parents of one student asked about their son's whereabouts and deposited a habeas corpus, the police denied having him in custody. Suspects were moved repeatedly to different police stations to confound the desperate relatives.[11] The repression reached high and low. The one-time prominent Peronist leader Cipriano Reyes was tortured in 1948 with an electric prod on suspicion of conspiring against Perón.[12] The torture regime became particularly grim when the protests against the Peronist government gathered force in 1952. When eight harbor workers refused to pay the dues for a memorial to the recently deceased Eva Perón, they were arrested, beaten, and hung by their thumbs for fifteen agonizing hours.[13]

The self-proclaimed Liberators of 1955 did not fare much better. Despite the rhetoric of having freed the country from its tyrant Perón, their repression of the Peronist Resistance was brutal. The democratically elected Frondizi government continued with the incarceration and mistreatment of thousands of political opponents. The military coup of 1966 would soon result in another wave of torture. Captured FAP guerrillas were tortured in 1968, and the proliferation of guerrilla organizations in 1970 turned torture into a routine practice.

A new repressive threshold was crossed when the knowledge about torture by law enforcement expanded among the military. The police were enlisted in the counterinsurgency efforts, and army intelligence officers were soon participating actively.[14] Nearly one hundred testimonies of torture during the Lanusse dictatorship were collected in May 1973.[15] These denunciations were made not only by Marxists and revolutionary Peronists, but also by right-wing Peronists.[16]

In 1973 the third Peronist government raised once more the hope that torture would be abolished. Within months of its installation, the first denunciations of torture and disappearance were made public. In September 1973, the revolutionary Peronist Sergio Maillmann was abducted by personnel of López Rega's Ministry of Social Welfare, tortured, and disappeared. Around the same time, the ERP member Alberto Alizalde was tortured by military personnel about his involvement in a guerrilla operation.[17] The Montoneros Maestre and Camps (Camps was one of the three survivors of the 1972 Trelew massacre) were abducted by federal police in May 1974. They reported having been tortured with a new device when they were forced into an ambulance: a portable electric prod.[18]

This brief historical review demonstrates that torture was endemic to Argentine society long before the 1976 coup, that it became applied to increasing numbers of Argentine citizens, and that the police were the principal State agents practicing torture. Particularly in 1976, large numbers of policemen were integrated into the military task forces because, as I was told by one former member, "the army didn't know how to work in the street."[19] The police had cultivated torture practices for more than six decades, and knew how to reach the limits of physical endurance without provoking death. Most secret detention centers were therefore located on police premises.

Despite the prominent role of the police in interrogating political opponents, torture acquired a new meaning in the hands of the military. Guerrilla combatants continued to be tortured for information, as had been done since 1968, but a new rationale emerged for the torture of noncombatants: they were not tortured for information, but to destroy their sociality. Drawn-out torture sessions of days, weeks, and even months aimed to dismantle persons socially. The Process of National Reorganization, intended for Argentine society as a whole, was being enacted on the souls of its captives. Torture was less a means to acquire information than to damage the mind, to traumatize the victims and alter their selves. Desocialization and traumatization were no longer the unintentional consequences of torture but became the primary objectives to accomplish a durable victory. No matter how much knowledge about withstanding torture had been accumulated in the Argentine popular consciousness during the previous six decades, nothing prepared people for the inferno they were to enter in 1976.

Torture Methods and Resistance to Torture

"If you talk I'll offer you an easy death, a shot; if not, a pig death through torture," an interrogator known as Texas used to tell his victims.[20] Torturers had infinite means of pain and power at their disposal, including the captives themselves. Everything at the torturer's hand could be turned into weaponry: a table, a chair, the walls, his fists, his voice, the captive's sexuality and convictions, and also other captives, partners, and children. Most torture methods were developed before 1976, and they are pitiful manifestations of the depths of humanity. Torture consisted of the infliction of physical, mental, and social pain, and sought the destruction of ego, self, and personhood.

The most common torture method consisted of tying a naked person by all fours to an iron bed frame, called a grill. The hands, feet, armpits, temples, lips, gums, teeth, nipples, genitals, and anus would be given shocks with an electric prod. The electric prod was the standard and preferred equipment in every interrogation because the pain was excruciating but left no visible marks on the body other than two small inflamed dots which went away over time.[21]

The electric prod (*picana*) was invented around 1934 by the Argentine police, and known by names such as the machine (*la máquina*), Carolina, Susana, and Margarita.[22] Sometimes, a metal ring would be slipped on a person's pinkie and another on his or her toe to increase the pain. A piece of cloth or rubber was stuffed in the mouth to prevent the victim from biting off his or her tongue. Regularly, the person would be drenched with water or forced to lie on a wet plastic sheet to enhance the intensity of the electric shocks.[23]

There were many instances of people being suspended from their wrists and ankles. Lifted from the cuffs that tied the hands behind one's back, the body's weight pulled the arms out of their sockets. Suspension and electricity were sometimes used in combination. Ana Cuadros Herrera was hung from her wrists while standing on her tiptoes. The floor was covered with water and coarse salt. Every time she touched the floor, she received a strong electric shock.[24] One person was forced to drink large quantities of water and was then given electric shocks. When water began to ooze from his body orifices even his torturers were so scared of his condition that they allowed him to recover before sending him to another torture center.[25]

Water was also used by itself as a means of torture. Many captives were brought to the verge of drowning. The so-called wet submarine involved holding a person's head under water until the moment of asphyxiation.[26] Sometimes, torturers banged the sides of the tub, causing internal bleeding and to rupturing ear drums. Another form of asphyxiation consisted of the dry submarine. A plastic bag was forced over a person's head and held tight until there was no oxygen left and the person nearly suffocated.

Beatings and blows to the head, abdomen, and joints with fists, sticks, and rubber truncheons were particularly common. A physician collaborating with the military explained to Jorge Watts that "hitting the joints made sense because it was difficult that a joint would break from a blow. It would have been easier to break my leg if they would have hit it in the middle than to break the knee. It produced a large swelling which made any movement very difficult. . . ."[27] This swelling became then a preferred target for electric shocks.

Sexual torture consisted generally of either forcing captives into humiliating sexual relations or genital torture making the captives associate pain, panic, and sexuality.[28] In Argentina, men and women were also frequently raped and sodomized, and forced to perform fellatio on their torturers. Objects would be thrust into the vagina and anus, and at times charged with an electric current.

There was also psychological torture. Many former captives agree that listening to someone being tortured is excruciating. Hearing the sound of a person gasping for air who is nearly drowned for hours on end, the screams of pain during sexual torture, and the pleas of mercy are "one of the worst tortures that a human being can suffer. . . ."[29]

Mock executions were another form of breaking people psychologically. Three days after his arrival in La Arana police station, Pablo Díaz was taken outside with several other captives. They were blindfolded. One person approached him and identified himself as the local priest. He told Pablo that they were going to be executed and asked if he wanted to go to confession. The firing squad was told to prepare, and then Pablo heard the discharges. "I was waiting for the blood to come out somewhere. I'm dead, I'm not dead, it's a second but this second lasts forever."[30]

The Montoneros assumed at first that torture should and could be resisted. Silence marked a victory over the enemy. A June 1975 article, entitled "Torture is a combat and it can be won," stated that "Torture hurts, but not the pain is unbearable but the situation and conditions in which we find ourselves."[31] Suggestions were given on how to mislead the captors and endure torture. Every guerrilla should develop a convincing story line (*un verso*) justifying his or her presence in a particular place. The more elaborate the story, the better. "One has to lie to and mislead the enemy; that is the way to fight them."[32] Torture victims should feign heart failure and exaggerate their pain. These instructions would allow guerrillas to earn a victory in the heart of the repressive apparatus. "The enemy may kill, torture, and abduct us, we may see comrades fall into their hands, but that doesn't mean that we lose the unbreakable will to win."[33]

Tellingly, the guerrilla organizations regarded torture in similar terms as the military, namely as the continuation of war in another theater of operations. They even spoke of the torture room as a battlefield in which a victory over the enemy could be achieved by resisting the interrogation.[34] Tragically enough, as Gasparini observes, winning the battle consisted for many tortured comrades in death rather than life. Death was a liberation from suffering rather than the end of life. "One had to endure the suffering before an enemy who didn't give death away. The victory was to earn one's death."[35]

The Montoneros abandoned this line of conduct in 1976. The torture practices had become so ferocious that resistance was impossible. Instead, members were ordered not to fall into enemy hands alive either through armed resistance or by swallowing a cyanide capsule. Suicide was the final sacrifice for the survival of the organization.

The PRT-ERP believed that resistance to torture was the mark of true revolutionaries whose faith prevented them from betraying comrades. The party was after all more important than its individual members. A secret internal PRT bulletin from August 1974 stated that "The high proletarian combat morale has to be demonstrated as much in the mass struggle as on the battlefield, in the torture chamber and in prison."[36] The enemy had to be defeated in the torture room by refusing to provide any information. A true revolutionary would rather die than betray his or her comrades. Only interested in protecting their organization, the PRT-ERP commanders ordered boundless sacrifice.

But could anyone prepare him or herself for torture when the interrogator's time was unlimited? Would reality not always defy the greatest imagination and most serious preparation? The prison cell will always look slightly different than imagined, the torturer's face unexpected, and the torture itself insurmountable.

Information Gathering

Information gathering was the principal rationalization for torture given to me by Argentine military. Torture was only an instrument, a technical means to expedite the interrogation. The typical justification was the hypothetical case of a guerrilla who had hidden a bomb in a nursery school. Torturing him into confession would save the children's lives. The principle behind this example was that if a lesser harm could prevent a greater harm from occurring then torture was morally justifiable.[37] General Osiris Villegas explained the inevitability of torture in counterinsurgency warfare as follows: "This war is very fast, very agile, very changeable. It's impossible. You seize an individual and you have to discover what he knows to avoid a greater damage somewhere else, he has to 'sing' as they say here, and this has to be done very quickly because you won't get anywhere if you take too much time."[38] General Tomás Sánchez de Bustamante confessed that it was very difficult "to object to a procedure that was successful and instead choose a more orthodox one, a more classic, more moral procedure that had failed repeatedly."[39] Torture served to pry open a hostile oppositional structure. Speedy information was needed to dismantle the subversive cells and prevent comrades from alerting one another.

However, the practice of torture and the information procured during the Argentine cultural war defied such facile rationalization. Generally, the interrogation was preceded by a "softening up" (*ablandar*) of the captive.[40] This softening up began already by blindfolding the abducted during their apprehension, and continued during the ride to the secret detention center. Persons would be repeatedly beaten, hit in the stomach, and stepped on while lying on the floor of a car. Once in the detention center, the person was taken to the torture room, and forced to undress. Without clothes, physically immobilized, and isolated from relatives and friends, a process of depersonalization was set in motion to enhance the feeling of helplessness.[41]

Clearly, expediency of information gathering was of little concern because the initial stage could take hours.[42] Instead, the softening up was intended to establish the ground rules of the relation between abductor and captive. The paradoxical silence of the beating interrogator served to turn the initial subject-subject relation into a subject-object relation of total dependency, one of captor and captive. The abducted victim had been a person with a home, family, name, and social status, and was now transformed into a non-person utterly isolated from family and friends, deprived of sight, immobilized, naked, and with a number instead of a name.

The torture began with the short command: "Start giving it to him." The electric prod touched the most sensitive areas of the body in search for a truth that was often not there. The interrogation itself was seldom directed at obtaining urgent, life-saving information. Many interrogations served to fill in the organigrams of guerrilla and front organizations, the political opposition, and human rights groups. Appearing in someone's address book could be grounds for torture to establish a possible involvement.[43] To which subversive organization do you belong? Who is your superior? Who are your comrades? Who are your friends? Where do they live? Where are the weapons hidden? With whom do you sleep? What is the address of Mario Firmenich? As if a sixteen-year-old high school student from La Plata would know the address of Argentina's most wanted Montonero commander. Such nonsensical questions were intended to transform the objectified captive into a reflexive object, who responded in the same immediate way to the interrogator's questions as his or her muscles contracted under the shocks of the electric prod. Body and movement, knowledge and voice, were entirely at the interrogator's disposal.

In many cases, the abducted had some background in political activism but was not a guerrilla combatant. Pablo Díaz was accused of belonging to a guerrilla organization, reading subversive magazines, and participating in the La Plata student protest. Before the first torture session began, his tormentors told him that they were going to connect him to a "truth machine" (*máquina de la verdad*). Pablo understood that they were going to administer a lie detector test, and eagerly consented because he had nothing to hide. Instead, they tortured him with an electric prod.[44] The electric prod/truth machine mirrored the state into which the torturers wanted Pablo Díaz to be transformed. Every electric discharge provoked a reflexive bodily reaction, and every question was to be answered truthfully.

In obvious contradiction, the objectified captive was told that he or she was a free subject and thus responsible for his or her own suffering. The rhetorical emphasis on information gathering served to separate knowledge from power, and substitute communication for interrogation. After all, so the torturers argued, if the detainee tells us what he or she knows then there will be no more torture. "Come on, give us the name of a kid and we leave you alone," the interrogator told Pablo Díaz.[45] Thus, he was blamed for his own pain. However, the torturer's simulated instrumental neutrality concealed that the hierarchical power relation, not the voluntary gift of knowledge, was the centerpiece of torture. Revealingly, Pablo Díaz was ordered to sign his confession blindfolded. However, he had succeeded in loosening his blindfold a bit, and saw that the sheet of paper was blank. So, he said that he could not sign what he had not read. One man grabbed him from behind, put a pen in his hand, and forced him to scribble across the paper.[46]

In sum, people in Argentina were generally not tortured for urgent life-saving information but to reveal their social networks; information that was often already known to the captors. The intelligence gathering was excellent, according to Major Ernesto Barreiro, an army intelligence officer in Córdoba during the dictatorship. "We had the files with political histories, photographs, and home addresses very, very well structured. We had things very well organized, in many at least, I'm not going to say one hundred percent, but we had lots of information, we had lots of information to begin with, lots. In Córdoba, for example, the organizations held many meetings, the photos appeared in the magazines, who they were, everything appeared, everything appeared. We had informers, there were informers, and excellent ones. . . . The intelligence was really very good."[47] In other words, everyone of the tens of thousands of people who went to a political rally of the Montoneros, who signed his or her name and address to a list for the founding of the Montoneros' Authentic Party, who went to a student protest, and who appeared in legal and illegal publications, became a potential target. They all had been spotted before the 1976 coup. Clearly, there was no utilitarian justification for torture in Argentina. Information was of less importance and urgency than the apologists of torture claimed.

Major Barreiro, who himself was accused of being the head of the interrogation team in Córdoba's La Perla secret detention center, even went so far as to deny the efficacy of torture. "I believe that, I believe that, I'd say that physical violence is an enemy of good information. I'm proud to have been one of the principal opponents to the use of physical violence. . . ."[48]

Barreiro insists that the best information is gathered through subtle methods, but admits that emotion sometimes overpowers reason. Maybe these emotions explain the traumatic experience of Graciela Geuna taken to La Perla on 10 June 1976. "They dragged me to the torture room. They undressed me and tied me to a bed frame. They used two electric prods, one of 220 volts to the body and another with a lower voltage to the face, eyes, lips and head. The one who was torturing me was the then Lieutenant Barreiro."[49]

Revenge, Invincibility, and Omnipotence

Torture was sometimes motivated by personal revenge. The infliction of pain was a retaliation for a loss suffered. One officer told a captured Montonero in late 1977: "And what were you thinking, that we were going to do nothing while almost all promotions of the Military Academy had casualities?"[50] As Major Barreiro clarifies: "When you are in front of a person who killed the son of your comrade with a bomb, or who shot a policeman with three shots in the back. . . . The sentiment is different, entirely different, totally different. I tell you this because I have seen really irrational attitudes because of this. . . ."[51] Barreiro explains how he arrived at an army unit in Córdoba whose commander Colonel Iribarren had been killed in April 1973. Iribarren was the head of intelligence of the Third Army Corps, and tried to resist a kidnapping attempt by the Montoneros.[52] "I arrived at a unit weighed down by a tremendous sentiment and the unit was, let's say, fighting for ninety-nine percent objectively against the subversion, but they reserved one percent to find the men who had killed Colonel Iribarren."[53]

One police officer was determined to find the four Montoneros who had assassinated his wife in Buenos Aires. She was taking the car out for a drive with her son and her mother. When she shifted into gear, the car exploded. The officer's wife was killed, his mother-in-law suffered lasting emotional damage, and his son had grave injuries to his limbs. The officer volunteered for particularly dangerous missions, eager to risk his life in the pursuit of revenge.[54]

The abovementioned examples harbor a specific target but there is another more diffuse level of revenge contributing to torture. This was revenge for the political violence inflicted on Argentine society. The guerrilla organizations were held responsible for destroying the Argentina of the Sunday afternoons with family and friends, the abundant barbecues, the evening strolls around the neighborhood, and the beer at a street-corner café. There was revenge for the permanent threat to their loved ones, for the "dirty work" they had to carry out, including the torture and assassination of political opponents. Many officers told me that they had resented carrying out the tasks ordered by their superiors. Trained in conventional warfare, they had been obliged to fight an invisible enemy.

Torture served also to give the task groups, intelligence officers, and policemen a feeling of power against an enemy portrayed as hiding in many disguises to destroy Argentine culture. The military's fear of the shadowy subversives—described to me by Colonel Daract as rats living in the sewers of Buenos Aires and emerging only at night to strike—was transformed into a visual and concrete enemy. Torture gave this invisible enemy an identity, albeit often a hooded and blindfolded one. Evil was contorting under the moves of the electric prod across the tied down body, and the torturer received a rush of invincibility.

Torture was a continuation as well as an inversion of war. Faced with the state of absolute dependency into which the victim had been forced, the torturer reconstructed the captive as his extension and contradiction. The victim had to respond to every command, to every movement of the torturer's hand, to act by reflex as if he were his captor's limb. At the same time, the captive was kept in a state of negation to the torturer to continue the process of imposition and subjugation. One policeman held a captive on a leash, making him bark like a dog.[55] This condition simultaneously dehumanized and encultured the captive. It asserted a continuous tension between difference and transcendence. It maintained the difference between victor and defeated, between self and other, but also enforced the transcendence of the torturer's self and cultural terms onto the captive. This contradiction continued to justify abuse.

Torture demonstrated the regime's omnipotence. Elaine Scarry has superbly analyzed the ways in which the many manifestations of pain become the insignia of power of a repressive political regime: "What by the one is experienced as a continual contraction is for the other a continual expansion, for the torturer's growing sense of self is carried outward on the prisoner's swelling pain."[56] The incontestable reality of physical pain becomes conferred on a regime needing repression to stay in power. A major rationale of torture is thus to imprint the regime's incontestability, and make clear that any resistance is futile.[57]

The presence of thousands of dehumanized captives in hundreds of secret detention centers enhanced the feeling of omnipotence for each and every member of the Argentine armed forces and police. In every zone and subzone, task groups and interrogators were extracting every detail about the revolutionary organizations and opposition groups, mapping their national networks, foreign contacts, and finances. The detention of great numbers of disappeared for years on end demonstrated the success of the antirevolutionary war. These captives were war trophies, the tangible proof of the superiority of the armed forces. Their torture proved that the cultural war could be won.

Blindfolding

Torture is a social complex whose form, method, and intensity correspond to different facets of the relation between captor and captive. A beating implies another social relation than rape. The social transgression of forced penetration is different from that of physical blows. The potential traumatization from one mistreatment or another differs so much from person to person that it is senseless to establish which abuse is worse. Still, a beating is socially unequivocal, while a rape confuses power and intimacy, and abuse and affection, by violently mimicking the sexual act between two lovers. Many social relations in the secret detention centers possessed this quality of simultaneously imitating and inverting social ties of everyday life. Physicians monitored life signs during torture, gynecologists delivered babies from blindfolded and handcuffed mothers, priests asked the condemned to confess information before execution, former guerrillas hunted after former comrades, and torturers married their victims.[58]

The beginning of a torture session already contained the shadows of the forceful abduction and the blows during the softening up stage. These past experiences forbode that captives were beyond outside help, that the future treatment could easily be worse, and that it could last forever. "Here, we have all the time in the world, time doesn't exist," said Navy Captain Pernía to Graciela Daleo.[59] The disappeared became isolated in a social space enclosed by the blindfold, the cell, the walls of the secret detention center, and the people they were forced to interact with.

Blindfolding was standard practice in the secret detention centers. The blindfold was justified by the military as functional in the counterinsurgency war because it prevented reprisals and a future prosecution of the perpetrators.[60] Be this as it may, the social and psychological reasons for blindfolding were far more important. The blindfold made the torturer faceless, thus implicitly appealing to a relationship of trust as there would exist between a surgeon and a patient. The captive's surrender was of course involuntary and therefore enhanced mistrust and suspicion. There was always the unexpected blow, the deprivation of food, and the imagined glance during the rare bath or shower. Each additional action by the torturer reestablished the terms of the relationship without erasing the physical and mental traces of previous actions, while anticipating new ones.

Blanca Buda, forty-six years old, was abducted on 30 March 1976. She had been a member of the social-democratic party Alianza Popular Revolucionario, and was detained for two years and nine months. A military court finally declared her innocent of belonging to a guerrilla organization and apologized for the mistaken arrest. On her first day of detention, her captors came to check on her in her cell and asked for her name: " 'My name is Blanca Buda! What do you want from me? I didn't kill anybody!' I received a tremendous kick against my legs just after they had opened the door violently. 'You treacherous daughter of a bitch! Shit Montonera, I'm gonna tear you to pieces!', said one of them while they shut the door with a blow."[61] The kick, the slur, the accusation, and the threat, all given within a few seconds, set the ground rules for the future meetings with her captors.

The blindfold itself served to define future relations as a torture device that could be loosened, tightened, repositioned, refreshed, and removed. Each action implied another social tie. Tightening betrayed a hostile guard, while a fresh blindfold meant empathy. Blindfolds or hoods used during a raid were often made from the captive's shirt or a bed sheet, and were replaced by a piece of cloth with an elastic band upon arrival in the secret detention center. Anticipating a longer stay, these blindfolds might be replaced with two wads of cotton attached with adhesive tape. Prolonged use of the blindfold could produce conjunctivitis and occasionally maggots.[62]

Blindfolding enhanced the pain of torture because one could not anticipate when and where the electric prod would strike. Graciela Daleo tried desperately to throw off her hood so that she could see to which parts of her body the electric current would be applied. She thus tried to influence, albeit in the smallest way, the conditions imposed on her.[63]

Finally, blindfolding served to disorient captives and reduce them to a state of helplessness which turned on them. The inability to see the material and social environment increased their confusion and delivered them physically, psychologically, and socially to their captors' whims. Mistrust gave way to a dependence on captors guiding them from one place to the next. Many captives recall their stooped entry into unknown detention centers, through passageways and down invisible stairways. Stooping was a protective posture exploited cruelly by the guards to enhance disorientation. Some would deliberately steer blindfolded captives toward walls and posts. Unable even to walk safely, their insecurity about themselves and their dependency on their captors was further increased. Personal autonomy was surrendered and nothing could be done to cope with the continued assault of the surrounding environment. With the ground rules of the captor-captive relation firmly implanted, the blindfolded were now subjected to the social world of their interrogators.

Interrogations were generally conducted by more than one person. One former captive conveyed to me the routine with which torturers went about their job, unaffected by the screams of pain. On one occasion, his blindfold fell off because of the blood running across his face. When he opened his eyes, he saw that one interrogator was quietly dipping his pastry into a cup of coffee, while his companion continued with the torture. Newspaper publisher Jacobo Timerman also noted a clear division of labor among his interrogators. "There was a person who often shouted his questions out loud, and there was someone who clearly operated the electric prod, but there was another person who pulled at my tongue, and placed an instrument in my mouth, I think, so that I couldn't grit my teeth or bite my tongue, and who also listened constantly to my heart."[64]

The social complexity of torture unfolds clearly in Timerman's description. Torture was conducted by a small group that specialized in their victim's various functions. One torturer dedicated himself to the nervous system by inflicting pain. Another focused on the mind and the information and political convictions hidden there, while the third made sure that the victim could continue to speak. Tormentor, interrogator, and paramedic were distinct social roles which the tortured recognized and responded to during brief periods of respite. The captive pleaded with the tormentor to loosen the handcuffs a bit, asked the interrogator what he really wanted, and requested a glass of water from the paramedic. Yet, all were torturers as they worked in a concerted effort on the blindfolded captive, highly aware of the fine line between damage and death.

The good guy-bad guy interrogation technique was another tested routine. One captor exploited social trust by relating to the captive as if a psychotherapist extending help, while the other enhanced fear by treating the captive as an object. Miriam Lewin was nineteen years old when she was abducted. "How are you Miriam, how are you doing? How much we have been looking for you," her abductor said sardonically when he forced her into the car.[65] He told her that nothing would happen to her if she collaborated, that he was not interested in her but in her friend Patricia. Patricia Palasuelo, the daughter of an air force brigadier, was accused of placing a bomb in the Cóndor building, the air force headquarters in Buenos Aires. Miriam's ordeal continued, "They untied my legs and raised a bit of the blindfold, and I could see that a man showed his genitals very close to me, and they told me: 'We're gonna pass you one by one, daughter of a bitch.'"[66] There were between eight and ten men in the torture room. They insulted Miriam Lewin and hit her. Her abductor caressed her hand in a protective gesture and told her, "Don't worry because nothing is gonna happen to you, if you collaborate nothing is gonna happen to you."[67] She was not raped but tortured with a dry submarine and an electric prod.

Humiliation was a crucial ingredient in establishing the parameters of social interaction between captors and captives. The abduction was humiliating in itself because the detained were degraded through beating and hooding, but humiliation involved especially the obstruction of bodily functions. Blanca Buda recalls her first hours in the secret detention center: "I felt like urinating. Probably, a reaction of fear. I tried to stand it all I could, without daring to call in order not to infuriate them, until I urinated on myself. I cried with desperation. With shame and pain, I understood the reason of the smells that hung in there."[68]

The captives' self-image conflicted harshly with the degrading behavior they were subjected to, and affected their self-esteem.[69] As Jean Améry sums up: "Whoever has succumbed to torture can no longer feel at home in the world. The shame of destruction cannot be erased. Trust in the world, which already collapsed in part at the first blow, but in the end, under torture, fully, will not be regained."[70] The ensuing damage to the self was further increased by the knowledge that others might have watched them or at least had heard their degradation. Future social relations with these witnesses, and with any other person in general, would always carry the burden of humiliation.

Sexual Torture

Sexual torture attacks simultaneously the captive's body, psyche, and sociality. Pain, humiliation, and shame are welded in a devastating assault on body, mind, self, sexuality, and identity. As Inger Agger concludes after treating abused refugees from many parts of the world, "the essential part of the sexual torture's traumatic and identity-damaging effect is the feeling of being an accomplice in an ambiguous situation which contains both aggressive and libidinal elements in a confusing mixture."[71] This ambiguity is driven to extremes in rape. Cathy Winkler has called rape a social murder. The rapist tries to sever body and self. He demands compliance and even approval, leaving a lasting and traumatizing imprint on his victim through his battery, penetration, insults, odor, terror, and humiliations.[72]

Sexual torture began in the Argentine secret detention centers always with forcing captives to undress. Nudity is generally associated with intimate settings such as the bedroom, the bathroom, and to a lesser extent, with a hospital or examination room. Forcing people to be without clothes violates cultural conventions of propriety and shame, and thus makes them feel degraded. Most disappeared were naked for months on end, and only received clothing when they were allowed to drop their blindfold and perform small tasks around the secret detention center.

The torture of the reproductive organs was standard practice in Argentina's secret detention centers. Anxieties over castration, impeded sexual and reproductive functioning, and the fear of no longer being a "real" man or an "honorable" woman were exploited in sexual torture.[73] As Marcelo Suárez-Orozco sums up the connection between the cultural war and the sexual torture of male captives: "In clandestine *quirófanos* [torture rooms] the ideological surgeons thus emasculated godless 'subversives,' *turning the feared enemy into passive, castrated beings.* . . . [and intended to create] a society of ruling *machos* and obedient, harmless *mansos* [tamed], castrated beings, that would not question orders but would just obey."[74]

The threat of rape was a most common form of sexual torture against women. Blanca Buda and her cellmates were warned in advance of the oncoming suffering. "Take notice that soon the torture will begin!" One of the torturers asked the captives: "What do you prefer: torture or that we screw you?"[75] In Blanca Buda's case, the men decided to torture her. However, one seventeen-year-old girl responded that she preferred being raped. She was gang-raped by ten to twelve men. Later, she was tortured anyway, but with an intensified brutality because, as one of the rapists said, "she had failed to hold high fundamental moral values."[76] This sadistic betrayal of an impossible choice showed the ambiguous relation between torturer and tortured. The girl was made to believe that she was an accomplice in her own rape, as if she engaged in consensual sexual intercourse. There is a perverse suggestion of pleasure in the violent gang rape that is psychologically highly confusing. Her subsequent torture complicated this relation even further as she was blamed for her torture by choosing to be raped. In the eyes of her tormentors/rapists, she had acted as a prostitute who needed punishment to put her on the right moral Christian course which the military junta had so self-righteously charted.

Rape occurs in almost all wars but is particularly likely to happen in counterinsurgency wars where women participate as guerrilla combatants. Littlewood suggests that these women are then regarded as legitimate targets of sexual violence and that their rape reduces them to a noncombatant status as women. In other words, rape redraws the boundaries between men and women blurred by guerrilla warfare, and elevates one's own women while degrading and dehumanizing the opponents' women.[77] Littlewood's interpretation can be extended further. The emphasis by the military junta on traditional family values, and the woman as mother and homemaker, contrasts sharply with the gang rape, the assault on the reproductive organs and finally, the kidnapping of newborn babies. The next chapter describes how attempts were made to transform these women into "model" women through rehabilitation programs and how stolen babies were raised by "model" military families.

The Torture of Families

Many captives tried to resist the disintegration of their sociality under torture through psychological splitting. Body and mind were temporarily dissociated, so that the captive could objectify his or her body. This survival technique became even more effective when the person succeeded in clutching to meaningful political or family ties, and thus maintained his or her projection in the world. The visualization of loved ones raised the personal defenses. "The guards didn't stop screaming at us and provoking us with their weapons. They threatened to kill our relatives. My mind held on to their memory. I saw them smiling, friendly. My husband's eyes accompanied me continuously with his deep and generous look," recalled Blanca Buda.[78]

But such daydreams could also turn into nightmares when torture took its toll with exhaustion and high fever. "I saw myself twenty years later. . . . I had returned to life after this lapse of time. One of my sons had died. I suffered his death as if it was real. My husband had remarried and had several children with his new wife. My other two children had forgotten me. There are no words to describe the pain I felt. I had loved them more than ever during these years. It was impossible that I meant nothing to them anymore."[79] The family ties were slipping from Blanca Buda, precisely what the torturers wanted. The self was nearing disintegration, and the desperation of abandonment was devastating.

Inside the Banfield center, Blanca Buda turned within herself. "Lost in a world without horizons, where everything turned spherical, my mind could no longer control things, space and time. My body had assumed a fetal position. I was swimming in a lukewarm and thick liquid inside a dark tube."[80] She tried desperately to find herself. At first by recovering her senses, smell, touch, sight and hearing. Later, she forced herself to remember, to go backwards to the past instead of forward to an uncertain future. "You have to recede every time more in years, wander in the love with your partner, in the smile of your children, in your first desire, in your first kiss! In mother, in the sweet smile of her half-open lips, rocking you in her arms, whispering a lullaby."[81] Finally, she regressed into her mother's womb, the ultimate abode of security and protection. She attempted to rebuild her life mentally from its inception, rediscovering her senses, and regaining trust.

These desires of maternal protection obtained an added significance when a mother was tortured to discover the whereabouts of her children. María Elisa Hachmann de Lande was tortured for several days but did not give in: "But if I gave life to my son, would I then bring him death?"[82] Her refusal to disclose her son's residence demonstrates that torture did not reduce victims completely to inert bodies consumed by pain. Tortured mothers like Ms. de Lande remained social beings, mothers defined by the relation with their sons and daughters. The intimate trust of the mother-child relation was unconditional and indestructible. Still, this strong attachment was at the same time a parent's weakest spot because there is no limit to human cruelty. Víctor Basterra was threatened by his torturers that if he would not talk, then they would strap his two-month-old daughter on his chest, while they would give him electric shocks.[83]

Norberto Liwski was told that he was soon going to accompany one of his daughters into the torture room. The youngest child was three and the eldest six. The attending physician told the interrogator that he could only use the electric prod on children that weighed more than twenty-five kgs.[84] In a psychological torment, Liwski was shown the soiled underpants of his little girls. "This went on and on, this torture of using the children in this way. At various occasions they told me that they had such control over my daughters that they had films of them on which I could ascertain myself—if I cared to see them—the degree of control they had over them."[85]

Nearly 250 boys and girls between the ages of thirteen and eighteen dis appeared, and many of them were tortured. Pablo Miguez, a boy of around thirteen years of age, had been abducted together with his mother Violeta. One witness testified about his emotional and physical state after he was taken with his mother to the torture room. "And when Pablito returns, he says: 'They tortured me,' and he was hurting all over, then the mother—who was a very strong woman of great human quality and moral strength—explained that they had tortured Pablito in front of her, and all this because Violeta had apparently not given them the title deed of her house. . . ."[86]

Children are particularly vulnerable to torture because the boundary between the inner and the outer world is still fragile. The torturer envelops and invades the child, literally and emotionally speaking, as an all-threatening environment. He breaks through the thin boundaries of the child's budding identity, easily fractures the inner defense shield, and saps the foundation of trust nurtured by the parents. Looking at the lacerations on his or her body, the child becomes shocked by its vulnerabilities and acquires a bodily fear of other human beings.

If Winnicott is right that infants do not remember when things went well, but only when things went wrong because "suddenly the continuity of their life was snapped. . . . ," then the tortured Argentine children became marked for life.[87] The traumatic experiences shook their confidence in other human beings, and thus affected their sociality in fundamental ways. This undermining of self and sociality was precisely what the torturers wanted to accomplish. In the case where the baby or infant was abducted, the adopted military parents would be able to raise the child anew. In the case where the children were released together with their parents, their relation would never be the same because the children would always doubt their parents' ability to protect them.

At the Navy Mechanics School (ESMA) secret detention center, torturers inserted a spoon into pregnant women to give electric shocks to the fetus.[88] Gladys de H. was six months pregnant when she was beaten, raped, and tortured with electric shocks in 1979. Her son Dario was born after her release but soon began to suffer from instability. A clinical exam determined that the electric shocks given during pregnancy had affected him during a critical stage of his fetal development.[89] Alicia Partnoy still remembers what Graciela Romero de Metz had told her after having been tortured while five months pregnant: "Each shock brought that terrible fear of miscarriage . . . and that pain, my pain, my baby's pain. I think it hurt more because I knew he was being hurt, because they were trying to kill him. . . . Sometimes I think it would have been better if I had lost him."[90] But she did not lose the baby. Her son was taken by an interrogator and Graciela disappeared.

María Luisa Sánchez de Vargas was abducted with her five-year-old daughter Josefina and her eighteen-month-old daughter Soledad on 12 June 1976. María Luisa succeeded in briefly meeting her husband in prison. Her husband told her that Josefina had been forced to watch him being tortured. After a couple of days the two children were taken to María Luisa's parents. María Luisa and her husband continued imprisoned, but several days later she was allowed to visit her parents. "I really believed that it was to please my old parents, to show them that I was alive and to allow me to renew contact with the children. But no, they took me to a funeral. And do you know whose funeral it was? It was that of my eldest child, my Josefina."[91]

What had happened? Only days after arriving at her grandparents' home, the five-year-old Josefina had taken her grandfather's gun from a drawer and killed herself. The emotional tie with her father, damaged by witnessing the torture session, was now cut definitely. The girl's image of her father as a loving, towering, and all-powerful protector must have been profoundly damaged by seeing him being humiliated and screaming in helpless despair. Josefina's suicide made her mother lose her oldest daughter and her youngest daughter lose her sister, while the father still figures on the list of the disappeared. Family ties were forever obliterated in one week. The impeded mourning for the disappeared husband and father lingered on, and the social trust of the surviving mother and daughter were permanently damaged.

Why this atrocious torture of babies and infants totally unrelated to the guerrilla insurgency? Marcelo Suárez-Orozco has argued that it served instrumental and symbolic purposes. The torture of children was an easy way to extract information from their parents. More important, torture served as a rite of separation intended to remove these children from their so-called subversive homes, sever the ties with their parents, and reintegrate them into the homes of upstanding childless military families.[92] Thus, Suárez-Orozco argues, the Argentine social landscape was re-organized according to the junta's image of an inspired Christian nation.[93] Torture was the transformation ritual needed for the transition of these children across the boundary separating the military from their enemies. Torture purified the children from their parents' bad influences, and made them receptive to the Christian values of their adopted families.

I believe that Suárez-Orozco's argument can be developed further by shifting the focus from the children to the bond between parents and children. Severance was a means and consequence rather than a goal. Placing parents in degrading situations, making them defenseless before their children, profoundly damages the trust between children and parents. The underlying objective was to alter their sociality. The children were not a target in themselves. After all, even though hundreds of children were placed in military families, many more were left with neighbors and relatives of the abducted. Not the children but the affective ties with their parents were the principal target. These ties were just as effectively cut by disappearing and assassinating the parents as by kidnapping children. Parents could not know if the children were really passed to the care of neighbors and relatives, and children were bewildered about the troubled and violent departure of their parents. Torture and forced separation attacked the emotional attachment of parents and children alike. Parents became loaded with guilt and children felt unprotected. The social trust of both was damaged and family ties wrecked, often irreparably.

The newspaper publisher Jacobo Timerman witnessed such devastation as the members of one family were tortured in each other's presence: "The entire affective world, constructed over the years with utmost difficulty, collapses with a kick in the father's genitals, a smack on the mother's face, an obscene insult to the sister, or the sexual violation of a daughter. Suddenly an entire culture based on familial love, devotion, the capacity for mutual sacrifice collapses."[94] From his cell, Timerman hears the father trying to get an apple to his children, and witnesses how the daughters try to win over a guard with the promise of an intimate relationship in exchange for sending an orange to their mother. Timerman also learns of the father's powerlessness, "that impotence that arises not from one's failure to do something in defense of one's children but from one's inability to extend a tender gesture."[95]

Listening to one's child screaming in pain, with all one's energy sapped by days of torture, physically and emotionally exhausted, unable even to shout for them to stop torturing one's son or daughter, and powerless to interfere in even the slightest way, must be one of the most devastating experiences in a human life. The child's pain summons a parental trust which cannot be acted upon. The inability to provide help under such circumstances produces an incredible anguish and disintegrates one's sense of community. Torture is therefore not the singular exertion of pain on one individual, but torture is physical, psychological, and social. Torture operates on multiple levels, on the body, the mind, family relations, political ties, and even society at large.

Traumatization and the Destruction of Sociality

The conquest of the mind was the third stage of Argentina's cultural war, following upon the demobilization of street crowds and the annihilation of the guerrilla insurgency and radicalized political opposition. The Argentine junta and most officers in active duty were willing to cross a moral boundary in the pursuit of a fundamental reorganization of their society. They felt torture to be the shortest road towards that goal. Ideologically and politically unwilling to follow democratic paths to achieve a stable society, they resorted to methods inadmissible by any moral standard, and especially by the Western values they claimed to defend. If a revolutionary war was fought over culture and spirit, so the reasoning went, then the battle would have to be waged in both arenas. As the Argentine military repeated frequently in public, the battle is fought on two fronts, the mental and the armed.

Mirroring the complementarity of war and torture, the interrogation room was known as the "operating theater" (*quirófano*).[96] The term refers both to an "operating theater" (*sala de operaciones*) in a hospital and to a battlefield or "operating theater" (*teatro de operaciones*). Thus, torture was the continuation of war into the bodies and minds of the enemy. Torture reenacted the cultural war on the captives in the secret detention centers, and made the "tumorous structure of subversion" visible and domitable.

The problem with a cultural war was that there was no decisive victory to be won because, as the Argentine military argued, subversive thought survives military defeat. "This war," said General Roberto Viola, "unlike classical war, has neither a beginning nor a final battle which crowns the victory. . . ."[97] Every triumph was only one step in a process instead of a definitive event. This processual nature of cultural warfare affected the meaning and use of torture. Torture was no longer an efficient means to achieve a decisive victory through speedy intelligence gathering, as the French had believed in Algeria; it became a prolonged operation deemed necessary to inculcate the cultural terms of the military junta's Process of National Reorganization. Torture became the continuation of war once public protest and guerrilla insurgency had been destroyed but revolutionary ideas survived.

Torture is generally interpreted in the scholarly literature as the infliction of great physical and mental pain. Most studies emphasize that torture intends to crush the victim's resistance by breaking his or her mind and body.[98] Elaine Scarry has advanced our understanding of torture considerably beyond the psychological approach with her groundbreaking analogy between torture and war. Torture no longer stands on its own but becomes related to the construction of the world, of society, culture, and self. Both war and torture injure and kill people, Scarry argues, and are displays of agency and power. Torture and war unmake the process of creation, while leaving physical, mental, social, and cultural traces. Finally, the torturer and the victorious armed forces transfer their cultural world on the victim and the defeated enemy respectively.[99]

Nothwithstanding the great insights offered by Scarry, her approach suffers from too great an emphasis on the finality of war and torture. She pays insufficient attention to the continuous processual destruction of people as social beings. My analysis of torture in Argentina reveals that the military junta and its torturers were after people's sociality, injuring the rock bottom of what makes human beings into social beings. Torture had lasting social consequences. As the physical pain subsided, the social damage remained. This damage became individuated and was shared with great difficulty with relatives and friends.[100] Such unshareability made the restoration of the damaged sociality so difficult because the person was cut loose from the outer world. When a person has lost faith in others, then this person stands utterly alone in the world as the ability to form firm social ties is crippled.

Torture in Argentina was aimed at destroying the politico-social by injuring people's sociality so that they would never again form political associations threatening the State. "You're never going to get involved any more, you'll see," so Pablo Díaz was told before one torture session.[101] At another occasion, he was told, "We're going to give you a session so that you won't forget. . . ."[102] Or, as Navy Captain Astiz told the Montonero Juan Gasparini who had already spent a year at the ESMA secret detention center: "with what has happened to you and with what you've seen, you're not going to get involved in any odd adventure anymore."[103] Torture was to imprint a lasting experience affecting the victims' political agency. Every future political action would be mentally related to the pain endured during the interrogation about such past activities, and those thoughts might have a paralyzing effect. People became traumatized in their social and political engagement with society. Their faith in other human beings, in relatives, friends, comrades, the community, and the state institutions became profoundly shaken.

Erik Erikson's insight into the development of trust helps us understand how torture affects people's sociality. Basic trust is constituted during the earliest stage of childhood when the baby learns to have confidence in its caretakers, and has the expectation that they will serve its needs and shield it from harm.[104] The mother and father protect the infant against threatening incursions from the outside world, and thus nurture faith in the family's benevolence. There are inevitable moments when the child's trust is frustrated and when the mother or father fails to provide relief from pain and discomfort, but such frustrations are generally surmounted and will lead to the development of a complete social being who does not feel threatened by the outside world.[105]

On this foundational trust established in the home, a social trust ensues that allows people to build relationships with the extended family, neighbors, friends, colleagues, and society at large.[106] Everyday practices need to continuously renew social trust, because persons cannot feed for the rest of their lives on the trust established in early childhood. Social trust is therefore not an inalienable part of the personal constitution but can disintegrate beyond recovery after undergoing violent experiences. Such experiences inflict permanent damage when people cannot accommodate them in an everyday world of safety and trust. Mistrust rules as terrifying memories keep intruding upon their relation to the world.[107]

Many torture victims have become forever distrustful of the social world, as has been amply documented in clinical studies. What made torture in Argentina during the 1976–1983 military dictatorship so pernicious was that the assault on social trust was not an aftereffect but a conscious objective after the guerrilla forces had been decimated in late 1976. The sociality of the noncombatant oppositional forces in Argentina had to be reshaped and a hierarchical social order reestablished. In this sense, torture reached as much into the heart of society as the repression of crowds and guerrilla organizations. Torture radiated from the individual to the social collectivity and destroyed Argentine society at its foundation by intervening in the dynamics of interpersonal relations. The military junta intended to reconstruct these relations from the bottom up, from the dyadic relations that make up society. In this sense, torture was a disciplinary practice by which the military impressed their idea of society onto the minds of their captives through forced resocialization, and by extension, on an Argentine people conscious of the dangers of oppositional politics.[108]

My study of torture in Argentina focuses therefore on the social universe in which people's sociality became injured and reconstructed. Torture sessions were not uniform ordeals of pain but social complexes with multifaceted relations between torturers and tortured. Clearly, there is no one reason why people were tortured in Argentina, even though the military have always maintained that gathering life-saving information was the only reason. Torture had at least nine reasons, some intentional, others implicit: (1) information gathering; (2) revenge; (3) display of invincibility; (4) demonstration of the State's omnipotence; (5) unmaking of the subverted Argentine society; (6) instilling obedience and subjugation; (7) materialization of the enduring victory by breaking the enemy's will to continue fighting; (8) destruction and reconstruction of sociality; and (9) traumatization.[109]

Torture was the third stage in a fundamental overhaul of Argentine society. The social traumatization of oppositional political forces, the dismantling of the rebellious and revolutionary self, the destruction of sociality and the resocialization of political prisoners and captives were the preferred means of cultural warfare. The deliberate alteration of the sociality of thousands of disappeared captives—namely, their capacity to make and sustain social bonds, their freedom to choose a particular social or political circle, and their faith in fellow human beings—tramples on the heart of a society which ultimately belongs to all and to no one in particular.

Chapter 12
Political Prisons and Secret Detention Centers: Dismantlement, Desocialization, and Rehabilitation

Jaime Dri's escape came as a deafening blow to the Argentine navy. Dri was a prominent Montonero held captive at the Navy Mechanics School in Buenos Aires. The former Peronist congressman had convinced his captors that he was willing to collaborate with Operation Latch (Operación Cerrojo). Operation Latch served to guard the harbors along Argentina's northern frontier against guerrilla incursions by using captives to detect their comrades. Dri was taken to Puerto Pilcomayo, at the confluence of the rivers Paraná and Pilcomayo, right opposite Asunción, the capital of Paraguay.

On Friday morning 19 July 1978, the thirty-six-year-old bald-headed Jaime Dri, known appropriately as *el Pelado*, is strolling with his twenty-year-old guard Alberto across the pier at Puerto Pilcomayo. Finding himself without cigarettes, the guard proposes to get them across the river, in Paraguay. Dri imagines a trap. He fears that they are testing his reliability as a collaborator. So, Dri warns him that crossing to Paraguay means abandoning their post, a breach of security that could get them into serious trouble. "It's only an instant. We go and come back," responds Alberto. "Yeah," says Dri, "you're right. It's only an instant. . . ." The guard wants to take a fast motorboat, but Dri suggests a barge. Barges are loaded with buses, cars, and trucks, and more important, their docking stage is further away from the customs house. "Are you going armed?" asks Dri. The guard confirms that he is carrying a pistol. Jaime Dri hints at possible trouble with the Paraguayan police if found out, so Alberto leaves his weapon behind.

Alberto and Jaime are the last passengers to board for the twenty-meter crossing. They get off, and Alberto wants to enter the first shop in sight to buy cigarettes. "Here, they sell the packets by the piece and much more expensive," says Dri. "Since we already came, let's go to Asunción, where they sell cartons and much cheaper." The guard agrees. They board a bus, and fifteen minutes later they are strolling through downtown Asunción. Suddenly, Dri spurts away. As he is about to turn a corner, he sees two policemen who are alerted by the chase. Dri begins to laugh loudly and pretends to be joking with his navy friend. The policemen also laugh, and continue on their way. But the guard catches up with Dri and grabs his arm. "*Pelado*, sonofabitch! You're escaping!" he screams. "Of course I'm escaping!" shouts Dri. He halts a cab, but the guard follows him into the rear seat. A fight ensues but Dri escapes and leaves Alberto and the cab driver squabbling over the fare.

When the navy hears of the getaway, it sends a four-man commando team to Paraguay to catch Dri. They are unsuccessful. Thanks to the intervention of Panamanian President Torrijo, Jaime Dri travels to Brazil, boards a plane to Panamá, and continues in late August 1978 to Europe to testify about the horrors of the Navy Mechanics School.[1]

Jaime Dri's escape was uncommon. Over ten thousand persons disappeared into the secret detention centers and were eventually assassinated and buried in mass graves. In addition only around a dozen captives escaped and thousands survived a short or prolonged disappearance to tell their stories of human degradation.[2] Some of them were moved to regular prisons and remained incarcerated till the rise of democracy, while the remainder of those thousands were eventually released after a positive assessment. The latter include maybe one hundred, but at least one group of over fifty former Montoneros who went through a lengthy "recuperation program" and were eventually set free.

Thousands of abducted citizens resurfaced after a disappearance of a few days or weeks. They had been interrogated by police and then allowed to return home, as happened to Lilia and Lucas Orfanó, who had been "locked up, terrorized, dying of fear, of the cold, and out on the floor" for fifteen days at the federal police headquarters.[3] If the Argentine military junta and its diplomats denied the disappearances, then why were disappeared Argentines set free?

The common explanation is that the released captives helped to spread fear. The stories of torture and abuse would give rise to a culture of fear and restrain others from engaging in political protest. Once released, many victims were so paralyzed with fear, so traumatized, that any political engagement had been sapped from them. Their testimonies certainly expanded into a culture of fear or as the torturer in the play *Mister Galíndez* stated: "You have to understand that for every job well done there are one thousand fellows paralyzed with fear. We act by irradiation. This is the great merit of our technique. . . ."[4]

Fear is spread most effectively when people believe that persecution is random. But why did the Argentine military take the risk of releasing political activists and fifty to one hundred guerrillas after they passed through a rehabilitation program when they might pick up arms again or engage anew in oppositional politics? This inconsistency can only be understood in relation to an even greater mystery: why were disappeared captives kept alive for months or even years in secret detention centers when they were already considered unfit for society?

Before addressing these questions, I describe the conditions to which political prisoners were subjected. The predicament of the disappeared is so overwhelming that many scholars neglect the fate of political prisoners. Yet, the social, psychological, and cultural dismantling of political prisoners resembled in many ways that of the disappeared captives. Inmates were tortured, subjugated, dehumanized, and desocialized in both penal regimes, thus revealing the continuation of the cultural war after arrest and abduction. As inmates of the Rawson maximum security prison were told repeatedly: "Nobody is going to leave alive from here. We're going to tear all of you apart. We're going to make you crazy, turn you into faggots, or you're going to commit suicide."[5] A joint analysis of political prisons and secret detention centers reveals that traumatization and resocialization were the principal objectives of the lengthy incarcerations.

Prisoners and Captives

The brunt of the 1976 military coup was immediately felt by the political prisoners incarcerated since the state of siege of November 1974. The prison regime worsened considerably and there was a concerted effort to break the prisoners physically, mentally, emotionally, and socially. During the first few months, prisoners were simply locked behind bars.[6] At the end of 1976, the prisoners became subjected to a devious disciplinary program. The Villa Devoto prison and the Rawson maximum security prison provide revealing cases.

According to the incarcerated psychologist and ERP member Carlos Samojedny, the male prisoners in Rawson were thoroughly interrogated in December 1976 about their family life, friendships, hobbies, religious beliefs, and political convictions.[7] This assessment served to reveal the prisoners' strengths and weaknesses, leadership qualities, and moral character. In September and October of 1977, the eight pavilions housing political prisoners were visited by eight wardens who observed the inmates, listened in on discussions and quarrels, but also struck up conversations about the military regime, the prison regulations, and especially about other prisoners. After these observers left, the prisoners were divided into three groups: G 1: unrecoverable (*irrecuperable*); G 2: semirecoverable (*semirecuperable*); and G 3: recoverable (*recuperable*).

Six pavilions were given the G 1 regime; one pavilion was designated as G 2 and one as G 3. Each group received a different treatment. For example, G 3 prisoners could listen to the prison radio channel, play soccer, and read books. There were between twenty and twenty-five recoverable prisoners in Rawson in a total population of about three hundred political inmates. They collaborated with the prison authorities.[8]

In April 1979, all eight pavilions were reclassified to the unrecoverable G 1 category. Each prisoner's conduct was periodically evaluated by an interdisciplinary board assessing his state of recoverability during lengthy questioning. With a carrot-and-stick method, prisoners would be promised better treatment if they showed remorse about having been a terrorist and decided to collaborate.[9]

The G 1, G 2, and G 3 categories were used in all prisons, including the women's ward in Villa Devoto. In Villa Devoto, G 3 prisoners could wear civilian clothing, were given more recreation time, and could do physical exercises. In contrast, G 1 women were locked in their cells most of the time, and could not share books, walk arm in arm, or embrace one another.

Captives of secret detention centers were also divided into the categories recoverable, semirecoverable, and unrecoverable. Still, there were four major differences between political prisoners and political captives. First, the former were officially acknowledged by the authorities while the latter were held in secret detention. Second, prisoners classified as unrecoverable were locked under the severest conditions, while unrecoverable captives were eventually assassinated. Third, prisoners seldom left the prison grounds, while captives were persuaded to collaborate with task groups in counterinsurgency operations. Four, recoverable prisoners were given a better treatment but remained incarcerated, while recoverable captives were sometimes enrolled in rehabilitation programs leading to their eventual release.

The boundary between political prisoners and disappeared captives was not impermeable. Captives could reappear as prisoners and some prisoners ended up disappeared. The reappearance could be ordered from the highest military echelons after persistent diplomatic pressure, but was also decided upon by lower military authorities. The disappeared captive was "whitewashed" (*blanqueado*), meaning that he or she was placed under the responsibility of the military junta, the National Executive Authority (Poder Ejecutivo Nacional), awaiting a trial which seldom took place. Sometimes, the captive became a stake in a tug-of-war between military forces, notably between army and navy, or between competing factions within the military, between legalists and hardliners. The newspaper publisher Jacobo Timerman believes that the legalist Generals Videla and Viola tried to convert his disappearance into a formal arrest but his hardline captors General Súarez Mason and Colonel Camps refused. Timerman spent thirty months in various secret detention centers. He was court-martialed but the case was dismissed for lack of evidence. Thanks to diplomatic pressure and a threat from Lieutenant-General Videla that he would resign from the presidency, Timerman was eventually expelled from Argentina after having been stripped of his citizenship.[10]

Legalization gave the disappeared a degree of protection from torture and execution but did not imply that they would be handed over to the courts. In fact, the military junta could override the justice system. When one political prisoner in Rawson complained that he had been sentenced to three years by a federal judge but had already been five years incarcerated in custody of the National Executive Authority, he was told bluntly: "But that has nothing to do with it. Imagine that you have one bill with the grocer and another with the baker. All right, you have already paid the grocer, but you still have a considerable debt with the baker. Calculate that you have at least five more years to go."[11]

Political Prisons

For many decades Argentina has had several well-known political prisons, including the Rawson prison in Chubut, the Río Gallegos prison even further south, the Villa Urquiza prison in Tucumán, Sierra Chica in Buenos Aires province, and the Villa Devoto prison near Buenos Aires.[12] Political prisoners were periodically moved. For example, Pedro Cazes Camarero was incarcerated between 1974 and 1983 in the following prisons: Río Gallegos, La Plata, Rawson, Sierra Chica, and Villa Devoto. These prisons also housed common criminals with long sentences, but political prisoners were generally held in separate quarters. More than five thousand persons were imprisoned during the dictatorship, adding to the thousands already penned up there since the 1974 state of siege.[13]

Maximum security prisons were particularly harsh. The regular cells in Rawson measured two by two meters. They contained two beds, a table and a bench, a chamber pot, and a small piece of furniture to keep personal belongings. The prisoners were under permanent surveillance through a small peephole in the cell door.[14] Solitary confinement in an empty cell of 2×0.8 meters and a ceiling at 4 meters was the most common punishment at Rawson. The floor was black and the walls were painted a dark gray to a height of 1.6 meters. There was one air hole with bars above the gray door. Without electric light, without heating in the freezing Patagonian winter, without a chamber pot, and only with a wet mattress, the isolation was total. To enhance the torment, prisoners were left naked in their cells and soaked at nightfall with a bucket of cold water.[15]

The conditions at Rawson prison changed several times during the military dictatorship. Physical torture and abuse were predominant between March 1976 and November 1978. As the human rights protests became stronger, the repression turned strictly psychological by November 1978. This psychological pressure led to a surge in suicides in 1979. Conditions relaxed in late 1980 when prisoners were allowed to read newspapers, receive mail, and were given paper and pencil.[16]

The prison authorities created an atmosphere devoid of physical, sensory, or mental stimulation. Confined to tiny cells, prisoners could only focus their eyes at a horizon one or two meters away. Their sight deteriorated through the years, obliging many to wear glasses. Walls, doors, bars, weapons, and the uniforms of the guards were all in drab gray colors. The omnipresence of gray turned into a visual punishment. When the female prisoners of Villa Devoto tried to break up the monotonous environment and asked for colored sewing material they were given thread in the colors black and white. When multicolored towels were handed out one day, they disassembled these thread by thread and made small dolls to decorate their cells.[17]

Guards tried their best to break prisoners into submission by confusing them through erratic rules and regulations, preventing them from settling into a prison routine, and meting out random punishment. "What did I feel at those moments?" asks one former inmate. "It is very difficult to describe, an infinite number of sentiments but above all a great impotence at being unable to do anything, absolutely nothing to get out of that situation, as well as much hatred and stubbornness."[18]

The prison regime was deliberately contradictory in matters of hygiene. Prisoners were exhorted to keep themselves, their cells, the latrines, and shower rooms clean, but were continuously frustrated in meeting even minimum standards. Rawson prisoners were forced to take a cold shower daily. They were not given any soap and had to stand still. They tried to avoid the freezing water by stepping aside but were immediately kicked under the cold spout and insulted for being dirty. Upon their return to the cell, they saw that the inspection team had thrown everything upside down. Those who had not been given a chance to visit the latrine found their chamber pot turned over with its feces splattered across the floor and mattress. Their feeling of human degradation was intensified by the profuse use of perfume by the prison guards.[19]

When Carlos Samojedny could no longer hold himself, he decided to defecate into his chamber pot: "suddenly the door opens: 'What are you doing?' They know, they see what I'm doing, I don't move, I look, there are three of them. 'Stand up!' I don't answer, I turn my head, I don't move. I boil inside. They look at me for a moment, 'Dirty!' screams one, he slams the door and they leave. . . ."[20] There were no chamber pots at the Villa María prison, so prisoners relieved themselves in a plastic bag and one inmate only ate the soft crumb of his bread and used the hard crust as a receptacle, throwing the urine out of the window. Another used the bread crumb to clean himself.[21]

After spending several years between prison walls, the inmates had internalized an impressive set of parallel rules and regulations corresponding each to a different guard. For example, one guard made prisoners form a line once the food arrived inside the pavilion, while another demanded that they stood in line before the food entered. Yet, each guard could suddenly change his personal rule, leaving prisoners disoriented. "The arbitrary sanction does not seek to impose discipline but to create panic. One cannot take any precaution in advance—nothing—to avoid it."[22] As in the case of torture, the guard's intention was to turn the prisoner into a shadow of himself, responding to his moves and even conditioning him to try to anticipate those moves.

Prisoners could therefore never settle into one routine, and found it increasingly hard to make personal decisions. Furthermore, they might come to accept the rules of conduct of the lenient or "good guard" as generous and humane, while condemning those of the "bad guard" as cruel.[23] Thus, the "permissive regime" became inculcated while the "repressive regime" was recognized as tyrannical. Such acceptance of the hierarchical prison world was regarded by the military prison authorities as an indication of a successful correctional education.

Broken individuals were prime targets for collaboration. The decision to collaborate and inform on other inmates occurred most often in the sick bay. The "good" doctor, nurse, or psychiatrist would tell the battered prisoner to stop his senseless suffering. Some broken prisoners did not recuperate from the brutal treatment and isolation. They had reached a stage of mental and especially social breakdown. They withdrew from the group into their cell, and refused to share anything. They did not eat well, began to hallucinate, and suffered from persecutory anxieties. Some prisoners were in such despair that they committed suicide.[24]

The prison regime was not only organized to break people individually but especially to destroy their sociality. This began by severing all ties with the outside world through a prison confinement far from home, and by restricting the contact with loved ones. Letters could at best be written once a week, and all correspondence passed through the hands of a censor. Parents could neither send nor receive drawings from their small children, thus cutting off the only viable means of communication available to them when visits were forbidden.

Visits were also exploited to create internal animosities among the prisoners. Recoverable prisoners were given more privileges than others. Unrecoverable G 1 mothers were not allowed to embrace their children.[25] Hilda Nava de Cuesta explains that the guards "put you in the courtyard for you to see. It was a way of saying, 'Look, if you show remorse for being a subversive, if you hand over people and collaborate with us, then you're going to embrace your child.' "[26] When her baby boy Mariano was eight months old, he was taken from her and passed to her parents. When he was one year old, she was able to see and touch him through the bars. Soon, the hardening prison regime forbade even such minimal physical contact and for four years she could only see him behind glass. "Small as he was, he began to cry and turned his back on me. He didn't want to be with me there anymore. He realized his powerlessness because of this window and became angry with me, he left annoyed, cried, he cried a lot. One time he began hitting the window, he wanted to break it."[27]

Inside prison walls, the guards tried to destroy the sociality by sowing dissension and placing insolvable dilemmas before inmates, for example by providing insufficient food. This problem had to be solved by the prisoner dispensing the meals. If he gave everybody a regular portion of soup or noodles, then he would be several servings short for the last few in line. He could ask for more food, but most likely the unlucky ones would go hungry for the night. If he decided to give everyone a smaller portion, then all ate but it meant that the next day they would receive the same inadequate amount.[28] Such dilemmas caused tensions within the group because whichever solution chosen was resented either by some or by all. Nevertheless, there were also acts of generosity in which a prisoner secretly passed food to a hungry comrade. Such a gift can be interpreted in functional terms as a survival strategy, an investment in social ties upon which one could draw on in hard times. Yet, it was just as much a way to recover one's own humanity and prove to oneself and each other that, despite the inhuman conditions, they were still human.

Isolated from the outside world and at odds with fellow inmates, the prison regime tried to take individual prisoners apart fiber by social fiber. What did such dismantling of sociality mean? It meant cutting every imaginable social tie which constituted prisoners as social beings. The guards understood intuitively that exchange is essential to sociality. Without exchange there is hardly any room left for a meaningful social relation, and without social relations people become pitiful shadows of themselves, surviving on the memory of past attachments. So, at times, the prison authorities forbade prisoners to share food, clothes, cigarettes, words, gestures, and glances. Inmates could also be isolated in solitary confinement for weeks on end. They could only maintain social relations with guards and torturers. Yet, these ties were perverted with mistrust, uncertainty, and abuse. Such relations damaged people's social trust. The taken for granted feeling that others will reciprocate in a social relationship was profoundly shaken.

Nevertheless, despite the ingenious ways to destroy people's sociality, the prisoners found ways to restore themselves as social beings. It was summoned through something as seemingly insignificant as a sneeze, a cough, or the clearing of the throat. These sounds betrayed the presence of others, and common bodily functions. Soon, several prisoners were making similar sounds as a form of corporal communication. Even the contact with the guards was exploited as an indirect means of communication. A prisoner asked to be taken to the bathroom. The guard denied it, but the following prisoner and the next one asked the same, both as a way of communicating a common need and as a subtle protest against the intolerable prison conditions.[29]

Despite the terrible prison conditions, the maltreatment, beatings, and sometimes executions, the political prisoners were better off than the disappeared. The inmates were at least acknowledged by the junta, and most survived their lengthy incarceration even though more than eighty prisoners were assassinated between 1976 and 1980.[30] Most disappeared prisoners instead ended up in a ditch or an unmarked grave or were dumped at sea after having spent months or years in a secret detention center or pit (*pozo*). Such a center was also known as a *chupadero*, which literally means a "place that sucks up people," but the free translation "black hole" seems more appropriate.

Secret Detention Centers

The first secret detention center was established in late 1974 at the police headquarters in San Miguel de Tucumán as part of the upcoming Operation Independence against the rural guerrilla insurgency. The first military center was the Escuelita de Famaillá in Tucumán province, run by the army beginning in February 1975. The last center opened sometime between August 1978 and February 1979 in Buenos Aires.[31] Most secret detention centers arose in 1976 and ceased to function between 1978 and 1979. The nearly eight-year-long operation of the Navy Mechanics School center between March 1976 and November 1983 was exceptional.

The 1984 CONADEP truth commission report listed 340 secret detention centers, a number updated in 2001 to 651 centers operative at one time or another.[32] There were many small and only a few large centers. Most centers had one or two rooms or a cellar where captives were held. The largest centers were the La Perla center in Córdoba, the Campo de Mayo army base, and the Navy Mechanics School in Buenos Aires. Through these centers passed respectively an estimated 2,200, 3,500, and 4,000 disappeared.[33]

The distribution of the centers followed the operational organization of Argentina into defense zones, subzones, and areas. Most subzones and areas ran their own centers because each task force jealously guarded its territory, and particularly its residents and material possessions. Information was the precious good that most directly brought the task force into existence, and war booty was its reward. Most captives were interrogated in the area of their abduction, held captive in a local center, and eventually buried in the area's mass graves.

Less than one-third of the centers were located on military bases and garrisons, while almost half existed in police buildings, stations, and precincts.[34] This distribution is understandable given that the police, unlike the military, had always played a prominent role in the repression of political opponents. The police possessed furthermore an elaborate infrastructure with cells and jails, and had a long and sorry tradition of brutal interrogation. The guards of the centers belonged generally to the gendarmery, the various police forces, or the federal penitentiary system. Conscript soldiers participated rarely.[35] Nevertheless, it is important to emphasize that military officers were in charge of all centers because the combined police forces were commanded by the armed forces.

Captives were given an identification number when entering a secret detention center. A card file was drawn up with their political affiliation and the names of family members. Sometimes a snapshot and fingerprints were taken. For example, the Navy Mechanics School gave all captives a number from one to one thousand, and would then start again at one. Each captive had a file containing his or her history, where the abduction had taken place, to which guerrilla or political organization he or she belonged, a life history written by the captive, and a final sentence. The letter T for *traslado* (literally: transfer) signified a death sentence. The letter L for *libertad* meant that the person would eventually regain his or her freedom.[36] In El Vesubio center, the letter P was placed before the identification number to designate that the person was a *perejil*, a wimp or a softy, and was thus not considered dangerous.[37]

Captives were held under degrading circumstances: naked, hooded, dirty, covered with sores, and with chronic infections and coughs. These subhuman conditions trampled on people's personal dignity and served to lower their self-esteem. The feeling of human degradation was enhanced when captives saw one another, emaciated, with dirty hair and an unkempt beard. Some walked with an awkward gait because of prolonged torture, dragging their exhausted bodies to the bathroom where they evacuated themselves in eternal fatigue. Such sights could not help but make each captive imagine that he looked the same, and that the deterioration of his mind would soon catch up with that of his body.

Just passing the day without being tortured could still be a major torment. The secret detention center at Campo de Mayo was located in several stables, and hooded captives were obliged to remain immobile in backbreaking positions: "we prisoners were made to sit on the floor with nothing to lean against from the moment we got up at six in the morning until eight in the evening when we went to bed. We spent fourteen hours a day in that position. . . . We couldn't utter a word, or even turn our heads." One captive had been forgotten by the torturers and he sat there immobile day in day out. When the mistake was found out, an interrogator "decided to 'transfer' him that week, as he was no longer of any interest to them. This man had been sitting there, hooded, without speaking or moving, for six months, awaiting death."[38]

Crucial for survival was first to figure out where one was being held, and what the unwritten rules of conduct were. This understanding gave captives a sense of mastery lost during torture, and helped them to anticipate what the guards might do next. If the guards walked slowly, then they came only to observe. If they walked fast, then torture was likely.[39] This learning process helped them to reconstitute a fragile self intent on survival, as if a new lease on life had been won. However, such hope was of course illusory because routines were broken deliberately to keep the hooded captives dangling from a thin thread that could pull them suddenly into a pit of despair with only one fatal exit.

All normal bodily functions were trampled. People slept naked on a cement floor or had to rest sitting because the cell had been cramped beyond capacity. Captives were prevented from maintaining their personal hygiene. There was not the contradictory prison regime where cleanliness was demanded but intentionally impeded. In the secret detention centers, lack of hygiene was a means to degrade captives and trespass on deeply engrained cultural notions of purity and shame. Going to the bathroom was always highly stressful because one never knew when permission was granted and whether one would be mistreated. At El Vesubio, the captives were taken to the latrine together, "all detainees of the place had to form some sort of little train, and some sadistic guards even made them hit against trees that were there. . . ."[40]

The continuing degradation assaulted and overwhelmed the captive's inner defenses which serve to screen incoming influences. Harmful intrusions could no longer be prevented and the person was at the mercy of his or her captors. The demolishing of these psychological boundaries mirrored the physical intrusions suffered during torture. Such dehumanization was in one particular instance transformed into animalization. One guard at the Club Atlético center had his eyes set on a Jewish captive. "He would make him wag his tail, bark like a dog, lick his boots. It was impressive how well he did it, he imitated a dog as if he really were one, because if he didn't satisfy the guard, he would carry on beating him. . . . Later he would change and make him be a cat. . . ."[41]

The disappeared captive was deindividualized and especially desocialized. The deindividualization was accomplished in ways resembling those of Nazi concentration camps. Captives were given numbers. Clocks were removed to deprive them of a sense of time. The boundaries between inner and outer were violated during physical and psychological torture, and shame barriers were torn down during body searches and bathroom visits.[42]

Torturers exploited the helplessness of their weakened captives to the extreme. Traumatized and barely able to cope in their uncertain environment, captives were so desperate for human contact that they clung to their captors, a social bond also pursued by the latter. "Both parties seem to feel some need of the other: for the torturer, it is a sense of omnipotence, without which he'd find it hard perhaps to exercise his profession—the torturer needs to be needed by the tortured; whereas the man who's tortured finds in his torturer a human voice, a dialogue for his situation, some partial exercise of his human condition—he asks for pity, to go to the bathroom, for another plate of soup, he asks for the result of a football game."[43]

Completely isolated from the world and their fellow-inmates, some went insane. The El Vesubio center had rooms with "broken people" shown as trophies to high-ranking officers.[44] These captives demonstrated the success of the desocialization process and presented a victory reaching into the minds of the enemy, the minds from which sprouted, according to the military, subversive ideas that changed the Argentine way of life, poisoned children, destroyed the family, and created chaos.

The routine regime in the secret detention centers resembled that of the political prisons during their harshest times. Captives were strictly forbidden to maintain social contacts. Their ties with the outer world had been radically cut because of their disappearance. Their inner world of identification with relatives and friends had been severely damaged or repressed through psychological splitting. Some captives became so withdrawn within themselves that they fled across the boundaries of life into death or madness. Jacobo Timerman contemplated both steps during his captivity. He often thought about committing suicide but always held back by treating suicide as a precious fruit, only to be consumed in his darkest hour. The thought of suicide could even give a feeling of empowerment because it placed the captive on an equal footing with the torturer as both surrendered to the use of violence.[45]

Suicide and madness were the symptoms of desocialization. They were antisocial responses to a total dismantling of a person who no longer desired to maintain existing relations or longed for a renewal of old ties. Such desires were assassinated in the secret detention centers, and only collaboration or a withdrawal into a private, psychotic world seemed the two forms of existence available.

Degradation, Collaboration, and Resistance

The labor union activist Luis Pérez was brought to the El Vesubio center in a deplorable state, "aside from being physically very beaten up, he was morally destroyed, didn't want to eat, didn't want to drink water, and didn't want to talk." One night, according to the testimony of Jorge Watts, he called for a doctor because of a broken rib. The physician examined him, and said he was fine. Later, "he became delirious, that is to say, asking for things, calling the guards, screaming, asking for water, something that was totally forbidden. . . ." Two guards arrived and kicked him until he stopped screaming. A few minutes later, he began again and was kicked continuously, "until there comes a moment that they give him an injection of, I don't know what, that calms him down for a little while, but later he began to scream again. They returned to kick him and after being in agony he died later on."[46] That day was the fortieth birthday of Luis Pérez.

The captive's conduct after his or her social death revealed the effect of the dismantling process. Luis Pérez resembled the so-called *Muselmänner* or walking dead in Nazi concentration camps who were also killed by lethal injection.[47] However, such total apathy was just as rare as a successful escape from a secret detention center. Between these two extremes there were many grades of collaboration and resistance.

Individuals received better treatment if they collaborated, even though the term collaboration carries an unintended overtone of voluntary choice. Captives could be forced to cooperate under death threats to them and their families. Collaboration could be passive or active. Active collaboration meant a direct involvement in repression and counterinsurgency. Passive collaboration consisted of carrying out household chores like sweeping, cleaning, cooking, and distributing food.

The Club Atlético center had a prisoner council whose members were allowed to move about without a blindfold, perform household chores, and take care of captives after torture. The group ate together, and took baths more frequently. At other places, they could watch television and smoke cigarettes, but could also be suddenly beaten up to dispel any hopes for the future.[48] Such passive collaboration allowed inmates to survive and provided opportunities to help others.

Some captives became involved in active collaboration. They accompanied task groups on their search missions, cruising the streets of Buenos Aires, Córdoba, La Plata, and Rosario. They were stationed at bus terminals, airports, harbors, ferries, and railway stations with the task of pointing out guerrillas and political activists. The collaborator was called a marker (*marcador*) or finger (*dedo*). Jaime Dri had feigned being such a collaborator.[49] Even children were involved in these operations. Five-year-old Josefina Vargas, who was to kill herself with her grandfather's gun a few days after having seen her father being tortured, was taken to the Mendoza bus terminal to identify comrades of her parents.[50]

The active collaboration reached sometimes even into the torture room. A captive physician at the ESMA center examined Víctor Basterra after he suffered a cardiac arrest, "and he said that given my condition they could continue with the torture; they hit me with sticks on my stomach. . . ."[51] One female captive, called Lucrecia, provided medical care to captives and could even influence the length of the torture sessions.[52]

The total disregard for human life by the executioners of the dirty war was shown nowhere more dramatically than in the treatment of pregnant women. Adriana Calvo de Laborde gave birth to a baby daughter on 15 April 1977 while she was being moved from the La Plata police station to the Banfield secret detention center in the company of two policemen and the captive nurse Lucrecia. As the police car was traveling at high speed to Buenos Aires, Adriana was feeling contractions. Although handcuffed, she succeeded in removing her underpants, and her baby was born on the back seat: "my baby was born well, she was very tiny, she was hanging from the umbilical cord because she had fallen from the seat. She was on the floor. I asked them to, please, hand her to me so that I could have her with me, but they didn't give her to me. Lucrecia asked for a rag to the one sitting in front, who cut a dirty rag and with that they tied the umbilical cord, and continued on their way. Three minutes had passed. My baby was crying, I continued with my hands behind my back, with my eyes covered. . . ."[53]

When they arrived at the Banfield center, the policemen parked the car, and left Adriana and her baby abandoned for two or three hours with the four car doors wide open. The baby continued to lie on the floor of the car, crying. Finally, the gynecologist Jorge Bergés arrived, cut the umbilical cord, and took Adriana to the detention center. He removed the placenta under a shower of insults, and ordered her to clean the floor, her clothes, and her baby.[54]

Even though captives had far fewer opportunities for acts of defiance than political prisoners, there were still sufficient instances for passive resistance. These were subtle ways to reverse the regime of dismantling imposed by the captors. Refusing to carry out a demand, pleading ignorance of a rule, deliberately misunderstanding an order, and even an inopportune glance at a guard were all acts that asserted the captives' agency, and more important, revealed that their sociality had not yet been fully destroyed.

There were also acts of resistance directed at maintaining group feelings. The embrace of a hooded female captive, an offer to get coffee, a gift of food and clothing, replacing a deteriorated blindfold, turning a bound, gagged, and sore victim on his or her other side, these and many more gestures of compassion could not return the captive's personal dignity but alleviated the suffering a bit and restored some faith in at least one human being.

The most active form of resistance was escape. There were a few spectacular getaways such as the one by Jaime Dri. The Montonero Horacio Domingo Maggio escaped from the ESMA on 17 March 1978 by jumping from a truck taking him elsewhere after thirteen months in captivity. Maggio was reincorporated in the guerrilla organization and participated in less than a month in the assassination of Miguel Tobías Padilla, an undersecretary at the Ministry of Economy. On 4 October 1978, Maggio had a fire fight with an army unit. He soon ran out of ammunition and refusing to surrender alive, began throwing stones at his assailants from a building under construction until they shot him dead. The corpse was taken to the ESMA, and its captives were forced to file by the bullet-ridden body to demonstrate the futility of escape.[55]

Rehabilitation and Resocialization

Allen Feldman has observed how the oral histories of torture in Northern Ireland pay much attention to the spatial order of incarceration. The suspect travels through police stations, interrogation centers, and prisons while the State inscribes its power on the captive's body. Feldman's analysis of the "architecture of coercion" significantly enhances our understanding of the complex relation between space and violence.[56] Argentine torture accounts pay an equally great attention to the topography of the secret detention centers, and could easily be analyzed in terms of Feldman's framework. However, my analysis is not concerned with the body but with sociality. The move of a captive from one space to another signaled changing social relations. Each successful passage meant for the captive another victory over death, and for the captors another step in the resocialization program. The Argentine accounts paint a social universe in which the captive's social transformation from "subversive" to "citizen" took place, as will be shown through an analysis of violence, space, and sociality in the Navy Mechanics School.

The secret detention center at the Navy Mechanics School, ESMA, was not an ordinary center. It has been called an elite center because of the professionalism of its task group and its specialization in the capture of high-ranking Montoneros. This assignment even led naval officers to Europe on search-and-destroy missions of the highest Montonero commanders. The ESMA also provided support to retired Admiral Massera's political career, and operated an elaborate rehabilitation program. The ESMA deserves close attention precisely because it reveals dimensions which remained underdeveloped in most other centers.

The ESMA was a complex sociospatial universe. Aside from the building for the technical training of NCO's from which its name was derived, the grounds contained other buildings such as the Naval War College, and the Naval Officers Mess (Casino de Oficiales). The secret detention center was located in the three-story Naval Officers Mess. It was comprised of three floors, a basement, a large attic, and a smaller second attic which used to hold the building's water tank. The first floor housed the offices of the ESMA task group. The private quarters of the naval officers were located on the second and third floor, and of course off-limits to captives. Around four thousand captives passed through the ESMA, of whom about two hundred were released.[57]

The ESMA's nerve center was a large room on the first floor known as the Gold Room (Dorado). Here, the intelligence team gathered information and the operational team planned its abductions. Here, the captive's entire journey through the secret detention center was conceived, from abduction to death or freedom.

The Basement (Sótano) was the place of entry for the captives into the world of the secret detention center, where the ground rules were established through lengthy torture, and an interrogation sought to extract information or simply break the captive without any immediate objective in mind. The Basement measured twelve by thirty-five meters, and was subdivided by movable partitions. In March 1976 it contained one dozen interrogation rooms, five torture rooms, an infirmary, one bathroom, a bedroom for the guards, a photography lab, and an office to forge documents. In October 1977, the basement was remodeled. The number of torture rooms was reduced to three, the interrogation rooms were removed, and the dark room was enlarged.

The remodeling implied a changing of relations between guards and inmates. A new space was added, called the Eggcup (Huevera). This room was made soundproof with carton eggcups and a rubber floor. It functioned as both a torture room and an audiovisual recording room. Next to the Eggcup, the recoverable captives ate and watched television. Carlos Muñoz testified that "one noticed that the image disappeared every time they were using the electric prod. Thus it seemed as if the electric prod was eating it. Thus, by the way the television image was being eaten, we could tell how much [electricity] they were giving."[58]

The Hood (Capucha) was located in the large attic. The electric light was on day and night. There was no heating and no ventilation. There were also three bathrooms and three showerrooms for the captives. A move from the Basement to the Hood marked the transition from dehumanization to desocialization. Captives were kept for extended periods in a state of vegetation, abandoned to themselves, their nightmares and fears. The people in the Hood were held in windowless cabins (*camarotes*) made of rubble-work and closed with hardboard doors. There were also narrow cubicles (*cuchas*) of 2 × 0.7 meters, and only seventy centimeters high, into which hooded, handcuffed, and shackled captives were shoved. Norma Arrostito, who had participated in the 1970 kidnapping of Lieutenant-General Aramburu, was kept there for two years, chained to a twenty-five-kilogram cannon ball, before being assassinated by lethal injection.

The major attic also housed the Large Storeroom (Pañol Grande) where the war booty was kept, anything from clothing to television sets and refrigerators. When we consider that material possessions are imbued with personal meaning for their owners, then the Large Storeroom mirrored the Hood. Personal identities were dismantled in both places, and the seizure of property forbode the destiny of their owners. In the description of one former captive: "One could smell death inside there. There were two large mounds of all sorts of clothing, whose bases were more than four meters wide and about three meters high. The dresses, pants, and shirts of thousands of disappeared were there."[59] The plunder of the ESMA task group was so extensive that it even set up a real estate agency to sell stolen property.

The life of an unrecoverable captive ended at the Little Hood (Capuchita). The Little Hood was located in the second and smaller attic of the Naval Officers Mess. It contained between fifteen and twenty tiny cubicles in which hooded captives were held before boarding a plane and being dumped at sea in the southern Atlantic ocean, that boundless dominion of the Argentine navy.[60]

Little is known about the rehabilitation programs of the Argentine military, in how many secret detention centers they functioned, and how many people passed through them successfully. There was only one official Resocialization Institute near Buenos Aires, which opened its doors in June 1977 to house remorseful guerrillas who had surrendered voluntarily. An investigative committee of the Organization of American States visited the Institute in September 1979 and found thirty-four inmates, including four of their children, receiving individual and group therapy to prepare them for a return to society.[61] Whatever the true extent of the secret rehabilitation programs, Jaime Dri has stated that the army, in the person of General Galtieri, sought to incorporate Montoneros into its nationalist political project because they were after all Catholics and nationalists, while the navy left dozens of Montoneros alive to work in Admiral Massera's political campaign.[62]

Recoverable captives suffered, endured, and survived the entire trajectory from abduction to liberation, from the Basement to the Hood to home, always by way of torture, disappearance, and lengthy incarceration. Each space had its own codes and social relations, and the passage to another space implied the access to small benefits. No longer blindfolded and shackled in a cubicle, they were now moved to a cell in the Hood. These privileges were for the captors an expression of the small steps toward total resocialization, toward the rebirth of a new Argentine citizen inculcated with Christian civilization, loyal to the Argentine State, and respectful of its authorities.

In August 1977 the Large Storeroom was transformed into the Fish Bowl (Pecera) with offices of hardboard and transparent acrylic panels. It was called the Fish Bowl because the captive workers were held alive as fish in an aquarium, and under constant surveillance by closed-circuit television and the eyes of the naval officers peering inside. When a captive responded well, he or she was ordered to carry out small tasks, such as translating and summarizing newspaper articles. The passage to the Fish Bowl entailed also a transition from dependency on guards to carrying out orders by officers. The captive was now part of the "staff." At the beginning, the captives' hoods were taken off inside the Fish Bowl, but the shackles were kept. As confidence increased, they were permanently without hoods and shackles.

Graciela Daleo, who worked as a typist, strongly rejects the term collaboration to describe her participation. She argues that the people in the Fish Bowl functioned as slave labor. Refusing such work would lead to certain death. "Thus, I took the following decision in there: within certain limits, I'm willing to survive here—that's why I told you that I was dead on the day they abducted me—and afterwards I'm going to recuperate my relation with life. . . ."[63]

The Fish Bowl contained a library with thousands of books stolen during house raids, a documentation center with newspapers and magazines, and a room with two teletypewriters. The possessions taken from the captives were now reappropriated under new circumstances. Captives were forced to use the knowledge stored in their books to assist their repressors. Furthermore, this inverted restoration of meaning was extended to the captives themselves. Captives were assigned tasks that drew on their professional skills. These tasks attempted to return the captives to their old professional identity with new values. At a certain moment, captives could even spend the night at home and return in the morning to continue with their work.[64] Persons working in the Fish Bowl were considered salvagable, and about 70 percent of them were eventually set free.[65]

In addition to the "staff," there was a "mini-staff" that had earned the highest degree of confidence.[66] According to several survivors and escapees, the ESMA began to appropriate the "gray matter" of former Montoneros for Massera's political campaign. Massera aspired to be a new Perón, and the think tank of captives commented on his speeches and infused them with a higher dosage of nationalist rhetoric.[67]

Even though recoverable captives might be working in the Fish Bowl, they were under constant scrutiny to test their social dismantlement. Graciela Daleo felt destroyed inside when a close fellow-captive was savagely tortured. She went to her small cell and only there allowed herself to cry because, "crying was a sign of weakness or that one had not recuperated, therefore, when one wanted to cry one did so secretly. . . ."[68] Likewise, Miriam Lewin could not demonstrate any emotion when she listened to others being tortured, "because the fact of being affected by the screams of torture is a symptom of not being recuperated. . . ."[69]

The captors tried to destroy the captive's social world in its spiritual, ideological, cultural, and emotional dimensions by making him or her believe that the only way to come out alive was by accepting the terms and rules set in the secret detention center. This conditioning entailed the imposition of the regime's worldview on the victim. The captors tried to reverse the process of revolutionary warfare which the revolutionaries had defined as "the conquest of the minds and hearts of the masses."[70] Dismantling and resocializing captives were the objectives of the counterconquest, while torture, disappearance, and human degradation were the preferred weapons. Torture struck at the social and the cultural through body and mind, with the social referring to the ability to associate with others and the cultural to the content of those associations.

Captives were ordered to write their life history as a decisive step in their social rebirth. These autobiographies were to be a self-critique. The disciplinary regime which forbade and punished any use of reflexive forms, such as "I think" and "I believe," now ordered such self-reflexivity to test the degree of resocialization. Miriam Lewin was still in the hands of the air force when asked to write her story: "I wrote a manuscript in which I revalued my life in a straight manner, and I showed remorse for having tried to commit suicide. . . ."[71] Her captors were so impressed that they ordered her to read her statement before a group of officers. The meeting was videotaped. A few weeks later, one officer came to her with good news: "You're reborn, kid. What you wrote fell really well, so we have decided to save your life. . . ."[72]

In another assessment, Miriam Lewin was asked what she thought about family, whether she believed in God, and in which historical era she would like to have lived. These interrogations reversed the objectification process established through torture. The captive could drop the blindfold, sit down, smoke a cigarette, and be called by his or her first name. This deceptive freedom contained great danger. A wrong answer under torture prolonged the torment but a wrong answer in what the interrogator perceived as an open conversation could mean that a person was not rehabilitated, was considered unfit for society, and would be assassinated. They asked Miriam Lewin where she would like to be taken. She asked to be sent to relatives in the U.S., but they added her to the ESMA "staff," working for Admiral Massera.

The final phase of the ESMA rehabilitation program consisted of a slow renewal of contact with the outside world, a hesitant step away from the surveillance of the captors. This meant that the captive was no longer disappeared, at least not for his or her relatives, because he or she was not granted a legal status as a political prisoner. Miriam Lewin's first step towards freedom was one phone call a month to her family. Later, she visited them in the presence of two officers, and eventually spent a night or weekend at home. When released in January 1979, she was forced to continue working for Admiral Massera's political campaign in his downtown Buenos Aires office.[73] She was threatened that if she fled, then the price would be paid by her relatives and her captive comrades at the ESMA.

A captive was considered recovered when the officers felt that he or she had acquired Western and Christian values, even though they never explained precisely what they meant. Sara Solarz de Osatinsky was asked about her life and given a large number of tests by a naval psychologist. Apparently, she passed the exam because she was allowed to leave the country, even though the naval officers made her understand that "they were the masters of life and death," and that they could take her life whenever they wanted.[74] Graciela Daleo observes that they wanted her to abandon feelings of social solidarity, and become a complete individualist. She was told repeatedly, "it's an individual process here, you have nothing to do with the rest, everything has to do with you. . . ."[75]

Even after release, the intrusion into the former captives' lives did not end. When visits to the ESMA were no longer needed, naval officers sometimes called their former captives, asking if they were doing well or in need of help. Three weeks after Elena Alfaro was freed from El Vesuvio center in November 1977, she gave birth to her son Luis Felipe. To her surprise, she received a visit in January 1979 from her former captor Colonel Franco Luque. Luque asked her why she had not yet baptized her son, and told her to do so. On 20 January 1979, her son was baptized with Colonel Luque as the godfather.[76]

Cultural War and Traumatization

The release of disappeared citizens and guerrillas by the Argentine military has often been explained as a sinister means to spread a culture of fear among the revolutionary insurgency and the Argentine people. This explanation is adequate to understand the freeing of the thousands detained briefly to ascertain whether they posed a real threat. However, the culture of fear argument fails to account for the predicament of either the more than ten thousand disappeared who were eventually assassinated or those released after spending an extended time in captivity. There are six reasons why thousands were not assassinated immediately and a number of captives were finally allowed to live.[77]

First, there were utilitarian reasons. Some captives might supply information to the counterinsurgency war. Others agreed to collaborate with the task groups. Again others were kept alive to extract ransom payments from desperate relatives. There were also captives, notably at the Navy Mechanics School, who were used as forced laborers. Furthermore, the continued presence of captives gave the secret detention centers a reason for existence by providing permanent tasks to guards and torturers. These utilitarian reasons have some explanatory value but do not explain the common pattern of an extended captivity of the already condemned.

Second, captives were war trophies, material proof of the military's superior force, while torture gave task groups the confidence that they were winning the fight against the revolutionary elements in society. The captives' pain embodied their victory, and the lasting posttraumatic aftereffects of the defeated secured their triumph.

Third, condemned captives served as guinea pigs to test the penal regime's effectiveness in dismantling and resocializing people. The political prisons and secret detention centers were institutional expressions of natural law structured along strictly authoritarian and hierarchical relations with military officers at the top and "subversives" at the bottom. The harsh regime was justified as a way to inculcate notions of hierarchy, order, discipline, and morality. The Process of National Reorganization, which was to guarantee the glorious future of Argentina, thus came to rest on the immoral pillars of abduction, torture, disappearance, assassination, and traumatization.

The treatment of political prisoners provides additional support for this third reason. They could not simply be done away with, so unrecoverable prisoners were subjected to a systematic resocialization aimed at inculcating notions of hierarchy, obedience, and dependency. Since these prisoners had been given up for society, they were not granted any restorative benefits as the dismantling reached completion. On the other hand, released captives were considered to have responded so favorably to the penal regime that they were believed to be recoverable for society. A select number were enrolled in rehabilitation programs.

Fourth, the freed captives proved for the Argentine military the soundness of their uncompromising antirevolutionary strategy and the success of their national reorganization program. If even revolutionaries could be resocialized into law-abiding citizens then they were a living proof that Argentine society could be remade in a similar fashion.

Fifth, the survivors confirmed for the military that they themselves held the highest moral standards, and acted upon their Christian belief in allowing captives to express remorse, ask for forgiveness, and gain redemption. There were certainly high-ranking officers, like the flamboyant Admiral Massera, who spoke about Christian values with rhetorical cynicism but others, such as the ascetic Lieutenant-General Videla, had deep religious convictions nurturing a self-righteous, holy war mentality.

Sixth, the extended suffering of already condemned captives can only be fully understood within the larger framework of the cultural war. The military were not simply after killing every subversive but continued their battle into the selves of prisoners and captives. The violent abduction, lengthy torture sessions, and subhuman regime during captivity dismantled people's sociality and left an indelible imprint on their bodies, minds, and selves. Traumatization was a sign of victory. The Argentine armed forces, and by extension the individual captors, confirmed their omnipotence by destroying their captives' will to fight and their ability to form political associations. Once this process was accomplished there was no more use for the traumatized, and if an individual proved stronger than the desocialization process then there was always the execution as a final proof of absolute power. For example, the legendary Montonera Norma Arrostito held her morale high for nearly two years at the Navy Mechanics School before she was assassinated.[78] Captives were thus assassinated either when they did not show any signs of desocialization or when desocialization was complete, when little of the person remained standing that could be crushed under the weight of captivity. Only those who recovered from the abuse were believed fit to contribute their talents to the New Republic.

The number of disappeared passing through some sort of rehabilitation program was small, maybe around one hundred, while more than ten thousand disappeared captives were assassinated. Still, these programs should not be dismissed as a cruel ploy to mislead the disappeared, as justifications to searching relatives, or a pretense of good intentions in the case officers would be brought to trial.[79] The resocialization of guerrillas and political activists was a way to reap a definite victory in the cultural war. In fact, the release of former guerrillas demonstrates why the dirty war was not just a counterinsurgency war but a cultural war. Resocialization was for the military proof that they had God and truth on their side, that Thomist thought was stronger than Marxist ideology, and that the natural order prevailed over the class struggle as the guiding framework of society.

The Argentine rehabilitation program consisted of four phases. The first phase was directed at disintegrating the old self. The abduction, softening up, interrogation, and torture accomplished a social death, as was described in chapters 10 and 11. The second phase, analyzed in this chapter, served to evaluate the person's conduct after social death. Some became apathetic, others collaborated, and again others resisted any attempt to destroy their personal and political identity. At this stage, decisions were made about life and death. The third phase accomplished a social rebirth through the construction of a new self. Potentially recoverable persons were allowed to drop their blindfold and ordered to carry out small tasks. Personal dignity was slowly restored with such privileges as ordinary clothes, better food, and bathroom facilities. At the Navy Mechanics School, captives were forced to perform tasks that coincided with their old profession. The final phase was the slow reincorporation into society by periodic visits to relatives or even a trip abroad. Captives were allowed a taste of life outside the secret detention center, yet remained under surveillance, while assessment talks with a supervising officer took place occasionally.[80] The ESMA rehabilitation program contains these four phases most clearly, but the first three were common elsewhere.

Was the resocialization of captives successful? Possibly the only real success stories, from a military point of view, were the three former Montoneras who married ESMA naval officers. Anita Dvatman collaborated actively with the ESMA task group in identifying former comrades, and eventually married its head of logistics Navy Lieutenant Jorge Radice. Marta Bazán came to marry the 1976–1978 commander of the Navy Mechanics School Rear-Admiral Rubén Chamorro. Finally, Lucy Changazzo had a long-term relationship with Navy Lieutenant Antonio Pernías, the very Pernías who had assassinated her husband.[81]

However, many "recovered" captives soon turned against their "educators" after they abandoned Argentine soil. Ana María Martí, María Alicia Milia de Pirles, and Sara Solarz de Osatinsky denounced the Argentine military in October 1979 before a European Interparliamentary Human

Rights Commission.[82] They had been part of a group of more than fifty former Montoneros held at the ESMA. Graciela Daleo and Andrés Castillo were about the last to be released, and also testified against their former captors.[83]

The dismantling of the enemy's self procured by the military, in part intentional and in part coincidental, reached its completion with the traumatization of the relatives of the disappeared. The traumatization was intended to paralyze relatives, to break their desire to protest against the established military order and its repressive apparatus. Relatives were expected to wallow in misery and withdraw within themselves in despair. However, this political paralysis failed to take effect as public protest became mobilized by deep-seated emotions between parents and children. These ties only strengthened through the military repression of the human rights movement, raising solidarity among searching relatives.

Part IV
Argentina's Nightmare:
The Forced Disappearance

Protest by Mothers and Grandmothers of the Plaza de Mayo, 28 April 1983.
Courtesy of *Diario Clarín*.

Chapter 13
The Disappearance:
Despair, Terror, and Fear

Each and every night, Elsa Sánchez de Oesterheld lies awake for hours agonizing about her disappeared husband and four daughters. "I believe that the disappearance is one of the most brutal things that can exist in today's war. It is the inhumane of the inhumane. I don't know how to express it. It's one of the most horrendous things because from one moment to the next a child disappears, a loved one, son, father, brother, whatever, husband, and this person has vanished into thin air without ever knowing what happened to him. It's very difficult to come to terms with. That's the anxiety, the despair, that in my personal case will obviously die with me."[1]

Elsa Sánchez de Oesterheld disapproved of the revolutionary ideals of her daughters and her husband, a well-known scriptwriter of science fiction. The four sisters became members of the Peronist Youth in 1973 and later joined the Montoneros. Their father Héctor Oesterheld became involved in the Montoneros as a press officer. According to his wife Elsa, he was interested in the political movement, saw his participation as an adventure, and wanted to accompany his daughters in their revolutionary quest. They went underground soon after the military coup. Elsa stayed at home and, for security reasons, was left in the dark about their hiding places.

Her eighteen-year-old daughter Beatriz was the first to disappear. She was working in a slum near San Isidro, a middle-class suburb of Buenos Aires, and was abducted on 19 June 1976. On 7 July, Ms. de Oesterheld received a phone call from an anguished police commissioner that he had received five dead bodies from the army, all between seventeen and nineteen years of age. Beatriz was among the dead. She had been assassinated five days earlier. The commissioner had been told to bury the bodies as unidentified persons in the cemetery of Virreyes but he could not reconcile himself with such cruel destiny. He called Ms. de Oesterheld and she retrieved her daughter's body the same day.

On 7 August 1976, her daughter Diana disappeared from her home in Tucumán province. There had been a political meeting, and the army had killed all participants, including Diana's husband. Diana (twenty-two years old) escaped but was never heard of again. On 3 June 1977, Elsa's husband Héctor disappeared. On 1 November 1977, her daughter Marina (seventeen years old) disappeared. Elsa de Oesterheld now had only her eldest daughter Esterlita left (twenty-four years old).

On 14 December 1977, Esterlita's three-year-old son Martín was abducted from his parents' home in Longchamps. Esterlita and her husband were not at home, but were killed when they arrived. Martín was taken to his grandfather Héctor at the Campo de Mayo secret detention center. That same evening, two young officers rang the doorbell of the home of Elsa de Oesterheld's parents, where Elsa was staying temporarily. They handed her the little boy. The officer had struck a friendship with Héctor Oesterheld and decided to disobey the order to leave the child in an orphanage.

Elsa was terrified, terrified that she also might be abducted and that then her grandson would be completely orphaned. Afraid to endanger him, she did not approach any human rights organization, and only sought contact with the grandmothers of the Plaza de Mayo in 1983. Since then she has been putting the pieces of her family's fate together, and testified in the 1985 trial of the junta members.

Elsa Sánchez de Oesterheld learned that her husband had been held captive by the First Army Corps at Campo de Mayo, and was assassinated in the town of Mercedes. She also heard that her daughter Diana was seven months pregnant when she was captured after the escape from her house in Tucumán. Her daughter Marina was also in an advanced stage of pregnancy when abducted. Elsa assumes that both daughters were assassinated after giving birth in captivity and that the babies were given away for adoption to military families.

Even though she now has the certainty that her husband and daughters died, her torment has not diminished since the disappearances first occurred: "It makes me have moments of really genuine despair. It is not death as such, but how they died. Because the fact of knowing the humiliation, torture, and horror our disappeared endured before dying makes me think that an execution, for example, would have been much more humane. . . . Death doesn't make me anxious because I know that my daughters, my husband, were at peace once they died. What worries me, what torments me, what makes me crazy is what happened before their death. This yes, when these thoughts come to me, which is usually at night, when one cannot sleep and begins to think and think. For fifteen years I have been brooding over this tragedy."[2]

The disappearance of Elsa de Oesterheld's entire family contains all the major elements suffered by tens of thousands of relatives: the abduction and disappearance of loved ones, the interminable search, the attempt to provide a proper burial, the years of silence in fear, the public testimony after the regime's fall, and a neverending anguish. The anguish and despair derive from a deep-seated feeling of having failed as parents to provide care and comfort to the disappeared children. Like Elsa de Oesterheld, many parents imagine their child being tortured and tormented to death—a mental image constructed from the many testimonies they have heard through the years. Each eyewitness account adds new details to their visualization and enhances their sense of helplessness. These parental emotions, together with unconscious guilt feelings, intensify the search. The incessant recreation of the loved one's death in thought, the insatiable desire to know every detail, and the awareness of its incomprehensibility are the makings of a posttraumatic response suffered by most surviving relatives, which hardened into psychological disorders for some but was transformed for many into a social trauma that strengthened their resolve to find the disappeared.

As desperate parents, husbands, wives, sisters, and brothers searched for their disappeared relatives, the military were assassinating them one by one. The military denied having them in custody and erected a façade of innocence concealing their deceit. Why did the Argentine military choose the forced disappearance as their method of repression? How did the abductions rupture the bond between parents and children, and what did those disappearances mean for the affected relatives embarking on an incessant search?

Disappearance Method

The disappearances in Argentina did not begin on the 24th of March 1976, the day of the coup. In Chapter 11, I mentioned that even in 1946 four students and one worker disappeared for several days and were moved repeatedly by the police to confuse the searching relatives.[3] In 1962, the Peronist unionists Felipe Vallese and Héctor Mendoza disappeared at the hands of the Buenos Aires police.[4] Still, disappearances were not yet a systematic repressive measure ordered secretly by the State authorities, not even during the 1966–1973 military dictatorship. Nevertheless, disappearances did occur in the early 1970s. The lawyer Néstor Martins and his client Nildo Zenteno Delgadillo were abducted by police on 16 December 1970 and were never heard of again. Three other persons were abducted by police in 1970, but they reappeared after some time.[5]

The number of disappeared political activists increased considerably in 1971. Twenty-five persons were abducted by police and held incommunicado for a period of time. Seven of them disappeared permanently, among whom Luis Pujals of the PRT-ERP.[6] The abductions became so common that the Catholic magazine *Criterio* wrote in May 1972: "Sometimes the process begins with the abduction of a person, who then either disappears—the list of 'disappeared' has grown long during these last years—or reappears after having been tortured during a lapse of time in which his whereabouts is officially unknown."[7]

The disappearance procedure that was to bring the 1976–1983 military juntas their worldwide notoriety had already crystallized by 1973: "abduction, torture, a silencing through death, and the disappearance of the principal evidence, namely the cadavers of the executed."[8] The leftist magazine *Militancia* described in 1973 a protocol to denounce disappearances. It recommended to immediately make the abduction public, and mobilize labor unions and political organizations. Next, a lawyer had to present a writ of habeas corpus obliging the authorities to notify within twenty-four hours whether or not the missing person had been detained.[9] In all, about six hundred abductions took place before the 1976 coup. The forced disappearance as a means of systematic repression was tested during the 1975 Operation Independence in Tucumán.[10]

The law, order, justice, and respect for individual rights proclaimed by the military junta on 24 March 1976 misled many people about the identity of the civilian squads abducting people in their Ford Falcons. The guerrillas were suspected, and so were right-wing parapolice organizations. Reliable information was scarce. The media did not report the disappearance of thousands of Argentines during the junta's first year because its Press Secretariat stated in April 1976 that "it is forbidden to inform, comment or make reference to themes related to subversive actions, the appearance of cadavers and corpses of subversive elements and/or members of the armed or security forces caused by those actions, except when reported by a responsible official source. This includes abducted or disappeared persons."[11]

The newspapers largely reproduced official communiqués about armed confrontations with guerrilla units.[12] The few times in which assassinations reached the front pages was when these deaths could be exploited politically. The assassination of three Pallotine priests and two seminarists on 4 July 1976 were blamed on the guerrillas but later proven to have been carried out by the ESMA task group.[13]

Short notices about abductions began to appear in 1977. In March 1977, *La Nación* mentioned the abduction of two men taken from their work "by eight persons dressed as civilians, two of them women, who only said that they were policemen."[14] Around the same time, the military orchestrated a semblance of due process by reporting the sentencing of guerrillas for the possession of weapons. The most devious deceit involved the occasional freeing of political prisoners, ostensibly "to make the spirit of justice prevail and as a contribution to pacification during the process of national reorganization."[15] For example, the Ministry of Interior declared at the turn of 1976 that during the first nine months of military rule, 1,546 persons had been released, and 114 foreigners expelled from the country.[16] Such figures gave the Argentine people the impression that the junta was meting out a correct military justice.

Even though the Argentine military denied having anything to do with the disappearances, they did disclose the method in private conversations. Just a few weeks after the 1976 coup, a naval officer told newspaper publisher Jacobo Timerman that the subversives had to be killed secretly and without a trial because otherwise the Pope would intervene on their behalf to commute the death sentence, "And we'd be allowing a twenty-year-old terrorist to remain alive and maybe receive amnesty in ten to fifteen years when a Parliament in this country might pass amnesty laws. Imagine, he'd be only thirty or thirty-five, the age of a good military or political leader, with the added appeal of having been a martyr in his youth. . . . But if we exterminate them all, there'll be fear for several generations." A flabbergasted Timerman asked, "What do you mean by all?" And the officer replied: "All . . . about twenty thousand people." And what about the Pope's reaction? "Not a trace or witness will remain."[17]

In another testimony, former police inspector Rodolfo Fernández disclosed a conversation among the Generals Harguindeguy, Videla, Viola, and Galtieri at the Ministry of Interior in 1976. Fernández overheard them saying that the main ideas behind the war doctrine were "the physical elimination of the so-called 'rootless subversion' and an ideological orientation along the principles of 'the defense of tradition, family and property.'"[18] Clearly, the practice of disappearances was a systematic, premeditated strategy based on a firm ideological foundation.

The Fate of the Disappeared

On 23 April 1976, seventeen-year-old Norberto Morresi tells his father Julio that he will return home late at night because he first has to run an errand and then attend a birthday party. Whenever he went out, Norberto would call his parents saying that he had arrived safely. On this particular evening, it is getting later and later, and Norberto does not call in. Julio and Irma Morresi are not worried. They assume that the animated birthday festivities must have made their son forget the time. Then, the telephone rings. "Why is Norberto not coming to the party? We have been waiting for him all evening." Julio becomes worried. He steps out the front door and looks in both directions. No Norberto. He grabs his coat and goes out into the street. He walks the tree-lined streets in his modest neighborhood and returns home very upset.

After a few endless hours, Julio decides to appeal for help from a retired police inspector. This inspector calls various police stations and hospitals. After about one hour, he contacts Julio and tells him that Norberto is nowhere to be found. He suggests that he is possibly passing the night in a hotel with a girlfriend. "We hardly slept that night, not knowing what to do," recalls Julio Morresi. "Daybreak came and neither Irma nor I had slept a wink all night, not knowing what to do, desperate you see, because we felt worse and worse as time passed. Until we received a phone call in the morning from someone who says, 'You are the parents of Norberto Morresi?', he says. 'Look, we don't know, but we are almost certain that he has been detained because we were waiting for him at a certain place.' I say, 'But how so? I made inquiries.' He says, 'No, this detention is complicated.' 'But who's talking?' He says, 'No, I hope you understand, but I can't give you my name, we are passing through a very delicate moment,' he says, 'because many comrades were caught yesterday.'"[19]

Where had Norberto been that evening? His father knew that his son was a member of the forbidden UES, the high school student organization controlled by the Montoneros, but he did not know that his errand on 23 April 1976 was the distribution of the illegal magazine *Evita Montonera*. Together with the thirty-four-year-old Montonero Luis María Roberto, he was detained in the Flores neighborhood in a Chevrolet station wagon loaded with the forbidden monthly. The two were obviously not combatants because no guerrilla would risk his life distributing magazines. By accident, a friend of Luis Roberto's wife had been passing in a bus when the detention occurred. She saw how the red-haired Luis and an adolescent boy were leaning eagle-spread against a Chevrolet, heads down.

What had happened to Norberto Morresi and Luis María Roberto? Luis Roberto's wife had heard her friend's eyewitness account but did not know who had been accompanying her husband. In turn, Julio and Irma Morresi had received an unidentified phone call. For all three, the trail of their loved ones ended at the intersection of Directorio street and the Perito Moreno highway between the Flores and Liniers neighborhoods of Buenos Aires.

Unbeknownst to the searching relatives, another piece of the trail was found two hours after the abduction. On an abandoned lot, the police of La Matanza found a partially burnt-out Chevrolet station wagon and two bodies: one adolescent with gun shot wounds in the lower abdomen and an adult with a head shot. Finger prints were taken and the two corpses were interred as unidentified persons in the General Villegas cemetery.[20] Only the First Army Corps and the Buenos Aires police knew what had happened between detention and assassination.

In a sense, the fate of Norberto Morresi and Luis María Roberto was uncommon. Most captives were sent to a secret detention center. Yet, in another sense, the fate of the two companions did not differ from that of most disappeared: the overwhelming majority would sooner or later be assassinated and their corpses destroyed. The ways in which the Argentine police and military disposed of the bodies were several, some reminding us of mass killings in other countries at other times.

One Sunday in May 1976, José Julián Solanille and a friend observed how army cars and trucks arrived at an open field near Córdoba. In the presence of Third Army Corps commander General Luciano Menéndez, soldiers began digging a pit of four-by-four meters. "The shots began when we were on the slope and we saw a hooded man running with his hands tied behind his back, who fell and got up until he was caught. There, below, the shots continued and other people were falling, also tied, and with black-painted glasses on their faces which stood out in the sun. They must have executed around fifty persons. . . ."[21] This story was corroborated by Lieutenant Ernesto Urien who had heard furthermore how the bodies were exhumed in 1978, deposited in oil drums and covered with lime. This operation occurred just before a fact-finding mission by the Organization of American States reached Córdoba.[22]

How did the disappeared die? A number of disappeared came to their end inside the secret detention centers. Some died accidentally and others deliberately from torture.[23] However, the majority was either shot at close range or dumped at sea while sedated.[24] The captives were generally hooded or blindfolded and then shot in the back of the head. Psychologically, this manner of killing is more acceptable and less traumatizing for the executioner than a face-to-face execution because the hood, blindfold, and turned back create an emotional distance. The executioner does not have to see the frightened, anguished expression, and can more easily rationalize the assassination as the necessary elimination of an enemy.[25]

Despite their denial of any involvement, the military could not ignore the fact that people were disappearing in Argentina. So they began to concoct plausible explanations. They would move several disappeared to a so-called recuperation center, give them food, dress their wounds, and improve their physical condition. After regaining a more civil appearance, they were shot. The bodies were then taken to another site and used to stage an armed confrontation. The press would be told that the army had won another victory over the terrorists. This explanation made perfect sense in the light of the political violence of 1974 and 1975. The military used a similar ploy to eliminate political prisoners. Relatives and the press would be informed that the prisoners had been on transport to another prison, when guerrillas attacked the convoy in an attempt to free them. Allegedly, the prisoners died during the failed escape attempt.[26]

Most disappeared were assassinated outside secret detention centers in order not to destroy the hopes of the captives. Nevertheless, the captives soon discovered that whoever was said to be transferred (*traslado*) to another center, was going to be assassinated. Some were indeed moved for further interrogation, but most transferees (*trasladados*) went to their final destination.

The term *traslado* was a euphemism for death. *Traslado* or transfer is a routine term used in Argentine cemeteries to describe the transfer of remains from one grave to another or from one cemetery to another. Possibly, the term *traslado* was used in a cynical reference to such a procedure. The secret detention centers were like cemeteries, the final station for most disappeared. They were already symbolically dead upon arrival, and their removal for assassination was thus nothing more than the substitution of one graveyard for another.

As in the case of Norberto Morresi and Luis María Roberto, the trail from abduction to assassination of the ESMA captives was compartmentalized. Witnesses could only provide pieces to the puzzle. The three Montoneras released from the ESMA in October 1979 gave the most complete account of the transfers. Group transfers occurred generally on Wednesdays and occasionally on Thursdays. The captives were told that they were going to be taken to other centers, to work camps near the Rawson prison or to be legalized as political prisoners. "A very tense climate reigned on the day of the transfers. We, the abducted, did not know whether or not it would be our turn that day. The guards took many more severe measures than usual. We couldn't go to the bathroom. Everyone of us had to remain strictly in his place, hooded and shackled, without making any attempt to see what was going on."[27] The Basement was completely vacated by 3:30 P.M. and, at about 5:00 P.M., the numbers of the transferees were called out. They were taken from their cells and cubicles in the Hood, formed in a single file, and taken one by one down the stairway to the Basement.

Another piece of the puzzle came from an unusual eyewitness. Sometime in February 1977, ESMA officers decided to transfer the Montonero Emilio Carlos Assales Bonazzola together with around one dozen captives. Once in the infirmary, they were given an injection to make them drowsy. They had been told that they would be taken to a place with better conditions, and that a vaccination was needed as a preventive measure. The next day, Assales Bonazzola awoke in his cubicle at the ESMA and told Juan Gasparini that he had been taken into a Fokker aircraft, but was told to step down before takeoff because he was demanded by a task force from Mendoza.[28]

The sedated captives were taken by truck to the Buenos Aires city airport Jorge Newbery, put aboard a Navy aircraft, and dumped in the ocean.[29] Many naval officers participated in these flights. Even special guests and high-ranking officers accompanied the crew for approval and moral support, watching as the bodies were dropped one by one.[30]

There were several details betraying the real destination of the transferees to the captives who stayed behind: the condemned departed with only the clothes on their backs; those very same clothes reappeared a few days later in the Large Storeroom where the war booty was kept; a metal box filled with shackles was unloaded after the transfer; and on the floor were "the marks of the bodies which had been dragged from the infirmary to the side door of the basement. The clearest marks were left by the rubber soles of shoes or slippers."[31] The accounts by former captives reveal significant pieces of the trajectory between abduction and death but contain blanks that can only be filled by the perpetrators.

The navy had always denied these death flights until 1995 when one traumatized navy captain began talking to the press, a breach of the code of silence which I discuss in this book's conclusion. However, I was already given some particulars about these death flights by Rear-Admiral Mayorga in 1990. This was the same Mayorga who had arrived in 1972 at the Trelew naval base just after sixteen guerrillas had been assassinated. Mayorga has always openly approved the death sentence for the guerrillas, but he disapproved of the disappearances. "As far as I'm concerned, they should have executed them at the River Plate [soccer stadium] with free Coca-Cola and on television. But one thing yes: with a signed order."[32] He believes that commanders must be responsible for their orders because orders given without written authorization undermine the legitimacy of the armed forces. Rear-Admiral Mayorga revealed the ESMA transfer procedure to me in the following way. "You would take a guerrilla, obtained the information, and decided in a small committee without a trial or signature whatever fate he was going to run. It is a lie that there were no verdicts. There were verdicts. But it is true that nobody ever signed the verdict. The death of any guerrilla was always decided by at least five persons. But one thing yes, five persons who like you and me, sitting like this, said, 'That one can't go on living.' What did they do? I tell you what happened in the navy, without any false sentiments. You will say, 'but did they. . .?' No, no, if not, I won't tell you anything and that's the end of it, isn't it? Very well, they injected them and threw them in the sea. They didn't . . . He didn't even know that he was going to die, I can assure you."[33] Did Mayorga intend to say with his last sentence that he had personally witnessed the body drops? Had he been aboard a Fokker cargo plane when thirty or forty people were thrown into the ocean?

The throwing of sedated captives out at sea was one way to make bodies disappear. Forensic anthropologists have estimated that between 2,000 and 3,500 army and navy captives met this fate.[34] Bodies were also abandoned along country roads, and there were secret detention centers which incinerated the corpses. Most often, they were cremated or interred in cemeteries as unidentified persons.

The unceremonial burial or cremation was the final act of dehumanization and desocialization. The dead persons were not acknowledged as human beings who deserved a proper ritual reincorporating them into society as deceased persons. In other words, the dumping of the dead denied their humanity, and disavowed their death as a loss to society, a loss which could not be commemorated by relatives and comrades. Such concealment served to doubly harm the surviving relatives. They had already been traumatized by the violent abduction of their hooded son, daughter, husband or wife, had been unable to find them, and would be traumatized again by the inability to bury or cremate them once the truth was found out.

The Violation of Parental Trust

In chapter 11, I explained how torture was aimed at traumatizing people and dismantling their self and sociality by destroying their social trust. This attack on social trust was also suffered by the relatives, and in particular by mothers who witnessed the abduction of a son or daughter. Children are raised with the notion of unconditional parental protection, which is most clearly expressed in physical holding to protect them from a hostile world.[35] Mothers and fathers seek to be physically close to their child so that it can be reassured of their protection by touching or at least hearing and seeing them. The threat of loss makes parents place their children's well-being ahead of their own.[36]

Whenever a task group forced its way into a home, the parents' concern went invariably first to the son or daughter, and only later to themselves and their spouse. Generally, the mother or father would go to the child's bedroom and stay at its side. When two men entered the home of Margarita Michelini, "my husband ran to take the baby because he thought that they might harm him. . . . they were armed, my son began to cry, I tried to calm him and at this moment I was ordered to come along, 'Get dressed, we have to leave,' and I told them to kill me right there, but I was not going to give them the baby. . . ."[37] The twelve-year-old daughter of Nélida Jauregui was awakened "with a machine-gun to her head and they wanted to take her away from me, so I embraced her and I told them that this was not going to be possible because she was a child and I took her to my bedroom. . . ."[38]

Nancy Chodorow has argued that, "Women get gratification from caring for an infant . . . because they experience either oneness with their infant or because they experience it as an extension of themselves."[39] I add that these feelings do not cease when the infant becomes an adult. This care is precisely what many mothers felt when they tried to protect their adolescent and adult children against the assault teams by remaining physically close to them. For a moment, they were again defenseless infants in need of maternal care. Whenever possible, fathers also tried to offer such protection but my analysis strongly suggests that fathers tended to attack the source of aggression verbally or even physically, while mothers would rather shield the child from violence.

As parents and children were led away together, they tried to remain physically close, constantly trying to touch one another. Iris Etelvina Pereyra de Avellaneda held on to her fourteen-year-old son Floreal. "I was holding him by the hand. At a certain moment they indicated that we had to lean against the top of a car. That was the last time I saw my son, looking at me while they were putting a blindfold on my eyes and a hood as well. I can still sense its filthy smell. We had our hands free and instinctively I searched for those of my son but I didn't find them. I then raised my voice asking for him, and the police commissioner answered unwillingly: 'I'll bring him right now.' And, in fact, they put us together in the same vehicle. They put us in the back seat. My son squeezed my right hand as if to give me courage. We remained silent."[40]

The protective feelings went also from child to parent. Twelve-year-old Zulema Lifsica de Chester protested loudly when the intruders threw her blindfolded mother on the floor: "My daughter saw this and began to scream that they shouldn't push her mother. Then they asked her: 'Why do you defend your mother?' She told them: 'Would you have liked it if someone did something to your mother?' to which she didn't receive an answer."[41] The girl was taken to her bedroom and interrogated about the hiding place of political pamphlets. The anguished mother heard the men's questions but not her daughter's replies and screamed: "'Where is my daughter? What's happening with my daughter?' until they finally throw us together in the hall."[42] Mother and daughter were separated once more and interrogated in their respective bedrooms.[43]

Parents will generally try to care for their children for the rest of their lives. First of all, the trust between parents and children is by definition intersubjective, and the desire to provide and receive trust does not cease when the infant grows into adulthood. Second, the age of the child matters little under traumatic circumstances as parents imagine their adolescent and adult children to be as infants in need of parental and particularly maternal protection.[44] Elsa Sánchez de Oesterheld asked herself in desperation: "What happened to those wonderful little girls? I speak of little girls even though they were women. This is, of course, a generic matter for all mothers who lost their children without knowing what happened to them."[45]

Just as Ms. de Oesterheld could only conceive of her daughters as little girls, so Luis José Bondone saw his mature sons as small children: "They were 'my children,' that small, soft thing that one takes in one's arms when they are so helpless. That sentiment came to me and I imagined them being mistreated and beaten by a cowardly, dirty, infamous hand, with their hands tied behind their backs, blindfolded."[46] It was the impotence at being unable to give this enduring care to the abducted child that was so traumatizing for parents during Argentina's dirty war.

Parental protection failed when adult and adolescent children endangered themselves through their political activism. While trust and protection coincide during the early stages of human development, they can become opposites after adolescence. The parental desire to isolate children from outside threats clashes with the need to raise them into independent adults. This made some mothers decide that it was better not to question their children's political judgment.

Matilde Herrera was shaking when her children told her that they had decided to join the outlawed People's Revolutionary Army (ERP) because she could now no longer shield them from the dangers they were facing. Yet she decided not to oppose their choice: "I knew that it was best not to argue with the children when they took such a decision. What I wanted most was that they wouldn't lose trust in me. One way or the other I was always at their side, and I thought that the worst I could do was to leave them unprotected, that they would feel abandoned by their mother. Society was already hostile enough to them."[47] The scales of trust and protection tipped for Matilde Herrera towards supplying a nurturing emotional environment as a last refuge from a threatening world, even when her fear of separation and her own political judgment told her that the armed struggle would end in certain death.

Other mothers chose safety over trust. This placed before them a different but equally desperate dilemma. They would have to avoid any further contact with their children and thus abandon them to an uncertain existence. Elsa Sánchez de Oesterheld decided not to follow her husband and four daughters into hiding. Like so many parents, she was left ignorant of their whereabouts. Each sign of life gave a moment of joy, but was always followed by weeks of worry.

These dilemmas were magnified when the child disappeared: waiting quietly for the abducted son or daughter to reappear was felt as abandonment, while active protest was regarded as endangering. These dilemmas became even more painful during an official media campaign carrying slogans such as: "How are you raising your child?" "Do you know what your child is doing at this precise moment?"[48] Intended to make parents aware of the education of their children and make them responsible for the company they kept, it produced tremendous guilt among parents of abducted children. Mothers were blamed for not giving a proper education that could have prevented their children from becoming involved with the guerrilla organizations. Parental emotions were mangled in a most cruel way, and feelings of shame and guilt were consciously manipulated. The military made parents believe that they were responsible for the violent death of their own children, the thankless burden of fighting a dirty war, and for now saddling them with the task to locate their missing children.

State Terror and the Culture of Fear

The state repression was so nebulous in the beginning that people denouncing a disappearance were not believed. "But nobody at that time knew who they were, groups with cars without license plates, civilians armed to the teeth, and well, but when one said, 'They took my son. Who? Eh, I don't know, I don't know. But how come you don't know? How were they dressed? They were dressed as civilians. Ah well, it were the terrorists, it was the Triple A.'"[49] María del Rosario de Cerruti was even doubted by her husband. They had spoken with a naval officer who swore on his nine-year-old daughter sitting at his side that he did not know anything about the disappearances. "My husband came back convinced, and I told him, 'You're a simple soul. You can't believe what the military are telling you. They're killing people, they're torturing them.'"[50]

A secretive State repression had descended on Argentine society employing terror to cow people into political submission. This culture of terror, to use Taussig's important concept, was inspired by a paranoid threat perception in an interplay of truth and illusion. A culture of terror developed, affecting victims as well as victimizers.[51] Anyone could be a potential enemy, so terror was regarded as both an effective and a preemptive means against the revolutionary subversion of Argentine society.

The culture of terror gave rise to a culture of fear. The relatives of the disappeared were afraid to tell anybody. "Many people concealed it out of fear, they concealed it," remembers Nora de Cortiñas whose son Gustavo remains disappeared since 15 April 1977. "I believe that fear was the most important reason, it was fear. There was great fear if there were other children because, when the disappearances began, they said in the same houses where they went, 'Good, don't do anything because if not, then we'll be back.'"[52] Victory and omnipotence were instilled as fear. Disappearance extended war and torture into civil society, into households and family ties. The feelings of anguish and uncertainty never left most relatives and thus condemned them to a mental and social state of war and torture.

Damaged homes and damaged selves go together. Many relatives did not undertake any immediate action, afraid to endanger the life of the missing family member and intimidated by the threats of the assault teams. Matilde Herrera: "The fact of the disappearance creates in the beginning a lack of resistance all around the disappeared person, because how are we going to do anything if maybe they are holding him captive somewhere?"[53] One mother spent seven months rocking in a chair.[54]

Matilde Herrera lost her entire family. First, her daughter Valeria, her son Martín, her daughter-in-law María Cristina, and her son-in-law Ricardo disappeared. Then, her son José and his wife Electra were abducted. "They were no more. None of them. They had become disappeared. I was left stunned. I couldn't cry. I continued to eat, sleep, and talk to friends. I knew that if I gave in to my pain, then I would have been unable to continue living. I didn't cry, because I sensed that if I would sit down and cry, then I would never ever be able to get back on my feet again."[55] Relatives of the disappeared, like Matilde Herrera, were trapped within their own unshareable anxiety. "The disappearance inserts you into a very large and dense fog from which one cannot escape because one assumes rationally the certainty of death, but some hope survives permanently in the unconscious."[56] The relatives were in a liminal space, emotionally suspended from the comings and goings of everyday life, and permanently cut loose from the rest of society in their suffering.

The military junta played a perverse game with its own population. They depicted public life as dangerous because of an invisible enemy who could strike anytime and anywhere. The enemy could be one's neighbor, an artist, a schoolteacher or a priest. They placed bombs in cinemas and subway stations, and even concealed explosive devices in innocent-looking gifts such as flowers or pen sets.[57] The Cardinals Aramburu and Primatesta wondered openly, "which forces are so powerful that they can operate freely in our society with total impunity and in total anonymity?"[58] Did they really not know that these all-powerful forces emanated from the military or were they sending a subtle message to the highest authorities?

State terror created two different kinds of fear: the fear of a harm known for generations (military repression, political proscription, torture, imprisonment) and the fear of an unknown threat, impossible to describe. People retreated from all walks of life perceived as dangerous. They were particularly suspicious of other people whose political convictions were unclear. The political violence of 1974 and 1975 had taught Argentines that one could be harmed through an unintentional association with the wrong people. A retreat into the home and among close relatives was therefore the safest response to an uncertain political climate.

The ultimate retreat was the collective denial that anything out of the ordinary was happening. As one Argentine acquaintance told me in March 1978, "I have never been arrested or maltreated by the police in Argentina. The talk in Europe about these so-called disappearances is all part of an orchestrated political campaign against Argentina." The Argentine scholars O'Donnell, Corradi, and Suárez-Orozco have argued persuasively that the climate of repression either made people live in a continued state of fear of injury or led to denial.[59] Argentines did not discuss politics openly. Journalists and newspaper editors censured themselves. Librarians and bookstore owners hid or destroyed "subversive" books. Cinemas did not feature certain foreign movies.

Guillermo O'Donnell and his wife Cecilia Galli conducted a very unusual research in 1978. They asked their middle-class friends how their lives had changed after the 1976 coup. They discovered that many interviewees suffered from a generalized, but often suppressed and displaced, fear making them withdraw within the family and concentrate on their work. Furthermore, they forbade their adolescent children from becoming involved in social associations that could not be monitored by family or school. People experienced this diminution of their social life as a profound loss, as if they had been amputated. After all, an active public life and a nurturing private life go together in Western culture. The classical Greek heritage has instilled the importance of the public sphere for the realization of a complete social existence, now denied by the Argentine military.[60]

The culture of fear nibbled away at Argentine society as people became afraid to talk to neighbors, make new friends, and socialize with colleagues, let alone engage in collective political action. People were even reluctant to join a theater or study group. "Getting together, in any of the manifold forms of sociability one takes for granted in more benign contexts, was suspect precisely because it meant getting together."[61] Social networks became impoverished and people were thrown back upon a diminishing circle of trusted relatives and long-time friends. Sometimes, even the closest relatives would turn their backs, as happened to Raquel Marizcurrena: "After my son and his wife disappeared, I never again heard from any of my seven sisters or my brother. They all avoided us. It has been seventeen years since I last saw them. They were terrified that the same thing would happen to them."[62] People were afraid to be near those who had been touched by a disappearance, recalls Julio Morresi, "me and my wife were sowing fear around us with our despair and anguish, because I realized that there were friends who were even afraid to talk to me."[63]

This social isolation was intensified by the official prohibition of informal social gatherings and political associations. "These laws splinter social and public ties, while press censorship keeps the majority ignorant of the processes in which they have been immersed."[64] This destruction of social life turned the similar plight of thousands of relatives into a personal calvary during the first year of military repression. A deep mistrust, ultimately more pernicious and tenacious than fear, engulfed Argentine society. After all, fear was soon overcome, as the mothers of the disappeared showed most dramatically, but mistrust was harder to dispel when founded on traumatic experiences whose consequences continued to haunt their sufferers. In the end, the traumatization of Argentine society proved to be more enduring than the culture of fear.

Appearance of the Disappeared

The inert body of Floreal Avellaneda, fourteen years old, was found floating close to the Uruguayan coast in May 1976. He had been abducted on 15 April 1976 together with his mother Iris Etelvina Pereyra de Avellaneda by the police searching for his father. When police asked Floreal's aunt if the boy was involved in anything, she said he was just a child. The lieutenant's answer made clear that children were treated as potential enemy combatants: "'Child. Look, in Tucumán there are kids who walk around armed and they are children,' he said, 'and to tell you the truth, I would distrust my own son because there are kids of fourteen, fifteen years old who are guerrillas,'"[65] After repeated torture at the Villa Martelli police station, Floreal's mother was taken to the Campo de Mayo secret detention center, and later to the Olmos prison. She was released in July 1978. Searching for her son, she discovered that he had been one of eight corpses recovered from the sea in mid-May 1976. An autopsy revealed that the fourteen-year-old Floreal had died from impalement.[66]

Despite attempts to conceal the execution of large numbers of missing Argentines, some information filtered through to society. After the eight mutilated bodies found along the Uruguayan coast, more bodies were located in the Paraná river. The director at the San Pedro cemetery wrote that the corpses were found, "blindfolded, gagged, and with their hands tied behind their backs with wire."[67] Between late 1977 and early 1978, around sixty bodies washed ashore on the beaches of Villa Gesell and Mar del Plata, many without hands and heads to prevent identification.[68]

An employee of the Judicial Morgue in Córdoba noticed how corpses were delivered in 1976, mostly by police but also by the military. "These corpses had the following characteristics: they had bullet wounds, some with a lot of perforations, sometimes as many as eighty, sometimes seventeen, for example. They all had painted fingers and bore clear marks of torture. They had marks on their hands as if they had been tied with cords. From time to time one would appear completely torn to pieces, split open."[69]

In June 1980, the employees of the Cordoban morgue were ordered to clear bodies from a hospital. The Dantesque scene at opening the storage room and the unwholesome working conditions prompted the staff to send a complaint to President Videla. "Some of the bodies had been stored for more than thirty days without any sort of refrigeration. There was a cloud of flies and the floor was covered in a layer about 10.5 centimetres deep in worms and larvae, which we cleared away with buckets and shovels. The only clothes we had were trousers, overalls, boots, and gloves, while some people had to do the work in their ordinary clothes. Mouth masks and caps were provided by the hospital administration thanks to the sub-director, as we did not have any. Despite all this we did not hesitate in carrying out the task as ordered. It should be noted that most of these bodies were of subversive delinquents."[70] The bodies were eventually buried in large pits at San Vicente cemetery.

Many people must have been aware of the many unnatural deaths and the attempts to conceal the bodies. Bus drivers, truck drivers, railroad workers, sailors, and mailmen traveling the roads and waterways of Argentina at odd hours must have noticed something and maybe told their wives and some close relatives. Conscript soldiers saw what was not destined for their eyes. Pathologists discovered the violent death of unidentified corpses, despite oral military orders not to perform autopsies on "subversives" and not to register the identity of persons killed in armed confrontations.[71] Hospital personnel saw bullet-ridden bodies, and even the proper authorities were sometimes caught unawares by ghastly discoveries. Gravediggers buried scores of unnamed dead, and army trucks arrived late at night at Argentina's cemeteries carrying containers full of naked, half-decomposed bodies of young people destined for cremation. These dead were not registered in the books. For example, at La Chacarita cemetery in Buenos Aires, there was a rapid decline in the official burial of unnamed bodies between 1974 and 1978, namely 70 (1974), 66 (1975), 1 (1976), 8 (1977), 0 (1978), and then slightly rising to 16 (1979) and 15 (1980). However, the number of registered cremations rose quickly: 13,120 (1974), 15,405 (1975), 20,500 (1976), 32,683 (1977), 30,094 (1978), 31,461 (1979), and declined again to 21,381 (1980).[72] Most of the cremated had died of natural causes, but the sudden increase in cremations after 1975 suggests that the remains of many disappeared were also disposed of in this manner.

In sum, many people in Argentina heard and saw the effects of the dirty war during the first year of the military dictatorship. Often, they could not identify the perpetrators, but they sensed that powerful forces were at work here. Intuitively, they hoped to remain far from these dangers, did not ask any questions, and tried as best as possible to carry on with their lives.[73]

Why Disappearances?

Many a country has its nightmare. Germany's nightmare is the Holocaust, China's the Great Leap Forward famine, and Argentina's nightmare is the forced disappearance. These societies suffered violence on so many levels that they have been troubled for many years by a collective trauma. Such traumatization did not happen all at once but people found themselves slowly enwrapped in a gripping reality beyond control and without escape. In Argentina, people began to disappear after having been abducted by unknown assailants. Newspapers failed to report the kidnappings, the authorities denied any involvement, and neighbors doubted the sincerity of the searching parents. A culture of fear arose affecting guerrilla combatants, political activists, despairing relatives, and Argentine society as a whole. A nightmare took hold of a defenseless Argentine people which suffered from its sequels for decades to come.

The practices of abduction, torture, and disappearance may have been originally designed as effective counterinsurgency methods but they were soon used to spread terror through Argentine society and unleash a repression extending beyond the military arena into the realms of family and self. This transposition from armed confrontations in the street and torture in secret detention centers to the privacy of the home and the intimacy of human existence reinforced the enmity in all four domains. Repressive measures rationalized as military expediency now became justified through this multipronged attack on the revolutionary and political opposition, producing a fall-out of fear that affected the entire Argentine society.

Until 1995, and after hundreds of disappeared had been exhumed and identified, the perpetrators of the dirty war still denied that the forced disappearances had been ordered by the junta. Yet, in a rare 1989 interview with the Armed Forces Supreme Council, one of the judges admitted in veiled terms to this ruthless practice. I had asked provocatively why the junta had not executed the guerrillas publicly. Rear-Admiral Eduardo Davion answered, while the other eight judges nodded in agreement: "If one would have done what you are asking, the reason why, then there would have been immediate revenge, not only on the executioner or those who presided the trial but also on their families. That is to say, the terror had also infused terror among the Armed Forces, and they responded with terror. This is the tremendous problem, the tremendous tragedy of this war."[74]

Brigadier Carlos Echeverria Martínez added in my second interview with the military supreme court that the Argentine military looked to the Americans, the French and especially the Israelis for inspiration on how to respond to the guerrilla insurgency, "they have one fundamental principle for this type of war which we perhaps also used: one can only fight terror by instilling a greater terror in the enemy. . . . And here we probably had to embark on that uncommon course that hurt and disgusted us all. If we wouldn't have more or less taken this road then Argentina would have been a bastion of Marxism at this moment."[75] Knowingly or unknowingly, he echoed Perón's exhortation in a letter to John William Cooke of 3 November 1956: "The more violent we are the better: one cannot beat terror, if not with another greater terror."[76]

Secrecy and terror are just two of the many explanations given for the disappearances and the destruction of the dead bodies. The CONADEP truth commission arrived at five reasons: (1) erase criminal evidence; (2) create uncertainty and false hopes among searching relatives; (3) stall investigations into the whereabouts of the disappeared; (4) paralyze public protest; and (5) prevent feelings of solidarity between the Argentine people and the searching relatives.[77] These reasons refer to the social and psychological consequences of disappearances, while lumping together different groups of victims. Instead, the forced disappearances constituted an overdetermined violent practice targeting many social dimensions, layers, and groups. The impact must therefore be traced into all these contexts while paying specific attention to the traumatization of Argentine society.

Why did the Argentine military junta decide upon disappearances rather than imprisonment or even execution? There is not one single explanation because the disappearances served several objectives at the same time and were aimed at different targets ranging from experienced guerrilla combatants to idealistic priests. Furthermore, the junta members themselves differed in their rationalization of the disappearance method. They had embarked on a cultural war with unconventional methods whose overall implications they failed to map in advance. Furthermore, the junta eagerly embraced several unexpected effects as beneficial to the war against subversion. The line between premeditation and opportunism is therefore hard to draw. So, in trying to uncover the rationale behind the disappearances, I make an analytical distinction between operational, judicial, political, symbolic, economic, historical, pedagogic, psychological, and social reasons, some intentional and others unforeseen yet condoned.

Operationally, the abductions allowed for an expediency of action not achieved by a formal procedure of arrest, an interrogation in the presence of a lawyer, and an arraignment in court. Even more important, the disappearance of guerrillas spread great confusion among the revolutionary organizations. General Virgilio Górriz explained this operational motive as follows: "[The guerrillas] carry out an operation, and lose two or three men. They end the operation. They leave and they don't know afterwards whether the others are dead, have been taken prisoner or something like that. Terror then turns against them. If one of them stays alive, then it is likely that they [the captors] will make him talk. So, this other man who holds all strings in his neighborhood sees himself obliged to leave, has to go abroad or something like that."[78] In sum, the guerrilla organizations were severely hampered when they did not know whether their combatants were dead or alive, had defected or deserted, were held up in traffic or were being tortured for information.

Judicially, the disappearances destroyed incriminating evidence. It became impossible to trace an abducted person when the kidnappers were disguised, their cars unmarked, the authorities denied having them in custody, and the bodies were cremated or buried in mass graves.

Politically, the disappearances misled national and world opinion, and hindered the mobilization of protest movements. Argentine diplomats and military authorities denied the disappearances and the existence of secret detention centers. A valuable lesson had been learnt from the adverse reactions to the mass arrests during Pinochet's first years in power. Unlike Chile, the Argentine junta was quickly recognized by foreign governments. Yet the Argentine military did at night what Pinochet's men had done during the day.

Symbolically, the destruction of the corpses prevented the slain from becoming martyrs. The embalmed body of Evita Perón had been disappeared for that same reason. In a country in which a visit to the national cemetery La Recoleta is one of the favorite weekend outings, the recovery of the dead would have given rise to numerous pilgrimages with clear political overtones.

Economically, the government feared that the international protest movement would harm foreign loans and investment. Such reaction would have been disastrous for the ambitious modernization of the Argentine economy.[79]

Historically, the Argentine military leaders knew that their reign would come to an end. They wanted to protect the reputation of the armed forces and secure their continued influence on Argentine society and politics. They believed that historical judgment could be influenced if relatives did not have a body to mourn and revolutionaries could not commemorate their dead. In other words, the disappearances served a conscious construction of a collective national memory.

Pedagogically, some military commanders held a rudimentary notion of reeducation. They wanted to punish the parents for not instilling patriotism, Christian values, and obedience to authority. They wanted to teach future parents not to make this mistake ever again. The military blamed the young generation's involvement in revolutionary politics on the parents. Hence, the bodies of the disappeared were not returned. Those parents did not deserve to mourn their dead, as one rear-admiral told me.

Psychologically, the annihilation of the corpses was a concrete measure of success for task force commanders and their men. Destroying these remains gave a sense of empowerment, in particular because the enemy had been defined as invisible, subterranean, and fed by foreign world powers. The corpses of the disappeared became the tally of war, and their eventual destiny a way to gauge the transition from war to victory.

Socially, the disappearances aimed at traumatizing the disappeared themselves, their relatives and Argentine society. After all, many disappeared were noncombatant but politically active citizens. Whether or not all social consequences had been thought through in advance, the armed forces decided to annihilate, traumatize, or resocialize a politically radicalized segment of society, instill fear and anguish in their relatives, and terrorize society. The traumatization manifested itself on the societal level as a culture of fear in which people shunned most informal contacts outside the family, and consciously cut all ties with relatives of disappeared persons. Many surviving relatives were at first paralyzed after an abduction because they had internalized the State terror as fear. People retreated so much within the home and within themselves that those who were not directly affected claimed that the disappearances did not take place at all.

Hannah Arendt's observation that totalitarian domination thrives on terror and loneliness can also be applied to Argentina. Arendt means by loneliness the state-induced isolation among people, because people devoid of social contact in the public realm are powerless. Such loneliness, in the public as well as the private domain, entails a loss of self because people require the company and trust of others to retain their self-confidence and self-worth.[80]

The Argentine military did not have the same grip on its population as the absolute rulers of Nazi Germany and the Soviet Union, but they did spread terror through the public and domestic spheres, and thus engendered loneliness among the relatives of the disappeared. Loneliness equaled abandonment. Surviving relatives felt deserted by a government failing to offer security, well-being and justice, abandoned by the Catholic Church which did not provide for its community of faithful, and abandoned by civil society, by relatives and friends. The practice of disappearance forced relatives into loneliness, precisely because of their emotional necessity to search for the disappeared. People shied away from them as if they were contagious. Each inquiry shut another door in their face, and each call for help was unanswered, thus effectively closing off one social realm after another.[81]

The denial of death was the most common response of people confronted with a disappearance. Argentine parents who saw their children being abducted alive, and heard stories about torture and assassination in secret detention centers, agonized about the fate of their loved ones, but hardly ever considered them to be dead. The hope that the loved one was still alive made the disappearance so tantalizing. Reality and fantasy were hard to disentangle as parents were thrown between hope for life and resignation to death. These parents composed and frequently readjusted their mental picture of how the lost child might have aged as years passed.[82] Mourning would deprive people of such hope, and was experienced as abandoning a child who might still be alive somewhere.

Sharing the anguish with others, so therapeutic for bereaved parents, could not be done during the first years of the dictatorship when the human rights movement did not yet draw wide support. A double stigma surrounded parents of the disappeared. First, there was the stigma that also envelops mourners. They are often shunned because their loss is regarded as a weakness believed to be contagious.[83] Second, people feared that their association might be politically dangerous. Had relatives been able to receive the final remains, and had they been allowed to conduct a proper ritual, then such social isolation would not have occurred. Now, the searching relatives had only each other to construct a sense of community, and they did so with remarkable strength. They overcame their initial posttraumatic paralysis and began searching actively for the disappeared, a search which would develop into a powerful oppositional movement to the military dictatorship.

Chapter 14
The Search:
Hope, Anguish, and Illusion

In July 1976, in the heart of the Argentine winter, Julio Morresi enters another bleak night to find his son Norberto who disappeared three months earlier. Through a labyrinth of contacts, he is sent to a place in Greater Buenos Aires between Quilmes and Bernal. Julio arrives late at night, stops his car and signals with his head lights. Lights off. Lights on. Lights off. Lights on. The response comes from a blinding searchlight. His eyes half-closed, his head tilted downward, Julio barely sees several men pointing their machine guns at him. "What are you doing? What are you looking for? Put your hands on the steering wheel!" Morresi mentions the name of the officer he has been sent to see. He is ordered to proceed, but does not know where.

In the pitch blackness of the moonless night Julio Morresi slowly makes his way and arrives at an open field. Another searchlight hits his face. A gate opens and he is ordered to enter. "I saw some types there, with beards, all with large weapons. 'How did you come here? Who sent you?' " Morresi saw the astonishment on the men's faces. He finally meets the commanding officer and gives his son's name. The officer checks a registry and says, "No. There's nobody with that name here," and orders Julio to leave immediately. "How?" asks Julio. " 'In the same way you came.' And I thought that I would never get out of there again. There, it must have been, let's say, it must have been five hundred meters, four hundred meters, it took me forever because I sensed the machine guns loading and felt that already, already there they were killing me." Hours later he arrives at home, exhausted. "Irma was waiting for me when I arrived home, desperate because I had gone alone. I tried not to tell her what I had been through so as not to bring her more distress than she already had. 'Eh, look, no, I didn't find out anything.' It was nearly dawn. I spent whole nights away like that."[1]

Julio Morresi is still uncertain whether or not he had visited a secret detention center, a temporary way station for the disappeared, or the hide-out of a task group. The danger was palpable, but the urge to find his son Norberto was greater. Each lead was checked, and each officer mentioned by relatives, friends, and acquaintances was approached. After his nightly visits to the most hidden of places, he procured information at the highest Argentine authorities. He succeeded in talking to a colonel holding office in the building of the suspended Buenos Aires City Council (Consejo Deliberante). The meeting was arranged by a retired lieutenant with whom Morresi had become friends at the Huracán soccer club.

Julio Morresi arrived at the monumental building, and was given a visi-tor's pass. He climbed the stairs, saw how intelligence personnel were mon-itoring the television stations, and finally entered the colonel's spacious office in the company of his friend.

"Tell me what happened," said the colonel. So I told him what happened. And with all [his] virulence, you looked at . . . I looked at this man, but I tell you as I told you before, that I tried to see from all sides if I could find the point of the . . . of the thread of . . . to, to arrive at the thread or needle in the haystack, trying to, to discover anything. After telling him everything, he says, "Good. Look, you have to do the following: you have to pretend that your son has cancer." I was listening and saying to myself, "What is he saying?" [The colonel continues:] "Pretend that he has cancer and that they have . . . that he is in an operating room and that there is a butcher and a doctor; pray that it will be the doctor who will be operating on him." And then I looked at, at the one with whom I had made a certain friendship and he took hold of his head and covered his, his face. Because he must have said, he himself must have said, "What is this sonofabitch saying?" Because then he real-ized that all his venom, his virulence came out of him [the colonel]. This man had stuck a dagger in my wound and had twisted it inside me. I say to him, "Pardon me." I say, "Sir, but do you know anything?" I said this because of what he had been telling me. "No, no, I am weighing the various possibilities and I am making a supposition. I don't know anything of what might ha—" And I say, "But how do you have the gall to . . . ," and because of my nerves the words couldn't come out but I had wanted to say, "You are a son of a thousand bitches." You see, tell him whatever barbarity. And then the other saw my condition because he thought that I was going to lose it. . . . I wanted to grab him by the throat and strangle him, but then anyone of those who were there would have taken their gun and killed me. There, for the first time in my life, the desire came over me to murder someone. I had been destroyed. And then one of them leaves [to get a glass of water], and the colonel gets up from his chair, touches me and says, "Come, come. Drink some-thing, drink some water." And within his cynicism he had realized my desperation and says, "Good, good, ciao, we'll see each other another day." He left and I, the other one tried to calm me, I couldn't speak. Something Irma doesn't know. They went to get a navy doctor who was there, and I took a sip of water and began to react, you see, I began to react.

Julio recovered and was given some coffee.

"And I remember that my despair was so great that day that I went to the river bank and I stayed there like two hours staring at the river and trying to react into coming home in one piece because if I came and Irma would see me like that, she would say, "What happened?" The thing is that Irma didn't know anything at all about this. With the passage of time I have told her. These are unfortunate things that happen to you in life. . . ."[2]

Julio Morresi was deliberately sent up more false trails and would have to swallow many more humiliations and callous remarks, as did thousands of other relatives. After recovering from the paralyzing news of a disappearance, relatives began to search and overcame their greatest fears. The search for the disappeared was generally conducted by the parents.[3] Their strength and courage were fed by the trust between parent and child. The disappearance made many people tap into nearly inexhaustible emotional reserves to continue the search. These reserves were nourished by bonds of attachment, feelings of trust, the desire to protect and provide care, as well as by a deep-seated guilt. Abandoning the search meant abandoning the disappeared to their suffering and this equaled killing their loved ones.

This chapter focuses on the myriad ways in which parents looked for the disappeared, and the devious manners in which the military deceived them. I pay particular attention to the manifestations of attachment, protection, and sacrifice to prove my point that the trust between parents and children, whether as infants or as adults, motivated the tenacious search and mobilized an opposition movement which eventually helped to overturn the military regime. Furthermore, I analyze the search for grandchildren as a combination of the transgenerational extension of trust and the reproduction of motherhood.

This chapter's larger issue is that a social trauma can release powerful political forces which do not shirk from facing ruthless, deadly regimes. The Argentine military who had so carefully and rationally planned the elimination of thousands of political opponents, and felt cocksure about its lasting success with the luminous idea to make them disappear, failed to understand the strength of family ties and the emotional bonds and feelings of trust and protection between parents and children.

Search and Betrayal

The search for a disappeared person began whenever possible at the scene of abduction. There, shocked parents asked neighbors when the raid had taken place, what the assailants looked like, how many cars and persons had been involved, in what condition their son or daughter was taken, and whether he or she had said something. Friends and comrades were also contacted. These inquiries yielded bits of the abduction scenario described in chapter 10. Since most disappeared were young people involved in some sort of political activity, many parents imagined that they had been detained by the police.

Julio Morresi discovered that not all captives were registered by the police in their entry books, but that there were several blank lines with dates but without names or numbers. He asked about this and was told: " 'Well, this all depends on the events. If they legalize them, then they are given numbers and if not, then they are erased, they are erased,' because it was written in pencil, 'they are erased and one continues with the list of numbered detainees.' "[4] Clearly, many persons passed through police stations on their way to the secret detention centers.

A fruitless search to the police stations made parents who had not received notice of an abduction think that maybe their son or daughter had fallen victim to a traffic accident. They called nearby hospitals, and some went to the morgue. Searching relatives also visited prisons because they had read in the newspaper that the government had legalized a number of detainees. However, prisons could not provide any information on illegally detained disappeared, so the relatives left empty-handed.

When these visits proved unsuccessful, relatives submitted a writ of habeas corpus to know whether and on what grounds a person was being held in custody. A court would check police detention records to ascertain whether or not the person had been arrested. The problem was that the military coup had suspended all constitutional rights. As General Sánchez de Bustamante declared in June 1980: "Terrorism is of such exception and importance that it calls for proportional rights. There are legal norms and guiding principles that do not apply here, for example the right of habeas corpus. The secrecy that must surround the special operations in this type of fighting implies that it cannot be revealed who has been caught and who must still be caught. A cloud of silence must surround everything. . . ."[5] In other words, the right of habeas corpus was intentionally denied, and the judiciary was unable to function properly.

Having exhausted the legal means of finding a disappeared person, many relatives tried informal channels. María Adela Antokoletz went to the parish priest for help in finding her son Daniel. He gave her a letter of introduction to the bishop of his diocese. The bishop refused to receive her. Instead, the bishop's secretary sent her to the Metropolitan Curia, where she was told to see Monsignor Grasselli, the military chaplain and private secretary of the military vicar.[6] Others soon learned by word of mouth that the chaplain was receiving searching relatives. The journey to Grasselli must have been daunting to many people because of the location of his small office.

The seat of the Military Vicariate is at the Stella Maris chapel situated on the grounds of Navy Headquarters. In the mid-1970s, when the guerrilla attacks on the military intensified, the navy built a large fence around its headquarters. Thus, relatives had to enter this building first before being able to see Grasselli. I took this route several times in 1989 when visiting Grasselli.

After passing through the main entrance and climbing the stairway to

Navy Headquarters, I arrived at the front desk. My arrival was announced to Monsignor Grasselli. I had to leave a piece of identification and was given a visitor's pass. An NCO and a security guard accompanied me through the large building. We passed through the security checkpoint with its metal detectors and I had to open my attaché case for inspection. We bypassed a second metal detector, walked down a stairway and left the building by the rear entrance. We crossed a parking lot, and entered the Vicariate. I took the stairway up to the second floor and was invited in by Monsignor Grasselli.

Thousands of people found their way to Grasselli within days or weeks of an abduction. They regarded him as an intermediary with the military, a man of God in whom they could put their faith and trust. Grasselli recalled the emotional state of his visitors during the 1984 trial against the junta commanders. When a judge asked him whether or not the declarations were true, Grasselli responded: "you, your honor, are receiving in this place testimonies of events that occurred eight years ago. What you are hearing, I heard after a few hours or a few days, and I can assure you that people were not play-acting."[7] According to Grasselli, there are people who say that he created the Mothers of the Plaza de Mayo because when the relatives asked him what to do, he told them to draw attention to their cause: "walk, ask, walk around streets and squares."[8] On the other hand, one testimony stated that Grasselli "told me it would be better if we kept quiet and did not make much fuss. . . ."[9]

Grasselli began receiving the first relatives in 1975 and as the numbers increased, he compiled a filing cabinet. Each card contained the name of the disappeared, the date and place of abduction, the name, address, and telephone number of the relative reporting the disappearance, the date of the first visit, the dates of follow-up visits, and a number referring to additional information kept in separate folders, like letters and writs of habeas corpus. The cabinet contains about 2,500 cards and is a who's who of the human rights movement. Emilio Mignone went there on 25 May 1976, eleven days after the disappearance of his daughter Mónica. Hebe de Bonafini went to see Grasselli on 2 and 7 March of 1977, one month before fourteen mothers staged their first protest at the Plaza de Mayo.

One decade later, Grasselli was called "an accomplice within the sinister machinery of genocidal repression" who with the permission of the military "created confusion, encouraged family members to keep up their hopes, and tempered their fighting spirit."[10] Also one decade later, Grasselli condemned the Church hierarchy for its weakness. "Thousands of lives could have been saved by a public denunciation. The protests should have been public instead of confidential."[11] Grasselli defended his own role by saying that he had facilitated the departure abroad of several families and a group of ESMA captives.[12]

Grasselli is a controversial figure uniting within himself the many contradictions also found among the highest ecclesiastical authorities. Grasselli kept an extensive file on the disappeared, consoled searching relatives, knew about torture at the Navy Mechanics School, condemns the weak attitude of Cardinal Aramburu, but did not speak out himself, allegedly to save the lives of the ESMA captives. Few Argentine bishops were outspoken. Bishops Tortolo, Bonamín, Medina, and Plaza were staunch defenders of the military, while Bishops Angelelli, Hesayne, Novak, and de Nevares accused them of human rights violations. However, most Argentine bishops and cardinals did not speak out either against or in favor of military repression. The complacency of Bishop Laguna in his periodic meetings with the junta, the passiveness of most Argentine bishops, and their half-hearted diplomacy were saturated with guilt and fear. "The military did their best to make the bishops, the Church, in a certain way responsible for the violence incited by the Third World Church, and that gave us also a guilt complex about not having been even firmer [with the Third World Church]," so I was told by Bishop Casaretto.[13]

The suspicious car accident killing Argentina's most outspoken Bishop Enrique Angelelli in August 1976 left a deep impression on the Church hierarchy. The bishops did not gather at Angelelli's funeral, either because they disagreed with his progressive stand or out of fear. The intimidation of the Argentine Church hierarchy had been successful. As former Bishop Jerónimo Podestá says: "When the Church doesn't react to the death of a bishop, they [the military] know that they have already won the battle, and that is what happened here."[14] Later investigations showed that Angelelli had been assassinated by the army.[15]

The number of searching relatives increased so rapidly after the March coup that the Ministry of Interior opened an office in August 1976 where people could register the disappearances.[16] People suffered from the verbal abuse by officials accusing them of being parents of subversives and were told that they should have taken better care of them before they disappeared.[17] When Patricia Roca de Estrada entered the Ministry of Interior for the first time in late 1976, "it was a bit like crossing the door to hell. We found there a completely unknown and gloomy world, because the only thing there were a lot of people, generally only crying women, which for us seemed like a pale shadow of the suffering of others. . . ."[18]

Occasionally, the government released deceptive information about their investigation into the disappearances. The Search for Missing Persons Division of the Federal Police (División Búsqueda de Personas Desaparecidas) announced in April 1978 that it had located 232 persons reported missing during the first three months of 1978.[19]

What is truly amazing is that the deception took place in the very offices of the highest ranking members of the armed forces. The commanders of the five army corps, the Minister of Interior, and even junta members, in particular Admiral Massera, would take the time to talk face-to-face to individual parents, assuring them that they would do everything in their power to find their missing son, daughter, or spouse.

Searching relatives also mustered the courage to go directly to Argentina's military bases. At times, the commanding officer listened patiently and then assured the mother or father that their child was not at the base, but had possibly gone abroad. Parents were also intimidated with subtle threats. They were told not to neglect their family, and to take good care of their remaining children. At other times, they were snubbed, openly insulted, or ignored. Graciela Fernández Meijide remembers the Cordoban woman María Casas who used to wait outside a garrison of the Third Army Corps to hear news about her disappeared daughter and two disappeared sons. "When the soldiers standing guard at that regiment saw this woman at the gate, waiting an entire day, in the rain, in the sun, in the cold, in the heat, and with ruined feet, they often ended up crying."[20] So many people made their way to the First Army Corps headquarters in Palermo that an office was opened to receive them.[21]

Some relatives even searched in mental hospitals in the belief that their son or daughter might have gone insane from torture. As late as 1989, I heard the story of an Argentine couple vacationing that year in San Cristóbal, Venezuela, who had seen a large, deranged man in his mid-thirties at the town square speaking with an Argentine accent. Several mothers showed photographs of their missing sons to these tourists to ascertain his identity. Julio Morresi also thought that his son Norberto might have been a victim of torture or brainwashing and was roaming the streets of Buenos Aires without knowing his real identity. Julio stopped his car numerous times, went in reverse, stepped out, and looked straight at a young man who had struck his eye. He adjusted the mental image of his son as the years advanced, not only older but also with or without a beard, with or without long hair. One day, he finally found a lead to his son.

In mid-1977, Julio Morresi was told by a shoe store owner that he knew an illegitimate daughter of Admiral Guzzetti who might help him find his son. A few days later, the woman called by phone, identified herself as Nélida, and asked Julio to come to her home at Guayaquil Street and José María Moreno Avenue in the Caballito neighborhood of Buenos Aires. Julio told her about the disappearance, and the many places he had searched. She did not make any promises but said she would check her contacts with the military.

Some time later, Nélida called. "Come! Come, because there's something!" Julio jumped in his car, ran several traffic lights, and arrived within three minutes at her door step. "'You? I just hung up the phone and you're already here!' I say to her, 'And what do you think?' 'Good,' she says, 'Good, don't raise your hopes too high, but it seems that we have found something.' I say, 'What?' me in my despair. 'No, no, no, we found something. Give me another piece of information about Norberto.'" Julio told her what he knew that might identify him. After several days, the woman told him to see a captain at the First Army Corps. The captain wrote down some information about Norberto, but told Julio never to come and see him again at the military base, but that he had to use Nélida as their intermediary.

One day, the woman called again and asked Julio to meet her in a shopping center in Caballito. He went there immediately, sat down, and she told him, " 'We found Norberto!' 'How?' 'Yes', she said, 'we found him,' she says, 'He is in a detention center.' I, in front of all this, you can't imagine. I didn't know whether to cry or laugh. 'Finally,' she said, 'finally we found something.' I wanted to, I don't know what, embrace, kiss this woman." She immediately tried to calm him down, saying that they might be under surveillance and that they had to maintain the highest degree of secrecy. Nélida explained that Norberto was held in the same cell as the son of a high-ranking officer and that he was therefore treated quite well. She emphasized that he could not tell anybody, not even his wife. "I say, 'No,' I say, I raised my hand, 'not to my wife? Why? You are a woman, a mother, and she may not know this?' She says, 'Good, only your wife and nobody else.' Just to tell you that we lived through this anguish and happiness the two of us; neither my mother-in-law, nor my brother-in-law who were living with us, nobody knew anything." Julio began to give the woman presents, and when his wife Irma finally met her, she embraced her crying, "She was our god, that's what that woman was at that moment. I believe that whatever that woman would have said, we would have done."

Several weeks after the first contact, Julio asked Nélida for some proof that Norberto was alive because in the midst of his hope he realized that he might be the victim of an extortion. They met days later, and she told Julio and Irma that through a guard at the secret detention center, she had heard that Norberto did not want to eat supper at night but preferred five or six green apples. "Well, with that piece of information she gave, Irma and I looked at each other and said: 'It's him! It's him! There's no doubt.' " Norberto was known for his voracious appetite for green apples. This was the living proof Julio and Irma had been waiting for.

Some time later, Julio and Irma received a desperate call. The woman told them that all captives at the secret detention center were going to be shot within one week, but that the officer's son was going to be spared. This was the chance to save Norberto. Nélida asked for money to buy a passport and bribe the guard. Julio owned a small second house, sold it far below its market value, and together with his savings, gave the woman around 25,000 U.S. dollars. Much more money was needed because the plan was to take Norberto and his cellmate in a jeep from the detention center, send them with false passports to Switzerland, place two dead bodies in the jeep, and then set the vehicle on fire. Julio gave Nélida more money but also asked for a letter from Norberto as proof that he was still alive. They were told that this was very difficult and that the guard was already risking his life on behalf of Norberto.

Julio began to change the little money he had left into Swiss francs because he was going to meet his son there. Nélida continued to demand money but also clothing. "Because nobody was to know, nobody of the family, and [Norberto] was going to a cold place, Irma spent all nights in bed knitting woolen clothing for him, pullovers, socks, vests, all through the night. Not during the day because then they would have asked: 'For whom are you knitting that?' So, she did the things of the house during the day and she knitted at night. I said, 'Irma, you're going to . . .' You could see her knitting with an enthusiasm, with a happiness. . . ." About two months had passed since the first contact. Norberto was about to be flown out of the country, so Julio asked one Friday for a letter from him. Nélida said that this was impossible, but Julio remained firm and asked for a piece of clothing, any kind of proof. She promised to have something by Tuesday.

On that particular Tuesday, Julio went to Nélida's apartment in Caballito but nobody answered the doorbell. He asked the doorman. He told Julio that the occupants had moved. " 'What do you mean, 'They moved'? When did they move?' The police almost got involved, because I grabbed the doorman by his throat because he didn't want to tell me where they had gone, and on what day. So, 'Police! Police!' I then took my car to get out of that situation and I left. They [the extortionists] had gone up in smoke. This was the time that Irma almost died. That was the worst moment through which Irma passed. She was torn to pieces, destroyed, mentally and physically, destroyed."[22]

Many more people were victimized by such schemes.[23] They were apparently so common that already in July 1976 *La Nación* newspaper carried a message from the Military Command of subzone 15 that warned "against false agents who, by charging large sums of money, promise parents of detainees allegedly held for a security check, to locate their whereabouts or places of detention." The communiqué further advised people to denounce such "individuals with a lack of professional ethic and social solidarity."[24] Implicitly, the army was thus admitting to the great number of disappearances, and that the extortionists came from their own ranks. Yet, people were afraid to denounce the extortion schemes. Despite everything, Julio and Irma Morresi still believed that Norberto might be alive because of the piece of evidence about his appetite for green apples.

Hope and Fantasy

The disappearance etched a silhouette in the home of searching family members. I have visited parents who maintained their daughter's room the way it was left two decades ago, and still changed the bedsheets every week. In another home, the housekeeper prepared every few days the favorite pudding of her employer's son. The dessert was left untouched in the refrigerator for him to savor if he would reappear. Many parents did not move to another house afraid that a returning son or daughter would be unable to find the new residence. One mother expressed the living inferno of waiting for a disappeared child as follows: "I don't imagine hell with spiked beds on which the condemned have to lie down, but with easy chairs on which one sits comfortably awaiting the mailman . . . who will bring news that will never arrive."[25]

When trail after trail and means after means had been exhausted, the uncanny crept into the everyday as parents imagined themselves in telepathic contact with their children. The need to be close and the desire to care for the missing son or daughter colored their perception of the world and made them enter the realm of fantasy. "I think and think, 'Where are you, my son? Are you in some place, maybe closer than I can imagine?' . . . What are you thinking, my dear, you who always thought so much? Who now occupies your thoughts? . . . Close your eyes, like I am doing now and think of me. I'm certain that in this way everything is going to pass very soon."[26] Estela Puccio Borrás held inner dialogues with her daughter Adriana: "Are you afraid, my little one? Are you tired? Are you awake or asleep? Did they hurt you? Did they cut your hair?"[27]

Some mothers believed they could give their children strength through telepathic communication. "Sometimes I seemed to hear Pablo's voice," recalls Graciela Fernández Meijide. "I lived as if hallucinating. When I was not doing something, some formal procedure or task for Pablo, I maintained even more that mental contact with him and I talked to him in thought. I told him 'Hold on, Pablo . . . , stay alive, Pablo . . .' I didn't know very well what Pablo had to endure but I imagined the horror of being alone, the anguish, the impotence. . . . I thought, 'Pablo must be having faith in us; he knows that we are going to get to him . . .', and . . . we couldn't. This still bothers me so much!"[28]

Matilde Saidler de Mellibovsky felt powerless when her daughter Graciela called by phone, as if from the grave, five days after her abduction. " 'Aunt! Aunt!' she said, 'It's me, Graciela!' 'No, my dear,' I said, 'it isn't your aunt, it's your mother, where are you? Where are you, my dear?' Then her voice changed: 'I'm very far away, I think I'm very far away.' I understood that it was going to be a very short phone call and I asked: 'When am I going to see you? Am I going to see you again?' And she said: 'No, no mother, never again.' I don't know which words came then, but she said with great emotion: 'Mother, I love you, I love you.' And I had the strength to tell her: 'And I adore you and am with you, wherever you are, I'm with you.' And they cut the communication. . . ."[29]

Even though many relatives had a premonition that the disappeared had been assassinated, it was difficult to reconcile oneself to the thought of such fatality because there was no body to grieve over. Mourning meant abandoning the disappeared and surrendering to the conditions created by the military junta. Julio Morresi always believed that his son was alive. "We always had the illusion that he could appear, without failing to realize that he might be dead. But we always kept in a corner of our heart [the hope] that he might appear some day."[30]

Likewise, the thought of giving up the search was experienced as abandoning the child once more, of violating again the trust between parent and child. Julio Morresi: "Because when a loved one dies of a disease or an accident and you tried to do something, then you know what happened and there comes a moment when you accept that it had to be that way. But you were searching for a loved one without knowing what had happened. You said that he was alive somewhere, because you were not going to kill him with your conscience by saying 'my son is dead.' I never ever thought that my son was dead, if not it would have given me the feeling that it was me who had killed him. But all this means that you were living a terrible anguish, that is the terrible anguish which lives in all homes of the disappeared."[31] In a convoluted way, the military implicated the surviving relatives emotionally in the death of the disappeared. Relatives could only begin to find some firm ground in life by giving up the disappeared as dead and thus enter a process of mourning. This emotional tangle became even more complex when the disappeared daughter was pregnant or had young children.

Disappeared Infants and Pregnant Mothers

Seeing one's infant son or daughter for the last time, crying inconsolably in the arms of gun-toting men as one was abducted and dragged away, must have been unbearable. Most often, the babies were given to the childless families of policemen, officers, or civilian collaborators. Some children disappeared after being given to neighbors. Such adoptive parents were sometimes forced to flee with the baby to another city after receiving threats from the assailants. Other infants ended up in an orphanage.[32]

The daughter-in-law of María Isabel Chorobik de Mariani was killed during a military assault on her home on 24 November 1976. Ms. de Mariani's son Daniel, a member of the Montoneros, escaped but was killed on 1 August 1977. Her granddaughter Clara Anahí was abducted. General Camps declared that the three-month-old girl had died in the attack but Ms. de Mariani heard from a retired policeman that the little girl had been adopted.[33] Just as Julio Morresi composed a mental image of his son that changed with the years, so Ms. de Mariani visualized the development of her granddaughter. The first teeth, the first steps, the first words, the first dress. She bought dolls for her granddaughter, and wrote on her fifth birthday: "I will find you, my Anahí, don't worry. Your little grandmother will recognize you because she carries you in her blood. You are the daughter of my dead son. . . . Anahí, my Anahí, our Anahí, have faith. We will find each other soon. Have faith in your little grandmother who has turned into steel to locate you but who will again be caring and warm when she finds you, my little one."[34]

Grandmothers displayed a social trust towards their grandchildren similar to that of their disappeared children. The transgenerational extension of trust and protection is rooted in the grandparent's own parental feelings. "We are involved in the desperate search for the disappeared children," observed Elida Galletti. "Mothers two times over, robbed even of the little sprouts of our children, the anguish is sometimes unbearable, and the absences hurt us deep. But we have to keep going, because we have to find them. We have to search for them today, tomorrow, and every day. At all hours."[35] Several grandmothers emphasized the need to let the disappeared grandchildren know that their parents had not betrayed their trust, as Reina Esses de Waisberg of the grandmothers of the Plaza de Mayo explains: "Every time we find a child it is as if I found mine. We fight so hard because the disappeared children have to know that they were not thrown away, that their mothers did not abandon them, that they were conceived with love."[36]

Nancy Chodorow's interpretation of motherhood can help us clarify the tenacious search of the grandmothers, especially in the case of finding the babies of disappeared pregnant daughters. According to Chodorow, mothers regard and raise daughters as extensions of themselves, while sons are stimulated towards differentiation, independence, and assertiveness.[37] This greater sense of oneness with daughters than with sons becomes particularly strong when the daughter is pregnant. The grandmother-grandchild bond is a complex whole of social strands and parental emotions that together provided the motivational forces for the search.

The grandchild is first of all the extension of the blood line. He or she projects the family into the future, remembers its history and continues its identity. Second, the grandchild is the child of the grandmother's daughter with all the feelings of love and tenderness which conception, pregnancy, and birth entail. The grandchild represents the successful passing on of motherhood. In fact, Matilde de Mellibovsky laments that her disappeared daughter could "not even leave in my arms her own image in the form of a son. . . ."[38] Thus, the grandmother feels a particular responsibility for the grandchild and will extend care and protection in the absence of the disappeared daughter. Third, the mother-child relation of the disappeared daughter and her infant is felt by the grandmother as a reflection of the attachment to her own daughter. The grandmother reproduces emotionally both her own mother-child relation as well as that of her disappeared daughter with that of the missing grandchild. The emotions and responsibilities evoked by these three social relations make grandmothers search relentlessly for their grandchildren.

There is a fourth, more hidden, motivation at play in finding the grand-child. Just as the violent abduction prevented the disappeared daughter from protecting her child, so the grandmother was helpless when her daughter was taken away. The unconscious guilt feelings associated with this failure of trust and protection made grandmothers determined not to have their grandchild run the same fate as their own son or daughter. In a way, the grandmothers were seeking a second chance at mothering, and vowed never to back down. Abandoning the search would imply giving them up to the kidnappers and adoptive families, just as they had been forced to surrender their own sons and daughters to the captors.

Babies were most often abducted together with their parents. This implied that the searching relatives were generally the parents of the adults and at the same time the infant's grandparents. On which search should they concentrate? This question arose in late 1977 among the mothers of the Plaza de Mayo when they received news that small children had been left abandoned in orphanages. Most grandmothers decided to dedicate their time to searching for their grandchild, either when the death of their own child was certain or when the disappeared son or daughter had been a member of a guerrilla organization. In the latter case, the grandmothers were politically aware enough to realize that their children had been assassinated. An additional reason was that inquiries about a disappeared adult were often met with hostility, while questions about a missing infant received more sympathy.[39]

The search for babies and infants was different from that of finding disappeared adults. Adults were either held captive or had been assassinated. Occasionally, a parent might receive a message from a released captive that their son or daughter had been seen alive in a secret detention center. Instead, babies and infants were most often in someone's private home.

What kept the hope of finding their grandchildren alive was that grandmothers had heard about the adoption of abducted infants, and that some were told by released captives of a successful delivery by their pregnant daughter.[40] Sometimes, an expecting daughter was allowed to call her mother to assure her that everything was fine.[41] Such messages of hope contrasted sharply with other information about the washing ashore of brutally assassinated adults, testimonies about executions, and the negative responses to writs of habeas corpus.

The grandmothers reasoned that their grandchildren had to be alive somewhere because if it was logical, according to military reasoning, to execute captured revolutionaries then it was illogical to have female captives carry their pregnancies to full term and then assassinate them together with their babies. A 1979 testimony by three released captives verified this reasoning: "With pain, we confirm that these [pregnant] women were almost certainly killed. The transfers meant only one thing: death. But the children are alive."[42] The grandmothers began to call them the "living disappeared" (*desaparecidos con vida*) to distinguish them from the adult disappeared who were privately presumed dead.[43]

In a very few cases, a baby was found shortly after its birth in captivity. Mirta Alonso de Hueravillo gave birth to a son in June 1977 at the Navy Mechanics School. She decided to mark her newborn behind the ear with a hot needle. Ten days after delivery, she was transferred, and most likely either shot or thrown into the sea. Her mother Ms. de Alonso succeeded in recovering the six-month-old baby boy from an orphanage in Buenos Aires thanks to the scar.[44]

At least one grandmother found her granddaughter, only to lose her again. Ms. Valenzi heard through a midwife that her disappeared daughter Silvia Mabel had given birth to a premature baby girl. She went immediately to the Quilmes Municipal Hospital and demanded to see her granddaughter. At first, the hospital director refused to admit that the baby was there, but later gave in when a nurse contradicted him. Although the director threatened the grandmother and told her never to return, the nurse allowed her to see her granddaughter gaining strength in an incubator. On her next visit, Ms. Valenzi was told that the baby had died. The word "deceased" had been written behind the baby's name in the birth register, and the mother's name had been erased crudely from the hospital records and was replaced by "NN" (no name or unidentified person). The midwife and nurse were abducted by police within two weeks of the birth. They remain disappeared.[45]

The precise number of disappeared babies and infants is as uncertain as that of the disappeared. The CONADEP truth commission wrote in 1984 that there were 147 disappeared children, including babies born in captivity.[46] The most thoroughly documented number is provided by Rita Arditti. In 1997, she arrived at 88 disappeared children, and 136 disappeared pregnant women.[47] The total number of disappeared babies, infants, and small children must thus be at least over two hundred.

Forced Adoptions and Grandparental Bonds

Why were babies, infants, and small children abducted and then adopted? General Vaquero made a revealing statement to Emilio Mignone when they discussed the disappearance of Mignone's daughter Mónica: "We have a big problem with the children of the subversives, and we have to find a way that the children of the subversives are not educated with hatred toward the military institutions."[48] The children had to be removed from a politicized family environment that had brought forth a rebellious generation. As judge Delia Pons told a group of grandmothers trying to recover one grandchild: "I, personally, am convinced that your children were terrorists. A terrorist is for me synonymous to a murderer. And I don't return children to murderers. Because it wouldn't be right. Because they wouldn't know how to raise them and because they don't have a right to raise them. I shall be unwavering in this. . . . They are in the hands of decent families who will know how to raise them in a way, I unfortunately have to say, that you didn't know how to raise your own children. Ladies . . . only over my dead body will you obtain custody of those children."[49]

The political motivation of the Argentine military provides only part of the explanation. The babies of the captives should be understood as war booty, both in symbolic and economic terms, as Matilde Herrera suggests: "it is a very sick thing to take possession of the most loved, the most intimate, of an enemy and put it in your house. That's to say, to keep your enemy's children as your personal things. . . ."[50] The victors appropriated the enemy's valuables as a manifestation of their power. The incorporation of the enemy's children suggested a lasting victory because it interrupted the social reproduction of the vanquished, and implied the termination of their social group for lack of descendants.

The Naval Hospital opened a waiting list for married navy officers who could not have children themselves.[51] According to Matilde Herrera, the prospective parents could choose babies from the photographs taken of their biological parents. They did not want to adopt children from the poor, lower classes but from intelligent, well-educated and well-fed white, middle class parents.[52] Raúl Vilariño, a former member of the ESMA task group, accused Navy Captain Astiz of selling babies and children for $700 to childless policemen and servicemen. He estimates that the navy task group sold a total of fifty-eight babies.[53] The ESMA even took in pregnant captives abducted by army and air force, a highly uncommon procedure given the strict divisions between the three forces.[54] Clearly, the appropriation of newborn babies was a deliberate policy.

Special facilities for pregnant captives were provided in at least three secret detention centers, namely the Navy Mechanics School, Campo de Mayo, and the Banfield center. ESMA director Captain Chamorro held guided tours for senior naval officers to boast about the excellent conditions under which pregnant captives were held. These "excellent" conditions consisted of a room with a window, a couple of mattresses, and the removal of chains and shackles during the final days before delivery.[55] The conditions at the Campo de Mayo Military Hospital were equally appalling. The eyes of the expecting mothers were covered with blindfolds or black sunglasses, yet they were given vitamins and were allowed to walk when they reached the seventh month. The deliveries were most often done by Caesarian section or accelerated with a serum to avoid hours of labor. The women were tied by hands and feet.[56]

The child abductions were not just motivated by the desire for appropriation but were also directed at the grandparent-grandchild bond. The grandparents were regarded as unfit to raise children. Their own children had turned into enemies of the Argentine state, and the grandchildren would follow in their step if the grandparents were allowed to educate them. The grandparents were punished by ostracizing them from the reproduction of society. The abduction and subsequent forced adoption of babies severed transgenerational ties, wove an entirely new web of bonds and affections, and created new identities and even new selves. Furthermore, the military knew that if grandparents suspected that their grandchildren were alive, then they would be held hostage to this situation, and be afraid to harm their own disappeared children through political protest.

How did the forced adoption of babies by members of the armed forces, the police, and civilian collaborators take place? Most commonly, the babies were registered under false pretense as their own natural-born children. Small children were also dropped first at orphanages as unidentified persons to confound searching relatives, and then adopted by a childless couple either ignorant of the child's real identity or in cahoots with the abductors.[57]

The ploy seemed foolproof but the Argentine military had greatly underestimated the strength of the personal attachment among grandparents, parents and (grand)children when they decided in late 1975 upon systematic, forced disappearances as the hard edge of their repression. What explains this blind spot?

One, the military had dehumanized their political enemies to such an extent that they could neither muster any empathy with the parents nor imagine the sentiments of grandparents who often disagreed politically with their own children. Two, the military expected the grandparents to withdraw in shame for having failed to educate their own sons and daughters into law-abiding citizens. Three, they believed that the trauma of disappearance would paralyze people emotionally, and could not imagine the collective forces that would arise from the common predicament of their social trauma. Four, they assumed that the repeated denial from the authorities would make people simply stop searching for the disappeared, and that they would accept the deceptive explanations given. Finally, it is likely that the military underestimated the strength of emotion because of a professional deformation. Military training is directed at controlling individual emotions freed under duress and at channeling these into coordinated moves and countermoves on the battlefield. The military junta must have made a rational assessment of the pros and cons of forced disappearances but, in their coldblooded battle plan, failed to take the feelings of the surviving relatives into account.

Unexpectedly, the disappearance set deep sentiments in motion which became the engine driving public protest. The parent-child and grandparent-grandchild bonds became the foundation of public resistance. These bonds constituted a political force imbued with personal meaning. As Nancy Chodorow has written perceptively, "These are the personal meanings that constitute psychic life and that also shape interpersonal relationships, personal projects, work, and constructions of cultural meanings and practices."[58] The disappearance of a child restructured people's inner lives and outer worlds. The tragedy befalling them changed their outlook on the world, their self-perception and social relations. Social trust made thousands of people search for relatives, create oppositional associations, and manifest their anger in public protest. Just as the disappeared felt totally abandoned, so the parents felt that they had forsaken their disappeared son or daughter. The use of diapers as headscarfs by mothers and grandmothers protesting the disappearance of their adult children and infant grandchildren was the most dramatic demonstration of those protective feelings.

The abduction of pregnant women, holding them captive till they delivered their babies, assassinating the young mothers, and then giving the babies away to childless military couples was one of the moral low points of Argentina's cultural war. The military commanders who masterminded this ploy never imagined that the babies born in captivity would come to haunt them even more than the disappeared and assassinated adults. The kidnapping of children was excluded from the general pardon given in 1989 and 1990. In June 1998 and December 1998 respectively, former junta members Lieutenant-General Videla and Admiral Massera were placed under house arrest, and more than a dozen others were to follow them.

Chapter 15
The Call for Truth: Defiance, Resistance, and Maternal Power

The recollection of my first meeting with the mothers of the Plaza de Mayo is vague. I have difficulty separating my earliest impression from later encounters, and even from the documentaries, newsreels, and the many photographs I have seen since then. I do remember walking along one of the fountains at the Plaza de Mayo in April 1978 where workers had cooled their tired feet during that momentous crowd mobilization of 17 October 1945. I also recall sitting on the glazed brickstone bench circling the fountain. Or was it a wooden bench closer to the statue of General Belgrano?

As I stood up to walk toward the Cabildo, the colonial town hall where Argentina's independence had been proclaimed on 25 May 1810, I was approached by three or four women walking swiftly towards me. "Where are our sons and daughters?" they said with desperation. "They took them but we don't know where they are!" I still remember my sense of bewilderment at being surrounded by these women, at the expressions on their faces, and the persistence in their asking. Taken aback, I said, "What do you mean: 'they took them away?'" I had great difficulty understanding them because they were looking around furtively while talking. As I tried to grasp what they said, our impromptu meeting was interrupted by a policeman and two civilians. The men spoke calmly but incessantly to the women while pushing them away from me.

Within a minute, they had all vanished. I stood as if nailed to the ground, unable to make sense of what had happened. I glanced around and strolled to the Cabildo absentminded, saw the pigeons circling the small pyramid commemorating the May Revolution against the Spanish colonizers, and watched the businessmen on their way to the banks and ministries surrounding the historic square. It seemed again another ordinary sunny day at the Plaza de Mayo in Buenos Aires.

The mothers of the Plaza de Mayo were the public face of the nonviolent resistance movement against the dictatorship, while the half dozen other human rights organizations worked in less visible ways. Theirs was a street protest. As one founding member said: "We decided to take to the streets, and it was the streets that taught us. That was what gave us our political strength."[1] The mothers had won the street, just as many oppositional crowds had done before them. It was the public protest of these mothers which would trigger large protest crowds against the military dictatorship and precipitate its fall from power.

This chapter focuses on the political response by searching relatives to the military terror tactics of forced disappearances, and the broadening of their protests into a large opposition movement. The military had sought to traumatize surviving relatives into passiveness. They did succeed in a number of individual cases, yet they provoked many more people to political action. Most relatives emerged from the culture of fear with an uncanny strength, became aware of the social trauma that enveloped them, and joined a growing human rights movement.

Public protest became a means to rework the anguish through collective action. The mothers of the disappeared experienced such coping with each successful Thursday protest at the Plaza de Mayo. "When everyone was terrorized we didn't stay at home crying—we went to the streets to confront them directly. We were mad but it was the only way to stay sane."[2] Clearly, the social trauma transformed individual suffering into political opposition and slowly gathered the support of broad layers of Argentine society.

Mothers of the Plaza de Mayo

The history of the mothers of the Plaza de Mayo is a chronicle of courage, betrayal, sorrow, tenacity, and resistance as well as a telling example of the transformation of a social trauma into political action. As a mother in search of a disappeared son or daughter walked the paths trodden by so many before, through police stations, prisons, and government offices, she could not help meeting others on a similar quest. One day in April 1977, during another fruitless wait at the military vicariate, Azucena Villaflor de De Vicenti proposed to several women to meet on the 30th of April at the Plaza de Mayo at eleven o'clock in the morning. The women realized that their sons and daughters had disappeared under similar circumstances, and that the joining of hands might yield better results.

According to María Adela Antokoletz, there were fifteen women at this first meeting. One of them was a young woman searching for her sister. The other women told her that it was too dangerous for her to come to the Plaza de Mayo as her young age might raise the suspicion of the police. The main square was empty on this chilly Saturday, so they agreed to return the following Friday at 3:30 P.M. The young woman stayed away and the fourteen remaining women met to draft a letter to President Videla. The group doubled after several Friday meetings until one woman proposed to meet on Thursdays because she felt Friday to be an unlucky day.[3]

The Plaza de Mayo was the most obvious place to meet because the presidential palace was located there and also the Ministry of Interior office where searching relatives went for information. These two reasons were reinforced by the symbolic significance of the Plaza de Mayo: these women moved their sorrow from the intimacy of their home to the most coveted square in Argentina and thus undermined the authoritarian state's control of public space. The public protest was an exteriorization of personal pain and the first open manifestation of a social trauma suffered by thousands.

The military authorities recognized the Plaza de Mayo's political and symbolic significance. They remodeled the square in 1977, adding fountains, flower beds, meadows, stone benches, and broad walkways.[4] They constricted its open spaces, transforming the square more into a park than a public place congenial to mass gatherings. The Plaza de Mayo became a place of rules, regulations, and proscriptions. People were not allowed to gather in groups or stage political manifestations. They could not sit on the grass, and had to remain confined to the walkways. In effect, this was both a form of crowd control, and an expression of the divine natural order which the Thomist military were so prone to imprint on the Argentine people. As urban architects of the Enlightenment had indicated, the organization of public space represented "the example of order, the happiness of order, the supremacy of order, the magnificence of order, the spectacle of order."[5]

In their early protest days, the mothers gathered at the wooden benches near the statue of General Belgrano, close to the presidential palace, to divide their tasks. After several months, around fifty women were attending the Thursday afternoon meetings, and were ordered by police to leave. Under the state of siege, there was a penalty of five to twelve years imprisonment for illicit association, and up to twenty-five years for the leaders.[6] Upon their refusal to leave, one policeman told them: "Well, you can only stay if you keep moving. You cannot stay here, you have to keep moving."[7]

And so they did. Groups of five or six women walked around the flowerbeds, their arms locked into one another. Soon, the intimidation began. The mothers were insulted, shoved, and arrested. They created new forms of resistance on the spot. On one occasion, when a woman was asked for her identity card, all other women presented their i.d.'s. With three hundred documents to review, the policeman had to tolerate their extended presence at the Plaza de Mayo. Thereafter, the police stopped asking for documents. The defiant act clogged not only the surveillance procedures but also made the mothers assume responsibility for each other, and thus strengthened their group solidarity.

Jennifer Schirmer has drawn attention to the encirclement of the pyramid at the square's center as a symbolic undermining of its grid pattern, thus providing an alternative to the political demonstrations which used to advance from different gathering points to the Plaza de Mayo.[8] The mothers reject the description of their protests as making rounds, but prefer to call them marches because a round is turned inwards while a march externalizes a protest towards a particular objective.[9] The progression from sitting at a bench and marching around the pyramid is of great importance because it transforms the protest from a passive into an active display, and extends the occupation of a place into the spatial appropriation. The inability to control the invasion of protesting citizens meant a loss of face for the military. The government even proposed to the mothers to move their protest to another square, to the Plaza San Martin or the Plaza Flores, but they did not give in.[10]

Several mothers have told me about their fears when Thursday arrived, fear about the civilian-clad policemen, the squad cars, and the threat of arrest. The fears manifested themselves in morning sickness, sweating, an upset stomach or dizzy spells. However, they all emphasized that these fears vanished once they were at the Plaza in the company of each other. This invigoration is a clear example of how personal experience can be transformed into group strength through the awareness of a social trauma. María del Rosario de Cerruti feels that the Plaza gives her strength. "It's a sentiment with great force, unbelievable. They may hurt, I may feel a lot of pain in my legs, but I don't feel anything when I'm marching. It's a sentiment of force, as if it feeds my strength at the square."[11] The group gave a protection that carried their personal courage forward. This encroachment on the authoritarian state at the Plaza de Mayo would soon branch out into other realms dominated by the Argentine military.

After claiming the Plaza de Mayo, the mothers broadened their protests into the halls of justice. The Argentine military had always cultivated an image of due process. However, on 19 April 1977, the Supreme Court declared the request of habeas corpus for 425 disappeared persons as beyond its jurisdiction, and argued that the complainants should direct their claims to the government.[12] On 28 June 1977, searching relatives presented 159 writs of habeas corpus to the court.[13] This barrage revealed the court's complicity in the repression. After several years of negative replies, the writ became a cynical means to expose the true face of military rule. So, fifty or sixty mothers would join hands to make one mass writ of habeas corpus to pester the judges. One of the last appeals united nine hundred requests for the whereabouts of the disappeared.[14]

In another move, the affected relatives submitted petitions supported by thousands of signatures. The first petition was presented on 15 October 1977. It was signed by twenty-four thousand civilians demanding an investigation into the disappearances, and was accompanied by a list with the names of 571 disappeared persons and 61 prisoners held without charge. This was the first public manifestation of the human rights movement as a whole. The mothers made a notable presence while other groups joined in during their vigil outside Congress as the delegation delivered the petition. Soon, the police moved in with great force, dispersing the mobilization with tear gas, and arresting about three hundred persons, including many mothers.[15]

How to bring word to the Argentine people about what was happening in their country? Officially, there was no censorship but reality was of course different. So, when the mothers approached newspapers to print ads calling attention to the plight of the disappeared, only *La Prensa* dared do so. On 5 October 1977, *La Prensa* published a passionate appeal signed by 237 mothers: "We ask nothing but the truth."[16]

Sometime in July or August of 1977, an attractive, athletic young man arrived with his sister at the Plaza de Mayo. His name was Gustavo Niño, and they were looking for their disappeared brother. Azucena de De Vicenti took a particular liking to the blond young man, and told him that it was dangerous to come to the Plaza de Mayo. So, Gustavo would wait at a corner nearby and only join the mothers and other relatives when they reassembled in a small hall at the Santa Cruz Church about forty blocks away. During one of these meetings, the idea arose to place another ad, more daring than the one of 5 October.

Signatures and donations were collected with great sacrifice. Particularly daunting was the condition imposed by the military government that all public denunciations had to be accompanied by the complainants' identity card numbers. On 8 December 1977, the day before the payment was due, four groups of three mothers departed after the Thursday afternoon protest for four churches in Buenos Aires city to collect the final names, numbers, and donations. The immense city had been divided into four zones to save the contributors a long trip. Nora de Cortiñas went with Azucena de De Vicenti to the Santa María Magdalena de Betánia church. Another group went to the Santa Cruz church in the San Cristóbal neighborhood.

Gustavo Niño and his sister showed up at the Santa Cruz church. He took out his wallet and apologized for only being able to contribute a small amount. Ostensibly, he showed a handful of banknotes to a number of individuals. Just after 8:00 P.M., when the meeting was about to end, "the blond angel" (*el angel rúbio*) as Niño became known, vanished from sight, leaving his sister behind. Gustavo Niño turned out to be no other than Navy Lieutenant Alfredo Astiz, a member of the ESMA task group. In the previous months, he had attended masses, meetings, and protests. He had ingratiated himself with the mothers when at one time he ran to their defense when the federal police were breaking up their protest at the Plaza de Mayo.

On 8 December 1977, when the group left the Santa Cruz church, they were accosted by several armed men who handcuffed them and dragged them by their hair to several passenger cars stationed nearby. Eight persons were abducted. They were taken to the ESMA secret detention center, interrogated, and tortured. Seven persons were "transferred" from the ESMA after ten days, among them the mothers María Eugenia Ponce de Bianco and María Esther Ballestrino de Careaga, and the French nun Alice Domon. All seven were assassinated. The eighth abducted person was Silvia Labayru, an ESMA captive who had been forced to pose as Astiz's sister. She eventually regained her freedom.

The mothers who had collected money in the other three churches were shocked by the abductions but Azucena de De Vicenti urged them to press on with the publication of the ad. The next day, *La Nación* received the payment for the ad signed by eight hundred mothers and wives demanding to know whether the disappeared were dead or alive.

On Saturday 10 December 1977, as Azucena Villaflor de De Vicenti was walking to a newspaper stand to buy *La Nación*, she was abducted by an ESMA task group. Later that day, three men who assisted the mothers with their protests and the French nun Léonie Duquet, who lived with the already abducted Alice Domon, were also taken.[17] The two French nuns had been helping the mothers and worked in a slum in Buenos Aires. One week after their abduction, a photo was delivered at the French embassy showing the nuns before an emblem of the Montoneros. The photo was accompanied by a letter by Alice Domon and a communiqué by the Montoneros. The ploy failed to fool the French authorities. Nevertheless, diplomatic pressure did not prevent the assassination of the French nuns at the Navy Mechanics School.[18]

The disappearance of Azucena Villaflor de De Vicenti, the founder and informal leader of the mothers, was a tremendous blow. The number of mothers returning to the Plaza de Mayo the next Thursday dwindled to less than forty. However, by this time, the group had acquired a social dynamic which overcame the loss of its most prominent member.

Maternal Power

When the mothers held their first demonstrations, the military junta was at a loss about how to react because they did not conceive of mothers as political actors. Derision was the first response. Lieutenant-General Videla remarked that they were crazy, and thus unworthy of interest to either the authorities, the press, or the Argentine people. They were outside existing sociopolitical patterns and therefore stigmatized as crazy. Still, there were other layers of meaning behind Videla's contempt.

The mothers of the Plaza de Mayo were cultural transgressors. They overstepped the gender divisions of traditional Argentine society, in which the public arena was a male and the house a female space. According to Nora de Cortiñas, they assumed a political role in public and politicized their domestic role at home: "We had to confront the military from that public square and we had to confront in our home the culture in which we had been raised. We had to confront a husband who sees that his wife arrives late at night, that his wife leaves and doesn't return that night because she remains in line at the Ministry of Interior, at the gate of a military base, at the door of a hospital, and doesn't return home."[19] Add to this the belief that women should be subordinate and docile, then we can understand better Videla's dismissal of these crying, protesting women as crazy. Women should suffer in private, not in public, as the hegemonic male ideology ordains in Latin America.[20]

On the level of male ideology, the designation of the mothers as crazy tied in with traditional Latin American notions about women as irrational, passionate, and thus susceptible to fits of hysteria when under duress. On the level of public life, their persistent presence at the Plaza de Mayo confirmed the belief that crowds and women resembled one another.[21] What would thus be more uncontrollable and dangerous than a crowd of distressed women?

The women utilized their role as mothers brilliantly in their resistance strategy. What was more natural than a mother wanting to know about the fate of her child? The mothers emphasized that they had no political motives or feminist sympathies, and presented themselves simply as housewives and mothers wanting news about their disappeared children. They traversed the public-domestic divide, so dominant in Latin American culture, in a reverse direction from the one used by the military assault teams which had invaded their homes. In a second transgressive act, they domesticized public space. They displayed photographs of their disappeared children, and covered their heads with gauze diapers as headscarfs because "it's going to make us feel better, closer to the children."[22] Such creative cultural strategies were all expressions of maternal protection and trust.

Why were women the main force of public protest? After all, men figured prominently in other human rights organizations. Today, the mothers give five explanations. One, their husbands had to work during the day while the women could dedicate themselves to visiting government offices, police stations, prisons, and military bases. Two, the women did not want their husbands present at the protests, afraid that they might run to their defense aggressively when their wives were being shoved around by the police. Three, the women claim a greater emotional resilience to cope with disappearances than their husbands, of whom several pined away in utter loneliness. A fourth explanation refers to the special bond between women and children forged during a painful delivery, impelling mothers to sacrifice themselves more readily. Matilde Herrera reflects about losing her three children: "I'm just someone who has lost in a brutal way the entire product of her insides. I think that a man can understand that, but I don't know if all men are able to feel it."[23] The fifth explanation is that mothers will seldom question their children's ways and are more forgiving than fathers of their missteps. Fathers tend to compete and argue more with their children about politics, and some fathers even blamed the disappearances on their children's own wrongdoing.

Another explanation is found in the special relation between mother and child in a traditional patriarchal society. The relegation of women to the domestic domain as homemakers and the domination of the public domain by men affect their selves. Nancy Chodorow has argued that women define themselves more in relational terms, as continuous with others, than men who define themselves as more independent and differentiated from the world.[24] This difference made mothers more prone to defy state repression almost recklessly. This is not to say that men did not search for their children, as the interminable journeys of Julio Morresi demonstrated, but men would more readily accept the military's total control of the public sphere and fear the infliction of even greater harm on their families.

The conduct of the mothers of the Plaza de Mayo was an expression of what Sara Ruddick has called "maternal thinking," that is the "unity of reflection, judgment, and emotion."[25] The mothers were not competing for power in the public domain but moved by maternal feelings to demand an accountability for their children's fate from the military authorities. This maternal appeal allowed them to feel an emotional kinship with one another which socialized their private pain, and impelled them towards joint action. By reliving their most anguished moments during their conversations, sharing their dreams and frustrations, facing together the blank walls of military bureaucracy, and scoring small victories with the placement of an ad or the presentation of a petition, the women coped with their social trauma and created a growing narrative which made some sense of the incomprehensible disappearances.

The mothers of the Plaza de Mayo consciously cultivated an ideological neutrality. This neutrality made them strike out on their own instead of joining the five existing human rights organizations which carried clear political or religious signatures.[26] The emphasis that they were not political actors but just mothers wanting to know about their children made it harder for the military to forbid their public outcries. The strategy to sow terror into the homes of people succeeded on the individual level but eventually failed politically as it was exactly the similarity of those paralyzing intimate feelings among a large group of people that impelled the relatives of the disappeared to public resistance. In other words, the social trauma formed the nucleus of the mothers' protest.

Resurgence of Human Rights Protests

The Argentine military were very concerned about the international perception of their regime. There had been a fact-finding mission by Amnesty

International in November 1976, and reports by the State Department and the Inter-American Commission on Human Rights of the Organization of American States accused the Argentine military of human rights violations. The Argentine ambassador to the U.S. began to lobby actively against these accusations in February 1977, and a public relations campaign was launched in Europe in September 1977 from a Pilot Center (Centro Piloto) in Paris set up by an ESMA task group that included Navy Lieutenant Alfredo Astiz.[27]

Only after the Argentine Episcopate declared in a pastoral letter of 7 May 1977 that dark forces had been released in Argentina engaging in torture, abduction, and disappearance did President Videla make a hesitant admission that some people might have disappeared because of excesses by the legal forces.[28] Precisely on the day of this declaration, Videla received the letter written by the fourteen mothers who had gathered at the Plaza de Mayo for the first time one week earlier.

Despite the December 1977 abduction of their informal leader Azucena Villaflor de De Vicenti, the mothers continued to maintain their presence at the Plaza de Mayo, in particular because of the upcoming Eleventh World Cup soccer tournament in June 1978. In the months before the tournament, passersby had criticized the mothers for damaging Argentina's reputation, and thus for being unpatriotic. Once again, the number of mothers protesting at the Plaza de Mayo declined, as it had in December 1977.

On Thursday 1 June 1978, at 3:30 P.M., the opening match of the World Cup soccer tournament was kicked off at the River Plate stadium in the notable presence of the three-man junta, Videla, Massera, and Agosti. At exactly the same time, about one hundred mothers began their usual march through the Plaza de Mayo.[29] It is unclear whether the time of the opening match had been scheduled before or after the mothers made their appearance in April 1977, but no foreign journalist missed the symbolic competition of the two events. Numerous foreign journalists had met the mothers and filmed their weekly protest march. They published critical articles about human rights violations which contributed to the mobilization of public opinion in Europe.

Encouraged by the growing foreign support, the human rights organizations handed a new petition to the military government on Thursday 21 December 1978 and were told that the government would respond the following Thursday.[30] One week later, there was an anxious crowd of over one thousand mothers at the Casa Rosada. After some negotiations, a four-woman delegation was allowed to enter. Meanwhile the mothers sounded their familiar chant: "We want our children, that they tell us where they are! That they tell the truth!" One army officer blurted out: "Daughters of bitches, they come to provoke us here, right under our noses, and they let them. They're all communists, mothers of subversives, and they dare to come and protest. If they would let me, I would clean the square very fast with the bursts of a machine gun. They wouldn't return."[31] The delegation returned empty-handed. They were told to come back next day for an answer.

The Plaza de Mayo was brimming with policemen when the delegation appeared at the presidential palace. Several hundred mothers had gathered on the steps of the Cathedral because no one was allowed to sit on the benches of the Plaza de Mayo. As two armored vehicles and an assault squadron with tear gas throwers entered the square, the church authorities ordered the Cathedral's heavy wooden doors closed to prevent the women from taking refuge there. The delegation of four women returned again empty-handed. They had been told that disappearances had to be reported through the proper channels at the courts and at the Ministry of Interior. The delegation was also given to understand that public manifestations were strictly forbidden. Immediately, riot police advanced, and detained a dozen mothers for several hours. The Plaza de Mayo was empty again, and it would remain empty the next Thursday and the Thursday thereafter. The mothers had lost temporary control over the Plaza, and it would take nine months before they could make their appearance again.[32]

In the first week of 1979, the police placed fences around the inner perimeter of the Plaza de Mayo to interrupt the free circulation of pedestrians. The fences were removed after some time but police maintained a noted presence throughout the year and prevented mothers from staging their weekly protest. Now, the women could only walk unassumingly along the square's outer rim, and rush furtively to its center before being taken away by police. With the mothers expelled from the Plaza de Mayo, military intelligence turned to the media in a concerted campaign to discredit the human rights organizations.

In order to discredit the Argentine human rights organizations, the military government accused them of links with the guerrilla organizations.[33] Obviously there were some common interests between the two, simply because the disappeared concerned both. The Montoneros maintained informal links to some mothers of the Plaza de Mayo but the guerrilla and human rights organizations always remained reluctant co-travelers pursuing different objectives.[34] The guerrillas wanted to conquer political space, while the human rights organizations were mainly interested in justice and due process.

According to General Díaz Bessone, the counterinsurgency war had been won militarily by late 1978, but the guerrilla organizations continued to fight with political means, in particular through an intense propaganda campaign denouncing Argentine human rights violations through conferences, publications, and propaganda.[35] The Montoneros also established "Argentina houses" in several European and Latin American capitals from which solidarity committees were organized for a worldwide human rights campaign.[36]

The human rights offensive gathered much strength after former disappeared captives returned alive from the secret detention centers. The testimonies in Paris, on 12 October 1979, of three women who had been considered recoverable by the ESMA task group, filled searching relatives with horror.[37] Still, the terrifying stories of these three Montoneras could be dismissed by the Argentine government as propaganda, but the investigation of the Inter-American Commission on Human Rights of the Organization of American States (OAS) could not. As if to defy the OAS investigation, the military government passed a law of defunction on 6 September 1979, the delegation's arrival date. The law declared that all persons who had disappeared between the beginning of the state of siege on 6 November 1974 and 6 September 1979 should be presumed dead.[38]

The line of people waiting to tell their story to the Commission formed at 9:30 A.M. and lasted till 10:00 P.M. More than one thousand forms for making a declaration had been handed out.[39] The mothers had utilized the OAS visit to register themselves on 22 August 1979 as a legal nonprofit organization, called the Mothers of the Plaza de Mayo Civilian Association (Asociación Civil Madres de Plaza de Mayo). As a result, provincial chapters were founded, thus expanding the movement across the entire country. At the time of the OAS visit, the Association comprised 150 mothers, and they all visited the OAS delegation.[40]

The delegation heard testimonies, spoke with the junta members, politicians, union leaders, members of the Roman Catholic Church, and human rights leaders. They also visited several prisons and military locations denounced as secret detention centers, such as the Navy Mechanics School. However, there were no captives there. The group of about fifty to sixty people had been taken secretly to an island near Tigre.[41]

The OAS Commission submitted a preliminary report to the Argentine government on 14 December 1979. The junta took too long to respond, so the Commission presented their final report on 11 April 1980. The findings came as a blow to the military junta and to the human rights organizations. The Commission accused the junta of gross human rights violations, confirmed the occurrence of thousands of disappearances, and concluded that most disappeared should be considered dead.[42] The delegation had not found any disappeared alive but did locate a large number of anonymous graves in the cemeteries of Greater Buenos Aires. María Adela Antokoletz commented: "A shiver shakes our hopes, something that everybody intuits but nobody dares to say. Notwithstanding the monstrosity that was proven to be true, we have more than ever the impression that the very worst has happened. And we find ourselves trapped between this terrible suspicion and the refusal to accept it."[43] The conclusions of the OAS commission were emotionally and politically unacceptable.[44] If the disappeared were dead, then on what charge had they been killed and why weren't the remains handed to their relatives?

Slowly, the Argentine people were becoming familiar with the plight of the disappeared. On 12 August 1980 the newspaper *Clarín* published an ad in which 175 well-known Argentines (among them writer Jorge Luis Borges and the cup-winning soccer coach César Luis Menotti) supported the demands of the human rights organizations. The issue of the disappeared became world news in 1980 when the Mothers of the Plaza de Mayo were nominated for the Nobel Peace Prize which was awarded instead on 13 October 1980 to the human rights leader Rodolfo Pérez Esquivel. The military government condemned the award as being politically motivated.[45]

Victory Crowds and Protest Crowds

The Argentine authorities had done their utmost to control public space since the 1976 coup. They did not entirely succeed in repressing the mothers at the Plaza de Mayo, but prevented the assembly of large crowds. There had been some limited strike activity in 1976 and 1977 but the protests occurred mostly on factory grounds. The only public crowds were religious crowds, such as the Corpus Cristi processions and the annual pilgrimages to Luján. The crowds celebrating the various victories of the Argentine team in June 1978 during the World Cup soccer tournament held in Argentina were the first large spontaneous crowds since 1976.

The first, somewhat hesitant, soccer celebration took place on Friday 2 June 1978 when cars brimming with supporters cruised along Corrientes Avenue in Buenos Aires. The second crowd on Tuesday 6 June began when cars with their joyous passengers left the River Plate stadium to savor another Argentine victory in downtown Buenos Aires. Soon, a massive pedestrian crowd gathered around the imposing obelisk at the intersection of Corrientes Avenue and the twenty-lane-wide 9 de Julio Avenue. Other festive crowds followed on 14, 18, and 21 June. Argentina beat the Netherlands in the finals on 25 June 1978, and won the World Cup. Hundreds of thousands of people congregated near the obelisk in the largest spontaneous crowd since 1976.

Its political significance did not escape the newspapers and the military junta. "The city center offered yesterday evening a spectacle that probably has never been seen," wrote one newspaper. "Everybody remembers of course other crowd gatherings in which large bass drums, whistles, and choruses stupefied the area of Plaza de Mayo, Avenida de Mayo, Diagonal Norte, and Corrientes. Those occasions were expressions of fanaticism, of a blind, irrational and arrogant sentiment. It's not worth emphasizing. But that of yesterday was something never seen before. One has to recognize how much the country has won, through the spirit of its people, when it can celebrate a sports victory, a world championship, with an unending parade of all sorts of vehicles, an ill-assorted crowd wearing, raising, and waving the Argentine flag, hailing the country, without disturbances, without affronts, and without violence."[46] Two years of military rule seemed to have domesticated the lawless, subversive, political crowds. The Argentine people had become a disciplined, civilized people, in the reporter's eyes.

President Videla expressed similar sentiments, remarking that "the Argentine people have given a supreme example of respect and order, something which I want to acknowledge explicitly. Our country has enjoyed in a spontaneous way, without incentives or pressures of any sort, an authentic festive climate that has surprised many visitors . . . [who had been misled] by a malicious international campaign."[47] He emphasized that the effervescence of mass gatherings had put the Argentine people in touch with their true self. The jubilant crowd had done its magic on the people by celebrating society itself. "The re-encounter with its traditional values, a people that feels proud of its past, which doesn't deny its present and takes on the immediate future with heroic optimism."[48]

The 1978 World Cup tournament had been an excellent occasion to test the mood of popular crowds. The Army High Command realized that the Argentine people had been left hungry for mass gatherings during the first years of the dictatorship. The military recognized the human need for association, and the importance of crowds as conduits for social sentiment. A secret assessment from 1979 stated that people and societies required three types of nourishment: food to satisfy bodily needs, spiritual nutrition (religion and moral beliefs) to guide people's inner lives, and mental nutrition to feed instincts and psychological appetites. These mental or "psychical foodstuffs [arrive] by way of 'incarnated' and expressive types of information like those offered by theater shows and crowd demonstrations."[49] In other words, people needed crowd events for emotional nourishment. The crucial issue was how to satisfy this appetite.

Orchestrated crowd events became favored by the military because they could be conditioned better and served as an antidote to revolutionary crowds by directing their raw energy into safe outlets. These events were regarded as necessary weapons of psychological warfare because "public performances, sport events, civil-military parades, and cultural competitions are in themselves very important means to influence the population, and these resources must be used permanently in the fight against subversion."[50]

This deliberate confluence of politics and sports through crowds became apparent at the 1979 World Championship Soccer tournament for youth teams, held in Japan. The Argentine team reaped the final victory on 7 September 1979, by coincidence the very day on which the Inter-American Commission on Human Rights began taking declarations at its office along Avenida de Mayo. The popular radio sportscaster José María Muñoz encouraged young celebrants to take possession of Avenida de Mayo and show the OAS delegation Argentina's real face. The jubilant adolescents were guided by police right past the long line of people waiting to give testimony, and were given a thumbs-up sign by Videla when they reached the presidential palace. Later that day, Videla met with an OAS commission visibly annoyed by the orchestrated show of patriotism.[51]

The jinni had been let out of the bottle. If the junta tolerated soccer crowds in 1978, endowed them with a political significance, and openly used them in 1979 for political ends, then other mass gatherings became hard to forbid. Labor unions and human rights organizations began to coopt nonpolitical crowds for their political purposes.

Around five hundred mothers presented a petition to the military government on 14 September 1979, and were determined to renew their weekly marches.[52] On Thursday 20 December 1979, more than two hundred mothers filed into the Plaza de Mayo. The police were completely taken by surprise. The mothers walked for one half hour around the pyramid, as they had done for the last time one year earlier.[53]

The labor movement raised its first public protest in April 1979 with a national strike. Although this act of defiance lacked mass support, it triggered a steady growth in public demonstrations by Argentine workers. There were ten street protests in 1979 and twenty-six in 1980.[54] The founding in November 1980 of the illegal union central CGT-Brasil, named after the street where it held office, intensified the labor protests.[55] Encouraged by the Polish Solidarity movement and Pope John Paul II's 1981 encyclical *Laborem Exercens* authorizing the right to strike, the oppositional Argentine union leaders used a religious crowd for their first major public protest against the military junta.[56]

Headed by CGT-Brasil union leaders Saúl Ubaldini and José Rodriguez, five thousand to ten thousand workers gathered on 7 November 1981 at the Vélez Sarsfield soccer stadium and walked the seven blocks to the San Cayetano church, the patron saint of Argentina's workers. The military authorities were uncertain how to respond because they had always encouraged religious processions. Argentine political life had come full circle. Street crowds had survived as the most enduring form of protest in Argentine twentieth-century political culture. After the religious service, a group of workers sang the national anthem, followed by the Peronist march, and finally by the shouts: "It'll end, it'll end, the military dictatorship." The police detained thirty workers but released them the same day.[57]

On 10 December 1981 at 3:30 P.M., the mothers began their first twenty-four-hour Resistance March. Hundreds of mothers walked slowly around the pyramid at Plaza de Mayo, taking turns, and attracting around one thousand sympathizers.[58] So, by late 1981, public space had been filled by human rights protests, pilgrimages, sport crowds, and labor mobilizations. The patches of white scarves became a recurring sight in many mass events in 1981. The presence of the mothers of the Plaza de Mayo reminded all that the fate of the thousands of disappeared stood at the center of the popular opposition to the dictatorship.

The street protests continued unabated in early 1982. The most signifi-cant protest crowd occurred on Tuesday 30 March when the CGT-Brasil union central called for the demonstration "Peace, Bread, and Work." The police sealed off the Plaza de Mayo, and arrested union leader Ubaldini and four hundred workers. They used tear gas and rubber bullets to dis-perse the crowd. A similar protest took place in Mendoza. Over two thou-sand people were arrested and a dozen workers were treated for gun shot wounds.[59] The Minister of Interior, General Alfredo Saint Jean, com-mented that the worker protests were "an exercise of subversion which the Government is not going to permit. We don't want another Cordobazo or Rosariazo."[60] By late March 1982, the military government had great diffi-culty in containing the expanding social and political unrest as well as the call for a peaceful transition to democracy similar to the 1980–1982 politi-cal "opening" in Brazil.

President Videla's successor General Viola took office in March 1981 but was ousted in December 1981 by General Galtieri. Galtieri inherited a country in crisis. The economy was suffering from capital flight, a skyrock-eting foreign debt, a declining gross domestic product, falling wages, high inflation, and a depreciation of the national currency by more than six hundred percent in 1981. The political parties united since July 1981 in the Multiparty Coalition (Multipartidaria) wanted some progress in the "political dialogue" mentioned first by President Videla in December 1977. This promise was tempered in April 1978 by Minister of Interior Har-guindeguy, and suffered a setback in September 1979 with the failed rebel-lion of General Luciano Menéndez. Finally, in March 1980, the historical moment arrived when Videla invited several prominent political leaders for informal talks. President Viola continued these talks in 1981 but the dia-logue was cut off abruptly by Galtieri.[61] The frustration of rising political expectations, growing labor unrest, defiant human rights protests, and the international accusation of gross human rights violations proved to be a volatile mixture.

President Galtieri decided on a bold move. He ordered the invasion of the Falkland Islands, known in Argentina as the Islas Malvinas. The opera-tion had been planned in late 1981 by Admiral Jorge Anaya, and was to take place in mid-1982. The national problems described above advanced the time table.[62] Galtieri hoped that the Argentine people would close ranks behind his historic move, that the economic and human rights prob-lems would receive less national and international attention, and that a conventional war would restore the military honor lost in the dirty war. Gal-tieri imagined himself treading in the footsteps of San Martin as Argenti-na's new liberator.

On 28 March 1982, an Argentine fleet sailed from Puerto Belgrano and troops landed on Friday 2 April on the Falkland/Malvinas Islands.[63] The Argentine people were ecstatic about the news that the islands, seized by the British in 1833, had been reincorporated in the national territory. On the day of the invasion, people began arriving spontaneously at the Plaza de Mayo to express their happiness. More than ten thousand people were present when President Galtieri appeared on the balcony of the Casa Rosada. People were singing, young couples held babies in their arms, and high school students cheered: "The Malvinas are Argentine!"

Galtieri could not hide his fascination with the crowd at his feet, and remarked to the Minister of Interior Alfredo Saint Jean, "Just imagine, they want me to talk! See how the square looks!" whereupon Saint Jean responded, "Enjoy it, chief. Enjoy it!"[64] Lieutenant-General Galtieri, known for his aspirations to become as popular as Perón, had been captured by the same fascination with crowds as so many Argentine rulers before him. The mass support raised his spirit, and would kindle him even further in the weeks to come as several impressive crowds took shape.

On Friday 9 April, at about six o'clock in the afternoon, a large crowd began gathering at the Plaza de Mayo. A radio station had summoned people to physically express their true sentiment to U.S. Secretary of State Alexander Haig, who was on a diplomatic mission to resolve the crisis. The people stayed at Plaza de Mayo throughout the night. By 11:00 A.M. on Saturday, the crowd had grown to 250,000 to 300,000 people. When Galtieri spoke from the balcony of the presidential palace, he was interrupted by the shout, "One feels it, one feels it, Perón is present."[65] The emotion associated with large crowds was foremost a Peronist sentiment after all, and Galtieri must have felt his great destiny was in the making.

The street mobilizations gained momentum after Haig's return visit on 18 April. An enthusiastic crowd brought home to Haig that Galtieri was supported by the Argentine people. One street crowd after another occurred throughout the country in the following weeks. Each immigrant community (Japanese, Korean, Uruguayan, Bolivian, Paraguayan, Italian, Spanish, and Armenian) organized its own show of support.

The largest crowds during the Falkland/Malvinas war were evoked by Pope John Paul II. Here, politics and religion mingled in a different manner than in the processions utilized by human rights and labor union protesters in 1981. An immense multitude gathered at the Basilica of the Virgin of Luján when the Pope held Mass on Friday the 11th of June. Later that day, a crowd assembled at the Plaza de Mayo when the Pope was holding talks with the military junta. Finally, an estimated two million people were present in the Palermo park of Buenos Aires when the Pope said his final Mass before returning to Rome.[66]

When the Pope left Argentina, the war was nearing its end. Argentina surrendered to Great Britain on Monday 14 June 1982. The capitulation was immediately followed by violent protests. The Argentine people were astounded. The national press, the junta, and the Minister of Foreign Affairs had been boasting for months about the military and diplomatic successes, when suddenly the curtain fell. Protesters flocked to the Plaza de Mayo. Cars were overturned, buses set afire, and barricades erected.

President Galtieri was to explain the dramatic unfolding of events from the balcony of the Casa Rosada at 7:00 P.M. but by that time the police was firing tear gas into an ebullient crowd of about five thousand people shouting slogans against the military.[67] Galtieri resigned the next day, and made way for the transitional government of General Reynaldo Bignone. The defeat in the south Atlantic was the immediate cause of the junta's fall from power, but the growing prewar protest crowds had been crucial in persuading Galtieri to embark on the ill-fated expedition while postwar street mobilizations hastened free elections.

Transition and Defeat

The mass mobilizations during the seventeen months of the transitional government were beyond control. The CGT-Brasil union central opened with a march to the San Cayetano church on 7 August 1982, and gathered fifteen thousand to thirty thousand workers on Wednesday 22 September 1982 at the Plaza de Mayo to listen to Ubaldini denouncing Argentina's social and economic situation. The street demonstrations held during the rest of 1982 are too many to mention but two human rights marches deserve special attention because they demonstrate the incredible accomplishment of the mothers of the Plaza de Mayo after five years of often isolated resistance, and reveal the military's fear of protest crowds as subverting the social order.

The human rights organizations planned a March for Life on 5 October 1982 which was immediately forbidden. An official communiqué stated that the government had been allowing political, social, and labor demonstrations since the 1st of July 1982 as a sign of a gradual political opening. However, such demonstrations should always be oriented towards the common good. The proposed "March for Life" was forbidden because it "aims to deepen the wounds caused by the terrorist war. . . . [and] risks making political use of a so human and respectable sentiment as pain. And it is precisely that, the politicization of a sentiment, which no government can or must protect."[68] The march was held anyway, and five thousand people walked part of the planned trajectory but could not reach the Plaza de Mayo because of an insurmountable force of assault vehicles, squad cars, police vans, water cannons, helicopters, and police, infantry, and cavalry forces.[69]

The most memorable crowd of 1982 during post-Falkland/Malvinas War times took place on Wednesday 16 December. The People's March for Democracy and National Reconstruction was organized by the CGT, the

Multiparty Coalition and the human rights movement.[70] Anxiety was high because police had a week earlier forced the twenty-four-hour Resistance March of the mothers to move from the Plaza de Mayo to a nearby intersection. On 16 December, the participating organizations gathered at different locations in downtown Buenos Aires, and then congregated at the Plaza de Mayo around 6:00 P.M. The 100,000 to 150,000 demonstrators were unstoppable. The crowd overflowed the Plaza de Mayo, listened to speakers praising the peaceful march towards democracy, and then departed.

Trouble began around 8:00 P.M. after most people had already left. Some young people tried to scale the security fence around the presidential palace and were detained by the Infantry Guard. Several protesters broke windows of the Casa Rosada, and three of them used a fence as a battering ram to force their way into the palace. The police responded with little restraint. The twenty-year-old Dalmiro Flores died from a gun shot in the stomach, sixty-five persons were wounded, and 120 arrests were made. In turn, thirty-five policemen were wounded. The disbanding protesters broke windows and telephone booths as they withdrew from the Plaza de Mayo.[71]

The year 1983 was election year. Numerous street manifestations were organized. Human rights organizations held marches to condemn the self-declared amnesty of the military, tried to submit petitions about the disappearances, and the mothers of the Plaza de Mayo organized their third resistance march, attracting thirty thousand people. The labor unions held general strikes and organized marches demanding peace, work and bread. Public opinion was turning rapidly against the military.

The times of omnipotence were over. A secret army directive urged officers not to race through traffic with sirens and policemen who attacked "with blows and kicks those vehicles which don't get out of the way fast enough. . . ."[72] The report further noticed a state of depression within the army. Army personnel felt discredited by the failures of the Process of National Reorganization, sensed a public hostility because of the Falkland/Malvinas defeat, and had a lack of confidence in the solutions offered by the transitional government. They were uncertain about the future, and felt a moral responsibility towards the victims and disappeared of the anti-revolutionary war.[73]

The Argentine military commanders who had taken power in March 1976, so cocksure of their ability to lead Argentina to greatness, were also anxious about their future. They felt defeated, not in the hills of Tucumán, the streets of Buenos Aires or the torture rooms of the secret detention centers, but in the south Atlantic by a NATO-backed British fleet, in the public arena by international human rights protests orchestrated by Argentine guerrillas in exile, and at the Plaza de Mayo by the weekly protests of a tenacious group of "crazy women."

The military had underestimated the deep attachment of parent and child. Any threat to this relation was experienced as the destruction of self, the world, and the meaning of life.[74] The searching relatives were moved to action by their personal attachments and the emptiness of life without the abducted loved ones. Their growing public presence, the resonance of their cause in Argentina and abroad, and the slow and painful discovery of bits of truth gave these searching relatives a sense of mastery over the posttraumatic reactions and proved the reality of the disappearances. Such confirmation of their traumatic experiences in the face of official denials, helped them cope with their social trauma. Personal sorrow was transformed into group protest, and expanded a small group of protesting mothers into large oppositional crowds.

What is crucial to understand about the human rights movement, and in particular about the mothers of the Plaza de Mayo, is that they worked through their social trauma through a symbolic and spatial expansion into the political arena. Their advance inverted the deep repression of the military, and thus regained a certain control over the domains wrested from them so violently. What was private and secret became public and open. As was explained in Chapters 10 and 11, the military dominated the public realm and intruded upon the most private of human domains: the home, the body, and the social. In an unexpected countermove, the mothers invaded the most public of all spaces in Argentina: the Plaza de Mayo.[75] The Nation's symbolic center, where presidents and dictators alike either basked in the cheers of their supporters or were scoffed by their detractors, was appropriated by mothers searching for their children.

Chapter 16
Recovery and Reburial of the Past: Democracy, Accountability, and Impunity

On 26 October 1983 I observed a large crowd from a window way up in a high rise near Constitución railway station in Buenos Aires. The crowd was estimated by police at more than 800,000 and by the organizers at 1.5 million people. Raúl Alfonsín was ending his campaign for the presidency of Argentina. The podium was located near the obelisk at the 9th of July Avenue where soccer celebrations had been held in 1978. Many young supporters were wearing white berets as a symbol of Alfonsín's UCR, the Radical Civic Union. I was struck by the relaxed atmosphere of the largely middle class crowd in the face of what was understood by all as a turning point in Argentine history.

Two days later, on 28 October, I walked through an equally sizable crowd of Peronist supporters accompanying the closing act of Italo Luder. This crowd had a different feel from the one two days before. It was a working class crowd and especially a Peronist crowd. Peronist songs were sung, and large bass drums sounded incessantly, imbuing the meeting with an electrifying tension I had not felt two days earlier. Old times seemed to have returned and also old vices were revived. When a column of young leftist Peronists tried to force its way to the stage, they were displaced in a brief scuffle by an even larger column of metal workers.[1] The 20 June 1973 violent confrontation at Ezeiza between the Peronist left and the Peronist right came briefly to mind, but fortunately the clash petered out. These were different times. These were times of hope that demanded a radical break with the past.

Raúl Alfonsín won 52 percent of the popular vote on the 30th of October 1983, while Luder received only 40 percent.[2] Alfonsín's victory was unexpected because polls had predicted a win for Luder who had already been president briefly in 1975. Most likely, many undecided voters had been swayed by the bad memories of the political chaos during the 1974–1976 Peronist government and the rumor about a secret pact between generals and Peronist union leaders that the military would not be brought to trial for human rights violations.[3] These politics of old contrasted sharply with Alfonsín's call for truth and justice and his message of hope for a better future.

On Saturday 10 December 1983, an immense crowd accompanied the open sedan driving President Raúl Alfonsín after his inauguration at Congress to the Casa Rosada at the Plaza de Mayo. On this sunny day, I saw a satisfied smile on an emotional Alfonsín from only a few paces away as he waved to the jubilant people along Avenida de Mayo. The military escort of grenadiers in ceremonial uniform reined in their horses with difficulty under the weight of the densely packed crowd. The significance of the crowd in Argentine political culture was impressed on me again as I thought back on my crowd baptism eight months earlier when I joined a human rights demonstration continuously intimidated by mounted policemen. The memory of one reporter went back much further: "Buenos Aires enjoyed yesterday a day of euphoria and emotion. . . . The bright and clear day served as an appropriate setting for the colorful expression of a people who enthusiastically took a leading role without disturbances, and without the aggressiveness characteristic of other crowd demonstrations from a dark past. It was a truly civil celebration."[4]

This celebration of freedom, democracy, and hope was however laced with anxiety about the fate of the disappeared. After Lieutenant-General Bignone had passed his baton of authority to Raúl Alfonsín and left the Casa Rosada by car, a member of the Mothers of the Plaza de Mayo Civilian Association slipped a piece of paper under the windshield wiper: "Cain, where is your brother?"[5] Five days later, on 15 December 1983, Raúl Alfonsín installed the National Commission on Disappeared Persons or CONADEP (Comisión Nacional sobre Desaparación de Personas) to discover whether there were still disappeared persons alive. He responded to the persistent rumors that the disappeared were still alive, hidden in some place unknown. For example, former police inspector Peregrino Fernández had declared in May 1983 that "one part of the detainees have been assassinated but another part can be found alive today, and is kept in clandestine detention centers, some of which have been built especially for that purpose."[6]

The CONADEP Truth Commission

The investigation of the CONADEP truth commission was severely hindered by the lack of cooperation from the armed forces.[7] The interim military government had declared in April 1983 that all disappeared were dead and had ordered the destruction of many incriminatory documents, and so would the army high command in November 1984. Moreover, the military simply denied that the forced disappearances had been a deliberate policy.[8] President Bignone also did his best to influence national opinion. He decreed a Law of National Pacification protecting guerrillas and officers from criminal prosecution for actions committed between 25 May 1973 and 17 June 1982. The document emphasized that "It must be brought to mind here that the Armed Forces have fought for the dignity of Man. Nevertheless, the cruel and cunning way in which the terrorist subversion waged the battle could, in the heat of the fight, have led to the occurrence of events incompatible with that intention."[9] In other words, the Argentine military admitted to war excesses but these were committed to achieve the greater good of a victory over the insurgency.

The military tried to impress the following four points on the Argentine people. One, the counterinsurgency war was a legitimate defense of the Argentine nation against a large guerrilla force supported by Cuba and the Soviet Union. This war had been won at the cost of the lives of hundreds of patriotic officers, soldiers, and policemen. Two, the military had halted the process of political disintegration, stimulated the economy, and combated corruption and nepotism. Three, the counterinsurgency war had been given a legal mandate in 1975 and was fought within the letter of the law. Torture and disappearances were not officially sanctioned, but were the inevitable excesses of war. Four, the armed forces were an inextricable part of Argentine society. They stood at the birth of the nation, had a constitutional right to existence, and should therefore not be put on trial.

The military tried to create a master narrative which failed to convince the Argentine people, not only because the litany of accomplishments was blatantly untrue (corruption, nepotism, and abuse of power soared during the dictatorship), but because the disappearances overshadowed everything else. Not just the truthful reconstruction of the traumatic past was at stake, but many people believed that there were still disappeared captives alive in secret camps.

Thus, memory construction and reality testing shared a discursive arena centered around the continued denial by the military and the persistent efforts of the CONADEP commission to document the disappearances as a carefully planned strategy. This dispute was initially an uneven fight because the military had had a head start in the politics of forgetting. They had gone to great lengths to obliterate the bodies of the disappeared and destroy any material and documentary evidence. In effect, they attempted to confine the repression to the discursive domain, putting their word against that of their victims.

This denial strategy became increasingly harder to maintain as the CONADEP truth commission progressed in its investigative work. Paradoxically, the deliberate attempt to deny and obliterate past offenses intensified the commission's resolve to uncover them. Delegations visited military bases, police stations, psychiatric hospitals, and sites denounced as secret detention centers. CONADEP commission member Magdalena Ruiz Guiñazu concluded that "unfortunately we have found nobody alive, not even in hospitals. We went to the Borda [psychiatric hospital] with relatives, examining patient by patient to see if we could find anyone. . . ."[10]

The CONADEP commission took over fourteen hundred depositions in Argentina, as well as hundreds of depositions abroad. It examined the records of morgues and cemeteries, opened mass graves, and carried out forensic investigations.[11] In the absence of much material evidence, the inquiry became above all a narrative reconstruction. The depositions were of great importance because they turned personal experience into public testimony. Excerpts were included in the commission's final report, and thus provided a narrative memory which gave emotional content to the dispassionate figures about the number of disappeared and the descriptions of secret detention centers.

The CONADEP commission's preliminary findings were presented to the Argentine people in the documentary "Never Again" (Nunca Más), broadcast on the evening of 4 July 1984.[12] The documentary began with the images of disappeared men, women, and children, and the voice of a narrator who said "Why this atrocious enigma?" Next, the commission's work was explained and the most shocking results presented, in particular that 8,800 persons had disappeared and that 172 babies and small children had been either abducted with their parents or born in captivity. The documentary had a tremendous impact on the viewers, and did much to shape public opinion. Shortly after the transmission, an explosive device was thrown at the television studio.[13]

Despite the documentary's persuasive narrative, there was also criticism about the way the opening question "Why this atrocious enigma?" had been answered. This criticism was framed in a collective memory debate among three different positions. The CONADEP commission and most human rights organizations explained the cultural war as a Manichean struggle between an idealistic younger generation and a repressive military apparatus. Good was pitted against evil. This interpretation was criticized by members of President Alfonsín's political party who presented their so-called two-demon theory. They observed that two evils had been responsible for the escalating violence. According to congressman Leopoldo Moreau, there "has been an armed struggle between two sectors to take power in which both equally demolished ethical values and were not fighting for democracy."[14]

The third interpretation came from the military. They also spoke of a struggle between good and evil, but represented the counterinsurgency war as the legitimate defense of Argentina's political sovereignty. The military rejected the documentary vehemently. One officer remarked: "According to the program, the disappeared were peaceful citizens, writers, workers, and housewives who knew nothing of politics. It seems that one day they were detained by the Armed Forces just like that, without rhyme or reason."[15] However, precisely this impression had been nurtured by the armed forces. The repression had been carried out with so much concealment, amidst denials, without trials and verdicts, and with the obstruction of the right of habeas corpus, that the documentary's image of sudden state terror was all the more convincing.

Two and a half months after the broadcast, the CONADEP truth commission presented its report *Never Again (Nunca Más)* to the government. An estimated seventy thousand persons accompanied the commission members on the evening of 20 September 1984 to the Casa Rosada under the motto "punishment for the guilty."[16] A short version of the report sold more than three hundred thousand copies to a horrified public. The *Never Again* summary was the first systematic effort to describe state terror for the Argentine people.[17]

"Many of the events described in this report will be hard to believe," opened chapter one.[18] The authors echoed the disbelief among many Argentines. All traumatic experiences are incomprehensible at heart but the tales of torture and abuse were particularly inconceivable because of the deceptive calmness of public life during the dictatorship. The terrifying accounts were hard to reconcile with the everyday experience of those who had not been touched personally by the repression. The prologue emphasized that the disappearances were a carefully planned witchhunt against innocent civilians. "The vast majority of them were innocent not only of any acts of terrorism, but even of belonging to the fighting units of the guerrilla organizations: these latter chose to fight it out, and either died in shootouts or committed suicide before they could be captured. Few of them were alive by the time they were in the hands of the repressive forces."[19]

The denial of due process made of course any question about innocence or guilt irrelevant, but the commission's reconstruction of the cultural war revolved forcefully around the moral contrast between innocent victims and abusive state authorities. Any mention of the victims' political affiliation was avoided in order not to cast doubt on the credibility of the testimonies, and to emphasize that the absence of due process made such information inappropriate. However, as has been explained in Chapters 9 and 10, even though most disappeared Argentines were not guerrilla combatants, many did belong to combative labor unions, front organizations of the guerrilla forces, and other political opposition groups that, right or wrong, fell within the enemy definition of the Argentine military and were thus regarded as justifiable targets.

The work of the CONADEP commission gave rise to a barrage of emotional testimonies in books, magazines, newspapers, and radio and television programs. The witnesses tried as much to come to grips with their own experiences as to inform the Argentine people. Their testimonies returned to them some control over life's destiny by assigning their suffering to the military and receiving the sympathy of their fellow-citizens. Furthermore, each revelation added to a growing narrative memory, showed another dark corner of state terror, and disproved the competing narrative constructed by the military.[20] Portions of the military discourse about the guerrilla threat remained in place, but the moral judgment of the Argentine people turned against them after learning of the indiscriminate counterinsurgency methods.[21]

How did the human rights movement react to the CONADEP report? The CONADEP's conclusion that the disappeared could be presumed dead was devastating. Conflicting parental feelings of protection and abandonment were stirred up as now the loss had to be mourned but the final rights of death could not be administered. Another issue that disturbed the emotions was the commission's conclusion that 8,960 persons had been disappeared during the 1976–1983 dictatorship. The human rights movement had always insisted on thirty thousand disappeared.[22] The accuracy of the latter number had become subordinate to its symbolic value. Thirty thousand disappeared was a political statement, and the figure of ten thousand was branded as a betrayal by the Alfonsín government, the CONADEP, and the human rights organization APDH (Permanent Assembly for Human Rights) which had provided much organizational support.

According to Graciela Fernández Meijide, a prominent member of the APDH responsible for the depositions department of the CONADEP commission, the number of thirty thousand disappeared was launched in Europe in 1977 by the Montoneros. The guerrilla organization wanted to leave the impression of their considerable strength by inflating the number of disappeared.[23] Instead, the CONADEP figure of 8,960 was based on depositions by relatives during times of democracy. Fernández Meijide believes that there may be a maximum of one thousand persons who did not enter the CONADEP lists, thus arriving at ten thousand disappeared and assassinated Argentines.[24]

The precise number of disappeared will never be known. Even twenty years after the dictatorship, there is substantial disagreement about the figures. The Undersecretary of Human Rights reported in September 2001 that the official count had reached fifteen thousand persons. However, the Argentine Forensic Anthropology Team which has been exhuming mass graves and investigated police archives, death registers, and cemetery records has arrived at around 9,150 confirmed disappeared.[25]

The CONADEP report left an indelible image on millions of Argentines. President Alfonsín came under tremendous pressure to bring the military to court. One obstacle was the Law of National Pacification, passed in September 1983 by the transitional military government, to provide amnesty to military personnel and guerrillas. On 18 December 1983 Alfonsín ordered the Supreme Council of the Armed Forces to try the nine commanders of the three military juntas that had ruled from 1976 to 1982. Nine days later, the self-amnesty law was abrogated in Congress.[26]

As if to provoke public opinion and defy the government, the military supreme court declared one day after Alfonsín had received the damaging CONADEP report that it could not pass sentence before the October 21 deadline. Faced with the unwillingness of the military court to judge its peers, the Federal Court of Appeals ruled that a civilian court could now take over the case.[27]

Trial and Conviction of the Commanders

The Buenos Aires Federal Court of Criminal Appeals selected the 670 strongest cases from the CONADEP report to prove that the nine junta members had designed and executed a secret plan to eliminate the guerrilla organizations by unlawful means. The prosecutors Julio Strassera and Luis Moreno Ocampo charged the defendants with 709 criminal offenses, including disappearance, torture, rape, theft, and murder.[28] The indictment was of historic significance, and more than 92 percent of the inhabitants of Buenos Aires approved of the trial.[29]

Public hearings began on 22 April 1985. The trial was presided over by six judges and observed by an audience of several hundred people. The testimonies of eight hundred witnesses were reproduced in a weekly publication (*El Diario del Juicio*) which sold sometimes over two hundred thousand copies a week. The hearings were broadcast on television but without sound so as not to incite the public hostility against the Argentine military any further. The mute images of the dictators sitting in the accused stand and the soundless sobs of the witnesses gave the images an unreal quality.[30]

The hegemony of the court suspended the memory competition between the military and the human rights movement.[31] Former captors and former captives were now placed on an equal footing before a court of law as defendants and plaintiffs, while the systematic questioning by judges, lawyers, and public defenders about the precise place and circumstance of torture and rape entailed a persuasive objectivity.[32] The nine former junta members expressed their contempt for the court by being absent during most of the testimonies or by chatting with one another, reading a book, laughing, snickering, and staring at the ceiling. Their attitude changed when the prosecution began its plea on 11 September 1985 and ended seven days later with the words "Never again!" The audience exploded with a standing ovation. The prosecutors smiled and embraced one another, while General Viola hurled angry words into the court room.[33]

After closing arguments had been read, the twenty-two lawyers of the defense council were heard. Lieutenant-General Videla refused to speak in his own defense but Admiral Massera did. His opening statement was as expected as revealing: "I have not come to defend myself. Nobody has to defend himself for having won a just war. And the war against terrorism was a just war. Nevertheless, I am put on trial here because we won that just war. If we would have lost it then we wouldn't have been here—neither you nor we—because the highest judges of this Chamber would have been replaced some time ago by turbulent people's tribunals, and a ferocious and irrecognizable Argentina would have replaced the old Fatherland. But here we are. Because we won the military war and lost the psychological war."[34] Here, in its most naked sense, the defendant's truth stood face to face with the prosecutor's truth, awaiting the ruling of the judges.

The verdict was read on 9 December 1985. The commanders were found guilty of organizing and ordering a secret criminal ground plan of systematic abduction, torture, disappearance, and assassination of Argentine civilians, and allowing subordinates ample freedom to decide about the fate of their victims in clear violation of due process.[35] Videla and Massera were given life sentences. Graffigna, Galtieri, Anaya, and Lami Dozo were acquitted, while Agosti, Lambruschini, and Viola were sentenced respectively to four and a half years, eight years, and seventeen years in prison.[36] A juridical truth had now been added to the competing narratives, and revived the dispute about the rendition of the past. Opposed memory constructions vied again for public attention.

How did the military respond to the successful efforts of the federal court and the human rights movement to convince the Argentine people that they had been victims of state terror? The military pursued three strategies: emphasizing that Argentina had been involved in a revolutionary war; discrediting the evidence about the disappearances; and portraying the convicted military commanders as martyrs. This reconstruction of the past did not replace other narratives but added yet another representation to the process of collective remembrance.

First, the military emphasized that Argentina had been in a state of war. The armed forces had the constitutional right to defend the country against an assault on its sovereignty. This message was repeated over and over. Second, the military dismissed the existence of systematic disappearances but, in the face of undeniable material proof, began to cast doubt on the quality of the evidence, the credibility of the testimonies, the political persuasion of the eyewitnesses, the forensic methodology, and the circumstances under which the deaths had taken place. The argument prepared by General Osiris Villegas in defense of General Ramón Camps provides an exemplary case of the military reasoning.[37]

General Villegas argued that many persons reported as disappeared were still alive. They were (1.) living in exile abroad; (2.) fighting as mercenaries in Algeria, Yemen, Lebanon, Nicaragua, and El Salvador; (3.) living under false names in Chile, Peru, and Brazil; (4.) had returned to Argentina illegally; or (5.) were known to be alive but had maliciously been reported missing.[38] Villegas could of course not deny that some people were really missing. According to Villegas, they were unidentified guerrillas who had died in combat or fallen victim to internal disputes. They were not really missing but were dead, and had been buried in unmarked graves. Villegas invoked the symbol of the unknown soldier to make his point.[39]

The third defense strategy of the military consisted of presenting themselves as victims of a political campaign. High-ranking officers did not tire of saying in public that the Alfonsín government tried to destroy the armed forces as an institution and trample on the martyrdom of hundreds of patriots who had lost their lives defending the nation. The military also encouraged solidarity organizations to express sympathy with their cause. The organization Relatives and Friends of the Victims of Subversion or FAMUS (Familiares y Amigos de los Muertos por la Subversión) was founded for that purpose in March 1987.[40]

Notwithstanding these three public strategies, high-ranking military officers were at a loss about how to respond to President Alfonsín's policy of curbing the political influence of the military, lowering the defense budget, reducing the number of troops, and prosecuting officers who had committed human rights violations. Increasingly, officers who had participated in counterinsurgency and intelligence operations were becoming disgruntled about their commanders' reluctance to protect them from criminal prosecution and their refusal to take open responsibility for the orders given during the cultural war.

Exhumations and Identifications

Eyewitness accounts formed the core evidence collected by the CONADEP commission and the prosecutor's case against the junta commanders because of the destruction of documents, the counterinsurgency practice of giving oral commands, and the incineration and mass burial of the bodies of the disappeared. A thorough forensic investigation of mass graves would have given greater credibility to the testimonies, but they were carried out with reluctance. There were serious technical, financial, political, and psychological problems surrounding forensic exhumations. The technical knowledge of Argentine forensic pathologists was below international standards, while the government did not supply enough money for extensive investigations. In addition, certain political, military, and human rights circles were opposing exhumations. Finally, the psychological toll of finally finding the disappeared, mutilated and assassinated by unidentifiable perpetrators, was very high. Nevertheless, forensic investigations came to play an increasingly important role in the contested narrative reconstruction of Argentina's cultural war. After all, exhumations could contest or support with hard scientific proof each of the conflicting judicial, military, and human rights renditions of the past.

The first exhumations were carried out in late October 1982 when foren-

sic experts were shocked to discover an estimated four hundred unidentified bodies at the cemetery of Grand Bourg near Buenos Aires. The
gruesome find was made during the exhumation of union leader Miguel
Angel Sosa who had disappeared in 1976. On the evening of 25 May 1976,
his naked body had been found floating in the river Reconquista. It showed
obvious signs of torture. The police established Sosa's identity, did not
notify his relatives, and buried him as an unidentified corpse. The 1982
exhumation was made at the request of relatives tipped off by an employee
at the Ministry of Interior.[41]

The excavation of mass graves continued reluctantly till December 1983
because the military were still in power. Unmarked graves were opened
with pick-axes and mechanical shovels, destroying important forensic
traces which could have led to positive identifications.[42] The display of piles
of bones and perforated skulls revealed to the stunned Argentines the horrors of the military regime as well as their own mortality and the chance
that they could have met the same fate. The unidentified remains were so
shocking because each parent imagined his child in the disassembled ribs,
the skull with the open jaw bone, and the pieces of clothing hanging
around the hips. Alfredo Galletti was already in a deep depression because
of his daughter's disappearance when he saw these images on television.
Watching exhumation after exhumation, he finally committed suicide.[43]

The turn to democracy gave free rein to the exhumations. Nearly every
day new disinterments were ordered by the courts as if impelled to come
face to face, time and again, with the incomprehensible. The appointment
of the CONADEP commission did much to improve the forensic approach
because of its invitation of foreign expertise. Crucial was the involvement
of Clyde Snow, one of the world's foremost forensic experts. In January
1985, he began training anthropology and medical students in state-of-the-
art techniques.[44] Snow demonstrated that a careful forensic examination
could establish the identity of the exhumed as well as the cause and circumstance of death. Furthermore, Snow could determine whether or not the
deceased had been pregnant, and whether or not she had given birth. Such
evidence gave surviving grandparents the hope to recover someday their
abducted grandchildren from the hands of the adopted parents.

Clyde Snow demonstrated this forensic technique on the second day of
the 1985 trial against the former commanders. Liliana Pereyra was twenty-
one years old when she was abducted on 5 October 1977. She was later seen
at the ESMA secret detention center in Buenos Aires. Two former captives
testified in October 1979 that Liliana had given birth to a baby boy in February 1978. After fifteen days, she was separated from her baby and taken
most likely to the Tactical Divers Navy Base in Mar del Plata. On 15 July
1978, two women and one man were killed in a shootout with the police,
according to an official communiqué. Liliana Pereyra was positively identi-

fied as one of the three slain guerrillas, but was nevertheless buried in an unmarked grave.

Clyde Snow and his team of Argentine forensic anthropology students carried out the exhumation of Liliana Pereyra in January 1985. Their exhumation established that she had been assassinated from less than one meter by seven bullets from a double-barrelled Ithaca shotgun of a type commonly used by police and military. Snow established from an examination of the pelvic bones that Liliana had given birth to a baby.[45] Liliana's baby, now a seven-year-old boy, was living somewhere unknown in Argentina.

The formation of the Argentine forensic anthropology team EAAF (Equipo Argentino de Antropología Forense), the availability of the latest forensic techniques, and the successful completion of the trial against the commanders added several new dimensions to the exhumations. Exhumations were no longer a reexperience of the traumatic death of unidentifiable disappeared but became a means of hope, of recovering abducted grandchildren and reestablishing the violently broken family ties. The forensic team began identifying the remains resting in mass graves and collecting proof about births in captivity. In addition, forensic evidence was gathered for various court cases against military officers. The repeated shocks of disclosure at the turn of 1983, the positive identifications in 1984, the collection of criminal evidence against the military in 1985 and the confirmation of births in captivity, gave the exhumations multiple meanings which were interpreted differently by various human rights organizations. These conflicts of interpretation were tied to the feelings of social trust that had impelled the relatives to search for the disappeared and defy military repression.

One would expect that all human rights organizations would wholeheartedly approve of the forensic efforts to identify the disappeared. After all, positive identifications gave the disappeared back their names, revealed life histories of political action, and thus would help raise the empathy from the rest of society for the victims of military repression. The surprise was great when one large faction of the Mothers of the Plaza de Mayo Civilian Association opposed the exhumations. This position made sense in 1983 and early 1984 when there was little political will to prosecute the guilty and remains could not be identified.[46] The opposition to forensic exhumations made less sense in later years, and can be explained by the way these mothers handled the social trauma of the disappearances and the contested memory construction of the past.

The Mothers of the Plaza de Mayo Civilian Association formulated its opposition to the exhumations in the second half of 1984 in terms of the ongoing memory construction about military repression. Reflecting on the intense soul-searching in 1984, Hebe de Bonafini said: "It cost us weeks and weeks of meetings at which there were many tears and much despair, because the profound Catholic formation of our people creates almost a need to have a dead body, a burial, and a Mass."[47] Most of the Association's members felt that, however painful, the wounds inflicted by the disappearances had to remain open to resist a national process of forgetting. "It has been eleven years of suffering, eleven years that have not been relieved in any sense. Many want the wound to dry so that we will forget. We want it to continue bleeding, because this is the only way that one continues to have strength to fight. . . . But, above all, it is necessary that this wound bleeds so that the murderers will be condemned, as they deserve to be, and that what has happened will not happen again."[48] In December 1984, the group of mothers headed by Hebe de Bonafini condemned the exhumations as a government scheme to have them accept the presumption of death of all disappeared, and thus silence their critical political voice.[49]

The leading figures of the Mothers of the Plaza de Mayo Civilian Association were well aware of the psychological toll of the enduring uncertainty to searching relatives. A team of psychotherapists stood by to provide counseling to mothers suffering from impaired mourning. Nevertheless, the Bonafini group continued to regard the exhumations as a sinister ploy to set in motion a mourning process that would achieve the resignation and depoliticization of all searching mothers and relatives. In particular, mourning would break the solidarity of the politicized Association's mothers and produce a reconciliatory attitude. Thus, exhumations and reburials would destroy the living memory of the disappeared, and inter them in an enclosed remembrance. "What are you going to protest when you accept the exhumations and the indemnification? In no way whatsoever, I don't want a dead body, what I want is the murderer!"[50] The Bonafini group preferred to appropriate public space with their weekly protest marches as living memorials to the repression. Reliving the pains and struggles of the past became their way of coping with their social trauma and, in the process, contributing to a social memory of state terror.

The chronic anxiety, the impaired mourning, and the continued hope that characterized the years between 1976 and 1983 had turned into anger and disillusionment by 1984 as more mass graves were discovered. Activism helped many mothers to cope with their grief, and submerge the personal and social trauma into protest and political action.[51] A majority began to embrace political ideas which many had opposed in the 1970s. They began to regard themselves as the embodiment of their children's ideals and struggles. Hebe de Bonafini commented about the revolutionary spirit of her two disappeared sons: "If they are not here, then I have to be them, to shout for them, vindicate them with honesty and return to them, even if it's only a slice of life."[52]

The tireless demonstrations of the Mothers of the Plaza de Mayo Civilian Association was one way of coping with the trauma of disappearance. It was the continued and unmourned reexperience of the disappearance which made these mothers try to take control of a world that had made them powerless at the moment of abduction. Every time a slogan was shouted, this power was exerted. Their conscious objective was to keep the memory of the disappeared alive, but a deeper motivation was their growing ability to cope with their traumatic memory through public rituals, the creation of a controlled and controlling narrative, and the transformation of suffering into action.

Most human rights organizations and a smaller faction within the Mothers of the Plaza de Mayo Civilian Association did not desire a collective memory based on chronic mourning. Many parents wanted to be reunited with their children, even if they had been reduced to a pile of bones. The years of uncertainty burdened many searching relatives with impaired mourning that continued after the 1983 fall of the military junta.[53] They remained in favor of the exhumations, and regarded the fight for the remains as a struggle about the survival of their legacy to Argentine history and society. The recovery of the dead confirmed that the disappearances had really taken place, and that Argentine society had to accept that the unbelievable was in fact true.

A tragic partition took place in January 1986 between the Mothers of the Plaza de Mayo headed by Hebe de Bonafini and the Mothers of the Plaza de Mayo Founding Line led by María Adela Antokoletz.[54] There were four reasons. One, the Bonafini group saw no real difference between the military junta and the Alfonsín government because both failed to provide an answer about the fate of the disappeared and protected the guilty from prosecution. The Founding Line group argued that, even though the Alfonsín administration had betrayed the cause of the disappeared by not prosecuting all perpetrators, it had brought the former junta commanders to trial and allowed human rights organizations to spread their message openly in society. The second reason for the split was a fundamental disagreement about the exhumations. The Founding Line supported the search for forensic evidence, while the Bonafini group rejected the exhumations. Three, the Founding Line disagreed with the provocative street politics championed by Hebe de Bonafini. Four, the Bonafini group sought the enduring remembrance of the disappeared by pursuing their political ideals, while the Founding Line proposed various commemorative means such as memorials, a national monument, and a museum and documentation center.[55]

Notwithstanding their rejection of the exhumations, the Bonafini group could not deny the political, historical, and judicial importance of the ongoing forensic investigations. The exhumations undermined the authority of the military by exposing their deceit and abuses. Together with the unending stream of testimonies by former captives, the call for punishment remained as strong in 1986 as during the 1985 trial of the commanders. The Alfonsín government worried that the prosecution of thousands of officers, NCOs, and policemen would destabilize the still fragile democracy. Military officers were becoming infuriated about being arraigned in court, the lackluster defense by their commanders-in-chief, the deteriorating wages, and the overall hostility from the surrounding society. Taunted and scoffed at in public, afraid to walk the streets in uniform, the Argentine military felt the brunt of the anger of the Argentine people for their years of repression.

Rebellion and Defense: Operation Dignity

By early 1985, more than two thousand complaints had been filed against six hundred and fifty officers.[56] The conviction of the former commanders-in-chief in December 1985 opened the likelihood for future trials of lower-ranked officers and NCOs who had carried out the repression. The joint chiefs of staff and the retired generals of the 1976–1983 dictatorship found themselves in an impossible situation. High-ranking military commanders had to carry on a public discourse of denial while acknowledging internally the patriotic repression executed by lower-ranked personnel.

At the same time, President Alfonsín was concerned about the cost to democracy of a resentful armed forces. The military felt that they had been singled out as the only culprit for the political violence of the 1970s. The trial against Montonero commander Mario Firmenich, arrested in Brazil and extradited to Argentina in October 1984, did little to appease them.[57] Alfonsín tried to press the military supreme court into making haste with indicting commanding officers to return to normalcy as soon as possible. Instead, in a terrible affront, the Supreme Council acquitted General Menéndez of the ruthless Third Army Corps of all charges. Federal courts now began taking over cases from military prosecutors, despite the refusal of several officers to testify.

Alfonsín decided to put an end to the bleak prospect of hundreds of trials and proposed the Final Stop law (Ley de Punto Final) which was accepted by Congress on 23 December 1986. The law placed a sixty-day statute of limitations on criminal complaints against individual officers. In an unexpected reaction, judges and legal clerks canceled their January vacation to file complaints against more than four hundred officers.[58]

Many of the accused were middle-rank officers (captains, majors, lieutenant-colonels) who had personally carried out the repressive operations as junior officers. These officers felt abandoned by their superiors in their efforts to stay out of the hands of the courts. They blamed the junta leaders for not providing any legal coverage to their repressive orders and no longer wanted to be held accountable. The very blood pact which had welded the complicity of high-ranking commanders and low-ranking members of the task forces had disintegrated. The chain of command was broken as angry officers vowed to protect their comrades from prosecution and the armed forces from its demise.[59]

Lieutenant-Colonel Santiago Alonso explained these concerns to me as follows: "We were convinced that the army would die if we didn't react, die as a spiritual entity, no? It wouldn't die as a physical entity or as a material infrastructure. It would die as a spiritual entity because the army is a spiritual entity, no? It has a soul. If comrades were betrayed, whatever their rank or grade had been in the war against the subversion, if they were abandoned to their own good luck before judges for carrying out acts of war— they had been given orders, they had been imparted orders, they didn't act on their own, and some even violated their own conscience—well, that would be the death of the army."[60]

The disgruntlement with the failing leadership of the armed forces comes to a burst a few days before Easter 1987. Major Ernesto Barreiro is summoned by a federal court on the charge of torturing prisoners at La Perla secret detention center.[61] He refuses to testify. When Barreiro fails to appear in court and the judge orders his arrest, Barreiro's comrades rise in rebellion. On Wednesday the 15th of April 1987, Major Barreiro takes refuge at the 14th Airborne Infantry Regiment in Córdoba. President Alfonsín is notified by the army commander that the units around Córdoba refuse to repress the rebels by force.[62]

Early the next morning, Lieutenant-Colonel Aldo Rico boards a flight to Buenos Aires. He is the commander of the 18th Infantry Regiment in San Javier, Misiones, and places himself at the head of the mutiny. Upon his arrival in Buenos Aires, Rico travels with a group of trusted men to the Campo de Mayo army base and takes the Infantry School by force. The men are dressed in fatigues and wear black camouflage makeup. They call themselves *carapintadas* or "painted faces" to distinguish themselves as warriors from the *uñas pintadas* or "painted nails," as they disparagingly call the army bureaucrats. Meanwhile, Barreiro leaves the Cordoban regiment secretly that evening, and hides at an army base in Tucumán province, while the mutiny spreads on Good Friday to four other military bases.[63]

What is so remarkable about the uprising is that none of the commanders of the six army bases in mutiny have been charged with human rights violations. For instance, their leader Lieutenant-Colonel Aldo Rico belongs to the Commandos, the army's prestigious special forces which fought with distinction in the Falkland/Malvinas War. Rico himself had been decorated for his merit during the war. What distinguishes them are their nationalist convictions, conservative Catholicism, anticommunism, and the belief that the counterinsurgency war was above all a cultural war. They all graduated from the Military Academy in 1964 and several belonged to the coterie of young officers surrounding the Catholic nationalist thinker Jordán Bruno Genta. Operation Dignity (Operación Dignidad), as Rico later baptized the mutiny, seeks to save the military from the humiliating trials, wants the press to stop harassing the armed forces, and demands the resignation of army commander General Ríos Ereñú for accepting the prosecution of officers. The rebels declare emphatically that they do not want to over-throw the government.[64]

On Saturday 18 April, large groups of people begin arriving spontane-ously at the Plaza de Mayo to express their support of democracy and to prevent a military coup through their massive outcry, while President Alfonsín is pondering how to resolve the crisis. In the evening, government officials ask the crowd to return the next day at noon for Alfonsín's public address. On Easter Sunday morning, a multitude of more than 400,000 people overflow the Plaza de Mayo. In addition, large crowds gather in doz-ens of other cities and towns in Argentina. It is not just the fear of a military coup or the defeat of democracy, but the reexperience of the traumas of the past, of the disappearances and military repression, which mobilizes people on Easter Sunday. What better way to express the popular disap-proval of the rebellion then to go to the squares of Argentina?

A day of hopeful signs between Rico and the Minister of Defense turns sour in the afternoon of Easter Sunday. The rebels demand to talk to Presi-dent Alfonsín in person. Alfonsín ascends the balcony of the presidential palace, and tells the expectant crowd that he will go to Campo de Mayo. The entire world should know, says Alfonsín, that with the massive popular presence at the Plaza de Mayo and everywhere else in Argentina "we are, in the first place, showing clearly the resolve to live in a democracy. In sec-ond place, we are showing that the force of a peaceful popular mobilization is stronger than violence."[65] Once more, the crowd at the Plaza de Mayo is given its place in history and used to legitimate the government's authority. Afraid that the people will accompany him en masse and provoke a violent reaction from the rebels, Alfonsín asks the people to wait at the Plaza de Mayo for his return.[66]

Alfonsín meets with Rico at five o'clock in the afternoon, and the rebel commander explains that their operation is not a military coup but that they want a political solution for the sequels of the counterinsurgency war and to begin a process of national reconciliation. Alfonsín announces that army commander Ríos Ereñú has asked for his retirement and he explains the new legislation he is about to submit to Congress. Rico feels that these conditions satisfy his main demands, and surrenders to the proper military authorities.[67]

As Alfonsín is leaving the reunion with Rico, he is stopped by an emo-tional Captain Breide Obeid: "Mister President, you have to understand us. . . . They ordered us to fight against the subversion, saying that we were defending society against the enemy. . . . We were not prepared for that type of a fight and they made us do things that we never dreamed of as military men. They said it was for our families." The captain continues to tell Alfonsín about the hardships during the Falkland/Malvinas War. "Immediately upon our return, they treated us as criminals, they hid us as if we were lepers. . . . The trials ended up crushing us. We didn't speak of anything else in the barracks. The generals didn't defend us, they didn't even take notice of our requests for reforms. . . . This is all, Mister President. I wanted to explain to you what I felt."[68]

Moved by the captain's words, Alfonsín returns victorious to the balcony of the Casa Rosada and wishes the people gathered at the Plaza de Mayo a "Happy Easter." Amid cheers, Alfonsín tells them that the rebels have ended their mutiny, and that they will be detained and submitted to justice. He adds that some of them are heroes from the Falkland/Malvinas War, and that they did not try to overthrow the government. Finally, concludes Alfonsín, "I ask all of you to return to your homes to kiss your children, and to celebrate Easter in peace in Argentina."[69] The price for this peace would be paid six weeks later.

On 4 June 1987, the government proposed the Due Obedience law (Ley de Obediencia Debida).[70] The law distinguished three levels of responsibility: the higher the rank, the greater the responsibility. Most indicted officers now became immune to prosecution because they had been carrying out orders from higher-ranked officers. Only theft, rape, and the abduction of children remained punishable.

What is the meaning of the 1987 Holy Week mutiny in relation to the cultural war? I believe that the mutiny was the eruption of a multiple social trauma within the military. The first social traumatization had occurred during the cultural war when individual officers decided to abuse people's most fundamental rights and lost their military honor in the process. The rebel officers blamed high-ranking commanders for making them fight a war for which they were ill-equipped. According to Major Ernesto Barreiro, "In general, we were not prepared for anything we did, we had to manage things by ourselves. This is the truth: we had to manage things alone."[71] The armed forces, its hierarchical command structure, its integrity and honor had been seriously damaged by the brutal cultural war, in the eyes of many officers. These ambivalent emotions about winning a dirty war which smeared their uniform led a submerged life because neither the military establishment nor Argentine society was receptive to their plight.

The second traumatization was the defeat on the Falkland/Malvinas Islands and the shameful return to Argentina. Lieutenant-Colonel Rico had spent five weeks as a prisoner-of-war of the British forces, and was shocked at his reception in Argentina. Instead of preparing a big welcome home, allowing the troops to parade through Buenos Aires, and commemorate the dead comrades left behind on the wind-swept Malvinas Islands, the war veterans "were hidden like lepers."[72] Aside from the posttraumatic stress disorder suffered by individual combatants, the military defeat and dishonorable arrival in Argentina cut deep wounds into the armed forces whose political, institutional, and emotional sequels can be best described as a social trauma.

The prosecution of hundreds of officers for human rights violations intensified the double traumatization. Lieutenant-Colonel Rico and his fellow rebels felt that their superiors failed to protect the armed forces against the humiliating trials and wanted their commanders to restore military honor by vindicating the cultural war.[73] Repeated public accusations obstructed the selective forgetting of memories which were particularly traumatizing because they could only be uttered at the expense of prosecution. In sum, the complex social trauma consisted of unresolved injuries of two wars enhanced by feelings of defenselessness against prosecution. The solution of this double social trauma was sought in a rebellious demonstration of power against the lackluster commanders, the persecutory government, and a thankless Argentine people.

The faith of the Argentine people in the rocky democratization process was tested again in January 1988. Once more, Lieutenant-Colonel Rico and almost three hundred rebels held the nation captive. However, the uprising at the 4th Infantry Regiment in Monte Caseros concerned largely Rico's unclear state of arrest, and failed to win much sympathy. Troops loyal to Alfonsín were ready to attack, and the rebels surrendered. Another uprising took place by officers and NCOs kindred in spirit to Rico. The Villa Martelli army base was taken in December 1988 by the ultranationalist Colonel Mohamed Alí Seineldín, a former instructor in counterinsurgency methods and a veteran of the Falkland/Malvinas War. He wanted to halt the budgetary and spiritual deterioration of the armed forces. The rebels surrendered after several days of negotiations and were duly arrested.[74]

With the principal rebel leaders behind bars, calm seemed to have returned to Argentina. However, on Monday 23 January 1989, at 6:15 in the morning, a truck forces its way through the front gate of the 3rd Infantry Regiment at La Tablada, followed by a string of vehicles. The assailants open fire and shout 'Long live Rico and Seineldín!' Another group attacks the base from the rear. A third group distributes pamphlets denouncing the Marxist subversion inside the Alfonsín government, and vindicating the dignity and honor of the armed forces. Provincial police surround the La Tablada base, while loyal infantry units start advancing from La Plata.

The counterattack begins around noon when two small tanks enter the army base, and set the building on fire where most assailants are concentrated. In the course of the day, it becomes clear that not sympathizers of Rico and Seineldín but about fifty leftist guerrillas have taken La Tablada. More army units arrive, and the base is retaken on Tuesday around noontime after more than thirty hours of pitched battle and at the cost of the lives of two policemen, nine armymen, and twenty-eight guerrillas.[75]

The guerrillas turned out to belong to the left-wing Everybody for the Fatherland Movement or MTP (Movimiento Todos por la Patria), and were an array of young workers, students, and veterans of Santucho's People's Revolutionary Army (ERP). The group believed that they had reliable information that a military coup was to begin on 24 January at the La

Tablada army base. They decided to make a preemptive strike, overtake the army base, proceed with several tanks to the Plaza de Mayo, and incite a popular mobilization against the conspirators.[76]

The La Tablada attack had been commanded by Enrique Gorriarán Merlo who had participated in the daring 1972 Rawson prison escape, risen in the ranks of the ERP, joined the Sandinista insurgents in 1979, and been responsible for the 1980 execution of former Nicaraguan dictator Anastasio Somoza. Gorriarán Merlo escaped from La Tablada, but more than a dozen guerrillas were captured alive, while others were detained later. The captives denounced the disappearance of three comrades captured alive, and the assassination of two others. One of the disappeared was the former ERP member and psychologist Carlos Samojedny, who had written so perceptively about the harsh maximum security prison regime of Rawson during the dictatorship.[77] On 5 October 1989, the verdict was read: thirteen persons received life sentences, seven persons were given prison terms from ten to twenty years. Gorriarán Merlo was eventually captured and given a life sentence in 1997.[78]

The Argentine armed forces benefited most from the La Tablada attack, despite their loss of lives. The divisive rebellions of 1987 and 1988 were temporarily forgotten, the military received the sympathy of the Argentine people and proved their value in defending democracy. Furthermore, the La Tablada attack placed the 1970s counterinsurgency war in a new light. Most people still condemned the brutal methods, but they became more understanding about the military's response.

Political unrest, and especially the economic crisis with its runaway inflation, made President Alfonsín not complete his term in December 1989. After losing the May 1989 presidential elections to the Peronist Carlos Saúl Menem, he stepped down in July 1989. Immediately, Menem joined the military in their plea for national reconciliation. He was of course aware of the public opposition to a sweeping amnesty of convicted and indicted officers, so he devised a clever strategy to prepare the Argentine people for the inevitable. Menem announced repeatedly that a presidential pardon was forthcoming but kept postponing the decision to exhaust the opposition. He accepted the many protest crowds stoically, and declared that he had the moral right to pardon the military because he endured torture and lengthy incarceration during the dictatorship.[79]

On 7 October 1989, President Menem pardoned the three junta members Galtieri, Anaya, and Lami Dozo, condemned in 1986 for waging the 1982 Falkland/Malvinas War, and 174 military officers and NCOs (including Rico and Seineldín) responsible for the 1987 and 1988 military rebellions. Menem also pardoned 39 retired military officers and 64 former guerrillas for their involvement in the political violence of the 1970s. Painfully, the list of pardoned guerrillas included twelve disappeared persons.[80]

In late May 1990, Carlos Menem made use once more of his tested formula to prepare the Argentine people for a second presidential pardon. He blamed the military and the guerrillas equally for the violence of the 1970s, and emphasized the need "to heal without more ado the bleeding wound of the Argentine body" to achieve national reconciliation.[81] Menem had embraced the two-demon theory of his predecessor Alfonsín, emphasizing the shared responsibility of the two armed parties locked in a spiral of violence. However, the Argentine people continued to have misgivings about Menem's determination to free the junta commanders. A July 1990 poll revealed that 70 percent of the respondents were against the pardon, a figure which declined only slightly to 63 percent in November 1990.[82]

As the Argentine people were resigning themselves to the president's solution of the "military problem," as Menem was prone to say, another rebellion took place. On 3 December 1990, at about three o'clock in the morning, fifty lower-rank officers and NCOs took army headquarters in Buenos Aires, while other rebel units occupied five more military installations. The uprising of around six hundred rebels would turn out to be the bloodiest but also the last of the military rebellions. The initiative had been taken largely by disgruntled NCOs who demanded higher wages, the dismissal of the army command, and the appointment of Colonel Seineldín as the new commander. President Menem had learned from Alfonsín's mistake. He refused to negotiate but repressed the rebellion. The killing of two officers, trying to wrest the Palermo infantry base from the rebels, made loyal troops break the unwritten rule not to fire on their own forces. The uprising was quelled by nine o'clock in the evening after two rebels, six loyalists, and five civilians had been killed. Hundreds of rebels were tried, while Colonel Seineldín was given a life sentence.[83]

Both Menem and the armed forces emerged strengthened from the conflict. The armed forces had once more shown their loyalty to the constitutional government, and President Menem had revealed himself as a determined national leader who was not going to tolerate any military insubordination. In Menem's eyes, the road to national reconciliation was open. On 29 December 1990 he pardoned the former junta members Videla, Viola, Agosti, Massera, Lambruschini, several generals, several right-wing Peronists, and Montonero commander Mario Firmenich as a final turning of the page in pursuit of national reconciliation.[84]

The wisdom of the presidential pardon was immediately questioned by politicians and human rights leaders. The human rights movement called for a "day of national protest and mourning" and invited the Argentine people to wear black bands and fill the squares of Argentina's cities. The call was heeded in many places. More than sixty thousand mourners gathered at the Plaza de Mayo. Former President Alfonsín had already in 1989 expressed his misgivings about the measures: "One cannot decree the amnesia of an entire society because every time anyone tried to sweep the past under the carpet, the past returned with a vengeance."[85] Alfonsín's words proved to be prophetic as exhumations continued to uncover new evidence of births in captivity, grandmothers intensified their search for their abducted grandchildren, and kidnapping charges were raised against the pardoned junta members.

Radicalization and Reburial

The 1987 Due Obedience Law and the 1989 and 1990 presidential pardons had a tremendous effect on the human rights movement. In particular, the Mothers of the Plaza de Mayo under the leadership of Hebe de Bonafini started on a path of ideological radicalization embracing the political project attributed to the disappeared. At last they acknowledged the political militancy of their disappeared children: "A step which cost the Mothers much was to realize that their children were political militants, revolutionary activists; the general discourse was at the beginning that my child hadn't done anything, and that they had taken him or her away because he or she was a teacher, an artist, or a lawyer."[86]

By late 1988, the idea arose that the mothers had to "socialize their maternity," and adopt the suffering of all victims of political violence in the world.[87] "When we understood that our children were not going to appear, we socialized motherhood and felt that we are the mothers of everybody, that all are our children."[88] Clearly, these mothers wanted to extend the maternal protection they had been unable to provide their own children at the hour of abduction to all victims of repression, and at the same time be faithful to their sons and daughters by embracing their radical political ideas. Trust and protection were the unconscious motives of their political position.

Their opposition to the exhumations remained as firm as ever through the years. "We know that they are exhuming cadavers. We are against those exhumations because we don't want our children to die. Our children cannot be enclosed in tombs, because they are free and revolutionary."[89] In the eyes of these mothers, exhumations became synonymous with spiritual and physical death, while the reburial of the identified skeletal remains destroyed the living memory of the disappeared. Political activism and the refusal to accept the death of their abducted children was their way of continuing a relationship with the assassinated disappeared.

Many searching relatives disagreed with the view that the exhumations depoliticized them. They turned the reburials into acts of political protest and collective mourning. These reburials allowed the bereaved to mourn their losses and were a last chance to protect the children they had been forced to abandon during their abduction. The thought that the disappeared had been dumped in mass graves, without any ritual or show of bereavement, was intolerable. A proper reburial was the ultimate demonstration of parental trust and protection. The reburials also restored the victims' public honor, reincorporated them into society as deceased members, politicized the recovered remains, and resurrected the ideals for which they had died.[90] Relatives were able to project their feelings on the bones, end their search, and concentrate on the political future.[91]

Julio and Irma Morresi found their son Norberto in 1989. They reburied him in the same grave as his companion Luis María Roberto who had died with him. "The truth, however hard it may be, will in the end bring tranquillity. I am no longer searching in that god-knows-where place . . . to see if it's Norberto, or visit a madhouse to see if he's there. I know, unfortunately, we have this little heap of bones at the Flores cemetery, no? It is like a ritual that we go there every Sunday to bring him even if it is only one flower. It is completely useless, but it helps spiritually. . . . We go there, we kiss the photo hanging on the niche, and it makes us feel good."[92]

The importance of finding the remains of a loved one was expressed in a moving way by Juan Gelman and Berta Schubaroff after forensic anthropologists had exhumed and identified their son Marcelo in 1989. "I kissed him again. I kissed all his bones, touched him, caressed him," said Berta Schubaroff. "But the emotion confounded with the pain, because once I found him, he turned out to be dead. So I cried the death of my son, and those thirteen years of search vanished. I can't relate to that period anymore."[93] Juan Gelman confessed to similar sentiments a few weeks later: "I feel that I have been able to rescue him from the fog."[94] I wonder through which fog Juan Gelman seized his son. The fog that drifts between the land of the living and the land of the dead? Or does he mean to say that he was finally able to deliver his son from the mists of oblivion?

The reburial of Marcelo Gelman had a strong emotional as well as a remarkable political significance. Berta Shubaroff decided to bury her son in a Jewish cemetery out of vindication, even though she never practiced the Jewish faith. She had become conscious of her Jewish heritage when she learnt that her son's tormentors had treated him as a "shit Jew" (*judío de mierda*), and she therefore wanted to demonstrate her forgotten identity openly through a Jewish reburial.[95] In another political act, a wake was held at the headquarters of the Buenos Aires press workers union. Marcelo Gelman was one of ninety disappeared journalists, and his reburial served to draw attention to their plight.

Reburials allowed parents to express their enduring loyalty to their deceased children by providing them with a proper resting-place and observing their departure with a culturally prescribed funeral. The torn fabric of society was restored by funerary rituals, the remains came to share sacred ground, and their souls were reconciled in the society of the dead, only to be recaptured periodically in annual remembrance or collective religious rites.[96] These purposes were served in Argentina for nearly two hundred identified and reburied disappeared. Their violent death accorded them a special position in society and turned the reburial from a ritual of restoration into a political manifestation.[97]

The rite of passage between life and death symbolized in funerals is analogous to the transition between war and peace. The military repression revolved centrally around the disappearance of their opponents and the paralysis of the searching relatives. The deliberate obstruction of funeral rites impedes a return to the normalcy of peace and a repair of the social fabric. The sorrow and rage of the living continued to trouble Argentine society throughout the 1990s. The uncertainty about thousands of unrecovered dead, the impunity and denial of their executors, the unending search for abducted children and the sequels of multiple social traumas continued to gnaw at the heart of the nation.

Conclusion: The Spirals of Violence and Trauma

"There are important details but it is difficult for me to talk about them. I think about them and I repress them. They were undressed while being unconscious and when the flight commander gave the order, depending on the location of the plane, the hatch was opened and they were thrown out naked, one by one. . . . As I was quite nervous about the situation, I almost fell and tumbled into the abyss. . . . I stumbled and they grabbed me."[1]

Captain Adolfo Francisco Scilingo never recovered from the shock. He began drinking excessively and took tranquilizers to remain on his feet. He also became troubled by a recurrent nightmare: he is flying across the south Atlantic, throwing naked bodies down the cargo door of an airplane. Suddenly, he stumbles and falls into the great sky below. Just before crashing into the ocean, he wakes up.[2] Scilingo's narrow escape from death in 1977 contributed to a posttraumatic stress disorder that would come to involve the entire Argentine society. Disturbed by constant nightmares, he lost his commission in the Navy. In March 1995, five years after President Menem had tried to bury the country's past with his last presidential pardon, Captain Scilingo broke the pact of silence of the Argentine military.[3]

Scilingo's confession gave a new turn to the disappearances. The Argentine people had heard about death flights before, but Scilingo's self-incriminating admission of guilt gave a sudden credibility to the inconceivable testimonies. His story also confirmed the feared truth that the remains of thousands of disappeared would never be found. Still, even though Scilingo filled in several unknowns, Argentine society continued to be divided about the rendition of the past.

The general awareness of the death flights reveals the complexity and polyphony of Argentina's collective trauma. Hundreds of officers, NCOs, and technicians were involved in the gruesome flights, while many high-ranking officers were aware of what was happening. With few exceptions, these perpetrators all denied the existence of the death flights. This denial was disputed by a handful of former captives who had witnessed the preparations. They provided the victims' perspective through public testimonies. Finally, there were thousands of people who agonized over the fall to death of their loved ones. These three groups have different social traumas. They may agree on the basic facts—the when, where, and how of the flights—but they have difficulty agreeing why captives were assassinated through air-drops. They cannot reconcile their diverse experiences because each social trauma contains gaps which the other cannot fill. The collective trauma of the Argentine people is therefore varied and heterogeneous, and divides society into many groups with their own rendition of events.

How do we know if Argentine society is suffering from multiple social traumas? Is the term social trauma not a too vague concept that obscures rather than advances our understanding of the social consequences of massive political violence? How can we establish whether or not the political violence and state terror of the 1970s led to the social traumatization of large groups of people? Finally, is there a direct or an indirect relation between massive violence and collective trauma in Argentina?

This concluding chapter elaborates the book's main argument, namely that between the 1950s and 1970s Argentina became involved in a spiral of violence mediated by the repeated social traumatization of political adversaries because of increasing attacks on multiple levels of Argentine society. Argentine society developed a violence-trauma-violence dynamic that culminated in the cultural war of the 1970s and was eventually halted through the outtraumatization of the guerrilla forces and the radicalized political left. The traumatizing sequels of this state terror helped bring down, in turn, the military regime through frequent street protests, national and international appeals for justice, and incessant calls for truth by people searching for disappeared relatives.

Political Violence and Collective Trauma

There is a common belief that violence can escalate by itself. In fact, the notion that violence has a logic of its own is deeply ingrained in Western culture, can be traced back to Greek tragedies like the *Oresteia* by Aeschylus, and is reflected in explanations of contemporary outbreaks of massive violence. Many scholars have also treated violence as an autonomous process, ranging from René Girard to anthropologists such as Allen Feldman, Valentine Daniel, and Michael Taussig.[4] Finally, Argentine writers, scholars, and politicians have also treated violence as a self-perpetuating process in the explanations of their country's troubled history. Recently, José Pablo Feinmann has argued that Argentine history has been poisoned by an interminable cycle of violence: "This is our history: it is woven out of violence and revenge, out of violence and counterviolence. Out of blood and out of revenge for spilled blood."[5] Clearly, the belief in an autonomous spiral of violence is firmly embedded in Western culture.

My study of half a century of Argentine political history has revealed that this general explanation does not hold true for Argentina because the escalating violence became mediated by a process of traumatization. As a matter of fact, I argue that the accumulation of the traumatic sequels of many acts of violence was crucial in perpetuating and escalating political violence. The mediation of massive violence by social trauma explains why state terror brought the increasing political violence to a halt in the late 1970s.[6] The spiral of violence burned itself out because one party outtraumatized the other, and was then struck itself from power by a human rights movement that arose from the outtraumatization.[7] The guerrilla forces had been decimated and demoralized, while the political opposition became paralyzed by military repression. The only public resistance came from relatives searching for their disappeared children.

The mounting violence and traumatization in Argentina were inflicted on several levels of social complexity, namely crowds, politico-military organizations, families, and the self. These different kinds of social relations relate to four domains: the public, politico-military, domestic, and personal. The practices and characteristics of one social level cannot be reduced to another, and violence and trauma in Argentine society did not necessarily appear in equal measures in all four of them. My focus on these four levels and domains corresponds to the places where political violence in Argentine society had been directed and trauma was suffered during the second half of the twentieth century.

Other societies may very well manifest a different constellation of levels and domains in times of upheaval. Such cross-cultural variation is inevitable because each level has certain unique characteristics and comprises practices that can only be observed and analyzed on that level of social interaction. The violence to the self through torture differs from the symbolic violence of curtailing the right of political expression or the violent repression of a protest crowd, but all three contribute to an overall climate of abuse and injury. Likewise, an armed confrontation between a military patrol and a guerrilla unit occurs on a different level of social complexity from a house raid and the abduction of its inhabitants. All these forms of violence do not necessarily come together. Counterinsurgency can also be conducted without systematic torture, and disappearances are not the only strategy available to spread confusion among enemy forces. Nevertheless, disappearances were a common practice in Argentina, and so were abduction, torture, guerrilla warfare, and the repression of protest crowds.

The historical coexistence of these different forms of violence created interlinkages that made the violence on one level spill over into another. These manifestations of violence have different historical and political origins, but they influenced and reinforced one another through time. Part I of this book has demonstrated how street crowds became a characteristic of Argentine political culture after 1945. These crowds at times provoked violent reactions from police and armed forces yet continued to crop up throughout the twentieth century. Part II analyzed how the Peronist Resistance arose during the late-1950s in the slipstream of the disenfranchised Peronist movement and the repressed Peronist crowds. The Peronist Resistance petered out after several years but its violent practices resurfaced again in 1970 with the birth of a guerrilla insurgency influenced by the Cuban revolution and encouraged by the outbreak of massive protest crowds. The political climate became harsher, the violence increased, and Argentine society became enveloped in a traumatizing grip. Protest crowds and guerrilla organizations fed on one another in a growing political radicalization, and violent insurgency met with intense police and military repression.

Part III analyzed the long historical roots of torture, disappearance, and state repression. The diverse forms of political violence described in Parts I to III developed interconnections that turned political violence and collective trauma into an overdetermined whole by the mid-1970s. At that time, the psychic, physical, social, political, and cultural became affected all together, thus traumatizing Argentine society as a whole, albeit not in equal ways. Argentina's military commanders decided to annihilate the guerrilla organizations, break the political culture of insurrectional crowd mobilizations, dismantle the political self and agency of critical sectors of society, and instill values of authority, discipline, and hierarchy. Although achieving their objectives in the short term, the Argentine military foundered on the thousands of people searching for disappeared family members. Part IV showed how the mothers of the disappeared staged street demonstrations as a tested form of political resistance. Parents defied state terror to protest the disappearance of their children, and gave rise to massive oppositional crowds that helped to topple the military regime.

With the previous delineation of the multilevel interconnections among violence and trauma, I want to emphasize that the political violence in Argentina did not simply beget more violence, but that the violence begot trauma, and trauma led to more violence. The decades of political disenfranchisement, military rule, nationwide repression, and finally the numerous casualties of armed combat, reprisal killings, and state terror traumatized Argentine society in multiple ways, affecting individuals as well as groups. There were many Argentines who suffered from an acute psychic trauma when subjected to violence and some developed posttraumatic disorders afterwards. Survivors of secret detention centers, parents of disappeared children, and military officers have all displayed symptoms associated with psychic traumas. This book has only addressed psychic traumas in passing, and concentrated on the traumatization of social groups.

The process of social traumatization came to affect increasingly more groups, just as violence did. The knowledge of a mother and father that their daughter had been tortured stirred them emotionally, changed the social dynamic of domestic life, affected the ties with friends and colleagues, and thus traumatized the family. In sum, massive political violence and social trauma arose together, contributed to each other's formation, and thus created a multilevel, overdetermined political context which damaged Argentine society as much as many individual lives. The escalating violence led to increasing degrees of social traumatization which stimulated more violence. The large-scale consequences of this destructive dynamic became hard to control.

This interactive process of violence and trauma makes the search for single causes of Argentine political violence a futile effort. I hope I have shown in this book that Argentine society was neither hit suddenly by an eruption of massive political violence nor traumatized all at once. There is not one moment or one event to which political violence and collective trauma can be traced. Rather, violence and trauma percolated through the various levels of society. Crowds were traumatized, and so were the military, the guerrillas, the captives, and the families. Even the lives of people who remained far from the political turbulence were affected.

Emotionally, I find it difficult to concede the term trauma to the Argentine military because I emphatically want to avoid a moral equation of perpetrators and sufferers. After all, individual torturers may have been troubled by the traumatic aftereffects of inflicting pain on their captives, but these symptoms were embedded in feelings of personal empowerment, the willingness to participate in repressive practices, and the pride of having defeated the enemy. The psychic traumas of perpetrators and survivors may very well have clinical similarities, but they entail different moral universes. Likewise, the social traumas of the armed forces and the human rights movement are morally, politically, and socially very different; nevertheless both groups have suffered the far-reaching consequences of decades of violence. For this reason, I use the term collective trauma for Argentine society as a whole, and social trauma as a group-specific condition. The collective trauma of victims, sufferers, survivors, and even of people who were neither involved nor directly affected by the violence, is thus socially complex and morally diverse.

My conclusion that Argentina became a traumatized society is not a foregone conclusion. Several authors have recently suggested that trauma may not be a universal response to excessive violence but a Western cultural construct, and that therefore not all societies will be traumatized by massive violence.[8] This question is of little concern in the case of Argentina. Psychoanalytic thought has penetrated Argentine culture as one of the foremost interpretive models about the human condition, and psychoanalysis continues to be the principal psychotherapy of victims of violence and repression. Concepts such as trauma, repression, neurosis, and the unconscious have pervaded popular speech and were even adopted, selectively, by the 1976–1983 military authorities.[9] Argentine people were thus predisposed towards understanding their suffering in terms of trauma, and this situation makes social trauma a congenial concept to interpret the socially disruptive consequences of political violence.

A social trauma is not an individual trauma writ large. The psychic traumas of guerrilla snipers, injured combatants, and survivors of torture do not inevitably add up to the social traumatization of guerrilla organizations, let alone to a traumatized Argentine society. Scores of Argentine guerrillas became personally traumatized after being tortured and some committed suicide afterwards. In turn, the guerrilla forces became socially traumatized after the massive assault by the Argentine task groups, the disintegration of their politico-military organization, and by the fear and mistrust that touched all members even if they did not suffer psychic traumas themselves. Likewise, numerous mothers neither personally underwent violence nor witnessed the abduction of their disappeared children—an experience which certainly qualifies as potentially traumatizing—but they still experienced a social trauma because of their collective predicament. A social trauma implies the existence of unique group processes triggered by excessive violence and collective losses. An examination of the differences between psychic and social traumas is necessary to give the term traumatized society a more precise meaning.

A personal brush with violence is generally stressful but not necessarily traumatic. An acute psychic trauma is a particular reaction to excessive violence, to experiences that overwhelm a person's ability to withstand or filter undesirable influences perceived as life-threatening. Psychic trauma makes people feel helpless before a violent event and prone to surrender to the enveloping danger. The psychologists Green and McNally distinguish three aspects to psychic trauma: the violent event, the sufferer's subjective perception, and his or her psychological reaction.[10] Perception and reaction determine whether or not excessive violence entails trauma. Physical violence is the most common cause of trauma, but a mock execution or watching others being hurt can be equally damaging.

Excessive violence can affect individuals but also groups. Major upheavals like wars and genocides have been said to provoke massive traumas because they leave entire communities and groups socially and emotionally defenseless.[11] Massive trauma is more than the sum total of individual suffering because it ruptures social bonds, destroys group identities, undermines people's sense of community, and entails cultural disorientation because taken for granted meanings become obsolete. A massive trauma is thus a wound to the social body and its cultural frame.[12] Sztompka has described a traumatizing sequence for societies which begins with a major social crisis (from genocide to economic collapse), continues with a cultural interpretation and narration of events, and then leads to disruptive collective conducts, opinions, and moods.[13] Massive traumas thus differ from psychic traumas by their manifestation on the social and cultural instead of the psychological level.

The joint analysis of political violence and collective trauma through decades of Argentine political history demonstrates another important difference between psychic and social traumas. An acute psychic trauma often entails passiveness, while a social trauma can lead to retaliatory violence, revenge, rebellion, and revolution as people accumulate injury upon injury. Social traumatization made Argentine political actors ready to act, to defend themselves against future traumatization, to redress past blows, and to preemptively attack potential threats. Such responses perpetuated the mutual reinforcement of violence and trauma.

In Argentina, there arose a tendency to surpass one's opponent's violence. The Argentine military, in particular, emphasized that terror could only be beaten by greater terror, thus raising the degrees of both violence and traumatization. They were intimately familiar with the vulnerabilities of their own citizens, and attacked there where the impact of their acts, and thus the traumatization, would be greatest. The military were successful in pushing the guerrilla organizations and political opposition to a breaking point of overtraumatization that exhausted the will to respond in kind, but they did not foresee the tenacity of parents searching for their disappeared children and the equally strong resolve of grandparents to find their grandchildren. These sentiments proved so strong that they set a broad opposition movement in motion that helped to topple the military regime.

The relation between violence and trauma does not end here because the debilitating consequences of an acute trauma can continue after the violent event ends. This is true both for psychic and social traumas. People can recover from an acute psychic trauma and nevertheless develop posttraumatic stress disorders (PTSD), sometimes even after dozens of years. Others may not have collapsed when they were subjected to violence, but can still suffer from PTSD later on.

The two most distinctive characteristics of a posttraumatic stress disorder are, alternatively, the frequent reliving of the original violent event and its avoidance through emotional withdrawal and dissociation.[14] The incessant recreation in disturbing recollections, nightmares, psychoses, and conducts are a desperate attempt to master the traumatic experience and erect proper defenses to contain the most painful recurring emotions. In turn, the progressive withdrawal into a restricted private world shuts out the most agonizing memories and allows a person to cope with his or her diminished personal and social capacities.[15] Compulsive acting-out prevents people from leaving their painful experiences behind and mourning their losses, while selective forgetting hinders working through past suffering.

Argentine society displayed such reenactment and reexperience in a most literal way during the 1970s. The violent repression of strikes and protest crowds, summary executions as well as the house raids and armed operations against guerrilla units, caused acute social traumas which provoked further crowd, working-class, and guerrilla violence.[16] Acute social traumas were followed by posttraumatic sequels that summoned more violence and caused new acute traumas in a violence-trauma-violence dynamic. Afflicted groups could not, so to say, lick their wounds and recover because new injuries were added at a growing pace, thus intermingling posttraumatic effects of past violence with the acute social traumas of new onslaughts. The political violence in Argentina increased through the decades, leaving a series of social traumas in its wake. Recurrent military repression, violent street protests, guerrilla attacks, deadly liquidations, revenge killings, and torture accumulated over time to increasing heights of intensity. A repertoire of violent practices developed that was reproduced with every new act. This spiraling violence advanced in conjunction with an accumulation of painful and unmourned experiences that constituted enduring social traumas. Each social trauma, which often began as an acute trauma and entailed a posttraumatic reaction, incited more violence. The various parties to the political conflict cultivated a collective sense of victimization, continued to remember their losses in belligerent terms, and never came to terms with the social traumas of the past. The brutal repression of the military dictatorship stopped the political violence of the insurgency at the cost of a society unable to work through its collective trauma when democracy was reinstalled in 1983.

There is a common assumption in the literature about psychic and collective trauma that individuals and societies alike need to repress traumatic events for extended periods before they are able to confront and mourn them. People resort to repression or dissociation to protect themselves from memories too painful and destabilizing to admit to consciousness.[17] Similar ideas have been expressed about genocides, massacres, and especially the Holocaust. "The traumatic event is repressed or denied and registers only belatedly (*nachträglich*) after the passage of a period of latency. This effect of belatedness has of course been a manifest aspect of the Holocaust. . . ."[18] Alexander and Margarete Mitscherlich, Adorno, Santner, Friedlander, LaCapra, and Segev, among others, have shown how the Holocaust was silenced for decades after the end of World War II, as much in Israel as in Europe (including Germany) and the U.S.A.[19] Clearly, there is a pervasive belief, founded principally on an interpretation of the Holocaust and its victims, that there exists a tendency to repress collective and personal traumatic memories.

McNally has severely criticized the notion of repression.[20] Clinical studies have shown that people may temporarily forget but do not repress traumatic memories. Generally, they do not suffer from amnesia, i.e. the inability to remember, but may have occupied their minds with other concerns, forgotten certain aspects of a traumatic event, or simply not encoded them in memory. In a similar vein, my analysis of Argentine political history shows that the decades-long silence that preceded the mourning of the Holocaust is not intrinsic to social trauma or caused by collective repression but dependent on specific political, national, and historical circumstances. The response to social trauma may be a lengthy silence, forgetting, and withdrawal, as in the case of the Holocaust during the 1950s and 1960s, but it can also be a repeated reliving, acting-out, and reexperiencing, as in the case of Argentina.

Part of the process of overcoming a trauma when the violence has ceased is the search for the meaning of past suffering. An individual may partially forget or not recall certain devastating experiences but that does not make the traumatic event go away.[21] Many traumatized people want to know every single detail of the harrowing events. This recurrent recollection is a way to come to grips with and adjust to the unknown and even the unknowable aspects of trauma, as Caruth has argued.[22] Some parts of a traumatic experience are recalled with incredible detail, including sensations of taste and smell, while others are never encoded and thus lost forever. A traumatizing event consists of so many new and overwhelming impressions that these can never be encoded in full.[23] In fact, Caruth argues in a reasoning that echoes that of the Holocaust scholars mentioned above: "The experience of trauma, the fact of latency, would thus seem to consist, not in the forgetting of a reality that can hence never be fully known, but in an inherent latency within the experience itself."[24] But does this latency also exist within a collective trauma experienced by a society composed of heterogeneous social groups with different ways of witnessing, encoding, remembering, and contributing to traumatic events?

Argentines who understood their violent experiences during the 1970s cultural war as a necessary political sacrifice coped much better than persons who felt themselves to have been victims of random persecution. Different social groups attributed other meanings to the same violent events, and transformed their experiences either into social traumas or collective glories. One group's victory became another group's defeat, and the suffering of a third group became opposed to the injuries of a fourth. The previous chapter demonstrated how the selective remembering and selective forgetting of officers, politicians, human rights advocates, and relatives of the disappeared led to ongoing public contests about what had really happened during the dictatorship as well as persistent attempts to bury the past. Thus, the differential recourse to meaning crystallized into irreconcilable historical, political, and moral positions which prevented the reconciliation of a traumatized Argentine society during post-dictatorship times.

The tenacious search for meaning ran aground on the emotional incomprehensibility of trauma. Psychic traumas are incomprehensible because they disassemble an internalized world of social trust. The knowledge that people had turned on one another during Argentina's cultural war goes against the grain of the social trust embedded in every human being. Traumatizing experiences can therefore not be integrated into the world of everyday life in which people are expected to interact with trust and understanding.[25] Argentina's social traumas remained incomprehensible at heart to both perpetrators and survivors after the end of military rule, albeit in different ways. The recurrent recollection of traumatic experiences was not a unitary process because different meanings were given to similar events. Each group emphasized certain experiences, disregarded others, and uncovered new injuries. Such continued exploration led to a polyphonic reconstruction of the past which pushed conflicting memories of violence and trauma to the forefront of each group's political concern. The persistence of adversary political groups in Argentina entailed the production of social memories that could not be integrated on a societal level but only on a group level.

If affected social groups keep returning incessantly to past sufferings in private conversations and public testimonies, enter into a contest about historical renditions, and continue to demand some sort of reckoning, then we may very well assume that these social groups have not yet overcome their social traumas. Scrutinizing the past is in Argentina an attempt to come to terms with those experiences. What other reason would there be to continuously recall extremely painful memories than to try to master them through repetition and reexperience? Such mastery is far from simple and straightforward, precisely because of the incomprehensible, unsolvable, and unknowable aspects of social traumas.

Now, people may not be able to describe the unknowable but they may at least draw the contours of the social traumas into which many experiences were inextricably absorbed. Argentine society began to notice the existence of these indescribable places after 1983 through the CONADEP truth commission, the trial of the former junta commanders, the amnesty legislation, the military rebellions, the presidential pardons, and the legislation about restitution payments. All these political reactions were attempts to come to grips with Argentine society's collective trauma.

Still, Argentina's social traumas could not be overcome with institutional measures such as truth commissions or criminal trials, important as they are in processes of reconciliation. The unknown and the incomprehensible kept intruding on Argentine society because of the polyphonic and polyexperiential construction of its collective trauma. New material evidence, unexpected revelations, and unprecedented confessions prevented a closure as gruesome deeds haunted their perpetrators and disturbed the survivors. Mass graves were opened, kidnapped children asked about their biological parents, and human rights organizations continued to clamor for justice. These returning intrusions from an unmourned past, the emotional responses they summoned forth, and the intense political debates and public protests they provoked, were the unmistakable characteristics of a traumatized society, a society that had not yet come to terms with the political violence that had plagued the Argentine people since the 1950s.

Although the political violence had ceased for nearly a decade when Argentina entered the 1990s, the society remained enwrapped in the unknowable, the inexplicable, and the incomprehensible of its cultural war. This preoccupation was driven underground at times of economic crisis and political instability, but it cropped up time and again in the face of sudden revelations. In the mid-1990s, when the wounds of the past seemed to have closed, the past returned with a vengeance as former perpetrators began to talk. Traumatizing experiences resurfaced and Argentine society realized that a national reconciliation was much further away than imagined.

Confession and Reckoning

Three months after the presidential pardon of December 1990, Lieutenant-General Videla received a letter from Captain Scilingo describing how he had hurled sedated prisoners from a plane. Scilingo expressed his anger at Videla's rejection that thousands of disappearances had taken place. This denial had converted him into a war criminal while he had only carried out orders, explained Scilingo. He added the threat that if Videla would not come forward, then he would disclose his secret. Videla did not care to write a response.[26]

Captain Scilingo was now faced with a dilemma. He could either confess in public and swallow the accusation of being a traitor to the navy or he could maintain the pact of silence and suffer the emotional consequences. Unlike the surviving victims who were weaving their gruesome accounts into Argentina's national memory, the perpetrators denied any involvement. There existed in Argentina a public space of solidarity among victims of repression and a private space of secrecy among perpetrators. This selective remembering functioned as much on the personal as on the social level. The military community continued to deny what had happened, refused to take responsibility for the repression, and thus abandoned some perpetrators to the whims of their posttraumatic stress disorders. This emotional strain became too great for officers like Captain Scilingo. They could no longer protect the armed forces from criminal prosecution at their own emotional expense when that institution turned its back on them.

Traumatized people, whether they are victims or perpetrators, need others to accept the reality of their harrowing experiences to be able to integrate them into consciousness.[27] Denial relegates those experiences to the world of fantasy. Officers like Scilingo were besieged by their own nightmares and by a society keen to make them pay in court. They felt doubly betrayed when their superiors failed to protect them against criminal prosecution.

The 1987 due obedience legislation, and the sweeping pardons in 1989 and 1990 only succeeded in keeping the lid on temporarily. With all the unresolved psychic and social traumas in Argentine society, the confessions of torture, point blank executions, and death flights were bound to erupt because such traumatizing experiences will eventually break through the façade of pretended innocence. Retired Navy Captain Scilingo's public confession on 2 March 1995 was such a catharsis of traumatic affects.[28] In less than two months, retired Sergeant Víctor Ibáñez confirmed Scilingo's confession. Just like Scilingo, Ibáñez had suffered from severe depressions because of his participation in the cultural war, and had been forced to retire from the army.[29]

Army Commander-in-Chief, General Martín Balza, decided that the time was ripe for a public apology. On the evening of 25 April 1995, General Balza declared that Argentina had been involved in a spiral of violence but that the restoration of law and order by military force did not justify the means employed. He took responsibility for the "mistakes" made by the army, and added that no officer would ever again be obliged to carry out immoral orders. General Balza made his historic televised statement to "start a painful dialogue about the past, something which has never taken place; a past hovering like a ghost over the collective conscience, returning hopelessly from the shadows where it occasionally hides, as has happened recently."[30] In other words, the collective trauma of the political violence had proven to be indomitable, and needed unburdening.

General Balza's confession was soon followed by similar admissions from the navy, the air force, and the police.[31] However, instead of deterring further confessions, the flood gates had been opened and several individuals came forward with their morbid recollections. These confessional outcrops disturbed the process of reconciliation which President Menem had tried to set in motion with his presidential pardons as Argentina continued to struggle with the unknowns of an unmourned past. There were more confirmations of the death flights, but also the first public admission that babies delivered by pregnant captives had been sold out of the Campo de Mayo secret detention center.[32] The June 1998 declaration by General Balza that the military junta had a standard procedure about how to separate guerrillas from their children shocked Argentine society even more.[33]

Apparently, the abduction of infants had been planned in the highest ranks. The seventy-two-year-old Lieutenant-General Videla was suddenly held in preventive custody on 9 June 1998. He was later put under house arrest on the charge of being responsible for the abduction of five babies born in secret detention centers.[34] Videla's coconspirator Admiral Massera was also charged and given house arrest on 7 December 1998.[35] The former junta members who had been held hostage by the continued protests of the tenacious mothers of the Plaza de Mayo were now held accountable for kidnapping the grandchildren of the equally tenacious grandmothers of the Plaza de Mayo.

The Grandmothers of the Plaza de Mayo

Captain Scilingo's confession, General Balza's mea culpa and the admission about the kidnapping of babies gave a new impetus to the forensic exhumations and the search by the grandmothers of the Plaza de Mayo for the disappeared grandchildren. The grandmothers arose from the mothers of the Plaza de Mayo. In October 1977, twelve grandmothers decided to organize a separate group under the leadership of María Isabel de Mariani.[36] Some mothers condemned the search for grandchildren which, in their eyes, detracted from the search for the children and seemed to presume that the latter were dead.[37]

For years, the search remained fruitless. The grandmothers visited juvenile courts to discover illegal adoptions, made trips abroad to solicit help, and continued with their weekly march at the Plaza de Mayo, shoulder to shoulder with the mothers. They also made contact with Argentine exiles living in Brazil. These former captives provided much valuable information about the identity of women who had given birth in captivity and how the babies had been taken away alive.[38] The grandmothers' persistence was rewarded in August 1979 when two children were located in Chile. Anatole Boris and Eva Lucía Julien Grisona, respectively six and four years old, had disappeared on 26 September 1976 in San Martín, Argentina, together with their Uruguayan parents. They were recognized in Valparaíso by Uruguayan exiles. With the consent of the paternal grandmother, the children remained with their adoptive parents.[39]

Little by little, the grandmothers began receiving information: a slip of paper with an address thrust in their hands during the Thursday afternoon protest march; an anonymous phone call about the sudden appearance of a baby without the mother having been pregnant; a nurse who talked about forged birth certificates at a maternity ward; a former captive who heard officers talk about the adoptions, and so forth. Upon receiving a tip, the grandmothers would survey the indicated home. They walked the streets, took photos at the playground, and sometimes even offered their services as a domestic.[40]

In March 1980 the first two Argentine children were located. Laura Malena Jotar Britos and her sister Tatiana were respectively three months and four years old when their parents were abducted on 17 October 1977. A police officer found the children one week later abandoned in the town of Billinghurst. The sisters were sent to two different orphanages, but were adopted together in March 1978 by a childless couple. The grandmothers of the Plaza de Mayo succeeded in finding the children after a careful journey through neighborhoods, orphanages, and courts.[41] What many had feared was now proven to be true. The Argentine military kidnapped babies and assassinated their parents, just as the Uruguayan military had done in the case of the Julien Grisona children.

The finding of Laura and Tatiana Jotar Britos raised one important problem: how could the grandparents prove that the children were really their biological grandchildren? In this particular case, the judge decided in terms of circumstantial evidence but the question remained urgent. How to establish the identity of children born in captivity? American genetic expertise became available in March 1984 to establish grandparentage through blood analysis. A National Genetic Data Bank (Banco Nacional de Datos Genéticos) was established in May 1987 preserving blood samples from grandparents and other close relatives searching for missing children.[42]

By August 1987, forty-two children had been located. Through the years, increasingly more people came forward with tips. In mid-1997, fifty-eight children had been found: eight were discovered to have been murdered during the cultural war, thirty-one were reunited with their biological families, thirteen remained with their adoptive parents, and six cases were pending in court. By December 2003, seventy-six children had been located.[43] Notwithstanding the successful restitution of many grandchildren to their biological relatives, the reestablishment of family ties was often complicated, in particular when the children were adolescents and adults, as in the case of Mariana Zaffaroni.

Mariana Zaffaroni was born in Argentina on 22 March 1975. She was the daughter of the political activists Jorge Zaffaroni and María Emilia Islas de Zaffaroni who had fled their native Uruguay in May 1973. The Zaffaronis were abducted on 27 September 1976. They had fallen victim to the secret 1975 Condor Agreement between Argentina, Uruguay, and Chile regulating the military cooperation against each other's political opponents. Neighbors pleaded with the task group to leave the eighteen-month-old Mariana to their care, but the entire family was taken. Jorge and María Emilia Zaffaroni were assassinated in the Orletti Motors secret detention center, while Mariana was taken home by the Argentine secret service agent Miguel Angel Furci. The little girl was registered with a forged birth certificate under the name Daniela Romina Furci.

Mariana was first located in January 1983 by her Uruguayan grandmothers through an anonymous tip. After more than a year, the court ordered a blood test but the Furcis abandoned Argentina in June 1984. An international search warrant was issued, and a campaign was launched to find Mariana. Her radiant eyes were soon peering from thousands of posters pasted on the walls of Buenos Aires and from the pages of newspapers in Argentina and abroad.

Seven years passed before the aging grandmothers finally located the Furci family in Buenos Aires in June 1992. Mariana was now seventeen years old. The long-awaited reunion could not have been more tragic. The maternal grandmother, María Ester Gatti, was overcome with confusion: "The happiness of seeing my granddaughter again, after so many years without her, merged into a feeling of sadness that she wasn't the daughter that I had spent so long looking for, too."[44] Mariana refused to have anything to do with her grandmothers. She insisted on calling herself Daniela Furci and told the judge that she wanted to remain with her adoptive parents. That same year, Mariana was given a writing assignment in high school with the title: "A Young Girl Applies for a Job." Mariana wrote a revealing essay.

The man in a gray uniform asked me: "Name, surname?" What was I to reply? That I had always been known as Daniela Furci, but now people said I was called Mariana Zaffaroni Islas? That the name given to me by my parents, now in jail for giving me it, is not legally my name? I would rather be an outlaw than a traitor, so I replied: "Daniela Romina Furci." "Nationality?" "I'm Argentinean, but I have two different backgrounds. One from my subversive Uruguayan parents, idealistic fighters in the dirty war fought in my country. The other from my Argentinean parents. My father fought on the other side. One day, I came to him. He had the choice between shooting me in the head and raising me as the child he couldn't have. His wish to be the best father in the world made him choose the second option. He is paying for it now as if he had killed me."[45]

Miguel Furci and his wife Adriana were given prison sentences of seven and three years, respectively. Mariana stayed with a relative of her adoptive father and returned to the Furci home when the adoptive mother was released after three months. Miguel Furci got out on parole after three years. Paradoxically, Mariana Zaffaroni claimed the restitution payment for being the child of disappeared parents.[46] Mariana Zaffaroni, or Daniela Furci as she prefers to be called, and her grandmothers María Ester Gatti and Marta Zaffaroni became victims of the same repressive regime and still ended up on opposite sides of the political divide, unable to renew the affective ties that had been so violently destroyed during her infancy.

The search for a common past made a group of adult children of disappeared parents form an organization in 1995, called Children for Identity and Justice, against Oblivion and Silence or HIJOS (Hijos por la Identidad y la Justicia, contra el Olvido y el Silencio). Many have no experiential recollection of the military repression, yet they are its living victims. They find support with one another by working through their social trauma through reading, talking, and protesting. HIJOS wants "to rewrite the story of our parents who were victims of these perpetrators and to maintain the spirit of struggle of our parents and that of other victims against the dictatorship."[47]

The past returns most visibly in their protest marches and public shaming of perpetrators. They trace the address of a retired officer or a former torturer, and then take up position in the street, posting signs: "Here lives a murderer." The house of the pilloried perpetrator is spray-painted with slogans, and his hidden past is divulged loudly by megaphone. Usually, television cameras are present to tape these so-called *escraches*, which sometimes turn into happenings involving thousands of people. The protests are intended to shame the perpetrators publicly, stigmatize them in their neighborhood, and ostracize them from Argentine society. Former junta members Videla and Massera have been picketed, and so have politicians and judges. Thus, these young people are adding a whole new dimension to the social traumas existing in Argentine society and the polyphony of memories of the years of repression.

According to the forensic anthropologist Darío Olmo, the children of the disappeared are less interested in recovering the remains of their assassinated parents but more in their lives. "They want to know more about their parents, they lost them so long ago and they were too small to fill that space with memories. So, they try to fill it, among other things, with information."[48] The surviving children try to establish contact with their parents' comrades, and want to hear how they died. It is their way of mastering their social trauma. They help to transmit an oral history of the violent 1970s, the ideals and deceptions, the abductions, torture, and disappearances, even though their historical reconstruction of the past will inevitably run into the incomprehensible and unknowable, qualities so characteristic of social traumas.

Unhealed Wounds and Contested Memories

The continued struggle about the remembrance of Argentina's cultural war and the best ways to commemorate the dead and the disappeared indicate that Argentine society has not yet come to terms with its past. According to Sztompka: "If we observe heated debates and public disputes in the media, at public meetings, or in political bodies; if values and judgments are strongly contested; if certain themes become obsessive for artistic expression through the movies, theatre, literature, and poetry; if social movements mobilize for the expression of cultural discontents, then we are certainly witnessing unhealed and potentially evolving trauma."[49] There are many signs that Argentina fits this description: the piecemeal confessions by military officers and the admission of guilt by military commanders in 1995, the 1998 house arrest of former junta members for their complicity in the kidnapping of infants, the institution of truth trials (*juicios de la verdad*) in 1999 calling pardoned officers to the witness stand to testify about the repression, and the derogation of the amnesty laws by the Argentine Congress in 2003. A final ruling by the Supreme Court may then make 1,180 pardoned Argentines once again vulnerable to prosecution.[50]

At the same time, there have been efforts to instill Argentine society with new renditions of the past. Buenos Aires proclaimed the 24th of March an annual Day of Memory to commemorate the 1976 military coup.[51] A large

Memory Park (Parque de la Memoria) was inaugurated in August 2001 along the Rio de la Plata river bank in Buenos Aires with a prominent "Monument to the Victims of State Terror" and a sinuous fissure traversing the park to symbolize the open wound left in Argentine society by the disappearances.[52] In April 2002, the secret detention center known as the Athletic Club (Club Atlético) was unearthed in Buenos Aires city near a highway overpass. Plans were made to turn the place into a site of memory.[53]

Many persons involved in social memory construction reiterate that they do not want Argentines to forget the horrors of the cultural war. Forgetting the past would be the second and final victory of the perpetrators, after having already succeeded in destroying the remains of many disappeared. The greater tragedy is that perpetrators always score a victory because the unknowable is a foundational element of any social trauma, as it is also in Argentina. In fact, the military junta intentionally inflicted a collective trauma on Argentine society to paralyze the forces of political opposition. Violence, trauma, and forgetting emerged simultaneously. Hence, social memory construction becomes an even more transcendent means to prevent forgetting, namely by filling the unknowable voids with narratives, debates, and commemorations.

These forms of social memory can bring some light to the incomprehensible, yet massive outbreaks of violence fail full human comprehension because meaning destruction and excess are at their center. Assaulted people and societies become disoriented, cannot comprehend, and fail to cope with the overwhelming atrocities. The fundamental obstruction to complete recall and comprehensive understanding make remembrance an interminable process. Remembrance is a desperate attempt to master and translate intolerable as well as unknowable traumatic experiences into narrative by articulating their meaning through repetition and reinterpretation.

The reliving of the past through ongoing trials, exhumations, and long overdue confessions and apologies are all attempts to master the multiple social traumas that besiege Argentine society. Clearly, people and societies cannot start afresh as if the past did not matter. There are never new beginnings, only new departures that drag along the burdens of the past. The aftermath of decades of violence has been an Argentine society traumatized by thousands of assassinated disappeared persons, the manifold number of relatives, friends, colleagues, and comrades who feel their absence, the survivors who bear the physical and mental scars of abuse, and the perpetrators who fell into the trap of omnipotence and came to feel the emotional consequences of their own violence.

Argentina's polyphonic social memory and the employment of different means, expressions, and narratives with which to remember the past complicate the attainment of a historical consensus and national reconciliation about its cultural war. The recurrent recollection of partial traumatic experiences will not unify discourse but enhance the antagonism within Argentine society. The persistence of hostile groups entails the production of social memories that cannot be integrated on the societal level but, instead, tend to further polarize into opposite positions. Just as psychologists have argued that personal memory is not one single faculty of the human mind but a dynamic constellation of different neural structures with distinct memory processes, so the collective memory of Argentine society consists of different social memories reproduced in different tempos, times, and ways in interaction with their context.[54] Different groups contribute different memories to Argentine society whose confrontation continuously produces new memory configurations.

Even memorials, monuments, and commemorations, which have played a significant role in mourning the Holocaust, have in Argentina increased rather than lessened its divisiveness. Contrary to Nora's suggestion that such embodied memories displace traumatic memories and thus relieve people from reliving a painful past, neither has history replaced memory in Argentina, nor has representation absorbed experience.[55] Young, Connerton, and LaCapra have pointed to the importance of commemorations, testimonies, historical studies, and even bodily practices for national reconciliation.[56] Memorial days create a shared history, allow people to exchange narratives about past sorrows, and enhance feelings of national identity. Yet, such ritualization of the past, and the mourning that ensues, are condemned by several sectors of Argentine society, notably segments of the human rights organizations and the armed forces, each of which are fraught with internal divisions. Argentine monuments, memorials, and commemorations are the expressions of political memory agendas and become therefore extensions, repetitions, and manifestations of social traumas rather than their substitutes.

Paradoxically, the polyphonic national memory complicates national reconciliation but also imposes a certain order on an incomprehensible past. Even conflictive remembrances, whether through trials, truth commissions, or testimonies, are all struggles with the incomprehensible and the unknowable aiming to reposition Argentine society in the flow of history. Such conflictive memories provide a certain antagonistic clarity, and reduce the enigma to historical narratives reorienting people in their collective and personal history. Eventually, narration will take the place of experience, even if that narration will reproduce the current antagonism founded on contrary experiences. Past episodes of violence will become increasingly appropriated by social memories, conflictive though they may be. This contested social memory returns to people a sense of control over the past and over their destiny as they now become engaged in a memory contest with an identifiable opponent with a clear contrary ideological and political discourse. Thus, the past will be ever more distant. The Argentine nation will eventually assume its violent history as a shared national tragedy, and allow the Argentine people to mourn their losses. The violence and trauma which kindled one another for half a century will retreat toward acceptance and reconciliation, and then be extinguished some long-awaited and distant day.

Appendix 1: Interview List

Poema Carbella de Akcelman
Lieutenant-Colonel Santiago Alonso
María Délia Antokoletz
Bishop José María Arancibia
Alcira Argumedo
Colonel Horacio Pantaleón Ballester
Dolores Barceló
Eduardo Barcesat
Major Ernesto Barreiro
Rodolfo J. Bernat
Presbyter Rafael Braun
Alfredo Bravo
Victor Bruschi
Bishop Rodolfo Bufano
Bishop Alcides Jorge Casaretto
General Juan Cazes
Pedro Cazes Camarero
General Carlos Horacio Cerdá
Mauricio Cohen Salama
Nora de Cortiñas
Graciela Beatriz Daleo
Colonel Guillermo Daract
Rear-Admiral Eduardo Davion
General Mariano De Nevares
Colonel Rafael B. De Piano
General Ramón Genaro Díaz Bessone
General Carlos Horacio Dominguez
Father Ruben Dri
Brigadier Carlos Ramón Echegoyen
Brigadier Carlos Echeverria Martínez
Renée Epelbaum
Father Luis Farinello
Graciela Fernández Meijide
Lorenza F. de Ferrari
Carlos A. Floria
General Ricardo Flouret
Lieutenant Rosendo Fraga
Rear-Admiral Juan Carlos Frías
Horacio González
General Virgilio Górriz

Military Chaplain Emilio T. Grasselli
Catalina S. de Guagnini
Juan Carlos Dante Gullo
María Elisa Hachmann de Lande
Jorge Enrique Hardoy
Matilde Herrera
Ernesto Luis Jauretche
Eduardo Y. Jozami
Archbishop Pio Laghi
Bishop Justo Oscar Laguna
Lieutenant-General Alejandro A. Lanusse
General Manuel A. Laprida
Simón Alberto Lázara
Jaime Malamud
Leonor Llames Massini de Barceló
Luis Mattini
Rear-Admiral Horacio Mayorga
Eduardo Menajovski
Rabbi Marshall T. Meyer
Emilio F. Mignone
José Enrique Miguens
José Miguez Bonino
Captain Federico Mittelbach
Mario Montoto
Luis Gabriel Moreno Ocampo
Julio Morresi
Bishop Jorge Novak
Bishop Emilio Ogñenovich
Lilia de Orfanó
Hebe Pastor de Bonafini
Roberto Perdía
Adolfo María Pérez Esquivel
Bishop Jerónimo Podestá
Rear-Admiral Nestor O. Pozzi Jáuregui
Father Patrick Rice
Lieutenant-Colonel Aldo Rico
Fernando Rivas
Admiral Isaac Francisco Rojas
María del Rosario de Cerruti
Juan José Salinas

General Tomás A. Sánchez de
  Bustamante
Elsa Sánchez de Oesterheld
Rear-Admiral Carlos A. Sánchez Sañudo
Brigadier Norberto Sciutto
Clyde Snow
Captain Luis Eduardo Tibiletti

Morris Tidball Binz
Fernando Vaca Narvaja
General Agusto José Vidal
General Osiris G. Villegas
Marcos Weinstein
Carlos Zamorano

Appendix 2: Acronyms

AAA (Alianza Anticomunista Argentina) Argentine Anti-Communist Alliance
ALN (Alianza Libertadora Nacionalista) Nationalist Liberating Alliance
APDH (Asamblea Permanente por los Derechos Humanos) Permanent Assembly for Human Rights
APRI (Agrupación Peronista de la Resistencia Insurreccional) Peronist Group of Insurrectional Resistence
ARP (Acción Revolucionaria Peronista) Peronist Revolutionary Action
CADHU (Comisión Argentina de Derechos Humanos) Argentine Human Rights Commission
CELS (Centro de Estudios Legales y Sociales) Center for Legal and Social Studies
CGE (Confederación General Económica) General Economic Confederation
CGT (Confederación General de Trabajo) General Labor Confederation
CGTA (Confederación General de Trabajo de los Argentinos) General Labor Confederation of the Argentines
CNP (Comando Nacional Peronista) Peronist National Command
CNT (Convención Nacional de Trabajadores) National Workers Confederation
COI (Central de Operaciones e Inteligencia) Intelligence and Operations Center
CONASE (Consejo Nacional de Seguridad) National Security Council
CONINTES Plan (Plan de Conmoción Interior del Estado) Plan of Internal Upheaval of the State
CORP (Central de Operaciones de la Resistencia Peronista) Peronist Resistance Operations Center
COSOFAM (Comisión de Solidaridad con Familiares de Presos y Desaparecidos) Solidarity Commission with Relatives of Prisoners and Disappeared
EAAF (Equipo Argentino de Antropología Forense), Argentine Forensic Anthropology Team
EGP (Ejército Guerrillero del Pueblo) People's Guerrilla Army
ELN (Ejército de Liberación Nacional) National Liberation Army
ENR (Ejército Nacional Revolucionario) National Revolutionary Army
ERP (Ejército Revolucionario del Pueblo) People's Revolutionary Army
ESMA (Escuela de Mecánica de la Armada) Navy Mechanics School
FAL (Fuerzas Armadas de Liberación) Liberation Armed Forces
FAMUS (Familiares y Amigos de los Muertos por la Subversión) Relatives and Friends of the Victims of Subversion
FAP (Fuerzas Armadas Peronistas) Peronist Armed Forces
FAR (Fuerzas Armadas Revolucionarias) Revolutionary Armed Forces
FARN (Fuerzas Armadas de la Revolución Nacional) Armed Forces of the National Revolution
FAS (Frente Antiimperialista y por el Socialismo) Anti-Imperialist and Pro-Socialist Front

FEDEFAM (Federación de Familiares de Detenidos Desaparecidos) Federation of Relatives of Disappeared Detainees
FORES (Foro de Estudios Sobre la Administración de Justicia) Forum for Research About the Administration of Justice
FREJULI (Frente Justicialista de Liberación) Justicialist Liberation Front
FRIP (Frente Revolucionario Indoamericano Popular) Indo-American Popular Revolutionary Front
FT (Fuerza de Tareas) Task Force
GAN (Gran Acuerdo Nacional) Great National Accord
GOU (Grupo de Oficiales Unidos) United Officers Group
GT (Grupo de Tareas) Task Group
HIJOS (Hijos por la Identidad y la Justicia, contra el Olvido y el Silencio) Children for Identity and Justice, Against Oblivion and Silence
JCR (Junta Coordinación Revolucionaria) Revolutionary Coordinating Council
JP (Juventud Peronista) Peronist Youth
JTP (Juventud Trabajadora Peronista) Peronist Working Youth
LADH (Liga Argentina por los Derechos del Hombre) Argentine League for the Rights of Man
MADES (Movimiento Argentino para la Defensa de la Soberania) Argentine Movement for the Defense of Sovereignty
MEDH (Movimiento Ecuménico por los Derechos Humanos) Ecumenical Movement for Human Rights
MJP (Movimiento de la Juventud Peronista) Peronist Youth Movement
MNRT (Movimiento Nacionalista Revolucionario Tacuara) Tacuara Revolutionary Nationalist Movement
MOPI (Movimiento Ortodoxo Peronista Independiente) Independent Orthodox Peronist Movement
MRP (Movimiento Revolucionario Peronista) Revolutionary Peronist Movement
MSB (Movimiento Sindical de Base) Grass Roots Union Movement
MTP (Movimiento Todos por la Patria) Everyone for the Fatherland Movement
OAS Organization of American States
OLA (Organización para la Liberación de Argentina) Argentine Liberation Organization
PCR (Partido Comunista Revolucionario) Revolutionary Communist Party
PLACINTARA (Plan de Capacidades Internas de la Armada) Navy Internal Capacity Plan
PRT (Partido Revolucionario de los Trabajadores) Workers Revolutionary Party
PSRN (Partido Socialista de la Revolución Nacional) Socialist Party of the National Revolution
SERPAJ (Servicio Paz e Justicia) Peace and Justice Service
SITRAC (Sindicato de Trabajadores de Concord) Concord Workers Union
SITRAM (Sindicato de Trabajadores de Materfer) Materfer Workers Union
SMATA (Sindicatos de Mecánicos y Afines del Transporte Automotor) Auto Workers and Mechanics Union
UCR (Unión Cívica Radical) Radical Civic Union
UES (Unión de Estudiantes Secundarios) Union of High School Students
UNBA (Universidad Nacional de Buenos Aires) National University of Buenos Aires
UOM (Unión Obrera Metalúrgica) Metal Workers Union
UTA (Unión Tranviarios Automotor) Transport Workers Union

Notes

Preface

1. Bonasso 1984:361.
2. Here I will not elaborate further on my research methodology but refer to already published work (Robben 1995, 1996).

Chapter 1. Changing the Course of History: Dignity, Emancipation, and Entrenchment

1. The forensic anthropologists worked for more than two years to remove all skeletons. Most of the dead came from the Banfield Pit secret detention center (Pozo de Banfield) operated by the Buenos Aires Provincial Police but under the direct command of the First Army Corps. Cemetery records reveal that the unidentified bodies were dumped periodically in the mass grave between April 1976 and September 1978 (Cohen Salama 1992:264–271; CONADEP [1984] 1986:151).
2. I have been struggling with the proper terms to describe the many violent deaths in this study. One solution would be to use the word killing for all forms of death. However, the word killing does not do justice to the horrendous circumstances under which many Argentines died and seems to suggest some degree of equity between killers and killed. I reserve therefore the word killing for combat situations, unclear causes of death, or as a synonym when a more defined term is apparent from the text. I use the word elimination for the violent death of someone considered representative of a particular political group, but who is not personally involved in any violent act. The term execution refers to the death of a person convicted of some wrongdoing. The penalty may have been imposed by a court of law or a military or guerrilla tribunal. The term assassination applies to a political killing. Officers were assassinated by guerrillas and most disappeared were assassinated by military and police forces. I have avoided the term murder. A murder is a nonpolitical death, such as in a robbery.
3. López Aufranc 1975:644.
4. Cited in Luna 1973:283–284.
5. Luna 1973:268. The unionist Cipriano Reyes has claimed that his incessant grass roots work among workers in Greater Buenos Aires was decisive for the 17 October mobilization (Reyes 1984:212–222).
6. Luna 1973:274–278.
7. Luna 1973:287.
8. Luna 1973:268.
9. Germani 1973.
10. Murmis and Portantiero [1971] 1987:95–100, 121–126.

11. Torre 1976, 1990:106–147; James 1988b.
12. The term mobilization has several meanings in Argentina, depending on the political context. In general, it refers to every form of political action by a part of the population, whether in the voting booth, on the work floor, in a neighborhood association, a political party, a resistance movement, or a street demonstration. The term mass mobilization is often regarded as synonymous with a working-class mobilization.

The term masses is also common in Argentina and indicates a multi-class majority of the Argentine population. A mass is a heterogeneous group of people sharing at least one main identity marker. The Peronists are thus a mass whose attachment to Perón overrides other social distinctions. A crowd is a physical expression of a mass. Due to the emphasis on crowds in Argentine political culture, the term mass mobilization most often refers to the assembly of people for a street demonstration. Throughout this book, I will use the term mass to denote a category of people (Peronists, Catholics, Marxists, workers, Argentines) who express their membership in public as a crowd. The term crowd refers to a physical gathering of people at a particular place.
13. James 1988a:31–33; 1988b; Torre 1990:124–125, 136; see also Matsushita 1987:292–295.
14. Luna 1973:279, 286.
15. James 1988a:33; see also Torre 1992:412.
16. James 1988b:452–453; Luna 1973:298; Page 1983:133.
17. Canetti 1966:329.
18. Neiburg 1992:75.
19. *La Prensa* 27 April, 5 and 9 May 1945.
20. *La Prensa* 20 September 1945.
21. *La Prensa* 20 September 1945.
22. Luna 1973:320.
23. Canetti 1966:29.
24. James 1988a:34–35.
25. These different interpretations played themselves out during the years immediately following 1945 as each party claimed responsibility for the crowd mobilization in its commemorative acts. Mariano Plotkin reveals how Perón appropriated and ritualized these anniversaries to nurture his charismatic bond with his following and erase the protagonism of his political competitors (Plotkin 1995:193–202, 217).
26. See the portrayal by vice-presidential candidate Enrique Mosca cited in Taylor (1979:117), the short story about "the feast of the monster" by the renowned writers Borges and Bioy Casares (1977:87–103), and the opinion of the Argentine communist party cited in Page (1983:135).
27. See McClelland 1989.
28. Ramos Mejía [1899] 1956:218.
29. See Munck 1987; Spalding 1977.
30. Sabato 1992:160. For the importance of violent crowds in other Latin American countries, see Arrom and Ortoll 1996.
31. Munck 1987:51.
32. Rock 1975:166; Babini 1967:14; see also Díaz Araujo 1988.
33. Page 1983:130. The loyalty of the police to Perón, the sympathy of a number of officers for Perón's nationalist-corporatist views, as well as the threat of uncontrollable worker protest, persuaded the military government to seek a compromise and decide against using violence to repress the crowd (Godio 1990:90; Torre 1976:37–38). Potash 1969:200, 281–282 suggests that guilt feelings about the unnec-

essary bloodshed during an attack led by Avalos on the Navy Mechanics School during a 1943 coup d'état made him decide to avoid a loss of lives on 17 October 1945.

34. Cited in Waisman 1987:170.

35. Page 1983:37.

36. Page 1983:45–49; Potash 1969:182–200; Rock 1987:246–249.

37. Page 1983:61–63; Potash 1969:209–248.

38. Crassweller 1987:86–89; Hodges 1991:51–62; Page 1983:35–37, 88–91. The alleged ideological affinities between Peronism and fascism have always been received with indignation by Peronist intellectuals (see Miguens 1988:42–46).

39. About Mussolini's acquaintance with Le Bon, see Moscovici 1985:63. About Perón's first-hand experience of Italian fascist rallies, see Crassweller 1987:87 and Page 1983:36.

40. Cooke 1973 1:21.

41. Perón [1957] 1985c:325.

42. There are many remarkable resemblances between Le Bon's book *The Crowd* and Perón's lecture course *Political Leadership*. For the influence of Ramos Mejía and Taine on Argentine nationalists, see Rock 1993:16.

43. Perón [1952] 1985a:37.

44. Perón [1952] 1985a:210.

45. The American journalist Ray Josephs noted Perón's fascination with crowds in 1944: "Long interested in mass psychology and in military strategy . . . Perón thinks Army techniques can be applied to the organization of the masses and that strategy is good preparation for Government administration" (Josephs 1945:159).

46. There are three main explanations for the rise of Peronism. Daniel James argues that Perón articulated in public the private feelings of exploitation and social exclusion experienced by the working class (James 1988a:31–33; 1988b). Gino Germani (1973) has argued that the political recruitment of impoverished rural migrants stood at the origin of Perón's political rise. Peter Smith (1972), and Murmis and Portantiero (1987) have stated that not recent migrants but traditional urban workers organized in labor unions were the decisive force (Torre 1990). Mora y Araujo and Llorente (1980) have nuanced the debate by demonstrating that the migrants came from the most developed provinces closest to Buenos Aires, and that they had had ample time to adapt to the urban environment. Madsen and Snow (1991) have emphasized the charismatic bonding between Perón and the rural migrants because of their despair and miserable living conditions in the urban slums.

47. Perón [1952] 1985a:37.

48. Cited in Luna 1973:295.

49. Perón [1952] 1985a:42.

50. Perón [1952] 1985a:209.

51. Luna 1973:293.

52. Luna 1973:295.

53. Sigal and Verón 1988:206–228.

54. *El Descamisado* 1974 39:2.

55. Luna, Navarro, Taylor, and Page regard this alleged protagonism as unfounded. Evita took refuge when Perón was arrested on 12 October, and only reunited with him on 18 October (Luna 1973:340–341; Navarro 1995:154–166; Taylor 1979:38, 73; Page 1983:134–135). The relation between Evita and the Peronist crowds will not be explored here, but the fabricated involvement of Evita in 17 October complied well with the public belief that there was a general similarity between women and crowds. Le Bon (1960 [1895]:35–36) and Ramos Mejía (1956 [1899]:12) had written that crowds were like women who were easily seduced, did

not reason much, were impulsive, and felt with a passion. For an historical analysis of the association of women and crowds, see Barrows 1981.

56. Caimari 1995:180–183.
57. Taylor 1979:88; Zuretti 1972:422.
58. Taylor 1979:108.
59. In October 1934, the Catholic Church organized the International Eucharistic Congress gathering nearly one million people. The people had been mobilized by parish priests (interview with former Bishop Jerónimo Podestá on 28 May 1990; see also Burdick 1995:33; Zuretti 1972:411).
60. Caimari 1995:237.
61. Cited in Page 1983:271.
62. Caimari 1995:283; Page 1983:272.
63. Cited in Frigerio 1984:28.
64. Perón [1952] 1985a:59–60.
65. Caimari 1995:282; Page 1983:290, 297–299; Rock 1987:314–315.
66. Rock 1987:315.
67. Perón 1973a:303–305, 309.
68. Page 1983:300; Potash 1980:173.
69. Burdick 1995:66–68.
70. Rock 1987:317; Torre and Riz 1993:260.
71. Cited in Page 1983:303.
72. Page 1983:303; Rock 1987:315.
73. República Argentina [1958] 1987:235.
74. Comisión de Afirmación 1985:46.
75. Frigerio 1984:56; Page 1983:307–309; Perón [1956] 1985b:66–68; Potash 1980:181–188.
76. Hugo Di Pietro cited in Frigerio 1984:56.
77. See U.S. Embassy report cited in Page 1983:309.
78. Frigerio 1984:56–57; Page 1983:310.
79. Cited in Page 1983:309.
80. Braun 1985:161; Lincoln 1989:117–127.
81. Editorial cited in Frigerio 1984:59.
82. Gillespie 1989:46; Goldar 1991:12; Rouquié 1987:114; Taylor 1979:56–57.
83. Page 1983:315.
84. Cited in Torre and Riz 1993:262.
85. Page 1983:325, 332; Potash 1980:200–202; Torre and Riz 1993:262–263; Rouquié 1987:116–120.
86. Potash 1980:197; Rouquié 1987:118–120; Torre and Riz 1993:262.
87. Perón [1956] 1985b:77; see also Crassweller 1987:288–289 and Page 1983:324.
88. James 1988a:50.
89. I do not aspire to provide a complete history of Argentine crowd demonstrations, but I shall concentrate on crowds that carry a manifest political meaning and are remembered by many Argentines as crucial turning points in Argentina's political history.
90. Canetti finds the essence of crowds in a corporal-emotional social cohesion which dispels people's natural fear of being touched (Canetti 1966:15).
91. Canetti 1966:29.
92. Canetti 1966:305.

Chapter 2. The Time of the Furnaces: Proscription, Compromise, and Insurrection

1. *La Nación* 24 September 1955.
2. *La Nación* 24 September 1955.

3. I will translate *Movimiento Peronista* throughout the book with Peronist Organization to avoid a confusion between the *movimiento Peronista* as a socio-political movement and the *Movimiento Peronista* as a formal political organization composed of a political, labor, women's, and youth branch (Gillespie 1982a:19).

4. Interview with Ernesto Jauretche on 6 April 1991.

5. Cooke 1973 1:34.

6. Page 1983:344–345; San Martino de Dromi 1988 1:79–80.

7. Anzorena 1989:25–35; Cichero 1992:236–251.

8. See Perón [1956] 1973b:380.

9. Perón [1956] 1973c:389; see also Cooke 1973 1:15; Perón [1956] 1973c:389–393.

10. Cooke 1973 1:143.

11. James 1988a:96.

12. Authoritarian Argentine governments would regularly assume full control over unruly institutions (*intervenir*), like labor unions and universities, by removing their presidents from office and replacing them with hand-picked inspectors-general (*interventor*) who might be civilian or military.

13. Juan Vigo cited in Munck 1987:148.

14. The total number of working days lost to strikes in the city of Buenos Aires from 1950 to 1954 averaged only 50 thousand per year, while the period 1956 to 1959 averaged 6.2 million per year (Munck 1987:138, 163).

15. San Martino de Dromi 1988 1:209.

16. *La Nación* 16 and 18 January 1959.

17. CNP report cited in Baschetti 1988:75.

18. *La Nación* 21 January 1959.

19. CNP report cited in Baschetti 1988:71.

20. CNP report cited in Baschetti 1988:77.

21. See Graham-Yooll 1989; Munck 1987:153.

22. San Martino de Dromi 1988 1:3, 144–148.

23. Munck 1987:163.

24. James 1988a:130.

25. Munck 1987:156.

26. Walsh [1969] 1986:144.

27. James 1988a:206.

28. James 1988a:142.

29. Brennan 1994:63–65. The Cordoban UOM union members were at first identified as *auténticos* (authentics) and later as *ortodoxos* (orthodoxes) because of their hard-line (*línea dura*) approach as opposed to *legalistas* (legalists) with their soft-line (*línea blanda*) style of integrationism and institutional pragmatism (Brennan 1994:66). For the sake of clarity, I have chosen to use the terms intransigents for hard-line Peronists—whether as a political majority in Córdoba or a minority in Buenos Aires—and the term integrationists for the soft-line Peronists.

30. Brennan 1994:56–63, 94–95; James 1988a:224–226.

31. Brennan 1994:69–73, 113–119.

32. Andrés Framini was running for the Unión Popular in Buenos Aires province, and had provocatively proposed the exiled Perón as his vice-governor. Perón's candidacy was of course unacceptable to the military, and his place was taken by Anglada (San Martino de Dromi 1988 1:116–118, 127–129).

33. The fall of Frondizi and the annulment of the elections prompted 62 Peronist unions, known as the "62 Organizations," to proclaim a radical program of nationalizations and expropriations at its national congress in the town of Huerta Grande (Baschetti 1988:118). This program illustrates clearly that the line between

intransigents and integrationists was not easily drawn. Union leaders were pragmatists who alternated their hit and negotiation tactics according to the political circumstances.

34. Rock 1987:344.
35. See Illia cited in San Martino de Dromi 1988 1:293.
36. See the proclamation by the Justicialist Party cited in Baschetti 1988:147.
37. James 1988a:195–197.
38. Page 1983:387–389.
39. James 1988a:177–179.
40. General Objectives of the Revolution cited in San Martino de Dromi 1988 1:336.
41. The economic plan of the Minister of Economy, Krieger Vasena, was successful. The Argentine peso was devalued by 40 percent, foreign capital was attracted, inflation was brought under control, unemployment remained low, wages fell only slightly, and the economy expanded (Rock 1987:346–348; W. Smith 1991:74–77).
42. San Martino de Dromi 1988 1:299–303.
43. San Martino de Dromi 1988 1:430–431.
44. W. Smith 1991:112–114; Munck 1987:162.
45. Brennan 1994:108–109; James 1988a:219; Perina 1983:179–181; W. Smith 1991:116–118.
46. Paseo Colón and Azopardo are two streets in Buenos Aires where the two rival union centrals had their offices.
47. The title referred to a quote from José Martí used by Che Guevara in his message to the January 1966 Tricontinental Conference in Havana: "Now is the time of the furnaces, and only light should be seen" (Guevara [1960] 1985:199).
48. Cited in Baschetti 1988:277–284.
49. Cited in Anzorena 1989:107.
50. See Perón cited in Baschetti 1988:285.
51. See Perón cited in Baschetti 1988:295.
52. W. Smith 1991:123–125.
53. James 1988a:253.
54. Gillespie 1982a:19.
55. Interview with Ernesto Jauretche on 6 April 1991.
56. Snow and Manzetti 1993:176.
57. Terán 1991:106–115.
58. Interview with Fernando Vaja Narvaja on 17 May 1990.
59. Cited in Baschetti 1988:222–223.
60. Statement by prisoners cited in Baschetti 1988:216; John William Cooke cited in Baschetti 1988:189–195.
61. Bra 1985:16.
62. The federal police were given a sudden chance to take revenge for the humiliation suffered one month earlier during their official homage to General Roca. That day the troops had been showered with coins from the roof of the Faculty of Exact Sciences located near Roca's statue (Botana, Braun, and Floria 1973:366; Roth 1985:20).
63. Bra 1985:10.
64. Cited in Moyano 1995:19.
65. Bra 1985:14.
66. See Delich 1974:53–56.
67. Cited in Lanusse 1977:128–129.
68. Carlos Villagra cited in Anzorena 1989:108.
69. Moyano 1995:116–118.

70. The suffix *azo* is used in the Spanish language as an augmentative, and in particular to constitute terms that express a blow or violent action, such as in *porrazo* (clubbing) and *arañazo* (scratch). See Moliner 1984:321 and Real Academia Española 1992:243.

71. Balvé and Balvé 1989:43. There exists a difference of opinion in the literature about the size of the price increase. Laclau (1970:15) mentions an increase of 537 percent from 27 to 172.50 pesos, while Lanusse (1977:19) talks about "a few pesos."

72. The universities in the northeastern provinces attracted many lower middle class students from the interior. Unlike most students in Buenos Aires who continued to live at home, the students from the interior were obliged to live in the university towns, and relied on the low-priced meals to make ends meet. Their vehement protest to the higher meal tickets should be understood as a reaction to the threat posed to their expectation of social improvement.

73. Balvé and Balvé 1989:34–40.

74. Gillespie 1982a:65.

75. Cited in Balvé and Balvé 1989:40.

76. Balvé and Balvé 1989:33–35.

77. Balvé and Balvé 1989:60.

78. Balvé and Balvé 1989:60–62, 83.

79. Balvé and Balvé 1989:97–111.

80. In defiance of martial law, the labor unions proceeded with their general strike on May 23. There were street demonstrations, and thousands of students, workers, and professionals accompanied the funeral procession of Luis Norberto Blanco along the eighty-seven blocks from his home to the cemetery (Balvé and Balvé 1989:145).

Chapter 3. A Breeze Turned into Hurricane: The Apogee of Crowd Mobilization

1. Lanusse 1977:xiv.

2. Cited in Lanusse 1977:16.

3. *El Combatiente* 1974 133:6.

4. *Nuevo Hombre* 1973 49:14.

5. See the CGTA declaration that the time had arrived for the working class to assume power through a two-pronged strategy of mass mobilizations and armed resistance (cited in Baschetti 1988:318).

6. Brennan 1994:142–148.

7. Lanusse 1977:23.

8. Alarcón 1989:56–59.

9. Alarcón 1989:60–62.

10. Balvé, Marín, and Murmis 1973:109.

11. Cited in Alarcón 1989:117.

12. Cited in Alarcón 1989:126.

13. Cited in Delich 1974:153.

14. Aside from my interviews with several protagonists, this description of the Cordobazo is based on the following sources: Alarcón 1989:72–144; Balvé, Marín, and Murmis 1973:109–148; Balvé and Balvé 1989:193–204; Brennan 1994:150–159; Delich 1974:156–185; W. Smith 1991:129.

15. Lanusse 1977:16.

16. These driving forces took on a special significance in Córdoba because of the dominance of foreign multinational corporations, the deteriorating economic

position of the middle class, rising unemployment in the labor-intensive industries, and the presence of combative, highly class-conscious auto workers (Laclau 1970:19; Balvé and Balvé 1989:253–260).

17. The rapid growth of the automobile industry in Córdoba since the mid-1950s had created a privileged segment of the Argentine working class. Years of higher salaries and rapid social mobility of former rural workers had given rise to social expectations which were threatened when the auto industry entered into crisis in the late 1960s. The national proscription of political parties and the corporatism of the provincial governor prevented the growing worker and middle class discontent from being expressed through institutional channels (Delich 1974:38–43; Lewis 1990:373–376; Munck 1987:173; W. Smith 1991:129–132).

18. Brennan and James emphasize that the understanding of the Cordobazo depends as much on those who were absent as on those who were present. The meager participation of the thousands of Fiat auto workers is as revealing as the leading role of the IKA-Renault workers. Clearly, the Cordobazo cannot simply be attributed to the relative deprivation of a privileged segment of modern industry, as Delich, Lewis, Munck, and Smith suggest, but can only be understood through a multidimensional analysis of national and plant-specific circumstances affecting broad layers of Cordoban society (Brennan 1994:141, 159–160; James 1988a:221–226).

19. Balvé, Marín, and Murmis 1973:120.

20. Cited in Alarcón 1989:117.

21. Cited in Alarcón 1989:119.

22. RC-8–3 1969:ii.

23. RC-8–2 1970 1:2–7.

24. RC-8–2 1970 1:2–7.

25. Villegas 1969.

26. W. Smith 1991:60.

27. RC-8–2 1970:1.

28. A 1969 army field manual placed crowds on a continuum from harmless to subversive. On one end stands a multitude (*muchedumbre*) of people waiting in a public place. Next comes the demonstration (*manifestación*) in which the participants have a common cause and constitute a psychological unity, as in a protest crowd. The mob (*turba*) is a disorganized, disorderly crowd. The mob can develop into a tumult (*tumulto*) which displays organized instead of erratic violence (RC-8–3 1969:ii–iii).

29. RC-8–3 1969:2–4, 22.

30. RC-8–3 1969:5.

31. RC-8–3 1969:94.

32. RC-8–3 1969:8–11.

33. RC-8–3 1969:11.

34. RC-8–3 1969:51.

35. Momboise 1973:383.

36. Botana, Braun, and Floria 1973:63.

37. Jacoby 1978 Anexo:89–101.

38. Balvé and Balvé 1989:208–238.

39. See Balvé and Balvé 1989:287, 315.

40. Brennan 1994:182–183, 198–204; James 1988a:224, 231–232; Munck 1987:177–179.

41. Anzorena 1988:157–159; Balvé, Marín, and Murmis 1973:12–16; Brennan 1994:171–179.

42. RC-8–3 1969:97.

43. Delich 1974:121–123.

44. Cited in Balvé, Marín, and Murmis 1973:23.

45. Uriburu speech of 7 March 1971 cited in Balvé, Marín, and Murmis 1973:24.

46. Balvé, Marín, and Murmis 1973:32, 46.

47. SITRAM union leader Páez cited in Balvé, Marín, and Murmis 1973:57.

48. Anzorena 1988:162–169; Balvé, Marín, and Murmis 1973:59–93, 182–187; Brennan 1994:190–193.

49. Moyano (1995:90) situates the peak of violent street protests during the 1969–1979 period in 1971. A careful survey of newspapers yielded the following distribution: 1969 (400 street protests), 1970 (225), 1971 (700), 1972 (350), 1973 (350), 1974 (100), 1975 (100), 1976 (80), while street protests are almost nonexistent in 1977 through 1979. William Smith (1991:134) provides a diagram of strikes and political demonstrations between 1966 and 1972. Although more detailed than the figure presented by Moyano, the graph suffers equally from a lack of attention to the quality of mass mobilizations.

50. Lanusse 1977:225; San Martino de Dromi 1988 1:484–493.

51. In the late 1960s, it was common military procedure that first the local, provincial and federal police would try to maintain public order. If they failed, then the National Gendarmery (Gendarmería Nacional) would be called upon to provide assistance. Once these repressive means had been exhausted, then the area would be declared an emergency zone and the army would be deployed. Lanusse changed this procedure in March 1971, allowing the army to move into action immediately (RC-8-3 1969:22–23; Lanusse 1977:10–11).

52. Page 1983:420–424; W. Smith 1988.

53. Anzorena 1988:204–206; Gillespie 1982a:114; Moyano 1995:68.

54. Brennan 1994:220.

55. Tambiah 1996:284, 293.

56. Tambiah 1996:280. Stanley Tambiah draws extensively on Le Bon and Canetti to explain the impulsiveness of crowds. He takes from Le Bon the insight that people in a crowd lose control over their intensified emotions and turn without restraint on others. He borrows from Canetti the idea of the boundless crowd leveling everything standing in the way of its growth, buildings as well as people (Tambiah 1996:297–298).

57. Stanley Tambiah, Veena Das, and Paul Brass have demonstrated that political calculation and emotional discharge are also at play in South Asian crowds. The collective violence is directed intentionally at the privileges of rival groups and is raised to excessive heights by a selective rage accumulated through the proper dynamics of the crowd. The crowd does not turn on others at random but selects its victims. In other words, collective violence is purposive but its intensity is not premeditated (Brass 1996:12–14, 1997:286; Das 1990a:28, 1990b:350; Tambiah 1996:281, 317).

58. In fact, most deaths were caused by police and military, while the violent crowds restricted themselves generally to the torching of buildings and the erecting of barricades in spontaneous outrage.

Chapter 4. Crowd Clashes: Euphoria, Disenchantment, and Rupture

1. Page 1983:437–440.

2. Lanusse 1977:305–309; San Martino de Dromi 1988 1:494.

3. Page 1983:441–442.

4. Cited in *La Nación* 20 November 1972.

5. Gillespie 1982a:72; Sigal and Verón 1988:228.

6. Rodolfo Galimberti had succeeded in uniting the various independent JP groups into the regional JP. The regional JP was organized territorially into seven regional organizations, with Galimberti as its national representative. Each regional organization was subdivided into zones, each zone into districts, and each district contained numerous local branches or basic units (*unidad básica*).

7. About the Fight and Return campaign, see Bonasso 1997:276.

8. The appointment of twenty-seven-year-old Juan Manuel Abal Medina was interpreted as a gesture by Perón to express his sympathy for both the youth branch and the armed wing of the Peronist movement. Juan Manuel was after all the brother of Fernando Luis Abal Medina, a founding member of the Montoneros who had died in September 1970 after a shoot-out with police.

9. Cámpora had earlier that year negotiated the transition to democracy with the Lanusse government on Perón's behalf. He had been the president of the Chamber of Deputies between 1948 and 1953, and stood on good terms with Perón's shock troops in the political fight with Lanusse, namely the Peronist Youth and the Montoneros (Crassweller 1987:353; Page 1983:444–446; San Martino de Dromi 1988 1:505).

10. See Perón cited in Anzorena 1988:216, 225.

11. Perón [1971] 1995:333.

12. The guerrilla organization had in 1972 coopted the Peronist Youth by recruiting behind the scene its principal national and regional leaders, including Galimberti (Anzorena 1989:167; Gillespie 1982a:120).

13. Cámpora received 49.56 percent of the popular vote. Balbín was the runner-up with 21.29 percent, while Brigadier Ezequiel Martínez received only 2.91 percent of the electoral vote (San Martino de Dromi 1988 1:511). Balbín's UCR ceded the victory to Cámpora making a run-off election unnecessary.

14. Cited in Anzorena 1988:233.

15. Bonasso 2000:101.

16. Crassweller 1987:355; Page 1983:453–455.

17. Page 1983:457.

18. Anzorena 1988:255–257; Bonasso 1997:506–509; Brennan 1994:245; Moyano 1995:71; Verbitsky 1986:20.

19. *La Nación* 21 June 1973.

20. Osinde had been head of intelligence during the Peronist government of the 1950s and became secretary of sports in López Rega's Ministry of Social Welfare in May 1973. A U.S. embassy report characterized Osinde as a "man with a Gestapo-like reputation" (cited in Potash 1996:501).

21. *La Nación* 21 June 1973; *La Prensa* 21 June 1973. A careful examination by Verbitsky in 1986 arrives at thirteen dead and 365 wounded (Verbitsky 1986:117–120).

22. Verbitsky 1986:153.

23. Verbitsky 1986:14.

24. See Peronist Youth communiqué cited in *Militancia* 1973 3:10.

25. See the joint statement by the FAR and Montoneros cited in *La Razón* 26 June 1973.

26. Sigal and Verón 1988:206–228. For an analysis of the Ezeiza events and the leader-crowd dynamic from a perspective of mass psychology, see Robben 1994.

27. *El Descamisado* 1974 39:2.

28. San Martino de Dromi 1988 2:9–10.

29. See Montoneros statement cited in *El Descamisado* 1973 9:17.

30. *Militancia* 1973 7:5; *El Descamisado* 1973 10:3.

31. *El Descamisado* 1973 16(special supplement):ii-vi.

32. But had Perón really seen the Peronist Youth columns? Tellingly, Perón returned inside the CGT building before the principal Peronist Youth, FAR, and Montoneros columns had passed (James 1988a:243).

33. *Las Bases* 1973 59:27.

34. Perón received 61.85 percent of the vote as candidate for the FREJULI coalition. Ricardo Balbín of the UCR received 24.42 percent (Graham-Yooll 1989:285).

35. *El Descamisado* 1973 22:2.

36. *El Descamisado* 1973 22:4.

37. *El Descamisado* 1973 22:4.

38. The social pact entailed that prices and salaries were frozen for two years, after a rise of 20 percent of the minimum wage as compensation for the 1972 inflation (Di Tella 1985:190–192; San Martino de Dromi 1988 2:126–127).

39. See the speech by Perón of early November 1973 reproduced in *El Descamisado* (1973 26:4). The new labor union law (Ley de Asociaciones Profesionales) gave legal status only to unions with the largest number of affiliates, and which represented an entire branch of industry. The legislation fit closely into Perón's larger political scheme to harness the labor movement, as he had done in the 1940s. The Cordoban Light and Power union was the first to feel the law's consequences when its affiliation with the national union central FATLYF was suspended on 8 November 1973 (Brennan 1994:254; Munck 1987:192; Roldán 1978:318–336; San Martino de Dromi 1988 2:129–130).

40. *El Descamisado* 1973 27:7.

41. San Martino de Dromi 1988 2:47–51.

42. *El Descamisado* 1974 36:2.

43. Cited in Graham-Yooll 1989:297.

44. Anzorena 1988:296.

45. The leaders of the JP and Montoneros were called *movimientistas* because of their belief in the revolutionary significance of a unified Peronist movement. A loyalist faction (la Lealtad) arose propagating a vertical obedience to Perón and rejecting the embrace of socialism. In Córdoba, the Sabino Navarro Column (*los alternativistas*) emerged which, together with the Peronismo de Base, rejected the growing vanguardism of the Montoneros and wanted a grass roots approach. On the other hand, the Columna de Recuperación Cooke-Pujadas accused the hegemonic movimientistas of opportunism and reformism, and proposed a more confrontational, vanguardist course of action (*Militancia* 1974 38:20–22).

46. *El Descamisado* 14 March 1974 extra edition: 2.

47. *El Peronista* 1974 2:2–3.

48. Gillespie 1982a:149.

49. *El Peronista* 1974 3:6.

50. *El Peronista* 1974 3:7.

51. Gillespie 1982a:148–150; *El Peronista* 1974 3:3; *La Prensa* 2 May 1974.

52. *De Frente* 1974 2:4.

53. Miguel Ragone of Salta and Alberto Martínez Baca of Mendoza were forced out of office in May and June of 1974. Jorge Cepernic of Salta followed later that year.

54. Jelin 1979:251.

55. Cited in Page 1983:491.

56. *La Nación* 4 July 1974.

57. Page 1983:493–494.

58. Bonasso 2000:168, 170–171.

59. See statement by Montonero leader Roberto Quieto cited in *La Causa Peronista* 1974 4:7–8.

60. Anzorena 1988:340–341; Brennan 1994:268–270, 292–295; Jelin 1979:245; Munck 1987:195–200; Page 1983:498; Pinetta 1986:77–80; Rock 1987:365. López Rega went to Spain, was arrested in Miami in March 1986, and extradited to Argentina. He died in preventive detention in June 1989.

61. Di Tella 1985:141–148, 325–328; Munck 1987:199–202.

62. See the 1977 and 1979 analyses by the Montonero leadership about the dialectics of mass and vanguard or, as it was also formulated: Peronism and Guevarism. The Montonero National Leadership admitted in the 1979 document that it had been a mistake to place a too singular emphasis on militarizing the organization at the expense of mass politics after Perón's death (*Vencer* 1979 2/3: iii–xii).

63. *La Nación* 20 April 1977; see also Brigadier-General Omar Graffigna cited in *La Prensa* 11 August 1980.

64. The Argentine military doctrine with respect to crowd control was derived mostly from American manuals developed during the 1960s. Compare, e.g., American field manual FM 19–15 (1964) and its Argentine adaptation (Taylor 1973).

65. Le Bon [1895] 1974:28–32.

66. Le Bon [1895] 1974:16. The study of mobs and riots by British historians disproved Le Bon's notion that popular crowds were destructive for pure violence's sake. Rudé debunked the myth that crowds consisted merely of drunks, derelicts, and criminals in his analysis of eighteenth- and nineteenth-century mobs in England and France. E. P. Thompson regarded rioting crowds as legitimate protests for social and economic justice in a moral economy under siege by an increasingly impersonal market economy, while Hobsbawm interpreted the violence of working class crowds as improvised forms of collective bargaining before their institutionalization in labor unions (Rudé 1964:195–234; Thompson 1971; Hobsbawm 1959:110–125). Brass (1996:16–21) concludes that these insights do not necessarily apply to riots in more recent times and that, despite Rudé's findings, criminal elements and the riffraff participate in most riots.

67. Similar concerns were expressed by nineteenth-century mass psychologists. The army was therefore regarded as the preeminent bulwark against the phantom of revolution. The army was the guardian of civilization, and a model for society. The psychologists considered mobs, churches, armies, and political parties comparable units of analysis because they all required the submission of individual interests to the greater good of the collectivity. Crowd manipulation techniques could thus be applied equally to popular crowds and armies. At the advent of World War I, Le Bon was cited widely by French, British, and American military strategists who came to regard the army as a disciplined crowd. French military commanders stated that war was the confrontation of armies with the objective of turning the enemy into a crowd. After all, an army in panic was nothing more than a disorganized crowd ((Barrows 1981:142–152; Moscovici 1985:156–169; Nye 1975:135–140).

68. Cited in Graham-Yooll 1989:417.

Chapter 5. Shots in the Night: Revenge, Revolution, and Insurgency

1. Walsh 1988:11; see Walsh (1995:25) about his support of the Liberating Revolution.

2. Walsh 1988:94.

3. Walsh 1988:99.

4. Cited in Cooke 1973 1:33.

5. Perón [1956] 1973c:395–396.

6. Perón [1956] 1973c:395–398. The respected Peronist intellectual Arturo Jauretche and Father Hernán Benítez, who was Evita's confessor, condemned

Perón's inflamed call for sabotage and violence in the strongest possible terms (correspondence cited in Cichero 1992:93, 103, 108, 282).

7. Proclamation cited in Verbitsky 1988:81.

8. There had been other isolated conspiracies in December 1955, but they never reached the level of organization of the June 1956 rebellion (Amaral 1993:78).

9. Interview with Admiral Rojas on 26 October 1990. The relatives of thirty-one persons executed after the Peronist rebellion, including General Valle and the eight men at José León Suárez, received damages from the Argentine government in March 2001.

10. Walsh 1988:148.

11. Admiral Rojas cited in *La Prensa* 12 June 1990.

12. Cited in Baschetti 1994:138.

13. Page 1983:346–348; Potash 1980:230–233.

14. Potash 1980:233–235.

15. Interview with Admiral Rojas on 26 October 1990.

16. Cited in Cooke 1973 1:13–14.

17. Perón [1956] 1973b:379.

18. James 1988a:63.

19. Amaral 1993:81; James 1988a:51.

20. Baschetti 1988:26–27; Perón 1973c:389–390; see also the testimonies of protagonists of the Peronist Resistance in Garulli et al. 2000.

21. Perón 1973c:391.

22. James 1988a:77–80.

23. Amaral 1993:79–81; Hodges 1991:73.

24. Baschetti 1988:29.

25. James 1988a:144.

26. Perón [1956] 1973c:393–394.

27. Cited in Cooke 1973 1:35.

28. Cooke 1973 2:376.

29. Perón [1956] 1973c:390, 392–393.

30. Cooke 1973 1:307. Cooke was greatly influenced by his friend Abraham Guillén, a veteran from the Spanish civil war living in exile in Argentina (Hodges 1991:74).

31. These organizations did not have the significance which their impressive names suggested, such as the CORP or Peronist Resistance Operations Center (Central de Operaciones de la Resistencia Peronista) headed by General Iñíguez himself, the MOPI or Independent Orthodox Peronist Movement (Movimiento Ortodoxo Peronista Independiente), and the APRI or Peronist Group of Insurrectional Resistance (Agrupación Peronista de la Resistencia Insurreccional) which in turn contained several commando organizations in the Federal Capital and Greater Buenos Aires engaging in guerrilla activities (Baschetti 1988:23).

32. Baschetti 1988:25–29; James 1988a:145.

33. James 1988a:146–147; Potash 1980:323.

34. Gillespie 1989:27–31.

35. Baschetti 1988:25–26; Gasparini 1988:19–25.

36. Cited in Anzorena 1989:40.

37. Anzorena 1989:33.

38. Anderson 1997:395–419.

39. Anderson 1997:419.

40. Guevara [1960] 1985:47.

41. Woddis 1972:185–211.

42. Debray 1967:15.

43. Debray 1973:51.
44. Cazes Camarero 1989:18.
45. Sebreli cited in Terán 1991:137.
46. Anderson 1997:308–311.
47. Rojo 1974:185.
48. Masetti was the editor-in-chief of the *Prensa Latina* until 1961. This news agency sought to present a voice different from the American-owned international press agencies, and counted Gabriel García Márquez and Rodolfo Walsh among its contributors. Walsh even worked as a decoder for the Cuban intelligence service (Anderson 1997:408; García Márquez 1983:62–64; Walsh 1995:121).
49. Anderson 1997:537–540.
50. Anderson 1997:546–549, 573–577.
51. Cited in Anderson 1997:576.
52. Anderson 1997:574; Mercier Vega 1969:115–117, 157–170; Rojo 1974:194–195.
53. Anderson 1997:575–579.
54. Anderson 1997:601; Gillespie 1982a:60; Mattini 1990:28–31.
55. Rojo 1974:198.
56. Most of them would be released in 1968. Two members remained in prison until their amnesty in 1973 (Anderson 1997:745–746).
57. Anderson 1997:587–593.
58. Gelman 1994:130.
59. Guevara's intentions about Argentina were clear. He told the Argentine Ciro Bustos in March 1967 about the principal reason for his Bolivian foco: "My strategic objective is the seizure of political power in Argentina. For this I want to form a group of Argentines, to prepare a couple of columns, season them in war for a year or two over here, and then enter" (Bustos quoting Guevara in Anderson 1997:709).
60. Gillespie 1989:36.
61. Gillespie 1989:56–57; Cooke 1973 2:333.
62. Gillespie 1989:73–78.
63. Baschetti 1988:242.
64. Gillespie 1989:35–36.
65. See 26 July 1960 speech by Castro cited in Anderson 1997:476.
66. Marini 1965.
67. These general ideas about the duty to defend the nation have become known as the National Security Doctrine. Brazilian and Argentine officers were its foremost intellectual authors (Calvo 1979:16–20). National security included a concern with legal, political, industrial, technological, scientific, regional, and military development. National defense, i.e. the protection of the national territory, was only one of its many aspects (Guglialmelli 1969; Jaureguialzo 1972; Villegas 1969). Much was made in the 1980s of this National Security Doctrine in a string of Argentine publications (see CONADEP [1984] 1986:442–445; Duhalde 1983; Lázara 1988; Lozada et al. 1983, 1985). These authors attribute all evil of the dirty war to this doctrine, as if this ideological framework would inevitably lead to torture and disappearances. However, as Nunn (1992:xi) observes: "comparability of military thought and self-perception does not necessarily lead to similar political behavior." The great difference between Brazil and Argentina in the number of disappearances attests to the importance of the national political context in explaining military repression.
68. Nunn 1992:13–15, 28–30, 56–59.
69. Villegas 1976:5–6; see also Ruda 1965:87.
70. *Revista Militar* 1989 721:83.

71. Potash 1996:132. As General Osiris Villegas pointed out to me, "The spirit of the Constitution indicates that a citizen has the ethical obligation to defend his country. And because each citizen cannot defend it with a rifle under his arm it has to be defended by a military organization. That is why there is compulsory military service" (interview with General Villegas, 10 October 1990). Article 21 of the Constitution states that "Every Argentine citizen has the obligation to arm himself in defense of the Fatherland and this Constitution, in accordance with the laws which are ratified by Congress and the decrees dictated by the National Executive." The guerrilla organizations in the 1970s invoked the first part of the sentence as the legitimization for their call to arms, while the armed forces emphasized the second part, arguing that their counterinsurgency measures had always been approved by the government.

72. *Revista Militar* 1989 721:80.

73. Three other reasons mentioned were the need for measures to curb the growing political power of the Peronists, the poor state of the economy, and the government's inability to lead the country towards clear political and economic objectives (Proclamation of the Argentine Revolution cited in Verbitsky 1988:102–104).

74. Interview with General Villegas on 10 October 1990.

75. Interview with General Villegas on 10 October 1990.

76. The First Tricontinental Conference of the Peoples of Asia, Africa and Latin America in Havana took place in January 1966. The Organization of Latin American Solidarity conference was held in August 1967, also in Havana (Leoni Houssay 1980:171).

77. Goldar 1991:35.

78. Anderson 1997:677–684.

79. Guevara [1960] 1985:213.

80. Cited in Kenner and Petras 1972:250.

81. Baschetti 1988:297–299; Goldar 1990.

82. Goldar 1990:8.

83. Communiqué cited in Baschetti 1988:297.

84. The guerrillas were finally given prison sentences of five to seven years in 1971, three years after their capture. Some were released after completing their three-year term, while others were given amnesty on 25 May 1973 (Goldar 1990:20).

85. Ollier 1998:120.

Chapter 6. The Long Arm of Popular Justice: Punishment, Rebellion, and Sacrifice

1. *La Causa Peronista* 1974 9:29.

2. *La Causa Peronista* 1974 9:30.

3. *La Causa Peronista* 1974 9:31. The abduction is widely attributed to the Montoneros but several conspiracy theories circulated immediately after the kidnapping. Some believed that Aramburu had organized his own abduction, while others insisted that the inexperienced guerrillas carried out their operation with help from government circles wanting to protect President Onganía against a palace coup by Aramburu (Fernández Alvariño 1973; Méndez 1988; *La Prensa* 29 May 1990; see also Potash 1996:293–294).

4. Perón [1956] 1973c:396–397.

5. Lieutenant-General Pedro Aramburu heads the list of names on a plaque commemorating army losses during its "fight against the subversion." The plaque is prominently placed at the entrance of army headquarters in Buenos Aires. The

date next to Aramburu's name is not the day of execution (1 June 1970) but the day his body was found (16 July 1970).

6. For several excellent accounts of the political intricacies of the guerrilla organizations, see Gasparini 1988; Gillespie 1982a; Mattini 1990; Moyano 1995.

7. Farinello 1999:191.

8. See Schuman and Scott 1989.

9. In a fine study about the political radicalization of the Argentine youth, Ollier (1998) describes how many members of guerrilla organizations came from politicized families, had directly or indirectly experienced repression as either Peronists or anti-Peronists, and were influenced by a politicized Roman Catholic Church.

10. Andrés Castillo cited in Anzorena 1989:96. Many founding members of the Peronist guerrilla organizations had in the early 1960s participated as teenagers in nationalist Catholic organizations, such as Tacuara and Catholic Action.

11. Gillespie 1982a:48–51; Rock 1993:205–206.

12. The Movement was dissolved in August 1973 due to internal political and doctrinal divisions, and fell apart into three factions (Pontoriero 1991:112). The largest faction aligned itself in 1974 with the left-wing Peronists remaining loyal to Perón (la Lealtad). One small group sympathized with the Montoneros, and the third group aligned itself with Grass Roots Peronism (Peronismo de Base) (interview with Ruben Dri on 1 July 1991).

13. Burdick 1995:137–140; Pontoriero 1991:35; C. Smith, 1991:136–138.

14. Brieger 1991; Gillespie 1982a:53–58; Pontoriero 1991:28. For an excellent description of these missions under the leadership of Father Mugica, see Anguita and Caparrós 1997:25–29. See also Mugica 1973, and Firmenich's eulogy to Mugica in *El Peronista* 1974 5:2 after his violent death in 1974.

15. Cited in Anzorena 1989:133.

16. Unfortunately, the analysis of gender roles among male and female guerrillas is beyond the scope of this book. See Diana 1997 for an excellent testimonial account of female guerrillas.

17. Gillespie 1982b:419–422; Jauretche 1997:203–204; Lanusse 1977:133; Moyano 1995:112–113. Moyano (1995:113) concludes on the basis of the biographical data of guerrillas captured or killed between 1969 and 1979 that the guerrilla organizations in Argentina were largely composed of middle class young adults. For a different assessment, see Jauretche (1997:58).

18. Gillespie 1982a:95.

19. Gillespie 1982a:95–96; *La Prensa* 2 July 1970; *Militancia* 1973 4:8–9.

20. *Militancia* 1973 4:8.

21. Gillespie 1982a:96–97.

22. *Militancia* 1973 13:13.

23. Communiqués reproduced in Baschetti 1995:73–75.

24. Gillespie 1982a:96.

25. The Argentine guerrilla organizations took their tactical inspiration about a rural guerrilla insurgency largely from Guevara, about sabotage and the organization of armed groups from Perón, and about urban guerrilla warfare from Guillén and Marighela. These writings were read as eagerly by Marxist and Peronist guerrillas as by the Argentine intelligence services (Guillén 1965; Hodges 1973; Marighela 1971).

26. Anzorena 1988:118–121.

27. PEN 1979:39. Thirteen months earlier, on 26 June 1969, the FAR had carried out an anonymous fire-bombing of fifteen Minimax supermarkets as a protest against the visit of its owner, Nelson Rockefeller, to Argentina.

28. Gillespie 1982a:107–108.

29. Letter by Perón cited in Baschetti 1988:273–274.

30. Cited in Baschetti 1988:295.

31. *El Descamisado* 1974 41:29–31. The ENR was a tiny hit squad of the Descamisados, one of several small revolutionary Peronist groups operating in the early 1970s. The Descamisados had close ties with the CGT of the Argentines (CGTA), led by Raimundo Ongaro. As was explained in chapter 2, Ongaro and Vandor represented respectively the revolutionary and the integrationist wing of the Peronist union spectrum.

32. ENR declaration cited in Baschetti 1988:384–386.

33. Gillespie 1982a:108; *El Descamisado* 1974 41:31; *La Causa Peronista* 1974 8:25–29.

34. Perón's health was also a factor in the desire for a speedy change of the guard. He had been operated on in March 1970 to remove several tumors (Page 1983:414). Who could ever take the helm from Perón's hands? Evita had died in 1952, Cooke in 1968, and there was no other person alive with sufficient charisma and authority to replace Perón. Perón had said that if a suitable leader could not be found to succeed him, then an organization should assume the leadership of the Peronist movement (Perón [1971] 1995:333–334).

35. Gillespie 1982a:99.

36. Moyano 1995:27.

37. The PRT was a fusion of the Indo-American Popular Revolutionary Front or FRIP (Frente Revolucionario Indoamericano Popular) and the Trotskyist Palabra Obrero. The FRIP had been founded by two brothers of future PRT-ERP leader Mario Roberto Santucho. Palabra Obrero had been founded by Nahuel Moreno. The FRIP had pursued a spontaneous insurrection of the rural workers of Argentina's northern provinces, while the Palabra Obrero had sought to conquer key posts in the labor unions to launch a revolutionary general strike. The PRT at first pursued these insurrectionist approaches, and even rejected an armed struggle against the Onganía dictatorship in favor of a general strike (PRT 1966:41).

38. Mattini 1990:36–39; PRT 1973a:24–31; J. Santucho 1988:126–135, 149–150.

39. PRT 1973a:65–66, 73.

40. Interview with Cazes Camarero on 29 May 1991. In fact, in 1971 the PRT-ERP killed on their own admission a total of twelve policemen in the frequent attempts to steal their hand weapons (Díaz Bessone 1988:132).

41. Seoane 1991:124, 133.

42. This decision was greatly influenced by José Baxter. Baxter was trained in Cuba, and had an impressive record of armed action in Argentina, Uruguay, and Vietnam (Gillespie 1982a:50–51; Hodges 1973:9–10). Santucho and Baxter proposed a series of resolutions stating that the revolutionary war had already begun, that it was going to be a long battle, and that this war was neither restricted to a particular part of the country nor depended on the masses. The masses would be incorporated in increasing numbers in the course of the struggle (Mattini 1990:65–74).

43. Despite the lip service paid to the Leninist position that the military wing resided under the political direction of the party, the power balance shifted immediately from the political to the military wing as can be read from the financial basis of each organization. The PRT survived on the donations of workers, and the sale of the party's magazine *El Combatiente.* Instead, the ERP financed their armed operations with bank assaults and ransom payments, and even loaned money to the PRT (PRT 1973a:89–90, 145; Mattini 1990:74). Furthermore, in April 1971, the executive committee decided that all PRT party members were automatically ERP combatants, that they must train in the use of weapons, and be available to pass from the mass organizations to the guerrilla forces (PRT 1973a:172).

44. Mattini 1990:78.

45. To be precise: out of a total of 504 operations between 1970 and 1973, there were 272 mass actions (food distributions, factory occupations, intimidation of managers), 154 attacks against the police and army (principally to obtain weapons), 66 expropriations of vehicles, machines, and money, 7 attempts to free imprisoned comrades, and 5 abductions (PRT 1973b:16).

46. Díaz Bessone 1988:132–139; Gasparini 1988:33–34; Gillespie 1982a:109–110.

47. *El Combatiente* November 1971 64:2.

48. Moyano 1995:27.

49. There was an urgent call to attract more working class recruits. A short communication from Córdoba observed that 80 percent of the participants in the plenary union meetings were intellectuals and only 20 percent workers. The note warned that the revolutionary intelligentsia would lead the movement to defeat if this situation was not reversed (*El Combatiente* 1971 65:15–16).

50. Activist cited in Moyano 1995:117.

51. PRT 1973a:227.

52. Moyano 1995:90. A detailed comparison of incidents of armed struggle and collective protest between 1969 and 1979 demonstrates the relative independence of crowd and vanguard. Moyano (1995:88–90) describes how both developed along parallel lines between 1969 and 1973, but that the armed struggle peaked between 1974 and 1976 while collective protests declined. She argues that a guerrilla insurgency might actually have a dampening effect on popular protest because their actions might wrest concessions that preempt grass roots mobilizations in pursuit of labor demands. Furthermore, armed violence will summon repressive forces which will also strike at collective protests.

53. PRT 1973a:162.

54. Interview with Lieutenant-General Lanusse on 18 September 1990.

55. Moyano 1995:28; San Martino de Dromi 1988 1:370–389.

56. Moyano 1995:28. Ollier (1986:119) arrives at 282 operations in 1970, 603 in 1971, and 368 in 1972.

57. Moyano 1995:103.

58. PRT 1973a:166–223.

59. Urondo [1973] 1988:32–33. Official sources mention that there were "166 subversive delinquents and 83 common delinquents" at Rawson, but the line between a political and a common prisoner was not always drawn clearly (Cheren 1997:200).

60. Fernando Vaca Narvaja, who participated in the planning of the operation, told me that there was an alternative escape plan in case Santucho's plan failed. The guerrillas had dug a tunnel which they carefully sealed before making their daring escape. The tunnel was only discovered ten years later (interview with Vaca Narvaja on 13 December 1990).

61. See statements by Santucho, Osatinsky, and Vaca Narvaja cited in Tapia 1972:7–11.

62. Martínez [1973] 1997:79, 96–97; Mattini 1990:161–163; Tapia 1972:4–6.

63. Martínez [1973] 1997:80; Urondo [1973] 1988:53–60; *La Causa Peronista* 6:14–19. Enrique Gorriarán Merlo was one of the six guerrillas who escaped to Chile. He stated in a May 1997 interview that the Rawson escape was facilitated by a prison guard who had smuggled 14 pistols and a military uniform to the guerrillas for a considerable sum of money (Cheren 1997:15).

64. Navy officer cited in Tapia 1972:2.

65. Urondo [1973] 1988:59–76, 89.

66. Captain Sosa and Lieutenant Bravo cited in Urondo [1973] 1988:108.

67. Cited in Urondo [1973] 1988:111.
68. Urondo [1973] 1988.
69. Urondo [1973] 1988:225–231.
70. Interview with Rear-Admiral Mayorga on 3 October 1990.
71. Interview with Rear-Admiral Mayorga on 3 October 1990.
72. Interview with Lieutenant-General Lanusse on 18 September 1990; see also Lanusse 1977:296–298.
73. Interview with Vaca Narvaja on 13 December 1990.
74. Vaca Narvaja himself was almost captured in December 1982. The navy had just caught the only survivor of the Trelew massacre, René Haidar, and obliged him to invite Vaca Narvaja for a meeting on 16 December. Vaca Narvaja sensed by the tone of voice that something was wrong. He failed to show up, and Haidar disappeared (interviews with Vaca Narvaja on 2 October and 13 December 1990).
75. Interview with Vaca Narvaja on 13 December 1990.
76. Potash (1996:444–446) is still in doubt about the true course of events. I suspect that his conversations with the astute Lieutenant-General Lanusse have influenced him, and I believe that he underestimates the weight of the humiliations suffered by the navy at the time. Tomás Eloy Martínez also believes that the assassinations were ordered by high-ranking navy officers as a coup de grace after the Chilean government refused to extradite immediately the escapees from the Rawson prison (Martínez [1973] 1997:161–164).
77. Cheren 1997:166.
78. Interview with Rear-Admiral Mayorga on 3 October 1990.
79. Anzorena 1989:144.
80. Cheren 1997:202; Petric 1983:113–115; *Liberación* 1974 19:20–23. Quijada had been killed by Vítor Fernández Palmeiro. Palmeiro was an ERP guerrilla who had escaped from the Villa Devoto prison in February 1972, had participated in the Sallustro abduction in March 1972, and had been one of the four guerrillas hijacking the plane in August 1972 at which the six guerrilla leaders escaped from Rawson to Chile.
81. Navy communiqué cited in Cheren 1997:203.
82. Besançon 1981:221–222.
83. Guevara [1960] 1985:187.
84. PRT 1972:20.
85. PRT 1972:16.
86. PRT 1973a:139.
87. Debray 1973:249.
88. Arendt [1948] 1975:465.
89. *El Descamisado* 1973 17:5.
90. *El Descamisado* 1973 17:5.

Chapter 7. Revolution Postponed: Anger, Frustration, and Entitlement

1. Jauretche 1997:193.
2. Urondo [1973] 1988:21.
3. Díaz Bessone 1988:161–165.
4. Lanusse 1977:273, 328.
5. See Cámpora's argument before Congress on 26 May 1973 in Congreso Nacional 1974:38.
6. San Martino de Dromi 1988 2:33–39.
7. The fact that Norma Arrostito, one of the guerrillas who had participated in

the Aramburu abduction, had been acquitted in 1970 for lack of evidence was regarded as ample proof of the due process given to guerrillas.

8. Chant cited in Díaz Bessone 1988:160–161.

9. Cited in Potash 1996:503.

10. Díaz Bessone 1988:154.

11. PRT 1973a:233–246.

12. Mattini 1990:223.

13. The party had founded in early 1973 the Anti-Imperialist and Pro-Socialist Front or FAS (Frente Antiimperialista y por el Socialismo), the Grassroots Union Movement or MSB (Movimiento Sindical de Base), and the Soldarity Movement with Political Prisoners (Movimiento de Soldaridad con los Presos Polítícos) as legal front organizations (Mattini 1990:173, 190–191; J. Santucho 1988:206).

14. PEN 1979:151–152; *La Prensa* 7 September 1973.

15. For the condemnation of the assault by the government, the armed forces, Congress, labor unions and employer organizations, see *La Prensa* 7 September 1973.

16. *El Descamisado* 1973 17:30.

17. San Martino de Dromi 1988 2:51.

18. *El Combatiente* 1973 92:2.

19. Moyano 1995:59.

20. Moyano 1995:36.

21. Díaz Bessone 1988:203–205; *El Combatiente* 1974 106:10; *Estrella Roja* 1974 29 (supplement):2–3.

22. Cited in San Martino de Dromi 1988 2:53.

23. Cited in Anzorena 1988:296.

24. *El Combatiente* 1974 105:2.

25. Grassroots union leader Iscaro cited in Mattini 1990:277.

26. Mattini 1990:281–286.

27. M. Santucho [1974] 1988:41.

28. Mattini 1990:293–307.

29. The Triple A had at least 159 members, of which 66 were on active duty in the police and armed forces (Moyano 1995:83).

30. Moyano 1995:105. Ernesto Jauretche estimates that the Montoneros had fifteen thousand members in 1974, of which six thousand belonged to the military branch. Only six hundred of these six thousand were well-trained, armed combatants (Interview with Ernesto Jauretche on 27 April 1991).

31. *El Descamisado* 1973 22:6–7; see also the FAR-Montoneros joint communiqué cited in *Militancia* 1973 19:26–27. The Montonero leader Mario Firmenich reaffirmed this position in early September 1973 when asked if the Montoneros would abandon their arms now that Perón was about to assume the presidency: "In no way whatsoever: political power sprouts from the barrel of a gun. If we have arrived till here, then it has been to a large extent because we had the guns and used them; if we would abandon our weapons then we would have to retreat to a political position" (cited in *El Descamisado* 1973 17:3).

32. See Perón's televised addresses to the CGT on 30 July and to Argentina's provincial governors on 2 August 1973 cited in *El Descamisado* 1973 12:7–8.

33. Gillespie 1982a:172; *Las Bases* 1973 58:18–19.

34. Cited in *El Descamisado* 1973 17:4.

35. Montonero cited in Giussani 1987a:49.

36. *La Nación* 27 September 1973.

37. Verbitsky 1986:39–41.

38. *El Descamisado* 1973 19:3.

39. *El Descamisado* 1973 20:4; *La Nación* 27 September 1973.

40. Miguel Bonasso confided to his diary, only days after the assassination, that Montonero commander Mario Firmenich told him that the Montoneros had killed Rucci (Bonasso 2000:141; see also Gasparini 1990:70).

41. *La Nación* 27 September 1973.

42. *La Nación* 27 September 1973.

43. *El Descamisado* 1974 37:5–8.

44. *Militancia* 1973 18:4–5.

45. Gillespie 1982a:144; Jauretche 1997:206.

46. Cited in *El Descamisado* 1973 26:4.

47. Page 1983:340.

48. Page 1983:397–400; Pinetta 1986.

49. Pinetta 1986:50.

50. Gabetta 1983:209; Pinetta 1986:90.

51. *El Caudillo* 1973 1:2.

52. *El Caudillo* 1974 11:11.

53. Fernández 1983:10–12.

54. The links between the AAA and the Argentine military existed from the start and became closer through the years. Retired Lieutenant-Colonel Osinde had commanded the Ezeiza operation and was López Rega's secretary of sports, while Captain Mohamed Alí Seineldín, who had participated in the Ezeiza operation, was training Triple A commandos at the Campo de Mayo military base in 1975. In Córdoba, low-ranking army officers were involved in the Liberators of America Commando (Comando de Libertadores de América). A substantial number of former Triple A members would later participate in the dirty war (Amnesty International 1981:7; Armony 1997:219; Fernández 1983:17, 54; González Janzen 1986:37–38; Moyano 1995:83; J. Santucho 1988:202; Seoane and Muleiro 2001:32).

55. Moyano (1995:94–95) believes that Perón approved of the death squads, while San Martino de Dromi (1988 2:125), González Janzen (1986:112), and Pinetta (1986:62–63) argue against Perón's complicity.

56. Organizations similar to the Triple A were the Comando Libertadores de América in Córdoba and the Comando Anticomunista Mendoza in Mendoza (Anzorena 1988:322).

57. Moyano 1995:81–82, 56.

58. González Janzen 1986:16; Moyano 1995:84.

59. *El Caudillo* 1974 39:5.

60. Cited in *La Causa Peronista* 1974 6:27. I read the term "dirty war" for the first time in a right-wing Peronist magazine from March 1974 (*Cabildo* 1974 11:3), and later in September 1974 (*Cabildo* 1974 17:3), to describe the leftist guerrilla insurgency.

61. *La Causa Peronista* 1974 9:25–31.

62. *Militancia* 1974 33:10.

63. *El Descamisado* 1974 43:2.

64. *La Causa Peronista* 1974 1:14.

65. *Puro Pueblo* 1974 5:6.

66. *La Causa Peronista* 1974 3:8; *La Nación* 16 July 1974.

67. Cited in Gillespie 1982a:164.

68. Arendt [1948] 1975:332.

69. Interview with Vaca Narvaja on 31 May 1990.

70. *Evita Montonera* 1974 1:11.

71. Interview with Alcira Argumedo on 9 April 1991. See also Juan Gelman cited in Mero 1987:85–86.

72. Interview with Ernesto Jauretche on 20 April 1991.
73. Gasparini 1990:74–89; *La Nación* 20 September 1974.
74. Gillespie 1982a:180–181. The total capital of the Montoneros amounted to a staggering 150 million dollars in 1977. The money was deposited in Argentina, Spain, and Switzerland. The Argentine army succeeded in recouping 85 million dollars that same year (Gasparini 1986, 1990:65). The Montoneros invested the remaining ransom money in American, Mexican, and European banks, but eventually passed the capital into Cuban hands for safekeeping. Castro pressured the Montoneros into donating sums of money to Central and South American guerrilla organizations. By 1992, around fifty million dollars were returned to Jorge and Juan Born (Castañeda 1994:10–15).
75. The right-wing AAA also turned on the combative unions of Córdoba in a temporary alliance with the orthodox CGT union central and UOM metal workers' union central. Tosco's Light and Power union was another favorite target (Brennan 1994:287–291).
76. *La Nación* 2 November 1974. Villar was succeeded by Luis Margaride who continued the repressive regime of his predecessor. Margaride survived an attack on 23 December 1974 by an ERP hit squad launching a truck with explosives against his car (Gillespie 1982a:185; *Estrella Roja* 1975 47:13).
77. Gasparini 1988:257–262; Mero 1987:157.
78. Gasparini 1990:74; Gillespie 1982a:177–179; Moyano 1995:148–149.
79. *Evita Montonera* 1974 1:16.
80. *Evita Montonera* 1974 1:17.
81. Gillespie 1982a:210–211.
82. Gillespie (1982a:178) gives the figure of five thousand Montoneros under arms.
83. Gillespie 1982a:178; Moyano 1995:104.

Chapter 8. The Shadows of Death: Improvisation, Counterinsurgency, and Downfall

1. *La Prensa* 2 December 1974; see also ERP operational evaluation cited in PEN 1979:205.
2. See Anzorena 1988:324 for a list of names.
3. *Estrella Roja* 1974 40:2; see also *El Combatiente* 1974 137:2. See Walzer 1977:207–215 on the risks of reprisal killings.
4. Fraga 1988:68, 111.
5. *Che Guevara* 1975 2:21. The Argentine army anticipated an insurgency in Tucumán in a 1970 study which observed that northwest Argentina (Tucumán, Salta, Catamarca) offered the most suitable terrain for guerrilla warfare (Crawley 1970:53). The first military reconnaissance of rural Tucumán had already been carried out at the beginning of 1974.
6. Ollier 1998:163.
7. Mattini 1990:313–319; *Estrella Roja* 1974 35:12.
8. *Estrella Roja* 1974 35:3.
9. *Estrella Roja* 1974 35:3.
10. The distribution figures of *El Combatiente* and *Estrella Roja* were considered reliable indicators of the PRT-ERP's popularity. The production of *El Combatiente* almost doubled from 6,360 issues in January 1974 to 11,280 in September 1974. The edition of *Estrella Roja* increased from 11,400 to 14,330 issues in the same period (*Boletín Interno* September 1974 67:4). It is important to realize that both

periodicals were forbidden and that a substantial number of issues were given away rather than sold.

11. Fraga 1988:129.

12. CGE 1975a.

13. "The General Army Command will continue to execute the military operations necessary to neutralize and/or annihilate the actions of subversive elements operating in the Province of Tucumán" (PEN 1975a:1).

14. CGE 1975b Plan de acción sicológica nro. 1/75 anexo 1:3.

15. CGE 1975d.

16. The tour of duty policy was developed by American military psychiatrists to reduce the chances of combat trauma among servicemen fighting in Vietnam. The rotation system proved very successful on the battlefield, yet led to a high incidence of posttraumatic stress disorders upon return home (Grossman 1995:268–270).

17. CGE 1975c; Fraga 1988:134.

18. CGE 1975b Plan de acción sicológica nro. 1/75:2.

19. CGE 1975b Plan de acción sicológica nro. 1/75 anexo 1:3.

20. The counterinsurgency force involved a total of 3,750 men, of whom 2,500 belonged to the army, 250 to the national gendarmery, 200 to the federal police, and 800 to the provincial police (CJE 1978).

21. D'Andrea Mohr 1999:53.

22. FAMUS 1988:98.

23. CJE 1976:41.

24. CJE 1976:43.

25. FAMUS 1988:98–104.

26. CJE 1976:44.

27. CJE 1978.

28. FAMUS 1988:107.

29. Mattini 1990:427–429; Seoane 1991:262–264.

30. CGE 1975e.

31. FAMUS 1988:144–145.

32. *Estrella Roja* 1975 63:6.

33. FAMUS 1988:138–160; Seoane 1991:270–271.

34. *El Combatiente* 1975 186:6.

35. FAMUS 1988:181–183.

36. Bonasso 2000:213–216; FAMUS 1988:120; Gillespie 1982a:224. The Montoneros tried to establish a small foco of their own, north of San Miguel de Tucumán, in late 1975. This attempt collided with an ERP initiative to open a new front in the same area. In search of the Montoneros, the army captured the ERP guerrillas by accident (Mattini 1990:473).

37. PRT 1985:28; FAMUS 1988:200–201; CJE 1978. Forty-five men died in Tucumán according to the army, but this list includes thirteen men who died in a plane crash under poor weather conditions, two men who crashed with a small plane into a mountain side because of poor visibility, five men (including Captain Viola) who were executed in reprisal killings, and one man who died after trying to deactivate an explosive device. The list gives twenty-four combat casualties (FAMUS 1988:217–220). The number of deaths on the guerrilla side is unknown but the ERP admitted to suffering nineteen deaths between 15 July and 15 October 1975 (*Estrella Roja* 1975 63:2).

38. Díaz Bessone 1988:220–222; *El Combatiente* 1974 130:2; *La Nación* 12 August 1974.

39. The disappearance and execution of the fourteen guerrillas was confirmed in a 1983 court case against General Luciano Benjamín Menéndez (Seoane 1991:243).

40. Díaz Bessone 1988:218–219; Seoane 1991:242–243; *El Combatiente* 1974 130:2, 11; *El Combatiente* 1974 133:8–9; *Estrella Roja* 1974 39:18–19; *La Nación* 12 August 1974.

41. The ERP had already carried out some reprisal killings against the police in December 1973, but the suspected execution of fourteen guerrillas made them return to the practice in September 1974, this time against military officers (*Estrella Roja* 1974 40:2). The terms of reprisal were broadened in January 1975 to include civilians when the ERP executive committee decided that the assassination of revolutionary workers and union activists by the armed forces would be followed by the execution of businessmen, union leaders and government officials (*El Combatiente* 1975 151:2; *Estrella Roja* 1975 47:19).

42. *Estrella Roja* 1974 43:19.

43. Cited in Petric 1983:153.

44. Petric 1983:143–159; *La Prensa* 24 August 1975. The PRT-ERP denied that Larrabure was tortured, arguing that torture was not a tactic of guerrilla warfare. The guerrillas confessed that Larrabure had suffered from emotional instability, and had received medical treatment. Since the Argentine army did not want to exchange prisoners for Larrabure, the ERP offered him freedom if he would work for some time in an ERP weapons workshop. The major refused, and eventually hung himself (*El Combatiente* 1975 180:15 and 182:16).

45. *La Nación* 25 August 1975.

46. Between May 1973 and March 1976, there were 140 kidnappings by the Marxist and Peronist guerrilla organizations, against 85 for the period between January 1969 and May 1973. Ransom was in about half of the cases the reason for the kidnappings. The sixteen highest paying kidnappings, conducted between 1971 and 1975, grossed over one hundred million dollars. These victims were all executives of large corporations. American corporations adopted the quick payment of ransom as their standard policy (Purnell and Wainstein 1981:61). Public officials, prison personnel, businessmen, and professionals were often abducted to extract certain demands, such as a better prison regime, the rehiring of dismissed workers, or improved working conditions. Finally, military officers, politicians, union leaders, and foreign diplomats were abducted to make a political statement, such as happened in the case of Major Larrabure, Lieutenant-Colonel Ibarzábel, and the honorary British consul Stanley Sylvester (Moyano 1995:56–59).

47. Seoane 1991:332; *Estrella Roja* 1975 47:10.

48. Díaz Bessone 1988:295–298; *El Combatiente* 1975 164:16; *Estrella Roja* 1975 52(suppl.):4.

49. Mattini 1990:347–348, 392–393; *El Combatiente* 1975 158:5, 13, and 175:5. Another measure of mass penetration was through the PRT party's financial situation. The party's expenses came from donations and the sale of magazines, and were regarded as "an excellent barometer of the degree of growth and political connection of the organization to the masses" (*El Combatiente* 1973 83:10). Each member had to donate part of his monthly income for the revolutionary struggle. Budget deficits could on certain conditions be covered by the ransom payments extracted by the ERP through kidnappings (PRT 1977a:10–11; *El Combatiente* 1975 175:5, 10, and 180:4).

50. *El Combatiente* 1975 155:5.

51. Mattini 1990:385–388.

52. The assault was planned for 19 or 20 December 1975 but, ironically, had to be postponed because Air Force Brigadier Orlando Capellini arose in rebellion against the Peronist government on the 18th. Capellini wanted the armed forces to overthrow the Peronist government, but he did not receive any support for this premature coup.

53. Any estimate of guerrilla strength depends on whether or not one only counts combatants or also includes communication specialists, physicians, and so forth. Moyano (1995:104) mentions a figure of fifteen hundred ERP members in 1975. Her estimate is based on Mattini (1990). Surprisingly, army estimates were much lower. In the battle order of 28 October 1975, the total number of combatants organized in platoons or companies is estimated between 430 and 600 men (CGE 1975f anexo 1:appendix 4).

54. An ERP squad executed the informer Rafael Ranier on 13 January 1976 after he confessed working for the army intelligence service (*El Combatiente* 1976 200:5–6).

55. Herrero 1991:17–21; Mattini 1990:476–480; San Martino de Dromi 1988 2:110; Seoane 1991:276–286; *La Prensa* 24 December 1975. The Montoneros condemned the assault, because the ERP commanders knew that the attack had been betrayed. Furthermore, such large operations were incomprehensible given the strength of the armed forces. The Montoneros lectured the ERP that they should wage many small combats and avoid decisive battles (*Evita Montonera* 1976 11:26).

56. *El Combatiente* 1976 206:4.

57. *Nuevo Hombre* 1976 7:10.

58. Cited in Seoane 1991:286.

59. *Boletín Interno* July 1976 121:6.

60. Interview with Luis Mattini on 14 September 1990; PRT 1977a:33–34; J. Santucho 1988:221–225; *Combate* 1985 116/117:9–11. By late 1979, the PRT-ERP broke into two groups. Mattini headed one group which swore off the militarist strategy and dissolved the ERP. Former Ramón Rosa Jiménez Mountain Company commander Hugo Irurzún and Gorriarán Merlo went to Nicaragua to join the Sandinistas in their final drive to Managua. They assassinated former Nicaraguan dictator Anastasio Somoza Debayle in September 1980 in Paraguay. Gorriarán Merlo escaped but Irurzún was caught and died under torture (Andersen 1993:292–293; Blixen 1988:268–270; Seoane 1991:311–313).

61. Clausewitz [1832] 1984:87.

62. Gillespie 1982a:192.

63. Perón [1971] 1995:323.

64. *Liberación* 1974 23:11.

65. *Evita Montonera* 1975 3:28.

66. *Evita Montonera* 1975 2:34, 4:26, 8:25.

67. *Evita Montonera* 1975 8:25.

68. *Evita Montonera* 1975 5:36.

69. Gillespie 1982a:194–196.

70. Gillespie 1982a:197; *La Prensa* 29 August 1975.

71. Gillespie 1982a:197–200; *La Nación* 6 October 1975.

72. Interview with General Díaz Bessone on 12 June 1989.

73. Gillespie 1982a:200.

74. Gillespie 1982a:218–219; *Evita Montonera* 1976 12:14.

75. *Evita Montonera* 1976 11:16.

76. Gasparini 1988:83. Juan Carlos Alsogaray would be bayoneted to death a few months later in Tucumán.

77. *Evita Montonera* 1976 11:17. The term dirty war is explained further after the March 1976 coup. "This is a dirty war, like all wars waged by reactionary armies. It is not just dirty because it uses the people's sons to fight against their brothers and their interests, but because it doesn't even respect war conventions. The enemy assassinates the wounded, tortures and executes prisoners, and turns its brutality on the relatives of the people" (*Evita Montonera* 1976 12:32).

78. *Evita Montonera* 1976 12:32.
79. Critical intelligence reports by Walsh are cited in Baschetti 1994:206–240.
80. Cited in Baschetti 1994:225.
81. My description is based on the account by Walsh's companion Lilia Ferreyra in *Página/12* 24 March 1997; see also CONADEP 1986 [1984]:367–368.
82. *Evita Montonera* 1976 13:31.
83. *Evita Montonera* 1976 13:supplement; *Evita Montonera* 1976 14:50; *La Prensa* 19 and 20 June 1976.
84. Díaz Bessone 1988:328–329; *Evita Montonera* 1977 15:27; *La Nación* 3 July, 8 September and 16 December 1976; *La Prensa* 16 December 1976.
85. Gillespie 1982a:236; *Evita Montonera* 1977 15:7.
86. Gillespie 1982a:236–237; *La Nación* 19 February 1977; Díaz Bessone 1988:334–335.
87. *Evita Montonera* 1978 20:6.
88. CJE 1977, 10 May 1978 update, anexo 1, appendix 8:4.
89. CONADEP [1984] 1986:190; Gasparini 1988:173; Gillespie 1982a:258; Samojedny 1986:421–422; *Evita Montonera* 1978 21:7; *Vencer* 1978 0:38–45.
90. Montonero communiqué cited in PEN 1979:295; see also *Esquiú* 1978 19(955):5; *La Prensa* 2 August 1978. Lambruschini would become a member of the three-man junta in 1980.
91. Interview with Graciela Daleo on 24 October 1990.
92. Bonasso 2000:318; Gillespie 1982a:263–265.
93. Cited in Gasparini 1988:147.
94. Cited in Gasparini 1988:146.
95. The breakaway was a combination of personal fear, political ambition, a dispute for power and money, and strategic disagreements. They accused Mario Firmenich of militarism, triumphalism, elitism, sectarianism, and, probably most insulting, foquism (Larraquy and Caballero 2001:316–325; Mero 1987:170–171; *Humor* 1988 215:36).
96. Bonasso 1984:405; Gillespie 1982a:266–268.
97. Interviews with Ernesto Jauretche on 4 May 1991, and Fernando Vaca Narvaja on 27 November 1990.
98. Andersen (1993:117–118, 319–321) believes, on rather flimsy grounds, that Mario Firmenich was an army intelligence agent from 1970, and that he worked for intelligence battalion 601 during the 1976–1983 dictatorship.
99. A standard U.S. textbook recommended in 1973: "Guerrillas must be fought with guerrilla methods by specially trained units. The core of the counterguerrilla troops must be a highly mobile attacking force" (Momboisse 1973:493).
100. Girard [1972] 1992:47.
101. Arendt [1948] 1975:462–468.
102. Clausewitz [1832] 1984:75.

Chapter 9. The War of Cultures: Hierarchy Versus Equality, Christianity Versus Marxism

1. Speech by Videla on 4 April 1976, cited in Loveman and Davies 1989:198.
2. Cited in *La Nación* 14 December 1976; see almost identical pronouncements by Videla in *La Opinión* 30 May 1978, *La Nación* 31 August 1979, and *La Nación* 1 April 1980.
3. Scarry 1985:137. Ernesto Guevara meant precisely this when he wrote that the guerrilla fighter "is ready to die, not to defend an ideal, but rather to convert it

into reality. . . . to achieve an ideal, to establish a new society, to break the old molds of the outdated. . . ." (Guevara 1985:54).

4. Cited in *Somos* 11 April 1980.

5. *El Combatiente* 1976 219:8.

6. Interview with General Díaz Bessone on 24 July 1989. Díaz Bessone mentions only two conditions given by Aquinas for waging a just war. Besides approving of the right of a God-given authority to combat unjust violence and the right of self-defense, Aquinas also wrote about the importance of right intention, of acting with Christian charity towards enemies instead of just hurting and dominating them (Johnson 1975:39–41).

7. Interview with General Díaz Bessone on 12 June 1989.

8. Walzer 1977:21.

9. Walzer 1977:323.

10. Walzer 1977:252.

11. The reported cases of torture by guerrilla organizations are few, even though the history of communist and socialist regimes elsewhere in the world leaves us with few illusions that the Argentine revolutionaries would have been more benevolent rulers. Nevertheless, not the guerrilla organizations but the military dictatorship institutionalized torture as a practice of war.

12. Walzer 1977:176–182.

13. Corradi 1985:24–30; Cortés Conde 1993; Waisman 1987:36–47.

14. Fraga 1988:210–215; Scenna 1983:344–345; Seoane and Muleiro 2001:31–45.

15. Fraga 1988:233.

16. The military forced López Rega to step down as Minister of Social Welfare and commander of the federal police because of two army reports of May and July 1975 documenting his involvement in the Triple A death squads (Fraga 1988:168).

17. *La Nación* 26 October 1975.

18. Scenna 1983:343–345.

19. The first instigation to a coup occurred on 18 December 1975 when Air Force Brigadier Capellini rose in rebellion. He wanted the Peronist government to step down, the air force commander replaced, and army commander Videla to lead the country. The four-day rebellion failed in its principal aims, but air force commander Fautario was replaced by Brigadier Orlando Ramón Agosti, while Capellini was not even sanctioned. The legalists and the hardliners agreed on the need of a coup by late December 1975, and also agreed on the need of a cultural war, but they disagreed on the time frame of their intervention. The hardliners wanted an unlimited military reign, while Videla and Viola were proposing a transitional military government of three to five years followed by a gradual opening to democracy. Pressure from air force and navy made Videla give in to the hardliners to secure his place at the head of the military junta (Fraga 1988:246–247). It is important to note that both factions shared the belief that the disappearance and death of thousands of so-called subversives was needed. After the 1983 fall of the dictatorship, the softliners would conveniently blame the hardliners for the severity of the repression (Fraga 1988:207, 244, 252, 258; San Martino de Dromi 1988 2:110–111; Seoane and Muleiro 2001:57).

20. Seoane and Muleiro 2001:41–42, 68–71.

21. Fraga 1988:241.

22. Díaz Bessone 1988:325; Gillespie 1982a:225.

23. Deheza 1981:240–245; San Martino de Dromi 1988 2:189.

24. Communiqué cited in Graham-Yooll 1989:417; for in-depth analyses of the coup, see Deheza 1981 and Dearriba 2001.

25. General Feced cited in *La Nación* 16 August 1977.

26. Communications cited in Graham-Yooll 1989:417–426; San Martino de Dromi 1988 2:229–234.

27. The junta declared military rule for an undetermined period. The Minister of Planning, General Díaz Bessone, suggested in 1977 that a return to civilian rule might take place as late as 1991 (*La Nación* 6 September 1977).

28. Notary record cited in Verbitsky 1988:142–144.

29. Proclamation cited in Verbitsky 1988:147–149.

30. Proclamation cited in Verbitsky 1988:148.

31. See Lynch 1993:38–46; Oszlak 1990:45–84; Rock 1987:120–126.

32. A political program of the Process, written in 1978 by the lawyer Jaime Perriaux on request of the junta, distinguished four phases in Argentine history: (1) civil wars (1810–1853); (2) national organization and economic progress (1853–1916/ 1930); (3) economic stagnation and the alternation of military and civilian governments (1916/1930–1976); and finally (4) institutional innovation, political consolidation, economic progress, and historical revitalization (1976–). The text emphasized that Argentina had been the battlefield of the Third World War between Western Civilization and Marxism during the mid-1970s (Perriaux report cited in Vázquez 1985:167–168).

33. Record of Basic Objectives cited in Verbitsky 1988:145.

34. Interview with General Díaz Bessone on 26 June 1989.

35. Cited in Bourke 1972 7:112.

36. Bourke 1972 7:111; Maritain [1944] 1958b:36–38.

37. Genta 1976:412–413.

38. This concept of natural hierarchy makes General Díaz Bessone, and undoubtedly many of his peers, more critical of the French Revolution than the American Revolution. These two revolutions rest on different liberal traditions in which the first starts off from reason and the second from God (interview with General Díaz Bessone on 21 June 1989).

39. Exactly the same ideas can be found in Chateau-Jobert's book on counterrevolutionary guerrilla warfare, one of the texts used by the Argentine military. "Revolution is a permanent rebellion against the natural order which, on earth, places man in the first place. . . . It is a force of evil" (Chateau-Jobert 1977:12).

40. Bonasso 1984:56.

41. Cited in *La Prensa* 29 February 1980; see also Lieutenant-General Roberto Viola cited in *Clarín* 12 April 1980.

42. This obsession with the preservation of Western civilization and culture can also be found in the writings of Jacques Maritain. He lamented the disintegration of the metaphysical unity of Western culture, and regarded Thomism as the solution to the ills of Western civilization (Maritain [1931] 1958a:69).

43. The Argentine nationalists had in turn been inspired by conservative French theologians, such as Jean Ousset, Michel Crouzet, Georges Grasset, Jacques Maritain, and Etienne Gilson. Grasset was a military chaplain in Algeria and a spiritual guide of the OAS (Organisation de l'Armée Secrète) which waged a terror campaign on the Algerians (González Janzen 1986:55–57; Mignone 1988:94).

44. González Janzen 1986:61–65; Rock 1993:224–230; Vázquez 1985:190. The Catholic nationalist influence on the air force was particularly marked. For instance, Brigadier Capellini of the December 1975 rebellion was known to have been inspired by Genta, and so were the pilots fighting in the Falkland/Malvinas War of 1982 (Zuleta Álvarez 1975:766; González Janzen 1986:59).

45. Genta 1976:351.

46. Interview with Lieutenant-Colonel Santiago Alonso on 24 October 1989; interview with Lieutenant-Colonel Aldo Rico on 5 June 1990.

47. The Marxist guerrillas were keenly aware of the influence of these two ideologues on the military. Genta and Sacheri were both assassinated by the ERP in 1974.

48. Genta 1976:551. Even though Genta's thinking is only representative of the most nationalist and Thomist faction within the armed forces, his glorification of the military is by no means exceptional. The more moderate General Bolón Varela wrote that the patriotism of soldiers surpasses that of civilians. Soldiers have the privilege and sacred obligation to defend their country (Bolón Varela 1981:18–19).

49. First-lieutenants at the War Academy in 1978 were taught the fundamental opposition between the spiritual, Christian world view and the materialistic conceptions of life by communism and liberal capitalism (Escuela Superior de Guerra 1978:360).

50. The army had begun to pay attention to the moral and ideological preparation of its officers in 1974 (Directivas 1981). In 1976, Major Mohamed Alí Seineldín and then-Captain Santiago Alonso gave several courses of ethical-political instruction to the federal police and to army personnel at Campo de Mayo. These courses were intended to instill a proper fighting spirit.

51. Cited in CONADEP [1984] 1986:443; see similar statements by General Menéndez, *La Nación* 29 October 1977 and 3 November 1980.

52. *La Nación* 4 December 1976; Sarmiento [1845] 1986. Unfortunately, I cannot enter into a discursive analysis of public military rhetoric. For an interesting study of language during the dictatorship, see Feitlowitz 1998:19–62.

53. Cited in Goyret 1979:11.

54. Trinquier had commanded operations behind enemy lines in Vietnam between 1951 and 1954, and reported his experiences in American counterinsurgency training centers in Japan and Korea (Trinquier [1961] 1964:xiii).

55. Horne 1978:198; Trinquier [1961] 1964:30; *La Nación* 29 October 1977.

56. General Massu admitted later to the use of torture (Horne 1978:199). For a description of the French torture methods, see Trinquier [1961] 1964:21–22.

57. Horne 1978:201–207. The preferred torture methods were electric shocks, in particular to the genitals, holding a person's head under water close to asphyxiation, and pumping the victim's belly full of water.

58. Bignone 1992:40; Fraga 1988:23; General Camps cited in *La Prensa* 4 January 1981.

59. *La Prensa* 4 January 1981.

60. Horne 1978:198; Rock 1993:196; San Martino de Dromi 1988 1:144–148.

61. As early as 1960, Rear-Admiral Pozzi Jáuregui had given a series of talks to the joint staffs of the Argentine armed forces about guerrilla warfare (Pozzi Jáuregui 1983:197). See also Villegas 1962.

62. Anderson 1997:522; Fraga 1988:23; Loveman and Davies 1989:164; Mercier Vega 1969:86.

63. Anderson 1997:738; Armony 1997:158.

64. See similar statements by Lieutenant-General Videla (*La Nación* 1 April 1977), General Viola (*La Nación* 20 April 1977), and the unpublished manuscript by General Acdel Vilas cited in D'Andrea Mohr 1999:53.

65. *La Prensa* 4 January 1981.

66. Masi 1967:38; see also Villegas 1987:12.

67. Garasino 1970:8.

68. López Echagüe 1991:176.

69. This three-phase model was still accepted as accurate in 1977 by the intelligence experts General Martínez and General Jáuregui (*La Nación* 20 April 1977).

70. Leoni Houssay 1965:31–40.

71. *La Nación* 27 May 1978.
72. Cited in *La Nación* 8 September 1976.
73. Cited in *La Nación* 4 December 1976.
74. Leoni Houssay 1965:17.
75. Cited in *La Nación* 25 September 1979.
76. Cited in *La Nación* 15 March 1977.
77. Cited in *La Nación* 3 November 1980.
78. Generals Martínez and Jáuregui in *La Nación* 20 April 1977.
79. Proclamation cited in Verbitsky 1988:148.
80. Vilas 1976:9.
81. *El Combatiente* 1976 221:11.
82. Cited in *La Nación* 6 December 1976.
83. Cited in Simpson and Bennett 1985:66. General Saint-Jean denied in a 1977 interview ever having issued this threat, and accused the Montoneros of fabricating the quote (*Somos* 1977 38:19). Whether or not he uttered precisely these words, the main idea reflected military thinking. The following quote from Colonel Tedesco closely resembles Saint-Jean's pronouncement: "Their total eradication has to be achieved in 1977 with the undivided support of the population and the engagement of the forces of order. The support of this process must be integral and must eliminate the neutrals and the indifferents, because no one can remain absent from this fight" (*La Nación* 6 January 1977). Also, Vice-Admiral Lambruschini declared that, "The enemies are not just the terrorists, the impatient, those who place sectorial interests above national interests, the frightened, and the indifferent are also enemies of the Republic" (*La Nación* 4 December 1976).
84. For an elaboration of this argument see Robben 1999.
85. Cited in *La Nación* 18 December 1977.
86. Lieutenant-General Videla cited in *La Nación* 8 July 1976; see also Videla cited in *La Nación* 4 December 1976.
87. Cited in *Esquiú* 1976 844:15.
88. Cited in *La Nación* 14 December 1976. See also Videla in *La Nación* on 8 July 1976 and 13 November 1976; General Viola in *La Nación* 17 November 1976; and Generals Martínez and Jáuregui in *La Nación* 20 April 1977.
89. Agosti 1978:66–68.
90. Cited in *La Nación* 3 November 1976.
91. Cited in *La Nación* 5 August 1976.
92. Cited in *La Nación* 8 July 1978.
93. Cited in *La Nación* 19 September 1978.
94. Cited in *La Nación* 12 December 1976.
95. The military did not protect their own troops from persecution, torture, and disappearance. More than 135 conscript soldiers disappeared, some for being members of guerrilla organizations. General Díaz Bessone told me that he could never trust the conscripts assigned as his drivers. Others disappeared because of leftist sympathies or for having seen too much of the repression (CONADEP [1984] 1986: 355–362). The military did not protect each other's families. Jorge Landaburu, a retired brigadier and a one-time air force commander, moved heaven and earth when his daughter Adriana was abducted. Adriana was held captive by the navy and later assassinated (CONADEP [1984] 1986:238; see also the account by Adriana's mother, Puccio Borrás 1983). Emilio Mignone reported how Colonel Roualdes snapped at his sergeant announcing a colonel wanting to see him: " 'Tell him to go to hell.' And when he left, he said to me: 'Look, this man has a disappeared son, here, here below,' and he jumped, 'I have thirty-three children of military officers and not one of them is ever going to see them again. . . . I receive you

because you are a civilian and because you, you are not pestering me. But I don't receive them because they made a pledge not to ask for anyone and to shut up.'" (Interview with Emilio Mignone on 14 December 1989).

96. Cited in Vázquez 1985:239.

97. Cited in *La Nación* 24 April 1977.

98. *El Diario del Juicio* 1985 18:393.

99. CONADEP [1984] 1986:336.

100. Timerman 1981:98. General Luciano Menéndez went so far in his zeal to stamp out subversion that he forbade the teaching of modern mathematics in the high schools and universities of Córdoba in 1978. Modern mathematics denied the axioms of logic and, by stating that everything is relative, presented provisional structures instead of a coherent rationality (Vázquez 1985:204–206).

101. Cited in *La Nación* 4 December 1976. Even fashion carried the threat of subversion. For example, the miniskirt and string bikini undermined traditional dress codes. Thus, they were believed to give rise to hidden passions, lack of respect and modesty, to dissolve moral values, and to subvert people's defenses against the attacks of Marxism-Leninism (EMGE 1979b:74–75).

102. Boixadós 1977.

103. *El Diario del Juicio* 1985 31:585.

104. Cited in *La Nación* 23 October 1976.

105. Cited in *La Nación* 5 December 1979.

106. General Vilas cited in D'Andrea Mohr 1999:53.

107. Villegas 1976:25; Villegas 1987:12.

108. Cited in D'Andrea Mohr 1999:53–54.

Chapter 10. The Wheelworks of Repression: Assault, Abduction, and Annihilation

1. The museum opened its doors in October 1978 and was demolished in the mid-1990s. The museum was situated in the former house of the quartermaster-general of the Campo de Mayo army base. The initiative had been taken by General Bussi, the second commander of Military Institutes at the Campo de Mayo army base (Almirón 1999:203; Balza 2001:248; Bignone 1992:105).

2. Interrogator César Ernesto Segal cited in Almirón 1999:201.

3. Testimony of Sergeant Víctor Ibañez cited in Almirón 1999:201–204.

4. Masi 1967:39.

5. Interview with Brigadier Norberto Sciutto on 20 December 1989.

6. CGE 1975f:5; see also CJE 1977:6.

7. PEN 1975b.

8. Much was made after the fall of the military junta about the meaning of the word annihilation. Was the word intended in its vulgar meaning of physically killing the enemy or in its conventional military meaning of breaking the enemy's will to fight? Italo Luder declared at the 1985 trial that annihilation had the latter meaning, while General Osiris Villegas said in his legal defense of General Camps that the word annihilate means to exterminate (*El Diario del Juicio* 1985 1:2; Villegas 1990:44–45). Lieutenant-Colonel Aldo Rico agrees with Villegas. He argues that there are no material or territorial objectives in a war against irregular forces, so that the combatants themselves become the objective (cited in Hernández 1989a:47–48). The same idea can be found in U.S. counterinsurgency thinking: "The worst military mistake in fighting guerrillas has been to treat them as if they were conventional opponents. There are crucial differences between tactical operations against a conventional opponent and those against guerrillas. Against the lat-

ter, physical destruction of the enemy becomes relatively more important, control of key terrain less" (Momboisse 1973:486–487).

9. RC-9-1 army manual cited in D'Andrea Mohr 1999:74–75.

10. The PLACINTARA plan dates back to the CONINTES Plan of Internal Upheaval of the State from the 1950s and 1960s. It was updated for the last time in 1972 when the guerrilla organizations were well-established. The 1975 version did not undergo any substantial changes during the 1976–1983 dictatorship (*El Diario del Juicio* 1985 26:5–10).

11. CD 1975:4; CGE 1975f:2–3.

12. CGE 1975f:4; CGE 1976a; CGE1976b.

13. CJE 1979:3.

14. Zone 1 (Federal Capital, Buenos Aires province, and La Pampa) was controlled by the First Army Corps; Zone 2 (Formosa, Chaco, Santa Fe, Missiones, Corrientes, and Entre Ríos) by the Second Army Corps; Zone 3 (Jujuy, Salta, Tucumán, Catamarca, La Rioja, San Juan, Mendoza, Santiago del Estero, Córdoba, and San Luis) by the Third Army Corps; Zone 4 (the northern part of Greater Buenos Aires, the belt of suburbs and working class towns around the Federal Capital) by the Military Institutes; and Zone 5 (the southern part of Buenos Aires province, Neuquén, Rio Negro, Chubut, Santa Cruz, and Tierra del Fuego) was the operational theater of the Fifth Army Corps. A sixth zone was established on 1 January 1982 when the borders of Zone 1 and Zone 3 were redrawn, and the Fourth Army Corps was created. The new Defense Zone 4 comprised the provinces San Juan, Mendoza, Neuquén, San Luis, and La Pampa, and was controlled by the Fourth Army Corps. The old Zone 4 now became Zone 6 (Mittelbach 1986:10; CJE 1979 anexo 2–3).

15. Mittelbach 1986:9–11.

16. Fraga 1988:19; Mittelbach 1986:13.

17. Cited in Seoane and Muleiro (2001:52). Videla thus puts the responsibility for the dirty war on the Luder government, even though the military did not disclose the operational aspects of the fourth option. The plan to create a repressive structure parallel to the regular troops came, according to Seoane and Muleiro (2001:41–42) from General Hugo Miatello, the former head of the military intelligence service during the Lanusse dictatorship. Be this as it may, the idea of task groups disguised as civilians had already been practiced in 1972 by the navy.

18. See RC-8-1 1968:22–33.

19. *El Diario del Juicio* 1985 14:319.

20. *El Diario del Juicio* 1985 9:193.

21. Fernández 1983:23.

22. Cited in *La Prensa* 29 February 1980; Frontalini and Caiati 1984:33; Orsolini 1989:72; *El Diario del Juicio* 1985 18:393.

23. The term "patota" referred originally to a youth street gang, and came to refer in the 1960s to a group of policemen who specialized in torture and interrogation (Walsh 1995:286).

24. The COI in Zone 1 (Buenos Aires Province) consisted of two colonels, two lieutenant-colonels, and eight captains (CGE 1976c:6).

25. CGE 1976c:4.

26. CGE 1976c:5.

27. Mittelbach 1986:19–20.

28. Defense zone 4 is the only exception. Its relatively small size did not justify subzones but only areas.

29. Mittelbach 1986:13–14.

30. The larger area 3 fell under the jurisdiction of the army (Mittelbach 1986:28).

31. Bonasso 1984:118–120; CONADEP [1984] 1986:123–124; Gasparini 1986: 143; Martí, Milia, and Solarz [1979] 1995:19–22; *El Diario del Juicio* 1985 24:457, 32:3. According to Rear-Admiral Mayorga, there is nothing unique about Lieutenant Astiz: "Who is Lieutenant Astiz? Lieutenant Astiz is a Navy officer. There are three hundred Astices in the Navy, at least three hundred Astices, because the Navy made all officers pass through the task groups" (interview with Rear-Admiral Horacio Mayorga on 3 October 1990).

32. *Boletín Interno* 1974 68:2–3.

33. *Boletín Interno* 1974 73:4.

34. EMGE 1979a:60.

35. CONADEP [1984] 1986:284, 368.

36. Munck 1998:65–68.

37. CONADEP [1984] 1986:370.

38. Andersen 1993:179.

39. Andersen 1993:178–183; Munck 1987:212, 229; Munck 1998:80–85.

40. Whereas in October 1975 the principal enemies were the PRT-ERP and the Montoneros, in May 1976 the smaller organization Poder Obrero was added (CGE 1976c:1). I have not discussed the Poder Obrero because very little information is available about this organization.

41. Daleo and Castillo 1982:16; Mattini 1990:289.

42. CJE 1977 anexo 1:appendix 7.

43. CJE 1977 anexo 1:appendix 6.

44. Gasparini 1988:128.

45. Interview with Ernesto Jauretche on 20 April 1991. See a September 1977 internal Montonero document stating that the Montoneros had been taken by surprise by the abduction-torture-confession dynamic (*Vencer* 1979 2/3:xiv).

46. Interview with Ernesto Jauretche on 20 April 1991.

47. Guevara 1985:53.

48. Interview with Ernesto Jauretche on 27 April 1991.

49. Interview with Luis Mattini on 20 October 1990.

50. Diez 1987:86.

51. Cited in Seoane 1991:297.

52. Mattini 1990:498.

53. PRT 1985:31; Seoane 1991:299.

54. Diez 1987:102.

55. Mattini 1990:508; *El Combatiente* 1976 213:2.

56. Almirón 1999:200–203; Gillespie 1982a:241; Mattini 1990:503–505, 520–521; Seoane 1991:307–309.

57. Lenin [1904] 1978.

58. PRT 1985:38.

59. CJE 1977 anexo 1:5.

60. CJE 1977 anexo 1: appendix 1.

61. Gasparini 1988:153.

62. *El Diario del Juicio* 1985 21:412.

63. Interview with Mattini on 14 September 1990.

64. Interview with Cazes Camarero on 24 May 1991. Neither the Montoneros nor the PRT-ERP adopted the Algerian practice in which detained guerrillas were told to resist torture during forty-eight hours. After two days, their comrades had had enough time to hide in other locations and move the caches of armament. The PRT-ERP did not adopt this practice because they regarded it as a sign of ideological weakness and a lack of revolutionary faith. The guerrilla who resisted torture indefinitely represented the ideal human being, Guevara's New Man. The Monton-

eros did not institute the forty-eight hours practice arguing that the torture would not cease after two days.

65. *La Nación* 12 May 1977.

66. There was also intense repression in the countryside against the Agrarian Leagues advocating land reform to benefit the many impoverished peasants. See Feitlowitz (1998:110–148) for an account of the repression in Corrientes province.

67. Cited in *La Nación* 27 June 1977. See also the 1969 army manual RC-8-2 1969b 3:76.

68. CJE 1977 anexo 3:2.

69. CJE 1977 anexo 3:6.

70. In a publication by the Army High Command, the influence of students on labor protests is analyzed (EMGE 1979a). The military were strengthened in this conviction by Debray (1973:53) who had written that the university should be regarded as a political foco subsidiary to the military foco. It is at the university that theoretical debate was stimulated and guerrillas were recruited.

71. According to the CONADEP report, 10.61 percent of the disappeared in its sample were between the ages 16 and 20, 32.62 percent between 21 and 25, 25.90 percent between 26 and 30, and 12.26 percent between 31 and 35 years of age (CONADEP [1984] 1986:285). In other words, more than half of the disappeared were young adults in their twenties, many of whom were students.

72. Massera 1979:86–87; Timerman 1981:130; Mignone 1988:106–107.

73. CJE 1977 anexo 4:5.

74. CJE 1977 anexo 5.

75. CJE 1977 anexo 3.

76. RC-8-2 1969a 2:12.

77. CONADEP [1984] 1986:334; *El Diario del Juicio* 1985 3:5, 7:168.

78. Cited in *La Nación* 18 December 1977.

79. The Argentine League for the Rights of Man or LADH (Liga Argentina por los Derechos del Hombre) was popularly known as the Liga, the country's oldest human rights organization with close links to the communist party.

80. Interviews with Lilia Orfanó on 12 and 14 November 1990.

81. See Walsh (1995:289) for a description of a 1968 police raid which involved hooding and torturing two suspected thieves.

82. *Gendarmeria Nacional* 1972 8(47):62–66; M-8-1 1972. The armed and security forces also conducted house searches in entire neighborhoods, called *quinteos* (*quinto* means fifth). Every fifth house was searched for weapons and subversive books (*El Diario del Juicio* 1985 11:235).

83. CONADEP [1984] 1986:13.

84. M-8-1 1972:17.

85. *El Diario del Juicio* 1985 2:2.

86. *El Diario del Juicio* 1985 2:2.

87. *El Diario del Juicio* 1985 24:453.

88. M-8-1 1972:18.

89. M-8-1 1972:22.

90. M-8-1 1972:21.

91. *El Diario del Juicio* 1985 31:566.

92. *Gendarmeria Nacional* 1972 8(47):62–66.

93. M-8-1 1972:55.

94. M-8-1 1972:56.

95. *El Diario del Juicio* 1985 2:37.

96. CONADEP [1984] 1986:18.

97. Feldman 1991:97–98.

98. CONADEP [1984] 1986:11.
99. Piaget 1971:331.
100. Winnicott 1986.
101. The roots of this division lie in ancient Greek and Hebrew culture (Arendt 1958:22–78). A similar dichotomy can be found in contemporary Islamic and Mediterranean cultures. The opposition between public and private is elaborated in cultural values such as honor and shame, modesty and display, and loyalty and betrayal (see Peristiany 1965; Robben 1989a, 1989b).
102. Robben 1989b. See Feldman 1991:88–97 for a Foucaultean analysis of the transgression of the domestic sanctuary by the nighttime arrest of political suspects in Northern Ireland.
103. *El Diario del Juicio* 1985 32:594.
104. see Csikszentmihalyi and Rochberg-Halton 1981.
105. CGE 1975f anexo 4:2.
106. CONADEP [1984] 1986:280–281; *El Diario del Juicio* 1985 16:352.
107. Martí, Milia, and Solarz [1979] 1995:30.
108. *El Diario del Juicio* 1985 8:175.
109. see Robben 1989b.
110. *El Diario del Juicio* 1985 15:331.
111. CJE 1977 anexo 13. Detention card reproduced in Seoane and Ruiz Nuñez 1986:251.
112. Masi 1967:80.
113. Cited in *La Nación* 3 November 1976.

Chapter 11. The Operating Theater: Torture, Dehumanization, and Traumatization

1. Seoane and Ruiz Nuñez 1986:9; Lamas 1956:47–53.
2. Cited in Seoane and Ruiz Nuñez 1986:40.
3. Seoane and Ruiz Nuñez 1986:51.
4. *Boletín Interno* 1976 121:25; *Evita Montonera* 1976 13:32; *La Nación* 29 October 1977.
5. Seoane and Ruiz Nuñez 1986:135–140.
6. CONADEP [1984] 1986:319; Seoane and Ruiz Nuñez 1986:113, 142.
7. Cited in Seoane and Ruiz Nuñez 1986:159.
8. The use of torture by municipal, provincial, and federal police forces was a routine practice between the 1960s and 1980s, in times of dictatorship and democracy. See the descriptions of the torture of criminal and political suspects during the 1966–1973 dictatorship (Walsh 1995:290; Foro 1973:213–220). See Americas Watch 1991b for a report on police abuse during the late 1980s.
9. For a review of the testimonial literature from the early 1930s about torture during the Uriburu dictatorship, see Unamuno 1988.
10. Rodríguez Molas 1983, 1985a:81–103, 1985b:87–153; see also Peters 1985:105–114.
11. Lamas 1956:47–53.
12. Reyes 1987:156.
13. Feitlowitz 1998:33; Lamas 1956:120–122; Rodríguez Molas 1985a:117–121, 1985b:156.
14. Foro 1973:143.
15. Foro 1973.
16. *Las Bases* 1972 14:33.
17. *Militancia* 1973 15:13.

18. *El Peronista* 1974 2:43, 4:12; *Liberación* 1974 20:2.

19. Interview on 2 October 1990.

20. Gasparini 1988:149.

21. Foro 1973:147.

22. Feitlowitz 1998:57; Peters 1985:164; Rodríguez Molas 1985a:98.

23. *El Diario del Juicio* 1985 2:3, 45; 6:67.

24. *El Diario del Juicio* 1985 9:205.

25. CONADEP [1984] 1986:35.

26. *El Diario del Juicio* 1985 2:30.

27. *El Diario del Juicio* 1985 14:302.

28. Agger 1989:308.

29. *El Diario del Juicio* 1985 17:380.

30. *El Diario del Juicio* 1985 3:63; Seoane and Ruiz Nuñez 1986:162–163. For other examples of mock executions, see Samojedny 1986:398; *El Diario del Juicio* 1985 2:3, 3:60, 22:422, 24:453.

31. *Evita Montonera* 1975 5:20. According to an October 1975 article, 800–1,000 members had been tortured since the Montoneros went underground in September 1974, of whom 95 percent did not talk under torture, 4 percent supplied some information, and only 1 percent told everything they knew (*Evita Montonera* 1975 8:21).

32. *Evita Montonera* 1975 5:23.

33. *Evita Montonera* 1975 3:27. In her fascinating study of the Khalistan independence movement, Cynthia Mahmood observes in very much the same way that for Sikh militants, "A death conceived as martyrdom turns what looks like defeat into victory; the individual died, but in his or her bloody witness the truth lives on; the individual died, but the community to which he or she was linked continues" (Mahmood 1996:201).

34. The Montoneros were unforgiving of comrades who talked under torture. Fernando Haymal was executed on 6 September 1975 for causing the death of the important commander Marcos Osatinsky (*Evita Montonera* 1975 8:21). In February 1976, Montonero commander Roberto Quieto was given a death sentence in absentia after two dozen comrades had fallen into the hands of the police upon his capture on 28 December 1975 (*Evita Montonera* 1976 12:13).

35. Gasparini 1988:149.

36. *Boletín Interno* August 1974 66:2.

37. This rationalization fails to acknowledge the moral principle of surrender, namely that prisoners of war should not be harmed even if suspected of placing bombs. Furthermore, the hypothetical case ignores other solutions, such as vacating the school and using dogs to detect the device. It also ignores the problem of compliance. The uninvolved bystander cannot be differentiated from the guerrilla pleading innocence. Even nurserymaids might then become targets of torture, and their denial becomes then a justification for more torture (Shue 1978:135).

38. Interview with General Villegas on 5 November 1990.

39. Interview with General Sánchez de Bustamante on 6 December 1989. Villegas and Sánchez de Bustamante follow the instrumental reasoning of Brian Crozier who justified torture as the most effective means to acquire decisive information about a revolutionary organization (Crozier 1974:157–161).

40. The word *ablandar* (sofening up) is only one of many terms of the "lexicon of terror" analyzed so well by Feitlowitz (1998:51–62).

41. Kordon et al. 1992:442.

42. Charts were kept for each captive indicating the interrogator's nickname, the task group that had carried out the abduction, the case number, the time of

starting and finishing the interrogation, and the physical condition of the captive. There was also a Final Resolution form which indicated whether the captive was given a "final destination" (*destino final*), was imprisoned under the care of the National Executive Authority (Poder Ejecutivo Nacional), or some other resolution was taken (*otras*), such as freedom or forced exile (Simpson and Bennett 1985:90).

43. CONADEP [1984] 1986:61.
44. *El Diario del Juicio* 1985 3:63.
45. Cited in Seoane and Ruiz Nuñez 1986:160.
46. *El Diario del Juicio* 1985 3:63.
47. Interview with Major Ernesto Barreiro on 22 May 1990.
48. Interview with Major Ernesto Barreiro on 22 May 1990.
49. *El Diario del Juicio* 1985 27:6.
50. Gasparini 1988:125.
51. Interview with Major Ernesto Barreiro on 22 May 1990.
52. Gillespie 1982a:113.
53. Interview with Major Ernesto Barreiro on 22 May 1990.
54. *El Diario del Juicio* 1985 14:304.
55. CONADEP [1984] 1986:72.
56. Scarry 1985:56.
57. In her challenging study about Mozambique, Carolyn Nordstrom (1997) provides an intriguing account of how ordinary people undermined the claims to absolute power by the Renamo guerrilla organization by unmaking its violence through informal food exchanges, healing ceremonies, schooling, and creative expressions such as songs, poetry, and storytelling.
58. Suedfeld (1990:3) delineates four components to torture: (1) debility (induction of physical and mental weakness through brutal treatment); (2) dependency (tortured are at the whim of their captors); (3) dread (prisoners are kept in a state of anxiety and fear about their predicament); (4) disorientation (victims are prevented from developing coping strategies through frequent changes in torture methods and the confinement regime). These four components describe well the microsociological aspects of the relation between torturer and tortured but fail to place this dependency in a wider context which includes other torturers and other captives.
59. *El Diario del Juicio* 1985 22:422.
60. *El Diario del Juicio* 1985 2:39.
61. Buda 1988:35.
62. CONADEP [1984] 1986:58; *El Diario del Juicio* 1985 3:64.
63. *El Diario del Juicio* 1985 22:422.
64. *El Diario del Juicio* 1985 2:45.
65. *El Diario del Juicio* 1985 21:412.
66. *El Diario del Juicio* 1985 21:412.
67. *El Diario del Juicio* 1985 21:412.
68. Buda 1988:32.
69. Kordon et al. 1992:442–443.
70. Améry 1980:40.
71. Agger 1989:309; see also Lunde and Ortmann 1992.
72. Winkler 1991, 1995.
73. Agger 1989:313.
74. Suárez-Orozco 1987:241–242; italics in original.
75. Buda 1988:42.
76. Buda 1988:44.
77. Littlewood 1997:10–11. Littlewood mentions three other explanations for

the frequency of rape in war situations that are complementary to the idealization-degradation explanation: (1) the absence of any social constraints during war; (2) rape enhances male bonding among soldiers; and (3) war is conducive to rape because the first enhances arousal while the second seems to reduce anxiety.

78. Buda 1988:63.
79. Buda 1988:65.
80. Buda 1988:73.
81. Buda 1988:75.
82. Interview with María Elisa Hachmann de Lande on 23 April 1990.
83. *El Diario del Juicio* 1985 23:435.
84. See Jonsen and Sagan (1985) on the medical cooperation of physicians in torture.
85. *El Diario del Juicio* 1985 30:549.
86. *El Diario del Juicio* 1985 14:319.
87. Winnicott 1986:146.
88. Arditti 1999:22.
89. CONADEP [1984] 1986:305–306.
90. Partnoy 1986:54.
91. CONADEP [1984] 1986:308.
92. See also Gregory and Timerman (1986) for a Turnerian analysis of torture as a rite of passage.
93. Suárez-Orozco 1987:238.
94. Timerman 1981:148.
95. Timerman 1981:148–149.
96. CONADEP [1984] 1986:60.
97. Cited in *La Razón* 27 May 1979.
98. see e.g. Kordan et al. 1992; Stover and Nightingale 1985; Suedfeld 1990.
99. Scarry 1985:18–21, 61–63, 121–139.
100. Daniel 1996:143.
101. *El Diario del Juicio* 1985 3:63.
102. *El Diario del Juicio* 1985 3:63.
103. Gasparini 1986:142.
104. Winnicott 1986:36.
105. Bowlby 1981:292; Erikson 1951:219–221.
106. Bowlby 1981:414. Since I am concerned here with the anthropological rather than the psychological importance of basic trust, I will use the term social trust. Furthermore, although Erikson regarded basic trust as a universal stage of personal development, its manifestation has distinctly social and cultural dimensions because of the influence of family and environment on the child's budding self.
107. Gampel 2000:55; Robben 2000b:72–82.
108. Foucault (1979) has pioneered the study of disciplinary practices. He argued that the rise of a prison system in Europe made torture obsolete. However, Rejali (1994) argues that torture in many modern states often exists in conjunction with other disciplinary institutions.
109. Most psychological approaches isolate five major objectives of torture, namely information gathering, incrimination, indoctrination, intimidation, and the separation of captors and captives into two radically different groups (Suedfeld 1990:2–3). Although correct by themselves, these five rationales fail to capture the widening social dimensions of torture by focusing too narrowly on the torturer-tortured relation.

Chapter 12. Political Prisons and Secret Detention Centers: Dismantlement, Desocialization, and Rehabilitation

1. Bonasso 1984:371, 385–388, 397.
2. Rodolfo Mattarolo, Secretary of Human Rights, has given a figure of sixteen hundred survivors of secret detention centers, but the basis for this precise number is unclear (*Clarín* 11 December 2003).
3. Interview with Lilia Orfanó on 14 November 1990.
4. Pavlovsky 1986:47.
5. Samojedny 1986:560.
6. See the secret army order of 2 April 1976 cited in *La Voz* 22 July 1984.
7. Carlos Samojedny was detained on 11 August 1974 in Catamarca. He spent nine years in Rawson, and was later sent to Villa Devoto. He received his freedom on 18 June 1984.
8. Samojedny 1986:122–124, 309–313.
9. Gorini and Castelnovo 1986:48; Samojedny 1986:122–128, 165, 172, 309–313. The Rawson prison board was composed of the prison director, the assistant director, the head of security, a physician, a psychologist, and a psychiatrist.
10. Bignone 1992:91; Timerman 1981:29, 128.
11. Officer cited in Vázquez 1985:60–61.
12. The FAL (Liberation Armed Forces) kidnapped the head of psychiatry at the Villa Devoto prison, Hugo Norberto D'Aquila, in January 1973 to better understand the effects of the maximum security regime on political prisoners. The text of the interrogation was later published (FAL 1973).
13. The human rights organization APDH stated that 8,713 persons had been held as political prisoners between November 1974 and June 1979 (Fernández Meijide 1988:32). The CONADEP reported that 5,182 persons were arrested during the military dictatorship, adding to the 3,443 persons already imprisoned since November 1974 (CONADEP [1984] 1986:404). In November 1991, the Argentine Congress passed law 24.043 legislating the payment of damages for illegal detention to prisoners at the disposition of the National Executive Authority during the state of siege between November 1974 and December 1983. A total of 12,890 complaints were filed (*Clarín* 25 March 2001).
14. Samojedny 1986:42.
15. Samojedny 1986:40, 86.
16. Gavensky and Wagner 1985; Jauretche 1997:264; Samojedny 1986:54, 120.
17. Gavensky and Wagner 1985; Gorini and Castelnovo 1986:55.
18. Samojedny 1986:161.
19. Samojedny 1986:59, 74.
20. Samojedny 1986:66.
21. Bondone 1985:24.
22. Samojedny 1986:204.
23. The existence of permissive and repressive guards in each prison block was planned. Prisoners in Rawson who had been rotated through various pavilions discovered that the guards would play the "good guy" in one pavilion, and the "bad guy" in another (Samojedny 1986:238).
24. Samojedny 1986:240, 277; see for example the account of the suicide of Gabriel De Benedetti in Samojedny (1986:298–309).
25. Gorini and Castelnovo 1986:48–50.
26. Gorini and Castelnovo 1986:49.
27. Gorini and Castelnovo 1986:53.
28. Samojedny 1986:176.

29. Samojedny 1986:67, 77; for an analysis of acts of resistance by female inmates, see Nari and Fabre 2000.

30. Samojedny 1986:557.

31. CELS 1986:6; CONADEP [1984] 1986:198–200; Mittelbach 1986:20; *El Combatiente* 1975 173:suppl. 2–3.

32. CONADEP [1984] 1986:51. The annex to the 1984 report provides a list of 365 secret detention centers (CONADEP 1985). An update from 2001 raised the total number to 651 centers (*Clarín* 25 March 2001).

33. The CONADEP truth commission made a distinction between transit camps and prisoner assessment centers (CONADEP [1984] 1986:76). A similar distinction has been made between tactical centers (*chupaderos tácticos*) and lodging centers (*chupaderos de alojamiento*) (*El Diario del Juicio* 1985 14:309). Transit centers housed captives for short periods immediately after their abduction or just before their release or transfer to a prison. Captive assessment centers held inmates for extended periods until a decision was made on whether to assassinate them, release them, imprison them, or resocialize them. Since the majority of the centers were captive assessment centers, and torture and secret detention occurred in both places, I will use the general term secret detention center to describe both types. I avoid the often used term concentration camp to prevent a historical confusion with Nazi Germany.

34. Mittelbach 1986:20–23. The precise distribution of the secret detention centers is as follows: police (48.9%), army (23.3%), navy (5.6%), air force (2.2%), prisons (7.8%), national naval prefecture (1.1%), secret service or SIDE (1.1%), and other institutions (10%) (Mittelbach 1986:23).

35. CONADEP [1984] 1986:63.

36. *El Diario del Juicio* 1985 24:457.

37. In 1973, the term *perejil* was used by the Peronist left to describe someone who wavered between various currents of revolutionary Peronism (*Militancia* 1973 25:38). The military began to use the term in 1975 to describe sympathizers of the revolutionary left and those who had simply run along with the crowd without any strong ideological conviction. Another common explanation for the use of the term *perejil* is that the phonemics of *perejil* closely resemble the expression *Pérez el gil* or Pérez the jerk. Another explanation is that *perejil* is parsley, and parsley wilts as easily without water as these captives did under torture.

38. Both quotes in CONADEP [1984] 1986:59.

39. Buda 1988:45.

40. *El Diario del Juicio* 1985 14:312.

41. CONADEP [1984] 1986:72.

42. See Grubrich-Simitis 1981:421–422.

43. Timerman 1981:37–38.

44. CONADEP [1984] 1986:73; see Saporta and van der Kolk 1992:153–155.

45. Timerman 1981:91.

46. *El Diario del Juicio* 1985 14:303.

47. Lifton 1986:261.

48. *El Diario del Juicio* 1985 5:112, 7:161.

49. Bonasso 1984:119, 282; Daleo and Castillo 1982:36; Diez 1987:214.

50. CONADEP [1984] 1986:308.

51. *El Diario del Juicio* 1985 23:434.

52. *El Diario del Juicio* 1985 2:39.

53. *El Diario del Juicio* 1985 2:32.

54. *El Diario del Juicio* 1985 2:32; see also CONADEP [1984] 1986:290–292.

55. Daleo and Castillo 1982:48; Gasparini 1988:105; *Vencer* 1978 0:49–51. Clau-

dio Tamburrini, Carlos García, Daniel Rosomano, and Guillermo Fernández escaped on 24 March 1978 from the Mansión Seré secret detention center run by the air force (*El Diario del Juicio* 1985 7:162–163). Two other escapees are Oscar Alfredo González and Horacio Guillermo Cid de la Paz who fled on 18 February 1979 after more than two years in captivity (*Revolución Peronista* 1980 7:9). At least four captives escaped from the Campo de Mayo secret detention center, among them the Montonero Juan Carlos Scarpati (Almirón 1999:169).

56. Feldman 1991:122–127.

57. Graciela Daleo estimates that about four thousand captives passed through the ESMA, while Carlos Muñoz who worked in the photography lab where he placed the information about inmates on microfilm arrives at a figure of five thousand (*El Diario del Juicio* 1985 22:428, 24:457). The figure of five thousand was corroborated by Raúl Vilariño, a former ESMA task group member. Vilariño stated further that a total of two hundred captives had been released from the ESMA (Simpson and Bennett 1985:104).

58. *El Diario del Juicio* 1985 24:460.

59. Martí, Milia, and Solarz [1979] 1995:30.

60. CONADEP [1984] 1986:79–84; Martí, Milia, and Solarz [1979] 1995:23–33, 38; Paoletti 1987:156–159; *El Diario del Juicio* 1985 5:115–116. The cells and two torture rooms of the Little Hood were sometimes on loan to the air force, army, and navy intelligence services.

61. CIDH [1980] 1984:216–218; see also *La Nación* 1 and 6 December 1977.

62. *Vencer* 1979 1:26. See also Miriam Lewin (*El Diario del Juicio* 1985 21:413); Graciela Daleo (Daleo and Castillo 1982:5); Carlos Oscar Lorenzo (CONADEP [1984] 1986:251); and Carlos Gabetta (1983:45–46) about rehabilitation programs.

63. Interview with Graciela Daleo on 4 October 1990.

64. *El Diario del Juicio* 1985 21:415.

65. *El Diario del Juicio* 1985 5:115.

66. The names of the members of the staff and mini staff are listed in Uriarte 1992:186.

67. Gasparini 1988:106; Uriarte 1992:188; *Vencer* 1979 1:26. Simpson and Bennett (1985:291–293) regard the rehabilitation program as the brainchild of Navy Captain Jorge Acosta, the ESMA task group commander and Massera's principal military advisor until 1979. Supposedly, Acosta came up with the idea to enroll a select group of ESMA captives into a rehabilitation program, and have them work for Massera's political campaign upon the promise of eventual freedom. The problem with this explanation is that (1) several army centers also have been said to have resocialization programs; (2) it makes little sense to use captives when enough voluntary collaborators could have been found in Argentina; and (3) it seems unconvincing that Massera would entrust his political future to a group of captured Montoneros. Therefore, I believe that the political work of the ESMA captives was subordinate to the resocialization program explained in this chapter.

68. *El Diario del Juicio* 1985 22:424.

69. *El Diario del Juicio* 1985 21:415.

70. PRT 1972:16.

71. *El Diario del Juicio* 1985 21:413.

72. *El Diario del Juicio* 1985 21:413.

73. *El Diario del Juicio* 1985 21:416.

74. *El Diario del Juicio* 1985 27:2.

75. *El Diario del Juicio* 1985 22:429; see also *El Diario del Juicio* 1985 23:462–463.

76. *El Diario del Juicio* 1985 14:318.

77. Of course, my explanation cannot account for every single release. There

was considerable arbitrariness. Unrecoverable captives could be reclassified as recoverable and the other way around, depending on the political situation. Furthermore, defense zone commanders, task force commanders, and heads of intelligence had considerable freedom to make life-or-death decisions. Some were more hawkish than others, but all commanders kept many disappeared for extended periods in captivity and then assassinated them.

78. Martí, Milia, and Solarz [1979] 1995:52.

79. Already in 1970 an army field manual established that, "Prisoners only guilty of being members of an irregular force will need a complete reeducation and reorientation while they are detained. In time and in accordance with security, those who have shown the good will to cooperate may be considered to be set free on their word" (RC-8–2 1970:59).

80. It is striking that the four therapeutic interventions recommended by psychotherapists to restore torture victims—physical recuperation, psychological restoration, examination of past experiences, and reintegration into society—were also used in the Argentine resocialization programs (see Gonsalves et al. 1993:356).

81. Andersen 1993:266; Daleo and Castillo 1982:39.

82. Martí, Milia, and Solarz [1979] 1995:13–18.

83. Daleo and Castillo 1982.

Chapter 13. The Disappearance: Despair, Terror, and Fear

1. Interview with Elsa Sánchez de Oesterheld on 15 April 1991.

2. Interview with Elsa Sánchez de Oesterheld on 15 April 1991.

3. Even though many people disappeared into Stalin's Gulag in the 1930s, the Nazis were the first to use disappearances militarily. The Chief of the German High Command, Field Marshal Keitel, issued on 7 December 1941 the infamous Night and Fog decree (Nacht und Nebel) which sought to counter the resistance movement in Western Europe, notably in France. In a February 1942 directive, Keitel wrote: "the prisoners are to be transported to Germany secretly. . . . These measures will have a deterrent effect because (a) the prisoners will vanish without leaving a trace, (b) no information may be given as to their whereabouts or their fate" (cited in Amnesty International 1981:2).

4. Andersen 1993:45; Anguita and Caparrós 1997:66–70; Foro 1973:9. Felipe Vallese was also a member of a tiny Peronist resistance unit called the ELN or the National Liberation Army (Ejército de Liberación Nacional).

5. Cortázar cited in Cheren 1997:157; Foro 1973:9–10.

6. Foro 1973:10–12.

7. Botana, Braun, and Floria 1973:347. The disappearances became so common in 1972 that one human rights inquiry lost count, so it documented seventeen representative cases (Foro 1973:20–22). For a detailed description of a one-week ordeal of the torture and disappearance of one female captive, see Morello (1972) and *Primera Plana* 1972 10(483):34–38.

8. Foro 1973:10.

9. *Militancia* 1973 20:23.

10. CONADEP [1984] 1986:10–11; Machado 1974:97.

11. *La Prensa* 24 April 1976.

12. Officially, there was no censorship in Argentina, but the junta released a set of guidelines, known as *The Principles and Procedures To Be Followed by Mass Communications Media*, urging the press to foster Christian values and promote positive social models for the youth (guidelines cited in Simpson and Bennett 1985:234–235). Furthermore, dissident voices were intimidated and printshops which issued critical

books or magazines were occasionally set afire (interview with Emilio Mignone on 14 December 1989). All in all, this climate resulted in self-censorship within the media. *La Opinión* and the *Buenos Aires Herald* were the only two newspapers reporting some of the disappearances but their circulation was confined to the middle class in Buenos Aires.

13. CONADEP [1984] 1986:349–350; *La Nación* 5 and 10 July 1976.

14. *La Nación* 4 March 1977.

15. *La Nación* 15 November 1976.

16. *La Nación* 30 December 1976.

17. Timerman 1981:49–50. Similar statements were made in December 1977 by General Bignone and Admiral Fracasi (General Bignone cited by Ms. de Carlotto in Nosiglia 1985:133; Admiral Fracasi cited by Emilio Mignone in *El Diario del Juicio* 1985 18:392). The naval officer was referring to the May 1973 amnesty of political prisoners upon the installation of Héctor Cámpora as Argentina's president, and to Pope Paul VI's appeal to General Franco in September 1975 not to execute five arrested ETA members.

18. Fernández 1983:23.

19. Interview with Julio Morresi on 15 May 1990.

20. Cohen Salama 1992:228–232.

21. *El Diario del Juicio* 1985 6:2.

22. *El Diario del Juicio* 1985 11:233.

23. *El Diario del Juicio* 1985 3:71.

24. Cohen Salama 1992:271; Somigliana and Olmo 2002:27.

25. Grossman 1995:128.

26. CONADEP [1984] 1986:215–221.

27. Martí, Milia, and Solarz [1979] 1995:40.

28. Daleo and Castillo 1982:33–34; Gasparini 1988:106. Assales Bonazzola was seen in a secret detention center in Mendoza and never heard of again, but his testimony was brought out by surviving ESMA captives as they were released in 1979.

29. Martí, Milia, and Solarz [1979] 1995:40. The army also used this gruesome method of disposing of the disappeared. According to two testimonies, Hercules transport planes departed from the Campo de Mayo base at night, carrying forty to fifty sedated persons. Sergeant Víctor Ibañez has stated that captives were stabbed in the stomach just before throwing them off the planes to attract sharks and to prevent the bodies from floating to the surface (Sergeant Ibañez cited in Almirón 1999:177–184; CONADEP [1984] 1986:296–297).

30. Verbitsky 1995:59.

31. Martí, Milia, and Solarz [1979] 1995:43; see also *El Diario del Juicio* 1985 27:510.

32. *El Porteño* 1985 4:24.

33. Interview with Rear-Admiral Mayorga on 3 October 1990.

34. Somigliana and Olmo 2002:27.

35. Ruddick 1980:350; Winnicott 1986:145–146.

36. Weiss 1993:274–275.

37. *El Diario del Juicio* 1985 9:207.

38. *El Diario del Juicio* 1985 31:568.

39. Chodorow [1978] 1999a:85.

40. *El Diario del Juicio* 1985 2:2.

41. *El Diario del Juicio* 1985 32:594.

42. *El Diario del Juicio* 1985 32:594.

43. For other instances of parental and filial protection, see *El Diario del Juicio* 1985 2:30, 3:68, 8:171, 9:202, 14:312, 16:365, 29:536, 31:566–567.

44. Revealingly, most poems written by the mothers of the disappeared are about the childhood years of their sons and daughters, their innocence, compassion, and generosity. See Madres de Plaza de Mayo 1985.

45. Interview with Elsa Sánchez de Oesterheld on 15 April 1991.

46. Bondone 1985:30.

47. Herrera 1987:182.

48. Interview with Nora de Cortiñas on 23 October 1990.

49. Interview with Nora de Cortiñas on 23 October 1990.

50. Interview with María del Rosario de Cerruti on 16 April 1990.

51. Taussig 1987:121–122.

52. Interview with Nora de Cortiñas on 23 October 1990.

53. Interview with Matilde Herrera on 24 April 1990.

54. Sánchez 1985:163.

55. Herrera 1987:399.

56. Mellibovsky 1990:46.

57. Communiqué by the Army High Command cited in *La Nación* 28 August 1976.

58. *La Nación* 20 July 1976.

59. O'Donnell 1986; Corradi 1985:124; Suárez-Orozco 1992:243. In their important collection, Corradi, Weiss, and Garretón (1992) demonstrate that state terror was a continentwide cultural and political phenomenon in Latin America.

60. O'Donnell 1986.

61. O'Donnell 1986:254.

62. Cited in Arditti 1999:83.

63. Interview with Julio Morresi on 15 March 1990.

64. Salimovich, Lira, and Weinstein 1992:76.

65. *El Diario del Juicio* 1985 6:129.

66. Almirón 1999:194; CONADEP [1984] 1986:228.

67. CONADEP [1984] 1986:228.

68. CELS 1982:17–18.

69. Francisco Rubén Bossio cited in CONADEP [1984] 1986:232.

70. CONADEP [1984] 1986:231.

71. Cohen Salama 1992:34, 38.

72. CONADEP [1984] 1986:225–226.

73. Both the Argentine military and the revolutionaries loathed those large sections of the population that did not want to become involved in the armed confrontation because it undermined their belief in the justice of their cause. For a detailed discussion, see Robben 1999.

74. Interview with Rear-Admiral Eduardo Davion on 20 December 1989.

75. Interview with Brigadier Carlos Echeverria Martínez on 21 December 1989.

76. Cooke 1973:35.

77. CONADEP [1984] 1986:233–234.

78. Interview with General Virgilio Górriz on 20 December 1989.

79. Martínez de Hoz 1981:105–108.

80. Arendt [1948] 1975:474–477.

81. Many parents of disappeared children suffered from multiple psychological problems, such as crying fits, anxiety attacks, depression, emotional emptiness, profound sadness, insomnia, loss of appetite, psychosomatic disorders, and suicide attempts (Edelman and Kordon 1995:103; Sluzki 1990).

82. It is revealing that the list of disappeared compiled by the CONADEP did not provide the date of birth but the date of disappearance and the person's age at the time the report was published (CONADEP 1985).

83. Gorer 1965:131; Parkes 1972:8.

Chapter 14. The Search: Hope, Anguish, and Illusion

1. Interview with Julio Morresi on 29 March 1991.
2. Interview with Julio Morresi on 29 March 1991.
3. Grandparents, spouses, siblings, and sons and daughters were much less involved in the search of disappeared adults. Grandparents searched mainly for grandchildren. Spouses and siblings raised the suspicion of the military that they were likely to sympathize with the revolutionary organizations, and thus were reluctant to search actively. The relatively young age of most disappeared accounts for the small number of sons and daughters trying to locate their disappeared parents. Eighty-three percent of the disappeared were thirty-five years or younger (CONADEP [1984] 1986:285).
4. Interview with Julio Morresi on 29 March 1991.
5. Cited in Zamorano 1983:59.
6. Interview with María Adela Antokoletz on 9 November 1990.
7. *El Diario del Juicio* 1985 5:111.
8. Interview with military chaplain Grasselli on 4 September 1989.
9. CONADEP [1984] 1986:250.
10. Mignone 1988:14.
11. Interview with military chaplain Grasselli on 4 September 1989.
12. Gasparini 1988:206; Mignone 1988:13; *El Diario del Juicio* 1985 22:425.
13. Interview with Bishop Alcides Casaretto on 27 June 1990.
14. Interview with former Bishop Jerónimo Podestá on 1 June 1990.
15. Fernández 1983:63–66; Mignone 1988:138–145. The role of the Argentine ecclesiastical authorities during the dictatorship cannot be discussed here for limitations of space. For a discussion, see Burdick 1995:222–236, and Mignone 1988.
16. The first office at the Ministry of Interior where people could register the disappearances was located inside the Casa Rosada. Sometime in 1976, the office was moved to an annex where people had to wait inside, away from the gaze of tourists and fellow citizens (Bousquet 1982:20).
17. Bousquet 1982:45; Gabetta 1983:38–39.
18. *El Diario del Juicio* 1985 28:516.
19. *La Nación* 13 April 1978.
20. Cited in Ulla and Echave 1986:80.
21. Nosiglia 1985:102.
22. Interview with Julio Morresi on 29 March 1991.
23. See e.g. Puccio Borrás 1983:95.
24. *La Nación* 25 July 1976.
25. Mellibovsky 1990:251.
26. Hebe de Bonafini cited in Sánchez 1985:106–107.
27. Puccio Borrás 1983:92.
28. Cited in Ulla and Echave 1986:37–38.
29. Mellibovsky 1990:242.
30. Interview with Julio Morresi on 15 May 1990.
31. Interview with Julio Morresi on 29 March 1991.
32. Nosiglia 1985:158. There exists one documented political kidnapping case which occurred two years before the 1976 coup. The three-year-old Amaral García Hernández was abducted with his Uruguayan parents in Argentina in November 1974. The father was a former member of the Tupamaros guerrilla organization (Barros-Lémez 1987).

33. Nosiglia 1985:18–21.
34. Cited in Nosiglia 1985:14–15.
35. Cited in Nosiglia 1985:68.
36. Cited in Arditti 1999:92.
37. Chodorow [1978] 1999a:109. Nancy Chodorow has been criticized for over-simplifying gender differences and overgeneralizing the Western, middle class, nuclear family while ignoring single-mother households and the raising of children by homosexual partners. She has nuanced her thinking in later work (see Chodorow [1978] 1999a:xi). Be this as it may, her original 1978 interpretation fits very well the patriarchal Argentine society of the 1970s in which the traditional gender roles of working fathers and childrearing mothers were still very much in place.
38. Mellibovsky 1990:49.
39. Herrera and Tenembaum 1990:56.
40. For grandmothers receiving news about forced adoptions, see Nosiglia (1985:21, 42). For news about births in captivity, see Nosiglia 1985:40, 75, 87, 95, 118, 141, and Martí, Milia, and Solarz [1979] 1995:46–49.
41. Nosiglia 1985:117.
42. Martí, Milia, and Solarz [1979] 1995:45.
43. Arditti 1999:51.
44. Martí, Milia, and Solarz [1979] 1995:47.
45. CONADEP [1984] 1986:272, 294; Nosiglia 1985:87–90.
46. CONADEP [1984] 1986:286.
47. Arditti 1999:50.
48. *El Diario del Juicio* 1985 18:390; similar comments were made by Colonel Cerdá (*El Diario del Juicio* 1985 18:390) and General Ramón Camps (Nosiglia 1985:22).
49. Cited in Nosiglia 1985:106.
50. Interview with Matilde Herrera on 24 April 1990.
51. CONADEP [1984] 1986:289; Martí, Milia, and Solarz: 1995 [1979] 44–45.
52. Interview with Matilde Herrera on 24 April 1990.
53. Simpson and Bennett 1985:110.
54. Arditti 1999:24; Martí, Milia, and Solarz [1979] 1995:44.
55. CONADEP [1984] 1986:289; Martí, Milia, and Solarz [1979] 1995:44.
56. CONADEP [1984] 1986:294–295.
57. Nosiglia 1985:158.
58. Chodorow 1999b:240.

Chapter 15. The Call for Truth: Defiance, Resistance, and Maternal Power

1. María Adela Antokoletz cited in Simpson and Bennett 1985:169.
2. Aída de Suárez cited in Fisher 1989:60.
3. Interview with María Adela Antokoletz on 9 November 1990; see also Bonafini 1988:2–3; Mellibovsky 1990:36, 39–40. The precise pace at which the group of mothers grew is impossible to reconstruct but a compilation of figures makes it clear that the solid nucleus of fourteen women of April 1977 had grown into 50 to 100 mothers in July 1977. When the Mothers of the Plaza de Mayo Civilian Association filed for legal status on 22 August 1979, there were 150 members (Bonafini 1988:12; Bousquet 1982:52). Many mothers of disappeared children never joined the organization but did attend major marches.
4. *Buenos Aires Nos Cuenta* 1988 15:11, 56.
5. Jean-François Sobry cited in Schirmer 1994:186.
6. Fisher 1989:52.

7. Interview with Nora de Cortiñas on 23 October 1990.

8. Schirmer 1994:210.

9. Bonafini 1988:4.

10. Interview with Nora de Cortiñas on 16 November 1990.

11. Interview with María del Rosario de Cerruti on 9 April 1990.

12. *La Nación* 20 April 1977.

13. Bousquet 1982:59.

14. Interview with María del Rosario de Cerruti on 9 April 1990.

15. Interview with Nora de Cortiñas on 23 October 1990; Bonafini 1988:5; Bousquet 1982:63–70.

16. Bousquet 1982:71.

17. CONADEP [1984] 1986:129, 343; Sánchez 1985:149; Bousquet 1982:73; *Clarín* 8 December 2002.

18. Bousquet 1982:73–78, 84–85; CONADEP [1984] 1986:128–129, 343; interview with Nora de Cortiñas on 16 November 1990. For further details about the abduction and torture of the French nuns, see Gasparini 1986:127–138. In the 1960s, Alice Domon and Léonie Duquet had taught the catechism to children with Down's Syndrome. By an uncanny coincidence, one of the children was the son of future dictator Jorge Rafael Videla. Videla's son died in 1982 (Seoane and Muleiro 2001:334–337; Welty-Domon 1987:27–28).

19. Interview with Nora de Cortiñas on 6 November 1990; for similar views, see Jelin 1985:34; Navarro 1989; Oria 1987:81.

20. see Robben 1988.

21. See Chapter 1, note 55.

22. Sánchez 1985:141; Bonafini 1988:5. In early October 1977, the mothers took their plight to the only public crowd gathering allowed by the military: the annual pilgrimage to the Luján basilica. Someone proposed a white headscarf to be able to find each other in the crowd. Another proposed a gauze diaper. This is the most often told origin story of the white headscarf but there are several other versions. One account tells that the idea arose during the visit of U.S. Secretary of State Cyrus Vance in July 1977. Someone proposed wearing a white headscarf as the simplest way to recognize one another because Argentine women generally carried a white headscarf in their handbag (Mellibovsky 1990:106).

23. Cited in Gabetta 1983:57.

24. Chodorow [1978] 1999a:169.

25. Ruddick 1980:348.

26. The Argentine League for the Rights of Man, known as the Liga or LADH (Liga Argentina por los Derechos del Hombre) was founded in 1937, and had been closely linked to the communist party. Paradoxically, the Liga did not really confront the junta, in large part because of the strong economic ties between Argentina and the Soviet Union due to a U.S. agricultural boycott during the Soviet involvement in Afghanistan. Familiares, properly the Commission of Relatives of People Disappeared and Detained for Political Reasons (Comisión de Familiares de Desaparecidos y Detenidos por Razones Políticas), was founded in October 1976 as an off-shoot of the Liga, and was thus also regarded as politically tainted. The Permanent Assembly for Human Rights or APDH (Asamblea Permanente por los Derechos Humanos) was founded on 18 December 1975 by people with various political backgrounds (Peronist, UCR, socialist, Christian-democrat, communist), and therefore considered by many mothers as too much linked to the political establishment. The two remaining organizations were religious human rights groups. The Ecumenical Movement for Human Rights or MEDH (Movimiento Ecuménico por los Derechos Humanos) was organized by progressive Catholic and

Methodist clergy and laymen on 24 February 1976, while the 1971 Peace and Justice Service or SERPAJ (Servicio Paz y Justicia) was an international organization with branches in many Latin American countries linked to the progressive Catholic church. The Argentine branch was founded in 1974 by Nobel laureate-to-be Adolfo Pérez Esquivel. These two organizations were rejected because of their close ties to the church. I will not enter into the differences between individual human rights organizations because much has been written about their development, see Brysk 1994a:45–51 and Veiga 1985.

27. CONADEP [1984] 1986:133; Martí, Milia, and Solarz [1979] 1995:57–58. An analysis of the Argentine diplomatic offensive to counter the international condemnation of gross human rights violations by Argentina is beyond the scope of this book. For an in-depth study, see Guest 1990.

28. *La Nación* 8 May 1977.

29. Gilbert and Vitagliano 1998:83–85.

30. Bousquet 1982:120–124.

31. Both quotes in this paragraph cited in Bousquet 1982:125–126.

32. Bousquet 1982:128–131.

33. See army intelligence report CJE 1979 anexo 1:1–6.

34. Thelma Jara de Cabezas worked with the Mothers and Familiares. Vaca Narvaja's sister-in-law Patricia Lesgart organized the Montonero human rights campaign in Europe, and also had ties with the Mothers and other Argentine human rights organizations (interview with Fernando Vaca Narvaja on 27 November 1990; Bonasso 2000:312).

35. Díaz Bessone 1988:339; CJE 1979 anexo 10 (appendix 1):1.

36. FEDEFAM (Federación de Familiares de Detenidos Desaparecidos) was the Latin American organization. Its European counterpart was COSOFAM (Comisión de Solidaridad con Familiares de Presos y Desaparecidos). The PRT-ERP also became active in human rights, principally through the CADHU (Comisión Argentina de Derechos Humanos). The CADHU was a joint effort of Montoneros and PRT-ERP, represented in Europe by Lidia Massaferro and Rodolfo Matarollo respectively. CADHU had offices in Paris, Mexico, Rome, Geneva, and Washington, D.C. (Interview with Luis Mattini on 20 October 1990; Guest 1990:66–67).

37. Martí, Milia, and Solarz [1979] 1995:9–12.

38. "A person can be assumed dead when his or her disappearance from his or her permanent or temporary residence, without any further notice, has been reported officially between 6 November 1974, the date of the 'State of Siege' by decree no. 1.368/74, and the date of the present promulgation" (Law 22.068 cited in *La Prensa* 13 September 1979).

39. *La Prensa* 8 September 1979.

40. Bonafini 1988:12.

41. *El Diario del Juicio* 1985 5:116; 24:458; 26:488; 27:508.

42. CIDH [1980] 1984:289. The military government finally responded to the report on 29 April 1980. The response questioned the objectivity and impartiality of the report, its investigative methodology, its incriminating tone, preconceptions, mistaken assumptions, and improper inclusion of disputable cases and denunciations (Government of Argentina 1980:59–62).

43. María Adela Antokoletz cited in Bousquet 1982:161.

44. The prominent UCR leader Balbín provoked the anger of all human rights organizations when he declared just after the publication of the OAS report that "there are no disappeared persons; there are dead persons" (*La Nación* 22 April 1980; see also *La Nación* 7 May 1980).

45. *La Nación* 19 October 1980.

46. *La Prensa* 26 June 1978.
47. Cited in *La Nación* 30 June 1978.
48. Cited in *La Nación* 27 June 1978.
49. CJE 1979 anexo 9:5–6.
50. CJE 1979 anexo 9:7.
51. Bousquet 1982:153–157; Gasparini and Ponsico 1983:96–100; *La Prensa* 8 September 1979.
52. Bousquet 1982:158–159.
53. Bousquet 1982:164–165.
54. Munck 1998:88; Munck 1987:229.
55. San Martino de Dromi 1988 2:379. The participationist and collaborationist unions were organized in the Intersectional CNT-20 in April 1981, led by Jorge Triaca. The CNT-20 or the National Workers Confederation (Convención Nacional de Trabajadores) was transformed the next year in the CGT-Azopardo which had its headquarters along Azopardo street (San Martino de Dromi 1988 2:379).
56. Abós 1984:83.
57. Munck 1998:25–126; *La Nación* 7 and 8 November 1981.
58. Mellibovsky 1990:144–146. 10 December was chosen because it marked the thirty-third anniversary of the Universal Declaration of Human Rights. After the first Marcha de Resistencia in 1981, there was a ten-day hunger strike by a small group of mothers in the cathedral of Quilmes (Bonafini 1988:14).
59. *La Nación* 1 April 1982; *La Prensa* 31 March 1982.
60. Cited in *La Nación* 2 April 1982.
61. *La Nación* 21 December 1977, 26 April 1978, 29 September 1979, 7 March 1980.
62. Rock 1987:374–377; Torre and Riz 1993:336–338. The wish to reintegrate the Falkland/Malvinas Islands into the national territory had been expressed many times in the past. As recently as 5 April 1977, Admiral Massera had said that the junta was determined to recoup the islands in the near future (*La Nación* 6 April 1977).
63. The invasion had been preceded by failed diplomatic negotiations in February 1982, and the raising of the Argentine flag on South Georgia Island on 11 March by Argentine workers dismantling an abandoned whaling station. Captain Alfredo Astiz, who had in 1977 infiltrated the Mothers of the Plaza de Mayo, posed as one of the workers. The South Georgia Island was regained by the British on 25 April (San Martino de Dromi 1988 2:279–280).
64. *La Nación* 3 April 1982.
65. *La Nación* 10 and 11 April 1982.
66. *La Nación* 12 and 13 June 1982.
67. *La Nación* 16 June 1982.
68. *La Prensa* 5 October 1982.
69. *La Prensa* 6 October 1982.
70. The Mothers of the Plaza de Mayo had succeeded in making the Multiparty Coalition place the issue of the disappeared on its political agenda after much initial reluctance from the board members.
71. *La Prensa* 17 December 1982.
72. CJE 1983:6.
73. CJE 1983 anexo 5:2–3.
74. Klass 1989:152; Rosenblatt 1993:103; Rubin 1993:288.
75. In a paid ad, the pro-military Argentine Movement for the Defense of Sovereignty or MADES (Movimiento Argentino para la Defensa de la Soberania) accused the mothers of appropriating the Plaza de Mayo and disrespecting the symbols of the nation (*La Razón* 7 October 1982).

Chapter 16. Recovery and Reburial of the Past: Democracy, Accountability, and Impunity

1. *La Prensa* 27 and 29 October 1983.
2. CISEA 1984:436.
3. A declassified secret communiqué, sent in April 1983 by the American embassy in Argentina to the State Department, confirms the existence of this pact (*Clarín* 22 August 2002).
4. *La Prensa* 11 December 1983.
5. Bignone 1992:185; CISEA 1984:534.
6. *Paz y Justicia* 1983 11:5.
7. For this reason, the human rights organizations had initially wanted a bicameral congressional commission possessing the power to hear people under oath. Most human rights organizations came around eventually, with the exception of one faction within the Mothers of the Plaza de Mayo, headed by its president Hebe de Bonafini.
8. CONADEP [1984] 1986:264; *Boletín Público Ejército Argentino* 1984 4524:673; González Bombal 1995:205–206; San Martino de Dromi 1988 2:343, 360; *Somos* 1983 346:15.
9. *Tiempos Argentinos* 24 September 1983.
10. *El Diario del Juicio* 1985 7:156.
11. CONADEP [1984] 1986:428–437.
12. More than 1,640,000 people watched the broadcast, giving it a rating of 20.5 points, almost double the second most watched transmission, a tango program with a rating of 11.2 points (*Somos* 1984 408:8).
13. *Somos* 1984 408:6–8.
14. *Somos* 1984 408:11.
15. *Somos* 1984 408:11.
16. *Somos* 1984 419:26–28.
17. The CONADEP was of course not the first organization to investigate the disappearances. Amnesty International had carried out an investigation in 1976. The Association of the Bar of the City of New York had sent a mission to Argentina in 1979 (Schell et al. 1979). There was also the 1980 report of the Inter-American Commission on Human Rights of the Organization of American States. Finally, the CELS (Centro de Estudios Legales y Sociales) had been founded in 1980 by Argentine human rights lawyers to document the human rights abuses of the military government. Nevertheless, the CONADEP report surpasses previous investigations and publications by far in depth, breadth, and public exposure.

Several months after the appearance of the report, a 656-page supplement was published containing the names of 8,910 disappeared, their age on 15 October 1984, and the date of their disappearance (CONADEP 1985). The supplement also contained a list of the people seen alive in these centers by eyewitnesses. The inclusion of the age at the time of the appearance of the supplement suggested that the disappeared were considered to be alive until proven otherwise.
18. CONADEP [1984] 1986:9.
19. CONADEP [1984] 1986:4.
20. There were also critical reactions to the CONADEP report from a legal perspective. One sustained critique came from the conservative think tank FORES (Foro de Estudios Sobre la Administración de Justicia). Its report argued that the CONADEP commission ignored the increasing political violence before the 1976 coup, and the responsibility of the guerrilla organizations in paving the way for an illegal repression by attacking judges (Lynch and Carril 1985:18–28, 110–111).

21. A public poll of July 1984, before the appearance of the CONADEP report, revealed that 72 percent agreed that the guerrillas be tried in court, while only 13 percent replied that they should be killed (*Somos* 1984 408:20–21). These figures suggest, at least at this moment in time, that the Argentine people believed the military discourse about the guerrilla forces, but rejected the dirty war methods and wanted justice to run its course.

22. CONADEP [1984] 1986:447.

23. Rodolfo Walsh might have been one of the sources. In his first mimeographed report of December 1976, he arrived at nearly fifteen thousand disappearances for the first nine months of the military junta (Walsh 1995:408).

24. Interview with Graciela Fernández Meijide on 20 April 1990. Different sources gave different estimates throughout the dictatorship. The U.S. State Department mentioned 8,000 disappeared in September 1978 and 11,000 in 1979. The OAS Inter-American Commission on Human Rights affirmed 5,818 disappeared between 7 January 1975 and 30 May 1979, while the Argentine Minister of Interior, General Harguindeguy, admitted to 3,447 disappeared (*Somos* 1985 474:10). The APDH arrived at 7,940 disappearances between March 1976 and June 1979 (APDH 1988:32–33). Lieutenant-General Videla admitted in an unauthorized interview in 1998 to about five thousand disappeared (Seoane and Muleiro 2001:215). Alison Brysk has analyzed in detail this "politics of measurement" but does not venture to suggest a number herself (Brysk 1994b). Yet, in another publication, she refers to "tens of thousands" of disappeared (Brysk 1994a:1). In early 1995 Congress passed law 24.411 which offered damages to the relatives of persons who died or were disappeared because of military repression. By March 2001 complaints were registered for 1,637 deceased persons and 8,950 disappeared persons (*Clarín* 25 March 2001).

25. *Clarín* 8 September 2001; personal communication by Patricia Bernardi on 19 January 2004.

26. Amnesty International 1987:6, 10–11; Bignone 1992:174–176; Nino 1996:65–66.

27. San Martino de Dromi 1988 2:555–556.

28. Amnesty International 1987:18, 21–22; Camarasa, Felice, and González 1985:89–90; Montenegro 1986:41, 57.

29. *El Diario del Juicio* 1985 25:1.

30. It would take till 1998 before the tapes would be broadcast with a sound track on Argentine television (*Clarín* 11 December 1998).

31. González Bombal 1995:210–214.

32. The defense council considered the trial unconstitutional. For a summary statement of its argumentation, see De la Riestra 1989.

33. Ciancaglini and Granovsky 1986:126–135, 145–148; Montenegro 1986:43, 229; Nino 1996:84–87.

34. *El Diario del Juicio* 1985 20:5. Several arguments presented by defense council to dispute the trial's legitimacy were the same as those made against the Nuremberg trials: the trials were a justice of the victors, they dispensed post facto justice, the junta was deprived of the right to defend national sovereignty, and the junta members could not be charged as individuals for crimes of state (see Baird 1972:x).

35. Camara Nacional 1987 1:266.

36. Camara Nacional 1987 2:858–866.

37. General Villegas never pronounced his defense of General Camps because the case was taken away from the military supreme court and placed in the hands of the Federal Appeals Court of Buenos Aires (Villegas 1990:11).

38. Villegas 1990:182–184. Several of these arguments had been used in the

1980 response by the junta to the report of the Inter-American Commission on Human Rights (Government of Argentina 1980:59–62).

39. Interview with General Osiris Villegas on 5 November 1990; Villegas 1990:182–183.

40. This was not the first time that relatives of the military had mobilized themselves. On 22 November 1975, a large group of women pertaining to the Argentine Women for the Fatherland (Mujeres Argentinas por la Patria) paid homage to the victims of the guerrilla insurgency by placing roses (a symbol of slain blood) on white handkerchiefs with the names of the fallen at the side of the pyramid at the Plaza de Mayo (*La Nación* 23 November 1975).

41. Cohen Salama 1992:60–62; *Somos* 1982 319:11.

42. Cohen Salama 1992:85–87.

43. Mellibovsky 1990:58.

44. Cohen Salama 1992:120–122; CONADEP [1984] 1986:311.

45. Cohen Salama 1992:160–166; Martí, Milia, and Solarz [1979] 1995:48; *El Diario del Juicio* 1985 1:15.

46. *Somos* 1984 382:20.

47. *Madres* 1987 37:11.

48. *Madres* 1987 29:1.

49. *Madres* 1984 1:2.

50. Hebe de Bonafini cited in Diago 1988:157.

51. See Maxwell 1995.

52. Cited in Sánchez 1985:75.

53. Braun de Dunayevich and Pelento 1991; Edelman and Kordon 1995; Kaës 1991:160; Nicoletti 1988.

54. Around a dozen mothers split off from the Mothers of the Plaza de Mayo of about two hundred members. The parting faction called itself Founding Line (*Línea Fundadora*) because several of its members belonged to the original group of fourteen women that stood at the birth of the protest group in 1977. Aside from the reasons for the partition mentioned here, there was also a class element involved. Most members of the Founding Line belonged to the Argentine middle and upper class, while the members of the Bonafini group were mostly lower middle and working class (Guzman Bouvard 1994:162–163).

55. Interviews with María Adela Antokoletz (9 November 1990), Hebe de Bonafini (9 April 1990), María del Rosario de Cerruti (9 April 1990), Nora de Cortiñas (16 November 1990), and Renée Epelbaum (28 May 1990). Guzman Bouvard 1994:162–164; Mellibovsky 1990:191–192.

56. Americas Watch 1991a:45.

57. Mario Firmenich was sentenced to thirty years in prison in May 1987 (San Martino de Dromi 1988 2:547).

58. Americas Watch 1991a:48; López 1988:66; Nino 1996:90–94; San Martino de Dromi 1988 2:560–563.

59. See Lieutenant-Colonel Aldo Rico cited in Hernández 1989a:38.

60. Interview with Lieutenant-Colonel Santiago Alonso on 21 November 1989.

61. Chumbita 1990:17; Grecco and González 1988:32–33.

62. Interview with Major Ernesto Barreiro on 22 May 1990; Giussani 1987b:247–248.

63. Interview with Major Ernesto Barreiro on 22 May 1990; Grecco and González 1988:52, 69; López 1988:77.

64. López 1988:61, 77, 86; Norden 1996:117, 123.

65. Cited in Grecco and González 1988:197.

66. Giussani 1987b:255–258.

67. Interview with Lieutenant-Colonel Aldo Rico on 24 September 1990; Giussani 1987b:261–262.

68. Cited in Grecco and González 1988:224–225; for a slightly different rendition, see Giussani 1987b:262–263.

69. Cited in Grecco and González 1988:289.

70. Already in August 1983, Alfonsín had announced that he would not prosecute every member of the armed and security forces because many lower-ranked officers had acted under the due obedience pressure of their superiors. Alfonsín had arrived at this decision under the fear that the prosecution of all violators would provoke a furious reaction from the military (Giussani 1987b:238–239; Nino 1996:63–64).

71. Interview with Major Ernesto Barreiro on 22 May 1990.

72. Cited in Hernández 1989a:68.

73. See Lieutenant-Colonel Aldo Rico cited in Hernández 1989a:45.

74. The two 1988 rebellions concerned mostly internal issues within the armed forces that do not require further elaboration here. For their analysis, see Chumbita 1990:68–78, 108–120; López 1988:133–147; Norden 1996:130–135.

75. *Clarín* 25 January 1989; *La Nación* 24 January and 1 February 1989; *La Razón* 23 January 1989; *Página/12* 24 and 25 January, 16 February 1989.

76. *Página/12* 23 July and 26 September 1989; *La Nación* 12 September 1989. On 12 January 1989, the group denounced a conspiracy by Colonel Seineldín, presidential candidate Carlos Menem and union leader Lorenzo Miguel to stage an institutional coup against Alfonsín (*Página/12* 13 and 20 January 1989). Several conspiracy theories have circulated about the masterminds behind the La Tablada attack, in particular members of the Argentine intelligence service and the Alfonsín government (Hernández 1989b).

77. *Página/12* 16 February 1989; Americas Watch 1991a:78–80; Chumbita 1990:136.

78. *La Nación* 6 October 1989. Gorriarán Merlo and sixteen companions recovered their freedom on 20 May 2003 thanks to a presidential pardon.

79. *La Nación* 29 May, 2 July, 16 July 1989.

80. *La Nación, La Prensa, Página/12, Sur* 8 October 1989; *Página/12* 10 October 1989.

81. Cited in *La Nación* 17 June 1990; see *La Nación* 27 May 1990 for Menem's declaration about the shared responsibility of guerrillas and military.

82. *Página/12* 21 July and 21 November 1990.

83. *La Nación* 4 and 5 December 1990; *Página/12* 4, 5 and 6 December 1990; Norden 1996:149–154. Colonel Seineldín did not participate personally in the rebellion because he was undergoing a sixty-day arrest for his public criticism of President Menem. Still, Seineldín was regarded as the mastermind behind the uprising, and convicted. He was freed, together with seven other rebels, after a presidential pardon on 20 May 2003.

84. *La Nación* 30 and 31 December 1990; *Página/12* and *Sur* 30 December 1990. Brigadier-General Agosti had already been released on 8 May 1989 for completing his sentence, while awaiting his trial for overthrowing the constitutional government of María Estela Martínez de Perón. Agosti, Videla, and Massera were all three pardoned for the coup.

85. Cited in *La Nación* 10 October 1989.

86. Cited in Diago 1988:122.

87. *Madres* 1988 48:17.

88. Hebe de Bonafini cited in *Madres* 1989 53:17.

89. Hebe de Bonafini cited in *Página/12* 22 December 1989.

90. For an elaboration of the political significance of reburials, see Robben 2000a.

91. The belief that the relatives of reburied disappeared would forget the dirty war proved to be ungrounded. Many relatives who recovered their loved ones continue to be active in human rights organizations. They endorse exhumations and reburials, demand restitution payments, hold public commemorations, erect memorials, write memoirs, promote artistic expressions, compile archives, continue to search for abducted children, and pursue human rights issues (better housing, health facilities, and police training) by political means. These ways of remembering the traumatic past imply a societal desire to restore the symbolic order damaged by political violence and terror.

92. Interview with Julio Morresi on 29 March 1991.

93. Cited in Cohen Salama 1992:249.

94. Cited in Cohen Salama 1992:250.

95. Cohen Salama 1992:250.

96. See Hertz 1960:54.

97. Katherine Verdery (1999:25) has analyzed exhumations and reburials as manifestations of political transformation in postsocialist European states. A similar approach to Argentina would be fruitful but I have chosen to focus on the implications of reburials for understanding social trauma.

Conclusion: The Spirals of Violence and Trauma

1. Cited in Verbitsky 1995:58.

2. Verbitsky 1995:192.

3. There had been at least two earlier public confessions, one by a police inspector (Fernández 1983) and another by a corporal (Vilariño 1984). These testimonies did not raise the public storm of Scilingo's confession because Fernández and Vilariño were of low rank, and their declarations were made in 1983 amidst the grueling revelations of former disappeared.

4. Daniel 1996; Feldman 1991; Taussig 1987.

5. Feinmann 1999:76.

6. I shall not attempt to define the concept of violence here, even though Carolyn Nordstrom and myself have tried to do so in the past (Robben and Nordstrom 1995:6). For several different approaches to the concept of violence, see Nagengast 1994, Lutz and Nonini 1999, and Sluka 2000.

7. According to Girard, "the mimetic character of violence is so intense that once violence is installed in a community, it cannot burn itself out" (Girard [1972] 1992:81). Girard bases the self-perpetuating mechanism of the reverberating violence on the equivalence of the reciprocal blows, and he takes recourse to the sacrifice of a scapegoat to end the spiral of violence. In Argentina, instead, there was no scapegoating because the violence was generally targeted at recognizable political actors.

8. See Merridale 2000:326–333; Kirmayer 1996; Last 2000; Young 1995.

9. Plotkin 2001.

10. Green 1990:1633; McNally 2003a:78.

11. Benyakar 2003:117–124; Krystal 1968, 1985.

12. See Erikson 1995; Neal 1998; Sztompka 2000; Watson 1994. Massive trauma may be transmitted to other generations as memories of unmourned and unintegrated experiences of violence. However, McNally (2003a, 2003b) casts doubt on the existence of secondary psychic traumatization, even though studies have shown that children of Holocaust survivors have developed severe psychological problems,

such as extreme anxiety, low self-esteem, social withdrawal, impaired reality testing, and persecutory dreams (Bar-On 1995; Bergmann and Jucovy 1982; Grubrich-Simitis 1981). Irrespective of whether or not cumulative psychic trauma exists, the Argentine case demonstrates the existence of transgenerational social trauma.

13. Sztompka 2000.

14. The third characteristic consists of behavioral disturbances like insomnia, concentration problems, and exaggerated startle (McNally 2003b:230–231).

15. Brett 1993; Carlson 1997:26–34, 43–49; Krystal 1985; van der Kolk 1989. Allan Young has analyzed the medicalization of psychic trauma in an excellent historiography of the PTSD concept (Young 1995). PTSD is a diagnostic tool that relies heavily on symptomatology, but does not attempt to explain psychic trauma. A more comprehensive diagnosis has been proposed, inter alia, by Judith Herman who prefers the term "complex post-traumatic disorder" (Herman 1992:118–122).

16. Benyakar (2003:30, 60–61) provides an interesting clinical analysis of the psychic and social disruption caused by violent political conflicts. He rejects the term trauma to describe social reactions to disasters, preferring the term disruptive environment instead.

17. Brett 1993; Mitchell and Black 1995:118–122.

18. LaCapra 1998:9.

19. Mitscherlich and Mitscherlich 1975; Adorno [1959] 1986; Santner 1990:1–30; Friedlander 1993:1–21; LaCapra 1994: 205–223; Segev [1991] 2000.

20. McNally 2003a:190, 275.

21. See Schacter (1996: 218–233) for a psychological explanation of psychogenic amnesia, as well as the eventual chances of recall.

22. Caruth 1995:153.

23. Caruth (1995, 1996) suggests that the refusal to force the inexplicable into interpretational schemata, and instead to bear witness, to listen, and allow testimony to unfold itself with all its contradictions and enigmas, is an alternative way of remembering. Likewise, Culbertson (1995) draws attention to the importance of embodied memory (smells, sounds, movements, aches, numbness) which cannot be translated into narrative memory.

24. Caruth 1996:17.

25. Caruth 1995:153; Gampel 2000:50–55; Saporta and van der Kolk 1992:152.

26. Verbitsky 1995:42, 180.

27. Robben 1996.

28. Captain Scilingo did not survive his confession unscathed. He was attacked on 11 September 1997 by four men. The men forced him into their car, warned him to stop talking to the press, and then carved into his face the initials of the three journalists who had interviewed him. Soon after, Scilingo traveled to Spain to testify in a lawsuit at the court of judge Garzón. After his testimony, Scilingo was taken into preventive custody for his crimes and arraigned in July 2003 (Feitlowitz 1998:254–255; *New York Times* 12 September 1997; *Clarín* 2 July 2003).

29. Feitlowitz 1998:206.

30. *Clarín* 26 April 1995; see also Balza 2001:256–263.

31. The declarations by the commanders of the armed forces were not uniformly shared within the military. A group of seventy retired generals, many of them active during the dictatorship, defended the repression (*La Nación* 6 May 1995).

32. Feitlowitz 1998:193, 225–226, 236.

33. *El País* 13 June 1998; see also *Clarín* 24 January 1999, and Balza 2001:277.

34. *Clarín* 10 June 1998.

35. *Clarín* 7 December 1998. Since the arrests of Videla and Massera, other high-

ranking officers, NCOs, police commissioners, and several civilians have been accused of playing a role in the abduction of babies. By mid-2000, thirty-two persons had been charged with baby theft (*Clarín* 23 July 2000). One lieutenant-colonel was convicted in June 2001 and sentenced to nine and a half years (*Clarín* 29 June 2001).

36. The organization was first called Argentine Grandmothers with Disappeared Small Grandchildren (Abuelas Argentinas con Nietitos Desaparecidos). The name was changed to Grandmothers of the Plaza de Mayo (Abuelas de Plaza de Mayo) in late 1979 (Arditti 1999:187–188; Nosiglia 1985:148). They became registered as a legal nonprofit organization in July 1982.

37. Interview with Nora de Cortiñas on 16 November 1990; Arditti 1999:37, 52–53; Nosiglia 1985:44, 90.

38. Nosiglia 1985:150.

39. Arditti 1999:65–66; Bousquet 1982:133–136.

40. Arditti 1999:67; Arijón and Martínez 1997.

41. Abuelas 1987:99; Nosiglia 1985:171–175.

42. Arditti 1999:72–73; Nosiglia 1985:157–162.

43. Abuelas 1987:3; Arditti 1999:103; Arijón and Martínez 1997; *Clarín* 17 December 2003.

44. Arijón and Martínez 1997.

45. Arijón and Martínez 1997.

46. In 1995, Congress passed law 24.411 in which first-degree relatives of the disappeared or assassinated were entitled to $200,000 indemnification. In March 1998, already 655 million U.S. dollars had been paid to nearly eight thousand persons (Duhalde 1999:70). By March 2001, 8,950 requests were deposited on behalf of disappeared persons, while 1,637 requests were made for persons who were assassinated during the military repression (*Clarín* 25 March 2001).

47. *Hijos* website 2001; see also Gelman and La Madrid 1997, and De Mano en Mano 2002.

48. Cited in Gelman and La Madrid 1997:311.

49. Sztompka 2000:456.

50. *Clarín* 30 August 2003.

51. *Clarín* 13 March 2001.

52. *Clarín* 30 August 2001.

53. *Clarín* 8 May 2002.

54. See e.g. Schacter 1996:5.

55. Nora 1978, 1984.

56. Young 1993, 1994; Connerton 1989; LaCapra 1998:184–196.

Bibliography

Published Works

Abós, Alvaro. 1984. *Las organizaciones sindicales y el poder militar (1976–1983)*. Buenos Aires: Centro Editor de América Latina.

Abuelas de Plaza de Mayo. 1987. *Niños desaparecidos en la Argentina desde 1976*. Buenos Aires: Abuelas de Plaza de Mayo.

Adorno, Theodor W. 1986 [1959]. "What Does Coming to Terms with the Past Mean?" In *Bitburg in Moral and Political Perspective*, ed. Geoffrey H. Hartman, 114–29. Bloomington: Indiana University Press.

Agger, Inger. 1989. "Sexual Torture of Political Prisoners: An Overview." *Journal of Traumatic Stress* 2(3): 305–18.

Agosti, Orlando Ramón. 1978. *Discursos del Comandante en Jefe de la Fuerza Aerea Argentina Brigadier-General Orlando Ramón Agosti*. Buenos Aires: Author's edition.

Alarcón, Roque. 1989. *Cordobazo*. Buenos Aires: Editorial Enmarque.

Almirón, Fernando. 1999. *Campo Santo*. Buenos Aires: Editorial 21.

Amaral, Samuel. 1993. "El avión negro: Retórica y práctica de la violencia." In *Perón: Del exilio al poder*, ed. Samuel Amaral and Mariano Ben Plotkin, pp.69–94. Buenos Aires: Cántaro Editores.

Americas Watch. 1991a. *Truth and Partial Justice in Argentina: An Update*. New York: Human Rights Watch.

———. 1991b. *Police Violence in Argentina*. New York: Human Rights Watch.

Améry, Jean. 1980. *At the Mind's Limits: Contemplations by a Survivor on Auschwitz and Its Realities*. Bloomington: Indiana University Press.

Amnesty International. 1981. *"Disappearances": A Workbook*. New York: Amnesty International.

———. 1987. *Argentina: The Military Juntas and Human Rights*. London: Amnesty International.

Andersen, Martin Edward. 1993. *Dossier Secreto: Argentina's Desaparecidos and the Myth of the "Dirty War"*. Boulder, Colo.: Westview Press.

Anderson, Jon Lee. 1997. *Che Guevara: A Revolutionary Life*. New York: Grove Press.

Anguita, Eduardo and Martín Caparrós. 1997. *La Voluntad: Una historia de la militancia revolucionaria en la Argentina*. Vol. 1, *1966–1973*. Buenos Aires: Grupo Editorial Norma.

Anzorena, Oscar R. 1988. *Tiempo de violencia y utopía (1966–1976)*. Buenos Aires: Editorial Contrapunto.

———. 1989. *JP: Historia de la Juventud Peronista (1955–1988)*. Buenos Aires: Ediciones del Cordón.

Arditti, Rita. 1999. *Searching for Life: The Grandmothers of the Plaza de Mayo and the Disappeared Children of Argentina*. Berkeley: University of California Press.

Arendt, Hannah. 1958. *The Human Condition.* Chicago: University of Chicago Press.
———. 1975 [1948], *The Origins of Totalitarianism.* San Diego: Harcourt Brace.
Arijón, Gonzalo and Virginia Martínez. 1997. *For These Eyes.* Film distributed by First Run/Icarus Films, New York.
Armony, Ariel C. 1997. *Argentina, the United States, and the Anti-Communist Crusade in Central America, 1977–1984.* Athens: Ohio University Press.
Arrom, Silvia M. and Servando Ortoll. 1996. *Riots in the Cities: Popular Politics and the Urban Poor in Latin America, 1765–1910.* Wilmington, Del.: Scholarly Resources.
Babini, Nicolás. 1967. "Pesadilla de una siesta de verano." *Todo Es Historia* 5:8–22.
Baird, Jay W. 1972. "Introduction." In *From Nuremberg to My Lai*, ed. Jay W. Baird, vii–xvii. Lexington, Mass.: D.C. Heath.
Balvé, Beba C. and Beatriz S. Balvé. 1989. *El '69 huelga política de masas: Rosariazo, Cordobazo, Rosariazo.* Buenos Aires: Editorial Contrapunto.
Balvé, Beba C., Juan Carlos Marín, and Miguel Murmis. 1973. *Lucha de calles, Lucha de clases: Elementos para su análisis, Córdoba 1971–1969.* Buenos Aires: Rosa Blindada.
Balza, Martín Antonio. 2001. *Dejo constancia: Memorias de un general argentino.* Buenos Aires: Planeta.
Bar-On, Dan. 1995. *Fear and Hope: Three Generations of the Holocaust.* Cambridge, Mass.: Harvard University Press.
Barros-Lémez, Alvaro. 1987. *Amaral: Crónica de una vida.* Montevideo: Monte Sexto.
Barrows, Susanna. 1981. *Distorting Mirrors: Visions of the Crowd in Late Nineteenth-Century France.* New Haven, Conn.: Yale University Press.
Baschetti, Roberto, ed. 1988. *Documentos de la resistencia peronista, 1955–1970.* Buenos Aires: Puntosur Editores.
———. 1994. *Rodolfo Walsh, vivo.* Buenos Aires: Ediciones de la Flor.
———, ed. 1995. *De la guerilla peronista al gobierno popular: Documentos 1970–1973.* Buenos Aires: Editorial de la Campana.
———, ed. 1996. *De Cámpora a la ruptura: Documentos 1973–1976.* Buenos Aires: Editorial de la Campana.
Benyakar, Mordechai. 2003. *Lo disruptivo: Amenazas individuales y colectivas: el psiquismo ante guerras, terrorismos y catástrofes sociales.* Buenos Aires: Editorial Biblos.
Bergmann, Martin S. and Milton E. Jucovy. 1982. "Prelude." In *Generations of the Holocaust*, ed. Martin S. Bergmann and Milton E. Jucovy, 3–29. New York: Basic Books.
Besançon, Alain. 1981. *The Intellectual Origins of Leninism.* Oxford: Blackwell.
Bignone, Reynaldo B. A. 1992. *El último de facto: La liquidación del proceso: Memoria y testimonio.* Buenos Aires: Planeta.
Blixen, Samuel. 1988. *Treinta años de lucha popular: Conversaciones con Gorriarán Merlo.* Buenos Aires: Contrapunto.
Boixadós, Alberto. 1977. *Arte y subversión.* Buenos Aires: Editorial Areté.
Bolón Varela, Emilio. 1981. *Fundamentos de ética militar: Apuntes sobre el espíritu militar argentino.* Buenos Aires: Círculo Militar.
Bonafini, Hebe de. 1988. *Historia de las Madres de Plaza de Mayo.* Buenos Aires: Asociación Madres de Plaza de Mayo.
Bonasso, Miguel. 1984. *Recuerdo de la muerte.* Mexico City: Ediciones Era.
———. 1997. *El presidente que no fue: Los archivos ocultos del Peronismo.* Buenos Aires: Planeta.
———. 2000. *Diario de un clandestino.* Buenos Aires: Planeta.
Bondone, Luis José. 1985. *Con mis hijos en las cárceles del "proceso".* Buenos Aires: Editorial Anteo.
Borges, Jorge Luis and Adolfo Bioy Casares. 1977. *Nuevos cuentos de Bustos Domecq.* Buenos Aires: Ediciones Librería la Ciudad.

Botana, Natalio R., Rafael Braun, and Carlos A. Floria. 1973. *El régimen militar, 1966–1973.* Buenos Aires: Ediciones La Bastilla.

Bourke, Vernon J. 1972. "Thomas Aquinas, St." *The Encyclopedia of Philosophy,* 7: 105–116. New York: Macmillan and Free Press.

Bousquet, Jean-Pierre. 1982. *Las locas de la Plaza de Mayo.* Córdoba: El Cid.

Bowlby, John. 1981. *Attachment and Loss.* Vol. 1, *Attachment.* Harmondsworth: Penguin.

Bra, Gerardo. 1985. "La noche de los bastones largos: El garrote y la inteligencia." *Todo Es Historia* 223: 8–26.

Brass, Paul R. 1996. "Introduction: Discourses of Ethnicity, Communalism, and Violence." In *Riots and Pogroms,* ed. Paul R. Brass, 1–55. New York: New York University Press.

———. 1997. *Theft of an Idol: Text and Context in the Representation of Collective Violence.* Princeton, N.J.: Princeton University Press.

Braun de Dunayevich, Julia and María Lucila Pelento. 1991. "Las vicisitudes de la pulsión de saber en ciertos duelos especiales." In *Violencia de estado y psicoanálisis,* ed. Janine Puget and René Kaës, 79–91. Buenos Aires: Centro Editor de América Latina.

Braun, Herbert. 1985. *The Assassination of Gaitán: Public Life and Urban Violence in Colombia.* Madison: University of Wisconsin Press.

Brennan, James P. 1994. *The Labor Wars in Córdoba, 1955–1976: Ideology, Work, and Labor Politics in an Argentine Industrial City.* Cambridge, Mass.: Harvard University Press.

Brett, Elizabeth A. 1993. "Psychoanalytic Contributions to a Theory of Traumatic Stress." In *International Handbook of Traumatic Stress Syndromes,* ed. John P. Wilson and Beverley Raphael, 61–68. New York: Plenum Press.

Brieger, Pedro. 1991. "Sacerdotes para el Tercer Mundo, una frustrada experiencia de evangelización." *Todo Es Historia* 287: 10–28.

Brysk, Alison. 1994a. *The Politics of Human Rights in Argentina: Protest, Change, and Democratization.* Stanford, Calif.: Stanford University Press.

———. 1994b. "The Politics of Measurement: The Contested Count of the Disappeared in Argentina." *Human Rights Quarterly* 16: 676–692.

Buda, Blanca. 1988. *Cuerpo I-Zona IV (el infierno de Suárez Mason).* Buenos Aires: Editorial Contrapunto.

Burdick, Michael A. 1995. *For God and the Fatherland: Religion and Politics in Argentina.* Albany: State University of New York Press.

Caimari, Lila M. 1995. *Perón y la Iglesia Católica: Religión, estado, y sociedad en la Argentina (1943–1955).* Buenos Aires: Ariel.

Calvo, Roberto. 1979. *La doctrina militar de la seguridad nacional.* Caracas: CEDIAL.

Camara Nacional de Apelaciones en lo Criminal y Correccional Federal de la Capital Federal. 1987. *La sentencia.* 2 vols. Buenos Aires: Imprenta del Congreso de la Nación.

Camarasa, Jorge, Ruben Felice, and Daniel González. 1985. *El Juicio: Proceso al horror.* Buenos Aires: Sudamericana/Planeta.

Canetti, Elias. 1966. *Crowds and Power.* New York: Viking Press.

Carlson, Eve B. 1997. *Trauma Assessments: A Clinician's Guide.* New York: Guilford Press.

Caruth, Cathy. 1995. "Introduction." In *Trauma: Explorations in Memory,* ed. Cathy Caruth, 151–157. Baltimore: Johns Hopkins University Press.

———. 1996. *Unclaimed Experience: Trauma, Narrative, and History.* Baltimore: Johns Hopkins University Press.

Castañeda, Jorge G. 1994. *Utopia Unarmed: The Latin American Left After the Cold War.* New York: Vintage.

Cazes Camarero, Pedro. 1989. *El Che y la generación del '70.* Buenos Aires: Ediciones Dialéctica.

CELS. 1982. *Muertos por la represión.* Buenos Aires: Centro de Estudios Legales y Sociales.

―――. 1986. *Terrorismo de estado: 692 responsables.* Buenos Aires: Centro de Estudios Legales y Sociales.

Chateau-Jobert, Pierre. 1977. *La confrontación revolución-contrarrevolución.* Buenos Aires: Editorial Rioplatense.

Cheren, Liliana. 1997. *La masacre de Trelew 22 de Agosto de 1972: Institucionalización del terrorismo de estado.* Buenos Aires: Corregidor.

Chodorow, Nancy J. 1999a [1978]. *The Reproduction of Mothering: Psychoanalysis and the Sociology of Gender.* Berkeley: University of California Press.

―――. 1999b. *The Power of Feelings: Personal Meaning in Psychoanalysis, Gender, and Culture.* New Haven, Conn.: Yale University Press.

Chumbita, Hugo. 1990. *Los carapintada: Historia de un malentendido argentino.* Buenos Aires: Planeta.

Ciancaglini, Sergio and Martín Granovsky. 1986. *Crónicas del apocalipsis.* Buenos Aires: Editorial Contrapunto.

Cichero, Marta. 1992. *Cartas peligrosas de Perón.* Buenos Aires: Planeta.

CIDH. 1984 [1980], *El informe prohibido: Informe sobre la situación de los derechos humanos en Argentina.* Buenos Aires: OSEA and CELS.

CISEA. 1984. *Argentina 1983.* Buenos Aires: Centro Editor de América Latina.

CJE. 1976. *El ejército de Hoy.* Buenos Aires: Círculo Militar.

Clausewitz, Carl von. 1984 [1832]. *On War.* Princeton, N.J.: Princeton University Press.

Cohen Salama, Mauricio. 1992. *Tumbas anónimas: Informe sobre la identificación de restos de víctimas de la represión ilegal.* Buenos Aires: Catálogos Editora.

Comisión de Afirmación de la Revolución Libertadora. 1985. *A 30 años de la Revolución Libertadora.* Buenos Aires: Edición de la Comisión.

CONADEP. 1985. *Anexos del Informe de la Comisión Nacional sobre la Desaparición de Personas.* Buenos Aires: EUDEBA.

―――. 1986 [1984]. *Nunca Más: The Report of the Argentine National Commission on the Disappeared.* New York: Farrar Straus Giroux.

Congreso Nacional. 1974. *Diario de sesiones de la Cámara de Diputados.* Vol. 1, *3 May–5 July 1973.* Buenos Aires: Imprenta del Congreso.

Connerton, Paul. 1989. *How Societies Remember.* Cambridge: Cambridge University Press.

Cooke, John William. 1973. *Perón-Cooke correspondencia.* 2 vols. Buenos Aires: Granica Editor.

Corradi, Juan E. 1985. *The Fitful Republic: Economy, Society, and Politics in Argentina.* Boulder, Colo.: Westview Press.

Corradi, Juan E., Patricia Weiss Fagen, and Manuel Antonio Garretón, eds. 1992. *Fear at the Edge: State Terror and Resistance in Latin America.* Berkeley: University of California Press.

Cortés Conde, Roberto. 1993. "The Growth of the Argentine Economy, c. 1870–1914." In *Argentina Since Independence,* ed. Leslie Bethell, 47–77. Cambridge: Cambridge University Press.

Crassweller, Robert D. 1987. *Perón and the Enigmas of Argentina.* New York: W.W. Norton.

Crawley, Eduardo D. 1970. *Subversión y seguridad: La cuestión de la guerra de guerrillas en el contexto argentino.* Buenos Aires: Círculo Militar.

Crozier, Brian. 1974. *A Theory of Conflict.* London: Hamish Hamilton.

Csikszentmihalyi, Mihaly and Eugene Rochberg-Halton. 1981. *The Meaning of Things: Domestic Symbols and the Self.* Cambridge: Cambridge University Press.

Culbertson, Roberta. 1995. "Embodied Memory, Transcendence, and Telling: Recounting Trauma, Re-establishing the Self." *New Literary History* 26 (1): 169–195.

D'Andrea Mohr, José Luis. 1999. *Memoria debida.* Buenos Aires: Ediciones Colihue.

Daleo, Graciela and Andrés Ramón Castillo. 1982. *Informe.* Madrid: CADHU.

Daniel, E. Valentine. 1996. *Charred Lullabies: Chapters in an Anthropography of Violence.* Princeton, N.J.: Princeton University Press.

Das, Veena. 1990a. "Introduction: Communities, Riots, Survivors—The South Asian Experience." In Veena Das, *Mirrors of Violence: Communities, Riots and Survivors in South Asia,* 1–36. Delhi: Oxford University Press.

———. 1990b. "Our Work to Cry: Your Work to Listen." In Veena Das, *Mirrors of Violence: Communities, Riots and Survivors in South Asia,* 345–398. Delhi: Oxford University Press.

De la Riestra, Guillermo M. 1989. "La sentencia nula." *Revista Militar* 721: 51–59.

De Mano en Mano. 2002. *Situaciones 5: Mesa de escrache popular.* Buenos Aires: Ediciones De Mano en Mano.

Dearriba, Alberto. 2001. *El Golpe: 24 de marzo de 1976.* Buenos Aires: Editorial Sudamericana.

Debray, Régis. 1967. *Revolution in the Revolution? Armed Struggle and Political Struggle in Latin America.* New York: Grove Press.

———. 1973. *Strategy for Revolution.* Harmondsworth: Penguin.

Deheza, José A.. 1981. *Quiénes derrocaron a Isabel Perón?* Buenos Aires: Ediciones Cuenca del Plata.

Delich, Francisco J. 1974. *Crisis y protesta social: Córdoba, 1969–1973.* Buenos Aires: Siglo Veintiuno Argentina Editores.

Di Tella, Guido. 1985. *Perón-Perón, 1973–1976.* Buenos Aires: Hyspamérica Ediciones Argentina.

Diago, Alejandro. 1988. *Hebe: memoria y esperanza.* Buenos Aires: Ediciones Dialéctica.

Diana, Marta. 1997. *Mujeres guerrilleras: La militancia de los setenta en el testimonio de sus protagonistas femeninas.* Buenos Aires: Planeta.

Díaz Araujo, Enrique. 1988. *La semana trágica de 1919.* Vol. 2. Mendoza: Universidad Nacional de Cuyo.

Díaz Bessone, Ramón Genaro. 1988. *Guerra revolucionaria en la Argentina (1959–1978).* Buenos Aires: Círculo Militar.

Diez, Rolo. 1987. *Los compañeros.* Mexico City: Leega.

Directivas de Educación del Ejército. 1981. "La educación ético-espiritual en el Ejército." *Revista de Educación del Ejército* 36: 33–47.

Duhalde, Eduardo Luis. 1983. *El estado terrorista argentino.* Buenos Aires: Editorial El Caballito.

———. 1999. *El estado terrorista argentino: Quince años después, una mirada crítica.* Buenos Aires: Eudeba.

Edelman, Lucila and Diana Kordon. 1995. "Trauma y duelo: Conflicto y elaboración." In *La Impunidad: Una perspectiva psicosocial y clínica,* ed. Diana Kordon, Lucila Edelman, Darío Lagos, and Daniel Kersner, 101–110. Buenos Aires: Editorial Sudamericana.

EMGE (Estado Mayor General del Ejército). 1979a. "El marxismo actúa en distinctos ámbitos del quehacer nacional." *Revista de Educación del Ejército* 32: 35–62.

———. 1979b. "La subversión emplea distintos medios para lograr la penetración ideológica." *Revista de Educación del Ejército* 32: 63–77.

Erikson, Erik H. 1951. *Childhood and Society.* London: Imago.

Erikson, Kai. 1995. "Notes on Trauma and Community." In *Trauma: Explorations in Memory*, ed. Cathy Caruth, 183–199. Baltimore: John Hopkins University Press.

Escobar, Raúl Tomás. 1984. *Estrategia contrarrevolucionaria.* Buenos Aires: Editorial F.I.

Escuela Superior de Guerra. 1978. *Manual de historia militar.* Vol. 3. Buenos Aires: Escuela Superior de Guerra.

FAL. 1973. *Máxima peligrosidad.* Buenos Aires: Editorial Candela.

FAMUS. 1988. *Operación Independencia.* Buenos Aires: FAMUS.

Farinello, Luis. 1999. "Religión y rol social." In *Juventud e Identidad: III Congreso Internacional*, ed. Abuelas de Plaza de Mayo, 191–196. Buenos Aires: Espacio Editorial.

Feinmann, José Pablo. 1999. *La sangre derramada: Ensayo sobre la violencia política.* Buenos Aires: Ariel.

Feitlowitz, Marguerite. 1998. *A Lexicon of Terror: Argentina and the Legacies of Torture.* New York: Oxford University Press.

Feldman, Allen. 1991. *Formations of Violence: The Narrative of the Body and Political Terror in Northern Ireland.* Chicago: University of Chicago Press.

Fernández, Rodolfo Peregrino. 1983. *Autocrítica policial.* Buenos Aires: El Cid.

Fernández Alvariño, Próspero Germán. 1973. *Z. Argentina: El crímen del siglo.* Buenos Aires: Author's edition.

Fernández Meijide, Graciela. 1988. *Las cifras de la guerra sucia.* Buenos Aires: Asamblea Permanente por los Derechos Humanos.

Fisher, Jo. 1989. *Mothers of the Disappeared.* Boston: South End Press.

FM 19–15. 1964. *Civil Disturbances and Disasters.* Washington, D.C.: Department of the Army.

Foro de Buenos Aires por la Vigencia de los Derechos Humanos. 1973. *Proceso a la explotación y a la represión en la Argentina.* Buenos Aires: Foro de Buenos Aires por la Vigencia de los Derechos Humanos.

Foucault, Michel. 1979. *Discipline and Punish: The Birth of the Prison.* New York: Vintage Books.

Fraga, Rosendo. 1988. *Ejército: Del escarnio al poder (1973–1976).* Buenos Aires: Sudamericana/Planeta.

Friedlander, Saul. 1993. *Memory, History, and the Extermination of the Jews of Europe.* Bloomington: Indiana University Press.

Frigerio, José Oscar. 1984. "Perón contra la Iglesia." *Todo Es Historia* 210:9–64.

Frontalini, Daniel and Maria Cristina Caiati. 1984. *El mito de la "guerra sucia".* Buenos Aires: CELS.

Gabetta, Carlos. 1983. *Todos somos subversivos.* Buenos Aires: Editorial Bruguera.

Gampel, Yolanda, 2000. "Reflections on the Prevalence of the Uncanny in Social Violence." In *Cultures Under Siege: Collective Violence and Trauma*, ed. Antonius C. G. M. Robben and Marcelo M. Suárez-Orozco, 48–69. Cambridge: Cambridge University Press.

Garasino, Alberto Manuel. 1970. "Gobierno y subversión." *Estrategia* 2 (7): 5–12.

García Márquez, Gabriel. 1983. *Obra periodística.* Vol. 4, *De Europa y América (1955–1960).* Barcelona: Editorial Bruguera.

Garulli, Liliana, Liliana Caraballo, Noemi Charlier, and Mercedes Cafiero, 2000. *Nomeolvides: Memoria de la resistencia peronista 1955–1972.* Buenos Aires: Editorial Biblos.

Gasparini, Juan. 1986. *La pista suiza.* Buenos Aires: Editorial Legasa.

———. 1988. *Montoneros: Final de cuentas.* Buenos Aires: Puntosur.

———. 1990. *El crímen de Graiver.* Buenos Aires: Editorial Zeta.

Gasparini, Roberto and José Luis Ponsico. 1983. *El director técnico del proceso.* Buenos Aires: El Cid.

Gavensky, Marta and Gustavo Wagner. 1985. "Detenidos políticos: El espacio como alternativa de violencia." In *Historia de la tortura y el orden represivo en la Argentina: textos documentales,* ed. Ricardo Rodríguez Molas, 246–254. Buenos Aires: EUDEBA.

Gelman, Juan. 1994. *Cólera buey.* Buenos Aires: Seix Barral.

Gelman, Juan and Mara La Madrid. 1997. *Ni el flaco perdón de Dios: Hijos de desaparecidos.* Buenos Aires: Planeta.

Genta, Jordán B. 1976. *Acerca de la libertad de enseñar y de la enseñanza de la libertad. Libre examen y comunismo: Guerra contrarrevolucionaria.* Buenos Aires: Ediciones Dictio.

Germani, Gino. 1973. "El surgimiento del Peronismo: El rol de los obreros y de los migrantes internos." *Desarrollo Económico* 13 (51): 435–488.

Gilbert, Abel and Miguel Vitagliano. 1998. *El terror y la gloria: La vida, el fútbol y la política en la Argentina del Mundial '78.* Buenos Aires: Grupo Editorial Norma.

Gillespie, Richard. 1982a. *Soldiers of Perón: Argentina's Montoneros.* Oxford: Clarendon Press.

———. 1982b. "Armed Struggle in Argentina." *New Scholar* 8: 387–427.

———. 1989. *John William Cooke: El peronismo alternativo.* Buenos Aires: Cantaro Editores.

Girard, René. 1992 [1972]. *Violence and the Sacred.* Baltimore: Johns Hopkins University Press.

Giussani, Pablo. 1987a. *Montoneros: La soberbia armada.* Buenos Aires: Sudamericana-Planeta.

———. 1987b, *Por qué, doctor Alfonsín?* Buenos Aires: Sudamericana/Planeta.

Godio, Julio. 1990. *El movimiento obrero argentino, 1943–1955: Nacimiento y consolidación de una hegemonía nacionalista-laborista.* Buenos Aires: Editorial Legasa.

Goldar. 1990. "El enigma de Taco Ralo." *Todo Es Historia* 279: 6–29.

Goldar, Ernesto. 1991. "John William Cooke: De Perón al Che Guevara." *Todo Es Historia* 288: 10–40.

Gonsalves, Carlos J., Tato A. Torres, Yael Fischman, Jaime Ross, and Maria O. Vargas. 1993. "The Theory of Torture and the Treatment of Its Survivors: An Intervention Model." *Journal of Traumatic Stress* 6 (3): 351–365.

González Bombal, Inés. 1995. "Nunca Más": El Juicio más allá de los estrados." In *Juicio, castigos y memorias: Derechos humanos y justicia en la política argentina,* ed. Carlos H. Acuña, 193–216. Buenos Aires: Nueva Visión.

González Janzen, Ignacio. 1986. *La Triple-A.* Buenos Aires: Editorial Contrapunto.

Gorer, Geoffrey. 1965. *Death, Grief, and Mourning.* Garden City, N.Y.: Doubleday.

Gorini, Ulises and Oscar Castelnovo. 1986. *Lilí, presa política: Reportaje desde la cárcel.* Buenos Aires: Ediciones Antarca.

Government of Argentina. 1980. *Observations and Criticisms Made by the Government of Argentina with Regard to the Report of the Inter-American Commission on Human Rights on the Situation of Human Rights in Argentina (April 1980).* Washington, D.C.: OAS.

Goyret, Juan T. 1979. "Estudio preliminar." In André Beaufre, *La guerra revolucionaria: Las nuevas formas de la guerra,* 7–39. Buenos Aires: Editorial Almena.

Graham-Yooll, Andrew. 1989. *De Perón a Videla.* Buenos Aires: Editorial Legasa.

Grecco, Jorge and Gustavo González. 1988. *Felices Pascuas! Los hechos inéditos de la rebelión militar.* Buenos Aires: Planeta.

Green, Bonnie L. 1990. "Defining Trauma: Terminology and Generic Stressor Dimensions." *Journal of Applied Social Psychology* 20: 1632–1642.

Gregory, Steven and Daniel Timerman. 1986. "Rituals of the Modern State: The Case of Torture in Argentina." *Dialectical Anthropology* 11 (1): 63–72.

Grossman, Dave. 1995. *On Killing: The Psychological Cost of Learning to Kill in War and Society.* Boston: Little, Brown.

Grubrich-Simitis, Ilse. 1981. "Extreme Traumatization as Cumulative Trauma: Psychoanalytic Investigations of the Effects of Concentration Camp Experiences on Survivors and Their Children." *Psychoanalytic Study of the Child* 36: 415–450.

Guest, Iain. 1990. *Behind the Disappearances: Argentina's Dirty War Against Human Rights and the United Nations.* Philadelphia: University of Pennsylvania Press.

Guevara, Che. 1985 [1960]. *Guerrilla Warfare.* Lincoln: University of Nebraska Press.

Guglialmelli, Juan E.. 1969. "Fuerzas armadas y subversión interior." *Estrategia* 1(2):7–14.

Guillén, Abraham. 1965. *Teoría de la violencia: Guerra y lucha de clases.* Buenos Aires: Editorial Jamcana.

Guzman Bouvard, Marguerite. 1994. *Revolutionizing Motherhood: The Mothers of the Plaza de Mayo.* Wilmington, Del.: Scholarly Resources.

Harkness, Laurie Leydic. 1993. "Transgenerational Transmission of War-Related Trauma." In *International Handbook of Traumatic Stress Syndromes,* ed. John P. Wilson and Beverley Raphael, 635–643. New York: Plenum Press.

Herman, Judith Lewis. 1992. *Trauma and Recovery.* New York: Basic Books.

Hernández, Pablo. 1989a, *Conversaciones con el Teniente Coronel Aldo Rico: De Malvinas a la Operación Dignidad.* Buenos Aires: Editorial Fortaleza.

———. 1989b, *La Tablada: El regreso de los que no se fueron.* Buenos Aires: Editorial Fortaleza.

Herrera, Matilde. 1987. *José.* Buenos Aires: Editorial Contrapunto.

Herrera, Matilde and Ernesto Tenembaum. 1990. *Identidad: Despojo y restitución.* Buenos Aires: Editorial Contrapunto.

Herrero, Antonio Miguel. 1991. "Monte Chingolo: La última batalla del E.R.P." *Todo Es Historia* 24 (284):6–24.

Hertz, Robert. 1960. *Death and the Right Hand.* Aberdeen: Cohen and West.

Hobsbawm, E. J.. 1959. *Primitive Rebels: Studies in Archaic Forms of Social Movement in the 19th and 20th Centuries.* Manchester: Manchester University Press.

Hodges, Donald C. 1973. *Philosophy of the Urban Guerrilla: The Revolutionary Writings of Abraham Guillén.* New York: William Morrow.

———. 1991. *Argentina's "Dirty War": An Intellectual Biography.* Austin: University of Texas Press.

Horne, Alistair. 1978. *A Savage War of Peace: Algeria 1954–1962.* New York: The Viking Press.

Jacoby, Roberto. 1978. *Conciencia de clase y enfrentamientos sociales: Argentina 1969.* Serie Estudios 32. Buenos Aires: CICSO.

James, Daniel. 1988a. *Resistence and Integration: Peronism and the Argentine Working Class. 1946–1976.* Cambridge: Cambridge University Press.

James, Daniel. 1988b. "October 17th and 18th, 1945: Mass Protest, Peronism and the Argentine Working Class." *Journal of Social History* 22: 441–461.

Jaureguialzo, Juan María. 1972. "Seguridad Nacional." *Gendarmeria Nacional* 8 (47): 67–75.

Jauretche, Ernesto. 1997. *Violencia y política en los 70: No dejés que te la cuenten.* Buenos Aires: Ediciones del Pensamiento Nacional.

Jelin, Elizabeth. 1979. "Labour Conflicts under the Second Peronist Regime, Argentina 1973–76." *Development and Change* 10 (2): 233–257.

Jelin, Elizabeth. 1985. "Los movimientos sociales en la Argentina contemporánea: una introducción a su estudio." In *Los nuevos movimientos sociales 1. Mujeres. Rock nacional*, ed. Elizabeth Jelin, 13–40. Buenos Aires: Centro Editor de América Latina.

Johnson, James Turner. 1975. *Ideology, Reason, and the Limitation of War: Religious and Secular Concepts. 1200–1740*. Princeton, N.J.: Princeton University Press.

Jonsen, Albert R. and Leonard A. Sagan. 1992. "Torture and the Ethics of Medicine." In *The Breaking of Bodies and Minds: Torture, Psychiatric Abuse, and the Health Professions*, ed. Eric Stover and Elena O. Nightingale, 30–44. New York: W.H. Freeman.

Josephs, Ray. 1945. *Argentine Diary: The Inside Story of the Coming of Fascism*. London: Victor Gollancz.

Kaës, René. 1991. "Rupturas catastróficas y trabajo de la memoria: Notas para una investigación." In *Violencia de estado y psicoanálisis*, ed. Janine Puget and René Kaës, 137–163. Buenos Aires: Centro Editor de América Latina.

Kenner, Martin and James Petras, eds. 1972. *Fidel Castro Speaks*. Harmondsworth: Penguin.

Kirmayer, Laurence J. 1996. "Landscapes of Memory: Trauma, Narrative, and Dissociation." In *Tense Past: Cultural Essays in Trauma and Memory*, ed. Paul Antze and Michael Lambek, 173–198. New York: Routledge.

Klass, Dennis. 1989. "The Resolution of Parental Bereavement." In *Midlife Loss: Coping Strategies*, ed. Richard A. Kalish, 149–178. Newbury Park, Calif.: Sage Publications.

Kordon, Diana, Lucila Edelman, Darío Lagos, Elena Nicoletti, Daniel Kersner, and Mirta Groshaus. 1992. "Torture in Argentina." In *Torture and Its Consequences: Current Treatment Approaches*, ed. Metin Başoğlu, 433–451. Cambridge: Cambridge University Press.

Krystal, Henry. 1968. "Patterns of Psychological Damage." In *Massive Psychic Trauma*, ed. Henry Krystal, 1–7. New York: International Universities Press.

———. 1985. "Trauma and the Stimulus Barrier." *Psychoanalytic Inquiry* 5: 131–161.

LaCapra, Dominick. 1994. *Representing the Holocaust: History, Theory, Trauma*. Ithaca, N.Y.: Cornell University Press.

———. 1998. *History and Memory After Auschwitz*. Ithaca, N.Y.: Cornell University Press.

Laclau, Ernesto. 1970. "Argentina: Imperialist Strategy and the May Crisis." *New Left Review* 62: 3–21.

Lamas, Raúl. 1956. *Los torturadores: Crímenes y tormentos en las cárceles argentinas*. Buenos Aires: Editorial Lamas.

Lanusse, Alejandro A. 1977. *Mi testimónio*. Buenos Aires: Lasserre.

———. 1989. *Protagonista y testigo*. Buenos Aires: Marcelo Lugones.

Larraquy, Marcelo and Roberto Caballero. 2001. *Galimberti: De Perón a Susana, De Montoneros a la CIA*. Buenos Aires: Grupo Editorial Norma.

Last, Murray. 2000. "Reconciliation and Memory in Postwar Nigeria." In *Violence and Subjectivity*, ed. Veena Das, Arthur Kleinman, Mamphela Ramphele, and Pamela Reynolds, 315–332. Berkeley: University of California Press.

Lázara, Simón. 1988. *Poder militar: origen, apogeo y transición*. Buenos Aires: Editorial Legasa.

Le Bon, Gustave. 1960 [1895]. *The Crowd: A Study of the Popular Mind*. New York: Viking.

Lenin, Vladimir Illich. 1978 [1904]. *One Step Forward, Two Steps Back: The Crisis in Our Party*. Moscow: Progress Publications.

Leoni Houssay, Luis Alberto. 1965. *Qué es la guerra*. Buenos Aires: Editorial Columba.

———. 1980. *La conexión internacional del terrorismo*. Buenos Aires: Ediciones Depalma.

Lewis, Paul H. 1990. *The Crisis of Argentine Capitalism*. Chapel Hill: University of North Carolina Press.

Lifton, Robert Jay. 1986. *The Nazi Doctors: Medical Killing and the Psychology of Genocide*. New York: Basic Books.

Lincoln, Bruce. 1989. *Discourse and the Construction of Society: Comparative Studies of Myth, Ritual, and Classification*. New York: Oxford University Press.

Littlewood, Roland. 1997. "Military Rape." *Anthropology Today* 13 (2): 7–16.

López, Ernesto. 1988. *El último levantamiento*. Buenos Aires: Legasa.

López Aufranc, Alcides. 1975. "Oraciones fúnebres y guerra revolucionaria." *Administración Militar y Logística* 38 (453): 643–648.

López Echagüe, Hernán. 1991. *El enigma del General Bussi: De la Operación Independencia a la Operación Retorno*. Buenos Aires: Editorial Sudamericana.

Loveman, Brian and Thomas M. Davies, Jr., eds. 1989. *The Politics of Antipolitics: The Military in Latin America*. Lincoln: University of Nebraska Press.

Lozada, Salvador María, Julio J. Viaggio, Carlos Zamorano, and Eduardo S. Barcesat. 1983. *La ideología de la seguridad nacional*. Buenos Aires: El Cid.

Lozada, Salvador María, Julio J. Viaggio, Carlos Zamorano, and Eduardo S. Barcesat. 1985. *Inseguridad y desnacionalización: La "doctrina" de la seguridad nacional*. Buenos Aires: Ediciones Derechos del Hombre.

Luna, Félix. 1973. *El 45: Crónica de un año decisivo*. Buenos Aires: Editorial Sudamericana.

Lunde, Inge and Jørgen Ortmann. 1992. "Sexual Torture and the Treatment of Its Consequences." In *Torture and Its Consequences: Current Treatment Approaches*, ed. Metin Başoğlu, 310–329. Cambridge: Cambridge University Press.

Lutz, Catherine and Donald Nonini. 1999. "The Economies of Violence and the Violence of Economies." In *Anthropological Theory Today*, ed. Henrietta L. Moore, 73–113. Cambridge: Polity Press.

Lynch, Horacio M. and Enrique V. del Carril. 1985. *Definitivamente . . . Nunca Más (La otra cara del informe de la CONADEP)*. Buenos Aires: FORES.

Lynch, John. 1993. "From Independence to National Organization." In *Argentina Since Independence*, ed. Leslie Bethell, 1–46. Cambridge: Cambridge University Press.

M-8-1. 1972. *Procedimientos para las operaciones contra la subversión urbana: Ejército Argentino, Jefatura III—Operaciones* (Departamento Doctrina). Mimeographed.

Machado, Tristán González. 1974. "Los derechos humanos y la represión en América latina." *Cristianismo y Sociedad* 12 (40–41): 93–109.

Madres de Plaza de Mayo. 1985. *Cantos de vida, amor y libertad*. 3 vols. Buenos Aires: Rafael Cedeño.

Madsen, Douglas and Peter G. Snow. 1991. *The Charismatic Bond: Political Behavior in Time of Crisis*. Cambridge, Mass.: Harvard University Press.

Mahmood, Cynthia Keppley. 1996. *Fighting for Faith and Nation: Dialogues with Sikh Militants*. Philadelphia: University of Pennsylvania Press.

Marighela, Carlos. 1971. *For the Liberation of Brazil*. Harmondsworth: Penguin.

Marini, José Felipe. 1965. "La lucha por la América latina." *Revista del Círculo Militar* 65 (675): 113–117.

Maritain, Jacques. 1958a [1931]. *St. Thomas Aquinas*. New York: Meridian Books.

Maritain, Jacques. 1958b [1944]. *The Rights of Man*. London: Geoffrey Bles.

Martí, Ana María, María Alicia Milia de Pirles, and Sara Solarz de Osatinsky. 1995 [1979]. *ESMA "Trasladados": Testimonio de tres liberadas*. Buenos Aires: Abuelas de Plaza de Mayo.

Martínez de Hoz, José A. 1981. *Bases para una Argentina moderna, 1976–80*. Buenos Aires: Author's edition.

Martínez, Tomás Eloy. 1997 [1973]. *La pasión según Trelew.* Buenos Aires: Planeta.

Masi, Juan José. 1967. "Lucha contra la subversión." *Revista de la Escuela Superior de Guerra* 45 (373): 36–90.

Massera, Emilio E.. 1979. *El camino a la democracia.* Buenos Aires: El Cid.

Matsushita, Hiroshi. 1987. *Movimiento obrero argentino, 1930–1945: Sus proyecciones en los orígenes del peronismo.* Buenos Aires: Siglo Veinte.

Mattini, Luis. 1990. *Hombres y mujeres del PRT-ERP.* Buenos Aires: Editorial Contrapunto.

Maxwell, Carol J. 1995. "Coping with Bereavement Through Activism: Real Grief, Imagined Death, and Pseudo-Mourning Among Pro-Life Direct Activists." *Ethos* 23 (4): 437–452.

McClelland, J. S. 1989. *The Crowd and the Mob: From Plato to Canetti.* London: Unwin Hyman.

McNally, Richard J. 2003a. *Remembering Trauma.* Cambridge, Mass.: Harvard University Press.

McNally, Richard J. 2003b. "Progress and Controversy in the Study of Posttraumatic Stress Disorder." *Annual Review of Psychology* 54: 229–252.

Mellibovsky, Matilde. 1990. *Círculo de amor sobre la muerte.* Buenos Aires: Ediciones del Pensamiento Nacional.

Méndez, Eugenio. 1988. *Aramburu: el crimen imperfecto.* Buenos Aires: Sudamericana/Planeta.

Mercier Vega, Luis. 1969. *Guerrillas in Latin America: The Technique of the Counter-State.* London: Pall Mall Press.

Mero, Roberto. 1987. *Conversaciones con Juan Gelman: Contraderrota, Montoneros y la revolución perdida.* Buenos Aires: Editorial Contrapunto.

Merridale, Catherine. 2000. *Night of Stone: Death and Memory in Twentieth-Century Russia.* New York: Viking.

Mignone, Emilio F. 1988. *Witness to the Truth: The Complicity of Church and Dictatorship in Argentina.* Maryknoll, N,Y.: Orbis Books.

Miguens, José Enrique. 1988. "Actualización de la identidad justicialista" In *Racionalidad del peronismo,* ed. José Enrique Miguens and Frederick C. Turner, 9–51. Buenos Aires: Planeta.

Mitchell, Stephen A. and Margaret J. Black. 1995. *Freud and Beyond: A History of Modern Psychoanalytic Thought.* New York: Basic Books.

Mitscherlich, Alexander and Margarete Mitscherlich. 1975. *The Inability to Mourn: Principles of Collective Behavior.* New York: Grove Press.

Mittelbach, Federico. 1986. *Punto 30: Informe sobre desaparecidos.* Buenos Aires: Ediciones de la Urraca.

Moliner, María. 1984. *Diccionario de uso del Español.* Vol.1. Madrid: Editorial Gredos.

Momboisse, Raymond M.. 1973. *Riots, Revolts, and Insurrections.* Springfield, Ill.: Charles C. Thomas.

Montenegro, Nestor J. 1986. *Será justicia.* Buenos Aires: Editorial Distal.

Mora y Araujo, Manuel and Ignacio Llorente. 1980. *El voto peronista: Ensayos de sociología electoral argentina.* Buenos Aires: Sudamericana.

Morello, Norma. 1972. "Mis días en el mundo del terror." *CIAS* 21 (214): 26–31.

Moscovici, Serge. 1985. *The Age of the Crowd: A Historical Treatise on Mass Psychology.* Cambridge: Cambridge University Press.

Moyano, María José. 1995. *Argentina's Lost Patrol: Armed Struggle, 1969–1979.* New Haven, Conn.: Yale University Press.

Mugica, Carlos. 1973. *Peronismo y cristianismo.* Buenos Aires: Editorial Merlin.

Munck, Gerardo L. 1998. *Authoritarianism and Democratization: Soldiers and Workers in Argentina. 1976–1983.* University Park: Pennsylvania State University Press.

Munck, Ronaldo. 1987. *Argentina: From Anarchism to Peronism: Workers, Unions and Politics, 1855–1985.* London: Zed Books.

Murmis, Miguel and Juan Carlos Portantiero. 1987 [1971]. *Estudios sobre los orígenes del Peronismo.* Buenos Aires: Siglo Veintiuno Argentina.

Nagengast, Carole. 1994. "Violence, Terror, and the Crisis of the State." *Annual Review of Anthropology* 23: 109–136.

Nari, Marcela M. A., and Andrea M. Fabre, eds. 2000. *Voces de mujeres encarceladas.* Buenos Aires: Catálogos.

Navarro, Marysa. 1989. "The Personal Is Political: Las Madres de Plaza de Mayo." In *Power and Popular Protest: Latin American Social Movements,* ed. Susan Eckstein, 241–258. Berkeley: University of California Press.

Navarro, Marysa. 1995. "Evita y la crisis del 17 de Octubre de 1945: un ejemplo de la mitología peronista y antiperonista." In *El 17 de Octubre de 1945,* ed. Juan Carlos Torre, 149–170. Buenos Aires: Ariel.

Neal, Arthur G. 1999. *National Trauma and Collective Memory: Major Events in the American Century.* Armonk, N.Y.: M. E. Sharpe.

Neiburg, Federico G. 1992. "O 17 de outubro na Argentina: espaço e produção social do carismo." *Revista Brasileira de Ciências Sociais* 7 (20): 70–89.

Nicoletti, Elena. 1988. "Missing People: Defect of Signifying Ritual and Clinical Consequences." In *Psychological Effects of Political Repression,* ed. Diana Kordon, Lucila Edelman, and Equipo de Asistencia Psicológica de Madres de Plaza de Mayo, 113–122. Buenos Aires: Sudamericana/Planeta.

Nino, Carlos Santiago. 1996. *Radical Evil on Trial.* New Haven, Conn.: Yale University Press.

Nora, Pierre. 1978. "Mémoire collective." In *La nouvelle histoire,* ed. Jacques Le Goff, Roger Chartier, and Jacques Revel, 398–401. Paris: Retz-C.E.P.L.

———. 1984. "Entre mémoire et histoire: La problématique des lieux." In *Les lieux de mémoire,* vol. 1, *La république,* ed. Pierre Nora, xvii–xlii. Paris: Gallimard.

Norden, Deborah L. 1996. *Military Rebellion in Argentina: Between Coups and Consolidation.* Lincoln: University of Nebraska Press.

Nordstrom, Carolyn. 1997. *A Different Kind of War Story.* Philadelphia: University of Pennsylvania Press.

Nosiglia, Julio E. 1985. *Botín de guerra.* Buenos Aires: Cooperativa Tierra Fertil.

Nunn, Frederick M. 1992. *The Time of the Generals: Latin American Professional Militarism in World Perspective.* Lincoln: University of Nebraska Press.

Nye, Robert A.. 1975. *The Origins of Crowd Psychology: Gustave LeBon and the Crisis of Mass Democracy in the Third Republic.* London: Sage.

O'Donnell, Guillermo. 1986. "On the Fruitful Convergences of Hirschman's *Exit, Voice, and Loyalty* and *Shifting Involvements*: Reflections from the Recent Argentine Experience." In *Development, Democracy, and the Art of Trespassing: Essays in Honor of Albert O. Hirschman,* ed. Alejandro Foxley, Michael S. McPherson, and Guillermo O'Donnell, 249–268. Notre Dame, Ind.: University of Notre Dame Press.

Ollier, María Matilde. 1986. *El fenómeno insurreccional y la cultura política, 1969–1973.* Buenos Aires: Centro Editor de América Latina.

Ollier, María Matilde. 1998. *La creencia y la pasión: Privado, público, y político en la izquierda revolucionaria.* Buenos Aires: Ariel.

Oria, Piera Paola. 1987. *De la casa a la plaza.* Buenos Aires: Editorial Nueva América.

Orsolini, Mario. 1989. *Montoneros: Sus proyectos y sus planes.* Buenos Aires: Círculo Militar.

Oszlak, Oscar. 1990. *La formación del estado argentino.* Buenos Aires: Editorial de Belgrano.

Page, Joseph A. 1983. *Perón: A Biography.* New York: Random House.

Paoletti, Alipio. 1987. *Comos los Nazis, como en Vietnam.* Buenos Aires: Editorial Contrapunto.

Parkes, Colin Murray. 1972. *Bereavement: Studies of Grief in Adult Life.* New York: International Universities Press.

Partnoy, Alicia. 1986. *The Little School: Tales of Disappearance and Survival in Argentina.* Pittsburgh: Cleis Press

Pavlovsky, Eduardo. 1986. *El señor Galíndez y Pablo.* Buenos Aires: Ediciones Busqueda.

PEN (Poder Ejecutivo Nacional). 1979. *El terrorismo en la Argentina: Evolución de la delincuencia terrorista en la Argentina.* Buenos Aires: PEN.

Perina, Rubén M.. 1983. *Onganía, Levingston, Lanusse: Los militares en la política argentina.* Buenos Aires: Editorial de Belgrano.

Peristiani, J. G., ed. 1965. *Honor and Shame: The Values of Mediterranean Society.* London: Weidenfeld and Nicolson.

Perón, Juan Domingo. 1973a. *El gobierno, el estado y las organizaciones libres del pueblo.* Buenos Aires: Editorial de la Reconstrucción.

———. 1973b [1956]. "Directivas generales para todos los Peronistas." In *Perón-Cooke Correspondencia,* vol. 2, 378–384. Buenos Aires: Granica Editor.

———. 1973c [1956]. "Instrucciones generales para los dirigentes." In *Perón-Cooke Correspondencia,* vol. 2, 388–398. Buenos Aires: Granica Editor.

———. 1985a [1952]. "Conducción Política." *Obras Completas,* ed. Fermín Chávez, vol. 14. Buenos Aires: Editorial Docencia.

———. 1985b [1956]. "La fuerza es el derecho de las bestias." *Obras Completas,* vol. 21. Buenos Aires: Editorial Docencia.

———. 1985c [1957]. "Los vendepatria: Las pruebas de una traición." *Obras Completas,* vol. 22. Buenos Aires: Editorial Docencia.

———. 1995d [1971]. "Actualización política y doctrinaria para la toma del poder." In *De la guerrilla peronista al gobierno popular: Documentos 1970–1973,* ed. Roberto Baschetti, 303–339. Buenos Aires: Editorial de la Campana.

Peters, Edward. 1985. *Torture.* New York: Blackwell.

Petric, Antonio. 1983. *Así sangraba la Argentina: Sallustro, Quijaba, Larrabure.* Buenos Aires: Ediciones Depalma.

Piaget, Jean. 1950. *La construction du réel chez l'enfant.* Neuchâtel: Delachaux et Niestlé.

Pinetta, Santiago. 1986. *López Rega: El final de un brujo.* Buenos Aires: Editorial Abril.

Plotkin, Mariano Ben. 1995. "Rituales políticos, imágenes y carisma: La celebración del 17 de Octubre y el imaginario peronista 1945–1951." In *El 17 de Octubre de 1945,* ed. Juan Carlos Torre, 171–217. Buenos Aires: Ariel.

———. 2001. *Freud in the Pampas: The Emergence and Development of a Psychoanalytic Culture in Argentina.* Stanford, Calif.: Stanford University Press.

Pontoriero, Gustavo. 1991. *Sacerdotes para el Tercer Mundo: "el fermento en la masa" (1967–1976).* Buenos Aires: Centro Editor de América Latina.

Potash, Robert A. 1969. *The Army and Politics in Argentina. 1928–1945: Yrigoyen to Perón.* Stanford, Calif.: Stanford University Press.

———. 1980. *The Army and Politics in Argentina. 1945–1962: Perón to Frondizi.* London: Athlone.

———. 1996. *The Army and Politics in Argentina, 1962–1973: From Frondizi's Fall to the Peronist Restoration.* Stanford, Calif.: Stanford University Press.

Pozzi Jáuregui, Nestor O. 1983. *Expansión mundial marxista: sus causas y su respuesta.* Buenos Aires: Centro Naval.

PRT. 1966. *La lucha recien comienza.* Buenos Aires: Ediciones La Verdad.

———. 1972. *Pequeña burguesia y revolución: Moral y proletarización.* Buenos Aires: Ediciones El Combatiente.

————. 1973a, *Resoluciones del V Congreso y de los Comité Central y Comité Ejecutivo Posteriores.* Buenos Aires: Ediciones El Combatiente.

————. 1973b, *Hacia el VI Congreso.* Buenos Aires: Ediciones El Combatiente.

————. 1977a, *Crisis y revolución en América latina.* Buenos Aires: PRT.

————. 1977b, *Documentos del Comité Ejecutivo de Abril de 1977.* Madrid: PRT.

————. 1985. *Comité Central "20 aniversario".* Edition unknown.

Puccio Borrás, Estela. 1983. *Nunca es demasiado tarde.* Buenos Aires: El Cid.

Purnell, Susanna W. and Eleanor S. Wainstein. 1981. *The Problems of U.S. Businesses Operating Abroad in Terrorist Environments.* Santa Monica, Calif.: Rand.

Ramos Mejía, José María. 1956 [1899]. *Las multitudes argentinas.* Buenos Aires: Editorial Tor.

RC-8-1. 1968. *Operaciones no convencionales (fuerzas especiales).* Ejército Argentino: Instituto Geográfico Militar.

RC-8-2. 1969. *Operaciones contra fuerzas irregulares.* Vol. 2, *Operaciones de guerrilla y de contraguerrilla.* Ejército Argentino: Instituto Geográfico Militar.

————. 1969. *Operaciones contra fuerzas irregulares.* Vol. 3, *Guerra revolucionaria.* Ejército Argentino: Instituto Geográfico Militar.

————. 1970. *Operaciones Contra Fuerzas Irregulares.* Vol.1. Ejército Argentino: Instituto Geográfico Militar.

RC-8-3. 1969. *Operaciones contra la subversión urbana.* Ejército Argentino: Instituto Geográfico Militar.

Real Academia Española. 1992. *Diccionario de la lengua española.* Vol.1. Madrid: Real Academia Española.

Rejali, Darius M.. 1994. *Torture and Modernity: Self, Society, and State in Modern Iran.* Boulder, Colo.: Westview Press.

República Argentina. 1987 [1958]. *Libro Negro de la Segunda Tirania.* 4th ed. Buenos Aires: Comisión de Afirmación de la Revolución Libertadora.

Reyes, Cipriano. 1984. *Yo hice el 17 de octubre.* Buenos Aires: Centro Editor de América Latina.

Reyes, Cipriano. 1987. *La farsa del peronismo.* Buenos Aires: Sudamericana/Planeta.

Robben, Antonius C. G. M. 1988. "Conflicting Gender Conceptions in a Pluriform Fishing Economy: A Hermeneutic Perspective on Conjugal Relationships in Brazil." In *To Work and to Weep: Women in Fishing Economies,* ed. Jane H. Nadel-Klein and Dona Lee Davis, 106–129. St. John's, Newfoundland: Institute of Social and Economic Research, Memorial University of Newfoundland.

————. 1989a. *Sons of the Sea Goddess: Economic Practice and Discursive Conflict in Brazil.* New York: Columbia University Press.

————. 1989b. "Habits of the Home: Spatial Hegemony and the Structuration of House and Society in Brazil." *American Anthropologist* 91 (3): 570–588.

————. 1994. "Deadly Alliance: Leaders and Followings in Transactionalism and Mass Psychology." In *Transactions: Essays in Honor of Jeremy F. Boissevain,* ed. Jojada Verrips, 229–250. Amsterdam: Het Spinhuis.

————. 1995. "The Politics of Truth and Emotion among Victims and Perpetrators of Violence." In *Fieldwork Under Fire: Contemporary Studies of Violence and Survival,* ed. Carolyn Nordstrom and Antonius C. G. M. Robben, 81–103. Berkeley: University of California Press.

————. 1996. "Ethnographic Seduction, Transference, and Resistance in Dialogues About Terror and Violence in Argentina." *Ethos* 24 (1):71–106.

————. 1999. "The Fear of Indifference: Combatants' Anxieties About the Political Identity of Civilians During Argentina's 'Dirty War.'" In *Societies of Fear: The Legacy of Civil War, Violence and Terror in Latin America,* ed. Kees Koonings and Dirk Kruijt, 125–140. London: ZED Books.

————. 2000a. "State Terror in the Netherworld: Disappearance and Reburial in Argentina." In *Death Squad: The Anthropology of State Terror*, ed. Jeffrey A. Sluka, 91–113. Philadelphia: University of Pennsylvania Press.

————. "The Assault on Basic Trust: Disappearance, Protest, and Reburial in Argentina." In *Cultures Under Siege: Collective Violence and Trauma*, ed. Antonius C. G. M. Robben and Marcelo M. Suárez-Orozco, 70–101. Cambridge: Cambridge University Press.

Robben, Antonius C. G. M. and Carolyn Nordstrom. 1995. "The Anthropology and Ethnography of Violence and Sociopolitical Conflict." In *Fieldwork Under Fire: Contemporary Studies of Violence and Survival*, ed. Carolyn Nordstrom and Antonius C. G. M. Robben, 1–23. Berkeley: University of California Press.

Rock, David. 1975. *Politics in Argentina 1890–1930: The Rise and Fall of Radicalism.* Cambridge: Cambridge University Press.

————. 1987. *Argentina, 1516–1987: From Spanish Colonization to Alfonsín.* Berkeley: University of California Press.

————. 1993. *Authoritarian Argentina: The Nationalist Movement, Its History, and Its Impact.* Berkeley: University of California Press.

Rodríguez Molas, Ricardo. 1983. "Torturas, suplicios, y otras violencias." *Todo Es Historia* 192: 8–46.

————. 1985a. *Historia de la tortura y el orden represivo en la Argentina.* Buenos Aires: EUDEBA.

————, ed. 1985b. *Historia de la tortura y el orden represivo en la Argentina: Textos documentales.* Buenos Aires: EUDEBA.

Rojo, Ricardo. 1974. *Mi amigo, el Che.* Buenos Aires: Merayo Editor.

Roldán, Iris Martha. 1978. *Sindicatos y protesta social en la Argentina. Un estudio de caso: El Sindicato de Luz y Fuerza de Córdoba (1969–1974).* Amsterdam: CEDLA.

Rosenblatt, Paul C.. 1993. "Grief: The Social Context of Private Feelings." In *Handbook of Bereavement: Theory, Research, and Intervention*, ed. Margaret S. Stroebe, Wolfgang Stroebe, and Robert O. Hansson, 102–111. Cambridge: Cambridge University Press.

Roth, Roberto. 1985. "La noche de los bastones largos." *Todo Es Historia* 223:20.

Rouquié, Alain. 1987. *Poder militar y sociedad política en la Argentina. II—1943–1973.* Buenos Aires: Emecé Editores.

Rubin, Simon Shimshon. 1993. "The Death of a Child Is Forever: The Life Course Impact of Child Loss." In *Handbook of Bereavement: Theory, Research, and Intervention*, ed. Margaret S. Stroebe, Wolfgang Stroebe, and Robert O. Hansson, 285–299. Cambridge: Cambridge University Press.

Ruda, Osvaldo Jorge. 1965. "Psicología de la voluntad de lucha." *Revista del Círculo Militar* 65 (676): 81–90.

Ruddick, Sara. 1980. "Maternal Thinking." *Feminist Studies* 6 (2): 342–367.

Rudé, George. 1964. *The Crowd in History: A Study of Popular Disturbances in France and England. 1730–1848.* New York: John Wiley & Sons.

Sabato, Hilda. 1992. "Citizenship, Political Participation and the Formation of the Public Sphere in Buenos Aires 1850s–1880s." *Past and Present* 136: 139–163.

Salimovich, Sofia, Elizabeth Lira, and Eugenia Weinstein. 1992. "Victims of Fear: The Social Psychology of Repression". In *Fear at the Edge: State Terror and Resistance in Latin America*, ed. Juan E. Corradi, Patricia Weiss Fagen, and Manuel Antonio Garretón, 72–89. Berkeley: University of California Press.

Samojedny, Carlos J. 1986. *Psicologia y dialéctica del represor y el reprimido.* Buenos Aires: Roblanco.

San Martino de Dromi, María Laura. 1988. *Historia política argentina (1955–1988).* 2 vols. Buenos Aires: Editorial Astrea.

Sánchez, Matilde. 1985. *Historias de vida: Hebe de Bonafini.* Buenos Aires: Fraterna/del Nuevo Extremo.

Santner, Eric L. 1990. *Stranded Objects: Mourning, Memory, and Film in Postwar Germany.* Ithaca, N.Y.: Cornell University Press.

Santucho, Julio. 1988. *Los Ultimos Guevaristas: Surgimiento y eclipse del Ejército Revolucionario del Pueblo.* Buenos Aires: Puntosur.

Santucho, Mario Roberto. 1988 [1974], *Poder burgués y poder revolucionario.* Buenos Aires: Editorial 19 de Julio.

Saporta, José A. and Bessel A. van der Kolk. 1992. "Psychobiological Consequences of Severe Trauma." In *Torture and Its Consequences: Current Treatment Approaches,* ed. Metin Başoğlu, 151–181. Cambridge: Cambridge University Press.

Sarmiento, Domingo F. 1986 [1845], *Facundo o civilización y barbarie.* Buenos Aires: Biblioteca Ayacucho y Hyspamérica Ediciones Argentina.

Scarry, Elaine. 1985. *The Body in Pain: The Making and Unmaking of the World.* New York: Oxford University Press.

Scenna, Miguel Angel. 1983. *Los militares.* Buenos Aires: Editorial de Belgrano.

Schacter, Daniel L. 1996. *Searching for Memory: The Brain, the Mind, and the Past.* New York: Basic Books.

Schell Jr., Orville H., et al. 1979. "Report of the Mission of Lawyers to Argentina." *Record of the Association of the Bar of the City of New York* 34 (7): 473–503.

Schirmer, Jennifer. 1994. "The Claiming of Space and the Body Politic Within National-Security States: The Plaza de Mayo Madres and the Greenham Common Women." In *Remapping Memory: The Politics of TimeSpace,* ed. Jonathan Boyarin,185–220. Minneapolis: University of Minnesota Press.

Schuman, Howard and Jacqueline Scott. 1989. "Generations and Collective Memories." *American Sociological Review* 54: 359–381.

Segev, Tom. 2000 [1991], *The Seventh Million: The Israelis and the Holocaust.* New York: Henry Holt.

Seoane, María. 1991. *Todo o nada.* Buenos Aires: Planeta.

Seoane, María and Vicente Muleiro. 2001. *El dictador: La historia secreta y pública de Jorge Rafael Videla.* Buenos Aires: Editorial Sudamericana.

Seoane, María and Hector Ruiz Nuñez. 1986. *La noche de los lápices.* Buenos Aires: Editorial Contrapunto.

Shue, Henry. 1978. "Torture." *Philosophy and Public Affairs* 7 (2):124–143.

Sigal, Silvia and Eliseo Verón. 1988. *Perón o muerte: Los fundamentos discursivos del fenómeno Peronista.* Buenos Aires: Hyspamerica Ediciones Argentina.

Simpson, John and Jana Bennett. 1985. *The Disappeared and the Mothers of the Plaza.* New York: St. Martin's Press.

Sluka, Jeffrey A. 2000. "Introduction: State Terror and Anthropology." In *Death Squad: The Anthropology of State Terror,* ed. Jeffrey A. Sluka,1–45. Philadelphia: University of Pennsylvania Press.

Sluzki, Carlos E. 1990. "Disappeared: Semantic and Somatic Effects of Political Repression in a Family Seeking Therapy." *Family Process* 29: 131–143.

Smith, Christian. 1991. *The Emergence of Liberation Theology: Radical Religion and Social Movement Theory.* Chicago: University of Chicago Press.

Smith, Peter. 1972. "The Social Base of Peronism." *Hispanic American Historical Review* 52: 55–73.

Smith, Wayne. 1988. "El diálogo Perón-Lanusse." In *Racionalidad del peronismo,* ed. José Enrique Miguens and Frederick C. Turner, 117–166. Buenos Aires: Planeta.

Smith, William C. 1991. *Authoritarianism and the Crisis of the Argentine Political Economy.* Stanford, Calif.: Stanford University Press.

Snow, Peter G. and Luigi Manzetti. 1993. *Political Forces in Argentina.* Westport, Conn.: Praeger.

Somigiliana, Maco and Darío Olmo, 2002. "La huella del genocidio." *Encrucijadas* 2 (January): 22–35.

Spalding, Hobart. 1977. *Organized Labor in Latin America*. New York: Harper and Row.

Stover, Eric and Elena O. Nightingale. 1985. "Introduction: The Breaking of Bodies and Minds." In *The Breaking of Bodies and Minds: Torture, Psychiatric Abuse, and the Health Professions*, ed. Eric Stover and Elena O. Nightingale, 2–26. New York: W.H. Freeman.

Suárez-Orozco, Marcelo M.. 1987. "The Treatment of Children in the "Dirty War": Ideology, State Terrorism and the Abuse of Children in Argentina." In *Child Survival: Anthropological Perspectives on the Treatment and Maltreatment of Children*, ed. Nancy Scheper-Hughes, 227–246. Dordrecht: Reidel.

———. 1992. "A Grammar of Terror: Psychocultural Responses to State Terrorism in Dirty War and Post-Dirty War Argentina." In *The Paths to Domination, Resistance, and Terror*, ed. Carolyn Nordstrom and JoAnn Martin, 219–259. Berkeley: University of California Press.

Suedfeld, Peter. 1990. "Torture: A Brief Overview." In *Psychology and Torture*, ed. Peter Suedfeld, 1–11. New York: Hemisphere.

Sztompka, Piotr, 2000. "Cultural Trauma: The Other Face of Social Change." *European Journal of Social Theory* 3 (4): 449–466.

Tambiah, Stanley J. 1996. *Leveling Crowds: Ethnonationalist Conflicts and Collective Violence in South Asia*. Berkeley: University of California Press.

Tapia, José Carrasco. 1972. "La fuga que conmovió al continente." *Punto Final* 166: 1–15.

Taussig, Michael. 1987. *Shamanism, Colonialism, and the Wild Man: A Study in Terror and Healing*. Chicago: University of Chicago Press.

Taylor, J. M. 1979. *Eva Perón: The Myths of a Woman*. Chicago: University of Chicago Press.

Taylor, Maxwell. 1973. *Control de disturbios: Manual de contraguerrilla urbana*. Buenos Aires: Editorial Rioplatense.

Terán, Oscar. 1991. *Nuestros años sesentas: La formación de la nueva izquierda intelectual en la Argentina, 1956–1966*. Buenos Aires: Puntosur Editores.

Thompson, E. P. 1971. "The Moral Economy of the English Crowd in the Eighteenth Century." *Past and Present* 50:76–136.

Timerman, Jacobo. 1981. *Prisoner Without a Name, Cell Without a Number*. New York: Knopf.

Torre, Carlos de la. 1992. "The Ambiguous Meanings of Latin American Populisms." *Social Research* 59 (2): 385–414.

Torre, Juan Carlos. 1976. "Un capítulo en la historia del movimiento obrero argentino: La CGT y el 17 de Octubre de 1945." Ibero-American Language and Area Center Occasional Papers 22. New York: New York University.

———. 1990. *La vieja guardia sindical y Perón: Sobre los orígenes del Peronismo*. Buenos Aires: Editorial Sudamericana.

Torre, Juan Carlos and Liliana de Riz. 1993. "Argentina Since 1946." In *Argentina Since Independence*, ed. Leslie Bethell, 243–363. Cambridge: Cambridge University Press.

Trinquier, Roger. 1964 [1961]. *Modern Warfare: A French View of Counterinsurgency*. New York: Praeger.

Ulla, Noemí and Hugo Echave. 1986. *Después de la noche: Diálogo con Graciela Fernández Meijide*. Buenos Aires: Editorial Contrapunto.

Unamuno, Miguel. 1988. "La primera gran represión." *Todo Es Historia* 248: 6–33.

Uriarte, Claudio. 1992. *Almirante cero*. Buenos Aires: Planeta.

Urondo, Francisco. 1988 [1973]. *Trelew: La patria fusilada.* Buenos Aires: Editorial Contrapunto.

Van der Kolk, Bessel A. 1989. "The Compulsion to Repeat the Trauma: Re-Enactment, Revictimization, and Masochism." *Psychiatric Clinics of North America* 12 (2): 389–411.

Vázquez, Enrique. 1985. *PRN la última: Origen, apogeo y caída de la dictadura militar.* Buenos Aires: EUDEBA.

Veiga, Raúl. 1985. *Las organizaciones de derechos humanos.* Buenos Aires: Centro Editor de América Latina.

Verbitsky, Horacio. 1986. *Ezeiza.* Buenos Aires: Editorial Contrapunto.

———. 1988. *Medio siglo de proclamas militares.* Buenos Aires: Editora/12.

———. 1995. *El Vuelo.* Buenos Aires: Planeta.

Verdery, Katherine. 1999. *The Political Lives of Dead Bodies: Reburial and Postsocialist Change.* New York: Columbia University Press.

Vilariño, Raul. 1984. *Yo secuestré, maté y vi torturar en la Escuela de Mecánica de la Armada.* Buenos Aires: Perfil.

Vilas, Acdel Edgardo. 1976. "Reflexiones sobre la guerra subversiva." *Revista de la Escuela Superior de Guerra* 54 (427): 7–14.

Villegas, Osiris Guillermo. 1962. *Guerra revolucionaria comunista.* Buenos Aires: Círculo Militar.

———. 1969. *Políticas y estrategias para el desarrollo y la seguridad nacional.* Buenos Aires: Editorial Pleamar.

———. 1976. *No acuso, reflexiono.* Buenos Aires: Editorial Pleamar.

———. 1987. "La estrategia integral de la guerra subversiva." *Revista Militar* 716: 11–19.

———. 1990. *Testimonio de un alegato.* Buenos Aires: Author's edition.

Waisman, Carlos H. 1987. *Reversal of Development in Argentina: Postwar Counterrevolutionary Policies and Their Structural Consequences.* Princeton, N.J.: Princeton University Press.

Walsh, Rodolfo. 1986 [1969]. *Quién mató a Rosendo?* Buenos Aires: Ediciones de la Flor.

———. 1988 [1957]. *Operación massacre.* Buenos Aires: Ediciones de la Flor.

———. 1995. *El violento oficio de escribir: Obra periodística (1953–1977).* Buenos Aires: Planeta.

Walzer, Michael. 1977. *Just and Unjust Wars: A Moral Argument with Historical Illustrations.* New York: Basic Books.

Watson, Rubie S. 1994. "Memory, History, and Opposition Under State Socialism: An Introduction." In *Memory, History, and Opposition Under State Socialism,* ed. Rubie S. Watson, 1–20. Seattle: University of Washington Press.

Weiss, Robert S. 1993. "Loss and Recovery." In *Handbook of Bereavement: Theory, Research, and Intervention,* ed. Margaret S. Stroebe, Wolfgang Stroebe, and Robert O. Hansson, 271–284. Cambridge: Cambridge University Press.

Welty-Domon, Arlette. 1987. *Sor Alicia: Un sol de justicia.* Buenos Aires: Editorial Contrapunto.

Winkler, Cathy. 1991. "Rape as Social Murder." *Anthropology Today* 7 (3): 12–14.

———. 1995. "Ethnography of the Ethnographer." In *Fieldwork Under Fire: Contemporary Studies of Violence and Survival,* ed. Carolyn Nordstrom and Antonius C. G. M. Robben, 155–184. Berkeley: University of California Press.

Winnicott, D. W. 1986. *Home Is Where We Start From: Essays by a Psychoanalyst.* New York: W.W. Norton.

Woddis, Jack. 1972. *New Theories of Revolution: A Commentary on the Views of Frantz Fanon, Régis Debray, and Herbert Marcuse.* London: Lawrence and Wishart.

Young, Allan. 1995. *The Harmony of Illusions: Inventing Post-Traumatic Stress Disorder.* Princeton, N.J.: Princeton University Press.
Young, James E. 1993. *The Texture of Memory: Holocaust Memorials and Meaning.* New Haven, Conn.: Yale University Press.
Young, James E., ed. 1994. *The Art of Memory: Holocaust Memorials in History.* Munich: Prestel.
Zamorano, Carlos M.. 1985. "El sigilo en la legislación y en los actos gubernamentales como capítulo de la doctrina de la "Seguridad Nacional." In *La ideología de la seguridad nacional,* ed. Salvador María Lozada, Carlos M. Zamorano, Eduardo S. Barcesat, and Julio José Viaggio, pp. 27–59. Buenos Aires: El Cid.
Zuleta Álvarez, Enrique. 1975. *El nacionalismo argentino.* Buenos Aires: La Bastilla.
Zuretti, Juan Carlos. 1972. *Nueva historia eclesiástica argentina: Del Concilio de Trento al Vaticano Segundo.* Buenos Aires: Itinerarium.

Secret Decrees, Instructions, Orders, and Plans

CD (Consejo de Defensa). 1975. Directiva del Consejo de Defensa no. 1/75 (Lucha contra la subversión). 15 October.
CGE (Comandante General del Ejército). 1975a. Directiva del Comandante General del Ejército no. 333 (Para las operaciones contra la subversión en Tucumán) 23 January.
———. 1975b. Plan de Acción Sicológica No. 1/75 (Apoyo Problema Independencia). 5 February.
———. 1975c. Orden de Personal no. 591/75 (Refuerzo a la Vta Brigada de Infantería). 28 February.
———. 1975d. Orden de Personal no. 593/75 (Relevo). 20 March.
———. 1975e. Instrucciones no. 334 (Continuación de las operaciones en Tucumán). 18 September.
———. 1975f. Directiva del Comandante General del Ejército no. 404/75 (lucha contra la subversión). 28 October.
———. 1976a. Instrucciones no. 335 (Continuación de las operaciones en Tucumán). 5 April.
———. 1976b. Orden Especial no. 336/76 (Continuación de la Operación Independencia). 25 October.
———. 1976c. Orden Parcial no. 405/76 (Reestructuración de jurisdicciones y adecuación orgánica para intensificar las operaciones contra la subversión). 21 May.
CJE (Comandante en Jefe del Ejército). 1977. Directiva del Comandante en Jefe del Ejército no. 504/77 (Continuación de la ofensiva contra la subversión durante el período 1977/78), 20 April 1977. and 10 May 1978 update.
———. 1978. untitled evaluation of Operation Independence.
———. 1979. Directiva del Comandante en Jefe del Ejército no. 604/79 (Continuación de la ofensiva contra la subversión). 18 May 1979. and 24 December 1981 update.
———. 1983. Directiva del Comandante en Jefe del Ejército no. 704/83 (Operaciones del Ejército en el Marco Interno). 21 March.
PEN (Poder Ejecutivo Nacional). 1975a, Decreto "S" 261 del Poder Ejecutivo Nacional. 5 February.
PEN. 1975b, Decretos 2770/2771/2772. 6 October.

Newspapers and Magazines

Boletín Interno (PRT-ERP)
Boletín Público (Ejército Argentino)

Buenos Aires Nos Cuenta
Cabildo
Che Guevara
Clarín
Combate
De Frente
El Caudillo
El Combatiente
El Descamisado
El Diario del Juicio
El País (Spain)
El Peronista
El Porteño
Esquiú
Estrella Roja
Evita Montonera
Gendarmeria Nacional
Humor
La Causa Peronista
La Nación
La Opinión
La Prensa
La Razón
La Voz
Las Bases
Liberación
Madres
Militancia
New York Times
Nuevo Hombre
Página/12
Paz y Justicia
Primera Plana
Puro Pueblo
Revista Militar
Revolución Peronista
Somos
Sur
Tiempos Argentinos
Vencer

Index

Acknowledgments

The idea of studying political violence and trauma in Argentina arose at the University of Michigan, Ann Arbor. I want to thank my colleagues at the Michigan Society of Fellows and the Department of Anthropology for helping formulate my thoughts. The warm welcome and hospitality of Martin and Shirley Norton, Rodrigo Díaz-Pérez, Skip Rappaport, and Betty and Conrad Kottak made Ann Arbor a particularly wonderful place to be.

Research was made possible by a 1989–1990 grant from the National Science Foundation (BNS-8904324) and two grants from the Harry Frank Guggenheim Foundation between 1989 and 1991. I am deeply grateful to Karen Colvard of the Guggenheim Foundation for her unrelenting support and for inviting me to several stimulating conferences in Portugal, Great Britain, and the U.S., where high-powered intellectual discussions helped sharpen my ideas considerably. Short visits to Argentina in 1995, 2000, and 2002 were made possible by travel grants from the Netherlands Foundation for Scientific Research (NWO) and the Department of Anthropology at Utrecht University in the Netherlands.

This research would not have been possible without the willingness of the persons listed in Appendix A to discuss their own part in Argentina's painful past. I owe them a great and standing debt. Having said this, I must admit that I was always keenly aware of their personal and political stakes in my research. These journalists, lawyers, human rights activists, parents of the disappeared, former political prisoners and disappeared captives, bishops, priests, politicians, generals, admirals, brigadiers, and guerrilla commanders many times tried to have me accept their side of the story as the only historical truth. The juxtaposition of their accounts and a comparison with a vast number of written sources allowed me to weigh and contextualize their often conflicting renditions and interpretations.

Since I cannot mention every librarian and archivist by name, I want to thank them collectively for their indispensable help in providing me swiftly with the many materials I requested at the Biblioteca Nacional, Archivo General de la Nación, the libraries of the Congreso, Consejo Deliberante, Círculo Militar and the Instituto de Cultura Religiosa Superior, the archives of CELS, Abuelas de Plaza de Mayo, and Tribunales in Buenos

Aires, the CEDLA library in Amsterdam, the New York Public Library, the Hatcher Library at the University of Michigan, Ann Arbor, the Widener Library at Harvard University, Cambridge, and the Benson Latin American Collection at the University of Texas, Austin. In addition, Oscar Anzorena, Rodolfo Bernat, Renée Epelbaum, Luis Mattoni, Jaime Malamud, Bishop Jerónimo Podestá, Admiral Isaac Rojas, General Sánchez de Bustamante, and María Seoane allowed generous access to secret documents, clandestine magazines, and unpublished materials in their personal possession. I am obliged to the Archivo General de la Nación and to Ricardo Kirschbaum of the newspaper *Clarín* for the permission to reproduce several photographs from their archives.

There are a great many people without whose help this book would not have been written. Clyde Snow and Eric Stover believed in my research project from the beginning, and I hope that this book lives up to their expectations. The forensic anthropologists Patricia Bernardi, Morris Tidball Binz, Mimi Doretti, Darío Olmo, Luis Fondebrider, Alejandro Inchaurregui, and Maco Somigliana were the first to help me on my way in Buenos Aires. They were and continue to be wonderful company. I admire their ability to maintain in good spirits despite the often gruesome nature of their professional work. María Laura Fruniz and Silvana Boschi deserve a special mention. They transcribed all my taped interviews with great care and accuracy, taught me much about Argentine culture, and were always there with a listening ear after my return from another painful conversation.

I want to thank warmly the following persons for contributing in one way or another to my stay and fieldwork in Argentina: Jeremy Adelman, Paula Alonso, Oscar Anzorena, Susana Boscaro, Lila Caimari, Liliana Caradzoglu, Gisela Cramer, Rodrigo Díaz-Perez, Andrés Fontana, Moira Fradinger, Laura Ruiz Jiménez, Sonja Leferink, Marta Mántaras, and Mariano Plotkin. The talented anthropologists Sabina Frederic, Rosana Guber and Sergio Visacovsky became close friends after I completed my main field research. They have kept me up to date on Argentine politics, sent me numerous books, and always challenge me to think in new ways about Argentina's many enigmas.

My stay in Argentina would not have extended to more than two years without the friendship of Juan Astica and Liliana Fleurquin, my oldest Argentine friends Loly Etchegoyen and Santiago del Pino, and my jazz buddies Enrique and Célia Gorostiaga. Several visits to New York during fieldwork in Argentina became a real treat thanks to the hospitality of Marcela and the late George Nazzari. There are no words to express my gratitude to my dear and lifelong friends Lucas Assunção and Deborah Berlinck. After providing a home away from home in Rio de Janeiro during my fieldwork in Brazil, they extended this generosity to New York and Geneva.

Since intellectual debts are not easy to trace beyond publications, I want to thank the following persons for contributing their incisive ideas on the research design, oral presentations, unpublished papers, and chapter drafts: Juan Corradi, Valentine Daniel, Allen Feldman, Shepard Forman, Tanya Luhrmann, Catherine Merridale, Carolyn Nordstrom, Sherry Ortner, Roy Rappaport, David Rock, Riordan Roett, Nancy Scheper-Hughes, Jeff Sluka, Alfred Stepan, Marcelo Suárez-Orozco, Julie Taylor, and Eric Wolf. I want to thank my colleagues at the Department of Anthropology at Utrecht University for providing me with a nurturing intellectual environment and valuable time away from committee work to write this book.

I am greatly indebted to Robert Borofsky and Cynthia Mahmood for their encouragement, astute editorial comments, and sustained efforts to have this long book published. Both are committed to making anthropology address life's larger questions, and have been crucial in steering the discipline to the study areas of violence and trauma. A very special thanks and gratitude go to my editor Peter Agree. We have known each other for nearly twenty years, and he has always given me generous and wise advice about academic publishing. I therefore cherish this opportunity to finally publish this book under his inspiring editorship. I also want to thank Ellie Goldberg and Alison Anderson for copyediting the manuscript and guiding me skillfully through the final publishing stage.

My greatest debt and gratitude are to my wife Ellen Klinkers who has supported me during the dozen years it took me to write this book. She never tired of listening to another heart-wrenching story, and showed genuine enthusiasm when I finished yet another final draft. This book could certainly not have been written without her. I dedicate this book therefore to Ellen and to our two children Oscar and Sofia who accepted my absences as I was in Argentina or upstairs in my study. I appreciate and love them more than I can ever express.